Integrating Social Media into Business Practice, Applications, Management, and Models

In Lee
Western Illinois University, USA

A volume in the Advances in E-Business Research (AEBR) Book Series

BUSINESS SCIENCE Reference
An Imprint of IGI Global

Managing Director: Lindsay Johnston
Production Editor: Jennifer Yoder
Development Editor: Erin O'Dea
Acquisitions Editor: Kayla Wolfe
Typesetter: Michael Brehm
Cover Design: Jason Mull

Published in the United States of America by
Business Science Reference (an imprint of IGI Global)
701 E. Chocolate Avenue
Hershey PA, USA 17033
Tel: 717-533-8845
Fax: 717-533-8661
E-mail: cust@igi-global.com
Web site: http://www.igi-global.com

Library of Congress Cataloging-in-Publication Data

Integrating social media into business practice, applications, management, and models / In Lee, editor.
pages cm
Includes bibliographical references and index.
Summary: "This book provides the most up-to-date research findings and future directions for customer relationship management in contemporary enterprises, covering a wide range of topics such as management issues, innovative ideas, state-of-the-art business applications, and evaluation of social media products and services"-- Provided by publisher.
ISBN 978-1-4666-6182-0 (hardcover : alk. paper) -- ISBN 978-1-4666-6183-7 (ebook) -- ISBN 978-1-4666-6185-1 (print & perpetual access) 1. Business enterprises--Technological innovations. 2. Industrial management. 3. Business enterprises--Information technology. 4. Information technology--Management. I. Lee, In, 1958- editor of compilation.

HF1008.I4658 2014
302.23'1068--dc23

2014013709

This book is published in the IGI Global book series Advances in E-Business Research (AEBR) (ISSN: 1935-2700; eISSN: 1935-2719)

British Cataloguing in Publication Data
A Cataloguing in Publication record for this book is available from the British Library.

Advances in E-Business Research (AEBR) Book Series

In Lee
Western Illinois University, USA

ISSN: 1935-2700
EISSN: 1935-2719

Mission

Technology has played a vital role in the emergence of e-business and its applications incorporate strategies. These processes have aided in the use of electronic transactions via telecommunications networks for collaborating with business partners, buying and selling of goods and services, and customer service. Research in this field continues to develop into a wide range of topics, including marketing, psychology, information systems, accounting, economics, and computer science.

The **Advances in E-Business Research (AEBR) Book Series** provides multidisciplinary references for researchers and practitioners in this area. Instructors, researchers, and professionals interested in the most up-to-date research on the concepts, issues, applications, and trends in the e-business field will find this collection, or individual books, extremely useful. This collection contains the highest quality academic books that advance understanding of e-business and addresses the challenges faced by researchers and practitioners.

Coverage

- E-Business Strategies
- E-CRM
- Trends in E-business Models and Technologies
- Social Network
- Collaborative commerce
- Telework and Telecommuting
- Sustainable E-business
- Semantic Web
- E-Business Management
- Electronic Supply Chain Management

IGI Global is currently accepting manuscripts for publication within this series. To submit a proposal for a volume in this series, please contact our Acquisition Editors at Acquisitions@igi-global.com or visit: http://www.igi-global.com/publish/.

The Advances in E-Business Research (AEBR) Book Series (ISSN 1935-2700) is published by IGI Global, 701 E. Chocolate Avenue, Hershey, PA 17033-1240, USA, www.igi-global.com. This series is composed of titles available for purchase individually; each title is edited to be contextually exclusive from any other title within the series. For pricing and ordering information please visit http://www.igi-global.com/book-series/advances-business-research/37144. Postmaster: Send all address changes to above address.

Titles in this Series

For a list of additional titles in this series, please visit: www.igi-global.com

Electronic Payment Systems for Competitive Advantage in E-Commerce
Francisco Liébana-Cabanillas (University of Granada, Spain) Francisco Muñoz-Leiva (University of Granada, Spain) Juan Sánchez-Fernández (University of Granada, Spain) and Myriam Martínez-Fiestas (ESAN University, Perú)
Business Science Reference • copyright 2014 • 393pp • H/C (ISBN: 9781466651906) • US $215.00 (our price)

Trends in E-Business, E-Services, and E-Commerce Impact of Technology on Goods, Services, and Business Transactions
In Lee (Western Illinois University, USA)
Business Science Reference • copyright 2014 • 347pp • H/C (ISBN: 9781466645103) • US $185.00 (our price)

Interdisciplinary Perspectives on Business Convergence, Computing, and Legality
Reema Khurana (Institute of Management Technology-Ghaziabad, India) and Rashmi Aggarwal (Institute of Management Technology-Ghaziabad, India)
Business Science Reference • copyright 2013 • 354pp • H/C (ISBN: 9781466642096) • US $165.00 (our price)

Research and Development in E-Business through Service-Oriented Solutions
Katalin Tarnay (University of Pannonia, Hungary & Budapest University of Technology and Economics, Hungary) Sandor Imre (Budapest University of Technology and Economics, Hungary) and Lai Xu (Bournemouth University, UK)
Business Science Reference • copyright 2013 • 328pp • H/C (ISBN: 9781466641815) • US $185.00 (our price)

Mobile Services Industries, Technologies, and Applications in the Global Economy
In Lee (Western Illinois University, USA)
Information Science Reference • copyright 2013 • 368pp • H/C (ISBN: 9781466619814) • US $190.00 (our price)

Strategy, Adoption, and Competitive Advantage of Mobile Services in the Global Economy
In Lee (Western Illinois University, USA)
Information Science Reference • copyright 2013 • 451pp • H/C (ISBN: 9781466619395) • US $190.00 (our price)

Electronic Commerce Management for Business Activities and Global Enterprises Competitive Advantages
In Lee (Western Illinois University)
Business Science Reference • copyright 2012 • 516pp • H/C (ISBN: 9781466618008) • US $185.00 (our price)

Strategic and Pragmatic E-Business Implications for Future Business Practices
Karim Mohammed Rezaul (Glyndwr University, UK)
Business Science Reference • copyright 2012 • 496pp • H/C (ISBN: 9781466616196) • US $185.00 (our price)

IGI GLOBAL
DISSEMINATOR OF KNOWLEDGE
www.igi-global.com

701 E. Chocolate Ave., Hershey, PA 17033
Order online at www.igi-global.com or call 717-533-8845 x100
To place a standing order for titles released in this series, contact: cust@igi-global.com
Mon-Fri 8:00 am - 5:00 pm (est) or fax 24 hours a day 717-533-8661

Editorial Advisory Board

List of Reviewers

Table of Contents

Detailed Table of Contents

This chapter discusses conceptually with some anecdotal evidence how social media engagement by business firms can influence their strategic decision making. It suggests a model of influence and proposes a knowledge integration mechanism through which such influence materializes. Social media engagement by business firms has been steadily on the rise, with its application extending to a range of corporate functions beyond marketing and customer engagement, many of which can be construed as strategic. However, the potential influence of social media on strategy process or strategic decision making has not been fully explored. In addressing this gap, this chapter conceptually explores the likely influence of social media on the issue of strategic decision making and the mechanism of such influence. Embellished by some illustrative anecdotes from practice, this chapter suggests a plausible model whereby corporate social media engagement influences the strategy process in firms through the three key dimensions – environmental factors, strategic characteristics, and decision issue characteristics. In particular, social media engagement is conceived as ingraining knowledge creation and integration through socialization within an extended value network.

This chapter highlights how companies might use social media marketing to build brand credibility and, ultimately, consumer-based brand equity. By building brand credibility and equity through SMM, companies can connect with distinctly different consumer groups. Because consumers are adept integrators of marketing communication channels within and across media, companies with strong virtual communities may reap even greater results from the theoretical perspective of customer-based brand equity discussed within the chapter. Marketing scholars and practitioners alike may find this chapter of interest due to the growing desire by companies to develop strong bonds with consumers and their interest in effectively using social media as a marketing tool.

Given the estimated online advertising market in the United States of around 4 billion dollars and the current proliferation of social media Websites, this study focuses on reviewing the key theoretical and practical aspects related to viral advertising. It includes an overview of different aspects related to the nature, characteristics, and evaluation of viral advertising, especially focusing on what makes advertisements viral. After a review of the term viral advertising, the author discusses the key characteristics of viral ads, including the most used viral advertising appeals—humor and sexual—and also including a section regarding the importance of the message source on consumers' reaction towards an advertisement. The study also provides a discussion about consumer-generated advertising, a modern online advertising

in human resources, public relations, marketing, social media, and/or employee engagement. One new way that companies are extending internal communication is by developing the use of their company intranets. Intranets can support an organization by sharing accurate company information on a timely basis. This chapter describes how Lenovo has developed and uses its Lenovo Central intranet to engage employees in its mission and vision.

Organizations increasingly rely on corporate social networks and online communities to enhance socialization and knowledge sharing, collaboration, and value creation among coworkers. This chapter presents and analyzes results from a qualitative exploratory study conducted recently with a group of 24 graduate management students from a French business school. It contributes to a better understanding of how generation Y perceives the use of Social Networking (SN) applications inside businesses by drawing up a list of dos and don'ts. This study provides an ordered list of important adoption issues to consider when implementing and using CSN applications in businesses. It provides expectations and precautions for stakeholders to take into account for best use, compared to users (coworkers), managers, and the enterprise as a whole. A first list of guidelines, to favor the best adoption of these applications and to make their usage effective, is formulated.

The emergence of social media has provided a new and essential way to reach customers. In fact, in many industries, more and more firms are seeking to approach social media for business purposes; thus, it becomes essential to understand how social platforms can be managed for corporate decision-making. The aim of this chapter is to give a better understanding of social media in the strategic management field; no study to date has examined the role of social media in market-driven firms. In particular, a novel conceptual framework is proposed to show how the integrated management of social media provides several opportunities to market-driven firms. First of all, social media enables market-driven firms to acquire data and information that is useful for monitoring the competitive environment. In addition, social media allows firms to develop greater customer knowledge and to improve customer relationships by attracting new customers and by engaging old ones.

Social media technology is an innovative way for businesses to collaborate, network, and provide a mechanism for individuals to interact. When social media technology is used effectively, it can be a powerful tool for businesses to market themselves and obtain important data on their customers and competitors. Given the importance and public nature of today's consumer opinions, it is vital for companies to present themselves effectively on social media. Some companies and their employees are not familiar with this form of technology and do not realize the massive amount of data social media sites can generate. Therefore, companies need to develop a social media policy and educate their employees on how to analyze and respond to the data produced from social media. This chapter studies Web 2.0 tools and social media in today's business world and provides guidelines of adopting social media for organizations.

As a new emerging trend, social Customer Relationship Management (social CRM) can be defined as the business practice of promoting voluntary customer engagement activities driven by social media into the value creation process in order to build long-term co-beneficial relationships with target customers as the ultimate end-goal of customer relationship management. Following the spirit of social CRM, this chapter is intended to propose conceptual guidelines for the design of effective relational integrated marketing communications strategies, including message and media strategies, with particular focus on the promotion of opinion leaders' voluntary engaged efforts with others in a typical social network setting. By implanting the power of social media in relational integrated marketing communications strategies, marketers are able to put the "relationship" back into CRM in order to restore its true meaning – building better long-term relationships with customers.

This chapter introduces the role of Social Media (SM) in Knowledge-Based Organizations (KBOs), thus explaining the concept of KBOs, the difference between KBOs and non-KBOs, the concept of Knowledge Management (KM), the concept of SM, the importance of SM to KBOs, the application of SM in the KBOs, and the challenges of SM in the KBOs. This chapter explains the significance of SM for organizational development and adaptation to the business architecture in order to create knowledge integration environment in the KBOs. SM enables the creation of knowledge value chain to customize information and delivery for a technological business growth. Firms need to be connected to their technological business environment through SM because interacting with external sources of knowledge can effectively improve their capabilities about industry benchmark and competitive advantage. Understanding the role of SM in the KBOs will significantly enhance the organizational performance and achieve business goals in the global business environments.

This chapter reviews some of the major business applications of social media and discusses how social media applications are used to support business model improvement. Social media offers business organizations an array of innovative ways to interact with their employees, customers, partners, and other stakeholders. Consumers have easy ways of interacting with companies and their employees in real time with various social media embedded devices. Managers are realizing that social media affects a wide spectrum of business activities from building product or brand awareness to after-sales services.

Therefore, it is crucial for companies to analyze their social media applications, develop a plan to continually monitor their advancements, and quickly respond to the social media needs of customers. For practitioners, this chapter provides managerial guidelines for social media applications for business model improvement.

Preface

Since the late 2000s, social media has paved new ways of accessing customers for businesses and conducting business activities. Social media represents a variety of dynamic and community-based Web applications that place value on the power of distributed knowledge and provide users with rich interactive experiences. Social networking services such as Facebook, Google+, LinkedIn, and Twitter have created massive online communities of people who are willing to communicate and collaborate with each other. Social networking services have already had great impacts on the ways that people interact and businesses operate. For example, Amazon created social networks around book readership as a new initiative to attract potential book buyers. In addition to the social networking services, companies have recently shown significant interest in other social media applications such as context-based advertising, distributed file sharing, media sharing, and social bookmarking.

New organizations taking advantage of social media are also being developed, creating new markets. For example, Blade.org is a collaborative community-based organization initiated by IBM around its blade server technology. Social commerce intermediaries such as Groupon and LivingSocial provide discount information on the products/services to consumers. Various merchant reputation sites such as Yelp, Angie's List, and TripAdvisor create value to consumers based on user-generated content. With the widespread adoption of social media by customers, it became imperative for businesses to leverage social media technologies to stay competitive in the global economy.

Despite the lack of a comprehensive framework for the use of social media applications, companies are eager to use them. Managers are already active users of the various social media technologies, such as social networks and blogs. Managers are realizing that social media affects a wide spectrum of business activities from building product or brand awareness to after-sales services. Therefore, it is crucial for companies to analyze their social media applications, develop a plan to continually monitor their advancements, and quickly respond to the social media needs of customers.

Although a large volume of literature is already available on social media, many new ideas and social media applications are constantly emerging and provide potential opportunities and challenges for further research. In this light, it is imperative for researchers to take stock of the new knowledge on social media and stimulate further interest in this area. *Integrating Social Media into Business Practice, Applications, Management, and Models* provides a reference source for researchers and industry practitioners to develop their research ideas, theories, and practical experiences, and discuss challenges and opportunities in the social media area. This book is composed of 14 chapters in a wide variety of topics such as social media marketing, social CRM, social media case studies, and user behavior in social media. A brief introduction of each chapter follows:

Chapter 1, "User Involvement, Open Service Innovations, and Social Media: Lessons from a Case Study," by Ada Scupola and Hanne Westh Nicolajsen, investigates the use of social media to collect ideas from the users in the service innovation process. After a theoretical discussion of user involvement and more specifically user involvement using social media and blogs, the chapter reports the results from a field experiment at a university library. In the experiment, a blog was established to collect ideas for service innovations from the library users. The experiment shows that blogs may generate a modest but useful amount of ideas. The experiment furthermore reveals that blogs might be useful to provide the institution with an image of openness and willingness to listen to customer input.

Chapter 2, "Impact of General Social Media Experience on Usefulness for Business in the Workplace," by Donald L. Amoroso, Tsuneki Mukahi, and Mikako Ogawa, looks at the adoption of general social media applications on usefulness for business, comparing the factors that influence adoption at work between Japan and the United States. In Japan, ease of use and usefulness for collective knowledge in general social media are predictors of usefulness for business social media, and in the United States, only the usefulness for collective knowledge is a strong predictor of usefulness for business. The authors did not find behavioral intention to use social media in the workplace to be an important factor in predicting the usefulness of social media for business. The value of this research is its ability to understand the use of social media in the workplace.

Chapter 3, "Influence of Corporate Social Media in Strategic Decision Processes," by S. Venkataraman and Ranjan Das, discusses conceptually with some anecdotal evidence how social media engagement by business firms can influence their strategic decision making. It suggests a model of influence and proposes a knowledge integration mechanism through which such influence materializes. Social media engagement by business firms has been steadily on the rise, with its application extending to a range of corporate functions beyond marketing and customer engagement, many of which can be construed as strategic. However, the potential influence of social media on strategy process or strategic decision making has not been fully explored. In addressing this gap, this chapter conceptually explores the likely influence of social media on the issue of strategic decision making and the mechanism of such influence. Embellished by some illustrative anecdotes from practice, this chapter suggests a plausible model whereby corporate social media engagement influences the strategy process in firms through the three key dimensions – environmental factors, strategic characteristics, and decision issue characteristics.

Chapter 4, "Using the Power of Social Media Marketing to Build Consumer-Based Brand Equity," by Kelley O'Reilly and Karen M. Lancendorfer, highlights how companies might use social media marketing to build brand credibility and, ultimately, consumer-based brand equity. By building brand credibility and equity through SMM, companies can connect with distinctly different consumer groups. Because consumers are adept integrators of marketing communication channels within and across media, companies with strong virtual communities may reap even greater results from the theoretical perspective of customer-based brand equity discussed within the chapter. Marketing scholars and practitioners alike may find this chapter of interest due to the growing desire by companies to develop strong bonds with consumers and their interest in effectively using social media as a marketing tool.

Chapter 5, "Viral Advertising and the Implications of Social Media," by Maria Petrescu, reviews the key theoretical and practical aspects related to viral advertising. This chapter discusses the key characteristics of viral advertising, including the most-used viral advertising appeals—humor and sexuality—and includes a section regarding the importance of the message source on consumers' reactions towards an advertisement. This chapter also provides a discussion about consumer-generated advertising, a modern online advertising feature that leads to increased interaction and involvement from consumers. The last part of this chapter focuses on the monitoring and evaluating viral ads outcomes by using both traditional and social media-specific advertising measures. A few ideas related to future research directions are presented.

Chapter 6, "Social Media: The Issues, Benefits, and Strategies for Brands," by Jenny Rowley, Catherine Ashworth, and Jeff McCarthy, explores attitudes and approaches to the use of social media in relationship and community building. Two contrasting study contexts are addressed: the UK football sector and UK pure-play Small/Medium-Sized (SME) fashion retailers. After an introduction, the chapter summarises discussion and research on brands and their management in social media. This is followed by an outline of the two contexts for study. From this, the aims, objectives, and research methodology are drawn. The findings are then presented, and the ensuing discussion proposes a summary of the approaches to social media strategy adopted in the two case contexts. Four important foci are established, namely strategic marketing, marketing communication, brand and community, plus monitoring and evaluation. This results in a useful strategic framework empirically drawn from the in-depth data.

Chapter 7, "Greek Politicians and the Use of Online Technologies for Citizen Engagement," by Savvas Papagiannidis, Teta Stamati, and Hartmut Behr, examines how politicians utilise Internet technologies to create an online presence, the motivating and hindering factors for doing so, and the perceived significance such a presence can have. The authors present empirical data collected via in-depth interviews with Greek politicians taking part in the general elections of 2012. The findings suggest that although politicians are increasingly interested in engaging with citizens using online technologies, their efforts are not always focused on achieving measurable and tangible results. Consequently, they do not make full use of the potential online technologies offer. Instead, the authors conclude, online strategies need to be organised around predefined objectives and based on clear communication and engagement plans.

Chapter 8, "Using Social Media in the Workplace: How 'Lenovo Central' brings Employees Together," by Karen Mishra, Khaner Walker, and Aneil Mishra, examines the internal communication practices of Lenovo, a $34 billion Fortune Global 500 technology company, and the world's second-largest PC vendor. In particular, this study examines how this company uses social media as a method of internal communications in fostering employee engagement. Internal communications is generally led by marketing or PR professionals with expertise in human resources, public relations, marketing, social media, and/or employee engagement. One new way that companies are extending internal communication is by developing the use of their company intranets. Intranets can support an organization by sharing accurate company information on a timely basis. This chapter describes how Lenovo has developed and uses its *Lenovo Central* intranet to engage employees in its mission and vision.

Chapter 9, "How Generation Y Perceives Social Networking Applications in Corporate Environments," by Imed Boughzala, presents and analyzes results from a qualitative exploratory study conducted recently with a group of 24 graduate management students from a French business school. It contributes to a better understanding of how generation Y perceives the use of Social Networking (SN) applications inside businesses by drawing up a list of dos and don'ts. This study provides an ordered list of important adoption issues to consider when implementing and using CSN applications in businesses. It provides expectations and precautions for stakeholders to take into account. Further exploration in other settings and cultural contexts will be required to investigate more deeply the validity and generalization of these results.

Chapter 10, "Social Media Opportunities for Market-Driven Firms," by Elisa Arrigo, attempts to give a better understanding of social media in the strategic management field; no study to date has examined the role of social media in market-driven firms. In particular, a novel conceptual framework is proposed to show how the integrated management of social media provides several opportunities to market-driven firms. First of all, social media enables market-driven firms to acquire data and information that is useful for monitoring the competitive environment. In addition, social media allows one to develop greater customer knowledge and to improve customer relationships by attracting new customers and by engaging old ones.

Chapter 11, "Web 2.0 and Social Media in Today's Business World," by Edward T. Chen, studies Web 2.0 tools and social media in today's business world and provides guidelines of adopting social media for organizations. When social media technology is used effectively it can be a powerful tool for businesses to market themselves and obtain important data on their customers and competitors. Given the importance and public nature of today's consumer opinions, it is vital for companies to present themselves effectively on social media. Some companies and their employees are not familiar with this form of technology and do not realize the massive amount of data social media sites can generate. This chapter emphasizes that companies need to develop a social media policy and educate their employees on how to analyze and respond to the data produced from social media.

Chapter 12, "Re-Conceptualizing Relational Integrated Marketing Communications from the Perspective of Social CRM," by Kanghyun Yoon and Jeanetta Sims, proposes conceptual guidelines for the design of effective relational integrated marketing communications strategies, including message and media strategies, with particular focus on the promotion of opinion leaders' voluntary efforts with others in a typical social network setting. As a new emerging trend, social Customer Relationship Management (social CRM) can be defined as the business practice of promoting voluntary customer engagement activities driven by social media into the value creation process in order to build long-term co-beneficial relationships with target customers as the ultimate end-goal of customer relationship management. Following the spirit of social CRM, this chapter is intended to propose conceptual guidelines for the design of effective relational integrated marketing communications strategies, including message and media strategies, with particular focus on the promotion of opinion leaders' voluntary engaged efforts with others in a typical social network setting. By implanting the power of social media in relational integrated marketing communications strategies, marketers are able to put the "relationship" back into CRM in order to restore its true meaning – building better long-term relationships with customers.

Chapter 13, "The Role of Social Media in the Knowledge-Based Organizations," by Kijpokin Kasemsap, introduces the role of Social Media (SM) in Knowledge-Based Organizations (KBOs), thus explaining the concept of KBOs, the difference between KBOs and non-KBOs, the concept of Knowledge Management (KM), the concept of SM, the importance of SM to KBOs, the application of SM in the KBOs, and the challenges of SM in the KBOs. This chapter explains the significance of SM for organizational development and adaptation to the business architecture in order to create knowledge integration environment in the KBOs. SM enables the creation of knowledge value chain to customize information and delivery for a technological business growth. Firms need to be connected to their technological business environment through SM because interacting with external sources of knowledge can effectively improve their capabilities about industry benchmark and competitive advantage. Understanding the role of SM in the KBOs will significantly enhance the organizational performance and achieve business goals in the global business environments.

Chapter 14, "Social Media for Business Model Improvement," by In Lee, reviews some of the major business applications of social media and discusses how social media applications are used to support business model improvement. Social media offers business organizations an array of innovative ways to interact with their employees, customers, partners, and other stakeholders. Consumers have easy ways of interacting with companies and their employees in real time with various social media embedded devices. Managers are realizing that social media affects a wide spectrum of business activities from building product or brand awareness to after-sales services. Therefore, it is crucial for companies to analyze their social media applications, develop a plan to continually monitor their advancements, and quickly respond to the social media needs of customers. For practitioners, this chapter provides managerial guidelines for social media applications for business model improvement.

Integrating Social Media into Business Practice, Applications, Management, and Models is an excellent collection of the latest research and practices associated with theories, user behaviors, and practices in social media. While social media is an important subject of study for academic researchers, there is still a lack of comprehensive reference sources that provide the most up-to-date research findings and future directions for contemporary enterprises. This book fills this void by covering a wide range of topics, such as management issues, innovative ideas, state-of-the-art business applications, and evaluation of social media applications. As leading experts in the social media area, the contributors did an outstanding job of providing our readers with extensive coverage of the most important research topics – new concepts, management strategies, online user behavior, social media usage, and trends. The projected audience includes researchers, instructors, social media managers, and undergraduate/graduate students in various academic programs. I expect this book to give new insights for researchers, educators, and practitioners to better understand the important issues of social media research and technologies.

In Lee
Western Illinois University, USA

Acknowledgment

I sincerely thank Mehdi Khosrow-Pour, Jan Travers, and other members of IGI Global, whose support throughout the whole process from the inception of the initial idea to the final publication has been invaluable. I also would like to express my heartfelt gratitude to all authors and reviewers for their invaluable contributions and collaboration.

In Lee
Western Illinois University, USA

Chapter 1
User Involvement, Open Service Innovations, and Social Media:
Lessons from a Case Study

Ada Scupola
Roskilde University, Denmark

Hanne Westh Nicolajsen
Aalborg University – Copenhagen, Denmark

ABSTRACT

This chapter investigates the use of social media to collect ideas from the users in the service innovation process. After a theoretical discussion of user involvement and more specifically user involvement using social media and blogs, the chapter reports the results from a field experiment at a university library. In the experiment, a blog was established to collect ideas for service innovations from the library users. The experiment shows that blogs may generate a modest but useful amount of ideas. The experiment furthermore reveals that blogs might be useful to provide the institution with an image of openness and willingness to listen to customer input.

INTRODUCTION

Concepts like Open Innovation (Chesbrough, 2003) and User-driven Innovation (Alam & Perry, 2002) are receiving growing attention. The concepts indicate that innovation is not confined to internal organizational processes but involve interactive processes, where organizations interact with external partners including customers and users. Research within innovation has traditionally focused on innovation within the industrial sectors. However, service innovation is becoming increasingly important as services form a significant part of economical and societal activities.

Libraries, and especially research libraries, are facing considerable challenges as their services are getting increasingly digitalized (Carr, 2009) and the Internet poses a threat to the services they provide. Thus, libraries face challenges to innovate their services to stay competitive (Scupola and Nicolajsen, 2010;

DOI: 10.4018/978-1-4666-6182-0.ch001

Scupola and Nicolajsen, 2012). According to Brindley (2006) library service innovation must happen in close contact with the users. Rutherford (2008) argues that such user involvement can be supported through new social software. By drawing on Brindley (2006) and Rutherford (2008), the aim of this chapter is, to investigate the potentials of using social media in user driven innovation service innovation in academic libraries. In doing so we limit ourselves to focus on the ideation phase of the innovation process in which the involvement of users has been found to possess particular potentials (Alam and Perry 2002). Therefore, the following research question is addressed in this chapter: How can social media be used in academic libraries to involve users in the idea generation phase of the service innovation process?

In order to investigate the research question we conducted an in depth case study at Roskilde University Library (Yin, 1994). The research design consisted of three steps. First a pilot study investigating existing innovation processes and user involvement in the innovation process at Roskilde University Library was conducted; then a field experiment was conducted in which social media such as blogs were set up on the library web page to collect ideas from the users; finally the third step consisted of follow-up interviews and workshops to get feedback and evaluate the experiment's results. All in all, the blog was considered by the library management as a useful tool to communicate with the users and to generate a manageable amount of useful ideas.

The chapter is structured as follows. First, we theoretically discuss user involvement in service innovation and in particular user involvement through social media with focus on blogs. Then we present our research method and the analysis and results. Finally we provide a discussion of the results and some concluding remarks.

THEORETICAL BACKGROUND

User Involvement in Open Innovation

Chesbrough (2003, p.26) defines open innovation as "a paradigm that assumes that firms can and should use external ideas as well as internal ideas, and internal and external paths to market, as the firms look to advance their technology".

Later research has focused on user involvement in relation to innovation, also in service innovation (Alam and Perry, 2002). This has resulted in a more detailed understanding of different types of user involvement. For example the so-called 'lead users' are users who develop new products/services due to specific needs they meet before the rest of the market (von Hippel, 1986, Morrison et al. 2004). These lead users include users who investigate new design opportunities (Baldwin et al. 2006) whereas "Co-innovators" are advanced users that combine existing products in new ways (Chesbrough 2003). Often the resulting innovations are neither owned nor controlled by organizations. However organizations may potentially commercialize these innovations if they can develop the prototypes invented by users or the ideas generated by the users and (mass) produce them. In addition, organizations may proactively involve customers/users in the innovation process in several ways: for example by asking for their opinion through surveys, involving them in workshops or by using social media such as for example idea competitions (Alam and Perry, 2002, Nicolajsen and Scupola, 2011). In relation to this, Nambisan (2002, 2008) differentiates between three roles that customers may play: 1) as a source of innovation in the idea generation phase, 2) as co-creators in the development phase or 3) as potential users in the test or implementation phase. The three roles are rather different as are the requirements for both the organizations and the customers/users.

Alam and Perry (2002) have developed a ten stages model of the service innovation process, going from idea generation to implementation and marketing and present and discuss user involvement in each of these ten stages. They conclude that it is most profitable to involve users in the earlier and later innovation phases. The reason being that these phases are closest to the role as "service user". This role does not demand particular expertise from the customers, but only that the customer/user provides insights on their own needs and wishes or evaluates an existing or potential service. The phases in between are more work-intensive and typically demand professional qualifications. Research shows that if the users have to contribute in these stages, they either need a high professional level or they need further education or training (Nambisan, 2002; Alam & Perry, 2002). Educating the customer/user may be rather costly and it may easily become a risky investment, as it may be difficult to hold on to the collaboration (Nambisan, 2002). According to Alam (2006), customer activities in the ideation phase include describing needs, problems and solutions. Customers may suggest wanted features and preferences or they may evaluate existing services, lackings in the market or wishes for new services.

Several researchers (e.g. Narver et al., 2004; Alam, 2006; Magnusson, 2003) argue that the direct interaction between customer and employee provides the basis for getting ideas and an understanding of customers' needs. For example, Magnusson (2003) argues for the benefits of face-to face meetings between professionals and customers because face to face meetings may provide the professionals with insights into the customers' needs and understanding and, conversely, the users may get a better understanding of the requirements allowing them to suggest more realistic ideas. Customer-employee collaboration is fruitful as users' suggestions are found to be more creative and valuable than suggestions provided by expert professionals. On the other hand often there is a need for professional elaboration of the users' ideas to make them implementable (Magnusson, 2003). Other ways to get ideas from users include monitoring of user data such as complaints, returned products, observation of customer behavior in the so-called 'service encounter' (Narver, 2004, p.336), company visits or integration of customers in development teams (Alam, 2006), innovation labs or virtual communities (e.g. Prandelli et al., 2008).

At a more general level, the choice of method to involve customers need to be based on a number of considerations, such as whether there exists a desire to develop existing products/services or if there is a need for more radical developments, which again depends on the market - and on the situation in this market - of the organization in question. In this respect by looking at different types of input from users, Narver et al (2004) distinguish between responsive and proactive approaches. In the responsive approach the focus is on the conscious and expressible needs of the customer. In the proactive approach the focus is on the latent needs, which are unknown to the customer himself. These two different approaches are described as different by Narver et al (2004), though in reality it could be argued that they are not. The responsive approach leads primarily to incremental innovations. The proactive approach has per se the greatest potential to lead to radical innovations but the resulting ideas will be more difficult to implement.

Use of Technology to Support User Involvement

The use of technology provides both potentials and challenges for involving users in the innovation process. Prandelli et al. (2006) have for example identified 28 different web tools that can be used in the different stages of product innovation. These web based tools range from surveys and 'complaint areas' used in the idea generation phase to 'virtual product tests' in the product test phase. In addition, Prandelli et al. (2006) found that the web-based tools are mainly used by larger corporations, and are mainly used in the first and last stages of the innovation process and are mainly considered as substitutes for offline practices. Many of such tools have been investigated in other studies as well. For example, Franke and Piller (2004) describe the use of simple toolkits to create user-adjusted design of watches, while Piller and Ogawa (2006) report the use of idea competitions for t-shirts design and Franke et al (2008) describe user design of ski equipment. Virtual communities are another example where customers help organizations to innovate products or service development by using social media . Lego Mindstorm and online gaming are well known examples (Jeppesen and Molin, 2003). These communities may be user or company initiated. In both cases, user involvement is based on the users' own interest and prestige in the community. Some organizations develop online user communities for users to exchange knowledge, which can be seen as extensions of the services delivered as in the case of Netdoctor's baby club. The interaction between an organization's customers can be an important source of knowledge regarding customers' challenges, discontent and needs relevant for new service or new product development.

The Use of Blogs for User Involvement in the Ideation Phase

As discussed above, the Internet has created many opportunities for organizations to interact both directly and indirectly with their users (e.g. Prandelli et al., 2008). However, so far social media and especially blogs have received rather limited attention as a technology to collect and discuss ideas form users for service innovation, even though a few studies have investigated the potential of blogs for innovation especially in the field of new product development (e.g. Droge et al., 2010). A blogs is here defined as a Web site that contains an online journal with reflections, comments, and often hyperlinks provided by the contributors to the blog. Blogs were initially used by persons or organizations to chronologically write posts about a particular theme: their life, products etc. (Newson et al, 2009). However changes in the technology, growing experiences, combination with other tools, easy access to free platforms as well as an increasing acceptance and use of user-created content has opened up for new use forms including professional, medical, political, industrial and product related issues (see Droge et al., 2010). The possibility to comment what other has written has created a shift towards more interaction and discussion on the blogs, making them more interesting (Bar-Ilan, 2007 in Aharony, 2009). In addition, Kuhn (2007) argues that blogs' transparency and documentation leads to accountability as well as the blogs' easy and cheap access promotes equality. Anonymity may also be a factor of relevance as it may affect the content in good or bad ways. It might result in more inputs especially if the content concerns tabus (Tyler, 2002). On the other hand anonymity or lack of knowledge about the senders might provide challenges such as difficulties in understanding the input or it might result in irrelevant or harsh input. Despite the fact that the blog provides for interaction among users and between users and organization's members it may be argued that this sort of interaction is limited compared to a real life situation. The feedback mechanisms (comments) are there, but may be characterized as limited, as they are asynchronous (Lipnack and Stamp, 1997) and the number of participants is many and somewhat unlimited (Ibid.). The communication on the blog becomes partly impersonal - if the contributors are anonymous or if limited knowledge of the communicators exist. On the other hand, the blog with its written form provides for well-formulated thoughts and input as nothing is published until the communicator decides so. This capability is called "revisability" by Clark and Brennan (1991). It may be hypothesized that blogs could sustain both responsive and proactive approaches to idea generation.

RESEARCH METHOD

In order to investigate the research question we conducted an in depth case study at an academic library, Roskilde University Library (Yin, 1994). The research design employed in this study consists of three steps. First a pilot study investigating existing innovation processes and user involvement at Roskilde University Library was conducted to get an understanding of the innovation processes at the library and especially to understand whether and how library users were involved. The pilot study was then followed by a field experiment in which social media such as blogs were set up on the library web page to collect ideas from the users concerning library services innovations. The experiment and its specific set-up is described in detail in the following section. Finally the third step consisted of follow-up interviews and workshops with library personnel in order to get feedback and evaluate the experiment of using of social media to generate new ideas for library service innovations.

Semi-structured qualitative interviews as well as a number of meetings and workshops lasting between 1 and 2 hours with top managers, middle managers, and 'front-line' librarians were the main data collection methods used in the pilot study. Based on the results of the pilot study, showing that there was almost no direct involvement of the library users in the innovation process of the library services, an agreement was made between the researchers and the library management to conduct an experiment where social media should be used to collect ideas from the users. Given the library's previous experience with a blog used for internal communication and discussion of several topics of relevance to the library personnel, it was decided to implement a blog on the library webside, entitled "RUbminds". The establishment of the blog and its use to collect innovative ideas from the customers is here defined as a so-called field-experiment, that is an experiment carried out in a natural context rather than in a laboratory. In this type of experiment, some control over the experiment itself is lost (compared with the traditional laboratory experiment), but the advantage is that the "natural settings ensure that the results will tell us something useful about the real world, not just some contrived laboratory setting" (Green & Gerber, 2003, 94). In spite of being a rarely applied method in innovation research such field-experiments have been argued to possess the capability of providing practically applicable knowledge about innovation processes while solving real life innovation problems (Sørensen et al. 2010). Field experiments are similar to other practice oriented methods such as action research, action learning and reflexive practice (Baskerville and Wood-Harper, 1996). As already said, semi-structured interviews and workshops with the library employees that had been involved in the blog experiment were conducted to evaluate the experiment and the results obtained. Other data collection methods used in this study includes library reports, minutes of top management meetings as well as click stream analysis.

Roskilde University Library (RUB): Background

RUB is a research library situated at Roskilde university campus, which is a regional university in the outskirts of Copenhagen. The target users are the students and the academics of the university. However organizations and private persons may also use the library. The University has approximately 10,000 students and about 900 employees which are served by the employees at the library. About half of the library employees' are librarians. The library provides a lot of different services - some face-to-face, some in the form of e-services.

RUB offers information literacy teaching sessions on how to use the library databases and library resources. Another service provided by the library is online chat consultations with librarians.

The Experiment: RUbminds' Process

After having agreed with the library top management that the social media to be used to collect innovation ideas from the users had to be a blog, a small team was established to design and implement the blog. The team comprised four employees from different library departments as well as the authors of this chapter. The team met on an ongoing basis for a period of six months. In this period the blog was designed and set up and a small test was conducted by inviting a small group of computer mediated communication experts to look at the blog and provide some feedback before the launch of the blog to the public. This group of experts provided some suggestions that were incorporated in the final version. In addition we had lengthy discussions on how best to meet and engage the users in order to make them contribute with innovative ideas.

Different blog names and layouts were discussed inspired by other blogs regarding content, tone etc. After some discussions and meetings, a decision was made to formulate four topics within which innovative ideas were solicited. Such topics were formulated by the library personnel based on their innovation needs.

The topics were formulated in such a way as to get a feedback on the services provided by the library as well as on the library physical settings. The topics were formulated as questions on the blog: 1) "Do we comply with your wishes?"; 2) "If you should furnish the library….?"; 3) "Is RUB your favorite library?"; and 4) "The future of the library – give us your suggestions". It can be argued that the questions overlap, however the different formulations sought to motivate for different answers. In addition to the questions a small piece of text giving examples of the kind of input looked for was put on the first page of the blog.

The blog experiment was advertised in several ways both online and at the university campus. For example a direct link to the blog was put at the FrontPage of the library homepage; posters describing the blog experiment were hang in campus buildings and book markers with the blog address were handed out to the library users when they loaned books.

To motivate library users to participate in the experiment two gift vouchers were promised at the end of the experiment to two randomly drawn blog contributors. This was advertised on the main page of the blog. The blog experiment was conducted for a period of three months. To increase credibility of the initiative, the blog introduction also stated that the library would follow up on the ideas provided on the blog and report back on this to the users. During the experiment, the library employees had the possibility to comment and respond to the users' postings, since the idea was that the blog should function as a web-based interactive platform between the users and the employees. At the end of the experiment period, the ideas collected through the blog were analyzed and discussed by library management in relation to their relevance and implementation potential at a management meeting.

The success criterion for the field experiment was that the blog (the independent variable of the experiment) could function as a medium for idea generation by library users and that these ideas could result in implemented service innovation at the library (the dependent variable of the experiment). In this chapter we primarily look at the first part – how useful is the blog to involve users in the ideation phase from the perspective of the library.

ANALYSIS AND RESULTS

The blog, directly allowing library users to provide ideas for service innovation that could be shared instantaneously with many other users, has challenged the existing approach to innovation at the library. Underneath we first present the results of the pilot study briefly showing the traditional approach to innovation at RUB, then we present the outcome of the blog experiment and finally we provide some findings that show important side effects of the experiment at the library.

User Involvement in Service Innovation at RUB: The Traditional Way

The results of the pilot study show that the library's traditional approach to innovation processes is mainly based on the use of 'internal development plans' where most ideas come from top management, collaboration with external partners and competitors but also, even though to a lesser extent, from employees. Traditionally, users have not been directly involved in the innovation process at RUB, but have been only indirectly represented through the employees understanding of the users' wants and wishes, likes and dislikes. This understanding is gained through mainly face-to-face interactions in the provisions of services like courses on how to use the library resources, library consultation services and other services. These service provisions, even though not specifically focusing on innovation, are the basis for ad hoc and indirect collection of ideas on users' needs and wants. These inputs often result in small changes in the practices of the employees, or the ideas may be sent to top management for evaluation and further action. Such service encounters, traditional user satisfaction surveys and complaint/satisfaction boxes have been the main ways for the library to collect opinions and wishes from the users. Web-based interactive tools in the form of online chat had just recently been adopted at RUB on an experimental basis to establish contact with users. However, this type of customer contact was just a virtual version of the face-to-face encounter and at the time of the study still limitedly used. RUB thus had very little experience with social media at the time of the study. For RUB, meeting the users through a blog interface was new and different. Direct ways to involve users in the idea generation phase of the service innovation process had not been tried out at the library yet. Therefore, traditionally at RUB the users were only an indirect source of innovation and a source of limited importance.

The Results of the Experiment

During the short period in which the experiment was conducted, 1.011 visits were made to the blog and 2572 pages were looked at. On average, the visitors stayed for 1 minute and 35 seconds. A total of 27 "useful" ideas were provided during the period the experiment run. The ideas generated by the users on the blog were very different in nature and covered a wide range of topics as illustrated by the examples provided in Table 1. Some ideas are visions of a whole new way of seeing the function of the library - as for example the library as cultural event place. Some are suggestions for new services such as an EndNote course, others suggest big or small changes in the services already offered such as access to computers in the library reading areas. A few comments just criticize the present service offerings, without providing suggestions for improvements.

Library Assessment of the Results of the Blog Experiment

In interviews conducted after the three months experiment period evaluating the experiment process and the results, RUB management stated that the blog had been a good way to get input from the users and especially to communicate online with the users. According to the library

Table 1. Examples of ideas contributed to the blog

Examples of ideas contributed to the blog
• Suggestion for RUB to provide students and employees with short courses on End Notes software
• Suggestion to change copy machines so that the same copy card could be used both at the University and the Library, thus improving the copy services
• Suggestion to extend the time period users can keep the books loaned from other libraries through the Interlibrary Loan.
• Increase the number of full text resources provided in electronic form
• Establish a Silent room with computers
• Establish small rooms where student groups conducting project work could meet and work instead of only having open space areas
• Establishment of a cozy lounge area with newspapers, a coffee machine, sandwiches and candy
• Establish open air library services, outside the library building, including Internet access, shadow and shelter in the summer
• Decrease the noise level generated by the air condition system in the silent area

management some ideas provided suggestions for radical innovations, while others required incremental changes of what was presently done. Furthermore, a few ideas posted on the blog addressed problems that were well known to the library but that had been forgotten or put aside. Reading such ideas again on the blog and knowing that many potential users could read the comments posted on the blog and become aware of the problems, had motivated the library management to find a solution and to fix the problems that had been neglected in the past. In a way, the library personnel felt a pressure from the blog to do something about the implementation of the ideas, both those pointing to well-known problems as well as those pointing to problems/ideas that the library was not previously aware of. Some ideas needed further investigation before the library could evaluate to what extent they should implement them or not; a few were completely dropped due to implementation requirements such as the establishment of open-air library services during summer time.

For RUB, the relative low activity on the blog has been an advantage because the resources needed to manage the blog were contained. According to the blog manager, they would had probably closed the blog if they got overwhelmed by a huge number of posting/ideas that would have required a huge amount of resources both in terms of employees time to handle the blog and money/other resources to investigate and eventually implement the ideas suggested by the bloggers. As of today, all the suggested ideas have been implemented by RUB.

In addition, the blog manager said that the blog had had several internal positive spin-offs such as increased collaboration among employees of different departments both in order to find appropriate answers to the blogs' questions/postings and to investigate/implement solutions. The blog had overall increased collaboration and communication among the library employees. Finally, the blog gave the library also the image of an institution that was open to ideas and critique from the users.

In a top management meeting to evaluate the outcome from the blog experiment and the usefulness of the blog to communicate online with the library users and to generate ideas for innovation purposes, the library decided to keep the blog on their website because "The blog invites for open discussion of suggestions and opinions in opposition to just e-mails" (Minutes from a RUB meeting). The blog has been used by the library to engage into online communication, idea generation and discussion with the library users until not long ago, when it has been substituted by Facebook.

DISCUSSION

Our study shows that the blog is perceived by RUB management to be a useful social media to communicate with the library users and to engage them in the idea generation phase of the service innovation process. So our study supports, even though with big caution, the results of the study conducted by Droge et al. (2010) that found that blogs can be useful in the field of new product development. Most of the contributed ideas suggested incremental innovations; some provided more radical suggestions, while a few comments just criticized the present service offerings, without providing suggestions for improvements. This broadness of topics is in line with Alam (2006) who argues that input can have many different forms.

However, our experiment shows that it is difficult to engage a big amount of users to contribute ideas and therefore to generate a huge amount of ideas on the blog. There could be several reasons for this. For example,the library users might not really burn to provide ideas about how to improve the library services and they are in general uncritical of the services received. It could be that RUB users are in general satisfied with the quality of service received. Finally it could also be due to the technical characteristics of the blogs and in particular the design of the RUbminds blog.

Nevertheless, the ideas generated by the library users during the three months experiment were considered important by library management. Such ideas were an eye opener for the library concerning what services the library users might wish from them, and library management further investigated and implemented several of them. However, some ideas that required major changes in the library interior decoration or architecture were considered but put on stand-by by the library. For RUB the relative low activity on the blog was seen as an advantage because they could manage it with relatively low resources. This was also the reason for making the decision to keep it on the web page and continue to use it to engage into a dialogue with the users. The library received not many, but nevertheless good and valuable insights into what users like, dislike, what they need and some suggestions about what to do. Some ideas pointed to implementable solutions. Others pointed to problems or needs that needed further investigation. Some critiques and needs even needed further inquiry to understand what the problem was. These results are in line with what is argued by Magnusson et al. (2003). Finally the library felt obliged to take into serious consideration the ideas posted on the blog, due to the transparency, documentation and archiving function of the blog as also stated by Kuhn (2007).

FUTURE RESEARCH DIRECTIONS

Our study provides some useful insights about the use of social media in the idea generation phase of service innovations in one specific case organization, a university library. However, the study presents a number of limitations implying that the results have to be taken with caution. For example, the study has been conducted only in one organization. In addition, only one experiment was conducted, which lasted for a very limited time, making it difficult to generalize from these results. Finally, the results of the experiment could have also been influenced by the overall user statisfaction with the present quality of the services provided by the library.

In future research, more experiments in the same library could be conducted in order to validate the results obtained in this study. In addition, several experiments in several different libraries could also be conducted in order to understand the applicability and usefulness of blogs for user involvement in library service innovations. More importantly, this research could be continued by investigating user involvement through other social media such as facebook and twitter at the same library, other libraries and private sector as well. For example RUB has abandoned the blog, but it is using Facebook to engage the library users i stedet for. It could be nice to follow up on the use of Facebook for customer involvement in library services innovation at RUC and possibly make a comparison between using the blog and Facebook. Finally, more research in other service sectors as well could be carried out in order to fully exploit the potential of social media for user involvement in the service sector.

CONCLUSION

This chapter has investigated the use of social media such as blogs to involve users in the idea generation phase of the innovation process in library services.

The study found that blogs can indeed be used to involve the users and collect ideas concerning some specific themes. In our experiment, in fact, the blog has generated a modest, but according to the library management, a useful number of ideas. If the purpose is, however, to generate a huge number of ideas or engage a huge number of users, then our experiment shows that probably blogs are not a good tool. Blogs can eventually be used in combination with other more traditional tools for involving users in idea generation process of service innovations as for example future workshops or other social media tools such as facebook or twitter.

In addition, our results show that using social media such as blogs to collect innovation ideas from the users may generate a number of spin offs advantages such as increasing internal collaboration among the organization employees and giving the organization an image of a more "open to critique and new ideas" kind of organization.

ACKNOWLEDGMENT

We wish to thank the employees and management group at Roskilde University Library for their openness, collaboration, and support during the whole study. In addition, we would like to thank all the colleagues participating to the ICE project (http://ice-project.dk/) for interesting discussions and suggestions. Finally, and especially, we would like to thank the Danish Strategic Research Council for financial support for the ICE project, without which this study would not have been possible.

REFERENCES

Aharony. (2009). Librarians and information scientist in the blogosphere: An exploratory analysis. *Library and Information Science Research*, (31), 174-181.

Alam, I. (2006). Removing the fuzziness form the fuzzy front-end of service innovations through customer interactions. *Industrial Marketing Management*, *35*(4), 468–480. doi:10.1016/j.indmarman.2005.04.004

Alam, I., & Perry, C. (2002). A customer-oriented new service development process. *Journal of Services Marketing*, *16*(6), 515–534. doi:10.1108/08876040210443391

Baldwin, C., Hienerth, C., & von Hippel, E. (2006). How user innovations become commercial products: A theoretical investigation and case study. *Research Policy*, *35*(9), 1291–1313. doi:10.1016/j.respol.2006.04.012

Baskerville, R. &Wood-Harper, A.T. (1996). *A taxonomy of action research methods* (Working paper). Institute of Informatics and Management Accounting, Copenhagen Business School.

Brindley, L. (2006). Re-defining the library. *Library Hi Tech. Bradford*, *24*(4), 484–495. doi:10.1108/07378830610715356

Carr, P. L. (2009). From innovation to transformation: A review of the 2006-7 serials literature. *Library Resources & Technical Services*, *53*(1), 3–15. doi:10.5860/lrts.53n1.3

Chesbrough, H. W. (2003). *Open innovation: The new imperative for creating and profiting from technology*. Harvard Business School Press.

Droge, C., Stanko, M. A., & Pollitte, W. A. (2010). Lead Users and Early Adopters on the Web: The Role of New Technology Product Blogs. *Journal of Product Innovation Management*, *27*(1), 66–82. doi:10.1111/j.1540-5885.2009.00700.x

Franke, N., Keinz, P., & Schreier, M. (2008). Complementing mass customization toolkits with user communities: How peer input improves customer self-design. *Journal of Product Innovation Management*, *25*(6), 546–559. doi:10.1111/j.1540-5885.2008.00321.x

Franke, N., & Piller, F. (2004). Value creation by toolkits for user innovation and design: The case of the watch market. *Journal of Product Innovation Management*, *21*(6), 401–415. doi:10.1111/j.0737-6782.2004.00094.x

Green, D., & Gerber, A. (2003). The underprovision of experiments in political science. *The Annals of the American Academy of Political and Social Science*, *589*(1), 94–112. doi:10.1177/0002716203254763

Jeppesen, L. B., & Molin, M. (2003). Consumers as co-developers: Learning and innovation outside the firm. *Technology Analysis and Strategic Management*, *15*(3), 363–383. doi:10.1080/09537320310001601531

Kuhn, M. (2007). Interactivity and Prioritizing the Human: A code of Blogging Ethics. *Journal of Mass Media Ethics*, *22*(1), 18–36. doi:10.1080/08900520701315244

Magnusson, P. (2003). Benefits of involving users in service. *European Journal of Innovation Management*, *6*(4), 228–238. doi:10.1108/14601060310500940

Morrison, P. D., Roberts, J. H., & Midgley, D. F. (2004). The Nature of Lead Users and Measurement of Leading Edge Status. *Research Policy*, *33*(2), 351–362. doi:10.1016/j.respol.2003.09.007

Nambisan, S. (2002). Designing virtual customer environments for new product development: Toward a theory. *Academy of Management Review*, *27*(33), 392–413.

Nambisan, S., & Nambisan, P. (2008). How to Profit From a Better Virtual Customer Environment. *MIT Sloan Management Review*, *49*(3), 53–61.

Narver, J. C., Slater, S. F., & MacLachlan, D. L. (2004). Responsive and proactive market orientation and new-product success. *Journal of Product Innovation Management*, *21*(5), 334–347. doi:10.1111/j.0737-6782.2004.00086.x

Newson, A., Houghton, D., & Patten, J. (2009). *Blogging and other social media: Exploiting the technology and protecting the enterprise*. Ashgate.

Nicolajsen, H. W., & Scupola, A. (2011). Investigating issues and challenges for customer involvement in business services innovation. *Journal of Business and Industrial Marketing*, *26*(5), 368–376. doi:10.1108/08858621111144424

Ogawa, S., & Piller, F. T. (2006). Reducing the risks of new product development. *MIT Sloan Management Review*, *47*(2), 65–71.

Piller, F. T., & Walcher, D. (2006). Toolkits for Idea Competitions: A Novel Method to Integrate Users in New Product Development. *R & D Management*, *36*(3), 307–318. doi:10.1111/j.1467-9310.2006.00432.x

Prandelli, E., Sawhney, M., & Verona, G. (2008). *Collaborating with customers to innovate*. Edward Elgar. doi:10.4337/9781848442917

Prandelli, E., Verona, G., & Raccagni, D. (2006). Diffusion of Web-Based Product Innovation. *California Management*, *48*(4), 109–135. doi:10.2307/41166363

Rutherford, L. L. (2008). Building participative library services: The impact of social software use in public libraries. *Library Hi Tech*, *26*(3), 41. doi:10.1108/07378830810903337

Scupola, A., & Nicolajsen, H. W. (2010). Service innovation in academic libraries: Is there a place for the customers? *Library Management*, *31*(4/5), 304–318. doi:10.1108/01435121011046362

Scupola, A., & Nicolajsen, H. W. (2013). Library perceptions of using social software such as blogs in the idea generation phase of service innovations: Lessons from an experiment. In *Organizational Change and Information Systems - Working and living together in new ways (LNISO)* (pp. 137–145). Berlin: Springer. doi:10.1007/978-3-642-37228-5_14

Sørensen, F., Mattsson, J., & Sundbo, J. (2010). Experimental methods in innovation research. *Research Policy*, *39*(3), 313–320. doi:10.1016/j.respol.2010.01.006

Tyler, T. R. (2002). Is the internet changing social life? It seems the more things change, the more they stay the same. *The Journal of Social Issues*, *58*(1), 195–205. doi:10.1111/1540-4560.00256

von Hippel, E. (1986). Lead users: A source of novel product concepts. *Management Science*, *32*(7), 91–805. doi:10.1287/mnsc.32.7.791

Yin, R. K. (1994). *Case study research design and methods* (2nd ed., Vol. 5). Thousand Oaks, CA: Sage Publications.

ADDITIONAL READING

Boyd, D. M., & Ellison, N. B. (2007). Social network sites: Definition, history, and scholarship. *Journal of Computer-Mediated Communication*, *13*(1), 11. http://jcmc.indiana.edu/vol13/issue1/boyd.ellison.html doi:10.1111/j.1083-6101.2007.00393.x

Dabham, D. (2010). Moving the crowd at iStockphoto: The composition of the crowd and motivations for participation in a crowdsourcing application, *FirstMonday*. Retrieved from http://firstmonday.org/ojs/index.php/fm/article/view/2159/1969

Fraser, M., & Dutta, S. (2010). *Throwing Sheep in the Boardroom: How Online Social Networking Will Transform Your Life, Work and World*. Wiley.

Kaplan, A. M., & Haenlein, M. (2010). Users of the World Unite! The challenges and opportunities of Social Media. *Business Horizons*, *53*(1), 59–68. doi:10.1016/j.bushor.2009.09.003

Kietzmann, J. H., Hermkens, K., McCarthy, I. P., & Silvestre, B. S. (2011). Social Media? Get serious! Understanding the functional building blocks of social media. *Business Horizons*, *54*(3), 241–251. doi:10.1016/j.bushor.2011.01.005

Nicolajsen, H. W., & Scupola, A. (2012). Creating a new innovation practice and a different innovation orientation through implementation of an idea competition tool. In *Proceedings of SIGSVC Workshop. Sprouts: Working Papers on Information Systems*. Retrieved from http://sprouts.aisnet.org/12-26/

Sakkab, N. Y. (2002). *Connect & develop complements research & develop at P&G*. Research Technology Management.

Scupola, A. (2013, Forthcoming), A Design Methodology for User Driven Service Innovations. In Simonsen., C. Svabo, M. S. Strandvad, K. Samson, & M. Hertzum (Eds.) Situated Design Methods. MIT Press.

Smith, N., Wollan, R., & Zhou, C. (2011). The Social Media Management Handbook: Everything You Need To Know To Get Social Media Working. In *Your Business*. John Wiley & Sons.

KEY TERMS AND DEFINITIONS

Blogs: A blog is a Web site that contains an online journal with reflections, comments, and often hyperlinks provided by the contributors to the blog.

Open Innovation: A paradigm that assumes that firms can and should use external ideas as well as internal ideas, and internal and external paths to market, as the firms look to advance their technology or service offerings.

Service Innovation: A new or considerably changed service concept, client interaction channel, service delivery system or technological concept that leads to one or more new or improved service functions that are new to the firm.

Social Media: Internet-based applications that build on the ideological and technological foundations of Web 2.0, and that allow the creation and exchange of user-generated content.

User-Driven Innovation: A paradigm that has the user of the service /product in focus in the process of developing new service/product innovations.

Chapter 2
Impact of General Social Media Experience on Usefulness for Business in the Workplace

Donald L. Amoroso
Auburn University – Montgomery, USA

Tsuneki Mukahi
Chukyo University, Japan

Mikako Ogawa
Tokyo University of Marine Sciences and Technology, Japan

ABSTRACT

This chapter looks at the adoption of general social media applications on usefulness for business, comparing the factors that influence adoption at work between Japan and the United States. In Japan, ease of use and usefulness for collective knowledge in general social media are predictors of usefulness for business social media, and in the United States, only usefulness for collective knowledge is a strong predictor of usefulness for business. The authors did not find behavioral intention to use social media in the workplace to be an important factor in predicting the usefulness of social media for business. The value of this research is its ability to understand the use of social media in the workplace to include how the experience of social media impacts on the expectation of usefulness for business and how the impact of ease of use differs from Japanese to the United States because of cultural, technological, and market reasons.

INTRODUCTION

This research paper addresses the impact from general social media perception or experience to perception of social media usefulness at work in both Japan and the United States. Is there a difference? It appears that culture may have an impact on the use of social media. Social media is defined as "a group of Internet-based applications that build on the ideological and technological foundations of Web 2.0, and that allow the creation and exchange of User Generated Content" (Kaplan &

DOI: 10.4018/978-1-4666-6182-0.ch002

Haenlein, 2010). Kalamas, Mitchell, and Lester (2009) defined social media as, "a communication medium that is devoted to or characterized by interaction between participants or consumers of the medium".

The worldwide rapid diffusion and growing popularity, potential risks, negative impacts or controversial issues of social media exists. Das and Sahoo (2011) describe the impact of social networking on individuals: "The growing popularity of social networking sites (SNS) among the Internet users demands an introspection of personal and social behavior of human beings. Today 1.5 billion people across the world have their profiles in social networking sites. Everything looks nice when you create a profile on social networking site, but how you feel when someone starts blackmailing using your personal data. Your boss threatens to fire you for posting comments on SNS. You feel compulsive to check your profile during work hours. SNS becomes a reason for anxiety and addiction. It starts affecting personal relationship with spouse and family members. Such sites make private life and public life of an individual a digital document." However, it might be true that still many practitioners and researchers anticipate massive opportunities, positive impacts and abundant harvest from usage of social media in the workplace, even though the way to success is still ambiguous. Many people, especially the younger generation, have already had some experiences with social media at least in private settings. Before discussing effective and/or efficient usage of social media in the work place, it might be useful for us to clarify ordinary people's needs or expectation to social media in workplace.

Internal corporate use of social media has reported in articles, especially in big global companies such as IBM (2010) and Ernst & Young (Williamson, 2009). Social networking has increased collaboration at IBM. The article explained effects to increase collaboration in IBM by using internal social networking. The article showed preferable effects of implementing social networking to increase internal collaboration in a company (Greenberg, 2009). According to Williamson (2009), a partner at Ernst & Young and the company's Americans Inclusiveness Officer, communication with team members is the most important task for virtual team managers. For efficient and effective communication, managers inevitably use both traditional media and the latest innovative technologies. They should use not only e-mail and a company intranet but also 'a community home space', which seemed to be an equivalent word to 'social networking site', to help virtual team members connect with each other and engage in the team. Moreover Williamson (2009) pointed that telephone call, face to face meeting and an annual onsite company-wide event are also important to manage a global company. It means social media should be used as one of communication technologies in global work place and we should understand the country and cultural difference of social media.

One of the benefits of social media is the ability to reach a large group of people by tapping into the network. Each person has their own network and each node in the network taps into a completely different group of people. This creates a very large audience to reach people in general. Many of these social media services are familiar to the younger generation. Annetta (2008) explained that younger social media users spend an average of 6.5 hours a day using variety of media. Managers believe that younger workers are more likely to create high level of emotional engagement when using social media in the workplace. Robinson (2006) also discussed that the increased participation in the use of social media potentially leads to greater attendance by workers and potentially a higher recollection of while at work. Divol, Edelman, and Sarrazin (2012) found that companies invest millions of dollars in social media, with little understanding of how it influences consumers to favor their brands or buy their products. Without knowing how social media affects consumer behavior, companies run the risk of aiming it at the wrong targets, wasting time and money on ineffective efforts, and generally failing to harness its potential. Bennett, Owers, Pitt, and Tucker (2010) found that the business advantages and benefits of social networking in the workplace are still very much underappreciated and undervalued. Some organizations across the world have started to implement some of the facets of social networking technology and reap the business benefits (Hathi, 2010; Williamson, 2009).

As mentioned above, the use of social media has expanded and many people use different types of social media in their private life. Past studies showed that technology experience enhanced users' perception of ease of use of the technology (Venkatesh, 2000; Venkatesh & Davis, 1996). It is possible that the use of private general social media experience might have impact on the expectation of social media at the work place. Therefore, it is the purpose of this research to clarify the impacts from general social media perceptions or experiences to perception of social media usefulness at work in both Japan and United States. We came up with two broad research questions:

- What are the predictors for expectation to social media at workplace?
- What are the experience levels of general social media perception and country difference?

LITERATURE REVIEW

Social Media and the TAM Model

Davis (1989) proposed Technology Acceptance Model (TAM) and he showed that perceived usefulness and perceived ease of use were antecedents of user acceptance were user attitude and behavioral intention. From that time, tremendous researchers applied TAM. Since technology adoption is not only influenced by a user's own preferences, but also by the norms and beliefs of the cultural environment, technology adoption and consumer behavior is culturally specific and articulated within or in relation to specific cultures (Yang & Jolly, 2009).

Lee, Xiongb, and Hu (2012) analyzed users' attitudes and intentions in Facebook and clarified that ease of use had indirect impacts on the attitudes. They found that valence, the continuum of positive and negative emotions, has a direct strong relationship with perceived ease of use which, in turn, impacts perceived enjoyment of using social media, and then affecting attitude toward using Facebook. Perceived usefulness and perceived ease of use were not directly related to attitude toward using social media. This indicates the need to consider other factors in explaining intention to use social media.

Lin and Lu (2011) studied why people continue to join SNS and found that usefulness is one of the influential factors in people's continued use of SNS. Like Lee et al. (2012), perceived enjoyment had a strong impact on continued intention to use social media

Leng, Lada, and Muhammad (2011) analyzed SNS adoption in Malaysia using TAM. They showed that ease of use has an impact on usefulness and that usefulness has impacts on attitude and behavioral intention. Perceived ease of use was found to affect perceived usefulness which, in turn, was found to affect attitude toward social media, similar to Lee et al. (2012). Unlike Lee et al. (2012), Leng et al. (2011) found that perceived usefulness had a strong impact on behavioral intention to use social medial

Lin, Liu, and Kuo (2013) found that perceived usefulness has a moderating effect between attitudes toward using mobile technologies in Taiwan. They also found that perceived usefulness was affected in part by users' perceived ease of use. This indicates that the attitude of users to use general social media may be moderated in part by perceived usefulness and affected by perceived ease of use of that social media application.

The research by Venkatesh and Davis (1996) focused on understanding the determinants of perceived ease of use and usefulness and found a direct relationship between experience and ease of use. Those studies imply that TAM can be applied to social media studies and the social media acceptance may be affected by another information technology or communication media experience.

Social Media and Employees

The importance of embracing social networking as an effective business tool is summarized in Williamson (2009) and Amoroso and Orita (2010). Bennett et al. (2010) found that the main business benefits that social networking tools can have are:

- In the workplace, social networking tools promise to revitalize organizations by harnessing collective intelligence.
- Social networks, blogs, wikis, mashups and RSS feeds can facilitate networked conversations, information sharing and problem solving.
- Rigid hierarchies, corporate silos and walled-off R&D departments can be ripped down and replaced by transparent, open-ended "crowdsourcing" strategies that even bring customers into the collaborative dialogue.
- Power is shifting from executive C-suites to employee cubicles, from companies to customers, from monopolists to markets.
- The potential upside: improved morale, enhanced collective knowledge, increased productivity, sharpened strategic focus, greater innovation. And on the bottom line, higher profits.

Edosomwan, Prakasan, Kouame, Watson, and Seymour (2012) discussed the benefits of social media in business, as listed here, but mostly to promote communication. Social media helps to share project ideas, communicate with customers, receives feedback, and provides a good venue for discussions. Social media will also create brand awareness, but they found that the key factor for success is enabling conversation.

Kane, Robinson-Combre, and Berge (2010) explored how knowledge management and e-learning within an organization are tied together through social networking, thereby causing a strong impact on how people communicate, learn and share knowledge. They found that knowledge management, e-learning, and social networking met the needs of adult learners. Further, they showed why an organization should tap into social networking tools and activities while incorporating them into their knowledge management system to enhance their e-learning and other training activities. Hsu and Lin (2008) found that ease of use and enjoyment and knowledge sharing were positively related to attitude toward using blogging. Also, attitude toward using blogging and community identification (social factors) significantly influenced a blog users' intention to continue to use blogs, explaining 83% of the variance of intention to blog.

The use of social networking websites such as Facebook, MySpace, LinkedIn, and Twitter for recruiting, hiring, or terminating individuals is relatively new. Many questions about using these sites for HR practice have yet to be addressed, including questions about the validity and usefulness of information obtained on these sites, applicant perceptions of employers' use of these sites, and the legality of using these sites, among others. The study by Davison et al. (2011) describes issues associated with using social networking websites for recruiting, staffing/selection, and discipline/termination, and provides recommendations for future research studies in this area. Clark and Roberts (2010) found that employers were making decisions not to hire people based on the information posted on social networking sites. Few employers have policies in place to govern when and how these online character checks should be used and how to ensure that the information viewed is accurate. They explored how these inexpensive, informal online character checks are harmful to society.

Based on those studies, one of the important outcomes of social media is sharing information and knowledge based on social networking. If people use general social media and learn the usefulness for knowledge sharing before using social media at work place, they may expect strong value of using social media in the workplace.

Social Media and Consumers

Social media is used so much in the area of marketing to consumers. Schmidt and Ralph (2012) found that companies need to be able to determine which of the different social media the company should or should not use in marketing their products, services, and/or company. One of the most important uses of social media sites is data collection. It not only provides companies with the ability to obtain massive amounts of information from a wide range of places about their products, services, and company, it also gives them valuable information about their competitors. Divol et al. (2012) proposed a model where social media can be used to develop a customer-oriented process for marketing and sales. The important aspect of this research is the involvement of both consumers and employees at each level and that customers will provide feedback to employees in order to make changes in brand and product. Social media is also used in customer relationship management to connect with consumers and to get feedback.

Social customer relationship management (SCRM) is also a remarkable concept in marketing area. Kotadia (2009) defined social CRM as "the business strategy of engaging customers through social media with a goal of building trust and brand loyalty." Loyalty is an attitude towards a brand that inclines a customer to repurchase it and/or recommend it to others. Social CRM and social media are more about building trust and managing loyalty with customers than about managing relationships or transactions. Greenberg (2009) also found that customer relationship management is not a technology, but a philosophy and business strategy with business rules, processes and social characteristics to support a collaborative environment with the customer. Woodcock, Green, and Starkey (2011) discussed three hurdles of SCRM which pioneers in large companies faced; (1) organizational readiness, (2) over-hype and over-expectation and (3) project management failings. Research by Baird and Parasnis (2011) clarified perception gaps between consumer and business executives showing that companies have some misperceptions regarding why consumers interact with them via social media. However Woodcock et al. (2011) found that the benefits are centered on 'customer engagement' and are not peripheral but fundamental to driving business performance. In addition, SCRM can deliver insight that will help drive real customer centric innovation.

Corporate Social Responsibility

Kaupins and Park (2010) found that corporate social networking sites provide employees and employers with considerable opportunity to share information and become friends. Unfortunately, American and international laws do not directly address social networking site usage. The National Labor Relations Act, civil rights laws, and various common law doctrines such as employment at-will and defamation provides the pattern for future social networking laws. Ethical considerations such as productivity, security, goodwill, privacy, accuracy, and discipline fairness also affect future laws. Corporate policies on corporate social networking should balance the employer and employee's interests. Existing laws and ethical issues associated with social networking should impact social networking policies related to configuration, communication, discipline, and evaluation of policies. Chen (2009) examined the growing importance of networks for businesses and found that there are few theoretical studies on the social responsibilities of businesses in such networks, and how these responsibilities are affected by different types of networks.

Cross Country Aspects of Social Media at Workplace

Large global companies introduce social media for business in order to understand and help employees work with country difference of social media. We believe, as other researchers have found, that country differences might have an influence the development of consumers' personalities, which can, in turn, impact the formulation of innate differences, such as innovativeness. Kim, Benedetto and Lancioni (2011) found that consumer innovativeness, defined as the predisposition to buy new things, can differ from one country or culture to another. They found that the generic socio-psychological trait dimension of consumer innovativeness was influenced by the country; whereas the product difference dimension did not have an impact. Further, they found that United States consumers had a higher level of innovativeness than both Korean and Chinese consumers.

The value of more cross-national research in technology acceptance is increasing in the inevitable trend of globalization of markets. Many studies have found that cultural factors influence technology development adoption, system usage, task outcomes, mobile application development and technology management (Baker, Al-Gahtani & Hubona, 2010; Hung, Kang, Yen, Huang & Chen, 2012; Sherer, Kohli, Yao & Cederlund, 2011). Hofstede, Hofstede, and Minkov's work (2010) focused on the cultural dimensions of individualism, power distance, masculinity, uncertainty avoidance and long-term orientation. Individualism is defined as the degree to which a society emphasizes the role of the individual. Uncertainty avoidance is the extent to which people feel threatened by unstructured and ambiguity. Uncertainty avoidance might be a similar construct to risk avoidance and may influence the degree of consumer innovativeness. Pookulangare and Koesler (2011) found culture as a moderating variable on perceived ease of use to intention to use social networks. In an earlier study, Amoroso and Ogawa (2013) also found that perceived ease of use was statistically significant with consumers in the United States, whereas Japanese consumers did not feel the influence of complexity of mobile applications, instead rather enjoyed solving problems related to learning how to use such applications.

We found a number of similar studies analyzing the constructs in our model, examining technology adoption across multiple cultures in two or more countries. For example, Baker et al (2010) found a relationship between social influence factors and cognitive instrumental factors affecting technology adoption in Saudi Arabia. Hung et al. (2012) studied the use of email and instant messaging within Taiwan and United States and found that culture and communication tools jointly affect communication outcome variables individually. Huy et al. (2012) investigated e-commerce adoption by small and medium size enterprises (SMEs) in transition economies, such as Vietnam, finding a positive relationship between attitudes of managers towards innovation and adoption. Shin (2010) conducted a cross-cultural validation of technology adoption between Korea and the United States and found that differences were identified in terms of intrinsic and extrinsic dimensions and can be inferred that user's motivation in different contexts are an important explanatory variable when determining cross-national SNS site usage. Pookulangara and Koesler (2011) used individualism, uncertainty avoidance and long-term orientation as tree culture dimensions to design their cross-cultural research model. Hung et al (2012) focused on especially individualism/collectivism to analyze culture dimension of communication between U.S. and Taiwan. Shin and Choo (2012) conducted a survey in

Figure 1. Research model

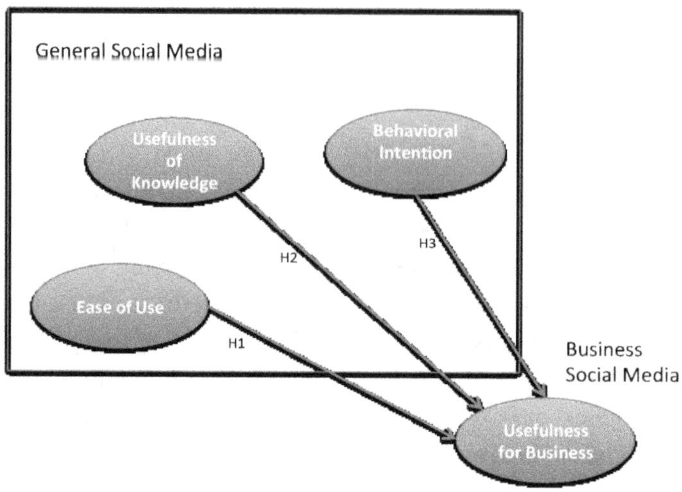

the United States and Korea to clarify country-specific differences in product value perceptions based on TRA and Hofstede et al.'s dimensions.

RESEARCH QUESTIONS AND HYPOTHESES

Based on existing studies, we sought to clarify the experience of general social media users, the expectation for workplace social media, and the country difference of the social media acceptance. This study focuses on experience levels of general social media perceptions and country difference. After review of previous models and their supported hypotheses on social media use and benefits in the workplace, we have developed the following research questions below and research model (see Figure 1). It was found that experience is important predictor of ease of use and usefulness (Venkatesh, 2000). They focused on understanding the determinants of perceived ease of use and usefulness and found a direct relationship between experience and ease of use. However they did not find that experience levels had any impact on the user's perception on usefulness.

We feel that experience may have a positive impact on not only ease of use but on usefulness with respect to social media adoption because social media users can learn not only how to use social media, but also how useful social media can be when users experience the communication and collection useful knowledge using social media. Therefore we hypothesize that the experience for social media utilization may have a direct effect on the expectation of usefulness for social media at the workplace.

RQ1: How does the experience of general social media impact on the expectation of usefulness for business?

People who use general social media can learn how to use social media in the workplace when they start to perceive that general social media is easy to use. Additionally, when they start to perceive that social media is useful and intend to use social media more, they will move over the application of social media to the workplace. It is possible that people who perceived ease of use for general social media expect usefulness for not only general social media but also for workplace social media.

H1: Ease of use for general social media will impact on the expectation of usefulness for business.

It is possible that people who perceived usefulness for general social media expect usefulness for social media at the workplace, especially the perception of usefulness for knowledge sharing may have strong impacts on expectation for usefulness for business.

H2: Usefulness for knowledge sharing in general social media will impact on the expectation of usefulness for business.

Based on the TAM model, ease of use and usefulness tend to have an impact on behavioral intention. Therefore, it is possible that people who intend to use social media expect usefulness for social media at workplace are based on their high perception of ease of use and usefulness. But the relationship between the behavioral intention and usefulness for business could be a spurious correlation because of the ease of use and the usefulness constructs.

H3: Behavioral intention for general social media will not impact on the expectation of usefulness for business.

According to the research about self-esteem, the level of self-esteem in North American is higher than Japan (Heine, et al. 2010). The self-esteem construct is a closely related concept to self-efficacy (Judge, Erez, Bono & Thoresen, 2002), and the self-efficacy concept is closely related to the concept of the ease of use (Clark & Roberts, 2010). Pookulangare and Koesler (2011) focused on a social networking environment and proposed the cultural difference had effect on self-efficacy, and the positive relationship between the self-efficacy and perceived ease of use based on some previous research studies (Das & Sahoo, 1989, Schmidt and Ralph, 2011).

We think that it is possible that level of the ease of use in the United States is higher than Japan, and the difference may have impact on the difference of causal models. The result is that it matters more in the Japanese culture because the consumers like complex applications. Hofstede, et al. (2010) found that countries that had a lower power-distance index, such as the United States rather than Japan, showed more of a need for self-expression and independence. They also found that countries that had more of an individualistic orientation (like the United States) rather than a more collectivistic culture would have a higher self-efficacy need and potentially a higher need for ease of use. Furthermore, the popular social media platform in the United States is different from Japan.

RQ2: How does the impact of ease of use differ from Japanese to United States because of cultural, technological and market reasons?

The research model in this study is a composition of variables and relationships in order to understand the theoretical underpinnings of the research model. Users' attitudes toward usefulness of knowledge was employed as an antecedent determinant that generated differences in behavioral intention and usefulness for business between American and Japanese social media users in this study. Ease of use in general social media and usefulness for collective knowledge in general social media was employed as an antecedent determinant that generate differences in behavioral intention in general social media and usefulness in business between American and Japanese social media users in this study (see Figure 1). We used the measure of usefulness for collective knowledge instead of the popular usefulness measure (Clark & Roberts, 2010); because collective intelligence is one of the business benefits, found by Amoroso and Orita (2010) and the experience of collecting useful knowledge in general social media may have an effect on expectation of social media for business.

METHODOLOGY

A survey to investigate the impact of social media in the workplace was developed using Survey-Monkey with twelve specific questions as derived from Amoroso et al. (2011), Amoroso and Orita (2010), and Ogawa, Amoroso, Mukahi, Tanabu, & Sato (2012). We adapted technology acceptance measures and developed new measures which are ease of use for general social media, usefulness for collective knowledge in general, behavioral intention in general social media, and usefulness for business social media. Reliability was checked by Cronbach Alpha and the construct validity by factor analysis. The survey was conducted at multiple universities with working students in the United States and Japan with 440 respondents completing the online survey. After considering response bias, 406 responses were utilized, yielding a 92.4% completion or usability rate with responses in Japan (n=210) and the United States (n=196). Although working university students comprised the primary sample, we observed the relationship between general social media experience and expectation of social media at work place. If we apply non-student office workers to the sample, we believe it is difficult to distinguish the effect of general social media experience from the effect of work place social media experience.

We looked at the types of reasons organizations why workers use social media, types of social media, and the purpose of social media use for respondents located in the United States and Japan (see Tables 1-4). We found that the most utilized social media was externally-focused toward the consumer, and the least utilized was the internally-focused employee social media. In both the United States and Japan, there was a high expected of social media for advertising products and/or services (78.6% in total). Consumer research (54.9%) was the second heaviest usage of social media in organizations followed by acquiring potential customers, which was significantly higher in the United States (63.3%). In general, marketing uses of social media were very strong.

The area of social media expectation that we are most interested in for this study is the internal corporate use of social media, the building of communities (31.5%) and meetings online (22.7%). Compared with the Japanese sample, the United States sample tended to use social networking sites and chat functions in order to communicate with friends outside of their own country (57.1% versus 17.6%). In both countries, business use of

Table 1. Comparison of social media means: Uses of social media

	Japan *n = 210*	US *n = 196*	Total *n = 406*	t-Test
Advertising	85.2	71.4	78.6	**
Research on users	52.9	57.1	54.9	*
Potential customers	30.0	63.3	46.1	**
Meetings online	17.6	28.1	22.7	**
Recruiting and hiring	36.7	39.8	38.2	*
Advertising	37.1	38.3	37.7	
Communities	29.0	34.2	31.5	*
Service provider	34.3	31.1	32.8	*

** t-test < 0.05, ** < 0.01*

Table 2. Comparison of social media means: Types of social media

	Japan *n = 210*	US *n = 196*	Total *n = 406*	t-Test
Social networking site	58.6	90.8	74.1	**
Blog	38.6	20.9	30.0	**
Chat	11.0	37.2	23.6	**
Photovideosharing	26.7	23.5	25.1	*
Message board	20.0	21.9	20.9	
Microblog	9.5	6.1	7.9	*

** t-test < 0.05, ** < 0.01*

Table 3. Comparison of social media means: Purposes of social media

	Japan *n = 210*	US *n = 196*	Total *n = 406*	t-Test
Pesonal use	80.1	69.4	74.9	**
Business use	19.4	28.0	23.5	**
Both	0.5	2.7	1.6	

** t-test < 0.05, ** < 0.01*

Table 4. Comparison of social media means: Reasons for using social media

	Japan *n = 210*	US *n = 196*	Total *n = 406*	t-Test
Friends in country	83.3	19.9	52.7	**
Friends in outside	17.6	57.1	36.7	**
Business in countriy	3.3	3.6	3.4	
Business in outside	1.9	11.2	6.4	**
Marketing	2.9	6.6	4.7	*
potential customers	1.4	5.6	3.4	*

** t-test < 0.05, ** < 0.01*

social media (23.5%) was far lower than personal use (74.9%). It is this area of social media use that we want to explore further in this research.

ANALYSIS

Measurement Model Evaluation

We found strong support for construct validity and reliability by examining Cronbach alpha reliability coefficients and by confirmatory factor analysis. The measurement scales for this instrument showed strong psychometric properties. All measurement scales showed relatively high Cronbach alpha coefficients (see Table 5) at α>=0.70 for all the measures with the exception of ease of use and usefulness for collecting knowledge in Japanese which is slightly below the lower bounds set for this study, near the α>=0.70. This pattern of high scale reliability is consistent with much of the prior research dealing with the technology acceptance model.

Average variance extracted (AVE), for assessing convergent and discriminant validity (Fornell and Larcker, 1981) is the sum of squared standardized loadings divided by the sum of squared standardized loadings plus the sum of indicator measurement error. Discriminant validity analysis refers to testing statistically whether two constructs differ; convergent validity tests through measuring the internal consistency within one construct, as Cronbach's alpha does, indicators for different constructs should not be so highly correlated as to lead one to conclude that they measure the same thing. This would happen if there were definitional overlaps between constructs. The average variance extracted (AVE) estimate (which measures the amount of variance captured by a construct in relation to the variance due to random measurement error, ranged from 0.312 to 0.898 for United States and Japanese participants. Convergent validity requires that AVE should be greater than 0.5. However, AVE score of Japanese usefulness for collective knowledge is low and the convergent validity of the measure is low. Discriminant validity requires that AVE should be greater than their squared correlation between two constructs. We calculated the squared correlation between each factors (see Table 6). For the Japanese sample, the squared correlation between ease of use and usefulness for business is lower

Table 5. Measurement model statistics

	Japan Sample			United States Sample		
Observed Indicator	Factor loadings	AVE	Cronbach alpha	Factor loadings	AVE	Cronbach alpha
My interaction with Social Media is clear and understandable.	0.574	0.461	0.612	0.781	0.67	0.796
I believe that it is easy to get Social Media to do what I want it to do	0.770			0.854		
Social Media aggregates individual actions into meaningful collective results.	0.482	0.312	0.686	0.704	0.662	0.905
Conversation in Social Media helps me generate ideas	0.613			0.836		
Social Media allows me to collaborate with others in cocreation of blogs, photos, similar projects.videos, and	0.444			0.804		
Social Media allows collective action to provide meaningful results	0.572			0.872		
Social Media facilitates sustained collaboration around a shared idea	0.652			0.842		
I intend to use Social Media in the next 3months.	0.964	0.873	0.953	0.949	0.898	0.963
I predict I would use Social Media in the next 3months.	0.940			0.969		
I plan to use Social Media in the next 3months.	0.898			0.925		
Using Social Media in my job would enable me to accomplish tasks more quickly	0.704	0.555	0.875	0.848	0.835	0.968
Using Social Media would improve my job performance	0.733			0.930		
Using Social Media in my job would increase my productivity.	0.828			0.949		
Using Social Media would enhance my effectiveness on the job.	0.838			0.957		
Using Social Media would make it easier to do my job.	0.554			0.913		
I would find Social Media useful in my job.	0.775			0.880		

Table 6. Squared correlations between each of the constructs

Japan	EOU	UK	BI	UB
EOU	0.461			
UK	0.277	0.312		
BI	0.049	0.114	0.873	
UB	0.734	0.192	0.062	0.555

USA	EOU	UK	BI	UB
EOU	0.670			
UK	0.263	0.662		
BI	0.265	0.172	0.898	
UB	0.073	0.329	0.027	0.835

**Scores on diagonal are AVE*

*Scores on diagonal are AVE

than AVE. We also found that the discriminant validity between ease of use and usefulness for business in Japan is low.

Measurement Equivalence Across Groups

The multiple group invariance tests have been suggested as a reliable method for determining measurement equivalent in a cross-cultural study (Myers, Calantone, Page & Taylor, 2000). This study undertook an application of multiple group invariance tests to determine the measurement equivalence between Japanese and United States samples. The chi-square difference tests and overall model fit indices were used to evaluate overall measurement structure consistency in this study.

We conducted the multiple group invariance tests for social media use samples across the countries of Japan and the United States, using a confirmatory factor analysis for Japan and United States individually. Second, the configural model was constructed and then we constrained all factor loadings between the two countries shown as invariance. Third, we calculated the difference between the configural and invariance models showing the difference (p-value). By examining the results of the chi-square difference test of factor invariance model against a configural model and model fit indices' changes, this study revealed the factor invariance model had a slight change in the model fit indices compared to the configural model for social media use. The results do not show significance at $p < 0.05$ and indicates that the factor correlations are invariant across the two countries. The data demonstrated that the measurements were invariant across the two country subjects, thus enabling the researchers to proceed to the structural model evaluation. We built the measures based on the results of confirmatory factor analysis and use the measures as variables for the structural model.

Hypotheses Testing

We generated two regression models for usefulness in business, one for Japan and the other for the United States sample. Table 7 provides the regression coefficients for each country's regression model. Both regression models showed strong

Table 7. Regression models for usefulness in business

	Japan			USA		
	Standardized Coefficients	t	p	Standardized Coefficients	t	p
EOU	0.285	3.890	0.000	-0.050	-0.663	0.508
UK	0.174	2.403	0.017	0.579	8.392	0.000
BI	0.083	1.238	0.217	-0.021	-0.285	0.776
R2	0.188			0.304		
Adjusted R2	0.176			0.293		
F	15.919			27.924		
p	0.000			0.000		

F-statistics at 15.919 and 27.924 respectively. The adjusted R^2 for the Japanese model is 17.6% and for the United States model 29.3%, showing the amount of variance explained. For the Japanese model, ease of use was found to be statistically significant in explaining usefulness in business ($p<0.000$). However, we did not find ease of use to be significant in the United States to explaining the usefulness of social media in business. Usefulness for knowledge of social media was found to be extremely significant ($P<0.000$) in the United States sample, but only mildly significant in the Japan sample ($p<0.017$). Behavioral intention to use social media was not found to be significant for either the Japanese or United States model.

Japan

We found that ease of use has significant impacts on usefulness in business; therefore H1 is supported. Since usefulness for knowledge sharing has significant positive impacts on usefulness in business, H2 is also supported. Since behavioral intention does not have significant impact on usefulness in business, H3 is supported.

United States

We found that ease of use does not have significant impact on usefulness in business; therefore H1 is not supported. Since usefulness for knowledge sharing has significant positive impacts on usefulness in business, H2 is supported. Since behavioral intention does not have significant impact on usefulness in business, H3 is supported.

Differences between Japan and the United States

Ease of use is a construct that has often been found to have a difference between the two countries (Amoroso & Ogawa, 2013). Because ease of use is a significant factor with Japanese consumers, we posit that the culture of Japan is much more technical than the United States, and as such Japanese consumers tend to view more complex applications as desirable and useful for working. We might even say that the more complex the social media application, the more useful for business. Social media usefulness for knowledge was found to be important to both the United States and Japan in terms of its impact on usefulness for business.

DISCUSSION

Significant Findings

In Japan, ease of use and usefulness for collective knowledge in general social media are predictors of usefulness for business social media. On the other hand, in the United States sample, only the usefulness for collective knowledge is a strong predictor of usefulness for business. These results mean, if the United States sample experienced that they could collect useful information in Facebook or another social media, they expect that social media is also useful in the business situation. In contrast, for Japanese respondents, not only collecting information but also perceived ease of use for Mixi, which is a popular social media in Japan, or another social media, are important for expectation for business social media. If Japanese companies apply social media at the work place, employees' perception of ease of use for general social media may be important. The difference of the two countries may be related to the difference of the score of ease of use. Our findings showed that usefulness for knowledge and ease of use scores are higher than Japan. Most usefulness for knowledge respondents perceive high ease of use for social media, therefore the ease of use may not important predictor of usefulness for business.

The results show that ease of use and usefulness for knowledge sharing using general social media has an impact on usefulness for business in Japan. In the United States, ease of use has an impact on usefulness for business. These results mean that the experience levels of general social media use enhances the expectation of social media for business. If an organization considers introducing social media for business, the organization should encourage employees to use social media effectively in their personal lives before introducing social media in the business units.

The results show that the impacts of ease of use differ from Japanese and the United States. In Japan, ease of use and usefulness for collective knowledge in general social media are predictors of usefulness for business social media. On the other hand, in the United States, only the usefulness for collective knowledge is a strong predictor of usefulness for business. These results mean, if the United States respondents could collect useful information in Facebook or another social media, they expect that social media is also useful in the business situation. In contrast, for Japanese, not only collecting information but also perceived ease of use for Mixi, which is a popular social media in Japan, or another social media are important for expectation for business social media. If Japanese companies apply social media at the work place, employees' perception of ease of use for general social media may be important.

Usefulness of the Findings

In the results of the factor analysis, the discriminant validity between ease of use and usefulness in the Japanese simple is lower than expected. For the Japanese employee, ease of use and usefulness for business might be almost one construct. However, our study shows that the causal structure is different between Japan and the United States, maybe due to cultural issues. In the results of factor analysis for the Japanese employee, the convergent validity for usefulness of collective knowledge is low. It is possible that, for Japanese respondents, meaning or role of collecting knowledge is different for United States respondents. In the summary of the reason for using social media, United States employees tended to use social media for communication with other persons who live overseas. The United States respondents have weaker but more diversified networks than the Japanese respondents. Granovetter (1973) argued that weak ties build wider relationships and are more effective for gathering diversified information. They may use the weak but diversified network for gathering diversified information and knowledge, and they perceived that social media was useful for collecting knowledge.

The question as to why the difference of ease of use exists between Japan and United States might be the effect on the difference of ease of use as a strong predictor for usefulness and self-esteem. In general, self-esteem of the United States respondents is higher than Japanese respondents and the difference may be reflected in ease of use. We found that in previous research (Amoroso and Ogawa, 2013) that self-efficacy, perception of external control, computer anxiety, perceived enjoyment and objective usability have strong effects on ease of use. The cultural, technological and market difference of social media between Japan and the United States for usefulness for knowledge may influence those predictor variables, and the predictor variables may also influence ease of use. These differences might have an impact on those predictors of ease of use. This study showed that general social media experience has an effect on perception of usefulness of social media for business. The relationship between experience and usefulness in social media is different from normal application software. This study also showed if companies introduce social media for business and their employees have a lot of experience with using social media, they might not be requested to provide much training for their employees.

Limitations

One of limitations of this study is related to the sample as we could not assess how the respondent was working. Because the sample contained some student respondents, we feel that those participants may not have had full-time employment, which might yield different results. We plan to conduct an additional study that will survey business employees directly in the organization. One reason for the lower convergent validity of the Japanese sample for usefulness for collective knowledge could be because this study did not use the normal usefulness measure but a measure of usefulness for collective knowledge. Collective knowledge is one of salient effects of social media. In future research, we will use another measure of usefulness and confirm these results. Also the discriminant validity between ease of use and usefulness in Japanese is low. Even though we found a significant path from ease of use to usefulness, we believe that both variables might be contained within one construct. The types of use of social media are different between Japan and United States samples. Even though cultural differences might be related to the selection of social media, we plan to select one type of social media and conduct an additional survey.

FUTURE RESEARCH

In this study, we conducted analysis using regression analysis. However, previous research showed that ease of use has an impact on behavioral intention through usefulness. We plan to confirm the relationship between those three constructs and usefulness in business using Structural Equation Modeling. Future research efforts will include examining social networking systems in specific organizations to ascertain how they are developed and how their configuration affects utilization. We would like to develop a specific employee adoption model for corporate-sponsored social networking systems to better understand why certain employees would use these systems and why others hesitate or find them not useful. In future studies, we plan to integrate the trust construct into further data collection efforts in order to analyze the impact of trust on social network system adoption within the workplace. As discussed above, the difference of ease of use is a key issue. The difference of how to use, purpose of use, kinds of social media and so on may effect on ease of use. We plan to analyze the causal model with these variables.

ACKNOWLEDGMENT

This study was partially supported by Japan Society of Promotion of Science KAKENHI (2530409) and with the help of the International Center for Innovation in Technologies (ICIT) at Kennesaw State University. We would like to thank all the above in writing.

REFERENCES

Amoroso, D., Amoroso, N., & Orita, A. (2011). Social Media Use by American-born versus Japanese-born Respondents: Is There a Difference? In Proceedings of National Conference JASMIN 2011. Matsuyama, Japan: Japan Society for Management Information.

Amoroso, D., & Orita, A. (2010). A Study of Anonymity of Social Media Use in Japan and the United States. In Proceedings of National Conference JASMIN 2010. Matsuyama, Japan: Japan Society for Management Information.

Amoroso, D. L., & Ogawa, M. (2013). Comparing Mobile and PC Internet Adoption Factors of Loyalty and Satisfaction with Online Shopping Consumers. *International Journal of E-Business Research*, *9*(2), 24–45. doi:10.4018/jebr.2013040103

Annetta, L. (2008). Video games in education: Why they should be used and how they are being used. *Theory into Practice*, *47*(3), 229–239. doi:10.1080/00405840802153940

Baird, C., & Parasnis, G. (2011). From social media to social customer relationship management. *Strategy and Leadership*, *39*(5), 30–37. doi:10.1108/10878571111161507

Baker, E. W., Al-Gahtani, S. S., & Hubona, G. S. (2010). Cultural impacts on acceptance and adoption of information technology in a developing Country. *Journal of Global Information Management*, *18*(3), 35–58. doi:10.4018/jgim.2010070102

Bennett, J., Owers, M., Pitt, M., & Tucker, M. (2010). Workplace impact of social networking. *Property Management*, *28*(3), 138–148. doi:10.1108/02637471011051282

Chen, S. (2009). Corporate Responsibilities in Internet-Enabled Social Networks. *Journal of Business Ethics*, *90*(S4), 523–536. doi:10.1007/s10551-010-0604-0

Clark, L., & Roberts, S. (2010). Employer's Use of Social Networking Sites: A Socially Irresponsible Practice. *Journal of Business Ethics*, *95*(4), 507–525. doi:10.1007/s10551-010-0436-y

Das, B., & Sahoo, J. (2011). Social Networking Sites – A Critical Analysis of Its Impact on Personal and Social Life. *International Journal of Business and Social Science*, *2*(14), 222–228.

Davis, F. (1989). Perceived usefulness, perceived ease of use, and user acceptance of information technology. *Management Information Systems Quarterly*, *13*(3), 319–340. doi:10.2307/249008

Davis, F., & Venkatesh, V. (2004). Toward Pre-prototype User Acceptance Testing of New Information Systems: Implications for Software Project Management. *IEEE Transactions on Engineering Management*, *51*(1), 31–46. doi:10.1109/TEM.2003.822468

Davison, H., Maraist, C., & Bing, M. (2011). Friend or Foe? The Promise and Pitfalls of Using Social Networking Sites for HR Decisions. *Journal of Business and Psychology*, *26*(2), 153–159. doi:10.1007/s10869-011-9215-8

Divol, R., Edelman, D., & Sarrazin, H. (2012). Demystifying social media. *McKinsey Quarterly*. Retrieved September 13, 2013, from http://www.mckinsey.com/insights/marketing_sales/demystifying_social_media

Edosomwan, S., Prakasan, K., Kouame, D., Watson, J., & Seymour, T. (2011). The History of Social Media and its Impact on Business. *Journal of Applied Management and Entrepreneurship*, *16*(3), 79–91.

Fornell, C., & Larcker, D. (1981). Evaluating Structural Equation Models with Unobservable Variables and Measurement Error. *JMR, Journal of Marketing Research*, *18*(1), 39–50. doi:10.2307/3151312

Granovetter, M. (1973). The Strength of Weak Ties. *American Journal of Sociology*, *78*(6), 1360–1380. doi:10.1086/225469

Greenberg, P. (2009). Time to Put a Stake in the Ground on Social CRM. *PGreenblog*. Retrieved from http://the56group.typepad.com/pgreenblog/2009/07/time-to-put-a-stake-in-the-ground-on-social-crm.html

Hathi, S. (2010). How social networking increase collaboration at IBM. *SCM Features*, *14*(1), 32–35.

Heine, S., Lehman, D., Markus, H., & Kitayama, S. (2010). Is there a universal need for positive self-regard? *Psychological Review*, *106*(4), 766–794. doi:10.1037/0033-295X.106.4.766 PMID:10560328

Hofstede, G., Hofstede, G., & Minkov, M. (2010). *Cultures and Organizations: Software of the Mind*. New York: McGraw-Hill.

Hsu, C., & Lin, J. (2008). Acceptance of blog usage: The roles of technology acceptance, social influence and knowledge sharing motivation. *Information & Management*, *45*(1), 65–74. doi:10.1016/j.im.2007.11.001

Hung, S.-Y., Kang, T.-C., Yen, D. C., Huang, A. H., & Chen, K. (2012). A Cross-Cultural Analysis of Communication Tools and Communication Outcomes. *Journal of Global Information Management*, *20*(3), 55–83. doi:10.4018/jgim.2012070103

Judge, T., Erez, A., Bono, J., & Thoresen, C. (2002). Are measures of self-esteem, neuroticisocial media, locus of control, and generalized self-efficacy indicators of a common core construct? *Journal of Personality and Social Psychology*, *83*(3), 693–710. doi:10.1037/0022-3514.83.3.693 PMID:12219863

Kalamas, M., Mitchell, T., & Lester, D. (2009). Modeling social media use: Bridging the communication gap in higher education. *Journal of Advertising Education*, *13*(1), 44–57.

Kane, K., Robinson-Combre, J., & Berge, Z. (2010). Tapping into social networking: Collaborating enhances both knowledge management and e-learning. *Journal of Information and Knowledge Management Systems*, *40*(1), 62–70.

Kaplan, A., & Haenlein, M. (2010). Users of the world, unite! The challenges and opportunities of Social Media. *Business Horizons*, *53*(1), 59–68. doi:10.1016/j.bushor.2009.09.003

Kaupins, G., & Park, S. (2010). Legal and Ethical Implications of Corporate Social Networks. *Employee Responsibilities and Rights Journal*, *23*(2), 83–99. doi:10.1007/s10672-010-9149-8

Kim, W., Benedetto, C. A. D., & Lancioni, R. A. (2011). The effects of country and gender differences on consumer innovativeness and decision processes in a highly globalized high-tech product market. *Asia Pacific Journal of Marketing and Logistics*, *23*(5), 714–744. doi:10.1108/13555851111183101

Kiron, D., Palmer, A., Phillips, N., & Kruschwitz, N. (2012a). What Managers Really Think About Social Business. *MIT Sloan Management Review*, *53*(4), 51–60.

Kiron, D., Palmer, A., Phillips, N., & Kruschwitz, N. (2012b). Social Business: What Companies Really Doing?, *MIT Sloan Management Review Research Report*.

Kotadia, H. (2009). *Definition: What is Social CRM?* Social CRM and Business.

Lee, W., Xiongb, L., & Hu, C. (2012). The Effect of Facebook Users' Arousal and Valence on Intention to Go to the Festival: Applying an Extension of the Technology Acceptance Model. *International Journal of Hospitality Management*, *31*(3), 819–827. doi:10.1016/j.ijhm.2011.09.018

Leng, G. S., Lada, S., & Muhammad, M. Z. (2011). An Exploration of Social Networking Sites (SNS) Adoption in Malaysia Using Technology Acceptance Model (TAM), Theory of Planned Behavior (TPB) and Intrinsic Motivation. *Journal of Internet Banking and Commerce*, *16*(2), 2–27.

Lin, F., Liu, C.-W., & Kuo, I.-H. (2013). Moderating Effect of Perceived Usefulness on the Relationship between Ease of Use, Attitude toward Use and Actual System Use. *International Journal of Organizational Innovation*, *5*(3), 180–191.

Lin, K.-Y., & Lu, H.-P. (2011). Why People Use Social Networking Sites: An Empirical Study Integrating Network Externalities and Motivation Theory. *Computers in Human Behavior*, *27*(3), 1152–1161. doi:10.1016/j.chb.2010.12.009

Moore, G., & Benbasat, I. (1991). Development of an Instrument to Measure the Perceptions of Adopting New Information Technology Innovation. *Information Systems Research*, *2*(3), 192–222. doi:10.1287/isre.2.3.192

Myers, M., Calantone, R., Page, T. Jr, & Taylor, C. (2000). Academic Insights: An Application of Multiple-Group Causal Models in Assessing Cross-Cultural Measurement Equivalence. *Journal of International Marketing*, *8*(4), 108–121. doi:10.1509/jimk.8.4.108.19790

Ogawa, M., Amoroso, D., Mukahi, T., Tanabu, M., & Sato, O. (2012). Social Media Use at Work: Comparison of the United States and Japan. In *Proceedings of National Conference JASMIN 2012*. Tokyo, Japan: Japan Society for Management Information.

Pookulangare, S., & Koesler, K. (2011). Cultural influence on consumers' usage of social networks and its impact on online purchase intentions. *Journal of Retailing and Consumer Services*, *18*(4), 348–354. doi:10.1016/j.jretconser.2011.03.003

Robinson, S. (2006). Using games and clickers to encourage students to study and participate. *Academy of Educational Leadership*, *11*(2), 25–29.

Schmidt, S., & Ralph, D. (2011). Social Media: More Available Marketing Tools. *Business Review (Federal Reserve Bank of Philadelphia)*, *18*(2), 37–43.

Shaw, S., & Fairhurst, D. (2008). Engaging a new generation of graduates. *Education + Training*, *50*(5), 366–378. doi:10.1108/00400910810889057

Sherer, S. A., Kohli, R., Yao, Y., & Cederlund, J. (2011). Do Cultural Differences Matter in IT Implementation? A Multinational's Experience with Collaborative Technology. *Journal of Global Information Management*, *19*(4), 1–17. doi:10.4018/jgim.2011100101

Venkatesh, V. (2000). Determinants of perceived ease of use: Integrating control, intrinsic motivation, and emotion into the technology acceptance model. *Information Systems Research*, *11*(4), 342–365. doi:10.1287/isre.11.4.342.11872

Venkatesh, V., & Davis, F. (1996). A model of the antecedents of perceived ease of use: Development and test. *Decision Sciences*, *27*(3), 451–481. doi:10.1111/j.1540-5915.1996.tb01822.x

Williamson, B. (2009, July 24). Managing at a distance. *Business Week*.

Woodcock, N., Green, A., & Starkey, M. (2011). Social CRM as a business strategy. *Journal of Database Marketing & Customer Strategy Management*, *18*(1), 50–64. doi:10.1057/dbm.2011.7

Yang, K., & Jolly, L. (2009). The Effects of Consumer Perceived Value and Subjective Norm on Mobile Data Service Adoption between American and Korean Consumers. *Journal of Retailing and Consumer Services*, *16*(6), 502–508. doi:10.1016/j.jretconser.2009.08.005

KEY TERMS AND DEFINITIONS

Behavioral Intention to Use Social Media: The perceptual measure of intention of workplace employees to use social media.

Business Use of Social Media: Use of social media based systems to achieve business goals and objectives, such as for marketing tools.

Collective Knowledge: Knowledge gained by adding two or more people's knowledge together.

Corporate Social Networking: The use of social media to support and enhance an organization's commitment to corporate social responsibility.

Corporate-Sponsored Social Media: Organizational approved and developed internal social media systems for employees.

Cross Country Aspects of Social Media: The differences between countries in the use of social media.

Cultural Aspects of Social Media: The infusion of cultural factors, such as individualism or long-term planning, on the use of social media.

Ease of Use: The lack of difficulty using social media programs and systems.

Expectation of Social Media Use: The predication of social media in the workplace to enhance job performance.

General Social Media: Social media that is used in the private sector by most consumers.

Social Media Systems: Internally developed social media-based information systems that are corporately maintained.

Team Enhancement: Ability to improve a team's overall performance using social media tools.

Usefulness for Knowledge: The ability of social media in the workplace to enhanced knowledge of one or more employees by sharing ideas.

Workplace Social Media: Social media used solely in the workplace by employees.

Chapter 3
Influence of Corporate Social Media in Strategic Decision Processes

S. Venkataraman
Indian Institute of Management Calcutta, India

Ranjan Das
Indian Institute of Management Calcutta, India

ABSTRACT

This chapter discusses conceptually with some anecdotal evidence how social media engagement by business firms can influence their strategic decision making. It suggests a model of influence and proposes a knowledge integration mechanism through which such influence materializes. Social media engagement by business firms has been steadily on the rise, with its application extending to a range of corporate functions beyond marketing and customer engagement, many of which can be construed as strategic. However, the potential influence of social media on strategy process or strategic decision making has not been fully explored. In addressing this gap, this chapter conceptually explores the likely influence of social media on the issue of strategic decision making and the mechanism of such influence. Embellished by some illustrative anecdotes from practice, this chapter suggests a plausible model whereby corporate social media engagement influences the strategy process in firms through the three key dimensions – environmental factors, strategic characteristics, and decision issue characteristics. In particular, social media engagement is conceived as ingraining knowledge creation and integration through socialization within an extended value network.

INTRODUCTION

The phenomenon of social media (SM) – manifest through internet based platforms such as Twitter, Facebook, Youtube, MySpace, Pinterest and other such platforms has grown exponentially across the world. This is particularly true for the current young and middle-aged population, who also hold significant spending power. Although SM platforms were initially more popular as avenues for personal level social networking and entertainment, in recent years SM has evolved to

DOI: 10.4018/978-1-4666-6182-0.ch003

become a part of a firm's operating environment, both external and internal. This is borne out by the increasing number of firms who appear to be engaging and investing in SM. According to an annual survey conducted by Burson-Marsteller (2012), the number of firms among Fortune 100 companies engaging in SM has steadily increased year on year to a level of 87% in 2011. In this context, this chapter explores whether and how this evolving environmental force could be an influence which can shape a firm's strategic agenda or strategic decision making - an agenda seen as pertinent to strategy process research (Hutzschenreuter & Kleindienst, 2006).

The increasing SM engagement by businesses has prompted the proliferation of several practitioner oriented books and internet web-logs (blogs) by several consultants and self-styled experts, as well as articles in many practitioner oriented journals. *Prima facie*, such practitioner accounts suggest that SM is making businesses re-orient themselves to their marketplace and to public sentiments on issues related to corporate citizenship and environment and in the way at least some firms are approaching their internal organization, especially customer facing functions. Anecdotes and case studies relating to SM also reveal that the SM experience is far from uniform among businesses.

Notwithstanding this burgeoning trend of SM application across sectors and disciplines, scholarly enquiry into this phenomenon is so far thin. Moreover, even the practitioner oriented literature in SM has trained its attention largely on its relevance to marketing, customer service and public relations/outreach. This is not surprising, since the natural and most apparent associations that SM platforms provide organizations are those with their customers, existing and potential. Nonetheless, a deeper perusal of the inherent attributes and characteristics of SM would reveal that its current use for marketing and customer engagement is probably only the tip of the iceberg. Though it is still early days, at least some bellwether firms like Dell, CISCO and Starbucks, have been quick to realize this latent potential and appear have moved to embed SM centrally into their functioning and operating culture so as to feed other important corporate and strategic objectives such as market education, sharing opinions on regulatory and policy matters, corporate responsibility related dissemination and new product ideas. Firms also appear to appreciate the tremendous power of SM to amplify messages and signals, and therefore make or mar reputations in double-quick time. Firms also realize that this forces the need for them to be strategic and smart in their responses on SM platforms. Despite possessing characteristics which can potentially position firms as distinct from their competitors and/or create competitive advantages through a variety of mechanisms, all which speak to SM's strategic potentiality, extant scholarly research has paid little attention to the relationship between SM and a firms' strategic decision making (SDM) or a firm's strategic agenda.

A quick perusal of some prominent general management/strategic management focused journals underscores this gap in SM related literature. The following table summarizes the search for social media, new media or Web 2.0 related articles, appearing from 2006-2010 (inclusive) in six prominent academic journals relating to the discipline of strategic management - all of them listed under the popular journals used by Financial Times in their research ranking of business schools. Practitioner oriented journals in this list were omitted for the purpose of this search.

Although only limited conclusions may be drawn from the above data, it is still interesting to note that till 2011, not a *single* SM related article has found visibility within this select space, exploring any relationship between SM and strategy content or strategy process.

The intent of this limited data is not to discount the importance of the SM related academic articles which have been published in other journals or presented at academic conferences – though not many, there are a handful of these, many cited

Table 1. SM related content in prominent international strategy journals: 2006-2010*

Journal	2006		2007		2008		2009		2010	
	Total	SM/ NM	Total	SM/ NM	Total	SM/ NM	Total	SM/ NM	Total	SM/ NM
Academy of management Journal	78	0	94	0	64	0	63	0	70	0
Academy of management Review	84	0	84	0	87	0	46	0	30	0
Administrative Science Quarterly	50	0	41	0	44	0	56	0	49	0
Journal of International Business Studies	68	0	97	0	94	0	119	0	137	0
Organization Science	51	0	61	0	54	0	64	0	73	0
Strategic Management Journal	62	0	73	0	77	0	73	0	76	0

Legend:
Total: Total articles including editorials and book reviews;
SM/NM: SM or New Media related articles
* Relevant content was adjudged by a scan of titles of articles and key words and the title of books reviewed in these publication, as presented in host databases such as Ebsco-Business Source Complete and Proquest Legacy/ ABI Inform Global.

in this essay (Baird & Fisher, 2005; Banbersta, 2010; Cooke & Buckley, 2008; Dadashzadeh, 2010; Fischer & Reuber, 2010; Gilbert & Karahalios, 2009; Hackworth & Kunz, 2010; Kaplan & Haenlein, 2010; Kwak, Lee, Park, & Moon, 2010; Porter & Donthu, 2008; Waters, Burnett, Lamm, & Lucas, 2009). Table 1 seeks to only underscore the limited point that academic literature relating SM to strategic management or SDM is scarce at present.

In contrast however, practice oriented journals such as California Management Review, Harvard Business Review and the Sloan Management Review and some leading business schools such as Harvard Business School, INSEAD, and London Business School are devoting research effort to this subject (Bonabeau, 2009; Dholakia & Durham, 2010; Edelman, 2010; Gaines Ross, 2010; Hoffman & Fodor, 2010; Karabell, 2010; McAfee, 2006; Nunes & Merrihue, 2007; Spenner, 2010; Tan, 2010). The current special forum initiative by IJEBR counts among the few such initiatives which are emerging from niche academic journals.

In this context of SM engagement by firms on the rise, of an increasing appreciation of the unique characteristics of this medium and of the utility of SM for purposes other than just customer engagement, and yet the limited attention accorded by academic literature to relating SM and strategic management, this chapter seeks to contribute to both the strategy discourse and the social media discourse by exploring the following questions:

1. Does the emerging phenomenon of social media have the potential to influence strategic decision making by firms?
2. What characteristics of SM support such influence? Through what dimensions of strategic decision making can one understand the potential and impact of social media (or new media) on the strategy process?

This chapter adopts a purely conceptual approach, and though quotes several examples from practice, does not purport to be a case-study based research. As an exploratory research, we have only attempted to use cases from practice, collated from secondary sources, more as anecdotes to extract some of the strategic orientations observed among firms with regard to SM, to illustrate some of its definitive characteristics and to some extent, buttress the model that we suggest for explicating the potential influence of SM on strategic decision making. With the phenomenon of corporate SM engagement still evolving, and academic research on SM still in a nascent stage, this research is more an attempt to explore the multiple strategic dimensions of SM for strategic decision making – as different from its more apparent and ventilated marketing related dimension.

The rest of the chapter is structured as follows. We first seek to elucidate the definitive characteristics of SM, particularly as relevant to business firms. Next, we briefly summarize, drawing out from extant strategic management research, the prominent dimensions of firms' strategic decision making (SDM) or strategy processes. Combining the characteristics of SM and the dimensions of SDM, we then proceed to suggest a model of SM influence on SDM. We finally pick one of these dimensions, the knowledge dimension, in an attempt to explicate in greater detail, the mechanism through which SM could likely influence SDM.

THE CHARACTERISTICS OF SOCIAL MEDIA

There are various kinds of SM platforms, differentiated based on their core utility, such as for social networking and sharing (such as Myspace and Facebook), for public sharing of videos and music (such as Youtube), sharing of pictures and photographs (such as Flickr), career oriented and professional networking (such as LinkedIn), corporate and personal weblogs (or blogs) to share thematic perspectives, hobbies etc, and microblogging such as Twitter (Fischer & Reuber, 2010). From the corporate perspective, the more interesting and popular SM services include Facebook, Twitter, Youtube, LinkedIn and blogging. (Aula, 2010; Burson-Marsteller, 2010).

While there appears to be no consensus or even a widely accepted definition of SM, the definitive characteristics of SM associated with socialization that emerge from its various definitions - *participation, relationships, collaboration, co-creation, and conversations* (Aula, 2010; Brogan, 2010; Kanter & Fine, 2010; Kaplan & Haenlein, 2010; O'Reilly, 2006) – are also very relevant to strategy process and strategy formulation in organizations (Van De Ven, 1992; Hendry, 2000; Mantere & Vaara, 2008; Prahalad & Ramaswamy, 2004; Wooldridge & Floyd, 1990). SM platforms can also be understood as amplifying the influence of online communities by "promoting deep relationships, allowing fast organization, improving the creation and synthesis of knowledge, and permitting better filtering of information" (Kane, Fichman, Gallaugher & Glaser, 2009)

SM in general and platforms like Twitter in particular, also exemplify the strength of weak ties (Gilbert & Karahalios, 2009; Granovetter, 1973), allowing organizations, as knowledge seekers to tap into personally distant sources for non-redundant information (Constant, Sproull, & Kiesler, 1996; Cross & Sproull, 2004), as they formulate strategies. Time and again, it is the collective power of these "weak ties" that has helped generate empathy and mobilize mass opinion – Apart from instances from the field of politics such as US President Obama's election in 2008 or more recently, the Egyptian revolution in 2011, cases are evident from the field of business- such as British Petroleum's 2009 oil spill in Gulf of Mexico or the case of United Airlines' ultimate official admission of responsibility in their careless handling of a passenger's expensive musical instrument.

There are several novel dimensions to corporate social media engagement, which *shifts the locus of control of corporate messaging away from the organization and towards customers and other stakeholders* (Burson-Marsteller, 2010). First, firms are simultaneously and continually connected to hundreds of stakeholders, in the manner of a value network extending well beyond an organization's formal boundaries (Allee, 2000; Fulk & DeSanctis, 1995; Normann & Ramirez, 1993). Second, SM networking is a mode of broadcasting where organizations are in little control of message flow or interpretation within and without the network, which frequently tests the integrity of thought, speech and action of corporate leaders, unlike with traditional media. Third, SM has the ability to squeeze time, space and *virtual strangers*, all into an open, real-time conversation, which can seriously influence global stakeholder opinions. Finally, the multiple times amplification and viral speed of global message transmission make SM a strategically potent but double-edged medium– it can make or mar reputations near- instantly.

Taken together, these novel attributes buttress SM's significant ability to mould impressions amongst firms' stakeholders, positively or negatively. In this manner, what SM seems to be effecting, is bringing the external environment and often even the internal environment (by facilitating a more engaged workforce) closer to the firm, by opening up a dynamic multi-way communication channel. In turn, a firm's environment is an important aspect frequently identified in strategy process research as an influential factor in strategic decision making (Pettigrew,1992).

Whether it is Best Buy deciding to offer free technical service through Twitter, or Transunion reducing tech support costs through investments in social media, or Starbucks dedicating effort and resources to collate, examine and implement customer ideas on their merits, or Dell Inc. investing in an SM centre and authorizing after specialized training over a few thousand of its employees to represent them on SM platforms or Gap Inc. having to revisit its rebranding on account of feedback on SM platforms – all of these measures and initiatives by the organizations concerned involve serious management consideration, monetary implications, and invariably, a change in the way certain things were so far being done. One can argue that many of these, if not all, are *strategic decisions*, when seen in the light of how extant literature has sought to define and understand strategic decisions. Strategic decisions have been variously described as involving "fundamental decisions which shape a firm's course or critically affect organizational survival" (Eisenhardt & Zbaracki, 1992), as an "organization-wide phenomenon" (Hart, 1992), or simply as "important (decisions), in terms of the actions taken, the resources committed or the precedents set"(Mintzberg, Raisinghani, & Theoret, 1976).

Seen in this perspective, it can be argued that the impact of SM is not just in the space of marketing and customer servicing. Even in those spaces and beyond, the process of engaging with customers, eliciting feedback, and deciding to action on customer ideas, feedback or complaints due to either respect accorded to stakeholders or fear of loss of reputation, involves devoting human, material and monetary resources. They also end up changing the mindset and cognition of employees, including the top management, in the process initiating a strategic change. In the absence of substantive peer reviewed academic literature, oft cited case studies in practitioner accounts emerge as the primary alternative to gain insights into how SM impacts business across various dimensions which can be deemed strategic. Table 2 presents a vignette of business related SM anecdotes to highlight several interesting SM related incidents and initiatives by business firms.

Table 2 serves to highlight several of the attributes of SM, already discussed, which have implications for not only the marketing or advertising dimension but extend to several other facets of business management, and therefore strategic management. It illustrates how SM is gainfully leveraged by firms for generating innovative ideas from outside, (eg: Dell. Starbucks, Rubbermaid). When such ideas generated from the market and a fan-base are then subject to rigorous internal tests and processes, supported also by a transparent and

Table 2. Strategic decisions and social media: Anecdotes

Case and Reference	Highlights	Dimension Related to Strategic Decision	Key Insights
Dell Inc (Binhammer, 2009; Chaney, 2009; Fidelman, 2011; Guglielmo, 2009; Thomas & Barlow, 2011)	Focused attempt at engaging customers through Twitter and Corporate blogs. What started as effort to address negative product and service feedback by listening to customers better, is now evolved to a 'culture' of genuine customer engagement, and idea generation and innovation through crowd-sourcing, through Dell's corporate blog-'Ideastorm'. Brain storming sessions held with network members. Over 40 product ideas implemented till date; Establishing an SM centre and an SM certification programme and training over 10,000 employees as of 2011.	To develop a mechanism and invest resources in SM to only understand and constantly track–what customers and the relevant market has to say about Dell. To not hide the problem of "exploding" Dell laptops in 2006, but acknowledge the problem, understand more dimensions of the problem, in working towards a solution. To action a "listen to the customer" philosophy, whereby a product is already "designed" by customers before its launch! Cost savings on market surveys. Commitment to and Investment in training and certifying a significant proportion of employees for SM engagement.	Leadership commitment to SM and visibility ; Staying relevant with messages and being honest with responses generates goodwill, as fast as negative reputation can spread due to poor customer engagement Leveraging the potential of SM for innovative idea generation and generate pre-launch loyalty.
Best Buy (Dunn, 2010; Thomas & Barlow, 2011)	Use of SM for employee empowerment and internal community development through multiple internal networking platforms similar to Facebook; Active presence on Twitter and blogging by Chief Executive Officer as well as Chief Marketing Officer -, responding to customers suggestions, sharing ideas and opinions on issues whether technical, related to Best Buy, or not related to Best Buy, to foster genuine community dynamics. Deploying hundreds of technically qualified sales professionals to offer technical advice, for free through "Twelpforce";	Fostering culture of using SM internally for bottom-up idea generation as well as *genuinely* and creating buy-in for strategic decisions, by seeking employee responses on important matters ; Not pricing advice rendered through 'Twelpforce', with a view to generating customer loyalty. Decision to developing some products in-house on pilot basis, through 'community' efforts – time and cost savings	Leadership commitment to SM and visibility. "Lethal generosity" (Israel, 2009) helps generate customer loyalty. Well managed internal SM networking fosters a virtuous cycle of transparency, trust and team work

continued on following page

open communication channel maintained with network members, they emerge with the advantage of starting off with a ready customer base. The fact that SM, if used internally, with intent and truly open culture, can serve to bolster internal commitment to firms' strategies and employee engagement is illustrated in the anecdotes of Zappos and Best Buy. The importance of leadership commitment and fostering a culture of openness in order for SM to be truly effective also emerges in the case of Dell and Zappos.

The ability of SM to build, break or manage reputations and external impressions is another key facet which the cases of British Petroleum, United Airlines, and Electronic Arts exemplify. What is interesting is also that not all the companies listed here are large corporations – underscoring the point that SM can work equally well for firms of differ-

Table 2. Continued

Case and Reference	Highlights	Dimension Related to Strategic Decision	Key Insights
Zappos (Chaney, 2009; Steinert-Threlkeld, 2009; Thomas & Barlow, 2011)	Creative use of SM – mainly Twitter for fostering a "happily engaged" work culture, and positive community dynamics, in keeping with the belief that 'happy employees result in happy customers"; Sharing Zappos work culture through Twitter as well posts on Youtube. SM supplemented by employee friendly policies and work conditions. Whether on SM or not, or whether it generates a sale for Zappos or not, employees spend time with anyone who requests help on the kind of merchandise which Zappos carries, Return on Investment (RoI) of SM not a priority. CEO, 24 year old Tony Hsieh very active on Twitter, engaging with public and employees, Twitter and had a followership of over 2.6 million fans on his Twitter page http://twitter.com/zappos as on September 10, 2012.. Zappos reaches USD 1 Bn revenues in less than 10 years of operations.	Decision to support a "happy", highly connected work culture through SM; related decision of commitment to transparency, inside and outside the organization. Opening up Zappos work culture and policies to the world through SM- creating a positive image for the brand as well as an attraction as a potential employer.	Leadership commitment to SM and visibility. Internal communication and employee engagement can be hugely facilitated by SM, if backed by transparency and sincerity in living core values.

continued on following page

ent sizes, although bigger size and consumer base are factors likely to engender a greater following on social media networks. The concept of "lethal generosity" (Israel, 2009), so often highlighted as important in engaging customer on an SM platform is another attribute which comes across effectively in the approaches of firms/brands such as H&R Block and Rubbermaid.

Having identified the definitive and inherent characteristics of SM and how these are relevant for firms' operating context, we now seek to identify the facets of strategic decision making that have a possible connect with the phenomenon that is SM. We attempt to do this in the next section, through a brief overview of strategy process/SDM.

STRATEGY PROCESS AND STRATEGIC DECISION MAKING

Strategy process and SDM have been discussed in academic research as having various dimensions and influenced by several aspects including managerial cognition (Hodgkinson & Johnson, 1994; Stubbart, 1989), organizational learning (Argyris, 1977; Dodgson, 1993; Levinthal & March, 1993; March, 1991), knowledge creation and integration (Cyert & Williams, 1993; Eisenhardt & Santos, 2002; Grant, 1996b; Nonaka, 1991; Nonaka, 1994; Nonaka & Toyama, 2003; Spender, 1996; Spender & Grant, 1996; Tsoukas & Vladimirou, 2001), innovation (Mezias & Glynn, 1993; Wolfe, 1994), corporate governance and stakeholder approach

Table 2. Continued

Case and Reference	Highlights	Dimension Related to Strategic Decision	Key Insights
Old spice (Old Spice, 2010; 2010a)	Humorous, witty, creative, attention riveting, and tasteful advertisements on Youtube, featuring actor Isaiah Mustafa, resulting not only in phenomenal fan following on Youtube, but also word-of-mouth publicity in other SM channels like Twitter and blogs. More importantly, the advertisements were followed up with *personalized*, elegant and sensitive video responses on Youtube to ordinary people (not just celebrities) who 'tweeted' or e-mailed or blogged elsewhere about the advertisement. Old spice also provided a voice mail message generator in Mustafa's voice which fans could use to create personalised outgoing messages on their phones. The campaign was discontinued after a while, before it got jaded; Old Spice sales increased by over 100% in the month following the initial Youtube advertisements.	Innovative approach to product promotion and marketing. Decision to invest effort and resources to establish a one-on-one connection even in the context of a typically one-to-many, broadcast type medium Strategic decision to stop the campaign and not overdo it, even when the campaign had tremendous followership	Real display of commitment to the principle of holding a conversation can harness the potential of SM; SM lends itself to more innovative ways of connecting with customers than what the SM platform features may themselves suggest; for instance before Old Spice, no one really used Youtube to respond to a one-on-one message on Twitter, and simultaneously broadcast such one-on-one message to create a wider fan following.
H&R Block (Thomas & Barlow, 2011)	Free tax advice in filing season through blogs during the busy tax filing season; Pro-active preparatory advice and tips in non-filing season; Product sales increase even though products were not actively promoted through the SM channels.	To provide free tax advice to even non-customers ; To utilize the firm's network of tax professionals for providing this service and steadily tightening the response time standards from 24hrs to 3 hrs.	'Lethal generosity' in SM platforms, if the generosity is sincere and about relevant information, can aid customer retention and customer acquisition. Relevant knowledge, freely shared pays back in other ways – in image building and trust generation, and *therefore*, in real revenues.

continued on following page

(Harrison & Freeman, 1999) and top management teams and their dynamics (Finkelstein & Hambrick, 1990; Hambrick & Mason, 1984; Stiles, 2001; Westley & Mintzberg, 1989). Though not an exhaustive listing, most of these influencers or moderators can be conceived as belonging to the inner or the outer contexts of the organization which have a bearing on the content and process of strategic choices and strategy formation (Pettigrew, 1992; Van De Ven, 1992).

Researchers who have conducted extensive reviews of the literature on strategic process - which covers both strategic decision making and strategy implementation, and attempted to integrate the myriad dimensions pertaining to this aspect of strategy, have highlighted somewhat similar

Table 2. Continued

Case and Reference	Highlights	Dimension Related to Strategic Decision	Key Insights
British Petroleum (BP) (Bean, 2010; Gaines-Ross, 2010; Shirey, 2010)	In the wake of a huge oil spill from a BP Platform off the Gulf of Mexico, BP displays less than exemplary sensitivity to environmental concerns, and refuses to adequately own up for the damage caused. A fake Twitter account posing as BP tweets sarcastic messages effectively parodying BP's apathy. Resultant huge groundswell, (followership of over 10 times more than followers of the official BP Twitter page) forces BPs hands to admit to lapses and thereafter take up subsequent damage control measures. The CEO, Tony Hayward who aggravated the situation by virtue of his insensitive comments in media, further amplified in SM sites, is also replaced by the Board of Directors.	Decision to come clean and own up responsibility for oil spill; Change in leadership	Impact of SM on corporate reputations, irrespective of whether an organization is active on SM or not highlights the viral potential of SM; Importance of alignment between professed values and real values in an SM dominated world; also lack of control of organizations over messaging, in an SM era.

continued on following page

aspects as the key influencers of the strategy process. For instance, Rajagopalan, Rasheed, & Dutta, (1993) suggest environment factors, organizational factors, and decision specific factors as the primary building blocks, with decision process characteristics process characteristics as a mediator (though not always) impacting strategy process outcomes. In this classification, the organizational factors include aspects such as top management characteristics, size, organization structure, slack etc, whereas environmental factors includes aspects such as environmental complexity, munificence, uncertainty etc. The dimension of decision specific factors includes issue complexity, issue urgency, decision motive and outcome risk or uncertainty.

Hutzschenreuter & Kleindienst (2006) use a slightly different taxonomy, summarizing the influences in terms of "the strategist, the issue and sequence of actions", and in turn grouped into three boxes - antecedents, strategy process and outcomes corresponding to various antecedents. They have attempted a more nuanced classification of influencing factors, separating static characteristics from dynamic characteristics. Accordingly static organizational factors (size, age etc), dynamic organizational characteristics (Business processes, routines etc), strategist static aspects (background, group heterogeneity) and strategist dynamic factors (cognitive dimension, individual disposition/ biases etc) are seen as impacting the strategic process outcomes differently

In analysing strategy processes, strategy can also be seen as "embedded" at multiple contextual levels of an organization – firm, sector, and economy- and reflecting the different processes at work at these levels (Pettigrew, 1992). Factoring these multiple-level processes are critical to understanding strategic decisions, as these processes constitute an important and rich source of infor-

Table 2. Continued

Case and Reference	Highlights	Dimension Related to Strategic Decision	Key Insights
Rubbermaid (Thomas & Barlow, 2011)	As the manufacturer of a wide and assorted range of household utility products, Rubbermaid's focus was on creating communities through SM platforms, mostly blogs, by offering helpful suggestions on matters of everyday utility to people – such as organizing space, closets etc. Discussions never focused on company products. Focus of SM engagement was always on thinking about what the customer wants. Rubbermaid queried target audience before they started, and figured that the latter preferred not be bombarded by product promotions. Once discussions commenced, the suggestions often came not from Rubbermaid employees, but from people on the network/ followers/fans. Started SM on a small scale, on select products, before expanding across a wider range, and different platforms, thereby also helping employees to learn from their small mistakes. Feedback from customers for product improvements; free fixes provided for products where defects were observed In the process, however, customers ended up using more Rubbermaid products, although they were never promoted by the company as such.	Not to even remotely promote its products product; on the contrary deciding to invest time, resources and effort in engaging general public, without any guarantee of immediate revenue payoffs. Clear focus on long term pay-offs.	Listening and empathising with customers is a critical skill for SM success. 'Lethal generosity' begets customer loyalty. A sure but small and slow start helps organization learning on SM engagement, rather than a precipitous start. 'In-the-face' product promotion is not likely to help an organization's cause on SM platforms.

continued on following page

mation and signals from the firm's internal and external context about aspects such as competition, market feedback, customer and public sensitivities, employee engagement, firm resources and other stakeholder sensitivities. Therefore, the ability of decision makers or the strategists to collect, filter and interpret data, messages and signals have a critical bearing on its strategy process and content (Makadok & Barney, 2001).

SOCIAL MEDIA INFLUENCE ON STRATEGIC DECISION MAKING: AN EXPLORATORY MODEL

Drawing from the above literature, of all the sub-dimensions, given that SM is essentially a communication medium, a platform for channelling and shaping opinions, *prima-facie*, the impact of SM on the strategy process is most likely to manifest through the sub-dimension of the "strategist" or

Table 2. Continued

Case and Reference	Highlights	Dimension Related to Strategic Decision	Key Insights
United Airlines (Chaney, 2009; Jackson, 2010)	United Airlines (United) reportedly ill-treats a customer by breaking his guitar in handling, and refuses to pay any compensation after months of follow-up. The frustrated customer, Dave Carroll, a professional musician, posts video on Youtube, titled "United Breaks Guitars", United does not react for a week, by which time the video goes viral, (chalking up over 7 million views in 2 years.) One week after the video, United hurried to offer a compensation settlement, which the musician refuses to accept. In the meantime, United's stock crashes, causing a stock value loss of nearly USD 180 million.	Decision to rescind earlier call of not compensating passenger. Delaying responding to Youtube video	With SM, customers have the power to message equally or more than the organization itself. In SM, the organization has absolutely no control over the there is no control over messaging
Electronic Arts Inc. (Owyang, 2011)	Spouse of exploited employee posts anonymous blog about unfair company practices and exploitation, which creates a groundswell of protest and negative publicity; Class action suits filed against the company and company is forced to settle large amounts as damages for unfair treatment of employees. (Owyang (2011); Santos, (2011))	Change in employment policies and practices; Change of CEO	Impact of SM on corporate reputation;
Starbucks (Sterne, 2010; Thomas & Barlow, 2011)	Idea generation by customers across a variety of areas.- over 65,000 ideas, under various stages of study, including many under implementation.	New products and variants, introduced based on customer suggestions Savings on market research.	Crowd-sourcing, and power of visible idea implementation Use of SM for innovation

the decision maker – whether belonging to the top echelons or middle management. However, there are potential effects which could manifest through the environmental and decision issue dimensions as well. Accordingly we proceed to suggest an exploratory model of SM influence on strategic decision making as represented in the Figure 1.

Figure 1 essentially projects the three key dimensions of strategy process – Environment, Strategist, and the Decision issue - as expounded in comprehensive literature reviews on the subject (Hutzschenreuter & Kleindienst, 2006; Pettigrew, 1992; Rajagopalan, Rasheed, & Dutta, 1993; Van De Ven, 1992b). In suggesting the mechanism for SM influence on strategic decision making, the above exploratory model suggests that there are aspects falling within each of these dimensions (identified within the perforated box in the middle of the diagram) that are prone to the influence of SM. At the same time, such influence of SM is not suggested as a necessary factor, and it is quite possible that in some cases, depending on the

Figure 1. SM influence on strategic decision making: An exploratory model
** Constructs adapted/combined from Hutzschenreuter & Kleindienst (2006) and Rajagopalan et al., (1993)*

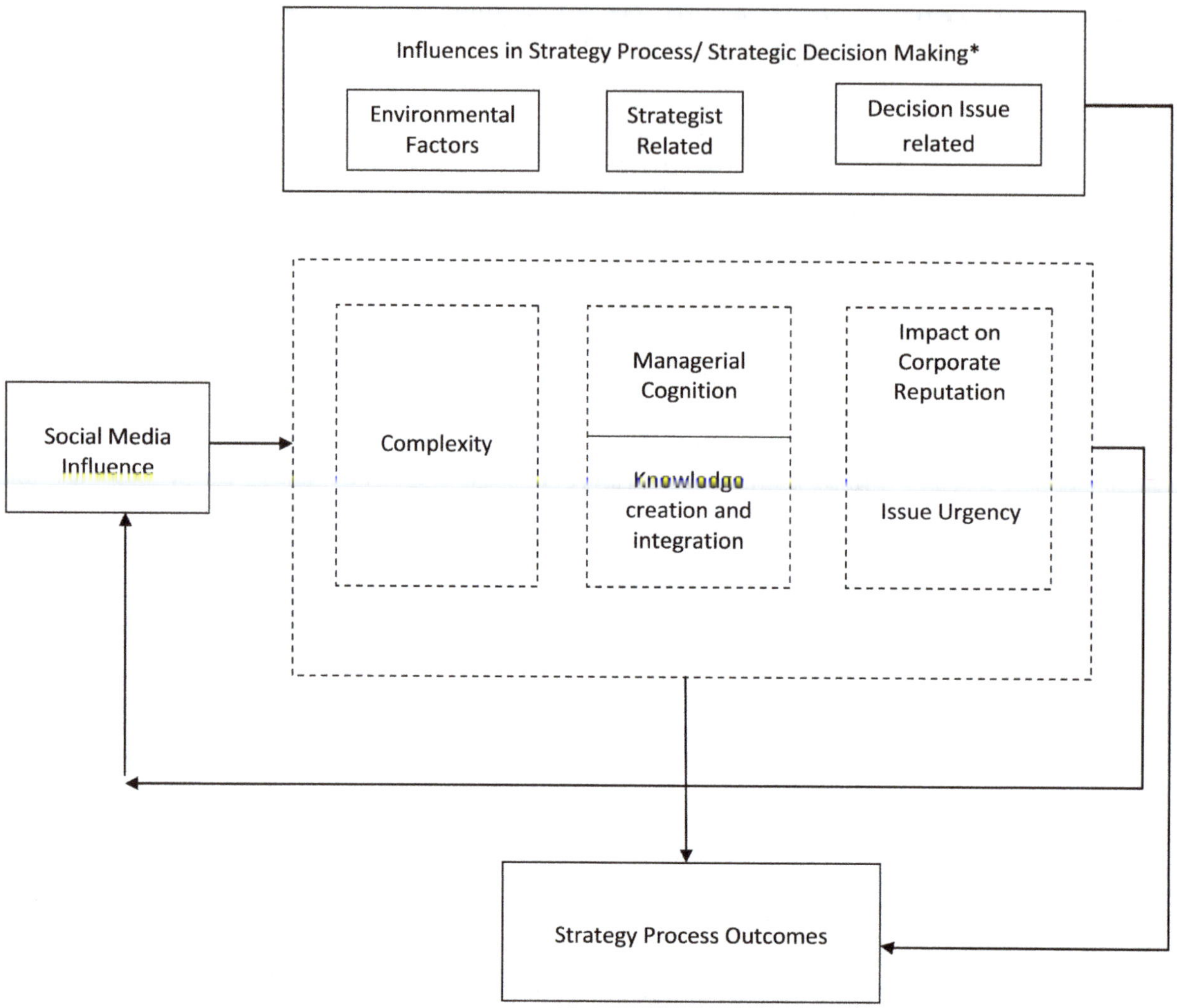

evolution of SM and/or the level of SM engagement of the firm, the strategic decision process side steps the influence of SM.

The influence of SM on the cognitive bases of strategists and their knowledge gathering and processing can be related to the effect of information and signals from the firm's internal and external context on sensemaking (Gioia & Chittipeddi, 1991; Weick, 1993; Weick, Sutcliffe, & Obstfeld, 2005), and therefore on strategic decisions. It can also be associated with the dynamics of organizational knowledge creation and with the knowledge based view of the firm (Eisenhardt & Santos, 2002; Grant, 1996a; Nonaka, 199, 1994; Nonaka & Toyama, 2003; Spender, 1996; Tsoukas & Vladimirou, 2001). While this process of information gathering and sensemaking by organizations and managers (the strategists) from their relevant internal and contexts is not a new feature and has evolved with the emergence of different kinds of technology and media, what is different in the context of SM is that it has now been revolutionized by the advent of SM, on account of its unique attributes outlined earlier in this chapter.

Similarly, due to its network characteristics, potential connection to a multitude of stakeholders, and rapid amplification characteristics, SM poses the ability – which could be an advantage or disadvantage as the case maybe – to render a strategic issue as urgent or demanding rapid response times from a firm. This is also often linked to the aspect of reputation management or impression management, both of which are considered as critical to strategy (Fombrun & Shanley, 1990; Gray & Balmer, 1998; O'Sullivan, 2000; Trammell & Keshelashvili, 2005; Weigelt & Camerer, 1988). In particular, the roles of communication and media in reputation management have been examined in literature (Deephouse, 2000). The reputational effects of SM are also exemplified in Table 2- positively in the case of Rubbermaid and Dell, and negatively in the case of British Petroleum and United Airlines.

Finally, SM can also potentially make a firm's environment more complex than it otherwise would be, by virtue of attracting more players into the contours of an issue, again due to its swift dissemination abilities and networked character. Issues tend to be discussed more publicly, rendered more visible on account of SM engagement, whether or not the firm in question is SM engaged or not. A result of this could be a faster-than-otherwise response from regulators or policy makers on matter of public sensitivity or national importance. This dimension is amply illustrated in the instances of British Petroleum and United Airlines, highlighted in Table 2.

The three mechanisms outlined above are only suggestive of the plausible ways through which SM can influence strategic decision making. Each of these mechanisms requires greater examination to explicate the manner of their influence. However, given the limitations of scope, we herein take up only one of the mechanisms, namely the knowledge dimension. Accordingly, in the next section, through the lens of knowledge creation, we highlight the likely mechanisms and process through which SM dynamics impact SDM in organizations.

KNOWLEDGE CREATION, KNOWLEDGE INTEGRATION, AND SOCIAL MEDIA

Since SM places emphasis on co-creation of knowledge and knowledge creation in turn is central to strategy and competitive advantage (Eisenhardt & Santos, 2002; Grant, 1996a, 1996b; Nonaka, 1991; Pfeffer & Sutton, 2000), the lens of knowledge creation lends itself to illuminating the processes through which SM impacts SDM.

In the context of an organization that is active on any SM platform, the management team is continually communicating with members on its primary network – for example, "fans" on Facebook, or "followers" on Twitter. The flow of messages makes up a stream of information on which an organization can act, once it is construed as knowledge, based on the organization's beliefs (Nonaka, 1994). Knowledge creation in an organization is driven by individual and social dimensions, as knowledge can only be created by individuals in a social setting, guided by their mental models. The centrality of individuals and social interaction to the organizational knowledge creation process, helps us conceive organization knowledge creation as "historically evolved collective understandings" (Tsoukas & Vladimirou, 2001) or as amplifying individual level knowledge to organizational levels (Nonaka, 1994)

Social interaction transforms individual, personal knowledge to legitimate organizational knowledge through a process of multi-level interaction which spans the value network rather than being limited to formal organizational boundaries (Nonaka, 1994). Further, defining organizational boundaries flexibly helps the knowledge creation process, as the shared experience and creative dialogue within the network funnels in the environmental knowledge into the firm, refining existing knowledge and creating new knowledge.

The three characteristics that emerge in this conceptualization of organizational knowledge creation – *individuals, social interaction, and the flexible conception of firm boundaries*- enlighten us about how SM engagement not just influences, but also becomes a knowledge creating routine in an organization. If members in a SM network are conceived as stakeholders in an organization, it can then be argued that for a firm operating in an SM connected world, the process of knowledge creation, as well as that of the Socialization-Externalization-Combination-Internalization (SECI) model of knowledge conversion (Nonaka, 1994; Nonaka & Toyama, 2003) is not only applicable, but even more amplified than in its original context of the "traditional" organizational model of the 1980's and 1990's.

The influential dimension of socialization in knowledge has continued to engage academic research (Brown & Duguid, 2001; Chua, 2002; Floyd & Wooldridge, 1999) and further, has extended to the influence of related aspects such as communities of practice (Duguid, 2005; Lee & Cole, 2003). From a strategy process perspective, of greater interest is how knowledge thus generated through SM gets integrated within an organization, and leads to strategic decision making and how organizations can exploit SM flexibly for knowledge generation and integration, in order to strategize for competitive advantage (Ilinitch, D'Aveni, & Lewin, 1996).

Extending the resource based view, Grant (1996a) makes a case for knowledge as the most strategically-important resource for a firm, reasoning that sustainability of competitive advantage requires resources which are idiosyncratic and therefore scarce, and not easily transferable or replicable. "If the strategically most important resource of the firm is knowledge and if knowledge resides in specialized form among individual organizational members, then the essence of organizational capability is the integration of individuals' specialized knowledge" (Grant, 1996a).

The distinction between knowledge integration and absolute knowledge becomes pertinent to gaining competitive advantage through SM, as any number of competing firms of equivalent stature and stakeholder following in a SM network may be able to access similar information and messages. However, what makes for competitive advantage is the manner in which such information is transformed to knowledge, the efficiency with which knowledge is integrated within the organization, and further in an externalization and socialization mode shared with the social network for feedback and signalling. By integrating knowledge from multiple sources in its external environment, a firm can influence its dynamic capabilities and thereby enhance the knowledge driven advantage (Nonaka & Toyama, 2003).

For knowledge integration to be effective in creating and sustaining competitive advantage, Grant (1996b) argues for the application and orientation to knowledge integration to be extensive and intense ("efficiency"), broad in scope, and flexible in approach. In a SM context, efficiency of knowledge integration can be interpreted as the extent to which an organization accesses and utilizes the expert knowledge and feedback available from the members in the SM network. The more an organization shares and externalizes, the more a piece of knowledge has scope for being refined and re-cycled to the network as new knowledge available to be integrated.

In a SM network, an organization has the choice of being in different modes of engagement. An organization could be a passive observer, only absorbing the messages and feedback on the network, but not engaging the network substantively; such predominant one-way communication would be of limited utility and likely result in limited network following as it does not conform to the "conversation" mode valued in good SM practice and often reduces SM engagement to little more than a helpdesk function. Examples of such passive SM practice by firms are many.

At the other end of the spectrum, like in the case of Dell or Best Buy, a firm could have dedicated people tracking the SM network, and actively engaging members to explore more of a highlighted problem, coordinating and following up to ensure that the problem is resolved, and moreover, voluntarily sharing the issue with the rest of the network to create greater connect and confidence. Organizations like Rubbermaid, Zappos, H&R Block or Proctor & Gamble provide free and useful information to the community on their network, irrespective of whether they are customers or not ("Beinggirl - Proctor and Gamble," 2011; Gaasterland, 2009; Steinert-Threlkeld, 2009; Thomas & Barlow, 2011). These engagements are strategic since they involve organizational commitment, investments and sometimes critical decisions (Mintzberg et al., 1976). While they may not be directly promoting a product or have an immediate impact on revenues, such engagement is instrumental in engaging and influencing relevant communities, usually generating tremendous goodwill, which on SM platforms spreads virally creating a virtuous cycle effect on brand recall and loyalty. Moreover, other network members feel encouraged to share information (Thomas & Barlow, 2011), and join agenda with the firm, and effectively become knowledge partners in supplementing the organization's own efforts – exemplifying highly efficient SM driven knowledge integration.

Knowledge gets created through socialization and externalization within a value network, and is continuously refined and integrated through combination and externalization; furthermore, its internalization closes the loop by prompting a strategic decision and effecting strategic action based on the new knowledge (Nonaka & Toyama, 2003), and this cycle is perpetuated within the value network.

The internalization leading to action is likely to be moderated by several organizational dimensions such as top management commitment, organizational culture, organization structure, industry membership, and orientation to network management. In particular, just as exemplified in instances of successful organizational knowledge management, integrating SM into the SDM process demands a deeper philosophical orientation towards SM and cultural assimilation (Alavi, Kayworth, & Leidner, 2006), in transcending from the knowledge of the 'what', 'why' and the 'how' of SM, to embedding the organization in a SM context - in a manner of going from the "surface to the soul", in bridging the "knowing-doing gap" (Pfeffer & Sutton, 2000; Prabhu, 2006).

CONCLUSION AND DIRECTIONS FOR FUTURE RESEARCH

This essay has sought to explore the strategic management dimensions of SM, specifically in terms of the influence that this emerging and evolving phenomenon could have on the aspect of strategic decision making (SDM). We have suggested that by virtue of its unique and powerful attributes, particularly those which make for speedy, multi-way, amplified and transparent communication, SM could potentially result in firms being more engaged with their environment. In an exploratory schematic model, we suggest that SM likely achieves this effect through its influence on imparting a sense of urgency strategic issues, reputation impact, and influencing the cognitive bases and knowledge integration of the decision makers and the organization.

We further used the lens of knowledge creation and integration in the context of a value network for explicating how strategic decision making is influenced by an evolving SM dominated environment. The striking parallels between the drivers of the knowledge process in firms and the context of value networks on one hand and the structural features and dynamics of SM on the other – socialization, sharing, collaboration, constant refinement of information, extended community as value network, and non-hierarchical, self organizing communities – suggest a strong linkage among SM dynamics, SM influence and strategy processes.

In exploring the manner of SM engagement by firms and relating SM's characteristics to SDM, our research sets the stage for a more incisive inquiry into the strategic dimensions of SM. By bridging strategic decision making processes and SM, this essay contributes by exploring a dimension sparsely addressed by scholarly literature in strategic management.

FUTURE RESEARCH DIRECTIONS

This essay has sought to explore whether the potentiality exist for SM to be seen as force which can impact strategic decision making in firms. While the arguments presented in the chapter affirm this notion, we believe that we have only scraped the tip of the ice-berg, particularly since this essay itself was developed on the back of several limitations, particularly that of a paucity of established SM related theories and the still evolving nature of corporate SM engagement. Nonetheless, we believe that our research serves to identify many areas which hold potential for future research, as expanded below

One, from a strategy perspective, there are several aspects of an organization that SM can potentially impact, although this essay has limited itself to SDM processes. Such specific areas include new product development, innovation, employee engagement, internal communication, corporate social responsibility and sustainability. SM applications are also evolving, and new applications emerging which firms are trying to leverage. Along with the evolution and maturing of SM in practice, a deeper investigation into some of these dimensions, marrying theories from sociology and other diverse fields can help shed light on the influence of SM. A maturing field will facilitate exploration through detailed case studies.

Two, this chapter has suggested that striking parallels exist between the processes that undergird good organizational knowledge management, and the processes that are central to effective and efficient SM engagement. Since knowledge management practices by firms are by now well established and documented, and SM is also being explored by many firms that espouse knowledge management, the ideas in this essay lend itself to a multiple case study based research, which can examine whether the ideas thrown up in this chapter find support from the field. Such a research may also serve to identify relevant influential factors which impinge on the dimension of managerial cognition and knowledge integration, other than what is already suggested in this essay.

Three, even within the dimension of strategy process and SDM, the model suggested in this chapter has only been partly expounded, and only one aspect, namely, the knowledge aspect, has been examined with in greater depth. For a more holistic and well grounded theoretical contribution to emerge, a further exploratory research is called for, with a well defined research framework and hypotheses, which can further be tested empirically. For instance, the influence of strategists' characteristics and decision issue characteristics calls for a more detailed inquiry - supported by case studies or cross-disciplinary theories, since academic literature in SM is at too embryonic a stage to offer any meaningful theoretical grounding.

Four, even as we suggest SM to hold a potential influence on the SDM process and suggest an exploratory model, we have not been able to examine whether SM would wield a *moderating* or a *mediating* influence on the key factors impinging on SDM. This is yet another aspect which calls for nuanced attention, in order to develop a strong theoretical basis for the influence of SM on strategy process.

Five, practitioners and researchers need to recognize the possibility of noises (Levinthal & March, 1993) being mixed up with the messages of value. There is also the aspect of how SM is handled internally within the firm – policies, rules, limitations, legal risks, the trust element– all of these having a bearing on how the risks and opportunities of SM are balanced. These SM dimensions related to strategic decisions call for further inquiry.

MANAGERIAL RELEVANCE

The business context of every organization has a unique character, which has to be central to how managers need to go about SM engagement. For the field of practice, this essay contributes by providing a knowledge based perspective of SM, and by highlighting its strategic potential.

In an environment where being on SM platforms is being see as fashionable, by many businesses, managers and leaders may tend to hastily jump onto the SM bandwagon sensing only its superficial aspects and viewing it as just another communication medium - in the process either not realizing its true potential, or worse, its dangers and negative reputation effects when inappropriately used. CEO's are still reported to be cautious in approaching SM (Burson_Marsteller, 2012), but yet SM possibly hold a key to strategic or competitive advantage for firms that are able to leverage it effectively and efficiently. The knowledge perspective presented in this chapter provides the arguments and even some principles for why and how business firms can use SM to their advantage. In tracing the processes which make SM relevant for strategy, this chapter not only delves beyond the more obvious marketing related applications of SM but also sensitizes that SM for strategic decision making is not just about its structural components – technologies, people and processes – it boils down to the core values, philosophies and the culture of the organization. Importantly, the chapter also highlights that SM lays bare and amplifies an organization's character, clarifying therefore that in working with this emerging phenomenon, it is important for organizations to learn to be transparent, genuinely empathetic, relevant (Thomas & Barlow, 2011) and responsible corporate citizens.

REFERENCES

Alavi, M., Kayworth, T. R., & Leidner, D. E. (2006). An Empirical Examination of the Influence of Organizational Culture on Knowledge Management Practices. *Journal of Management Information Systems*, *22*(3), 191–224. doi:10.2753/MIS0742-1222220307

Allee, V. (2000). Reconfiguring the value network. *The Journal of Business Strategy*, *21*(4), 36–39. doi:10.1108/eb040103

Argyris, C. (1977). Double loop learning in organizations. *Harvard Business Review*, *55*(5), 115–125.

Aula, P. (2010). Social media, reputation risk and ambient publicity management. *Strategy and Leadership*, *38*(6), 43–49. doi:10.1108/10878571011088069

Baird, D. E., & Fisher, M. (2005). Neomillennial User Experience Design Strategies: Utilizing Social Networking Media To Support Always on Learning Styles. *Journal of Educational Technology Systems*, *34*(1), 5–32. doi:10.2190/6WMW-47L0-M81Q-12G1

Banbersta, M. (2010, June). The success factors of the Social Network Sites Twitter. *Applied Sciences*.

Bean, J. (2010). BP: Delivering on the brand promise (?). *Slideshare.net*. Retrieved May 3, 2011, from http://www.slideshare.net/JustinC-Bean/bp-a-marketing-case-study

Beinggirl - Proctor and Gamble. (2011). *Beinggirl.co.in*. Retrieved May 3, 2011, from http://www.beinggirl.co.in/main/home.php

Binhammer, R. (2009). How Dell took social media mainstream. Smartblogs.com/socialmedia. Retrieved May 3, 2011, from http://smartblogs.com/socialmedia/2009/10/02/how-dell-took-social-media-mainstream/

Bonabeau, E. (2009). Decisions 2.0: The power of collective intelligence. *MIT Sloan Management Review*, *50*(2), 45–52.

Brogan, C. (2010). Social media 101. In *Media*. Hoboken, NJ: John Wiley & Sons.

Brown, J. S., & Duguid, P. (2001). Knowledge and organization: A social-practice perspective. *Organization Science*, *12*(2), 198–213. doi:10.1287/orsc.12.2.198.10116

Burson-Marsteller. (2010). Burson-Marsteller 2010 Fortune Global 100 Social Media Study. *The Burson-Marsteller Blog*. Retrieved April 7, 2011, from http://www.burson-marsteller.com/Innovation_and_insights/blogs_and_podcasts/BM_Blog/Lists/Posts/Post.aspx?ID=160

Burson-Marsteller. (2012). Burson-Marsteller 2011 Fortune Global 100 Social Media Study - Update. *The Burson-Marsteller Blog*. Retrieved July 4, 2012, from http://www.burson-marsteller.com/Innovation_and_insights/blogs_and_podcasts/BM_Blog/default.aspx

Chaney, P. (2009). *The Digital Handshake: Seven Proven Strategies to Grow Your Business Using Social Media*. Hoboken, NJ: John Wiley & Sons Inc.

Chua, A. (2002). The influence of social interaction on knowledge creation. *Journal of Intellectual Capital*, *3*(4), 375–392. doi:10.1108/14691930210448297

Constant, D., Sproull, L., & Kiesler, S. (1996). The kindness of strangers: The usefulness of electronic weak ties for technical advice. *Organization Science*, *7*(2), 119–135. doi:10.1287/orsc.7.2.119

Cooke, M., & Buckley, N. (2008). Web 2. 0, social networks and the future of market research. *International Journal of Market Research*, *50*(2), 267–293.

Cross, R., & Sproull, L. (2004). More Than an Answer: Information Relationships for Actionable Knowledge. *Organization Science*, *15*(4), 446–462. doi:10.1287/orsc.1040.0075

Cyert, R. M., & Williams, J. R. (1993). Organizations, decision making and strategy: Overview and comment. *Strategic Management Journal*, *14*(S2), 5–10. doi:10.1002/smj.4250141003

Dadashzadeh, M. (2010). Social Media In Government : From e-Govemment To eGovemance. *Journal of Business and Economic Research*, *8*(11), 81–87.

Deephouse, D. L. (2000). Media Reputation as a Strategic Resource: An Integration of Mass Communication and Resource-Based Theories. *Journal of Management*, *26*(6), 1091–1112. doi:10.1177/014920630002600602

Dholakia, U. M., & Durham, E. (2010). One Café Chain's Facebook Experiment. *Harvard Business Review*, *88*(3), 26.

Dodgson, M. (1993). Organizational learning: A review of some literatures. *Organization Studies*, *14*(3), 375–394. doi:10.1177/017084069301400303

Duguid, P. (2005). The Art of Knowing: Social and Tacit Dimensions of Knowledge and the Limits of the Community of Practice. *The Information Society*, *21*(2), 109–118. doi:10.1080/01972240590925311

Dunn, B. J. (2010, December). How I Did It … Best Buy's CEO on Learning to Love Social Media. *Harvard Business Review*.

Edelman, D. (2010, December). Branding in The Digital Age: You're Spending Your Money In All the Wrong Places. *Harvard Business Review*.

Eisenhardt, K. M., & Santos, F. M. (2002). Knowledge-Based View: A New Theory of Strategy? In A. M. Pettigrew, H. Thomas, & R. Whittington (Eds.), *Handbook of Strategy and Management* (pp. 139–164). London: Sage Publications Ltd.

Eisenhardt, K. M., & Zbaracki, M. J. (1992). Strategic decision making. *Strategic Management Journal*, *13*(S2), 17–37. doi:10.1002/smj.4250130904

Fidelman, M. (2011). 5 Reasons Why Dell Is The World's Most Social Company. www.businessinsider.com. Retrieved June 11, 2011, from http://www.businessinsider.com/is-dell-the-worlds-most-social-company-scorecard-2011-6?utm_source=twbutton&utm_medium=social&utm_term=&utm_content=&utm_campaign=sai-contributor

Finkelstein, S., & Hambrick, D. C. (1990). Top-management-team tenure and organizational outcomes: The moderating role of managerial discretion. *Administrative Science Quarterly*, *35*(3), 484–503. doi:10.2307/2393314

Fischer, E., & Reuber, A. R. (2010). Social interaction via new social media: (How) can interactions on Twitter affect effectual thinking and behavior? *Journal of Business Venturing*, *26*(1), 1–18. doi:10.1016/j.jbusvent.2010.09.002

Floyd, S. W., & Wooldridge, B. (1999). Knowledge Creation and Social Networks in Corporate Entrepreneurship: The Renewal of Organizational Capability. *Entrepreneurship. Theory into Practice*, *23*(3).

Fombrun, C., & Shanley, M. (1990). What's in a name? Reputation building and corporate strategy. *Academy of Management Journal*, *33*(2), 233–258. doi:10.2307/256324

Fulk, J., & DeSanctis, G. (1995). Electronic Communication and Changing Organizational Forms. *Organization Science*, *6*(4), 337–349. doi:10.1287/orsc.6.4.337

Gaasterland, M. (2009). Most products are like tampons. *Blog: Social Media Tactics You can Trust*. Retrieved from http://www.michielgaasterland.com/case-studies/most-products-are-like-tampons/

Gaines-Ross, L. (2010, December). Reputation Warfare. *Harvard Business Review*, 70–77.

Gilbert, E., & Karahalios, K. (2009). Predicting tie strength with social media. In Proceedings of the 27th International Conference on Human Factors in Computing Systems (CHI '09). ACM.

Gioia, D. A., & Chittipeddi, K. (1991). Sensemaking and sense-giving in strategic change initiation. *Strategic Management Journal*, *12*(6), 433–448. doi:10.1002/smj.4250120604

Granovetter, M. (1973). The strength of weak ties. *American Journal of Sociology*, *78*(6), 1360–1380. doi:10.1086/225469

Grant, R. M. (1996a). Toward a knowledge-based theory of the firm. *Strategic Management Journal*, *17*(Winter Special), 109–122.

Grant, R. M. (1996b). Prospering in dynamically-competitive environments: Organizational capability as knowledge integration. *Organization Science*, *7*(4), 375–387. doi:10.1287/orsc.7.4.375

Gray, E. R., & Balmer, J. M. T. (1998). Managing Corporate Image and Corporate Reputation. *Long Range Planning*, *31*(5), 695–702. doi:10.1016/S0024-6301(98)00074-0

Guglielmo, C. (2009). Dell Rings Up $6.5 Million in Sales Using Twitter. *Bloomberg.com*. Retrieved May 3, 2011, from http://www.bloomberg.com/apps/news?pid=newsarchive&sid=akXzD_6YNHCk

Hackworth, B. A., & Kunz, M. B. (2010). Health care and social media: Building relationships via social networks. *Academy of Health Care Management Journal*, *6*(1), 55–69.

Hambrick, D. C., & Mason, P. A. (1984). Upper echelons: The organization as a reflection of its top managers. *Academy of Management Review*, *9*(2), 193–206.

Harrison, J. S., & Freeman, R. E. (1999). Stakeholders, Social Responsibility, and Performance: Empirical Evidence and Theoretical Perspectives. *Academy of Management Journal*, *42*(5), 479–485. doi:10.2307/256971

Hart, S. L. (1992). An integrative framework for strategy-making processes. *Academy of Management Review*, *17*(2), 327–351.

Hendry, J. (2000). Strategic decision making, discourse, and strategy as social practice. *Journal of Management Studies*, *37*(7), 955–978. doi:10.1111/1467-6486.00212

Hodgkinson, G. P., & Johnson, G. (1994). Exploring the Mental Models of Competitive Strategists: The Case for a Processual Approach. *Journal of Management Studies*, *31*(4), 525–552. doi:10.1111/j.1467-6486.1994.tb00629.x

Hoffman, D. L., & Fodor, M. (2010). Can You Measure the ROI of Your Social Media Marketing? *MIT Sloan Management Review*, *52*(1), 41–49.

Hutzschenreuter, T., & Kleindienst, I. (2006). Strategy-Process Research: What Have We Learned and What Is Still to Be Explored. *Journal of Management*, *32*(5), 673–720. doi:10.1177/0149206306291485

Ilinitch, A. Y., D'Aveni, R. A., & Lewin, A. Y. (1996). New organizational forms and strategies for managing in hypercompetitive environments. *Organization Science*, *7*(3), 211–220. doi:10.1287/orsc.7.3.211

Israel, S. (2009). *Twitterville: How businesses can thrive in the new global neighborhoods*. Penguin.

Jackson, T. (2010). Case Study: United Airlines Loses Millions on Social Media. *Social Media Risk.com*. Retrieved May 3, 2011, from http://socialmediarisk.com/2010/03/case-study-united-airlines-loses-millions-on-social-media/

Kane, G. C., Fichman, R. G., Gallaugher, J., & Glaser, J. (2009). Community Relations 2.0. *Harvard Business Review*, *87*(11), 45–50. PMID:19891388

Kanter, B., & Fine, A. H. (2010). The networked nonprofit. In *Seven*. San Francisco: Jossey-Bass, John Wiley & Sons.

Kaplan, A. M., & Haenlein, M. (2010). Users of the world, unite! The challenges and opportunities of Social Media. *Business Horizons*, *53*(1), 59–68. doi:10.1016/j.bushor.2009.09.003

Karabell, S. (2010). Just a pretty face(book)? Social media tries to come of age. *INSEAD Knowledge*. Retrieved March 17, 2011, from http://knowledge.insead.edu/contents/social-networking-wpp-google.cfm?vid=419

Kwak, H., Lee, C., Park, H., & Moon, S. (2010). What is Twitter, a social network or a news media? In Proceedings of the 19th International Conference on World Wide Web (pp. 591–600). Academic Press. doi:10.1145/1772690.1772751

Lee, G. K., & Cole, R. E. (2003). From a firm-based to a community-based model of knowledge creation: The case of the Linux kernel development. *Organization Science*, *14*(6), 633–649. doi:10.1287/orsc.14.6.633.24866

Levinthal, D. A., & March, J. G. (1993). The myopia of learning. *Strategic Management Journal*, *14*(S2), 95–112. doi:10.1002/smj.4250141009

Makadok, R., & Barney, J. B. (2001). Strategic factor market intelligence: An application of information economics to strategy formulation and competitor intelligence. *Management Science*, *47*(12), 1621–1638. doi:10.1287/mnsc.47.12.1621.10245

Mantere, S., & Vaara, E. (2008). On the Problem of Participation in Strategy: A Critical Discursive Perspective. *Organization Science*, *19*(2), 341–358. doi:10.1287/orsc.1070.0296

March, J. G. (1991). Exploration and exploitation in organizational learning. *Organization Science*, *2*(1), 71–87. doi:10.1287/orsc.2.1.71

McAfee, A. P. (2006, Spring). Enterprise 2.0: The dawn of emergent collaboration. *MIT Sloan Management Review*, 21–28.

Mezias, S. J., & Glynn, M. A. (1993). The three faces of corporate renewal: Institution, revolution, and evolution. *Strategic Management Journal*, *14*(2), 77–101. doi:10.1002/smj.4250140202

Mintzberg, H., Raisinghani, D., & Theoret, A. (1976). The structure of unstructured decision processes. *Administrative Science Quarterly*, *21*(2), 246–275. doi:10.2307/2392045

Nonaka, I. (1991, November-December). The knowledge-creating company. *Harvard Business Review*, 96–104.

Nonaka, I. (1994). A dynamic theory of organizational knowledge creation. *Organization Science*, *5*(1), 14–37. doi:10.1287/orsc.5.1.14

Nonaka, I., & Toyama, R. (2003). The knowledge-creating theory revisited: Knowledge creation as a synthesizing process. *Knowledge Management Research & Practice*, *1*(1), 2–10. doi:10.1057/palgrave.kmrp.8500001

Normann, R., & Ramirez, R. (1993, July-August). From value chain to value constellation: Designing interactive strategy. *Harvard Business Review*, 65–77. PMID:10127040

Nunes, P. F., & Merrihue, J. (2007). *The Continuing Power of Mass Advertising The Continuing Power of Mass Advertising*. MIT Sloan Management Review.

O'Reilly, T. (2006). Web 2.0 Compact Definition: Trying Again. *O'Reilly Radar Blog*. Retrieved April 8, 2011, from http://radar.oreilly.com/2006/12/web-20-compact-definition-tryi.html 05-04-2011

O'Sullivan, B. (2000). What you don't know won't hurt me. *Human Communication Research*, *26*(3), 403–431.

Old Spice. (2010a). Old Spice: The Man Your Man Could Smell Like. *Youtube.com*. Retrieved May 23, 2011, from http://www.youtube.com/watch?v=owGykVbfgUE

Old Spice. (2010b). Re: @kevinrose. *Youtube.com*. Retrieved May 23, 2011, from http://www.youtube.com/playlist?p=PL484F058C3EAF7FA6

Owyang, J. (2011). A Chronology Of Brands That Got Punk'D By Social. *Web Strategy*. Retrieved May 17, 2011, from http://www.web-strategist.com/blog/2008/05/02/a-chonology-of-brands-that-got-punkd-by-social-media/

Pettigrew, A. M. (1992). The character and significance of strategy process research. *Strategic Management Journal*, *13*(S2), 5–16. doi:10.1002/smj.4250130903

Pfeffer, J., & Sutton, R. I. (2000). The Knowing-Doing Gap: How Smart Companies Turn Knowledge into Action. *Administrative Science Quarterly*, *46*, 558.

Porter, C. E., & Donthu, N. (2008). Cultivating Trust and Harvesting Value in Virtual Communities. *Management Science*, *54*(1), 113–128. doi:10.1287/mnsc.1070.0765

Prabhu, D. (2006). KM Tigers. *Inside Knowledge*, *9*(9).

Prahalad, C. K., & Ramaswamy, V. (2004). Co-creating unique value with customers. *Strategy and Leadership*, *32*(3), 4–9. doi:10.1108/10878570410699249

Rajagopalan, N., Rasheed, A. M. A., & Dutta, D. K. (1993). Strategic decision processes: Critical review and future directions. *Journal of Management*, *19*(2), 349–384. doi:10.1177/014920639301900207

Santos, S. (2011). Why Social Media is Disruptive. www.thesocialcustomer.com. Retrieved May 17, 2011, from http://thesocialcustomer.com/shawn-santos/34382/why-social-media-disruptive

Shirey, T. (2010). BP and Social Media. *Webpage-FX Weekly*. Retrieved May 3, 2011, from http://www.webpagefx.com/blog/business-advice/bp-and-social-media/

Silva, C. (2010, May). Social Media Customer Leaders: Some Early Performance Data. *Harvard Business Review*.

Spender, J. C. (1996). Making knowledge the basis of a dynamic theory of the firm. *Strategic Management Journal*, *17*(S2), 45–62. doi:10.1002/smj.4250171106

Spender, J. C., & Grant, R. M. (1996). Knowledge and the firm: Overview. *Strategic Management Journal*, *17*(S2), 5–9. doi:10.1002/smj.4250171103

Spenner, P. (2010, December). Why You Need a New-Media Ringmaster. *Harvard Business Review*, 78–80.

Steinert-Threlkeld, T. (2009). Following Zappos.com. *ZDNet*. Retrieved May 3, 2011, from http://www.jmorganmarketing.com/wp-content/uploads/2010/01/ZDNet-Zappos-SR.pdf

Sterne, J. (2010). Social Media Metrics: How to Measure and Optimize Your Marketing Investment. In *Media* (Vol. 3). Hoboken, NJ: John Wiley & Sons.

Stiles, P. (2001). The Impact of the Board on Strategy: An Empirical Examination. *Journal of Management Studies*, *38*(5), 627–650. doi:10.1111/1467-6486.00252

Stubbart, C. I. (1989). Managerial cognition: A missing link in strategic management research. *Journal of Management Studies*, *26*(4), 325–347. doi:10.1111/j.1467-6486.1989.tb00732.x

Tan, K. (2010). Why social media are absolutely crucial to businesses. *INSEAD Knowledge*. Retrieved March 17, 2011, from http://knowledge.insead.edu/contents/networking-social-media-crampton-100513.cfm?vid=415

Thomas, D., & Barlow, M. (2011). *The executive's guide to enterprise social media strategy*. Hoboken, NJ: John Wiley & Sons Inc.

Trammell, K. D., & Keshelashvili, A. (2005). Examining the New Influencers: A Self-Presentation Study of A-List Blogs. *Journalism & Mass Communication Quarterly*, *82*(4), 968–982. doi:10.1177/107769900508200413

Tsoukas, H., & Vladimirou, E. (2001). What is organizational knowledge? *Journal of Management Studies*, *38*(7), 973–993. doi:10.1111/1467-6486.00268

Van De Ven, A. H. (1992). Suggestions for studying strategy process: A research note. *Strategic Management Journal*, *13*(S1), 169–191. doi:10.1002/smj.4250131013

Waters, R. D., Burnett, E., Lamm, A., & Lucas, J. (2009). Engaging stakeholders through social networking: How nonprofit organizations are using Facebook. *Public Relations Review*, *35*(2), 102–106. doi:10.1016/j.pubrev.2009.01.006

Weick, K. E. (1993). The Collapse of Sensemaking in Organizations: The Mann Gulch Disaster. *Administrative Science Quarterly*, *38*(4), 628. doi:10.2307/2393339

Weick, K. E., Sutcliffe, K. M., & Obstfeld, D. (2005). Organizing and the process of sensemaking. *Organization Science*, *16*(4), 409–421. doi:10.1287/orsc.1050.0133

Weigelt, K., & Camerer, C. (1988). Reputation and corporate strategy: A review of recent theory and applications. *Strategic Management Journal*, *9*(5), 443–454. doi:10.1002/smj.4250090505

Westley, F., & Mintzberg, H. (1989). Visionary leadership and strategic management. *Strategic Management Journal*, *10*(S1), 17–32. doi:10.1002/smj.4250100704

Wolfe, R. A. (1994). Organizational Innovation: Review, Critique and Suggested Research Directions. *Journal of Management Studies*, *31*(3), 405–431. doi:10.1111/j.1467-6486.1994.tb00624.x

Wooldridge, B., & Floyd, S. W. (1990). The strategy process, middle management involvement, and organizational performance. *Strategic Management Journal*, *11*(3), 231–241. doi:10.1002/smj.4250110305

KEY TERMS AND DEFINITIONS

Impression Management: The process by which people or organizations seek to control the impressions others form of them. This is an important concept in inter-personal behavior.

Managerial Cognition: How managers in organizations model reality and how such models influence their behaviors.

Resource Based View: A view, often construed as a theory, that argues that a firm dervises competitive advantage primarily by virtue of access to a bundle of tangible or intangible resources that typically have attributes that may be described as valuable, rare, inimitable, and organized/not easily transferable.

Stakeholders: A set of people who influence and are also influenced by, an organization's actions. Typically refers to shareholders, employees, customers, suppliers, community, the Government and regulatory agencies.

Weak Ties: A concept in social networking. Refers typically to the relationship between two individuals where interaction is infrequent or irregular.

Chapter 4
Using the Power of Social Media Marketing to Build Consumer-Based Brand Equity

Kelley O'Reilly
Western Michigan University, USA

Karen M. Lancendorfer
Western Michigan University, USA

ABSTRACT

This chapter highlights how companies might use social media marketing to build brand credibility and, ultimately, consumer-based brand equity. By building brand credibility and equity through SMM, companies can connect with distinctly different consumer groups. Because consumers are adept integrators of marketing communication channels within and across media, companies with strong virtual communities may reap even greater results from the theoretical perspective of customer-based brand equity discussed within the chapter. Marketing scholars and practitioners alike may find this chapter of interest due to the growing desire by companies to develop strong bonds with consumers and their interest in effectively using social media as a marketing tool.

INTRODUCTION

This chapter highlights an approach for developing consumer-based brand equity via social media marketing (SMM). SMM can provide a relatively inexpensive way to connect with interested consumers, leverage their connected "friends," and tap into valuable social intelligence via crowdsourcing and other passive means. By using the suggestions provided in this chapter, practitioners may be better positioned to maximize and refine their ongoing social media marketing efforts for better effect to create brand equity and increase traditional market share. As a means to provide context, this topic is viewed through the strategic lenses of Relationship Marketing and Consumer-based Brand Equity, and views SMM as a tactical action.

Marketing has often been epitomized as the singular act of exchange (Bagozzi, 1974). The exchange or transaction was the "be-all, end-all" moment. When money changed hands, the

DOI: 10.4018/978-1-4666-6182-0.ch004

Figure 1. Traditional direct channel approach

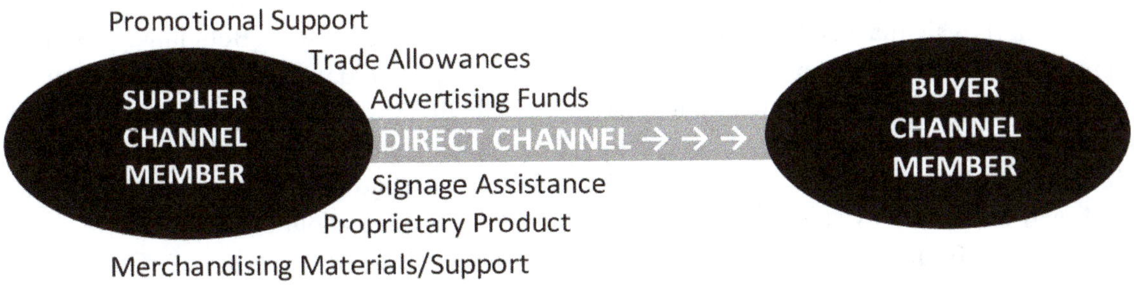

exchange was complete. Many of us came to understand this phenomenon through the teachings of Porter (1987) and a supplier-centric view that concretely and systematically helped to dissect the supply chain, diagnose gaps, and maximize the firm's interest through a strategic process of financial impact and outcome scenarios. Viewed this way, the marketing concept (or the idea of exchange) was easy to grasp. *I make something, I price it, I promote it, and I distribute it to the customer*. Figuratively, the moment of exchange was the point in time when that product left the sellers' hands and was placed in the buyers' hands.

However, this view has since evolved. In 2004, The American Marketing Association (AMA) modified its definition of marketing to "Marketing is an organizational function and a set of processes for creating, communicating, and delivering value to customers and for managing customer *relationships* in ways that benefit the organization and its stakeholders" (AMA, 2008; emphasis added). Since then, the concept of relationship marketing (RM) has become accepted as a more modern view of marketing (Harker & Egan, 2006). This modern view shifts our understanding of the company consumer dyad, with contemporary marketing researchers proclaiming that customers can no longer be viewed as being in endless supply and passive in regard to decision making – no longer can we take a "one size fits all" approach to the simple manipulation of McCarthy's (1960) 4Ps: Product, Price, Place and Promotion, as was the case for decades using a transactional approach to marketing. From this perspective, RM can be viewed as a paradigm shift for marketers who desire to move beyond a transactional approach toward more of a relational one (Grönroos, 1994; Gummesson, 1994).

If we dig deeper into RM, traditional RM efforts typically begin with the direct channel partners being the focal point for planning, investment, and program support as shown in Figure 1. In this context, funding, support and attention by the selling partner all serve as 'accelerants' for the relationship development with the buying partner. Thus relationship strength is evidenced through increased commitment and trust among direct channel partners via an enduring desire to continue as partners and/or partner dependency. Because relationship development commonly begins with the direct channel partners, traditional approaches to RM are commonly "inside out." In other words, attention is inward on direct channel partners with little attention given initially to indirect or "outside" channel members. The actions the supplier takes toward the direct channel buyer are designed to "insulate" the relationship against competitive threat and strengthen both desire and dependency to remain partners. Because in most circumstances resources are limited, funding and support of any outside, or indirect channel members typically occurs only after direct channel relationships are perceived to be stable and secure.

Coincidentally, many firms now use an unique application of SMM to enhance their relationship marketing efforts which has resulted in an "outside in" approach to channel development. This "outside in" activity is often necessitated by market conditions such as competitor size and influence. For instance when a company lacks the financial strength and credibility to compete head-on to drive awareness from direct channel members this approach is often embraced. This "outside in" strategic approach demonstrates the distinctive power of SMM which allows even small market players to establish, build, and ultimately extend relationships with both indirect and direct channel partners. Marketing scholars and practitioners alike may find this application of SMM of interest due to the growing desire by smaller companies to develop strong relationships with key channel partners and their interest in effectively using alternative marketing tools such as social media in their marketing efforts.

BACKGROUND

Key Literature on Relationship Marketing

To examine SMM's application in this context, the literature on relationship marketing, consumer-based brand equity and current thought on social media marketing are used as a backdrop for this chapter.

Relationship marketing (RM) is concerned with creating improved shareholder value through the development of appropriate relationships with key customers and customer segments. The strategic perspective of RM as a process of acquiring, retaining, and partnering with customers is well established in the marketing literature (Frow & Payne, 2007; Parvatiyar & Sheth, 2001; Payne & Frow, 2005; Reinartz, Krafft, & Hoyer 2004; Verhoef & Langerak, 2002). In essence, RM initiatives strive to deliver dual creation of value for the firm and the customer, and are reliant on the notion that RM activities should enhance company performance (Boulding, Staelin, Ehret, & Johnston, 2005; Osarenkhoe, 2006; Parvatiyar & Sheth, 2001). With a dual creation approach, enhancing the relationship "is not so much about advertising and conventional brand-related activities, but rather about building processes to support the customer experience" (Frow & Payne, 2007, p. 91).

At the core of RM is the relationship between the firm and customer. This relationship, by definition, exists for a reason and requires reciprocal exchange and benefits to all participants. As a process phenomenon, the relationship will evolve and change over time because of the interactions occurring *between* participants (Czepiel, 1990; Hinde, 1979). It is these interactions between company and customer where value is created and delivered over time as the relationship with the customer develops (Grönroos, 1997). The creation of value (or value co-creation between company and customer) "[...] requires an ability to engage 'the extended enterprise' by managing *across* and *within* customer and supplier value creation processes" (Payne, Storbacka, & Frow, 2008, p. 93, emphasis in original).

Today it is generally accepted that relationships can be formed via various communication channels (e.g. face-to-face, or virtually online). It is these online channels that have proved both appealing and challenging for marketers. Considering that many marketing programs have been traditionally crafted to drive purchases of the product or service, managing brands more holistically is particularly salient against the backdrop of the social media landscape and phenomenon of virtual communities. To be successful in these new communities online, marketers must acknowledge the role of the consumer as co-creator of brand meaning if they hope to establish strong associations between the consumer and brand (Brown, Kozinets, & Sherry, 2003; Fournier & Avery, 2011).

Figure 2. Building brand equity through SMM

Key Literature on Consumer-Based Brand Equity

Brand equity is of interest to marketers because it is positively correlated to favorable responses from consumers to an element of the marketing mix (Keller, 1993). Understanding how to build brand equity from the 'ground up' is of practical value to managers since it will aid in refining the marketing mix elements. Defined as, "the differential effect of brand knowledge on consumer response to the marketing of the brand" (p. 8), it is desirable to establish strong connections and involvement between the consumer and the brand. These connections often start at consumer engagement whereby marketers attempt to influence and encourage consumers to interact with and about the brand (Schultz & Peltier, 2013), with often positive results. A number of brands have shown an improvement in business performance as a result of consumer engagement. According to the ENGAGEMENTdb Study by Wetpaint/Altimeter Group (Li, 2009), "the most valuable brands in the world are experiencing a direct correlation between top financial performance and deep social media engagement" (p. 1).

In this way, we can view consumer engagement as the first step towards building brand equity. It should be noted that consumer loyalty and retention are often positively correlated with increased levels of consumer engagement (Vivek, Beatty, & Morgan, 2012). Therefore, this linear process of building consumer-based brand equity from the ground up is illustrated in Figure 2.

"Building brand equity requires creating a familiar brand name and a positive brand image – that is favorable, strong, and [has] unique brand associations" (Keller, 1993, p. 17). However, because too many marketing programs have been solely focused on driving purchases, it is important for marketing teams to step back and consider their efforts more holistically; particularly in the context of virtual communities and SMM. As means of example, "Facebook is the dominant social-networking site, [over] 1 billion registered users. Facebook accounts for 90 percent of all time spent on social-networking sites" (Lipsman, Mudd, Rich, & Bruich, 2012, p. 40). To establish strong associations between the consumer and brand will require marketers to acknowledge and embrace the role of the consumer as co-creators of brand meaning (Brown et al., 2003; Fournier & Avery, 2011).

Virtual brand communities have the ability to influence community members, speed up communications between members, provide robust access to member opinions and evaluations, and provide opportunities for interaction (Algesheimer, Dholakia, & Herrmann, 2005) thereby contributing to the growth of brand equity through SMM. Thus, once consumers are aware and engaged with a brand they are in a position to communicate their opinions to other consumers (Hoffman & Fodor, 2010). Therefore,

> *highly engaging social media campaigns involving user-generated content [will] likely generate commitment on the part of the consumer, reinforcing loyalty to the brand and making the customer more likely to commit additional effort to support the brand in the future (Hoffman and Fodor, 2010, p. 46).*

This suggests that the traditional top-down approach to marketing should be abandoned in favor of more participatory and interactive cooperation between marketer and consumer (Christodoulides, Jevons, & Bonhomme, 2012). This will create stronger brand associations, thereby improving consumer-based brand equity.

Key Literature on Social Media Marketing

Social media is best understood as an Internet marketing medium that offers one-to-one methods for meeting and interacting with companies and other customers. Its relative importance to marketers is fast outstripping that of traditional media since it is inexpensive and can quickly get marketing messages to prospects through interactive discussions and rapid word-of-mouth (Owyang, 2009). Social media tools are moving into a golden time as more and more consumers, born into the "Internet generation" reach their 20s, 30s and beyond. Research tells us that this generation "…socializes more online, downloads more entertainment media, and consults the Web for a wider range of purposes than do present adults or young people of the previous generation" (Herring, 2008, p. 71). Indeed, it seems this is "…a generation [that] is growing up in an era where digital media are part of the taken-for-granted social and cultural fabric of learning, play, and social communication" (Ito, Davidson, Jenkins, Lee, Eisenberg, & Weiss, 2008, p. vii).

"In the social media environment, every time a person uses an application designed by or about the company, the company gains increased exposure to its brand, often in highly relevant contexts" (Hoffman & Fodor, 2010, p. 46). This creates a distinct shift in control of brands across contexts whereby, "Consumers are now the individuals broadcasting personal or second-hand stories to their social networks and the world. They are a brand's storytellers and the new brand ambassadors" (Booth & Matic, 2011, p. 185). Interestingly, a consumer's relationship with a specific brand has been shown to be an "antecedent to his or her identification with the brand community" (Algesheimer, Dholakia, & Herrmann, 2005, p. 30). Authenticity is an important part of building and maintaining a successful brand because it forms a unique brand identity and provides a strong, favorable association (Gundlach & Neville, 2012). Additionally, Algesheimer et al. (2005) suggest that member's various behavioral intentions translate into actual behaviors – which provides empirical support for advocates favoring the building of brand communities.

Companies who take a proactive stance to social media, commonly empower employees to talk, listen, and respond to what consumers post on social media (Smith, Fischer, & Yongjian, 2012). Because marketer created content may encourage more sharing online, user-generated content can be indicative of brand engagement and word-of-mouth. Therefore these co-created brand environments (Fournier & Avery, 2011) reward social media marketing strategies that "*put the brand to work for the customers* by satisfying their needs to create, consume, connect and control in the social Web" (Hoffman & Fodor, 2010, p. 49, italics in original). New technologies have made this very easy as, "…new low-cost digital production tools mean that amateur and casual media creators can author, edit, and distribute video and other rich media forms that were once prohibitively expensive to produce and share with others" (Ito et al., 2008, p. viii).

BEST PRACTICES FOR MAXIMIZING SMM INITIATIVES

When the Internet was first gaining ground as a mainstream marketing tool, companies quickly jumped on board with little or no strategic thought or plan. This resulted in many sub-optimal static websites that did little to build brand equity or engage consumers. Today, the same phenomenon appears to be taking place with SMM as companies implement SMM, often with little forethought as to why, where, and how these initiatives can best be harnessed for building consumer-based brand equity. The following section is intended as a guideline for marketing practitioners to help differentiate between the varying SMM opportunities and how they might be used.

Understanding How to Use SMM for Different Marketing Intents

Recognizing the power of positive consumer-based brand equity and its link to brand loyalty and engagement, companies will benefit from brand recognition, a positive brand image, and unique brand connections (Keller, 1993). For many companies, this means moving beyond the experimentation phase of 'trying every social media outlet' and looking at the 'mix within the mix' of social media. While 86% of marketers indicate that social media is important for their business, experienced marketers recognize that each social media platform is distinct (Social Media Examiner, 2013). For instance, if we consider the top five social media platforms used by marketers (Facebook, Twitter, LinkedIn, blogging and YouTube), each of these platforms delivers an audience with unique goals and attitudes towards online participation, sharing and collaborating with companies (Smith et al., 2012). Table 1 highlights the primary social media marketing sites, number of users, and marketing trends moving forward.

The Use of 'Loyals' to Draw Others to Company Online Web Assets

As is common in many companies, online social media is used much like advertising – create compelling messages that draw interested potential buyers to the brand. In this way, social media is used as a draw to the brand. This strategy is supported by research which reports "increased exposure" as the top benefit of social media marketing (Social Media Examiner, 2013). From the same report, other benefits include increasing traffic, providing marketplace insight, and developing loyal fans - in fact, most marketers now recognize that developing loyal brand fans ranks higher in importance that generating leads. In fact, "when a brand focuses on acquiring and engaging fans, it can benefit from a significant secondary effect – exposure among friends of fans that often surpasses reach among fans" (Lipsman, Mudd, Rich, & Bruich, 2012). Because one of the primary benefits of social media marketing is increasing exposure, SMM can have a significant positive effect on the effort to drive fan exposure → engagement → loyalty → influence → equity.

This notion is supported by recent research that suggests that consumers loyal to the brand can be used to influence and draw others to the brand. As highlighted in previous research, "Enroll existing, long tenured customers who already have an affirmative relationship with the brand" (Algesheimer et al., 2005, p. 30), and then drive them to the online experience. Additionally, Lipsman et al. (2012) suggest that "friends of fans typically represent a much larger set of consumers (34 times larger on average, for the top 100 brand pages) and can receive social-media brand impressions by way of their friends." This highlights that those loyal to a brand on a particular SMM site can influence potentially dozens of connections that might also benefit and be interested in the web assets of a particular company.

The Value of Using SMM for Social Intelligence

Lastly, this chapter highlights our perspective that SMM is about the web of people, not the web of brands. Social media enables an interactive stream of communication with consumers rather than a one-sided brand push (Hennig-Thurau, Malthouse, Friege, Gensler, Lobschat, Rangaswamy, & Skiera, 2010). As such, marketers need to recognize that they are not always welcome

Table 1. Primary social media platforms, users, and trends

Social Media	Description	Users[1]	Trend	Marketer Context[2]
Facebook *(facebook.com)*	Facebook is an online social networking service.	1.15B Ranked #1 for users, and #1 by marketers.	↑	• Facebook is a social networking site. • Facebook is most used platform for SMM. • Facebook is used more commonly by B2C marketers. • Only 37% of marketers believe that their Facebook marketing is effective.
Google+ *(google.com)*	*Google+* aims to make sharing on the web more like sharing in real life with Circles, Events and Hangouts.	343M (active) Ranked #2 for users, and #6 by marketers.	↑	• Google+ is a social media networking site. • 1 in 4 marketers have no plans to use Google+. • Male marketers are more likely to use Google+ than female marketers.
YouTube *(youtube.com)*	A site to share videos.	1B Ranked #3 for users, and #5 by marketers.	↑	• Significant cross-over with Google+ users. • For third year, YouTube is the top platform where marketers plan to increase spending.
Twitter *(twitter.com)*	Twitter is a real-time information network that connects users to the latest stories, ideas, opinions and news. At the heart of Twitter are small bursts of information (140 characters) called "Tweets".	500M Ranked #4 for users, and #2 by marketers.	↓	• Two-thirds of marketers plan to increase their Twitter activities; however this is down from last year. • Younger marketers are more likely to use Instagram than Twitter. • Most popular bookmarking sites are Twitter, Pinterest, Reddit and StumbleUpon.
LinkedIn *(linkedin.com)*	A social networking website for people in professional occupations.	238M Ranked #5 for users, and #3 by marketers.	↑	• LinkedIn is a social networking site. • LinkedIn is used more commonly by B2B marketers.
Tumblr *(tumblr.com)*	Tumblr is a blogging platform that allows users to post text, images, videos, links, quotes and audio to their short-form blog.	216.3M	↑	• Tumblr is a blogging platform. • Blogging is rapidly gaining favor with SMM marketers with two-thirds indicating that they will increase efforts in this area.
Instagram *(instagram.com)*	A community where you can capture and share photos.	130M	↑	• Instagram is a photo-sharing site. • B2C marketers are significantly more likely to use Instagram. • Younger marketers are far more likely to use this type of platform. • Marketers with more than 5 years of SMM experience are likely to increase their efforts here.
Yelp *(yelp.com)*	A site where users write and publish unsolicited reviews.	100M	↑	• Yelp is a social networking review site.
Flicker *(flickr.com)*	An image hosting and video hosting website.	87M	↓	• Flickr is a photo and video sharing site.
Pinterest *(pinterest.com)*	Pinterest is a pinboard-style photo-sharing website that allows users to create and manage theme-based image collections such as events, interests, and hobbies.	70M	↑	• Pinterest is a photo-sharing website. • Pinterest seems more suited to B2C marketers. • Female marketers use Pinterest more than male marketers.

continued on following page

Table 1. Continued

Social Media	Description	Users[1]	Trend	Marketer Context[2]
Living Social *(livingsocial.com)*	LivingSocial is a local marketplace to buy and share things to do in your city.	70M	↓	• Living social is a daily deal site. • Daily deal sites can be beneficial to brand marketers due to "pay on performance" model; however, 80% of marketers are not planning on using daily deal sites for their marketing efforts in coming year.
Reddit *(reddit.com)*	Is a social news and entertainment bookmarking website where registered users submit content in the form of either a link or text.	69.9M	↑	• Reddit and Digg are the top social bookmarking sites with the most power for marketing and managing traffic en masse. • Social bookmarking sites continue to rapidly decline to only 10% use by marketers in 2013.
Groupon *(groupon.com)*	Groupon is a deal-of-the-day website that features discounted gift certificates usable at local or national companies.	41.7M	↓	• Groupon is a daily deal site. • Use by marketers of daily deal sites is declining.
Twitter Vine *(vine.com)*	Is a mobile service that lets you capture and share short looping videos. Like Tweets, videos on Vine are short (6 seconds or less).	40M	↑	• Twitter vine is a social bookmarking site that is new and upward trending.
Foursquare *(foursquare.com)*	Foursquare is a free app that helps consumers and their friends make the most of where they are.	33M	↓	• Foursquare is a geo-location site. • Foursquare provides marketers with tools to engage customers at their "point-of-need." • Forums and geo-location sites are in strong decline. • Male marketers are more likely to use than female marketers.
StumbleUpon *(stumbleupon.com)*	Founded in 2001, was one of the first sites to become wildly popular by helping people find amusing, weird, and useful things on the internet.	25M	↓	• Stumbleupon is a bookmarking site. • Formerly owned by eBay and struggling to regain momentum after redesign. • Not significant for marketers today.
Digg *(digg.com)*	Digg is a news aggregator with an editorially driven front page	10M	↓	• Digg is a bookmarking site. • 2012 redesign and relaunch of Digg Reader. • Questionable as to whether site can stay relevant.
Delicious *(delicious.com)*	Delicious is a free tool to save, organize, and remember the links you find interesting on the web.	~5M	↓	• Delicious is a bookmarking site. • Formerly del.ico.us.com • Relaunch and redesign in 2011, 2012. • Not significant for SMM.
Quora *(quora.com)*	Quora is a question and answer site that encourages people "in the know" to answer the queries of others.	2.9M	↓	• Quora is a Q&A site. • Quora is not a significant site for SMM.

[1]Source: http://expandedramblings.com
[2]Source: http://www.socialmediaexaminer.com/social-media-marketing-industry-report-2013/

in the social web when their only goal is to sell and blatantly promote their goods (Fournier & Avery, 2011). Instead marketers can participate (albeit sometimes passively) as a way to better understand their consumers, which in turn can help them understand the relative strength of their consumer-based brand equity. Here the brand realizes that it needs to listen and respond to its audience on a more connected level (Qualman, 2009). According to Keller (2008), the "power of a brand lies in what customers have learned, felt, seen and heard about the brand" (p. 48) and SMM sites provide a valuable conduit for companies to better explore their brands' relative strengths and weaknesses. As noted by Jill Brittlebank, director of strategy at e-Dialog, social media can provide a useful source of intelligence for marketers. "By listening to what the communities on social networks are saying," she says, "you can find out what is interesting and relevant to them" (Clawson, 2012, p. 8). But often brands and marketers forget that "if you would like your customers to engage with you, you need to give them a reason for doing so" (Kaplan & Haenlein, 2010, p. 66). Only after you have actually listened to your consumers to find out what they are interested in and what they want to talk about, are you able to engage the customers on their level.

Termed "social intelligence," it's a relatively new discipline that "combines social media data with traditional customer data sources" as a means of developing better actionable market decisions (Walters, 2013, p. 14) or a so-called "database of intentions" thereby forecasting future consumer behavior (Hennig-Thurau et al., 2010). When combined with other customer data, it allows companies to manage real time (or near real time) conversations with customers in order to deliver information that is timely and relevant via those same social media channels (Stone & Woodcock, 2013; Veeck, 2013; Walters, 2013). This "real-time" component is important because data that sits without analysis for a long time loses its relevance (Qualman, 2009). Further, research has shown that the more rapid the response to the consumer, the more valuable that information is considered to be (Weiss, Lurie, & MacInnis, 2008). And here it's all about the consumer. Companies have the opportunity through social media to extend their brand's personality and engage with consumers, but it's on their terms and through their chosen channels (Stone & Woodcock, 2013). This is where many companies have gone astray, as they struggle to make their social media initiatives engaging and truly valuable to consumers (Schultz & Peltier 2013).

One step in the social intelligence process is the activity of social listening or social media monitoring. Forrester Research, Inc. (2011, p. 4) defines social listening as "programs that utilize social media to monitor, measure, and respond to customer conversations and feedback online."

We monitor social media because it provides unsolicited and unbiased consumer opinions about our products and brands in real time. If a brand, messaging or product problem is identified by bloggers, we can fix the problem quickly before it gets too widespread. Also, positive comments help us understand early on if something is working particularly well – Christine Stasiw Lazarchuk, Director, Global Market Research, Ford Motor Company (Aberdeen, 2008, p. 10).

Companies who engage in social listening have the opportunity to "have an active hand in owning their brand's story" (Booth & Matic, 2011, p. 185). Social listening provides benefits to firms in terms of customer service through anticipation of problems and the ability to communicate instantly with customers, as well as crisis and reputation management (Grimes, 2013; Sinickas, 2010/2011). It can also assist with recruiting, product development, public relations strategies, and of course, word of mouth (Qualman, 2009).

This opportunity, however, comes with some caveats. Research shows that the information obtained from engaging in social listening activities is highly dependent on "where" we listen (i.e., selectively monitoring only a single social media site) and how the data is analyzed (Schweidel & Moe, 2012). In this respect it is important to remember that comments posted on social media sites may not represent your entire audience (Sinickas 2010/2011). According to Sinickas (2010/2011), a best practice is to "look at social media monitoring as a way to identify emerging trends, and then add questions to existing surveys to see how prevalent those perceptions are" (p. 11).

One of the biggest challenges that has arisen with the advent of social listening is the influx of "big data". With many organizations already struggling to integrate multiple relevant data sources into one consistent, consumer-focused experience, social media monitoring/listening brings with it an additional challenge (Walters, 2013). With a little bit of modification however, a model for the analysis of social media data already exists, and can be applied by practitioners. Compiled from research by Veeck (2013), and Walters (2013), the following represents five steps to help organize your social listening efforts:

- **Step 1. Make a Plan:** A key element of social media monitoring is the development of a problem definition and objectives that form the basis of a carefully designed plan of action (Veeck, 2013). What do you want to achieve through the social listening activity? Without a plan of action, "listening to a customer and understanding the customer's opinion about your products and services in a strategic vacuum is worthless" (Walters, 2013, p. 15). To be effective the plan should include both those actions needed and the costs involved in implementation.
- **Step 2. Identify and Collect the Data:** Here it's important that you identify both key search terms and social media data sources in order to get the most complete picture, without getting bogged down. With so much information available on social media, companies must carefully determine which data is relevant and which is not. To start a search, some obvious terms would include the brand name, as well as competitors' brand names and product class (Veeck, 2013). Next, with the increasing growth of Web 2.0 technologies, there are numerous social media sites that can provide consumer-generated data. Technologies that support this task include web crawlers that systematically download relevant posts from key sites, as well as word taxonomies that map key terms from text data (Bastone, 2010). Veeck (2013) provides a succinct list:
    - social network sites (e.g., Facebook);
    - video-sharing sites (e.g., YouTube);
    - photo-sharing sites (e.g., Flickr);
    - product and service review sites (e.g., Yelp);
    - Web-based communities (e.g., Chowhound);
    - blogs (e.g., Gardenista); and
    - microblogs (e.g., Twitter).
- **Step 3. Organize and Analyze the Data to Extract Meaning:** With the abundance of data on the Web, more and more companies are being asked to extract and deliver value from new so-called "big data". Measurement must be very specific, so selecting the right measures and analyses are important to link the data back to the desired outcomes (Grimes, 2013). A number of analytical tools can help assess social media content to identify key themes in "beliefs, ideas, concepts, definitions, [and] behaviors" (Veeck, 2013). Sentiment analysis can also assist here to help managers track conversations similarly to the way they might track day to day stock fluctuations (Bastone, 2010).
- **Step 4. Integrate:** Although the data gathered in Steps 2 and 3 is valuable, by

integrating the social listening data with other data sources, deeper insights can be gleaned (Walters, 2013). For example, companies may supplement their current tracking studies by using social listening (when combining brand sentiment and automated text analysis) (Schweidel, Moe, & Boudreaux, 2011). "Thanks to new search and analysis tools created for social media, you can connect click-throughs that lead to sales. You can track changes in sentiment in discussions about your organization. You can correlate sales to social media channels and campaigns. You can show the ROI" (Brogan & Bastone, 2014, p. 8.).

- **Step 5. Strategize:** As with any research, the most important step is the final action of using the findings to develop actionable recommendations based on the research objectives (from Step 1) (Veeck, 2013). Here the goal is to "create a framework for action" (Grimes, 2013) that aligns with your company's goals.

Another benefit of the social intelligence process is the opportunity to identify "influencers" who may be open to spreading positive messages about your brand. Discussed as fan influence earlier in the chapter, the identification of "social media users who are both influential and particularly interested in the company's product or service category" (Kumar & Mirchandani, 2012, p. 55), provides the opportunity to engage those consumers more fully with the brand as brand advocates. Fans and advocates tend to "evangelize" brands they love, thereby promulgating early adoption messages (Stone & Woodcock, 2013). As brand advocates, these influencers have the ability to influence the attitudes and behaviors of consumers who share their networks.

And that's a good thing. According to a 2012 Nielsen survey, 70% of consumers trust online reviews, while 92% of consumers trust recommendations from family and friends. Further, consumers rely on content from others to form opinions before making purchase decisions (Ertimur & Gilly, 2012). But it's not simply enough to identify these enthusiasts and to monitor their conversations. A brand must communicate to these high-value consumers the value of the brand/consumer relationship (i.e., what makes the relationship worthwhile to both parties), and then enlist those influencers (through incentives) to spread positive WOM (Osterholm, 2013). Here social media provides the vehicle to manage the brand networks and loyalty programs (Stone & Woodcock, 2013) and to determine "how" to "influence the influencers". "The incentives offered to influencers can be tangible (such as discounts or freebies), intangible (such as recognition in a social network) or both" (Kumar & Mirchandani, 2012, p. 57).

Some companies are taking the next step beyond social intelligence. In a recent survey conducted by Forrester Research, Inc. (2011), 64% of 200 US-based marketers at medium and large companies indicated that they are incorporating customer ideas into process or product improvements. Known as User-Generated Content (UGC), its content that is "created outside of professional routines and practices" (Kaplan & Haenlein, 2010, p. 61). Coming in various forms from customer product or service reviews, blog posts, comments on a forum, Twitter tweets, sites such as Wikipedia where users contribute to articles, Facebook posts, or even some videos on YouTube, etc., etc., UGC can be of benefit to companies because it aggregates the large pool of online talent, and facilitating collaboration through UGC tends to be a low cost endeavor (Liu-Thompkins & Rogerson, 2012). Further, brand advocates as discussed above are more likely to be creators of UGC (Liu-Thompkins & Rogerson, 2012). Research also has shown that consumer involvement with UGC can positively impact consumer-based brand equity; as brand equity increases, the more positive effect it has on co-creation and the community (Christodoulides, Jevons, & Bonhomme, 2012). It should be noted however that while UGC is content developed by consumers, much of UGC is "produced in a co-created brand environment" in which marketers can and should engage with consumers (Fournier & Avery, 2011; Smith et al., 2012, p. 106).

Crowdsourcing is one form of UGC that provides opportunities for marketers, especially in the new product development phase and subsequent product marketing. Crowdsourcing is an "online, distributed problem solving and production model largely in use for business. It leverages the collective intelligence of online communities by soliciting ideas and solutions for an organization from these communities through the form of an open call" (Brabham, 2010, p. 2). Here the activity of co-creation allows the consumer to collaborate with the company and other consumers in order to generate value (Christodoulides et al., 2012). Utilization of crowdsourcing in the product development phase has resulted in improved profitability from reduced new product failures and quicker speed to market (Stone & Woodcock, 2013). And a number of companies have turned to crowdsourcing as a means of engaging their consumers on a deeper level.

Coca-Cola has used its 50 million+ person Facebook community to help mold a new marketing strategy while also collaborating on product development projects with its customers (Seb, 2012). Elsewhere, companies such as Mountain Dew, Pizza Hut, and Doritos have asked consumers to design new ad campaigns. Recently, P&G initiated a "My Talking Stain Commercial Contest" inviting consumers to create their own ads for the product. Harnessing the Relationship Marketing and WOM literatures, the campaign effectively inspired consumers' creativity and started an authentic dialogue with consumers (Ertimur & Gilly, 2012).

In each of these cases, the companies had fans within their social media networks that were passionate about the brand and its products. Here the openness and flexibility of social media allowed social media marketers to tap into a group with a clear desire to become part of the product design and marketing process (Smith, 2012). However, as with any new business proposition, crowdsourcing is not a panacea to solve every problem. One study determined that the best scenario was actually to utilize crowdsourcing to gather ideas from consumers that could then be used to complement the ideas generated internally by company professionals (Poetz & Schreier, 2012).

Guidelines for Implementing a SMM Strategy

To aid companies in implementing SMM initiatives, the following tips are offered as a means to guide marketers in formulating, implementing and evaluating a SMM strategy.

Tip 1: Integrate SMM Holistically

Understanding that SMM is one element within an integrated marketing communications plan, it is vital that marketers *integrate* SMM with ongoing marketing activities and strategies to ensure a cohesive brand message and approach. All too often companies jump on board with SMM as a tactical tool. Because managers tend to be older than many lower-level staffers, they perceive these younger staff members as universally better informed of the intricacies and trends of SMM. While there may in fact be generational differences in regard to understanding and using SMM, what managers offer to the SMM puzzle that young interns or low-level staffers can't yet recognize is the overall strategic contribution that SMM can make to the corporate and brand positioning. In this way, SMM must be viewed as another brand-building mechanism. How tightly SMM programs, activities, and strategies are intertwined with overall IMC efforts will largely determine the effectiveness of SMM as a brand-building tool. For this reason, managers should not create SMM campaigns in isolation of their other marketing efforts and should stay intimately involved with the campaign planning, implementation, and evaluation.

Tip 2: Conduct On-Going Research

As highlighted in this chapter, not all SMM is created equal. Consider the evolution of television broadcasting as a good example to predict where SMM may be headed. In the early years of television, very few stations were broadcast and the consumer targeting was very broad and general. For most advertisers, the target was defined as "those watching television in the evenings." As additional stations were added via cable and now satellite options, there are literally hundreds (if not thousands) of consumer options for entertainment and this has created a micro-targeting approach for many advertisers. This evolution can help us to understand SMM as well. Initially, Facebook appealed to anyone interested in connecting with others socially via the Internet. Today, as more and more sites pop up, their operational function (what they are used for) and who they are targeting has become more refined and narrow. This phenomenon will continue, and marketers need to closely watch the trends and audience numbers for various SMM options to ensure they are correctly targeting via the more effective avenues. In this way, it is critical to recognize and understand the differences between social media, bookmarking, blogging and geo-location sites, and for whom these sites appeal most.

Tip 3: Identify Role Models

Because of the velocity of trends and proliferation of SMM choices, marketers may be leery of their ability to determine, formulate, and ultimately implement sound SMM campaigns. One way to help companies robustly develop and compete in the SMM space is for companies to identify a group of peer companies outside of their own industry. In this way, marketing managers can identify with peer-companies who are targeting similar customers and positioning their brands in a complementary manner to their own brand. By watching these peer-companies, marketing managers can observe, learn, and expand their own approaches to new customer campaign ideas that might help further brand-building within their own firms. By selecting and "following/liking" a peer-group of firms and paying attention to their iterative marketing efforts, companies can more easily monitor marketplace changes and develop new ideas to improve their own efforts. This strategy can be particularly helpful for companies that have traditionally only followed their own industry closely, but have not looked beyond their core industry. Without a look beyond your own industry, managers can get lulled into believing that just because a fellow competitor is doing some form of SMM, that you must follow suit. We recommend that marketers expand their view in order to recognize broader marketplace changes, SMM trends, and audience preference.

Tip 4: Measure Quantitatively and Qualitatively

As discussed in this chapter, driving "likes" of your brand and engaging the friends of loyal customers in your SMM efforts can be as effective as measuring purchase results. In this way, it is vital to measure the effectiveness of SMM via both quantitative and qualitative measures. From the quantitative standpoint, full cadres of analytic tools are available for use that allow managers to measure and evaluate their SMM efforts through rigorous financial analysis. In this way, SMM should be viewed like any other paid media placement and should be planned with spending allocations based on strategic goals and measurable ROI targets. Just because most SMM is relatively inexpensive doesn't mean it automatically makes sense for your brand. Likewise, from a qualitative perspective, SMM can positively contribute to your brand building efforts but the beneficial results may be embedded in more qualitative themes. Measures such as pass-along comments, the tone of online consumer reviews of your products, and the number of "likes" can all be used as softer measures that provide a directional gauge for your efforts. These qualitative measures also tend to provide a leading indicator of the harder quantitative results that will likely follow. Therefore, qualitative measures can be as valuable to a manager's strategic planning and assessment as quantitative results and ROI calculations. With these two approaches for measuring results, you will have the proper data and logic to determine if an SMM option can replace other media in your arsenal.

Tip 5: Use an Expert "Intern"

As mentioned, SMM trends, new sites, and audience preferences are changing at an amazing pace. With this rate of change it can be difficult to stay on top of SMM options. While it was suggested earlier in this chapter to "follow/like" peer companies that you identify with and that are doing a good job targeting the same customer groups as your firm; likewise, you must take action to keep your own firm abreast of new SMM developments. This can sound daunting and expensive, but we recommend solving this challenge with inexpensive social media "gurus" or interns. By hiring an intern (or a few) to surf the web and explore, experience, and evaluate current SMM options, you will give a young professional(s) the chance to develop expertise in the SMM space (and your industry) while providing you with up-to-date reports on what's trending up (and down), what's buzzing in the industry, and who is doing it best. So while keeping up to date on SMM can sound daunting, a young 20-something can help you navigate and determine what SMM to try next. Additionally, this position can provide weekly trending reports and keep your entire team up-to-date on new sites and trending developments within existing sites, which can increase the expertise of the team as a whole.

Tip 6: Create a Web Policy

As soon as your company ventures into SMM, you will notice a curious thing – you will begin to hear the chatter of your customers more clearly, more loudly, and often more critically. The Internet is the great liaison between companies and the customers they serve, and therefore, SMM will activate customer feedback that is typically faster, harsher, and less private. Because we recommend that you have someone monitoring all of your web assets as they relate to SMM, it is vital that these individuals know how to handle critical feedback and what actions they should take when they come across an inaccuracy in an online customer review of your product/service. When a customer publicly posts a story about a gross-injustice experienced at the hands of your firm or brand, should you react? If misinformation is posted about your firm or brand, should you reply? These questions and dozens more like it must be contemplated in advance and captured via a web policy for your employees so they know how to monitor user-generated content on your site and across related social media sites. Don't assume your employees will know how to handle customer inquiries, complaints, and viral misinformation on the web. We do not recommend deleting messages, reviews, or posts that are negative since customers value balanced information that is neither too positive or negative (O'Reilly & Marx, 2011); therefore, your web policy should provide guidance to employees so that they respond appropriately and do not embroil your brand in a debate of opinion fought via keyboard. Ensure that your employees know what is expected, what they should do, and who they should contact if something pops up that they do not know how to handle.

Evaluating the Likelihood of SMM Success

It's important to remember that in the deployment of any SMM initiative that a combination of both strategic actions and organizational capabilities must be considered. According to the consulting firm, Aberdeen Group (2008), a SMM Strategy requires "not only the need to create new cross-functional, enterprise-wide business processes to collect, manage, and share information with relevant stakeholders, as well as to measure success, but also the need to educate employees about the value …and why it should matter to them in the context of their specific areas of accountability" (p. 9).

Accordingly, as a further aid to companies to help them identify their firms' likelihood of success in implementing SMM initiatives, the following suggestions are offered:

Understand Your Own Bias for Online vs. Offline Programs

Commonly senior management determines strategic corporate direction. While this is not inherently problematic, consideration must be given to the decision-makers own characteristics and biases. For instance, managers in their 40s or 50s may not appreciate the value of mobile marketing or new SMM developments. Therefore, leaders should understand their own biases and invite the views of customers and/or employees so that a wide range of consumer types provide feedback regarding how best to interact with customers. Additionally for those who tend to favor the ease of online and potential for SMM to be a robust method of brand-building, we would caution and advise the same: invite the views of customers and/or employees so that a wide range of consumer types provide feedback regarding how best to interact with customers. To truly build brand value for the firm and equity from customers requires a give-and-take that will be likely to reward balanced approaches to online and offline marketing efforts.

Can Company Systems Fully Integrate Online and Offline Marketing Activities?

If the computer systems of a firm are unable to effectively integrate with all customer-facing initiatives (whether online or offline), priority should be to upgrade the system to make integration possible. Without a fully-integrated system, SMM will be silo-based and unlikely to optimally deliver new and compelling value to customers. Optimal brand-building through SMM will enable brand engagement between customers and the firm; and typically the firms' website will be the bridge that links these two stakeholder groups together. Without a solid IT platform that is capable of integrating all functions, particularly in this age of big data and analytics, good consumer perceptions of the firm online can be instantly destroyed when a click through to the company's website is met with "denial of service" failures due to a weak IT platform, spotty security, or unanticipated demand.

Is the Organizational Culture Open To Honest Feedback?

Because SMM typically involves two-way communication with customers, organizations will quickly begin to harvest both positive and negative input from the marketplace. For some organizations this will be received positively and viewed as a means to develop improvement strategies that focus on the cares and concerns of its current customers. For other firms, negative feedback may be met with a less open culture. Make sure your firm is ready for 'honest' feedback from consumers and that processes and procedures are in place to receive, respond, and act on suggestions from customers. Research tells us that the quickest way to shut down customer feedback is to do nothing or worse yet, delete feedback from your forums or threaded discussion boards that don't meet your own version of the brand's strengths. Firms should be ready for the good, the bad, and the ugly of online communications since for many customers, the Internet provides a large dose of "keyboard courage" which may be a jagged pill for some marketing managers to swallow. If you are not ready for negative feedback, you are not ready for SMM initiatives.

What Benefits Does the Company Expect to Derive from SMM?

Unmanaged, SMM can alter the balance between building relationships with customers and creating cost savings through streamlined transactions and automated e-marketing. In essence, the power of the one-to-one relationship can easily be converted into an efficient and effective exchange between the customer and the company's computer. While customers do in fact value the benefits of electronic exchange (Porter & Donthu, 2008), we believe the benefits of combining human interaction and accessibility with electronic systems outweigh a purely electronic exchange. Therefore, if the only desire for SMM rests with minimizing overhead or automating customer touch points, SMM is unlikely to deliver optimally. To maximize the likelihood of success take the time to ensure that the benefits of SMM exposure and brand building align with the corporate strategic positioning and differentiation.

How Will the Company Measure SMM Success?

By understanding upfront how SMM success will be measured, managers can thoughtfully consider if the benefits are likely to outweigh the costs. If the measure of success is simply a decrease in traditional (offline) marketing spending, how are changes in consumer interaction, response rates, referrals, or loyalty considered in a cost/benefit analysis? Reduced costs are only of value with concurrent value-added increases in customer behavior like engagement of customers fans and friends, repeat purchases, referrals, or increased job averages.

FUTURE RESEARCH DIRECTIONS

The nature of e-Business applications, like SMM, will continue to hold great promise as well as challenges for practitioners. Understanding the role that people, business processes, and technology play as a conduit between firm and customer is key. Therefore, we suggest that future research on SMM should be viewed from a cross-disciplinary lens that considers research from information systems, marketing, management, and psychology to name but a few. To effectively bridge this research divide requires a holistic look at the combination of people, processes, and technology as key drivers of SMM innovation and change.

CONCLUSION

The advent of social media requires practitioners today to shift their thinking; away from a one-way, push model, to a scenario where consumers are actively involved with companies and increasingly connected to other consumers through a variety of channels. The locus of control has now shifted to the consumer, and firms must both actively listen to consumers and agree to engage in open, two-way conversations to succeed (Stone & Woodcock, 2013). In order to utilize the opportunities provided by new media, managers must thoroughly understand the tools available to them.

This chapter has highlighted an approach for developing consumer-based brand equity via social media marketing (SMM). SMM offers companies the opportunity to become a more active partner "in the conversation" with empowered consumers through social media exposure, the engagement of loyal fan and brand advocate networks, and tapping into valuable market intelligence via social listening and crowdsourcing. With only 20% of U.S. companies focusing marketing efforts on consumer-centric social media strategies (Forrester, 2011), the time is right for insightful practitioners to commit to the deeper interactions with consumers through SMM that correlate with increased brand equity and better financial performance.

REFERENCES

Aberdeen Group. (2008). *Social media monitoring and analysis: Generating consumer insights from online conversation*. Retrieved September 1, 2013 from http://robertoigarza.files.wordpress.com/2008/10/rep-social-media-monitoring-and-analysis-aberdeen-group-2008.pdf

Algesheimer, R., Dholakia, U. M., & Herrmann, A. (2005). The social influence of brand community: Evidence from European car clubs. *Journal of Marketing*, *69*(3), 19–34. doi:10.1509/jmkg.69.3.19.66363

Bagozzi, R. P. (1974). Marketing as an organized behavioral system of exchange. *Journal of Marketing*, *38*(4), 77–81. doi:10.2307/1250397

Bastone, J. (2010, August 17). Evaluate social media by listening, leveraging and engaging. *Direct: Magazine of Direct Marketing*. Retrieved February 12, 2014 from http://www.chiefmarketer.com/web-marketing/evaluate-social-media-by-listening-leveraging-and-engaging-17082010

Booth, N., & Matic, J. A. (2011). Mapping and leveraging influencers in social media to shape corporate brand perceptions. *Corporate Communications: An International Journal*, *16*(3), 184–191. doi:10.1108/13563281111156853

Boulding, W., Staelin, R., Ehret, M., & Johnston, W. J. (2005). A customer relationship management roadmap: What is known, potential pitfalls, and where to go. *Journal of Marketing*, *69*(4), 155–166. doi:10.1509/jmkg.2005.69.4.155

Brabham, D. C. (2010, November). The effectiveness of crowdsourcing public participation in a planning context. *SSRN Working Paper Series*.

Brogan, C., & Bastone, J. (2014). Acting on customer intelligence from social media. *AMA Marketing Effectiveness Online Seminar Series*. Retrieved February 12, 2014 from https://www.sas.com/offices/NA/canada/en/resources/white-paper/wp_21122.pdf

Brown, S., Kozinets, R. V., & Sherry, J. F. Jr. (2003). Teaching old brands new tricks: Retro branding and the revival of brand meaning. *Journal of Marketing*, *67*(3), 19–33. doi:10.1509/jmkg.67.3.19.18657

Castronovo, C., & Huang, L. (2012). Social media in an alternative marketing communication model. *Journal of Marketing Development and Competitiveness*, *6*(1), 117–134.

Christodoulides, G., Jevons, C., & Bonhomme, J. (2012). Memo to marketers: Quantitative evidence for change. How user-generated content really affects brands. *Journal of Advertising Research*, *52*(1), 53–64. doi:10.2501/JAR-52-1-053-064

Clawson, T. (2012, July 11). Email's social evolution. *Marketing*, S8-S9.

Czepiel, J. A. (1990). Service encounters and service relationships: Implications for research. *Journal of Business Research*, *20*(1), 13–21. doi:10.1016/0148-2963(90)90038-F

Ertimur, B., & Gilly, M. C. (2012). So Whaddya think? Consumers create ads and other consumers critique them. *Journal of Interactive Marketing*, *26*(3), 115–130. doi:10.1016/j.intmar.2011.10.002

Forrester Research, Inc. (2011). *Listening and engaging in the digital marketing age*. Retrieved August 31, 2013 from http://i.dell.com/sites/content/corporate/secure/en/Documents/listening-and-engaging-in-the-digital-marketing-age.pdf

Fournier, S., & Avery, J. (2011). The uninvited brand. *Business Horizons*, *54*(3), 193–207. doi:10.1016/j.bushor.2011.01.001

Frow, P., & Payne, A. (2007). Special issue papers. Towards the 'perfect' customer experience. *Brand Management*, *15*(2), 89–101. doi:10.1057/palgrave.bm.2550120

Grimes, S. (2013). The rise and stall of social media listening. *Information Week*, *1361*, 5–6.

Grönoos, C. (1994). From Marketing Mix to Relationship Marketing: Towards a paradigm shift in marketing. *Management Decision*, *32*(2), 4–20. doi:10.1108/00251749410054774

Grönroos, C. (1997). Value-driven relational marketing: From products to resources and competencies. *Journal of Marketing Management*, *13*(5), 407–419. doi:10.1080/0267257X.1997.9964482

Gummesson, E. (1994). Making relationship marketing operational. *International Journal of Service Industry Management*, *5*(5), 5–20. doi:10.1108/09564239410074349

Gundlach, H., & Neville, B. (2012). Authenticity: Further theoretical and practical development. *Journal of Brand Management*, *19*(6), 484–499. doi:10.1057/bm.2011.51

Harker, M. J., & Egan, J. (2006). The past, present and future of relationship marketing. *Journal of Marketing Management*, *22*(1-2), 215–242. doi:10.1362/026725706776022326

Hennig-Thurau, T., Malthouse, E., Friege, C., Gensler, S., Lobschat, L., Rangaswamy, A., & Skiera, B. (2010). The impact of new media on customer relationships. *Journal of Service Research*, *13*(3), 311–330. doi:10.1177/1094670510375460

Herring, S. C. (2008). Questioning the generational divide: Technological exoticism and adult constructions of online youth identity. In D. Buckingham (Ed.), *Youth, Identity, and Digital Media* (pp. 71–92). Cambridge, MA: The MIT Press.

Hinde, R. A. (1979). *Towards understanding relationships*. London, UK: Academic Press.

Hoffman, D. L., & Fodor, M. (2010). Can you measure the ROI of your social media marketing? *MIT Sloan Management Review*, *52*(1), 41–49.

Ito, M., Davidson, C., Jenkins, H., Lee, C., Eisenberg, M., & Weiss, J. (2008). Youth online authorship. In D. Buckingham (Ed.), *Youth, identity, and digital media*. Cambridge, MA: The MIT Press.

Kaplan, A. M., & Haenlein, M. (2010). Users of the world, unite! The challenges and opportunities of social media. *Business Horizons*, *53*(1), 59–68. doi:10.1016/j.bushor.2009.09.003

Keller, K. L. (1993). Conceptualizing, measuring, and managing customer-based brand equity. *Journal of Marketing*, *57*(1), 1–22. doi:10.2307/1252054

Keller, K. L. (2009). Building strong brands in a modern marketing communications environment. *Journal of Marketing Communications*, *15*(2), 139–155. doi:10.1080/13527260902757530

Kumar, V., & Mirchandani, R. (2012). Increasing the ROI of social media marketing. *MIT Sloan Management Review*, *54*(1), 55–61.

Li, C. (2009). *The world's most valuable brands. Who's most engaged? ENGAGEMENTdb: Ranking the top 100 global brands*. Retrieved February 9, 2014 from http://www.altimetergroup.com/2009/07/engagementdb.html

Lipsman, A., Mudd, G., Rich, M., & Bruich, S. (2012, March). The power of like: How brands reach (and influence) fans through social media. *Journal of Advertising Research*, *52*(1), 40–52. doi:10.2501/JAR-52-1-040-052

Liu-Thompkins, Y., & Rogerson, M. (2012). Rising to stardom: An empirical investigation of the diffusion of user-generated content. *Journal of Interactive Marketing*, *26*(2), 71–82. doi:10.1016/j.intmar.2011.11.003

McCarthy, E. J. (1960). *Basic marketing*. Columbus, OH: McGraw-Hill/Irwin.

Nielsen. (2012). *Global consumers' trust in 'earned' advertising grows in importance*. Retrieved September 1, 2013 from http://www.nielsen.com/us/en/press-room/2012/nielsen-global-consumers-trust-in-earned-advertising-grows.html

O'Reilly, K., & Marx, S. (2011). How young, technical consumers determine online WOM credibility. *Qualitative Market Research: An International Journal*, *14*(4), 330–359. doi:10.1108/13522751111163191

Osarenkhoe, A. (2006). Customer-centric strategy: A longitudinal study of implementation of a customer relationship management solution. *International Journal of Technology Marketing*, *1*, 115–144.

Osterholm, J. (2013). *Brand fandom: The modern market mavens of the digital age*. Retrieved August 31, 2013 from http://odmgrp.com/blog/2013/01/24/brand-fandom-the-modern-market-mavens-of-the-digital-age/

Owyang, J. (2009). *The future of the social web: In five eras*. Retrieved April 24, 2012 from http://www.web-strategist.com/blog/2009/04/27/future-of-the-social-web/

Parvatiyar, A., & Sheth, J. N. (2001). Customer relationship management: Emerging practice, process, and discipline. *Journal of Economic and Social Research*, *3*(2), 1–34.

Payne, A., & Frow, P. (2005). A strategic framework for customer relationship management. *Journal of Marketing*, *69*(4), 167–176. doi:10.1509/jmkg.2005.69.4.167

Payne, A. F., Storbacka, K., & Frow, P. (2008). Managing the co-creation of value. *Journal of the Academy of Marketing Science*, *36*(1), 83–96. doi:10.1007/s11747-007-0070-0

Poetz, M. K., & Schreier, M. (2012). The value of crowdsourcing: Can users really compete with professionals in generating new product ideas? *Journal of Product Innovation Management*, *29*(2), 245–256. doi:10.1111/j.1540-5885.2011.00893.x

Porter, C. E., & Donthu, N. (2008). Cultivating trust and harvesting value in virtual communities. *Management Science*, *54*(1), 113–128. doi:10.1287/mnsc.1070.0765

Porter, M. E. (1987). From competitive advantage to corporate strategy. *Harvard Business Review*, *65*, 43–59.

Qualman, E. (2009). *Socialnomics: How social media transforms the way we live and do business*. John Wiley & Sons, Incorporated.

Reinartz, W., Krafft, M., & Hoyer, W. D. (2004). The customer relationship management process: Its measurement and impact on performance. *JMR, Journal of Marketing Research*, *41*(3), 293–305. doi:10.1509/jmkr.41.3.293.35991

Schultz, D. E. (1999). Integrated marketing communications and how it relates to traditional media advertising. In J. P. Jones (Ed.), *The Advertising Business: Operations, Creativity, Media Planning, Integrated Communications* (pp. 325–338). London, UK: Sage. doi:10.4135/9781452231440.n34

Schultz, D. E., & Peltier, J. (2013). Social media's slippery slope: challenges, opportunities and future research directions. *Journal of Research in Interactive Marketing*, *7*(2), 86–99. doi:10.1108/JRIM-12-2012-0054

Schweidel, D. A., & Moe, W. W. (2012, October). The perils of 'selective listening' in social media monitoring: Sentiment and venue choice in social media posting behavior. *SSRN Working Paper Series*.

Schweidel, D. A., Moe, W. W., & Boudreaux, C. (2011). *Social media intelligence: Measuring brand sentiment from online conversations*. Retrieved February 12, 2014 from http://ssrn.com/abstract=1874892 or http://dx.doi.org/10.2139/ssrn.1874892

Seb, J. (2012, November 15). Brands delve deeper into crowdsourcing. *Marketing Week*, 6.

Sinickas, A. (2010/2011). Who needs surveys when you can scan social media? *SCM*, *15*(1), 11.

Smith, A. (2012, April 20). Three amazing crowdsourcing campaigns. *Social Media Today*. Retrieved September 1, 2013 from http://socialmediatoday.com/alex-smith/492666/three-amazing-crowdsourcing-campaigns

Smith, A. N., Fischer, E., & Yongjian, C. (2012). How does brand-related user-generated content differ across YouTube, Facebook, and Twitter? *Journal of Interactive Marketing*, *26*(2), 102–113. doi:10.1016/j.intmar.2012.01.002

Social Media Examiner. (2013). Retrieved January 3, 2014 from http://www.socialmediaexaminer.com/social-media-marketing-industry-report-2013/

Stone, M., & Woodcock, N. (2013). Social intelligence in customer engagement. *Journal of Strategic Marketing*, *21*(5), 394–401. doi:10.1080/0965254X.2013.801613

Veeck, A. (2013, October). Beyond monitoring: Analyzing the content of social media data. *Quirks*, 74-75.

Verhoef, P. C., & Langerak, F. (2002). Eleven misconceptions about customer relationship management. *Business Strategy Review*, *13*(4), 70–76. doi:10.1111/1467-8616.00235

Vivek, S. D., Beatty, S. E., & Morgan, R. M. (2012). Customer engagement: Exploring customer relationships beyond purchase. *Journal of Marketing Theory and Practice*, *20*(2), 127–145. doi:10.2753/MTP1069-6679200201

Walters, S. (2013). Beyond listening: Six steps for integrating and acting on social media. *Business Intelligence Journal*, *18*(1), 13–17.

Weiss, A. M., Lurie, N. H., & MacInnis, D. J. (2008). Listening to strangers: Whose responses are valuable, how valuable are they, and why? *JMR, Journal of Marketing Research*, *45*(4), 425–436. doi:10.1509/jmkr.45.4.425

ADDITIONAL READING

Bowden, J. L. H. (2009). The process of customer engagement: A conceptual framework. *Journal of Marketing Theory and Practice*, *7*(1), 63–74. doi:10.2753/MTP1069-6679170105

Churchill, G. A. Jr. (1979). A paradigm for developing better measures in marketing. *JMR, Journal of Marketing Research*, *16*(February), 64–73. doi:10.2307/3150876

Court, D., Gordon, J., & Perrey, J. (2012). Measuring marketing's worth. *The McKinsey Quarterly*, *3*, 113–118.

de Vries, L., Gensler, S., & Leeflang, P. S. H. (2012). Popularity of brand posts on brand fan pages: An investigation of the effects of social media. *Journal of Interactive Marketing*, *26*(2), 83–91. doi:10.1016/j.intmar.2012.01.003

Divol, R., Edelman, D., & Sarrazin, H. (2012). Demystifying social media. *The McKinsey Quarterly*, *2*, 66–77.

Gabrielli, V., & Balboni, B. (2010). SME practice towards integrated marketing communications. *Marketing Intelligence & Planning*, *28*(3), 275–290. doi:10.1108/02634501011041426

Keller, K. L. (2010). Brand equity management in a multichannel, multimedia retail environment. *Journal of Interactive Marketing*, *24*(2), 58–70. doi:10.1016/j.intmar.2010.03.001

Kerr, B. (2009). Shopping for loyalty: An executive's wish list. *Journal of Consumer Marketing*, *26*(1), 49–51. doi:10.1108/07363760910927046

Kumar, V., Aksoy, L., Donkers, B., Venkatesan, R., Wiesel, T., & Tillmanns, S. (2010). Undervalued or overvalued customers: Capturing total customer engagement value. *Journal of Service Research*, *13*(3), 297–310. doi:10.1177/1094670510375602

LaPointe, P. (2011). The rock in the pond: How online buzz and offline WOM can make a strong message even more powerful. *Journal of Advertising Research*, *51*(3), 456–457. doi:10.2501/JAR-51-3-456-457

LaPointe, P. (2012). Measuring Facebook's impact on marketing: The proverbial hits the fan. *Journal of Advertising Research*, *52*(3), 286–287. doi:10.2501/JAR-52-3-286-287

McAlexander, J. H., Schouten, J. W., & Koenig, H. F. (2002). Building brand community. *Journal of Marketing*, *66*(January), 38–54. doi:10.1509/jmkg.66.1.38.18451

Morgan, R. M., & Hunt, S. D. (1994). The commitment-trust theory of relationship marketing. *Journal of Marketing*, *58*(July), 20–38. doi:10.2307/1252308

Naylor, R. W., Lamberton, C. P., & West, P. M. (2012). Beyond the like button: The impact of mere virtual presence on brand evaluations and purchase intentions in social media settings. *Journal of Marketing*, *76*(6), 105–120. doi:10.1509/jm.11.0105

Nelson-Field, K., Riebe, E., & Sharp, B. (2012). What's not to like? Can a Facebook fan base give a brand the advertising reach it needs? *Journal of Advertising Research*, *52*(2), 262–269. doi:10.2501/JAR-52-2-262-269

Pomirleanu, N., Schibrowsky, J. E., Peltier, J. W., & Nill, A. (2013). Internet marketing research: A review of the literature. *Journal of Research in Interactive Marketing*, *7*(3), 166–181. doi:10.1108/JRIM-01-2013-0006

Porter, C. E., Donthu, N., MacElroy, W. H., & Wydra, D. (2011). How to foster and sustain engagement in virtual communities. *California Management Review*, *53*(4), 80–110. doi:10.1525/cmr.2011.53.4.80

Quinton, S., & Harridge-March, S. (2010). Relationships in online communities: The potential for marketers. *Journal of Research in Interactive Marketing*, *4*(1), 59–73. doi:10.1108/17505931011033560

Reichheld, F. F. (2011). The one number you need. *Harvard Business Review*, *81*(December), 46–54.

Sawhney, M., Verona, G., & Prandelli, E. (2005). Collaborating to create: The internet as a platform for customer engagement in product innovation. *Journal of Interactive Marketing*, *19*(4), 4–17. doi:10.1002/dir.20046

Schultz, D. E., & Block, M. P. (2012). Rethinking brand loyalty in an age in interactivity. *Journal of Brand Management*, *1*(3), 21–39.

Singh, S., & Sonnenburg, S. (2012). Brand performances in social media. *Journal of Interactive Marketing*, *26*(4), 189–197. doi:10.1016/j.intmar.2012.04.001

Sonnier, G. P., McAlister, L., & Ritz, O. J. (2011). A dynamic model of the effect of online communications on firm sales. *Marketing Science*, *30*(4), 702–716. doi:10.1287/mksc.1110.0642

Trueman, M., Cornelius, N., & Wallace, J. (2012). Building brand value online: Exploring relationships between company and city brands. *European Journal of Marketing*, *46*(7/8), 1013–1031. doi:10.1108/03090561211230179

Williams, R. L., & Cothrell, J. (2000). Four smart ways to run online communities. *Sloan Management Review*, *41*(4), 81–91.

KEY TERMS AND DEFINITIONS

Consumer Engagement: Consumer engagement is the interaction of customers with one another, with a company or a brand that is typically either consumer- or company-led. It is typically seen as the phase occurring after a customer is exposed to a certain marketing message.

Consumer Exposure: Consumer exposure represents both the reach and frequency of company messages that are typically delivered via a marketing campaign and/or media. These campaigns are designed to market specific services or products to a target customer or customer group.

Consumer Loyalty: Customer loyalty is typically expressed as the byproduct of attracting the right customer, getting them to buy more and often, which then can result in the customer recommending other customers to your brand.

Consumer-Based Brand Equity: The positive effect of all types of knowledge a consumer has about a brand that favorably impacts the consumer's response to the brands' marketing.

Integrated Marketing Communications (IMC): IMC requires that marketers evaluate different communication options from a perspective of horizontal and vertical coordination, that is, both across and within media with a particular focus on the coordination of consumer messaging across all communication channels.

Social Bookmarking Site: A social bookmarking site allows users to add, annotate, edit, and share bookmarks with others.

Social Media Marketing: Social media marketing is best understood as the marketing activities taking place on an Internet platform (e.g. Facebook) that offers one-to-one opportunities for meeting and interacting with companies and other customers.

Social Media: Social media is best understood as an Internet platform that offers one-to-one methods for meeting and interacting with companies and other customers.

Social Networking Site: A social networking site is a website or platform that allows individuals or companies to view and connect with their social network as well as the networks of others.

Chapter 5
Viral Advertising and the Implications of Social Media

Maria Petrescu
Nova Southeastern University, USA

ABSTRACT

Given the estimated online advertising market in the United States of around 4 billion dollars and the current proliferation of social media Websites, this study focuses on reviewing the key theoretical and practical aspects related to viral advertising. It includes an overview of different aspects related to the nature, characteristics, and evaluation of viral advertising, especially focusing on what makes advertisements viral. After a review of the term viral advertising, the author discusses the key characteristics of viral ads, including the most used viral advertising appeals—humor and sexual—and also including a section regarding the importance of the message source on consumers' reaction towards an advertisement. The study also provides a discussion about consumer-generated advertising, a modern online advertising feature that leads to increased interaction and involvement from consumers. The last part of this chapter focuses on the monitoring and evaluating viral ads outcomes by using both traditional and social media specific advertising measures. The author also presents a few ideas related to future research directions and information that might prove useful for advertising research and practice.

INTRODUCTION

Ever since the creation of the Internet, business research has focused on its impact and influence in the creation of the new media and of a new marketing paradigm. Research has shown that the Internet has affected different aspects of business processes, including key marketing aspects such as pricing, retailing and advertising (Datta, Chowdhury & Chakraborty, 2005; Rust & Oliver, 1994). Technology and other factors have significantly evolved and positively affect consumer behavior, due to a more efficient information exchange and interactivity (Johnson, Bruner II & Kumar, 2006; Keller, 2009). The widespread use of the Internet not only in the U.S., but also across the globe, has helped managers realize the advantages of this new technology, able to complement traditional word-of-mouth communication and to add an online viral way of communication with and among consumers (Datta et al., 2005).

DOI: 10.4018/978-1-4666-6182-0.ch005

The main benefits of online marketing are its capacity of reaching fast and with low-expenses a large segment of consumers, as well as its interactivity, leading to marketing efficiencies. In this context, researchers and practitioners have noted the evolution of advertising from involuntary to voluntary, placing the consumer in control regarding not only the media choice, but also the delivery process of advertising (Keller, 2009; Rust & Oliver, 1994). Thanks to the benefits of new technologies and communication platforms, modern advertising benefits from more interaction, targeted communication, increased reach and better monitoring and evaluation (Kozinets, de Valck, Wojnicki & Wilner, 2010).

Researchers and practitioners have noted that consumers are getting more involved with online viral advertising campaigns that encourage individuals to pass along a marketing message to others by Internet or e-mail. In this context, world-renowned companies and brands, such as Nike, Budweiser, Ford, GMC, Levi's and De Beers have successfully used viral advertising in social media (Borroff 2000; Morrissey 2008; Rechtin 2009; Solman 2008a, 2008b; Thompson 2010). In this case of Internet media, consumers value the non-commercial, non-pushy, personal sources of advertising information and messages received from their peers (Kirby and Marsden 2006; Steyer et al. 2007).

The trend regarding online video advertising is positive, with estimations that in the U.S. it will increase from $1.1 billion in 2009 to $4.1 billion in 2013 (Tsai 2009). Moreover, the positive evolution and the widespread reach of social media websites are significant. For example, in 2013 more than 1 billion unique users were visiting YouTube each month, with over 6 billion hours of video watched monthly. However, research regarding viral marketing and social media has been sparse, with a rather limited understanding of the viral process, both from the point of view of researchers and practitioners (Allsop, Bassett and Hoskins 2007; Borroff 2000; Steyer et al. 2007).

Given the current state of research, we intend to focus on studying aspects related to the nature, characteristics and evaluation of viral advertising, by analyzing how viral advertising works and the contexts in which it performs best. We start with a short history of the viral term and the definition of viral advertising. The study then focuses on the key characteristics of viral ads, as shown by practice and research, with specific discussions related to viral advertising appeals, including the most used, humorous and sexual appeals. Consumer generated advertising is another topic of interest in this context, especially in relation to the various types of social media platforms available for marketers and considering the significant success of recent user-generated ads. The last part of this chapter focuses on the monitoring and evaluation of viral ads outcomes, an important step in assessing the success of a campaign and making potentially necessary adjustments to the strategy.

VIRAL ADVERTISING HISTORY AND DEFINITION

The origin of the term viral marketing is attributed to articles published in the 90s, when the Internet was starting to develop significantly, though there are different sources that receive credit for the term. Many published works attribute the formulation of the term "viral marketing" to Jurvetson and Draper (1997). The two authors used the term "viral marketing" to describe the free email service that Hotmail was providing at that time. In order to promote its services and spread the word about the availability of free email accounts, a message was included each sent e-mail from Hotmail noting that the company provides a free service available to anyone. Jurvetson and Draper's definition of viral marketing is one of the most cited in the literature on viral marketing (Bampo et al. 2008; Cruz and Fill 2008; Datta et al. 2005; Fattah 2000; Swanepoel, Lye and Rugimbana 2009; Petrescu and Korgaonkar 2011).

Other studies cite Harvard professor Rayport as mentioning the term in 1996 (Kirby and Marsden 2006; Shukla 2010), while others mention an even earlier use of the term in 1989, in a PC User magazine article referring to Apple computers - Macintosh (Kirby and Marsden 2006).

In this context, Jurvetson and Draper (1997) defined viral marketing as online word-of-mouth that is enhanced by the use of social networks. Other authors consider that viral marketing is the email use for word-of-mouth referral endorsement from one customer to other prospective customers. Moreover, viral marketing is also defined as the process of encouraging individuals to pass along favorable marketing information received online (Dobele et al. 2005) and as marketing techniques that use pre-existing social networks to produce exponential increases in brand awareness (Datta et al. 2005). Other studies consider viral marketing any form of electronic, online form of word-of-mouth (Anderson 2008; Cruz and Fill 2008). Bampo et al. (2008) define viral marketing as a strategy that encourages individuals to propagate a message, while Welker (2002) defines viral communication as cost reduced transmission of messages through environments that allow exponentially increasing diffusion of the message.

In the modern context of marketing and the Internet, there are many new terms used by marketing research and practitioners. Many of these terms are used interchangeably, even though the concepts of viral advertising, viral marketing, buzz marketing or electronic word-of-mouth each have their own meaning and characteristics (Petrescu and Korgaonkar 2011). Thereof, viral advertising is a term distinct of other concepts used in connection to marketing and the Internet.

Well-known (and seen) viral advertising examples are the "Whassup?" viral ads from Budweiser, the Blendtec advertisements for blenders or the Trojan condoms' 2004 "Sex Olympics", downloaded more than 40 million times (Reid 2005). All of them rely on consumers transmitting the message to their peers within their social circle, either through email or, even more efficiently, through social networks. Viral advertising is controlled by consumers, who need to like the ad enough not only to be convinced to buy the product, but also to pass the message to their family, friends and other members of their social network.

The widespread use of the Internet offers a significantly increased potential of an advertisement becoming viral and having a high and fast diffusion rate. Viral advertising refers to online ads that become viral because consumers take action and actively participate in their diffusion. While sometimes companies pay for their creation, other times they can be user generated; however a key distinction from traditional advertising is represented by unpaid distribution from consumer to consumer. Viral advertising can be transmitted in different forms, such as the link of a video ad from, for example, YouTube, sent through e-mail or social media. In the diffusion from peer to peer intervene the advantages of the Internet and of modern social networking websites, since online peer-to-peer transmission of an ad is much faster and with a much wider reach.

Viral advertising is personal and even though it comes from an identified sponsor, in the peer-to-peer transmission process, companies do not pay for the ad's distribution. Most of the classical viral advertising examples circulating online are ads created and paid by the sponsor brand, launched on the company's website or on social media websites such as YouTube. However, after this phase, consumers receive the link to the advertisement or copy the entire ad and forward it through e-mails, blogs, webpages and social media profiles.

Given the distinction of viral advertising from other terms and especially viral marketing, it is important to clarify its definition. Porter and Golan (2006) define viral advertising as "unpaid peer-to-peer communication of provocative content originating from an identified sponsor using the Internet to persuade or influence an audience to pass along the content to others" (p.29). Viral advertising is seen as contagious advertising messages transmitted from peer to peer in order to increase brand awareness (Kirby and Marsden 2006). In this context, we define viral advertising as unpaid electronic (e-mail, web or social media) distribution of business or user generated advertisements from consumer to consumer, based on distinct advertisement characteristics and appeals, such as ad content likeability, entertainment and controversial characteristics (Petrescu and Korgaonkar 2011).

Regarding the viral advertising characteristics and appeals, research and practice has discussed different aspects, such as a catchy and cool message, controversial content, significant entertainment and higher engagement levels, including a significant use of humorous appeals (Cruz and Fill 2008; Porter and Golan 2006; Swanepoel et al. 2009; Wasserman 2009).

Since viral advertising presents huge benefits for many companies, especially due to low costs and wide diffusion, it is important to study which circumstances enhance its potential, from different types of ad appeals to sender and receiver characteristics.

CONTEXT AND CHARACTERISTICS OF VIRAL ADS

As in the case of traditional advertising, viral advertising also has a significant number of factors that influence it and make it more efficient. Nevertheless, there are key characteristics, such as ad appeals, that are essential in helping an advertisement become viral. Also, some brands can benefit more than others from the effects of viral ads, while companies need to focus, at the same time, on finding the right target in the social network. In this context, we focus on the types of products that can better benefit from the effects of viral ads and the key characteristics of the ad source.

Types of Products

Previous research has shown that the use of peer-to-peer communication is more efficient when consumers need to choose among similar products and brands. In the case of low-differentiation brands and products, viral advertising can help consumers notice the brand and the product and become more interested in trying it (Derbaix and Vanhamme 2003; Larceneux 2007). The efficiency of peer-to-peer communication in the context has been proven by word-of-mouth research, especially for credence and experience goods (Cruz and Fill 2008; Datta et al. 2005; Derbaix and Vanhamme 2003; Hung 2007).

In the context of a widespread use of social media, viral advertising is an attractive tool of promotion and information, especially for companies that are not yet well-known and established, and need to take advantage of a low-cost advertising solution. For products and brands that do not benefit of a "wow" factor, viral advertising has the capacity to create a significant amount of buzz on the market, as long as marketing specialists are able to come up with an advertisement with viral potential (Kirby and Marsden 2006). Viral advertising is, thereof, an unconventional marketing technique that can significantly help small businesses with low budget campaigns, but with unique and compelling messages (Porter and Golan 2006; Swanepoel et al. 2009).

While the success of viral advertising used by well established brands, such as Budweiser and Levi's, shows that viral ads work well for any company, in the current highly competitive global market, where low-differentiation can become a problem, viral advertising can add a cool factor to a product otherwise indistinguishable from its competitors.

While initially marketers estimated that more "interesting" or "cool" brands or categories of products will have a greater opportunity to become successful in a viral environment, studies have shown that any type of brand or product can achieve viral success. What is more important is to have good creative, advertising appeals that attract consumers, make the ad stand-out and determine consumers to forward it (Southgate, Westoby and Page 2010).

The best example in this case is also a classical one, related to the viral ads created by Blendtec. While blenders are definitely not the best example of products with a "cool" factor and able to generate consumer buzz or significant differentiation between brands, Blendtec's viral advertising campaign "Will it blend" was a significant success. It brought significant success and exposure for the brand, by just using video advertisements that show Blendtec blenders being put to work with different "unblendable" products, from CDs to phones. The videos are both company and user generated and were able to get significant consumer attention and involvement for a type of product that usually does not elicit consumers' affective involvement and interest.

In this context, viral advertising fits in the context of a pulling marketing strategy, when the advertiser wants to raise attention, create emotions and make consumers associate the good feeling experienced due to the content of the ad with the otherwise uninteresting brand (Porter and Golan 2006; Shukla 2010).

At the same time, as we will see in the following, the source of the ad influences consumers' reaction to the advertisement, the way they process the information and their intentions to forward an advertisement.

Ad Source

Among the antecedents of attitude toward the ad, researchers include elements such as source credibility and attitude toward the source (Chiu et al. 2007; Cruz and Fill 2008; Lutz, MacKenzie, and Belch 1983; MacKenzie and Lutz 1989). In the context of viral advertising, we discuss about ad source not from the point of view of the sponsor of the ad – the advertising company, but as the consumer (peer) who recommends or talks about an advertisement.

Research related to word-of-mouth noted the impact of interpersonal information sources, on marketplace choices and even on purchasing decisions (Feick and Price 1987; Gilly et al. 1998; Phelps et al. 2004). Researchers also wrote about the importance of sources of information selection, how and from where the information is obtained, in order to understand consumers' responses to marketing and communications (MacInnis and Jaworski 1989; Stewart and Pavlou 2002). In the context of Internet marketing and advertising, personal sources with higher credibility have been found to have a higher impact on consumers' responses and purchasing behavior. Cruz and Fill (2008) showed that if a source is perceived as credible, the messages it transmits are more likely to be acted upon.

Researchers also found that personal sources of information are important for consumers, especially when discussing about new or high-risk products or brands present in a low-differentiation context (Feick and Price 1987; Gilly et al. 1998). Interpersonal sources have a higher influence on consumer behavior because they are perceived as having no personal hidden intentions and nothing to gain from the product or brand recommendations they make (Chiu et al. 2007; Feick and Price 1987). Under these circumstances, messages received from known sources are perceived as more credible (Chiu et al. 2007; Phelps et al. 2004). For these reasons, peer-to-peer communication is considered more credible than commercial communications because it comes from "people like me", that usually have a better image and higher trust potential than a marketer (Allsop et al. 2007).

In viral studies, researchers found that when product or marketing information comes via an e-mail from a person the consumer knows, the receiver is more likely to pass along this information and forward the e-mail to other consumers (Phelps et al. 2004). Of course, when the e-mail originates from an unknown and low credibility source, and it is an unsolicited e-mail, consumers usually delete them or at least do not forward them. Researchers conclude that individuals are more willing to pass along marketing messages if they come from an interpersonal source, rather than a commercial source, especially because they tend to trust more those who are similar to them (Chiu et al. 2007; Phelps et al. 2004).

The better, more trustworthy and closer the relationship between source and receiver, the more likely consumers are to evaluate the senders as credible and dependable, leading to a positive attitude toward the message. Thereof, an advertisement received from a known and/or credible interpersonal source, such as a family member, friend, Facebook contact or any other credible person has the potential to lead to a more positive attitude toward the ad and to a higher chance of forwarding the message.

VIRAL ADS APPEALS: EMOTIONS, SEX, HUMOR

The key characteristics of viral advertising shown by previous research and practice include "commercial-free" traits, especially the capacity of entertaining and engaging consumers, rather than focusing on a call to action (Cruz and Fill 2008). The most effective viral ads are focused on entertaining, creating emotions and generating product or brand awareness, not on transmitting traditional advertising messages and a list of factual information about the product. In this context, emotional ads focus on the emotions that individuals will experience seeing the ads and by using or owning a product. Traditional advertising characteristics, such enjoyment, involvement and branding, which are used in assessing the potential success for offline TV advertising awareness, can also predict viral potential, along with distinctiveness and perceived likelihood to pass along to others, some of the key determinants of viral advertising (Southgate, Westoby and Page 2010).

From this point of view, studies have shown that advertisements targeting more the emotional side of consumers tend to create more favorable attitudes toward the ad than advertising containing a lot of information (Batra and Ray 1986; Muehling and McCann 1993). In addition, previous research has shown that consumers' attitude toward the ad may be improved by the use of humorous appeals and by making the ads more likeable (Chattopadhyay and Basu 1990, Gelb and Pickett 1983; Muehling and McCann 1993). Other types of ad appeals, such as sexual appeals, have been shown to produce favorable attitudes toward the ad, lead to higher sales (Muehling and McCann 1993; Severn et al. 1990), and even outperform the effects of humor (Duncan and Nelson 1985).

Unlike logical arguments, emotions require less effort from the viewer, are more interesting, increase attention to the ad, are easier to recall and can lead more rapidly to a change in behavior (Tellis 2004), which prove to be extremely important elements for viral advertising and intention to forward. Viral ads need to be emotional or funny enough to determine if consumers will send it to their social network (Porter and Golan 2006; Tsai 2009) and build an emotional connection between the campaign and the recipient (Dobele et al. 2007). For example, some of the most shared ads in 2013 were based on consumers' emotional reactions, including Dove's "Real Beauty Sketches" (4.24 million shares), Budweiser's "Brotherhood" (2.72 million shares) and Ram Trucks' "Farmer" (1.88 million shares) (Nudd, 2013; Wassserman, 2013). The ads from Budweiser and Ram, together with the emotion-based "The Scarecrow" ad from Chipotle were also included among the most unforgettable ads of 2013 by Forbes (Smith 2013), while Dove and Chipotle were mentioned among the best by USA Today (Horovitz 2013).

Involvement and enjoyment are emotional outcomes that can make a viral advertisement very effective in the online environment and to have a positive impact on the brand. Research has shown that, in order to have an impact on brand attitudes, an advertisement must attach good memories to the brand (Southgate, Westoby and Page, 2010).

However, it is rather difficult to estimate how consumers will react to the advertisement's appeal, especially in the viral context, where consumers not only need to see the ad, but also forward it. Traditional advertising tools are not usually efficient in pre-testing the potential success of a viral advertisement, though some tools, such as the Millward Brown Link solution, have been shown to work. This is a pre-test tool that includes around 150 25-minute interviews about an advertisement within the target segment (Southgate, Westoby and Page 2010).

Despite the difficulty of using traditional tools, there are already a few successful characteristics and appeals proven successful by viral advertising research and practice. According to a study performed by Porter and Golan (2006), besides funny and humorous ads, other types of appeal use by viral advertisers include sex, nudity and violence. Practice shows that humor and sexual appeal are widely used in successful viral ads, therefore te analyze the two of the most used ad appeals in high-quality viral advertising.

Humor

Advertising research has shown that humor is one of the most widely used message techniques even in traditional advertising, covering as much as 24.4% of prime-time television advertising in the United States (Alden et al. 1993; Brown, Bhadury, and Pope 2010; Weinberger and Gulas 1992). At the same time, some of the most memorable viral ads launched on the U.S. market are based on a humorous appeal, from the "Whassup" Budweiser commercials, to Old Spice and Doritos. In viral context, humorous advertising appeal is one of the most frequently encountered, due to its capacity to spark strong emotions and elicit action (Phelps et al. 2004). For example, some of the most viewed and shared ads of 2013 included some type of humorous appeal, including Geico's "Hump Day"; Kmart's "Ship My Pants", PooPourri's "Girls Don't Poop" and Doritos' "Goat 4 Sale" (Nudd 2013; Smith 2013; Wasserman 2013). Of course, just showing how personal and subjective reaction to humor is, some of these humorous and successful ads were also included by experts among the worst advertisements of the year (Horovitz 2013).

While there is a widespread use of humor in advertising, conclusions are sometimes contradictory and nuanced, since humor is a complex concept by different contextual elements, including type of humor, medium, placement and audience. Research and practice have generally shown that humor has a significant positive effect on attention and recall, potential to increase processing and comprehension, as well as the capacity to increase positive attitudes towards the brand (Chattopadhyay and Basu 1989; Scott et al. 1990; Sternthal and Craig 1973; Weinberger and Gulas 1992). Humor improves attitude toward the ad, increases liking of the ad and reduces irritation experienced from the commercial (Duncan and Nelson 1985; Speck 1987; Weinberger and Gulas 1992).

The key positive effects of humor on advertising, and especially its impact on consumers' direct involvement with the forwarding and viewing of viral ads, come from its capacity to improve consumers' mood, creating joy, satisfaction, and positive feelings then transferred to the advertised brand (Cline et al. 2003).

Since viral advertising is based on consumers transmitting ads to other consumers, the context demands that consumers find a true appeal in the ad, provocative content worth forwarding to others. As a look over the most successful viral ads of the last years shows, most of the viral ads have some form of humor. Porter and Golan (2006) underline the fact that humor is a universal appeal for making content viral, utilized in most viral ads.

The importance of humor in the viral advertising context comes from the fact that consumers are more willing to forward advertising that is engaging, entertaining and creates feelings of good (Chiu et al. 2007; Dobele et al. 2005; Phelps et al. 2004; Stanbouli 2003). This type of emotional appeal is important under online conditions, where viral ads need to be emotional or funny enough to justify their forwarding to the social network. Since funny ads create joy, feelings of good and happiness, they are more likely to be forwarded to others. The main reason for consumers to forward humorous ads is to make individuals around them feel as good as they felt when they saw the humorous ad.

Besides humorous appeals, sexual content is another appeal element used in viral advertisements, including in a combination of the two. In the next section, we present an overview of sexual appeals in advertising.

Sexual Appeals

Advertising that incorporates sexual appeals is based on brand information using sexual content, and includes nudity or sexually suggestive images (Bello, Pitts and Etzel 1983; Reichert, Heckler and Jackson 2001). Researchers have noted that the use of sexual appeals in advertising has been increasing in the USA during the last decades, especially regarding the insertion of graphic content (LaTour and Henthorne 1994; Liu, Cheng and Li 2009; Severn et al. 1990).

Especially in the context of viral advertising, the key objectives of using sexual appeals are to attract attention, generate interest and create market buzz. From this point of view, advertising studies have shown that sexual appeals have potential benefits for advertisements in becoming viral, since sexually charged ads attract significant initial attention and also retain this attention for longer periods of time (Liu et al. 2009). Moreover, the use of sexual content also elicits emotional responses, including excitement and arousal (Liu et al. 2009; Lombardot 2007; Reichert et al. 2001).

Sexual appeals and nudity are among the characteristics that motivate consumers to pass along content online. In the context in websites and social media, it is relatively easier than in traditional media to distribute advertising with sexual appeals, since the regulations regarding the use of sexual content are less restrictive. Moreover, it is easier to target and propagate the message to the right segment of consumers, in order to avoid negative reactions from the public. In this sense, for sexually charged ads to become successful viral ads, they need to be provocative and appeal common human motivations.

The fact that ads with sexual content attract attention and interest is essential in the context of viral advertising, since the online advertising competition is high and diverse. In this context, sexual appeals can contribute to the improvement of ad recall and recognition, and create emotional responses (Reichert et al. 2001). Consumers react more positively to sexually oriented ads, usually rating them as more entertaining, interesting and original than non-sexual ads, resulting in favorable predispositions toward the ad and greater purchase intentions (Severn et al. 1990). The influence of sex appeals on behavioral intention is especially important in the context of viral advertising, where sexual content has the potential to increase forward intentions. For example, articles on viral advertising note the success of online ads deemed too controversial for television, but who create huge audiences through online viral means, including Agent Provocateur, featuring artist Kylie Minogue, a Chanel ad with actress Keira Knightly and a Mercedes-Benz ad featuring model Kate Upton.

Despite the significant benefits of sexual appeals for viral advertising, there is another aspect that marketers need to consider: the gratuitous use of sexual images in ads tends to be penalized by some consumers, especially of feminine gender (Dahl, Sengupta and Vohs 2009). This happens especially when advertisers use sexual appeals that have no relation to the ad and are not relevant to the brand and the context.

For example, a widely seen, but controversial, commercial from 2013 was GoDaddy's "Perfect Match" ad, featured during the SuperBowl and then gone viral on YouTube. The ad features supermodel Bar Refaeli, who represents the "sexy" side of GoDaddy, and Walter, a geeky guy who represents the techy side, who end-up kissing in the ad in a very close-up and awkward kiss. The advertisement received over 11 million views only on YouTube, and over 1 million views for an "extended" version with scenes that were not shown on TV. However, it was mentioned by consumers and critics among the worst ads of 2013, due to its uncomfortable and awkward use of the sexual-appeal (Horovitz 2013). Nevertheless, other advertisements from GoDaddy, especially the sexually charged ads featuring Danica Patrick for a couple of years, were very successful, widely seen online and led to increased traffic on the website do to their "teaser" characteristics. They did not, however, feature such controversial sexual images that could have made viewers uncomfortable.

These examples show that there are other potential disadvantages in using sexually charged ads, such as the potential to detour the attention from the brand message to the sexual content, making the consumer miss the key information of the ad. In this case, the ad might not lead to a positive attitude toward the brand (Severn et al. 1990). However, in the context of viral advertising, these potentially risky issues might not be that important, since the key objective is for consumers to forward the ad and generate market buzz. And even the controversial sexually charged ads that received criticism, such as GoDaddy's, were able to generate millions of views and shares after their launch, therefore create buzz around the brand.

In consequence, in the case of both humorous and sexual appeals, advertisers need to consider not only the relevance and execution of the appeal type, but also aspects related to cultural and demographic differences and preferences, in order to make sure the use of a strong or controversial emotional appeal does not generate significant negative effects and does not make consumers act negatively towards the ad.

CONSUMER GENERATED ADVERTISING

Research related to word-of-mouth also noted the importance of information sources, especially interpersonal, in the diffusion of information, marketplace choices and even in purchasing decisions (Feick and Price 1987; Gilly et al. 1998; Phelps et al. 2004). Researchers also wrote about the importance of sources of information selection, how and from where the information is obtained, in order to understand consumers' responses to marketing and communications (MacInnis and Jaworski 1989; Stewart and Pavlou 2002).

Generally, personal and higher credibility sources have been found to have a higher impact on consumers' responses and purchasing behavior. In the modern marketing world, specialists recommend a careful balance between control and impartiality in marketing initiatives, in order to achieve more credibility (Cruz and Fill 2008). In viral studies, researchers found that when product or marketing information comes via an e-mail from a person the consumer knows, the receiver is more likely to pass along this information and forward the e-mail to other consumers (Phelps et al. 2004).

Besides the importance of the message source, as previously discussed, a significant viral advertising strategy includes user-generated ads. In this context, Internet-based advertising has the advantage of benefiting from a high interactivity potential (Johnson, Bruner and Kumar 2006) that involves consumers not only in the following and forwarding the ad, but also in its creation. Due to the interactive potential of the Internet, the presentation and promotion of advertising content assumes a mutual interaction between consumers and marketers (Stewart and Pavlou 2002). In this context, consumer-generated viral ads come as a response to Internet users looking for more interactive marketing communications (Stanbouli 2003).

Interactive marketing communications can present significant benefits for a brand, since they encourage attitude formation and behavioral decisions, especially when combined with off-line channels (Keller 2009. These online interactions can also contribute to strengthening brand attachment and improving the relationships consumers have with brands.

In order to increase interactivity in their advertising strategy, many companies have resorted lately to user-generated advertising campaigns, involving consumers in the creation of advertising. Such an example is represented by Doritos, a brand that has been running for several years an advertising competition for its fans. The best, and usually the funniest ads, receive prizes and are shown during the SuperBowl and on the web. Besides the millions of views the benefit from through traditional media, the advertisements also receive millions of clicks online, on the campaign's website and on YouTube. For example, Doritos' "Goat 4 Sale" advertisement was one of the most viewed, and appreciated by critics, consumer-generated commercial in 2013.

Besides the benefits and millions of responses that these initiatives can bring for large companies, smaller and less-known brands can also involve their customers and other consumers in the creation of advertising content. Encouraging the development of user-generated advertisements can lead not only to higher level of interactivity and involvement from the part of consumers, but can also improve the level of quality and creativity of ads, as well as their diffusion on social media platforms.

SOCIAL NETWORKS AND VIRAL BENEFITS

Social network theory (SNT) seeks to explain how networks work and analyzes the complex set of relationships within a network of individuals or organizations (Scott 2000; Wasserman and Faust 1994). Social network analysis views social relationships in terms of nodes and ties: nodes are the individual actors within the networks, and ties are the relationships between the actors. It studies networks as a function of different indices, including direction, frequency of relations, size, centrality and density of a network.

Mark Granovetter (1983) popularized an information diffusion model focused on the strength of weak ties that serve as bridges between network segments. Strong ties express the reciprocal social relationships, while weak ties refer to loosely connected individuals. He noticed that tie strength depends on three factors: frequency of contact, reciprocity, and friendship. According to Granovetter (1983), weak ties create more opportunities for individuals to share information and lead to greater levels of social capital. Granovetter (1983) also noted that future research should focus on the network idea, study the interactions and developments within networks, rather than consider only the individual and static analyses.

In recent years, the Internet has encouraged the constantly developing extent of network interaction, especially in the modern social media websites. This also applies in the case of viral networks, since the spread of viral information in the community is achieved through social networks (Tuten 2008). Social networks are extremely important for viral advertising, no matter if we are discussing about social media websites, or about more traditional social networks of friends and relatives. Liu-Thompkins (2012) found that the positive outcome for a viral advertisement is related to the number of seeds used to start a viral campaign, however, this is not always an essential condition. When the viral message has a high quality, the need to use a large number of seeds diminishes significantly, which makes viral advertising accessible even to small businesses who cannot afford large seeding budgets, but who are able to target the right social network.

Researchers found that social networks and social ties are important in information dissemination and propagation, including both weak and strong ties (Brown and Reingen 1987; Datta et al. 2005). Social networks such as Facebook and LinkedIn allow the establishment of links connecting family members, friends and peers (Tuten 2008). Weimann (1983) found that information becomes influential due to strong ties within the group, which are more likely to be used and perceived more credible than weak ties. Brown and Reingen (1987) conclude that weak ties allow and promote the dissemination of information between groups, while strong ties are much more influential in word-of-mouth, referral behavior and promote the flow of communication between the members of a group.

In the context of word-of-mouth and viral communication between consumers, strong ties represent the key influential points in the group with constant social influence on consumer choices, as stable and permanent socialization agents, while weak ties allow individuals to extend their information sources to outside groups, in certain moments and specific conditions.

Since Granovetter (1983) estimated that stronger ties lead to greater credibility of the sender, we can expect that consumers will put a greater value on word-of-mouth and referrals coming from persons with strong ties within their social networks. Moreover, the electronic word-of-mouth literature also found that stronger and more credible sources lead to more e-mails open and read coming from these sources, and to more forwarded messages.

Chiu et al. (2007) assessed that, in the context of word-of-mouth, consumers trust more their strong ties than their weak ties, leading to a greater influence from strong ties on consumers' purchase decisions. In addition, researchers found that most individuals do not forward information to persons they do not know, socially or virtually, which depends on the strength of their relationship (Huang, Lin and Lin 2009). Smith et al. (2007) also demonstrated that moderately and highly connected respondents are more likely to forward marketing messages.

Liu-Thompkins (2012) also found that it is more efficient to start a viral campaign with consumers who have a strong tie with the viral message originator. Individuals with strong ties are more strongly influenced by the message source, and they will be more likely to forward the message to other consumers. In this context, even using consumers with a large number of connections might not always be efficient for a viral campaign. The social cost of maintaining a large network leads to weaker average connection, which can lead to a reduced influence on further generations of consumers (Liu-Thompkins 2012). An efficient seeding and diffusion strategy focuses on reaching a large number of easily influenced individuals, rather than targeting a small number of highly connected hubs in a social network.

Another aspect related to social networks and diffusion strategy notes the fact that a heterogeneous group of consumers, with various interests and social relations can be more beneficial in the diffusion process. When members of a network share too few or too many common interests, diffusion outcome does not reach its high potential, while a heterogeneous group of consumers can improve the possibility of reaching a more diverse consumer population (Liu-Thompkins 2012).

Related to the use of social networks and modern social media websites, researchers also found that there are structural differences in the media used to spread electronic word-of-mouth. For example, studies have shown that Generation Y members are more heavily engaged with social networking media and Generation X members focus more on email. No matter the differences between generations regarding the use of Internet tools and platforms, research notes that motivations and behaviors are rather similar, with a few differences related to technology skills or attitudes toward technology (Strutton, Taylor and Thompson 2011).

Nevertheless, given the complex aspects related to the seeding and diffusion of a message in a social network and its varying potential for success or failure, constant monitoring of an advertisement's online evolution is absolutely necessary in order to evaluate its performance in the network. Aspects related to monitoring and evaluating viral advertising are further discussed in the next section.

VIRAL ADVERTISING MONITORING AND EVALUATION

Research and practitioner articles have discussed so far some of the key objectives of viral advertising, such as building widespread brand awareness, generating consumer interest, product trials and, bottom line, sales (Keller 2009; Kirby 2006). Viral advertising has been noted for its potential to lead to higher sales, all in record time and with low advertising costs (Dobele et al. 2007; Fattah 2000).

Viral advertising can contribute to a boost in the level of brand awareness, an increase in consumer-driven interest and even helps businesses reach beyond a business' core target market (Kirby 2006). Nevertheless, a key benefit is its contribution in adding to the bottom line, in terms of response and increased recommendation rates (Kirby 2006). Viral advertising is also able to motivate and lead consumers to product trial and acquisition (Ferguson 2008).

Practice examples have shown viral ads' potential to lead to better exposure and increased sale. The "Will it blend" commercials from Blendtec have led to an estimated 800% increase in sales (Truong 2010), while Old Spice's "Smell like a man, man" campaign has been a success in terms of reach, being viewed more than 40 million times. Also, according to The Nielsen Co. and data from SymphonyIRI Group, sales of Old Spice body wash featured in the viral ads increased 11% over 12 months (O'Leary and Wasserman 2010).

Viral ads have the ability to create buzz, brand awareness, and contribute to the bottom-line numbers, leading to increased sales. Since consumers participating in the viral process like the advertisements so much that they forward them to other individuals, the effects of viral ads can also affect consumers' purchase behavior.

Under these circumstances, it is important for marketers to consider measures that can contribute to the monitoring and evaluation of viral advertising results. On the one hand, this is rather difficult in the online viral environment, where consumers are in control regarding the diffusion of the message and where traditional objectives and evaluation methods need to be adapted. On the other hand, social media websites allow for easier collection of some metrics, such as number of views and clicks.

Research has noted the importance of incorporating in the evaluation of viral advertising not only classical evaluation measures, such as awareness and reach, but also different attitudinal and behavioral responses, such as ad conversion rates, product and brand preference and sales creation or increase (Bampo 2008; Cruz and Fill 2008).

Regarding the monitoring and evaluation of viral advertising, there are different types of measures that can be used to assess the efficiency of a viral campaign in social media, including, but not limited to websites such as Facebook, YouTube, Pinterest, Google Plus and Flickr.

The first type of measures that advertisers can use is related to consumer reach, similar to traditional advertising. In this case, practitioners can utilize measures such as number of impressions or views of the advertisement, depending on the type of ad.

A second type of measures used to evaluate viral advertising results is related to consumer involvement, and can use metrics such as number of "likes", number of comments or number of subscribers. For a better assessment, different types of ratios can also be used, such as the number of ad views vs. the number of "likes" or comments.

A third type of evaluation metrics refers to the basis of a viral campaign, determining consumers to forward an advertisement. In this case, marketers can use measures such as number of shares, number of reposts, number of video embedding on other webpages, number of references or links toward the advertising page.

Nevertheless, traditional bottom-line and behavioral measures can also be used in assessing the effectiveness of viral advertisements and their impact on business metrics. While not a very easy task, marketers can establish the relationship between the viral ad and sales, in order to assess whether the ad lead to increases in sales. In this case, other factors need to be considered, including promotions and other types of brand communications that might affect results. Other types of data collection procedures can be used, including surveys and experiments, to estimate traditional advertising attitudinal and behavioral factors, such as attitude toward the ad, attitude toward the brand, ad and brand recall and purchase intentions. Moreover, marketers can also assess consumers' viral intentions, meaning their intention to forward an ad.

FUTURE RESEARCH DIRECTIONS

Future studies on viral advertising can focus on detailing the place of viral advertising in the general advertising framework, and its potential contribution to the integrated marketing strategy of a business. While we noted the positive influence of humor and sexual appeals in the viral process, future research can analyze the relationship between viral advertising success and other content related factors, such as advertisement controversy, or other types of appeals, including surprise, shock or violence.

Regarding the significant number of social media websites and the specific profile of each of them, it would also be interesting to find out which of them are more efficient for viral ads placement and under which circumstances. Different elements discussed by advertising researchers and managers, such as variations based on the creator of the ad and importance of user-generated advertising, diffusion of viral public announcement ads and differences based on different demographic and cultural characteristics are some of the points that can be advantageous and practical for future advertising research.

Nevertheless, it can also be beneficial, especially for practitioners, to formulate specific profiles of consumers more prone to be influenced and to forward viral advertisements, for different types of content and advertising appeals. From a more technical point of view, in an online world providing more social media options every day, it would be interesting to find the best social networking platforms to launch viral advertisements and the best options as a function of the ad or product type.

CONCLUSION

Given the current proliferation of social media websites, the hundreds of millions of social media users and the millions of views that some viral ads receive in social media, this study focused on underlining the key theoretical and practical aspects related to viral advertising. We presented an overview of different aspects related to the nature, characteristics and evaluation of viral advertising, especially focusing on what makes advertisements viral.

After a clarification of the term viral advertising, we focused on the key characteristics of viral ads, as shown by practice and research, with specific discussions related to viral advertising appeals. We presented an overview related to the success of emotions in viral advertising, no matter if we are discussing about sentimental advertisements, or those using humorous and sexual appeals to arouse consumer interest. We also noted that, despite initial evaluations, viral advertising can work for any type of product, not just for cool and interesting brands.

The discussion about consumer generated advertising was another modern advertising topic taken into consideration, given the importance of various types of social media platforms for consumers. Nevertheless, we showed that the source of the message and the creator of the message are important factors in a viral campaign and, from this point of view, consumers are much more comfortable and more likely to like an advertisement if it comes from a peer.

The last part of this chapter focused on the monitoring and evaluating viral ads outcomes, including both traditional and social media specific advertising measures. This is extremely important in a very dynamic and volatile context as the one related to viral advertising, where an ad can quickly become a success or can generate significant negative feedback, all factors that might require adjustments to the viral strategy and reaction from the brand.

Overall, the study shows the key characteristics of viral advertising and underlines both its similarities and common elements with traditional advertising, but also its specific traits and advantages due to online communications and social media.

REFERENCES

Alden, D. L., Hoyer, W. D., & Lee, C. (1993). Identifying global and culture-specific dimensions of humor in advertising: A multinational analysis. *Journal of Marketing*, *57*(2), 64–75. doi:10.2307/1252027

Allsop, D. T., Bassett, B. R., & Hoskins, J. A. (2007). Word of mouth research: Principles and applications. *Journal of Advertising Research*, *47*(4), 398–411. doi:10.2501/S0021849907070419

Anderson, S. (2008). Using social networks to market. *Rough Notes*, *151*(2), 114–115.

Bampo, M., Ewing, M. T., Mather, D. R., Stewart, D., & Wallace, M. (2008). The effects of the social structure of digital networks on viral marketing performance. *Information Systems Research*, *19*(3), 273–290. doi:10.1287/isre.1070.0152

Batra, R., & Ray, M. L. (1986). Affective responses mediating acceptance of advertising. *The Journal of Consumer Research*, *13*(2), 234–249. doi:10.1086/209063

Bello, D. C., Etzel, M. J., & Pits, R. E. (1983). The communication effects of controversial sexual content in television programs and commercials. *Journal of Advertising*, *3*(12), 32–42. doi:10.1080/00913367.1983.10672846

Borroff, R. (2000). Viral Marketing. *Precision Marketing*, *20*, 12.

Brown, J. J., & Reingen, P. H. (1987). Social ties and word-of-mouth referral behavior. *The Journal of Consumer Research*, *14*(3), 350–362. doi:10.1086/209118

Brown, M. R., Bhadury, R. K., & Pope, N. K. L. (2010). The impact of comedic violence on viral advertising effectiveness. *Journal of Advertising*, *39*(1), 49–65. doi:10.2753/JOA0091-3367390104

Chattopadhyay, A., & Basu, K. (1990). Humor in advertising: The moderating role of prior brand evaluation. *JMR, Journal of Marketing Research*, *27*(4), 466–476. doi:10.2307/3172631

Chiu, H.-C., Hsieh, Y.-C., Kao, Y.-H., & Lee, M. (2007). The determinants of email receivers' disseminating behaviors on the internet. *Journal of Advertising Research*, *47*(4), 524–534. doi:10.2501/S0021849907070547

Cline, T. W., Altsech, M. B., & Kellaris, J. J. (2003). When does humor enhance or inhibit ad responses? The moderating role of the need for humor. *Journal of Advertising*, *32*(3), 31–45. doi:10.1080/00913367.2003.10639134

Cruz, D., & Fill, C. (2008). Evaluating viral marketing: Isolating the key criteria. *Marketing Intelligence & Planning*, *26*(7), 743–758. doi:10.1108/02634500810916690

Dahl, D. W., Sengupta, J., & Vohs, K. D. (2009). Sex in advertising: Gender differences and the role of relationship commitment. *The Journal of Consumer Research*, *36*(2), 215–231. doi:10.1086/597158

Datta, P. R., Chowdhury, D. N., & Chakraborty, B. R. (2005). Viral marketing: New form of word-of-mouth through internet. *Business Review (Federal Reserve Bank of Philadelphia)*, *3*(2), 69–75.

Derbaix, C., & Vanhamme, J. (2003). Inducing word-of-mouth by eliciting surprise – A pilot investigation. *Journal of Economic Psychology*, *24*(1), 99–116. doi:10.1016/S0167-4870(02)00157-5

Dobele, A., Lindgreen, A., Beverland, M., Vanhamme, J., & van Wijk, R. (2007). Why pass on viral messages? Because they connect emotionally. *Business Horizons*, *50*(4), 291–304. doi:10.1016/j.bushor.2007.01.004

Dobele, A., Toleman, D., & Beverland, M. (2005). Controlled infection! Spreading the brand message through viral marketing. *Business Horizons*, *48*(2), 143–149. doi:10.1016/j.bushor.2004.10.011

Duncan, C. P., & Nelson, J. E. (1985). Effects of humor in a radio advertising experiment. *Journal of Advertising*, *14*(2), 33–64. doi:10.1080/00913367.1985.10672944

Fattah, H. M. (2000). Viral marketing is nothing new. *Technology Marketing Intelligence*, *20*(10), 1–4.

Feick, L. F., & Price, L. L. (1987). The market maven: A diffuser of marketplace information. *Journal of Marketing*, *51*(1), 83–97. doi:10.2307/1251146

Ferguson, R. (2008). Word of mouth and viral marketing: Taking the temperature of the hottest trends in marketing. *Journal of Consumer Marketing*, *25*(3), 179–182. doi:10.1108/07363760810870671

Gelb, B. D., & Pickett, C. M. (1983). Attitude-toward-the-ad: Links to humor and to advertising effectiveness. *Journal of Advertising*, *12*(2), 34–42. doi:10.1080/00913367.1983.10672838

Granovetter, M. (1983). The strength of weak ties: A network theory revisited. *Sociological Theory*, *1*, 201–233. doi:10.2307/202051

Horovitz, B. (2013). *Horovitz: Best and worst ads of 2013*. Retrieved 6th January 2014 from http://www.usatoday.com/story/money/business/2013/12/23/top-five-ads-of-2013-commercials-advertisements-year-end/4045173/

Huang, C.-C., Lin, T.-C., & Lin, K.-J. (2009). Factors affecting pass-along email intentions (Paels), integrating the social capital and social cognition theories. *Electronic Commerce Research and Applications*, *8*(3), 160–169. doi:10.1016/j.elerap.2008.11.001

Hung, K. H., & Li, S. Y. (2007). The influence of eWOM on virtual consumer communities: Social capital, consumer learning, and behavioral outcomes. *Journal of Advertising Research*, *47*(4), 485–495. doi:10.2501/S002184990707050X

Johnson, G. J., Bruner, G. C. II, & Kumar, A. (2006). Interactivity and its facets revisited: Theory and empirical test. *Journal of Advertising*, *35*(4), 35–52. doi:10.2753/JOA0091-3367350403

Jurvetson, S., & Draper, T. (1997). *Viral marketing phenomenon explained.* Retrieved April 15th, 2013, from http://www.dfj.com/news/article_26.shtml

Keller, K. L. (2009). Building strong brands in a modern marketing communications environment. *Journal of Marketing Communications*, *15*(2), 139–155. doi:10.1080/13527260902757530

Kirby, J., & Marsden, P. (2006). *Connected marketing: The viral, buzz and word of mouth revolution.* Oxford, UK: Elsevier.

Kozinets, R. V., de Valck, K., Wojnicki, A. C., & Wilner, S. J. (2010). Networked narratives: Understanding word-of-mouth marketing in online communities. *Journal of Marketing*, *74*(2), 71–89. doi:10.1509/jmkg.74.2.71

Larceneux, F. (2007). Buzz et recommandations sur internet: Quels effets sur le box-office? *Recherche et Applications en Marketing*, *22*(3), 45–64. doi:10.1177/076737010702200304

LaTour, M. S., & Henthorne, T. L. (1994). Ethical judgments of sexual appeals in print advertising. *Journal of Advertising*, *23*(3), 81–91. doi:10.1080/00913367.1994.10673453

Liu, F., Cheng, H., & Li, J. (2009). Consumer responses to sex appeal advertising: A cross-cultural study. *International Marketing Review*, *26*(4/5), 501–520. doi:10.1108/02651330910972002

Liu-Thompkins, Y. (2012). Seeding viral content: The role of message and network factors. *Journal of Advertising Research*, *52*(4), 465–478. doi:10.2501/JAR-52-4-465-478

Lombardot, É. (2007). La nudité en publicité: Quelle influence sur l'attention portée à l'annonce et la fonction mémorielle de la marque? *Recherche et Applications en Marketing*, *22*(4), 23–41. doi:10.1177/076737010702200401

Lutz, R. J., MacKenzie, S. B., & Belch, G. (1983). Attitude toward the ad as a mediator of advertising effectiveness: Determinants and consequences. *Advances in Consumer Research. Association for Consumer Research (U. S.)*, *10*, 532–539.

MacInnis, D., & Jaworski, B. (1988). Information processing from advertisements: Toward an integrative framework. *Journal of Marketing*, *53*(4), 1–23. doi:10.2307/1251376

MacKenzie, S. B., & Lutz, R. J. (1989). An empirical examination of the structural antecedents of attitude toward the ad in an advertising pretesting context. *Journal of Marketing*, *53*(2), 48–65. doi:10.2307/1251413

MacKenzie, S. B., Lutz, R. J., & Belch, G. (1986). The role of attitude toward the ad as a mediator of advertising effectiveness: A test of competing explanations. *JMR, Journal of Marketing Research*, *23*(2), 130–143. doi:10.2307/3151660

Morrissey, B. (2008). Viral video hits blur the authenticity line. *Adweek*, *49*(37), 8.

Muehling, D. D., & McCann, M. (1993). Attitude toward the ad: A review. *Journal of Current Issues and Research in Advertising*, *15*(2), 25–58. doi:10.1080/10641734.1993.10505002

Nudd, T. (2013). The 20 most viral ads of 2013. *Adweek*. Retrieved 5th January 2014 from www.adweek.com/news-gallery/20-most-viral-ads-2013-154000#intro

O'Leary, N., & Wasserman, T. (2010). Old Spice campaign smells like a sales success, too. *Brand Week*. Retrieved April 13th 2013, from http://www.brandweek.com/bw/content_display/news-and-features/direct/e3i45f1c709df-0501927f56568a2acd5c7b

Petrescu, M., & Korgaonkar, P. (2011). Viral advertising: Definitional review and synthesis. *Journal of Internet Commerce*, *10*(3), 208–226. doi:10.1080/15332861.2011.596007

Phelps, J. E., Lewis, R., Mobilio, L., Perry, D., & Raman, N. (2004). Viral marketing or electronic word-of-mouth advertising: Examining consumer responses and motivations to pass along e-mail. *Journal of Advertising Research*, *44*(4), 333–348.

Porter, L., & Golan, G. J. (2006). From Subservient Chickens to Brawny Men: A comparison of viral advertising to television advertising. *Journal of Interactive Advertising*, *6*(2), 30–38.

Rayport, J. F. (1996). The virus of marketing. *Fast Company*. Retrieved May 20th 2013, from http://www.fastcompany.com/magazine/06/virus.html

Rechtin, M. (2009). Fiesta viral marketing: First, Ford built awareness of its upcoming small car, next, it shows off features. *Automotive News*, *84*, 6–7.

Reichert, T., Heckler, S. E., & Jackson, S. (2001). The effects of sexual social marketing appeals on cognitive processing and persuasion. *Journal of Advertising*, *30*(1), 13–27. doi:10.1080/00913367.2001.10673628

Reid, A. (2005, February). Viral advertising campaigns. *Campaign*, 14.

Rust, R. T., & Oliver, R. W. (1994). The death of advertising. *Journal of Advertising*, *23*(4), 71–77. doi:10.1080/00913367.1943.10673460

Scott, C. M., Klein, D., & Bryant, J. (1990). Consumer response to humor in advertising: A series of field studies using behavioral observation. *The Journal of Consumer Research*, *16*(4), 498–501. doi:10.1086/209235

Scott, J. (2000). *Social network analysis: A handbook* (2nd ed.). London: Sage Publications.

Severn, J., Belch, G. E., & Belch, M. A. (1990). The effects of sexual and non-sexual advertising appeals and information level on cognitive processing and communication effectiveness. *Journal of Advertising*, *19*(1), 14–22. doi:10.1080/00913367.1990.10673176

Shukla, T. (2010). Factors affecting 'internet marketing' campaigns with reference to viral and permission marketing. *The IUP Journal of Management Research*, *9*(1), 26–37.

Smith, J. (2013). The most unforgettable ad campaigns of 2013. *Forbes*. Retrieved 5th January 2014 from www.forbes.com/sites/jacquelynsmith/2013/12/17/the-most-unforgettable-ad-campaigns-of-2013/print/

Smith, T., Coyle, J. R., Lightfoot, E., & Scott, A. (2007). Reconsidering models of influence: The relationship between consumer social networks and word-of-mouth effectiveness. *Journal of Advertising Research*, *47*(4), 387–397. doi:10.2501/S0021849907070407

Solman, G. (2008a). Levi's likes the style of new viral videos. *Brandweek*, *49*(20), 4.

Solman, G. (2008b). Viral video success changes Levi's plans. *Adweek*, *49*(17), 6.

Southgate, D., Westoby, N., & Page, G. (2010). Creative determinants of viral video viewing. *International Journal of Advertising*, *29*(3), 349–368. doi:10.2501/S0265048710201221

Stanbouli, K. (2003). Marketing viral et publicité. *Revue Française du Marketing*, *192/193*, 97–106.

Sternthal, B., & Craig, S. (1973). Humor in advertising. *Journal of Marketing*, *37*(4), 12–18. doi:10.2307/1250353

Stewart, D. W., & Pavlou, P. A. (2002). From consumer response to active consumer: Measuring the effectiveness of interactive media. *Journal of the Academy of Marketing Science*, *30*(4), 376–396. doi:10.1177/009207002236912

Steyer, A., Garcia-Bardidia, R., & Quester, P. (2007). Modélisation de la structure sociale des groupes de discussion sur internet: Implications pour le contrôle du marketing viral. *Recherche et Applications en Marketing*, *22*(3), 29–44. doi:10.1177/076737010702200303

Strutton, D., Taylor, D. G., & Thompson, K. (2011). Investigating generational differences in e-WOM behaviors: For advertising purposes, does X = Y? *International Journal of Advertising*, *30*(4), 559–586. doi:10.2501/IJA-30-4-559-586

Swanepoel, C., Lye, A., & Rugimbana, R. (2009). Virally inspired: A review of the theory of viral stealth marketing. *Australasian Marketing Journal*, *17*(1), 9–15. doi:10.1016/j.ausmj.2009.01.005

Tellis, G. J. (2004). *Effective advertising: Understanding when, how, and why advertising works*. Thousand Oaks, CA: Sage Publications.

Thompson, C. (2010). To click with youth, GMC pitches go viral. *Automotive News*, *84*, 4.

Truong, H. (2010). The top ten successful viral ads of all time by AdAge. *DigiWave*. Retrieved 11th March 2013, from http://www.thedigiwave.com/2010/11/top-ten-viral-ads-of-all-time.html

Tsai, J. (2009). Video is more than viral: Forget YouTube sensations and wardrobe malfunctions. *CRM Magazine*, *13*, 36–42.

Tuten, T. L. (2008). *Advertising 2.0: Social media marketing in a web 2.0 world*. Westport, CT: Praeger.

Wasserman, S., & Faust, K. (1994). *Social network analysis: Methods and applications*. Cambridge University Press. doi:10.1017/CBO9780511815478

Wasserman, T. (2009). Marketing innovation of the decade: Viral videos. *Adweek*, *50*(44), 24.

Wasserman, T. (2013). *The most-shared ads of 2013*. Retrieved 5th January 2014 from www.mashable.com/2013/11/21/these-are-the-most-shared-ads-of-2013/

Weimann, G. (1983). The strength of weak conversational ties in the flow of information and influence. *Social Networks*, *5*(3), 245–267. doi:10.1016/0378-8733(83)90027-8

Weinberger, M. G., & Gulas, C. S. (1992). The impact of humor in advertising: A review. *Journal of Advertising*, *21*(4), 35–59. doi:10.1080/00913367.1992.10673384

Welker, C. B. (2002). The paradigm of viral communication. *Information Services & Use*, *22*, 3–8.

ADDITIONAL READING

Barefoot, D., & Szabo, J. (2010). *Friends with benefits. A social media marketing handbook*. No Starch Press.

Bickart, B., & Schindler, R. M. (2002). Expanding the scope of word of mouth: Consumer-to-consumer information on the Internet. *Advances in Consumer Research. Association for Consumer Research (U. S.)*, *29*, 428–430.

Breazeale, M. (2009). Word of mouse. an assessment of electronic word-of-mouth research. *International Journal of Market Research*, *51*(3), 297–318. doi:10.2501/S1470785309200566

Brodin, O. (2000). Les communautés virtuelles: Un potentiel marketing encore peu exploré. *Décisions Marketing*, *21*, 47–56.

Dellarocas, C. (2003). The digitization of word of mouth: Promise and challenges of online feedback mechanisms. *Management Science*, *49*(10), 1407–1424. doi:10.1287/mnsc.49.10.1407.17308

Gladwell, M. (2000). *The tipping point*. Boston: Little, Brown and Co.

Godes, D., & Mayzlin, D. (2004). Using online conversations to study word-of-mouth communication. *Marketing Science*, *23*(4), 545–560. doi:10.1287/mksc.1040.0071

Godin, S. (2000). *Unleashing the Ideavirus*. Do You Zoom, Inc.

Goldenberg, J., Libai, B., & Muller, E. (2001). Talk of the network: A complex systems look at the underlying process of word-of-mouth. *Marketing Letters*, *12*(3), 211–223. doi:10.1023/A:1011122126881

Gruen, T. W., Osmonbekov, T., & Czaplewski, A. J. (2006). eWom: The impact of customer-to-customer online know-how exchange on customer value and loyalty. *Journal of Business Research*, *59*(4), 449–456. doi:10.1016/j.jbusres.2005.10.004

Helm, S. (2000). Viral marketing: Establishing customer relationship by word-of-mouse. *Electronic Markets*, *10*(3), 158–161. doi:10.1080/10196780050177053

Hennig-Thurau, T., Gwinner, K. P., Walsh, G., & Gremler, D. D. (2004). Electronic word-of-mouth via consumer-opinion platforms: What motivates consumers to articulate themselves on the Internet? *Journal of Interactive Marketing*, *18*(1), 38–52. doi:10.1002/dir.10073

Henricks, M. (1998). Spread the word: Advertising by word-of-mouth. *Entrepreneur*, *26*(2), 120–126.

Hogan, J. E., Lemon, K. N., & Libai, B. (2004). Quantifying the ripple: Word-of-mouth and advertising effectiveness. *Journal of Advertising Research*, *44*(3), 271–280. doi:10.1017/S0021849904040243

Horovitz, B. (2009). Pistachio industry hopes risqué ad campaign goes viral. *USA Today*, Oct. 5, 02B.

Keller, E. (2007). Unleashing the power of word of mouth: Creating brand advocacy to drive growth. *Journal of Advertising Research*, *47*(4), 448–452. doi:10.2501/S0021849907070468

Laughlin, J. D., & MacDonald, J. B. (2010). Identifying market mavens online by their social behaviors in community generated media. *Academy of Marketing Studies Journal*, *14*(1), 55–70.

Newman, P. J. Jr. (1999). When windows replace walls: Investigating virtual word of mouth exchanges and constructing multilogue profiles. *Advances in Consumer Research. Association for Consumer Research (U. S.)*, *26*, 653–654.

Niederhoffer, K., Mooth, R., Wiesenfeld, D., & Gordon, J. (2007). The origin and impact of cpg new-product buzz: Emerging trends and implications. *Journal of Advertising Research*, *47*(4), 420–426. doi:10.2501/S0021849907070432

Norman, A. T., & Russell, C. A. (2006). The pass-along effect: investigating word-of-mouth effects on online survey procedures. *Journal of Computer-Mediated Communication, 11*(4). Retrieved on April 20th 2013, from http://jcmc.indiana.edu/vol11/issue4/norman.html

Perkins, B. (2009). The power of viral revenge. *Computerworld*, July 20 – July 27, 40.

Plummer, J., Rappaport, S., Hall, T., & Barocci, R. (2007). *The online advertising playbook: proven strategies and tested tactics from the Advertising Research Foundation*. Hoboken, New Jersey: John Wiley & Sons, Inc.

Riegner, C. (2007). Word of mouth on the web: The impact of Web 2.0 on consumer purchase decisions. *Journal of Advertising Research*, *47*(4), 436–447. doi:10.2501/S0021849907070456

Shimp, T. A., Wood, S. L., & Smarandescu, L. (2007). Self-generated advertisements: Testimonials and the perils of consumer exaggeration. *Journal of Advertising Research*, *47*(4), 453–461. doi:10.2501/S002184990707047X

Thomas, G. M. (2004). Building the buzz in the hive mind. *Journal of Consumer Behaviour*, *4*(1), 64–72. doi:10.1002/cb.158

Villanueva, J., Yoo, S., & Hanssens, D. M. (2008). The impact of marketing-induced versus word-of-mouth customer acquisition on customer equity growth. *JMR, Journal of Marketing Research*, *45*(1), 48–60. doi:10.1509/jmkr.45.1.48

Watts, D. J., & Peretti, J. (2007). Viral marketing for the real world. *Harvard Business Review*, *85*, 22–23.

KEY TERMS AND DEFINITIONS

Consumer Buzz: Consumer-to-consumer communications regarding a company or brand resulting from viral marketing strategies.

Electronic Word-of-Mouth: Online consumer-to-consumer communication regarding a brand or product.

Humorous Advertising Appeals: Use of funny content and messages as the basis of an advertisement.

Sexual Advertising Appeals: Use of sexually charged content and messages or nudity in an advertisement.

Social Media: Broad range of online platforms, such as social networking sites, brand-sponsored virtual worlds, open virtual worlds, video and photo communities, and social news.

Social Network: Relationships and interactions between friends, colleagues, and other personal or online contacts.

Viral Advertising: Unpaid electronic distribution of business or user generated advertisements from consumer to consumer.

Viral Marketing: Online and offline marketing activities performed to influence consumers to pass along commercial messages.

Word-of-Mouth: Non-commercial, oral, person-to-person communication about a brand or product between consumers.

Chapter 6
Social Media:
The Issues, Benefits, and Strategies for Brands

Jennifer Rowley
Manchester Metropolitan University, UK

Catherine J. Ashworth
Manchester Metropolitan University, UK

Jeff McCarthy
Manchester Metropolitan University, UK

ABSTRACT

On the basis of qualitative research conducted in two different case contexts, this chapter explores attitudes and approaches to the use of social media in relationship and community building. Two contrasting study contexts are addressed: the UK football sector and UK pure-play Small/Medium-Sized (SME) fashion retailers. After an introduction, the chapter summarises discussion and research on brands and their management in social media. This is followed by an outline of the two contexts for study. From this, the aims, objectives, and research methodology are drawn. The findings are then presented, and the ensuing discussion proposes a summary of the approaches to social media strategy adopted in the two case contexts. Four important foci are established, namely strategic marketing, marketing communication, brand and community, plus monitoring and evaluation. This results in a useful strategic framework empirically drawn from the in-depth data. Finally, suggestions for future research precede a conclusion.

INTRODUCTION

Social media sites have become an important digital meeting place for friends and acquaintances, and their reach has grown significantly in the last few years (Halliday and Vrusias, 2011; Harrigan, 2011). Social media is a broad term often used to encapsulate the applications that enable increasingly popular social cyber-activities, such as blogging, micro-blogging, social networking, photo-sharing and video-sharing (Centeno *et al*., 2009). Almost 1.9 billion global consumers are currently engaged with social media (Kemp, 2014); and Facebook itself hosts around 1.19

DOI: 10.4018/978-1-4666-6182-0.ch006

Figure 1. Active global users by social media platform (Drawn from statistics in Kemp, 2014)

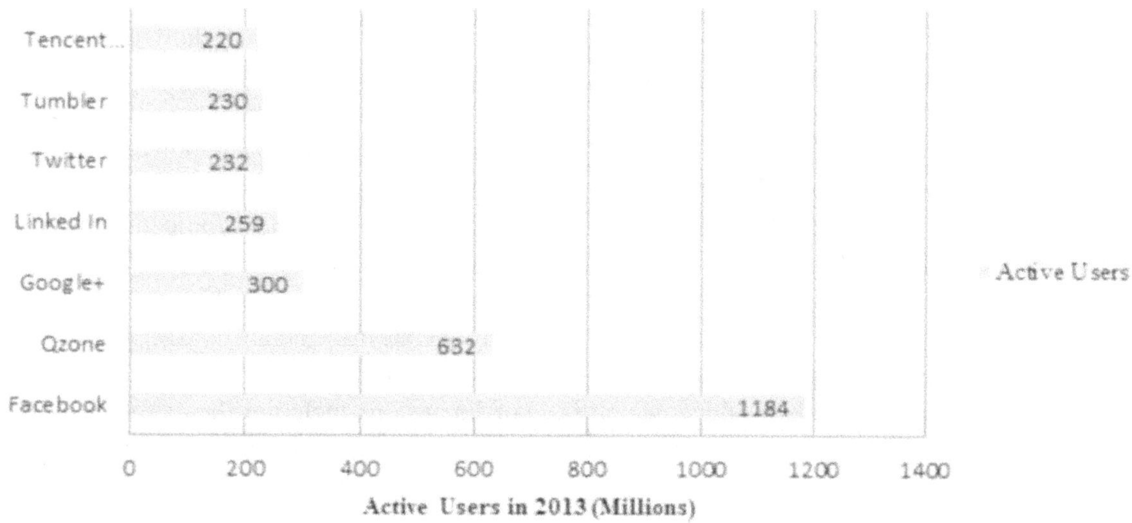

billion active users each month for commercial, leisure and social purposes (Facebook.com, 2014). Currently, Facebook is the main platform globally for active social media users (Kemp, 2014) and this can be seen in Figure 1. With average users spending over six hours per month on Facebook, this presents a highly receptive target audience in the social media domain.

The UK has the highest internet penetration of all countries with 87% of the national population connected (Kemp, 2014). This is high compared to the USA (80%), Western Europe (78%) and Eastern/Central Europe (54%). The UK is also an international leader in terms of social media penetration, with 76%, closely followed by Germany (74%), with France (68%) and Italy (54%) both lagging behind in the technology race. Around one-third of European online adults participate in Facebook conversations. UK consumer Facebook penetration is even higher – with over 50% of the population engaged (Social Bakers, 2014) - emphasising the potential of social media in the context of brand communication innovation. With the average user connected to over 80 community pages, Facebook represents a key avenue for triadic communication on a consumer-to-consumer (C2C), consumer-to-business (C2B) and business to-consumer (B2C) basis (Ashworth, 2013). However, academics have typically focused on the consumer-business social media dyad (Larson and Watson, 2011), rather than offering any wider understanding. Twitter, on the other hand, which amassed around 232 million users in just seven years is now struggling to widen its audience as quickly (Evening Herald, 2014); and growth is only significant in developing markets such as Saudi Arabia. Presently, 77% of monthly active users of Twitter are outside the US. The number of daily active Twitter users is about 100 million and the average daily tweets stands at 500 million (Inforrms, 2013) – thus still making this an interesting platform for global brand communications. In the UK there are around 13 million active Twitter users each month, with 2.5 million of these tweeting daily. However, the Twitter figures should be considered carefully, as reliable statistics are hard to come by (Inforrms, 2013).

On account of the large and rapidly increasing audiences associated with social media sites, marketers have become increasingly interested in the potential that computer-mediated communication offers for interacting and communicating with both current and prospective customers. Positive communications via social media provide opportunities for building brand visibility, awareness and value (Gummerus *et al.*, 2012). Conversely, negative comments from social media pose threats to the reputation of a brand given the speed and reach of electronic word-of-mouth (eWOM) communications (Colliander and Wien, 2013). According to Shang *et al.* (2006), experiences in a virtual community, such as a social media site, may be a significant part of the consumer experience of a brand. In particular, social media engagement is found to produce strong-tie relationships, which enhance customer acquisition and retention, as well as building brand credibility (Ashworth, 2013). As Coulter and Roggeveen (2012) state, "The implication for social network marketers is to foster closer customer relationships by "following their followers", rather than merely churning out one-way communications" (p.895).

This chapter compares research findings conducted in two different case contexts in which there is potential for relationship and community building through social media which will, in turn, build brand presence, ubiquity and equity. The two study contexts are the UK football sector representing the large-scale organisation perspective (LSE), and UK pure-play small/medium-sized (SME) fashion retailers representing the independent, small firm view. There is no single international definition of a small firm due to the wide diversity of businesses operating in the marketplace (www.dti.gov.uk, 2007). Since the focus of this study is UK-based, the UK government's Department of Trade and Industry (DTI) definition of a small to medium-sized business is adopted. The DTI define a small firm as one which is an independent trading organisation, with no parent company and less than 250 employees (small: 0-49; medium: 50-249 employees). Varying widely in size and capacity for growth/development, small firms are characterised by "independence of action, differing organizational [sic] structures, and varied management styles" (Churchill and Lewis, 1983, p. 30). The multiplicity of vibrant small businesses has long been recognised as a significant contributor to a dynamic economy in the UK (Brown *et al.*, 1977). In particular, a strong SME sector remains vital to a flexible and buoyant economy, creating jobs, providing the foundations for future large companies and contributing to the UK's long-term growth and international competitiveness. Within this small firm context, pure-play enterprises are those which do not hold a high street presence and only operate in the online domain. The football and fashion sectors are therefore different on a number of dimensions, including the size of the businesses, the equity of their brand and the centrality of 'traditional' digital marketing to their business, plus the extent to which their customer base sees itself as a brand community, or 'tribe'. This is important because recent consumer-oriented research suggests that tribes and communities may need to be addressed differently from a marketing perspective (Goulding *et al.*, 2013). Both contexts consider the attitudes towards and the strategic approaches to the adoption and use of social media at a sectoral level. These two contexts represent areas in which the authors have recently undertaken research into social media strategies.

In the process of this study, the researchers noted some interesting differences between managers' perceptions of the issues and benefits of social media and the approaches being adopted in the two sectors. In particular, the UK football sector has been hesitant in its adoption of social media, whereas the pure-play SME fashion retailers in our study have embraced social media wholeheartedly, and could be viewed as exemplars of good practice. Accordingly, in this chapter, we take the opportunity to compare and contrast findings from these two sectors, and use this analysis to propose two models which, respectively, identify and summarise the key foci of a social media strategy, and the impact of effective engagement in social media. Findings and conceptual developments discussed in this chapter are empirically drawn from the in-depth data generated.

The chapter first reviews the research and key practitioner literature on brands and their management in social media. Next, the differing football and fashion pure-play research contexts are discussed. This is followed by a summary of the aims, objectives and research methodology, to explain the research strategy for generating in-depth data into social media in the two contrasting UK case study contexts: football clubs, and pure-play fashion retailers. The findings for the football and fashion sectors are then summarised. These are then followed by a discussion section which compares and contrasts the findings from the two research contexts, as a basis for summarising the contrasting approaches to social media brand strategies, and proposes the four foci of social media brand strategy. Finally, the chapter concludes with a summary of the strategic options available to organisations in the social media age, and offers recommendations for practitioners and suggestions for further research.

BACKGROUND

Social media are seen as offering both opportunities and challenges as a potential channel through which businesses can communicate or interact with their customers and potential customers. On the positive side, social media are viewed as channels through which organisations can promote their products, services and brands, provided that they behave in such a way as their (commercial) presence in what is regarded as a social space is deemed appropriate (Boyd and Ellison, 2008; Harrigan, 2011). Many commentators suggest that social media are good arenas through which customer relationships (all of B2C, C2B and C2C) can be cultivated, which, in turn, lead to the strengthening of bonds between the organisation and its customers (Ashworth, 2013; Coulter & Roggeveen, 2012; Kim & Jin, 2006), resulting in increased brand loyalty and the creation of brand communities. In addition, contributions from the more established literature on online communities suggest that empowering customers is crucial to these online relationships and is central to effective community building (Thorbjornsen *et al.*, 2002; Rowley *et al.*, 2007). Similarly Sicilia and Palazon (2008) point to the importance of offering consumers functional, social and experiential value in online community building.

On the negative side, Fournier and Avery (2011, p. 193) argue that commercialisation of brands is neither well received nor welcomed in social media because "the Web was created not to sell branded products, but to link people together in collective conversational webs". However, technology breakthroughs impact upon brand management and, with Twitter and Facebook, the consumer is in effect given considerable power to decide for themselves whether to interact with a brand or receive their updates (Fournier and Avery, 2011; Curran *et al.*, 2011). SMEs in particular have been slow to react to the changes and opportunities presented by social media and as such they are severely limiting their ability to capitalize on new opportunities (Parrott *et al.*, 2010).Traditional marketing has focussed on mass-market push strategies whereby the firm orchestrates communications. Recent research (Larson and Watson, 2011) discusses the concept of dyadic communications which are enabled in the social media context. Here the traditional mass-market push strategy of uni-directional conversation is replaced by business-consumer (B2C) and consumer-to-business (C2B) interaction. Indeed Larson and Watson (2011) identify this as the key social media dyad. Social media offers the opportunity for two-way relationships (Lipsman *et al.*, 2012) and as such enables increased communications/noise about a brand. However, little research exists beyond the consumer perspective – despite the potential opportunities provided for industry and sectoral practitioners.

The particular characteristic of social media of most concern and interest to organisations is the speed with which opinions can be communicated between members of a consumer community (Hennig-Thurau *et al.*, 2004). These opinions can be regarded as a form of electronic word-of-mouth (eWOM) and may impact on customers' attitudes and behaviours in respect of an organisation or a brand. As such, virtual consumer communities might become threats to companies, because enterprises have no control over negative messages from unsatisfied customers on the internet (Maclaran and Catterall, 2002; Muniz and O'Guinn, 2001).

Concerns over the negative impact on the brand have led various commentators to discuss the potential for a power struggle between consumers and organisations in relation to the control of the brand (Bernoff and Li, 2008; Fisher and Smith, 2011), with negative brand hijack the most sinister outcome (O'Guinn and Muňiz, 2005). In seeking resolutions to this situation, Christodoulides *et al.* (2009), for example, suggest that post-internet branding is about facilitating conversations around the brand, and the co-creation of meaning, which, in turn has consequences for established tenets of branding and marketing theory (Fisher and Smith, 2011). Large brands are often in a position to respond to negative brand noise by investing significant resources into their social media brand presence, effectively drowning out other voices. In contrast, smaller-sized, independent and niche brand enterprises may benefit from the agility and flexibility to personalise communications in order to strengthen brand and relationship ties via more natural and effective communications with target consumers (Ashworth, 2013).

The recent emergence of 'urban tribes' (e.g. Watters, 2004) offer strong social groups which provide an alternative focus to traditional family structures; and in this context, the considerable retail, marketing and branding opportunities for entrepreneurialism in the online community sector are highlighted. Goulding *et al.* (2013), following a five-year ethnographic study, emphasize the benefits of communal consumption and explain that brand managers can effectively leverage subcultures and brand communities, or 'tribes', in order to offer products and services as learning resources that facilitate tribal practices to generate and sustain consumer engagement. However, recent research (Colliander and Wien, 2013) suggests that consumers who counter negative messages are not necessarily loyal to nor advocates of the brand, as formerly assumed, but rather motivated by a need for self-enhancement. This means that unless organisations can really engage the community then the brand will struggle to build long-term relationships and will also fail to maximise value from social media; and thus commercialisation of the platform will be highly limited. This situation is exacerbated by the fact that the impact of social media is very difficult to evaluate clearly (Peters *et al.*, 2013).

Georgi and Mink (2013) advocate that consumers require the opportunity to engage in online consumer-to-consumer interactions (e-CCI) in innovative business models (i.e. on Facebook) in order to build sustainability into the venture. This means that the simple dyadic social media communications advocated earlier by Larson and Watson (2011) are insufficient in the context of brand management. These understandings emphasise the point that it is important *not* to view brand presence in social media in isolation, and to understand the contribution of social media within the wider marketing and branding context to brand equity (Bruhn *et al.*, 2012). For example, in a recent study Bruhn *et al.* (2012) examined the relative impact of social media and traditional media in brand equity creation, and found that whilst both traditional communications and social media communications have a significant impact on brand equity, their contributions are different. Social media influence brand image, whilst traditional media have a stronger impact on brand awareness. Furthermore, firm-created social media communication has an important impact on functional brand image, whereas user-generated social media communication exerts a major influence on hedonic brand image. The evidence base is growing on the importance of social media to the long-term viability of firms, yet there has been very limited prior empirical research into social media and its use from the enterprise perspective (Kim and Jin 2006; Chan and Ngai, 2011).

In summary, the question of whether and how social media may be used to leverage consumer engagement into profitable relationships has yet to be explored (Schultz and Pettier, 2013). This is important since a limited right to content creation is likely to prevent relationships from forming (Tikkanen *et al.*, 2009). Forming only weak relationships is likely to directly impact on brand equity and integrity, thus impacting negatively on future commercialisation opportunities. Consequently, more research is required in order to understand "ultimate marketing strategies" employed in the social media context (Erdoğmuşa and Çiçek, 2012, p. 1359).

UK FOOTBALL AND FASHION SECTOR ISSUES IN SOCIAL MEDIA BRAND MANAGEMENT

In order to contextualise the study, this section addresses the football and fashion sectors. The UK football sector is dealt with first and the SME fashion context is considered next.

UK Football Context

Football is big business, both nationally and often internationally. The latest report into football finance (Deloitte, 2012) shows the top 20 clubs earned €4.4 billion in combined revenues (2010/11). In the same period, English Premier League (EPL) average club revenues rose to £114 million, totalling £2.27 billion across the sector. Football League (FL) clubs achieved a total of £6.3 billion in combined revenues. However, despite their size, these clubs are not well prepared to manage the social media presence of their brand, because many have limited experience of, or autonomy in relation to, the management of their brand presence (McCarthy *et al.*, 2014). Most professional UK clubs have their website hosted and managed via the Football League interactive (FLi) network, which is run as a managed portal, and whilst standardization of participating club website presence ensures consistency across the sector, it acts as a constraint on innovation and entrepreneurialism by individual clubs, such as developing a dynamic social media presence. This has led to social media innovations around football and its communities taking place independently of the clubs. Both unofficial football websites and football-related content on social media sites such as Facebook and Twitter have grown exponentially in popularity in recent years.

Another very important aspect of the football sector is the fans (McLean & Wainwright, 2009), who not only contribute to the success of 'their' club through brand support and commercial transactions, but also have strong opinions about their club, which they are often keen to share as part of the tribal bonding process with other fans. Indeed, the relationship between football fans and their club involves much more than transaction-based customer relationships (Healy and McDonagh, 2012). Being a fan involves 'doing' something, such as evoking a shared sense of emotional attachment to their club (Abosag *et al.*, 2012). For many fans, their club-related consumption is, to varying degrees, part of their self-identity (Tapp and Clowes, 2002) and they exhibit social and cultural attachment to clubs (Supporters Direct and Substance, 2010). In addition, fans also identify with other fans, leading to a strong sense of community amongst sports and football fans (Sweeney, 2010; Underwood *et al.*, 2001), with sports fans having a unique relationship with the team they support and thereby having a unique relationship with the club's brand (Bühler and Nufer, 2010; Chadwick and Beech, 2007). However, some commentators have argued that the recent climate of commercialism is making this relationship more precarious and endangering the historic link between club and its fan community (Chadwick and Beech, 2007; Chadwick *et al.*, 2008). More specifically, in the context of social media, McLean and Wainwright (2009) discovered fan dialogue on an unofficial club forum site for Newcastle United FC was restricted due to corporate interests and subsequent media manipulation by the club; this resulted in further alienation of already disaffected supporters. The risk here is the long term effect on the brand of sustained customer disengagement and attrition. Despite these issues and risks to the long term viability of the sector, a gap in the research persists from the management perspective.

In summary, UK football clubs are large, driven organisations, with high profile brands and committed communities of fans (McCarthy *et al.*, 2014). These fans often have strong opinions that they enjoy airing regarding the clubs', their management, and 'their' team's performance, and many are highly active in social media. It would appear that football clubs have much to gain from a carefully pitched and effective social media marketing and engagement strategy. Therefore, UK football clubs present an ideal context in which to conduct research on brand presence in social media.

UK SME Fashion Context

The fashion sector is highly important to the British economy. Household consumption on clothing and footwear is € 59 billion and British consumers spend about € 900 on fashion, slightly above the EU-27 average of € 700 per year. The UK fashion and textile sectors as a whole employ an estimated 600, 000 people, making the United Kingdom the third-largest fashion employer in the EU-27, surpassed only by Italy and Germany (Fashion United, 2013). Fashion retail employment remains stable making this a critical sector to the economy, given that circa 435,000 people are active in textile, clothing and footwear retailing in the UK at any given time.

The online retail (e-retail/e-tail) market continues to grow whilst the high street is in stagnation or decline. Indeed, e-commerce remains one of the fastest growing markets in Europe. Online retailers in only three countries (UK, Germany then France) accounted for 71% of total European online sales (2008-2012) making the UK, as leader, a focal location for investigation. Fashion pure-players/independents now take over 20% of the UK fashion market, having increased from just 2% only a few years ago. This dramatic shift in the retail landscape makes this an important context for research.

SMEs are critical contexts for study in the fashion domain as they have an important role in maintaining the diversity and richness of the shopping experience (Ashworth, 2012). However, smaller sized firms are widely recognised to be constrained in their activities by their limited resources in finance, marketing and strategic planning, and thus adopt different marketing strategies to larger organisations (De Burgh *et al.* 2000; Fillis *et al.*, 2003). Yet, marketing competencies are essential to sound business practice, and may be pivotal to survival for retail SMEs in general and pure-players in particular given the current sustained global downturn and the hostility of the retail sector (Ashworth, 2012). Despite the critical need for understanding there has been very little theoretical progress made in this area to date (Simpson *et al.*, 2012). Small business research is further complicated by the diverse and highly fragmented nature of SMEs and the business environments in which they operate, plus the many problems specific to small business research - such as access to key informants and the availability of financial and other company data (Curran and Blackburn, 2001). These issues are exacerbated in the context of pure-play enterprises given that no formal database or sample frame for study exists and little research has been conducted into this context (Ashworth, 2012).

Rapid consumer migration to social platforms is driving organisations to engage with new technology to facilitate online marketing effectiveness, as static online content does not motivate repeat traffic (Sicilia and Palazon, 2008; Rohm *et al.*, 2013). Social media empowers consumers to be active players and may assist in building customer relationships. It also has the potential to reinforce network effects, yet few retailers have embraced effective social media strategies and there is little academic understanding of this issue from the enterprise perspective (Kim and Jin, 2006; Chan and Ngai, 2011; Hopkins, 2012). Smaller retailers therefore need to understand the parameters for generating and sustaining communications (Sicilia and Palazon 2008), via innovations in social media, that can lead to strong relationships, differentiation and ultimately, competitive advantage in order to secure the diversity of the 'super high-street' and to keep pace with consumer migration to the virtual social platform.

In summary, new technology from a small business perspective, such as social media, presents an additional challenge to the resource constraints and marketing capabilities of the SME. Consequently, the potential opportunities offered by social media have put a fresh and more urgent focus on effective online marketing communications given the speed of consumer adoption in both the developed and developing worlds. Pure-play small business fashion/apparel retailers are highly dependent on the web presence of their brand (Ashworth, 2012). In addition, some have embraced the potential for building online communities through their web presence to develop internationalisation of the customer base and advance enterprise growth (e.g. Foscht *et al.*, 2006). Businesses in this sector are unlikely to be able to survive and flourish if they ignore social media, and its associated challenges or opportunities, in relation to their brands. Therefore, pure-play smaller-sized fashion retailers (e-SMEs) present an ideal and interesting context in which to conduct research on brand presence in social media and knowledge is now required to better understand the issues in this sector.

The research methodology is discussed next.

METHOD

Research design is the "framework for collection and analysis of data" (Bryman and Bell, 2007, p.731) which best provides for the study to meet objectives (Easterby-Smith *et al.*, 2002). Since there is little previous research on the management of brand presence in social media, this study adopted an exploratory approach, based on multiple case study design (Gummesson, 2005; 2006) across two important UK industry sectors, namely football and fashion.

Aim and Objectives

The aim of the research summarised in this section, and reported more fully in Ashworth (2013) and McCarthy *et al.* (2014) is to develop an understanding of managers' perceptions of the issues of and strategies adopted to brand management in a social media age.

The objectives of this research were to:

- Gather insights into the issues that football club management and fashion pure-players perceive in relation to developing a social media strategy.
- Explore the value and/or potential benefits of social media strategy from the practitioner perspective.
- Identify any differences in strategic approaches towards social media strategy between the sectors in order to understand and contextualise the implications and impact from a brand management perspective.

Research Strategy

Qualitative research outputs are "of more relevance and interest to management practitioners" than quantitative (Cassell *et al.*, 2006, p.163) and case studies are most useful in the context of social media research (Urquhart and Vaast, 2012). Indeed, the advantage of the case study approach is that it investigates a contemporary phenomenon in its context (Yin, 2009), whilst a multi-case study design generates more varied and richer empirical evidence that can provide a basis for deeper and more meaningful analytical comparison (Eisenhardt and Graebner, 2007). Football cases were selected as they offered a two-pronged view of social media given that two clubs were already engaging social media and two were yet to engage. However, their social media engagement was limited. In contrast, the SME pure-play fashion sector was selected as it is an area where consumers and businesses are increasingly active online. An in-depth and rich perspective was secured as participants had significant time operating in the football/fashion domains. As such the key informants provided high levels of experience in the field in order to better contextualise and bring communicative validation to the social media domain (Creswell and Miller, 2000) highlighted in this study.

In total, eight cases were explored in-depth, comprising: four football clubs (Cases A-D) and four independent pure-play e-retailers (Cases E-H). Data gathered from the key informants in the eight sector-specific cases were then supplemented by secondary data in order to balance the wider experiential view. In this study the concept of "good fit" (Gummesson, 2000, p. 93) is adhered to in order to build greater credibility into the findings.

Data on the cases was gathered through a combination of desk research, based on documents and websites, and in-depth guided interviews. Desk research was undertaken in order to familiarize the research team with the case companies and aspects of their online presence. Tracking the case companies online and via various media was useful in the first instance to contextualise the social media activity; and latterly, to confirm insights gained from the key stakeholder interviews. Desk research focused on: branded social media presence of the cases (where this existed); any unofficial social media sites related to each case; selected digital relationship marketing communications, key media and industry websites; plus, industry reports.

An inductive approach that used guided interviews to generate qualitative data was employed (Saunders *et al.*, 2007). Since previous research on social media strategy from a management perspective, in general, and in the context of football clubs and the fashion retail sector, in particular, is limited, it was important to adopt an approach that would provide in-depth insights, and be flexible and exploratory in order to fully examine industry phenomena (Bryman and Bell, 2011). Depth interviews were therefore selected as they offer reliable evidence in management research (McCracken, 1988). Adopting a high-interest stakeholder perspective through the selection of football marketing/brand managers and e-retail owner-managers as participants ensured a sample of credible native speakers (Johnson and Weller, 2002).

To support the research design in the football sector, given their nascent level of social media marketing development, cases were chosen on the basis of their activity (2 cases) and inactivity (2 cases). In the fashion sector theoretical sampling, following advice from industry experts, was utilized in order to identify highly social media active cases. This comprised first movers online, who had been operating for many years in the e-retail domain (2 cases), and comparatively new entrants who had been operating transactional cyberstores for just a few years online (2 cases). This enabled a richer understanding of the social media landscape in both sectors. The online presence of cases was then tracked for some time in order to gauge the level of marketspace activity. Final case selection in the fashion industry was on the basis that each pure-play e-retailer was highly social media active. The strong level of social media activity highlighted that small firms are much more open and active in their social media communications and much more agile and flexible in responding to marketspace opportunities arising from online community engagement, and hence presented appropriate cases for learning (Eisenhardt, 1989).

Interview schedules were designed to draw out interviewees' views on social media strategy and any associated challenges, plus their perceptions of the benefits and value of social media. Interviews typically lasted one and a half hours, with the longest running over two hours. The interviews were recorded, transcribed, stored electronically and supplemented by field notes. The data generated was coded and scripts were analysed via thematic template analysis (King, 1998). Within-case analysis preceded across-case analysis (Patton, 2002; Perry, 1998) in order to identify emergent themes, content and key issues related to the research aim in order to "allow commonalities to emerge" (Stavros and Westberg, 2009, p. 312) within sectors. Participant checking was used during the stages of transcript approval in the first cases in order to validate the initial coding. Key themes and differences were then identified at across case-level in order to enhance validity of the study (Creswell and Miller, 2000). Findings were then conceptually developed – since in qualitative research "the account must offer conceptualization and condensation or the researcher has not contributed interpretation and meaning" (Gummesson, 2005, p.315). Conceptual developments reported in the next sections are inductively developed from the data generated in this study.

The participating football and fashion cases are briefly considered next.

Summary of Football Cases

The football cases involved interviews with four senior managers who had responsibility variously for marketing, branding, and web presence. Four UK football cases were selected. All of the case clubs were significant players in either the EPL or the (UK) Football League. Clubs were selected to achieve diversity in their recent fates regarding league status, spectator attendance levels, and revenue.

Case A is a large club in terms of attendance at matches, size of fan base, and revenue. In addition, it has experienced promotion to and relegation from the EPL. It makes some limited use of social media. Case B is a medium-sized club in terms of attendance, fan base, and revenue, and has also experienced a mix of promotion and relegation. Case B had no official social media presence on external platforms, such as Facebook. Case C also had no official social media presence at the time of research. Therefore, the gap created by a lack of official social media presence on Facebook and Twitter by cases B and C, was already being filled by the club's supporters setting up their own unofficial presence and gaining fans and followers. Both cases regarded this as a missed opportunity to be addressed. Like case B, case C is also a medium-sized club, in terms of attendance and fan base, but has less of an international profile than A or B. Due to EPL status the club enjoys higher revenue than a club of similar size may traditionally expect and thus has a strong focus on commercialisation. In terms of revenue, Case D is smaller than the other three clubs, but attendance and fan base are similar to Case C, although their fan base is more international. Case D resided in the second tier at the time of data gathering – but made some minimal use of social media. In summary, in common with all EPL and FLi football clubs at the time of the research, every case was very much in the infancy of any social media presence or how to respond to the challenge of this new media landscape.

Summary of Pure-Play SME Fashion E-Retail Cases

In contrast to the somewhat nascent stage of development and reluctance to engage social media in the football sector, the SME pure-play fashion e-retailers had more wholly embraced social media as a brand communication strategy.

Case E had been online for the longest period having operated for over 15 years online. They had developed their own e-retail shopping basket before off the shelf solutions were available and thus had significant e-retail experience to draw upon. Case E had also grown with the changing face of social media: from initially posting on target segment bulletin boards in the late nineties, to engaging with MySpace, Bebo and Facebook in the new millennium as the social media landscape developed. Case F had been operating online for the shortest period with just over three years e-retail experience. However, Case F had the fastest growth profile having reached over £1m turnover within the first 12 months of operation. Case F has sustained a strong growth profile from a zero start despite the aggressive economic retail climate and is now one of the leading independent online fashion retailers targeting the teens/twenties market. In addition, the participating marketing director from Case F had extensive previous e-retail experience in established organisations (e.g. Tesco, Next etc). This case utilised social media from enterprise start-up in order to develop a critical mass of customers and so quickly spread eWOM as an integral viral marketing strategy. The two remaining cases (Cases G and H) were 'industry best' award winners for their online activities. These companies had focussed on developing brand engagement via BeBo/MySpace initially but later switched their social media efforts to Facebook and Twitter as target audiences migrated platforms. All the fashion cases utilised a good variety of social media marketing tactics in order to engage target audiences (e.g. style guides, competitions, lifestyle commentary, promotions etc). Each case therefore represented a useful context for learning (Eisenhardt, 1989). Moreover, given early perceived success from social media activities, the fashion participants unanimously advocated the importance of social media to future brand strategy and business development.

FINDINGS: ISSUES AND BENEFITS OF SOCIAL MEDIA IN THE UK FOOTBALL AND FASHION SECTORS

The findings of this study are presented next. Firstly, findings from the football sector are addressed and latterly, the fashion sector results are provided. An examination of the differences between sectors can be found in the discussion section later.

Issues from the Football Sector

The research revealed that interviewees' concerns regarding the social media presence of their brand centred on three key issues: control of conversation, fan engagement, and commercialisation. Participants' perceived challenges in each of these areas, but were also starting to experiment with potential responses to those challenges.

First, clubs were concerned about the impact of social media on their control of the conversations associated with the club, and also, ultimately on the club's brand identity and image. They were particularly worried about unfavourable comments about the club, or offensive language, and a shared awareness that these comments were being posted on unofficial websites, in social media sites, as well as being shared face-to-face. There was a particular concern regarding the potential for negative comments within the official club website, and it was felt that a social media area on their official website might impact negatively on the club's brand reputation and equity. On the other hand, it was acknowledged that, as one interviewee said:

These supporters are saying it in the pubs, or on the terraces, or in the shops, wherever they meet and congregate. So denying them that space on the website doesn't mean that those views will go away. (Marketing Manager)

Notwithstanding their concerns regarding control, there was a general recognition that in order to tap into the passion of fans it is necessary to accept that views expressed by fans will not always be what the club wants to hear. Interviewees all discussed the need to release some control of the conversation if official sites are to accommodate and facilitate such fan debate, and were aware of the need to progress towards an understanding of appropriate controls. It was seen as particularly important to exercise control in three areas: the potential for hijacking of the online conversation by rival club supporters; fans expressions of their views on the club chairman, manager, players or staff in general; and, the management of and responsibility within clubs for social media content and engagement with fans.

The second collection of issues was associated with fan engagement. Overall, there was a sense that there was no real effort to know the customer. Specifically, there was weak development of digital customer relationship management, plus a lack of strategy and tactics to encourage fan interaction. For example, interviewees reported that a lack of systems integration and data warehousing contributes to a limited view of customer behaviour and a fragmented approach to relationship marketing communications. As one interviewee suggested:

...we have a single customer view of some sort which is still very much in its embryonic stage... our email providers aren't plugged into that single customer viewpoint yet... Did they click through on the email, did they shop off-site, did they browse around the site, how much did they spend online... you know, we don't capture any of that information at the moment and that... isn't plugged into the central database... (Head of Customer Operations)

However, there was recognition that social media had the future potential to generate real-time customer insight, which could form the basis for more sophisticated relationship marketing activity. Strategic direction and impact of social media had thus yet to be realised by the football clubs.

All clubs agreed that their official site (e.g. www.nufc.co.uk) was lacking opportunities for fan engagement and interaction, and that this was likely to cause fans to migrate to unofficial sites (e.g. www.nufc.com, or www.skysports.com), with concomitant consequences for clubs' ability to communicate with fans, and manage the customer relationship online. References to clubs "missing a trick", "playing at it" and "scratching the surface" were evidence of a reticent approach.

... from what I've seen of it in the rest of the football industry I'm not convinced anybody is doing it particularly well. When you look at other industries and other uses of Twitter particularly, I think that we're miles behind. (Head of Customer Operations)

In particular, there was an understanding that this lack of opportunity for interaction meant that clubs were not capitalising on football's tribal nature and the opportunity that it provides to create a community around a team brand, and an awareness that this needed to be addressed. Clubs were currently experimenting with social media practices that would facilitate the sharing of experience between, for example, supporters in a specific location, and responding to concerns raised in discussions on unofficial social media sites.

The final recurrent theme was commercialisation. Social media was seen as a driver of traffic to the official site which is monetised via advertising revenue and sales of commercial products, such as online player TV, ticketing and merchandise. Clubs are aware fans may consider social media as their space (private or public), yet there is pressure to use them as a commercial space if they are to allocate resource. Interviewees were aware of this tension, as suggested by the following quotes:

... the danger is that you make it overtly commercial. That's the big, big issue. (Marketing Manager)

We have to be a little bit careful that we don't push them [fans] into finding information elsewhere in terms of the stuff we put out from a Club point of view. (Marketing Manager)

However, clubs still have to develop a perspective on their web presence (that pervades their website and any social media engagement) that goes beyond revenue generation to a more sophisticated approach to brand building. For example, both interviews and desk research showed that clubs lack imagination and creativity in the content that they are posting on social media sites, and were simply duplicating official website headlines and providing links back to those stories, thus potentially adding little value to the brand.

Football Sector Benefits

Despite their tardiness and concerns regarding their engagement with social media, all interviewees acknowledged that there were benefits that their club might accrue from an effective social media strategy. These were seen to be in the areas of content, interaction, community, and revenue generation.

First, social media was viewed as an opportunity to share content with fans. For example, clubs A and D have activated a Twitter profile, though it was acknowledged these are duplicating the current news feeds of the official site. Given their commercial agreement with FLi and its reliance on advertising revenue, Twitter was viewed as an opportunity to drive traffic to the official club website. Desk research of the branded Facebook pages and Twitter profiles for cases A and D confirmed that no unique content is being posted. It was simply duplication of existing official website headlines and links back to those full stories on the respective official sites. However, research has shown that used more imaginatively and effectively, the value of Twitter is proven in driving traffic back to the sites responsible for the original tweet, in addition to facilitating extensive (viral) re-tweeting (Kwak *et al.*, 2010). By failing to engage with customer pull, and resisting the move to social media, clubs are potentially limiting the development of the brand and missing the opportunity to build brand equity and drive revenues for the club. Avoidance of fresh and original content is also likely to lead to further customer attrition from official sites and to limit the opportunity for enhancing relationship ties with the fan base.

Notwithstanding their conservative approach to social media, all clubs appreciated that football was unique in its ability to create a unifying interest around a team brand and recognised that the way to drive traffic was to engage fans through their passion for the club. For the future, they acknowledged the importance of enabling engagement in a proactive manner, rather than simply responding to discussion or duplicating existing official site content. Clubs hope this would overcome the limitations of their current generic 'push' communication, despite the absence of targeted and appropriate communications. It was suggested that social media offered real-time customer insight, enabling more sophisticated relationship marketing activity – yet none of the participants had ventured down this route. The current findings therefore strongly suggest the potential for commercial gain in relation to employing social media in the football sector in line with Beer (2008). Interviewees also articulated an intuitive understanding of the benefits of engaging with online communities that exist around their club in the form of social media (Schau *et al.*, 2009).

Interviewees also discussed the potential role of social media in building the fan community, by offering fans a chance to show their 'badge of honour' and being given the opportunity to share experiences. Clubs were considering allowing fans to connect with fellow supporters in a specific location, and acting as facilitators in community growth and belonging. Also, regarding match day experience, clubs have been willing to successfully respond to concerns raised in discussions on unofficial social media sites, not by participating in the conversation but by introducing initiatives at the stadia.

Finally, club's interest in social media is driven by its potential for revenue generation:

As you get used to people's user habits and their profile, of who they are, you can get even more sophisticated. So I think that's how you commercialise the [social media] element. But it's the club shop window and if people are only passing once a week, then you've got a 1 in 7 chance of making a sale. If they're coming on 5 or 6 times a week - that has surely got to uplift your opportunity. (Marketing Manager)

As exemplified above, attracting higher and more frequent traffic in order to improve page impressions on the official site is regarded as important in increasing advertising and other commercial revenue streams.

Issues and benefits of findings from the pure-play fashion sector are explained next.

Issues from the Pure-Play SME Fashion E-Retail Sector

The research revealed that participant's initial concerns regarding the social media presence of their brand echoed those voiced by the football sector interviewees. In other words, organisations in both sectors exhibited caution when faced with a new medium, especially one in which people could talk about their brand. However, interviewees in this sector were much more relaxed in relation to control of conversations, and more positive and certain about the considerable opportunities for both community engagement and the commercial aspects of brand building and positive brand advocacy. Indeed, each e-retail case highlighted significant financial improvements from social media engagement, which cemented a strong commitment to increasing levels of brand development via social media communications in future marketing strategy. The only challenge in developing their social media presence that the participating e-retailers perceived related to resource constraints (i.e. staff time). The first movers admitted they initially had concerns relating to the 'unknown potential/effect' of social media at the outset, but any worries were quickly redressed as a result of positive experiences. Consequently, each e-retail case was increasing planned activity and experimentation with social media in order to keep pace with customer migration and opportunities arising within online social space. They were also very confident of the brand advocacy provided by their consumers in social space. Positive communications and consumer endorsements coming through social media are seen to build brand image and identity in a credible and constructive way. They were also seen to build relationships and enhance engagement in the fashion sector.

Grounded in their engagement with social media, as indicated above, the e-retailers perceived few issues and, instead, saw social media as having a very positive impact on their business in terms of both customer retention and acquisition. Improved market intelligence gathered through social media, based on real-time data, enabled more effective target marketing, leading in turn to customer conversations, in which customers are keen to collaborate to defend the brand online:

If you've got an open group, customers find you and join. They could express their discontent - but in practice we never see any of that negative branding at all... (Marketing Director & Shareholder)

It just happened to us once in the last five years. Even before we responded; lots of our existing customers came out in our defence and said: "That really isn't our experience". So it works in our favour, which is a good thing, because people can then see others have had a good experience. It's much more credible when it [the defence/endorsement] comes direct from happy customers... (Founder & Managing Director)

Concerns were expressed about customer engagement, but the e-retailers managed this process by making a significant effort to understand customers in real-time and to comprehend subtle nuances and changes which offered opportunities for research and market development, customer relationship building, and to encourage customer interaction.

It gives lower costs in market research, lower costs in promotion, and a lot more advertising impact... (Co-Founder & Marketing Director)

Positive customer contributions encourage e-shopping with new and existing customers... helps build and sustain the brand ... improves conversion rates... (Marketing Director & Shareholder)

Company engagement with Facebook groups is also perceived to enable better access to consumer tribes/sub-cultures and emergent 'scenes', such as new music genres/lifestyles, such that the SME e-retailers are using social media strategically and successfully from very early on in their online/community encounters:

Found we could research very easily on Facebook ... looking at people online, what they're talking about, getting excited about. That really helped us when 'Steampunk' took off. It helped us launch our own products into that category quickly, we were the first – so we rapidly became established in the community ... now it's one of our best revenue streams... (Founder & Managing Director)

In addition, SME e-retailers were also seeking direct commercial gain from their social media investments. They saw social media as a driver of traffic to their website, for both existing and new customers.

Because information is shared fluidly and it's an open system: once you've joined the network it generates a lot of word-of-mouth and eWOM. It has a very positive impact... (Marketing Director & Shareholder)

In terms of content, the e-retailers were actively feeding the social space with a variety of relevant communications focused on information and entertainment. The emphasis for the e-retail sector was to create communications which were timely and appropriate for each target segment's needs and which involved a good variety of messages. Simply posting product/brand information was not perceived as sufficient to generate interactivity, relationships or engagement with consumers. Participants agreed that considerable creativity and thought had to be put into generating engaging social media communications across a number of levels in terms of information, entertainment and lifestyle related content to satisfy hedonic and functional needs (Sicilia and Palazon, 2008; Georgi and Mink, 2013).

Benefits from the Pure-Play SME Fashion E-Retail Sector

On the basis of their experience with social media, the e-retailers were able to report positively on the benefits that accrue from their social media strategies. Indeed, engaging with social media is unanimously perceived to contribute positively to the sustainability (Ashworth, 2013) of the e-SME retail enterprise:

It gives you lower costs in market research, lower costs in promotion, and a lot more advertising impact ... customers come to you, then recommend new people ... [so] you grow your business organically. (Marketing Director & Shareholder)

Facebook in particular is used as a primary platform for communications, interactivity and engagement; whilst Twitter acts as the secondary and supporting element to further develop brand ubiquity across target groups. The ease and speed of social media interactions means the costs of customer acquisition and retention are minimised which assists with cash flow and enables better financial management for the small firm. In addition, there was a strong recognition of the importance of 'pull' rather than 'push' content, as a means of attracting and engaging customers. This process was, in turn, seen as offering additional routes to brand and market development. In particular, failing to engage consumers online was seen to limit WOM and eWOM opportunities and, it was recognised that for the small firm, this would mean that more resources have to be pumped into traditional (and less effective) marketing communications in order to build brand ubiquity, further constraining enterprise resources and thus limiting the longer term development of the firm.

In addition, the benefits of customer interaction and engagement (Coulter & Roggeveen, 2012) were recognised and discussed. For a pure-play business, the main mode of customer interaction is online and hence such interaction is pivotal (Ashworth, 2013). For example, interviewees stated that by engaging in social media e-retailers are more able to meet niche/market needs online as enterprises are better informed:

All this extra exposure means more customers and more sales right across our target groups. There would be no way for us to do that from a small high street store, or just through search engine optimisation (SEO) as a small firm... (Founder & Managing Director)

Importantly also, e-retail dialogue is expected to be shared three-ways in order to be most effective. This means active participation is required and encouraged on a C2C, C2B and B2C basis in order to maximise communication and branding opportunities for the firm in the social media context. Thus the current findings from the fashion sector challenge the social media dyad advocated by Larson and Watson (2011) in favour of a more triadic approach (Ashworth, 2013). Interviewees also perceived this three-way (triadic) interaction as forming the foundation for building more durable community bonds:

The influence of these online communities is definitely growing in the consumer groups we target. That justifies our strategy to continue with social media as a marketing mechanism... (Marketing Director & Shareholder)

Finally, interviewees reported on the considerable benefits that they are accruing from effective social media strategies. Each case clearly highlighted that the organisational value derived from social media involves a positive impact on the bottom line. That the small enterprises explored in this study are able to effectively measure and monitor social media impact – and then to successfully feed this back into strategy - is an interesting finding given the difficulties in social media measurement highlighted earlier by Peters *et al.* (2013). The consensus from participants is that the effective engagement of social media has a tangible, positive effect on enquiries, conversion rates and orders, exemplified below:

I certainly say if you're on Facebook and you're active, I would be extremely surprised if you didn't quickly see an increase in enquiries and sales and customers... (Founder & Managing Director)

We've seen a significant increase in traffic and repeat visitors since implementing social shopping and believe this community atmosphere has been integral in improving our success online... (Marketing Director & Shareholder)

Significant improvements in the performance of the site - including a 162% increase in conversion rates since engaging in the social shopping community... (Company Director)

The next section discusses the findings in the context of brand management taking into account the practitioner viewpoint and sectoral differences in social media marketing strategy.

DISCUSSION

As the findings demonstrate there are considerable perceived and real advantages to be gained from implementing an effective social media strategy in the commercial world. However, what transpires from the profiles and findings from the two different sectors is that their uses of social media, and the resultant impact on the company and customer, are very different.

In the first instance the communications strategy is polarised between the two sectors: push (football) versus pull (e-retail). This clearly has an impact on the opportunity for interactivity, which has a knock-on effect with relationship ties and community engagement. In addition, the commercial focus for football clubs is highly controlled and uni-directional messaging combines with a hard-sell approach focussed on commercialisation. However, this has the limiting effect of driving customers away to unofficial sites and thus restricting opportunities for engagement, relationship-building and ultimately, revenue generation. This has an impact on the further commercialisation of the football websites and thus potentially affects additional investments in social media. On the other hand, fashion e-retailers employ a soft-sell approach with an open and triadic system of communications (B2C, C2C and C2B) to maximise WOM and eWOM, providing flexibility, agility and variety of communications. This has the benefit of maximising traffic and engagement, building brand advocacy and strengthening relationship ties; which in turn offers better opportunities for customer acquisition and retention, whilst maximising cross and up-selling. This also encourages further investment in social media strategy by the firm.

It is perhaps a little too easy to leap to the conclusion that with their confidence in the benefits of social media to their bottom line and the sustainability of their business that the pure-play SME fashion retailers provide a model of best practice for others to follow. And, conversely, that the UK football sector, characterised by large organisations with 'big' brands, has been surprisingly lumbering and cautious in its engagement with social media, particularly given their ready-made 'communities'. However, it is more fruitful to view these two exemplars at opposite ends of a spectrum in terms of their social media activities and strategy.

Table 1 summarises the approaches to social media strategy adopted by the UK football sector and pure-play SME retailers, in terms of the four identified foci. The four foci are: strategic marketing, marketing communication, brand and community, plus monitoring and evaluation. For each of the four foci a summary of the approach adopted is offered, accompanied by a summary of the impact of that approach. The final row of Table 1 summarises the value creation opportunity that emerges from the adopted strategies.

We describe these polaric approaches in terms of four different foci which impact directly on the value creation opportunities of the organisation. These are summarised in Figure 2 next:

The dimensions of Figure 2 are briefly explained next.

1. **Strategic Marketing:** The overall strategic approach adopted by the organisation to its social media marketing activities, characterised here in terms of the balance between push and hard-sell versus pull and relationship marketing.

Table 1. Approaches to social media strategy & resultant impact

	Theme	Football Club Approach	Impact	SME Fashion E-retailing Approach	Impact
Strategic Approaches	**Strategic Marketing Focus**	• Sales and push marketing approach • Hard sell • Random and mostly un-related products	• Minimal engagement • Leads to weak-tie relationships • Fan/customer disengagement • Traffic limited • Customer attrition	• Relationship and pull marketing approach • Soft sell • Value-adding and related products only	• Intense customer engagement • Leads to stronger-tie relationships • Stronger ability for cross/up-selling • Traffic growth
	Marcomms Focus	• Strong focus on uni-directional messaging • Closed and tightly controlled network	• Customer defection to unofficial sites • Stagnant/decreasing community • Negative WOM/ eWOM • High customer acquisition costs	• Engagement strategy and triadic communication • Open and flexible network	• B2C, C2C & C2B engagement • Strong & positive WOM & eWOM • Growing community • Minimal customer acquisition costs
	Brand and Community Focus	• Create brand identity in-house • Only interested in promoting the business/ brand • Exert strict control over community messaging	• Limited detailed understanding of consumer, thus defection • Limited opportunity for research • Limited dialogue with fans • Limited customer retention	• Brand identity built via co-creation with consumers • Embed within the community • Join, lead & engage the community	• Maximise research & new product opportunities • Maximise understanding of consumer • Maximise communication effectiveness • Strong customer retention
	Monitoring and Evaluation Focus	• Business statistics & KPIs • Quantitative analysis	• Lack of impact from quantitative data • High marketing & customer acquisition costs	• Listening and watching community activity • Qualitative analysis •	• Low costs for market research • Low customer acquisition costs • High customer retention • Minimal marketing costs
Overall Impact	**Value Creation Opportunity**	• Focus on value creation for the organisation, little focus on the customer/fan • Inflexible strategy leads to inability to meet objectives here	• Opportunities missed from arms-length strategy • Limited opportunity for advantage • Sales not maximised	• Value creation for the customer, niche & community • Flexible strategy leads to value creation for the firm and continuous improvement	• New markets/ opportunities identified from close customer contact • First mover advantage • Sales maximised

Source: Table 1 is inductively developed from the football and fashion sector empirical case data.

2. **Marketing Communications:** The strategic approach adopted to marketing communications through the various different social media channels including, pivotally, messages, content, and approach taken to the encouragement of customer conversations and interaction, characterised here in terms of sales-orientated versus market-oriented.

3. **Brand and Community:** The strategic approach adopted to brand development, control and ownership, including the attitude towards community engagement with the brand, characterised here in terms of in-house control versus co-creation and building community embeddedness.

Figure 2. Strategic considerations for social media

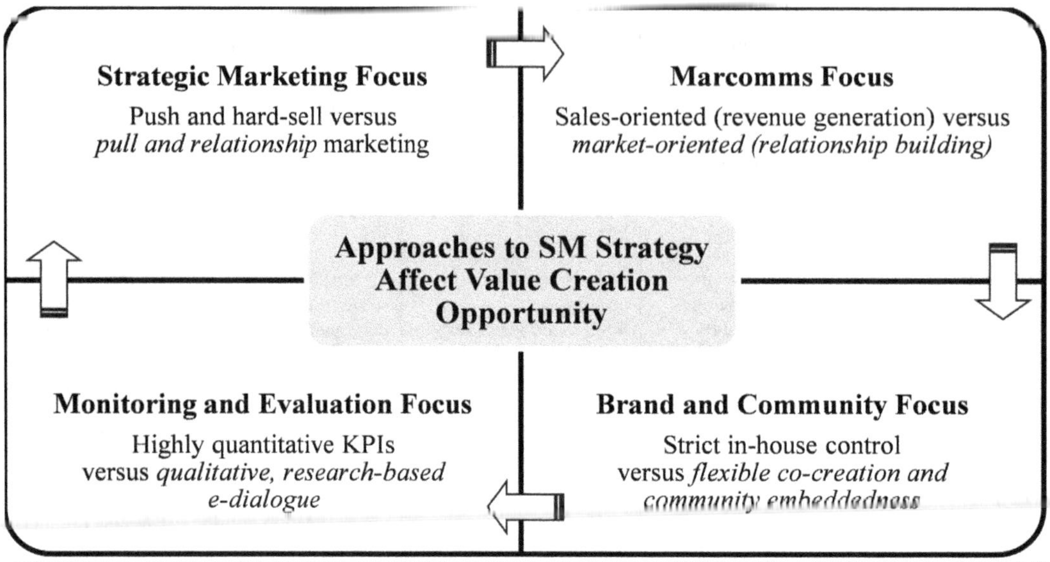

Note to Figure 2:
In order to *maximise opportunities and impact* from the implementation of social media strategy, the discerning enterprise should *follow the arrowed path* (in *italics*) around the matrix.

Source: Concepts inductively developed from the fashion and football sector case data.

4. **Monitoring and Evaluation:** The strategic approach adopted to monitoring and evaluation of social media strategies, characterised here in terms of quantitative KPI's versus qualitative enquiry-based e-dialogue.

The arrows in Figure 2 signify that each focus impacts on the others, and in particular that with an effectively managed strategic process, the development of an organisation's social media strategy is a cyclical process. Most importantly, these different foci should not be viewed as a series of stand-alone activities or strategic considerations which operate independently, notwithstanding that they may be the responsibility of different departments depending on the size of the organisation concerned. Optimally, the strategic marketing focus will be linked to organisational objectives and strategies, and will, in turn, influence the other three foci, but in reality some organisations are likely to be more successful with this alignment than others. In addition, where there is alignment of marketing across channels, the organisations' social media strategy in the context of each of these four foci will be influenced by its overall stance on marketing and its degree of market orientation. Importantly, Table 1 is not intended to imply that there are only two options, as represented here by our two case contexts. Many organisations will lay between these two extremes, in, for example, the balance that they strike between sales and push marketing and relationship marketing, and this will have consequences for the most appropriate behaviour for them to adopt in respect of the other foci – and bearing in mind their target market.

Different organisations will adopt different social media strategies, as they perceive appropriate for their organisation, brands, products and service, customers and marketplace. Nevertheless, it is appropriate to conclude this discussion by returning

Table 2. Seven key benefits accrued from effective social media strategy

Key Benefit	Explanation
1. Enhanced Opportunity for E-Dialogue	Social media engagement enables an enhanced opportunity for an open e-dialogue which is construed as more credible, believable and trustworthy than traditional push tactics.
2. Deeper Understanding of Target Customers	A deeper understanding of target/niche consumers enables the e-retailer to get closer to the customer, which reinforces positive e-dialogue and network effects.
3. Increased Exposure & Reach	This broader web-of-communications increases exposure to customers, which again reinforces network effects, so stimulating increasing levels of e-dialogue amongst existing and potential customers and improving reach.
4. Low Cost Customer Acquisition & High Retention	E-dialogue between existing and potential customers with the brand builds credibility and encourages new prospect attention, enhancing low cost customer acquisition opportunities, and increasing both customer retention and positive referrals.
5. Reduced Market Research Costs & Improved Real Time Data	Social media engagement provides useful real-time market research data, and at the same time reduces market research costs.
6. Communication Effectiveness Improved	Social media engagement maximises communication effectiveness and reduces marketing costs.
7. Positive Impact on Sales Revenues	Social media engagement promotes both new and repeat sales and ultimately, supports business survival.

Source: Established from SME pure-play fashion industry empirical case data (See: Ashworth, 2013).

to the exemplar of the approach to social media adopted by the pure-play SME fashion retailers, since it illustrates the potential of social media strategies to promote the success of a business, and the value of its brands. The findings for this case support seven key benefits identified and explained in Table 2 next:

These findings support Boyd Thomas *et al's* (2007) and Coulter and Roggeveen's (2012) views that communication via social media can indeed create communal bonds and relationship ties between consumers. Customer collaboration to defend the brand is much more credible and believable to e-shoppers than a direct/corporate response (Ashworth, 2013). This, in turn is consistent with the growing online consumer behaviour literature which suggests that consumers are more willing to shop online with brands they feel they can trust (e.g. Bauer *et al.* 2002; Kim and Jones, 2009; Hahn and Kim, 2009).

FUTURE RESEARCH DIRECTIONS

The studies reported in this chapter were conducted in specific sectors and at a specific point in time, and thus encompass important viewpoints stretching from the early days of social media marketing. There is considerable potential for further research in this area, including in other sectors (embracing, for example large and smaller organizations, and those with established brands, and those still engaged in developing their brand), at other times, and in other countries and different cultural settings given the fragmented take up by consumers and industry in different global locations – and bearing in mind the inherent opportunities offered by rapidly developing markets, such as BRIC and MINT countries.

CONCLUSION

This chapter acknowledges the challenges that social media poses for brands, and reports on research which addresses two contemporaneous but separate and highly divergent market sectors. The chapter explains and summarises the impact of their associated approaches to social media strategy. Whilst even within sectors there are differences between organisations, of particular interest is the nature of the sector in determining attitudes to social media. The UK football sector, with its large and highly profitable organisations, high profile brands and committed and vociferous brand (or fan) communities has regarded social media with some apprehension, and exhibited nervousness in committing to developing an effective social media presence. They also view social media as threatening traffic flow to their web site, as well as being potentially damaging to the brand, managers and players via negative online communications and hence having potential to reduce their commercial revenues. The football sector therefore seeks to heavily control social media communications – which may impact severely on the success of those conversations.

An interesting question that surfaces in the face of this comparison is 'why are these profiles so different?' Possible answers may lie in the relative size, agility and flexibility of the organisations, the organisational structure, the role of marketing within the organisation, the level of the brand equity, the innovativeness and entrepreneurial nature of the sector, or the level of prior engagement with digital marketing and online communities. But, this is only speculation. More research, across a larger number of sectors and organisations is necessary in order to provide an answer to this question. Such research would also offer deeper and more extensive insights into the match between organisational strategies and objectives, and the various foci within a social media strategy and their corresponding impacts in terms of customer acquisition and retention, plus brand building and the strength of relationship-ties developed.

Finally, in both sectors, despite the more hesitant response amongst UK football clubs, there is awareness of the threat (Maclaran and Catterall, 2012) and possible benefits of negative messages combined with positive engagement of consumer advocate responses, plus the need to respond to the shifting balance of power in relation to brands (Bernoff and Li, 2008: Fisher and Smith, 2011) and brand communications in social space. The pure-play SME fashion retailers demonstrate the value of facilitating conversations around the brand, and engaging in co-creation of brand meaning and experiences (Christodoulides *et al.*, 2009; Goulding *et al.*, 2013). Different organizations will also likely prioritise different objectives for their social media strategy. Some organizations, may focus on the 'public relations' element of social media strategies with a view to promoting and protecting their brand and reputation. Others will seek to be more proactive in welcoming and cultivating member or customer contribution (co-creation) to building both the brand image, brand experience and brand defence. However, what is clear is that given the global trend towards migration of consumers to social media platforms, all organizations will need to consider the role of their social media strategy as an element of their defence against competition and for building protective and durable barriers and relationships in social space, and thus to strike an appropriate balance between revenue generation and brand building through their social media and web presence.

REFERENCES

Abosag, I., Roper, S., & Hind, D. (2012). Examining the relationship between brand emotion and brand extension among supporters of professional football clubs. *European Journal of Marketing*, *46*(9), 1233–1251. doi:10.1108/03090561211247810

Ashworth, C. J. (2012). Marketing and organisational development in e-SMEs: Understanding survival and sustainability in growth-oriented and comfort-zone pure-play enterprises in the fashion retail industry. *The International Entrepreneurship and Management Journal*, *8*(2), 165–201. doi:10.1007/s11365-011-0171-6

Ashworth, C. J. (2013). Empowering small firms: Value and impact of social media communication innovation in pure-play SME retail marketing. Paper presented at the EURAM Conference 2013. Istanbul, Turkey.

Bauer, H. H., Grether, M., & Leach, M. (2002). Building customer relations over the internet. *Industrial Marketing Management Journal*, *31*(2), 155–163. doi:10.1016/S0019-8501(01)00186-9

Beer, D. (2008). Social network(ing) sites… revisiting the story so far: A response to Danah Boyd & Nicole Ellison. *Journal of Computer-Mediated Communication*, *13*(2), 516–529. doi:10.1111/j.1083-6101.2008.00408.x

Bernoff, J., & Li, C. (2008). Harnessing the power of the oh-so-social-web. *MIT Sloan Management Review*, *49*(3), 36–42.

Boyd, D. M., & Ellison, N. B. (2008). Social network sites: Definition, history and scholarship. *Journal of Computer-Mediated Communication*, *13*(2), 210–230.

Brown, R., Hayton, J., Sandy, C., & Brown, P. (1977). *Small businesses - Strategy for survival*. London: Wilton House Publications.

Bruhn, M., Schoenmueller, V., & Schafer, D. B. (2012). Are social media replacing traditional media in terms of brand equity creation? *Management Research Review*, *35*(9), 770–790. doi:10.1108/01409171211255948

Bryman, A., & Bell, E. (2007). *Business research methods*. Oxford, UK: Oxford University Press.

Bryman, B., & Bell, E. (2011). *Business research methods* (3rd ed.). Oxford, UK: Oxford University Press.

Bühler, A., & Nufer, G. (2010). *Relationship marketing in sports*. Oxford, UK: Butterworth-Heinemann.

Cassell, C., Buehring, A., Symon, G., & Johnson, P. (2006). Qualitative methods in management research: An introduction to the themed issue. *Management Decision*, *44*(2), 161–166. doi:10.1108/00251740610650166

Centeno, C., Wainer, L., Misuraca, G., Punie, Y., & Broster, D. (2009). *Key findings, future prospects, and policy challenges. Joint Research Centre Institute for Prospective Technological Studies*. Luxembourg: Office for Official Publications for the European Communities.

Chadwick, S., & Beech, J. (2007). Introduction: The marketing of sport. In *The marketing of sport* (pp. 3–22). Harlow, UK: Pearson Education.

Chadwick, S., Garford, W., Guimaraes, G., & O'Reilly, D. (2008). The formation, organisation and management of MyFootballClub: Implications for marketing practice. *Journal of Direct. Data and Digital Marketing Practice*, *10*(2), 150–160. doi:10.1057/dddmp.2008.29

Chan, Y. Y. Y., & Ngai, E. W. T. (2011). Conceptualising electronic word-of-mouth activity: An input-process-output perspective. *Marketing Intelligence & Planning*, *29*(5), 488–516. doi:10.1108/02634501111153692

Christodoulides, G. (2009). Branding in the post-internet era. *Marketing Theory*, *9*(1), 141–144. doi:10.1177/1470593108100071

Churchill, N. C., & Lewis, V. L. (1983, May-June). The five stages of small business growth. *Harvard Business Review*, 30–50.

Colliander, J., & Wien, A. H. (2013). Trash talk rebuffed: consumers' defense of companies criticized in online communities. *European Journal of Marketing*, *47*(10), 1733–1757. doi:10.1108/EJM-04-2011-0191

Coulter, K. S., & Roggeveen, A. (2012). Like it or not: Consumer responses to word-of-mouth communications in online social networks. *Management Research Review*, *35*(9), 878–899. doi:10.1108/01409171211256587

Creswell, J. W., & Miller, D. L. (2000). Determining validity in qualitative inquiry. *Theory into Practice*, *39*(3), 124–130. doi:10.1207/s15430421tip3903_2

Curran, J., & Blackburn, R. A. (2001). *Researching the Small Enterprise*. London: Sage Publications.

Curran, K., O'Hara, K., & O'Brien, S. (2011). The role of Twitter in the world of business. *International Journal of Business Data Communications and Networking*, *7*(3), 1–15. doi:10.4018/jbdcn.2011070101

De Burgh, H., Carson, D., & Gilmore, A. (2000). SME marketing management competencies. *International Business Review*, *9*(3), 363–382. doi:10.1016/S0969-5931(00)00006-8

Deloitte. (2012). *Fan power: Football money league*. Sports Business Group.

DTI. (2007). *What does the DTI recognise as a small and medium-sized enterprise (SME)?* Department of Trade and Industry. Retrieved from http://www.dti.gov.uk

Easterby-Smith, M., Thorpe, R., & Lowe, A. (2002). *Management research - An introduction*. London: Sage Publications.

Eisenhardt, K. M. (1989). Building theories from case study research. *Academy of Management Review*, *14*, 532–550.

Eisenhardt, K. M., & Graebner, M. A. (2007). Theory building from cases: Opportunities and challenges. *Academy of Management Journal*, *50*(1), 25–32. doi:10.5465/AMJ.2007.24160888

Erdoğmuşa, İ. E., & Çiçek, M. (2012). The impact of social media marketing on brand loyalty. *Procedia: Social and Behavioral Sciences*, *58*, 1353–1360. doi:10.1016/j.sbspro.2012.09.1119

Evening Herald. (2014, February 8). *Twitter usage drops*. Retrieved from http://www.herald.ie/lifestyle/twitter-usage-drops-29989318.html

Facebook. (2013). *Over 1 billion people now on Facebook*. Retrieved from https://www.facebook.com

Fashion United. (2013). Retrieved from http://www.fashionunited.co.uk/facts-and-figures-in-the-uk-fashion-industry

Fillis, I., Johansson, U., & Wagner, B. (2003). A conceptualisation of the opportunities and barriers to e-business development in the smaller firm. *Journal of Small Business and Enterprise Development*, *10*(3), 336–344. doi:10.1108/14626000310489808

Fisher, D., & Smith, S. (2011). Co-creation is chaotic: What it means for marketing when no one has control. *Marketing Theory*, *11*(3), 325–250. doi:10.1177/1470593111408179

Foscht, T., Swoboda, B., & Morschett, D. (2006). Electronic commerce-based internationalisation of small, niche-oriented retailing companies: The case of Blue Tomato and the snowboard industry. *International Journal of Retail & Distribution Management*, *34*(7), 556–572. doi:10.1108/09590550610673626

Fournier, S., & Avery, J. (2011). The uninvited brand. *Business Horizons*, *54*(3), 193–207. doi:10.1016/j.bushor.2011.01.001

Georgi, D., & Mink, M. (2013). eCCIq: The quality of electronic customer-to customer interaction. *Journal of Retailing and Consumer Services*, *20*(1), 11–19. doi:10.1016/j.jretconser.2012.08.002

Goulding, C., Shankar, A., & Canniford, R. (2013). Learning to be tribal: Facilitating the formation of consumer tribes. *European Journal of Marketing*, *47*(5/6), 813–832. doi:10.1108/03090561311306886

Gummerus, J., Veronica, L., Weman, E., & Pihlstrom, M. (2012). Customer engagement in a Facebook brand community. *Management Research Review*, *35*(9), 857–877. doi:10.1108/01409171211256578

Gummesson, E. (2000). *Qualitative methods in management research*. London: Sage Publications.

Gummesson, E. (2005). Qualitative research in marketing: Road-map for a wilderness of complexity and unpredictability. *European Journal of Marketing*, *39*(3/4), 309–327. doi:10.1108/03090560510581791

Gummesson, E. (2006). Qualitative research in management: Addressing complexity, context and persona. *Management Decision*, *44*(2), 167–179. doi:10.1108/00251740610650175

Hahn, K. H., & Kim, J. (2009). The effect of offline brand trust and perceived internet confidence on online shopping intention in the integrated multichannel context. *International Journal of Retail & Distribution Management*, *37*(2), 126–141. doi:10.1108/09590550910934272

Halliday, S., & Vrusias, B. (2011). The spread and spread of word of web: Towards understanding how marketers can interact with social networks. Paper presented at the Academy of Marketing Conference 2011. Liverpool, UK.

Harrigan, P. (2011). Modelling CRM in the social media age. Paper presented at the Academy of Marketing Conference 2011. Liverpool, UK.

Healy, J. C., & McDonagh, P. (2013). Consumer roles in brand culture and value co-creation in virtual communities. *Journal of Business Research*, *66*(9), 1528–1540. doi:10.1016/j.jbusres.2012.09.014

Hennig-Thurau, T., Gwinner, K. P., Walsh, G., & Gremler, D. D. (2004). Electronic word-of-mouth via consumer-opinion platforms: What motivates consumers to articulate themselves on the internet? *Journal of Interactive Marketing*, *18*(1), 38–52. doi:10.1002/dir.10073

Hopkins, J. L. (2012). Can Facebook be an effective mechanism for generating growth and value in small businesses? *Journal of Systems and Information Technology*, *14*(2), 131–141. doi:10.1108/13287261211232153

Inforrm. (2013). Social media: more Twitter usage statistics. *International Forum for Responsible Media (Inforrm)*. Retrieved from http://inforrm.wordpress.com/2013/11/19/social-media-more-twitter-usage-statistics

Johnson, J. C., & Weller, S. C. (2002). Elicitation techniques for interviewing. In J. F. Gubrium, & J. A. Holstein (Eds.), *Handbook of interview research: Context and method* (pp. 491–514). London: Sage Publications.

Kemp, S. (2014). *Social, digital & mobile worldwide in 2014*. Retrieved from http://wearesocial.net/blog/2014/01/social-digital-mobile-world-wide-2014

Kim, H.-S., & Jin, B. (2006). Exploratory study of virtual communities of apparel retailers. *Journal of Fashion Marketing and Management*, *10*(1), 41–55. doi:10.1108/13612020610651114

Kim, S., & Jones, C. (2009). Online shopping and moderating role of offline brand trust. *Direct Marketing: An International Journal*, *3*(4), 282–300. doi:10.1108/17505930911000874

King, N. (1998). Template analysis. In G. Symon, & C. Cassell (Eds.), *Qualitative methods and analysis in organisational research: A practical guide*. London: Sage Publications.

Kwak, H., Changhyun, L., Park, H., & Moon, S. (2010). What is Twitter, a social network or a news media? Paper presented at the World Wide Web (WWW) Conference. Raleigh, NC. doi:10.1145/1772690.1772751

Larson, K., & Watson, R. T. (2011). The value of social media: Toward measuring social media strategies. Paper presented at the 32nd International Conference on Information Systems (ICIS). Shanghai, China.

Lipsman, A., Mudd, G., Rich, M., & Bruich, S. (2012, March). The power of like: How brands reach (and influence) fans through social media marketing. *Journal of Advertising Research*, *52*(1), 40–52. doi:10.2501/JAR-52-1-040-052

Maclaren, P., & Catterall, M. (2012). Researching the social web: Marketing information from virtual communities. *Marketing Intelligence & Planning*, *20*(6), 319–326. doi:10.1108/02634500210445374

McCarthy, J., Rowley, J., Ashworth, C. J., & Pioch, E. (2014). Managing brand presence through social media: The case of UK football clubs. *Internet Research*, *24*(2), 181–204. doi:10.1108/IntR-08-2012-0154

McCracken, G. (1988). *The long interview*. Newbury Park, CA: Sage Publications. doi:10.4135/9781412986229

McLean, R., & Wainwright, D. (2009). Social networks, football fans, fantasy and reality: How corporate and media interests are invading our life world. *Journal of Information. Culture and Ethics*, *7*(1), 54–71.

Muniz, A. M. Jr, & O'Guinn, T. C. (2001). Brand community. *The Journal of Consumer Research*, *27*(4), 412–431. doi:10.1086/319618

O'Guinn, T. C., & Muñiz, A. M. Jr. (2005). Communcal consumption and the brand. In D. G. Mick, & S. Ratneshwar (Eds.), *Inside consumption: Frontiers of research on consumer motives*. London: Routledge.

Parrott, G., Roomi, M. A., & Holliman, D. (2010). An analysis of marketing programmes adopted by regional small and medium-sized enterprises. *Journal of Small Business and Enterprise Development*, *17*(2), 184–203. doi:10.1108/14626001011041201

Patton, M. Q. (2002). *Qualitative research & evaluation methods* (3rd ed.). London: Sage.

Perry, C. (1998). Processes of a case study methodology for postgraduate research in marketing. *European Journal of Marketing*, *32*(9/10), 785–802. doi:10.1108/03090569810232237

Peters, K., Chen, Y., Kaplan, A. M., Ognibeni, B., & Pauwels, K. (2013). Social media metrics - A framework and guidelines for managing social media. *Journal of Interactive Marketing*, *27*(4), 281–298. doi:10.1016/j.intmar.2013.09.007

Rohm, A., Velitchka, D., Kaltcheva, G., & Milne, R. (2013). A mixed-method approach to examining brand-consumer interactions driven by social media. *Journal of Research in Interactive Marketing*, *7*(4), 295–311. doi:10.1108/JRIM-01-2013-0009

Rowley, J., Kupiec-Teahan, B., & Leeming, E. (2007). Customer community and co-creation: A case study. *Marketing Intelligence & Planning*, *25*(2), 136–146. doi:10.1108/02634500710737924

Saunders, M., Lewis, P., & Thornill, A. (2007). *Research methods for business students* (4th ed.). Harlow, UK: Pearson.

Schau, H. J., Muñiz, A. M. Jr, & Arnould, E. J. (2009). How brand community practices create value. *Journal of Marketing*, *73*(5), 30–51. doi:10.1509/jmkg.73.5.30

Schultz, D. E., & Peltier, J. (2013). Social media's slippery slope: Challenges, opportunities and future research directions. *Journal of Research in Interactive Marketing*, *7*(2), 86–99. doi:10.1108/JRIM-12-2012-0054

Shang, R.-A., Chen, Y.-C., & Liao, H.-J. (2006). The value of participation in virtual consumer communities on brand loyalty. *Internet Research*, *16*(4), 365–379. doi:10.1108/10662240610690025

Sicilia, M., & Palazon, M. (2008). Brand communities on the internet: A case study of Coca-Cola's Spanish virtual community. *Corporate Communications: An International Journal*, *13*(3), 255–270. doi:10.1108/13563280810893643

Simpson, M., Padmore, J., & Newman, N. (2012). Towards a new model of success and performance in SMEs. *International Journal of Entrepreneurial Behaviour & Research*, *18*(3), 264–285. doi:10.1108/13552551211227675

Social Bakers. (2014). *United Kingdom Facebook Statistics Online*. Retrieved from http://www.socialbakers.com/facebook-statistics/united-kingdom

Stavros, C., & Westberg, K. (2009). Using triangulation and multiple case studies to advance relationship marketing theory. *Qualitative Market Research: An International Journal*, *12*(3), 307–320. doi:10.1108/13522750910963827

Supporters Direct and Substance. (2010). *The Social and Community Value of Football*. Author.

Sweeney, J. (2010). *Man United – into the red*. Retrieved from http://www.bbc.co.uk/iplayer/episode/b00snmrj/Panorama_Man_United_Into_the_Red/

Tapp, A., & Clowes, J. (2002). From carefree casuals to professional wanderers: Segmentation possibilities for football supporters. *European Journal of Marketing*, *36*(11/12), 1248–1269. doi:10.1108/03090560210445164

Thorbjørnsen, H., Supphellen, M., Nysveen, H., & Pedersen, P. E. (2002). Building brand relationships online: A comparison of two interactive applications. *Journal of Interactive Marketing*, *16*(3), 17–34. doi:10.1002/dir.10034

Tikkanen, H., Hietanen, J., Henttonen, T., & Rokka, J. (2009). Exploring virtual worlds: Success factors in virtual world marketing. *Management Decision*, *47*(8), 1357–1381. doi:10.1108/00251740910984596

Underwood, R., Bond, E., & Baer, R. (2001). Building service brands via social identity: Lessons from the sports marketplace. *Journal of Marketing Theory and Practice*, *9*(1), 1–13.

Urquhart, C., & Vaast, E. (2012). Building social media theory from case studies: A new frontier for IS research. Paper presented at the 31st International Conference on Information Systems. Orlando, FL.

Watters, E. (2004). *Urban tribes: A generation redefines friendship, family, and commitment*. London: Bloomsbury Publishing.

Yin, R. K. (2009). *Case study research: Design and methods* (4th ed.). London: Sage.

ADDITIONAL READING

Ashworth, C. J., Schmidt, R. A., Pioch, E. A., & Hallsworth, A. (2006). Web-weaving: An approach to sustainable e-retail and online advantage in lingerie fashion marketing. *International Journal of Retail and Distribution Management*, *34*(6), 497–511. doi:10.1108/09590550610667074

Ashworth, C. J., Schmidt, R. A., Pioch, E. A., & Hallsworth, A. (2006). An approach to sustainable 'fashion' e-retail: A five-stage evolutionary strategy for 'clicks-and-mortar' and 'pure-play' enterprises. *Journal of Retailing and Consumer Services*, *13*(4), 289–299. doi:10.1016/j.jretconser.2005.08.018

Barnes, D., Hinton, M., & Mieczkowska, S. (2004). Avoiding the fate of the dotbombs: Lessons from three surviving dotcom start-ups. *Journal of Small Business and Enterprise Development*, *11*(3), 329–337. doi:10.1108/14626000410551582

Brown, R. (2009). *Public relations and the social web: How to use social media and web 2.0 in communications*. London: Kogan Page.

Champoux, V., Durgee, J., & McGlynn, L. (2012). Corporate Facebook pages: When "fans" attack. *The Journal of Business Strategy*, *33*(2), 22–30. doi:10.1108/02756661211206717

Christodoulides, G., Chernatony, L. D., Furrer, O., Shiu, E., & Abimbola, T. (2006). Conceptualising and measuring the equity of online brands. *Journal of Marketing Management*, *22*(7-8), 799–825. doi:10.1362/026725706778612149

Colliander, J., & Wien, A. H. (2013). Trash talk rebuffed: Consumers' defense of companies criticized in online communities. *European Journal of Marketing*, *47*(10), 1733–1757. doi:10.1108/EJM-04-2011-0191

Cova, B., Kozinets, R. V., & Shankar, A. (2007). *Consumer Tribes*. Oxford: Elsevier.

Curran, J., & Blackburn, R. A. (2001). *Researching the small enterprise*. London: Sage.

De Souza, C. S., & Preece, J. (2004). A framework for analyzing and understanding online communities. *Interacting with Computers, the Interdisciplinary Journal of Human-Computer Interaction*, 16(3), 579-610.

Dholakia, R. R., & Zhao, M. (2009). Retail web site interactivity: How does it influence customer satisfaction and behavioral intentions? *International Journal of Retail & Distribution Management*, *37*(10), 821–838. doi:10.1108/09590550910988011

Doherty, N. F., & Ellis-Chadwick, F. (2009). Exploring the drivers, scope and perceived success of e-commerce strategies in the UK retail sector. *European Journal of Marketing*, *43*(9/10), 1246–1262. doi:10.1108/03090560910976474

Fill, C. (2009). *Marketing communications: Interactivity, communities and content* (5th ed.). Harlow: Pearson.

Hansson, L., Wrangmo, A., & Solberg, K. S. (2013). Optimal ways for companies to use Facebook as a marketing channel. *Journal of Information. Communication and Ethics in Society*, *11*(2), 112–126. doi:10.1108/JICES-12-2012-0024

Heller Baird, C., & Parasnis, G. (2011). From social media to social CRM: Reinventing the customer relationship. *Strategy and Leadership*, *39*(6), 27–34. doi:10.1108/10878571111176600

Jahn, B., & Kunz, W. (2012). How to transform consumers into fans of your brand. *Journal of Service Management*, *23*(3), 344–361. doi:10.1108/09564231211248444

Kilian, T., Hennigs, N., & Langner, S. (2012). Do Millennials read books or blogs? Introducing a media usage typology of the internet generation. *Journal of Consumer Marketing*, *29*(2), 114–124. doi:10.1108/07363761211206366

Kozinets, R. V. (1999). E-tribalised marketing? The strategic implications of virtual communities on consumption. *European Management Journal, 17*(3), 252–264. doi:10.1016/S0263-2373(99)00004-3

O'Toole, T. (2003). E-relationships - emergence and the small firm. *Marketing Intelligence & Planning, 21*(2), 115–122. doi:10.1108/02634500310465434

Phillips, D., & Young, P. (2010). *Online public relations*. London: Kogan Page.

Poynter, R. (2010). *The handbook of online and social media research*. Chichester: John Wiley and Sons Ltd.

Ruane, L., & Wallace, E. (2013). Generation Y females online: Insights from brand narratives. *Qualitative Market Research: An International Journal, 16*(3), 315–335. doi:10.1108/13522751311326125

Safko, L. (2010). *The social media bible: Tactics, tools and strategies for business success*. Hoboken, NJ: Wiley.

Sashi, C. M. (2012). Customer engagement, buyer-seller relationships, and social media. *Management Decision, 50*(2), 253–272. doi:10.1108/00251741211203551

Shao, G. (2009). Understanding the appeal of user-generated media: A uses and gratification perspective. *Internet Research, 19*(1), 7–25. doi:10.1108/10662240910927795

Tikkanen, H., Hietanen, J., Henttonen, T., & Rokka, J. (2009). Exploring virtual worlds: Success factors in virtual world marketing. *Management Decision, 47*(8), 1357–1381. doi:10.1108/00251740910984596

Toral, S. L., Martinez-Torres, R. M., Barrero, F., & Cortes, F. (2009). An empirical study of the driving forces behind online communities. *Internet Research, 19*(4), 378–392. doi:10.1108/10662240910981353

Williams, D. E. (2009). The evolution of e-tailing. *International Review of Retail, Distribution and Consumer Research, 19*(3), 219–249. doi:10.1080/09593960903233657

Wipperfürth, A. (2005). *Brand hijack: Marketing without marketing*. New York: Portfolio.

KEY TERMS AND DEFINITIONS

Brand Community: A collection of customers that identify with a specific brand, and possibly with each other, thereby increasing the perceived value of the brand.

Consumer Tribe: A group of consumers who identify closely with one another, have shared experiences and emotions, plus engage in collective social actions on/offline which can be facilitated through a variety of brands, products/services or activities.

Customer Acquisition: The processes associated with attracting customers to a brand or organisation for the first time.

Customer Retention: The processes associated with encouraging customers to repeatedly engage with an organisation and become behaviourally and attitudinally loyal.

Electronic Word-of-Mouth (eWOM): Communications, typically between consumers, regarding incidents, events, organisations, experiences and brands, using the Internet and social media.

Pure-Play Retailing: Retailing online, whereby the retailer only has a cyberstore presence (virtual presence) and no high street store (i.e. no physical presence). However, the pure-player may have a multiple cyberstore presence online, thus operating an e-portfolio.

SMEs: Small and medium sized enterprises.

Social Media Marketing: Marketing that uses social media for one or two way communicationor two way communications with customers. Increasingly this is interpreted to also mean three way communications on a B2C, C2B and C2C basis.

Social Media: The applications that enable social communication activities via the Internet, such as blogging, micro-blogging, social networking, photo-sharing and video-sharing.

Virtual Community: An online community in which community members communicate with each other remotely over the Internet.

Chapter 7
Greek Politicians and the Use of Online Technologies for Citizen Engagement

Savvas Papagiannidis
Newcastle University, UK

Teta Stamati
National and Kapodistrian University of Athens, Greece

Hartmut Behr
Newcastle University, UK

ABSTRACT

This chapter examines how politicians utilise Internet technologies to create an online presence, the motivating and hindering factors for doing so, and the perceived significance such a presence can have. The authors present empirical data collected via in-depth interviews with Greek politicians taking part in the general elections of 2012. The findings suggest that although politicians are increasingly interested in engaging with citizens using online technologies, their efforts are not always focused on achieving measurable and tangible results. Consequently, they do not make full use of the potential online technologies offer. Instead, the authors conclude, online strategies need to be organised around predefined objectives and based on clear communication and engagement plans.

1. INTRODUCTION

Although political parties and their affiliated politicians may have often reacted slowly in grasping and adopting technological developments, they are gradually recognising the importance that online technologies have and the opportunities and challenges they may give rise to. An example of this can be seen in Barack Obama's presidential campaign and the way social media were utilised (Luck, Beaton, & Moffatt, 2010; Sevin, Kimball, & Khalil). Having a web site and organising a page on Facebook, which were considered an innovation just a few years ago, are now becoming an essential ingredient of any campaign, as they enable not only the promotion of the candidate,

DOI: 10.4018/978-1-4666-6182-0.ch007

but also more active engagement with voters. Undertaken effectively, online campaigning can yield great returns. Undertaken poorly, it can backfire, creating irreversible damage to a candidate's profile. It is not unusual to come across web sites, blogs, Facebook pages and other online spaces created just for the sake of campaigning, signalling to visitors the lack of real interest in and understanding of such technologies by the candidates. Such late efforts would have a limited impact anyway. This work's main objective is to study how politicians use their Internet presence (e.g. their web sites and social media) to engage with citizens during different circumstances. More specifically, the questions it sets out to answer are firstly what is the perceived significance of establishing an online presence for politicians and what are the motivating and hindering factors for doing so, secondly what is the role of social media within the context of a politician's online presence and thirdly how do politicians form their online presence strategies and how do they plan and implement their engagement plans.

2. LITERATURE REVIEW

2.1 Using the Internet to Engage Citizens

Political marketing has grown as a discipline over the past two decades, attracting the interest of marketers, political scientists and communication experts (Yannas, 2005) (for an account of its emergence and development see Scammell, 1999; Shama, 1976). Wring (1997, p.653) suggests that political marketing is concerned with a "party's or candidate's use of opinion research and environmental analysis to produce and promote a competitive offering which will help realise organisational aims and satisfy groups of electors in exchange for their votes." In other words, it aims to identify what the voters want so a value proposition resulting in a favoured voted can be put forward. Maarek's (1995) agrees with the above statement, but goes a step forward, explicitly referring to the use of offline and online approaches. He defines it as "the use of online and offline advertising, marketing and promotion techniques to influence individual voters to cast their vote in favour of a specific political party or candidate" (Maarek, 1995, p.15). For O'Cass (1996) political marketing promotes and enables parties, candidates and voters to participate in a constructive dialogue for both specific and broader societal development and utilisation of social and economic goals. Finally, Hughes and Dann (2009, p.244) adapting the 2007 commercial marketing definition of the American Marketing Association defined political marketing as "a set of activities, processes or political institutions used by political organisations, candidates and individuals to create, communicate, deliver and exchange promises of value with voter consumers, political party stakeholders and society at large." Arguably, the above mentioned definitions consider political marketing as having an important role to play, not just in terms of communicating political views, but also facilitating the democratic process. Still, from an online perspective, prior to social media, the role of political marketing was mostly confined to influencing voting intentions and not sensing the political environment via direct interactions with users. For instance, in the Greek context, Papagiannidis et al (2012) found that users tended to visit the websites of favoured candidates, reinforcing their positive perceptions of them, while as far as the websites themselves and their content and the services provided were concerned there was room for improvement.

Although political marketing is considered as having much potential to fulfil, it has also seen its share of criticism. Dean and Croft (2001) maintained that many of the more detailed criticisms made of marketing in politics echo a broader questioning of the role of marketing in society as a whole, calling for an examination of the relevance of any current broad marketing formulae and their applicability to politics. Even if one were to accept political marketing as a potential valid and needed multi-disciplinary research area, the way this has developed over the past few years has also attracted criticism. Considering political marketing as a methodology transfer is to leave aside its role as an intervention and as a change agent in politics (Moloney, 2004). Much criticism revolves about the commercialisation of the political and voting process (Henneberg, 2004). Despite this often holding true in practice, it is a rather narrow outlook. In fact, following the seminal work of Vargo and Lusch (2004) challenging the dominant logic in marketing, Butler and Harris (2009) argue that "marketing emphasises intangible resources, the co-creation of value and relationships. It is a view that regards the model of exchange that was inherited from economics as outmoded, and proposes building marketing on the foundations of human knowledge and skill, information and connectivity, and relationships." The above naturally lend themselves to political marketing theorists and practitioners, especially those operating in the online environment. One could actually use the exact same words to describe any social networking application. Also, O'Shaughnessy (2001) suggests that the impact of political marketing is not directly analogous to its effectiveness in business, because of differences between a business context and a political one.

When it comes to online political marketing and the work undertaken with regards to how candidates and parties formulate strategies and organise their online presence, previous studies typically took place in the context of a particular country, undertaking comparisons of such presences. For example, there exist cases for Australia (Van Onselen & Van Onselen, 2008), Germany (Gibson, Rommele, & Ward, 2003), Greece (Coursaris & Papagiannidis, 2009; Lappas, Chatzopoulos, & Yannas, 2008), India (Gadekar, Thakur, & Ang, 2011), Italy (Newell, 2001), Malaysia (Hassan & Li, 2005), Netherlands (Utz, 2009), New Zealand (Conway & Dorner, 2004), Spain (Sampedro & Perez, 2008), United Kingdom (Bowers-Brown & Gunter, 2002; Jackson, 2006), United States (Warnick, Xenos, Endres, & Gastil, 2005). The focus tended to be on evaluating and comparing web sites using frameworks such as that of Fogg *et al* (2001) or Gibson and Ward (2000). Although these may provide useful insights as to how web sites are utilised by political parties and politicians, they can answer questions about "what" users can potentially do in these electronic spaces, rather than "why", while they may not fully capture activities that take place on social networking sites, especially when such activities are fragmented across many different networks. Equally importantly, the Internet does not create an entirely new political order, although to understand its role requires that we understand much else about the social processes that surround it (Agre, 2002).

2.2 Developing a Social Media Conceptual Framework

"Social media employ mobile and web-based technologies to create highly interactive platforms via which individuals and communities share, co-create, discuss, and modify user-generated content." (Kietzmann, Hermkens, McCarthy, & Silvestre, 2011) Despite social media being a recent phenomenon, studies on the use of social media by political parties, politicians and citizens have already started emerging (e.g. see Farrell & Drezner, 2008; H. Gil De Zúñiga, Puig-I-Abril, & Rojas, 2009; Homero Gil de Zúñiga, Veenstra, Vraga, & Shah, 2010; Grant, Moon, & Grant, 2010; Kalnes, 2009). Kietzmann *et al* (2011) proposed a framework (Figure 1) that defines social media by using seven functional building blocks. The proposed blocks make it possible to deconstruct the social media user experience. User experience more generally refers to technology that fulfils more than just instrumental needs in a way that acknowledges its use as a subjective, situated, complex and

Figure 1. Social media framework. Adopted from (Kietzmann et al., 2011)

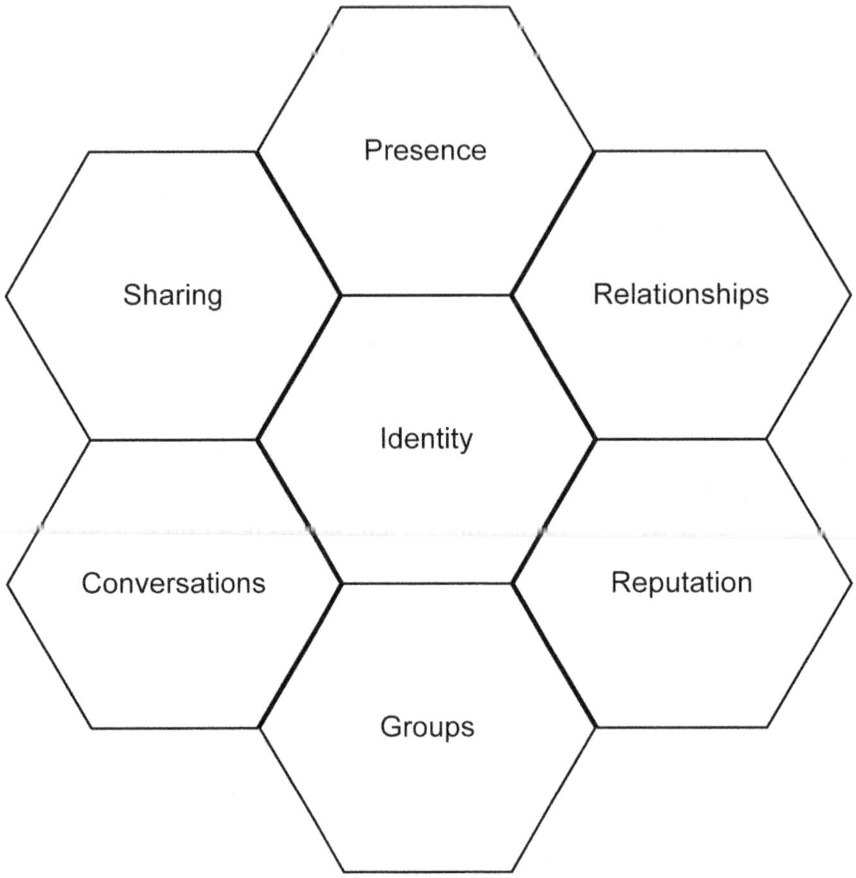

dynamic encounter and it is a consequence of a user's internal state, the characteristics of the designed system and the context or the environment within which the interaction occurs (Hassenzahl & Tractinsky, 2006). The blocks are neither mutually exclusive, nor do they all have to be present in a social media activity, i.e. each social activity will consist of a subset of the blocks depending on the approach adopted.

More specifically, the *identity* block represents the extent to which users reveal their identities in a social media setting. For a politician it would not just make sense to reveal their true identity in order to capitalise on any potential gains, but it would actually be expected. Exposed camouflaged accounts could potentially have devastating event effects for those involved. For politicians identity would be more about constructing a representative of the politician identity that users could relate to. The second block, *conversations*, represents the extent to which politicians communicate with other users in a social media setting. This could be in the form of personally looking after their accounts or having a team manage them on their behalf. The latter may offer a more consistent and professional approach, but it limits the personal contact voters have with politicians. This in turn may affect the *presence* block, which represents the extent to which users can know if other users, and in particular the politicians, are accessible, either offline or online. For the offline aspect this could take the form of posting one's physical presence or to state the politician's online availability using statuses such as 'Online', 'Offline' or 'Away' etc. The fourth block, *sharing*, represents the extent to which users exchange, distribute, and receive content. Biographical and multimedia content such as photos and audio-visual clips are consistently featured across virtually all politicians' personal web sites. Social media offer the possibility of maximising the impact such content can have by linking to it or embedding on third party sites. For example, a politician may post transcripts of speeches on Scribd, photos on Flickr and videos on YouTube that can be then embedded by his voters on their own sites and profiles, in turn influencing their own followers and friends and creating a viral effect. The *relationships* block represents the extent to which users can be related to other users. It may refer to formally stated relationships, e.g. adding someone to one's friends list on Facebook, or to informally ad hoc relationships, e.g. simply reading regularly one's blog posts. The *groups* block represents the extent to which users can form communities and sub-communities of interest. Friends and followers of a politician form an implicit group in their own right. Kietzmann *et al* (2011) refer to Dunbar (1992), who theorised that people have a cognitive limit which restricts the number of stable social relationships they can have with other people to about 150. A relationship between a politician and a follower does not need to have the intensity, frequency and depth that personal relationships have. The relationship and groups blocks could be coupled together to form a *network* block. Finally, the r*eputation* block is the extent to which users can identify the standing of others, including themselves, in a social media setting. Various metrics (e.g. 'Likes', comments by users on posts, views of videos) could be potentially used to measure how engaged a politician is with friends and followers on a social media platform.

2.3 Adapting the Social Media Framework to Online Political Presence

Applying the social media honeycomb to politicians' online activities in the same way in which was applied by Kietzmann *et al* (2011) would be limiting the ability to holistically consider the activities undertaken. Instead, it is proposed that an adapted framework (as shown in Figure 2) which incorporates a few notable differences is used. First of all, the identity block has been extended to explicitly include an image and personal brand building aspect. Secondly, the groups and relationship blocks have been merged into a new *network* block. This is because although there may be one main group revolving around the politician, namely those typically interested in and voting for him/her, users could also form relationships among themselves. Thirdly, the reputation block has been extended to include an influence aspect to highlight that it is not just important to have a good reputation, but that it has to be an influential one. Having influence encourages and facilitates engagement and sharing. Ultimately, influence can lead to earning votes. The more followers engage and share, the more influential the politician becomes on the network. For engagement we adopt the definition by Hutchins et al (1985), which considers engagement as taking place when a user experiences direct interaction with the objects in a domain, leading to a feeling of involvement directly with a world of objects. In addition to the above, a new block, *content*, has been added. Without it there can be few longitudinal opportunities for sharing, influencing and engaging one's network. Finally, the new layout aims to separate the actors from the processes and also to illustrate the fact that these processes are bi-directional, i.e. not only can the politician affect the network, but also the network can affect the politician, which is in alignment with o'Cass' (1996) view that political marketing promotes and enables parties, candidates and voters to participate

Figure 2. Online political presence framework. Adapted from (Kietzmann et al., 2011)

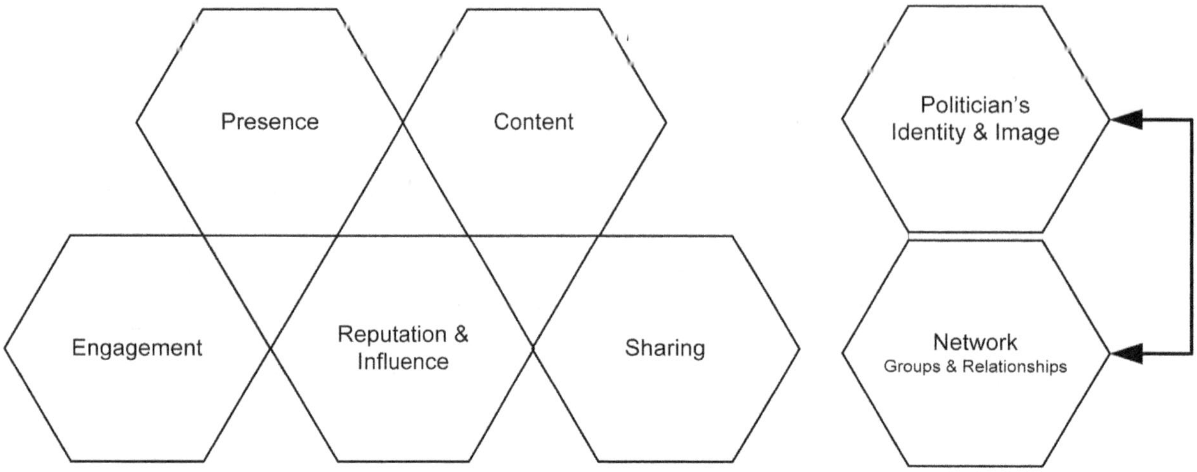

in a constructive dialogue for both specific and broader societal development and the utilisation of social and economic goals. It is also in alignment with the definition of social media put forward earlier, which refers to the co-creation of value by the users themselves. Online users are considered external actors, the party and the politician's team are internal actors that can affect the politician's online presence.

3. METHODOLOGY

3.1 Research Context

This work took place in Greece in the first half of 2012. Greece was selected for a number of reasons. In 2010, Greece found herself in the epicentre of a global sovereign debt crisis, which sparked a great deal of interest in politics and much anger towards politicians. The unrest reached its high point in May 2011 when citizens organised gatherings in many major cities using Facebook and other social media. In Athens, there was so much tension outside the Greek Parliament that Members of Parliament (MPs) and the cabinet could not reach it without a police escort and assistance. After the summer of 2011, given the economic and political circumstances and the fact that the government at that point had already seen half of its time in office gone, elections were thought to be just a matter of time, with parties and candidates reported to be preparing for them. A transition government supported by three parties was formed in November 2011, which led the country to elections 6 months later, after having completed a series of pre-agreed tasks, such as completing the restructuring of the Greek debt. Two national general elections took place, one on the 6th of May 2012 and then, after failing to form a coalition government, on the 17th of June 2012. Consequently, timing-wise, this was an excellent opportunity to study how politicians perceived the benefits and challenges of engaging with citizens, both in terms of communicating with citizens during harsh conditions and in terms of how they prepare their election campaigns. In addition, findings from previous studies could be drawn upon, as interestingly, given its size, Greece has actually offered the stage for many studies in the area of political marketing. Finally, from a pragmatic and methodological point of view, accessing politicians and collecting data, a major obstacle for such studies, was possible for the selected country.

3.2 Data Collection and Analysis

Data was collected via cross-sectional semi-structured interviews with politicians. Interview questions revolved around the key constructs in the conceptual framework. The interview guide was tested and piloted before data collection commenced (Adams, Khan, Raeside, & White, 2007). Revisions were made in order to ensure the reliability and validity of the data collected. The interview guide enabled the collection of data that could be compared across the interviews conducted (Guthrie, 2010). The questions asked were grouped into two main groups, namely questions about the politician's online presence, and secondly questions about the actors involved in the establishment and maintenance of these online properties. The above questions were complemented by demographic questions, in particular about the participant's political career and ICT skills/usage. Interviews took place between mid April 2012 and mid June 2012, i.e. a period of about 2 months. Each interview lasted approximately 1 ½ hours, typically taking place in the participant's office. Interviews were conducted in Greek so that participants' ability to communicate effectively was not impaired by having to speak in a language with which they were less familiar (Bryman & Bell, 2011). Transcripts and notes were also recorded in Greek. These were then coded appropriately and analysed thematically, with key themes emerging compared across the data collected in relation to the set research questions. The findings were then translated into English.

3.3 Sampling

A purposive sampling approach was adopted. Despite the difficulties in obtaining access to politicians, especially during a very busy time for them, much effort was invested in organising a representative sample, both in terms of political affiliations and personal demographics. In total 16 interviews were conducted with 12 male and 4 female politicians with an average age of 52 years. All participants were highly educated, having completed higher education studies, with 3 of them also holding Masters degrees and 4 of them having completed Doctorate degrees. In terms of the ICT skills they reported (on a 5 point scale with higher numbers indicating more advanced skills) an average score of 2.9 for both ICT applications and Internet applications. They also reported a lower average score of 2.3 for social media skills. In terms of their experience they reported having used ICT applications for about 11 years on average, Internet applications for 10 years and social media for about 3 years. The relative shorter exposure they have had to social media may explain why they reported lower scores for their social media skills. When it came to which social networks participants mostly used, Facebook, Twitter and YouTube typically featured prominently in the lists provided, with Google+ and LinkedIn also mentioned. 12 of the participants had a web site, 11 a Facebook presence, 6 a Twitter account and 5 of them a YouTube channel. Finally, when it came to the participants' political affiliations, 5 out of the 7 parties that exceeded the 3% minimum threshold to enter the Greek Parliament and elected MPs were represented in our sample. 5 candidates had not been elected before. The rest had an average of about 6.3 years of service as MPs. Six of the participants had previously served as Ministers or held other key government positions.

4. RESULTS

4.1 Online Political Presence

The first set of questions examined the construction of the participants' online political identity, its perceived significance, the motivating and hindering factors and the perceived impact and influence this had. Numbers in parentheses indicate views of specific participants.

- **Significance of Online Presence:** Virtually all participants agreed that online communications are of importance or great importance, with a few expressing the view that this is likely to intensify in the future. This may not just apply to the younger users, as one of the participants suggested, but also to older people too (3). Public figures are expected to have an online presence as this constitutes an important communication medium (15). The participants' online presence was constructed around this view, revolving primarily around two axes. On the one side, there was a utilitarian facet aiming to provide information about the background and activities of the politician, not just for those who voted in favour, but also for the undecided ones. On the other side, interactivity was considered to be an important, aspect aiming to involve users as much as possible and establishing a dialogue with them.
- **Motivating and Hindering Factors:** The majority of the participants reported that direct communication with citizens and the ability to interact with them directly were the main motivating factors for having an online presence. The second most important motivating factor was the ability to instantly make information available. Having an online presence was also considered important when it came to self-promotion and branding, especially in relation to electoral campaigning. Other factors mentioned included widening political participation, the low cost of communication, responding to opposing views and during times of crisis by offering instant responses when needed. On the other hand, the amount of personal time and effort needed was considered a key hindering factor. Having the necessary know-how and skills (both in terms of personal skills and team skills) was perceived as an equally important factor. This also included the ability to package content in the right format so that this is appropriate for online media, as otherwise it would not be effective. In addition participants also expressed a concern about posting online more generally, as everything that is made available is difficult to be retracted in the future. Moreover, the financial cost was reported as a significant hindering factor. Finally, one of the participants mentioned that ideology as an opposing factor for adopting an online political presence in the context of online political marketing.
- **Online Strategy and Decision Making:** Participants referred to their reliance on communication experts and external agencies consulted with regards to their online presence and associated strategies. They stated the importance of being personally involved and explicitly mentioned that they would often be the final decision makers. Best practice as manifested in big campaigns, such as that of President Obama, was also mentioned as an influential factor. Two of the participants reported that they did not have a specific strategy, but relied on personal, spontaneous and direct communication with citizens, while one of the participants suggested that regular exposure to mass media meant that having an online presence was not necessary so far. As far the target audience is concerned, demographic characteristics such as age were not mentioned as frequently as may have been expected, following stereotypes of online users being of a young age. The majority reported that their prime target audience are those in their constituencies, with everyone also being important albeit in secondary place. Attending to voters and convincing the undecided was also considered of importance.

- **Impact and Influence:** The politician's responses in relation to the influence of their online presence were correlated to the views they held about their online presence itself. The underlying view was that as long as a presence was established and relevant information became available, much of the objective set was met. This was also based on comments, typically positive, received by users. However, there was little evidence of a structured approach to measuring engagement and influence, by liaising with the users themselves. Views on measuring the engagement and the impact of one's online political presence fell into three main categories. In the first there were those who used quantitative (such as number of friends/followers, likes etc.) and qualitative performance indicators (such as comments) to gauge the impact their presence has online. In the second category there were 2 participants who were not interested in measuring the impact or did not do it, while in the final category there were those who believe that their effectiveness is projected in being elected or not. In terms of how frequent monitoring is, the majority of those who had an online presence mentioned that during election times they review metrics more often, even on a daily basis. However, during normal periods monitoring is less frequent, e.g. monthly or even quarterly.

4.2 Online Communication Channels

11/16 participants had had a web site on average for about 5 years. The majority stated that they were the ones who had the initial idea, although colleagues and friends and family also played an important and encouraging role. The motivations for establishing a web site were in alignment with those of having an online presence more generally, with the web site acting as an information repository. Interestingly, a third of those that had a web site stated that they established it because they did not have a choice not to do so or because of how marketing and communications had developed over time. Hindering factors for establishing and maintaining a web site included finding the necessary time to invest, the on-going costs of maintenance and the quality management of the content posted. Web sites were updated regularly, often with the politician being personally involved in the process. Although this varied from case to case typically the majority got involved at least once a week. Personal involvement increased during pre-election periods, indicating that participants considered the web site a valuable promotional tool. In addition to having a web site, about 2/3 of the participants reported that they also send out newsletters typically a few times a month, but this became more frequent during the pre-election periods. This was partly attributed to the low impact newsletters have and the limited scope for interaction. Politicians mostly monitored the process. Email as a communication method was also used by virtually all participants. Emails were typically answered by those in the team of each politician, unless it was something that they needed to be personally involved in. The volume of email communications typically increased during pre-election period.

4.3 Social Media

This set of questions examined how active participants were online, in the context of their online political presence. Only 4 of the 16 participants had not adopted social media practices. Among the rest, 9 had initiated this. The main motivation was the ability to directly interact with online users and communicate with them. Competitiveness among candidates, the importance of social media as a campaigning tool and positive results of other colleagues were also mentioned as significant motivating factors. On the other hand, similarly to having a web site and maintaining an online presence more generally, the necessary time and associated costs were reported as hindering factors. What was different compared to web sites was that social media require extra effort to monitor and respond to what was written by other users, but also to ensure that what the politician posted was correct, as trivial mistakes could have a negative impact. In addition, one of the participants mentioned that communication via social media often felt as a distant approach to communicating with friends. Participants used both quantitative and qualitative measures revolving around usage to get a feeling of engagement and influence without, though, reporting specific performance indicators. About half of those engaged thought they were doing well, mostly via increasing interest and positive feedback, while the other half were split between feeling there was scope for improvement or were not interested in measuring the impact of social media as such. Participants were personally active regularly, with the majority stating their involvement daily or at least 3-5 times a week.

4.4 Team Support

The questions about the participant's team aimed to explore the role teams played and identify their contributions. On average, support teams consisted of 3 members of staff, who had to deal with political communication, understand politics, offer specialised support (e.g. legal or financial), be involved in marketing and campaigning, deal with social aspects and support the IT function. Virtually all candidates reported making personal choices, taking into consideration the candidate's CV, their prior experience and in a few cases recommendations by others. Participants reported taking into consideration their teams' recommendations and views, but this often depended on the decision that had to be made. Participants perceived their teams as being very influential in the majority of cases, albeit there were also 5 cases where this would depend a great deal on what was discussed and 2 cases in which the team had no influence at all. For those that reported that their staff was not considered influential, this could be explained by their "team" consisting of a single individual who was undertaking personal assistance tasks. Consequently, the scope of influence was narrow. Despite ICT support only featuring twice in the responses provided about the tasks each team undertakes, participants responded that their teams were influential when it came to planning the online strategy and implementing it. This may be due to an implicit arrangement that online activities are just the means for undertaking other wider ones, such as communicating with citizens. The three most important networks were Facebook, Twitter and YouTube.

4.5 Party Support

The question regarding the support participants received with regards to their political presence sparked a range of interesting responses. In a small number of cases (3) participants answered based on their underlying ideology, either suggesting a wider opposition to political marketing or believing that party involvement would have compromised their independence. Others reported parties having started looking into this more actively, especially after the first general election in May, in order to coordinate individual activities better. More generally, political parties offered some general guidelines and support in the form of materials, activities which not surprisingly intensified during the pre-elections time. Still, participants were ultimately responsible for organising their presence and campaigning. Peer support and attending seminars about political communication were quoted as being useful. In terms of the influence exerted by parties, participants responded that they had to abide by the general guidelines and directions given by the parties but there was still scope to instil one's individual perspective, especially when it came to dealing with local constituencies. When it came to party support for organising politicians' online political presence and the influence parties exerted, this was considered very limited and low respectively. With no substantive support provided, politicians had to organise their own online activities, which ultimately gave them a great deal of scope and flexibility.

4.6 Elections and Online Presence

This set of questions aimed to explore the participants' views when it came to the role of their online presence with regards to their elections campaign. Almost everyone suggested that having an online presence in the context of one's election campaign was important or very important. In many cases the team or trusted individuals made recommendations regarding the strategy to follow online, although the final decision was always for the candidate to make. The campaigns targeted both those voting favourably for the candidates, but also those who were still undecided, as was the case for the participants' online presence before and after the election period. However, given the circumstances the emphasis was more towards converting interest into votes. Two participants from smaller constituencies suggested that social media may be more useful for larger constituencies as candidates in those need to reach far more people, while in their constituencies physical presence and personal contact were necessary. Participants reiterated the motivations and hindering factors that were mentioned about having an online presence without adding any further items to the list. This also applied to their beliefs about the influence of their online presence during the pre-election time, which interestingly was not linked directly to voting. Instead, the focus, as during the normal period, was on communicating and interacting with voters. Given that many of the views that participants expressed regarding their online presence during the elections time and a normal period were in alignment, one would expect there not to be a fundamental difference in terms of how they perceived and approached the activities that need to be undertaken during the pre-election period. Indeed, this was reflected on their comments, suggesting a more intense period, but not a period during when different types of activities were undertaken. Two participants actually felt there was no real difference, with only one believing the opposite.

5. DISCUSSION

5.1 Ideology, Marketing, and Market Orientation

Before proceeding with the discussion of the findings in relation to the four research questions, it is worth highlighting the difference in attitude towards political 'marketing' that participants had, depending on their political ideology. A clear distinction could be seen when positioning participants from right to left, with attitudes progressively becoming negative as one moved towards the left. This could be attributed to the connotations that the term 'marketing' carries. Despite the negative and opposing views towards political marketing, their respective parties have a presence on the Internet. It is also worth noting the difference between *political marketing orientation*, which refers to activities such as image management, voter opinion research, and advertisement creation, carried out principally during the run-up to an election, and *political market orientation*, which is characterised by all party members feeling a responsibility for taking part in the development and implementation of strategies and the policy portfolio (Ormrod, 2005). Past research found ND and PASOK exhibiting elements of market orientation, although the two parties were not fully market-oriented, as they focused almost exclusively on short-term voter desires and failed to fulfil their pre-election promises (Kotzaivazoglou, 2011). On a politician level such elements of market orientation appeared to correspond to the individual's marketing orientation, as expressed by the responses of the participants affiliated to these two parties.

5.2 Perceived Benefits and Challenges of an Internet Presence

There was an overall positive attitude towards having an online presence, especially for larger constituencies such as those in Athens. This is in alignment with previous work about Greek politicians and the use of mobile phone SMS, which found that candidates from the constituencies of Attica and Thessaloniki used this form of communication more than their colleagues in the rest of the country (Mylona, 2008). The ability to directly communicate and interact with users was considered the most important benefit, especially for those who did not have much exposure to mass media, such as national television and radio. Even those who regularly featured on mass media have started recognising the importance of online communications. For instance, one of the participants stated: "My online presence does not really exist. Due to my exposure on mass media there has not been a great need to develop my digital voice. I understand that times are changing and there is a digital society out there that we need to listen to and a society that needs to listen to us. I accept it, but I am not fully certain yet as to how to go about it. Sometimes it is better to abstain from doing something than do it naively." (12) The quote also summarises two more findings, namely that participants felt the pressure to be involved online because there was now an expectation from society to do so and also that, as another participant put it, "there is little point in having an online presence for the sake of having an online presence." (9) Especially when it came to social media, there was an even greater need to do things properly: "The goal is to initiate conversations and quick responses… I do not want to create accounts just for them to exist. I ought to follow them." (2) The question then arising is how realistic it is to expect politicians to do things "properly" and follow best practice when there are not enough resources invested and there is also a lack of technical expertise and know-how. The similarities between the challenges faced by politicians and small and medium enterprises (SMEs) or e-government initiatives are striking (e.g. see Beatty, Shim, & Jones, 2001; Dholakia & Kshetri, 2004; Moon, 2002). Potentially, research findings from IT and web technology adoption studies could inform online political marketing practice.

Responses suggest an inclination towards a utilitarian approach to communicating, in which the politicians aim to distribute information promoting themselves and their affiliated parties. Despite the occasional reference to interactions there was little evidence to suggest that this takes place systematically. This is not surprising if one considers the amount of time and effort such interactions would require. Given that on average teams consisted of only 3 staff and the tasks that need to be undertaken, there is little available time to invest in developing such interactions. Consistently the main two hindering factors of developing an online presence were time and associated costs. To address the above, political parties could facilitate the establishment of a political presence for their politicians, benefiting from economies of scale. For example, they could organise an online communications team centrally, tasked to organise, help implement and coordinate politicians' online activities. This should not be in the form of creating online clones that would counteract any potential benefits, but distinct entities. Central support could both lower costs for everyone involved and also lift the quality of the user's experience. The party could also feed content, making accounts feel more active, freeing time for politicians and their teams to invest in instilling a personal feeling to their presence and interacting more with users. In other words, the party could take over the "utilitarian" side of the communication, focusing on distributing accurate, consistent and timely information, and the politician the "hedonic" side, focusing on interaction. In the context of this study there was evidence of this happening between the elections of May the 6th and June the 17th. In the first case one of the parties started organising seminars for its candidates, while another party appointed a member of staff tasked to overlook the party's social media efforts. Such efforts, though, were probably undertaken too late in the process to have any significant impact.

Social media were found to be an important part of politicians' online presence, with participants appreciating the different role they can play in relation to the other available forms of online communication. The low barriers for entering the social media arena could partly address the challenges faced with establishing an online presence. For instance, creating a Facebook or Twitter account is instant, does not incur any costs and can provide rich functionality. On the other hand, establishing a web site requires a great deal of preparation, incurs development and maintenance fees and may not be as (inter)active as one would like it to be. The last point may not be just because of the features that a web site can provide to users, but also communities around web sites need to be created from scratch. This is not the case with social media, on which communities of interest exist and can be tapped into by politicians. If undertaken effectively, social media investments can amplify a politician's communication efforts. If not, though, they can also amplify negative perceptions, causing much damage. This is not the case with web sites, which are more controlled spaces and have a lower potential reach. Consequently politicians and those involved in engaging online users via social media need to gradually become more vocal and visible, familiarising themselves first with the *modus operandi*. In this way valuable experience and know-how can be gained first, minimising the early risks.

5.3 Online Engagement: Strategy and Operations

Politicians were heavily involved in forming online strategies after consulting their teams and specialists. Again, these mostly revolved around communicating without specific performance indicators put in place in advance. This meant that measuring the effectiveness of the strategy was not possible. Quantitative metrics and qualitative feedback may have been taken into consideration, but without a structured approach these do not suffice. Specific targets would have driven a process of optimisation underpinned by regular reviews. Otherwise, a false feeling of success could create complacency, hindering any further development. To reverse the argument, success breeds success and not operationalising strategies systematically would only lead towards a self-fulfilling prophecy.

Perhaps more importantly, grounding a strategy in communication only does not clearly acknowledge the role of political marketing in both offering the tools for environmental analysis and satisfying electors in exchange for their votes (Wring, 1997). Attracting additional votes was only explicitly mentioned in a couple of instances, e.g.: "all methods for attracting votes and being in touch with the public are only measured by the final outcome: will the Greek people decide to have you represent them in Parliament?" (7) As a strategy this could be conceptualised simply as a two stage process. In the first step the politician engages with online users, creating a relationship. Over time this relationship develops and in the second stage it results in sufficient influence for the user to vote for the politicians. The evidence suggests that most of the effort is invested in the first stage, but not enough in the second. Taking into consideration the Greek context and that participants of this study had on average about 6 years of service in Parliament, one could argue that for participants to be successful in getting elected other forms of political engagement and influence have been historically more important and effective. Still, as participants acknowledged, the growing importance of online technologies suggests that these technologies need to be more woven into the political engagement fabric. This may not be a matter of choice any more. An online presence cannot by itself create a competitive advantage. However, it can act as a catalytic factor in communicating any existing political advantages politicians may have.

The answer to how deployment could take place may be that instead of focusing on "communication" activities politicians can focus on "citizen relationship management" (CRM) activities. Similar to customer relationship management, politicians could aim to develop longitudinal in-depth relationships that revolve around the citizens and not themselves. Two key elements of strategic marketing theory regarding customer orientation, namely leading and following, could be used to define three postures that parties and, potentially, politicians could adapt (Henneberg, 2008). Convinced Ideologists adopt a rigid content-based approach towards policy-making and a leading stance, while the Tactical Populists adopt a catch-all approach and a following stance. The third posture, i.e. the Relationship Builder, a mixture of leading and following, focuses on longer-term relationships, away from a purely transactional approach and could form the basis of such a strategy. The three stances could correspond to the product-, sales- and market- oriented typology that Strömbäck (2007) puts forward. The Convinced Ideologist corresponds to a product-oriented view that perceives the party's ideas and policies to be the best and consequently expects voters to acknowledge this by voting for it. The Tactical Populist would use market intelligence to identify what voters want and aim to satisfy them. The Relationship Builder, though, does not correspond to the sales-orientation in which a party believes in its own ideas, but appreciates that these need be sold to the voters. The party does not adapt to their views, but aims to make voters want what it offers. An alternative way to conceptualise this is as a move from a product strategy towards a customer-oriented one, rather than a sales strategy. Within the online environment, such strategies have been successfully adopted by electronic retailers, who could profile customers aiming to provide a personalised experience, which resonates with the analysis of Towner and Dulio (2012). This experience could be the last stage of this strategic transformation, with citizens involved in the democratic process, by interacting with politicians for a purpose. This is not to say that currently interactions have no purpose or meaning, but that interaction is moved to the centre of the online stage.

Another crucial element for a successful strategy could be more actively involving users in a many-to-many dialogue, co-creating the value and experience they get by participating politically online. Politicians' Facebook pages, for example, could become a natural place for constructive discussion, with the politician facilitating the process, e.g. by suggesting a topical issue for discussion and then providing feedback to the community as to how the views expressed influenced his/her thinking and actions. Users could feel more engaged and valued, with the politician obtaining helpful feedback that could be acted upon accordingly, making him/her more responsive to the issues that are of interest for the electoral body. This is analogous to the proposition that Prahalad and Ramaswamy (2004) make in the commercial setting, suggesting that companies must escape the firm-centric view and aim to co-create value with their customers via an obsessive focus on personalised interactions, which will need managers to move beyond their product-centred thinking and focus on the experiences that customers will seek to co-create. In other words, politicians need to move away from a politician-centred approach and focus more on the interaction and engagement with citizens. However, this only limits the exchange within pre-defined boundaries. Prahalad and Ramaswamy (ibid) take the argument a step further: "We need to challenge the traditional, distinct roles of both the consumer and the company and examine the impact of a convergence of the roles of production and consumption; or the convergence of the roles of the company and the consumer." (p.7) Breaking down the distinction between the "politician" and the "citizen" or "voter" can have fundamental repercussions not just for political participation, but for the democracy itself. Citizens will not just delegate political responsibility via casting their votes for their preferred candidates, but actively and continually be involved in politics. Online technologies, such as social media, can provide the means for taking direct participation and political engagement to a whole new level.

5.4 Revisiting the Conceptual Framework: Online Engagement as a Process

Based on the evidence collected and the analysis undertaken, the initially proposed engagement process could be extended as shown in Figure 3. The network block is split into 4 actors: the politician, the support team, the party and the online users. In this chapter we have not considered the online users, which could be a future research project. Actors interact with the rest of the actors via the online presence (which consists of the blocks as shown in Figure 2), except for the party. The role of the party is mainly to feed information on a regular basis as previously discussed. The politician can engage and influence users, who in turn can feed back to the politician and the team. This feedback is taken into consideration and acted upon by the politician, either by bringing it for discussion at a party or Parliament level. The process is an iterative one, with the politician updating users with any progress on the issues discussed. This process instills a political purpose in having a web site or a social media presence, beyond just building a personal image and aiming to influence undecided voters closer to the elections. When this purpose starts being fulfilled, online users could share the information and updates with their networks, inviting them to join the online dialogue, amplifying the reach and influence of the politicians' online presence.

Figure 3. The revised online political engagement and influence process

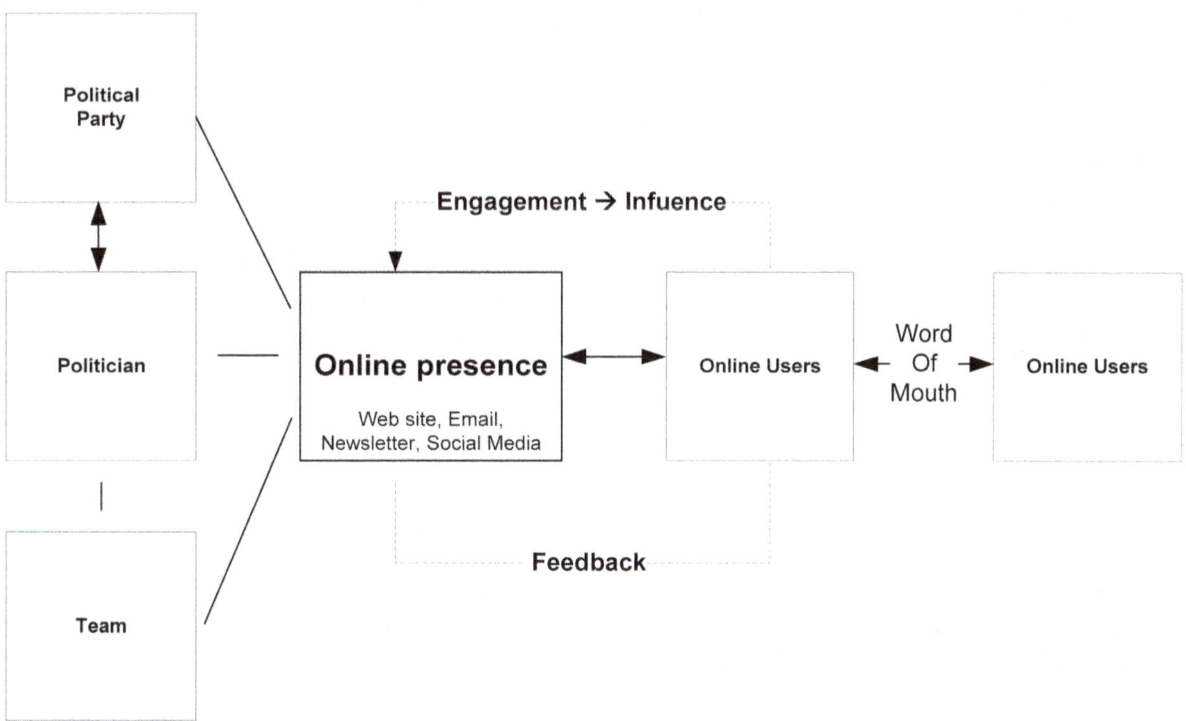

6. CONCLUSION

Applying marketing principles to political communication and engagement is a growing trend that has been fuelled by the relative ease of adopting online technologies and establishing a presence in social media. This work studied how politicians use such technologies and in particular social media to engage with citizens as part of their wider online presence strategy. A number of motivating and hindering factors were identified as playing an important role, typically irrespective of the circumstances in which online activities take place. The main finding of this work is that although politicians consider online technologies an increasingly useful means for communicating with citizens, their online efforts and activities are not always structured towards sustaining engagement and longitudinal relationships that can result in influence and impact. Social media pose new and different types of challenges that require more regular and active personal involvement by the politicians themselves compared to having a personal web site. The promised benefit is the direct communication with the citizens, which can bring interactivity to a whole new level compared to that stakeholders typically enjoyed on politicians' web sites. To fulfil their goal social media strategies need to be integrated at the core of a politician's online presence and not just approached as a separate entity or 'add-on'.

REFERENCES

Adams, J., Khan, H. T. A., Raeside, R., & White, D. (2007). *Research Methods for Graduate Business and Social Science Students*. New Delhi: Response.

Agre, P. E. (2002). Real-Time Politics: The Internet and the Political Process. *The Information Society*, *18*(5), 311–331. doi:10.1080/01972240290075174

Beatty, R. C., Shim, J. P., & Jones, M. C. (2001). Factors influencing corporate web site adoption: A time-based assessment. *Information & Management*, *38*(6), 337–354. doi:10.1016/S0378-7206(00)00064-1

Bowers-Brown, J., & Gunter, B. (2002). Political parties' use of the Web during the 2001 general election. *Aslib Proceedings*, *54*(3), 166–176. doi:10.1108/00012530210441719

Bryman, A., & Bell, E. (2011). *Business research methods*. Oxford, UK: Oxford University Press.

Butler, P., & Harris, P. (2009). Considerations on the evolution of political marketing theory. *Marketing Theory*, *9*(2), 149–164. doi:10.1177/1470593109103022

Conway, M., & Dorner, D. (2004). An evaluation of New Zealand political party websites. *Information Research, 9*(4).

Coursaris, C., & Papagiannidis, S. (2009). Online political marketing in Greece: An evaluation of the 2007 national elections and two case studies. *Computers in Human Behavior*, *25*(4), 853–861. doi:10.1016/j.chb.2008.10.002

Dean, D., & Croft, R. (2001). Friends and relations: Long-term approaches to political campaigning. *European Journal of Marketing*, *35*(11/12), 1197–1216. doi:10.1108/EUM0000000006482

Dholakia, R. R., & Kshetri, N. (2004). Factors Impacting the Adoption of the Internet among SMEs. *Small Business Economics*, *23*(4), 311–322. doi:10.1023/B:SBEJ.0000032036.90353.1f

Dunbar, R. I. M. (1992). Neocortex size as a constraint on group size in primates. *Journal of Human Evolution*, *22*(6), 469–493. doi:10.1016/0047-2484(92)90081-J

Farrell, H., & Drezner, D. W. (2008). The power and politics of blogs. *Public Choice*, *134*(1-2), 15–30. doi:10.1007/s11127-007-9198-1

Fogg, B. J., Marshall, J., Laraki, O., Osipovich, A., Varma, C., Fang, N., et al. (2001). *What makes Web sites credible? A report on a large quantitative study.* Paper presented at the SIGCHI Conference on Human Factors in Computing Systems. Seattle, WA. doi:10.1145/365024.36503710.1145/365024.365037

Gadekar, R., Thakur, K., & Ang, P. H. (2011). Web sites for e-electioneering in Maharashtra and Gujarat, India. *Internet Research, 21*(4), 435–457. doi:10.1108/10662241111158317

Gibson, R., & Ward, S. (2000). A proposed methodology for studying the function and effectiveness of party and candidate websites. *Social Science Computer Review, 18*(3), 301–319. doi:10.1177/089443930001800306

Gibson, R. K., Rommele, A., & Ward, S. (2003). German Parties and Internet Campaigning in the 2002 Federal Election. *German Politics, 12*(1), 79–108. doi:10.1080/09644000412331307534

Gil De Zúñiga, H., Puig-I-Abril, E., & Rojas, H. (2009). Weblogs, traditional sources online and political participation: An assessment of how the internet is changing the political environment. *New Media & Society, 11*(4), 553–574. doi:10.1177/1461444809102960

Gil de Zúñiga, H., Veenstra, A., Vraga, E., & Shah, D. (2010). Digital Democracy: Reimagining Pathways to Political Participation. *Journal of Information Technology & Politics, 7*(1), 36–51. doi:10.1080/19331680903316742

Grant, W. J., Moon, B., & Grant, J. B. (2010). Digital Dialogue? Australian Politicians' use of the Social Network Tool Twitter. *Australian Journal of Political Science, 45*(4), 579–604. doi:10.1080/10361146.2010.517176

Guthrie, G. (2010). *Basic Research Methods.* New Delhi: SAGE Publications.

Hassan, S., & Li, F. (2005). Evaluating the usability and content usefulness of web sites: A benchmarking approach. *Journal of Electronic Commerce in Organizations, 3*(2), 46–67. doi:10.4018/jeco.2005040104

Hassenzahl, M., & Tractinsky, N. (2006). User experience – A research agenda. *Behaviour & Information Technology, 25*(2), 91–97. doi:10.1080/01449290500330331

Henneberg, S. C. (2004). The views of an advocatus dei: Political marketing and its critics. *Journal of Public Affairs, 4*(3), 225–243. doi:10.1002/pa.187

Henneberg, S. C. (2008). Leading or Following? *Journal of Political Marketing, 5*(3), 29–46. doi:10.1300/J199v05n03_02

Hughes, A., & Dann, S. (2009). Political marketing and stakeholder engagement. *Marketing Theory, 9*(2), 243–256. doi:10.1177/1470593109103070

Hutchins, E. L. D., Hollan, J., & Norman, D. A. (1985). Direct Manipulation Interfaces. *Human-Computer Interaction, 1*(4), 311–338. doi:10.1207/s15327051hci0104_2

Jackson, N. (2006). Dipping their big toe into the blogosphere: The use of weblogs by the political parties in the 2005 general election. *ASLIB Proceedings: New Information Perspectives, 58*(4), 292-303.

Kalnes, Ø. (2009). Norwegian Parties and Web 2.0. *Journal of Information Technology & Politics, 6*(3-4), 251–266. doi:10.1080/19331680903041845

Kietzmann, J. H., Hermkens, K., McCarthy, I. P., & Silvestre, B. S. (2011). Social media? Get serious! Understanding the functional building blocks of social media. *Business Horizons, 54*(3), 241–251. doi:10.1016/j.bushor.2011.01.005

Kotzaivazoglou, I. (2011). Political marketing in the Greek context: Does market orientation exist? *International Review on Public and Nonprofit Marketing*, *8*(1), 41–56. doi:10.1007/s12208-011-0070-0

Lappas, G., Chatzopoulos, S., & Yannas, P. (2008). Parliamentary Candidates Running on the Web for the 2004 Greek National Elections. *Journal of Political Marketing*, *7*(3-4), 256–277. doi:10.1080/15377850802008327

Luck, E. M., Beaton, J., & Moffatt, J. J. (2010). *The social media (r)evolution: Obama's political campaign.* Paper presented at the 2010 Global Marketing Conference. Tokyo, Japan.

Maarek, P. (1995). *Political Marketing and Communication.* John Libbey & LTD Publishers.

Moloney, K. (2004). *Is Political Marketing New Words or New Practice in UK Politics?* Paper presented at the PSA Conference. Lincoln, UK.

Moon, M. J. (2002). The Evolution of E-Government among Municipalities: Rhetoric or Reality? *Public Administration Review*, *62*(4), 424–433. doi:10.1111/0033-3352.00196

Mylona, I. (2008). SMS in Everyday Political Marketing in Greece. *Journal of Political Marketing*, *7*(3-4), 278–294. doi:10.1080/15377850802008335

Newell, J. L. (2001). Italian Political Parties on the Web. *The Harvard International Journal of Press/Politics*, *6*(4), 60–87. doi:10.1177/108118001129172341

O'Cass, A. (1996). Political marketing and the marketing concept. *European Journal of Marketing*, *30*(10/11), 37–53. doi:10.1108/03090569610149782

O'Shaughnessy, N. J. (2001). The marketing of political marketing. *European Journal of Marketing*, *35*(9/10), 1047–1057. doi:10.1108/03090560110401956

Ormrod, R. P. (2005). A Conceptual Model of Political Market Orientation. *Journal of Nonprofit & Public Sector Marketing*, *14*(1-2), 47–64. doi:10.1300/J054v14n01_04

Papagiannidis, S., Coursaris, C., & Bourlakis, M. (2012). Do websites influence the nature of voting intentions? The case of two national elections in Greece. *Computers in Human Behavior*, *28*(2), 300–307. doi:10.1016/j.chb.2011.09.013

Prahalad, C. K., & Ramaswamy, V. (2004). Co-creation experiences: The next practice in value creation. *Journal of Interactive Marketing*, *18*(3), 5–14. doi:10.1002/dir.20015

Sampedro, V., & Perez, F. S. (2008). The 2008 Spanish General Elections: Antagonistic Bi-polarization Geared by Presidential Debates, Partisanship,and Media Interests. *The International Journal of Press/Politics*, *13*(3), 336–344. doi:10.1177/1940161208319293

Scammell, M. (1999). Political Marketing: Lessons for Political Science. *Political Studies*, *47*(4), 718–739. doi:10.1111/1467-9248.00228

Sevin, E., Kimball, S., & Khalil, M. (2011). Listening to president Obama: A short examination of obama's communication practices. *The American Behavioral Scientist*, *55*(6), 803–812. doi:10.1177/0002764211406847

Shama, A. (1976). The marketing of political candidates. *Journal of the Academy of Marketing Science*, *4*(4), 764–777. doi:10.1007/BF02729836

Strömbäck, J. (2007). Political Marketing and Professionalized Campaigning. *Journal of Political Marketing*, *6*(2-3), 49–67. doi:10.1300/J199v06n02_04

Towner, T. L., & Dulio, D. A. (2012). New Media and Political Marketing in the United States: 2012 and Beyond. *Journal of Political Marketing*, *11*(1-2), 95–119. doi:10.1080/15377857.2012.642748

Utz, S. (2009). The (potential) benefits of campaigning via social network sites. *Journal of Computer-Mediated Communication*, *14*(2), 221–243. doi:10.1111/j.1083-6101.2009.01438.x

Van Onselen, A., & Van Onselen, P. (2008). On message or out of touch? Secure web sites and political campaigning in Australia. *Australian Journal of Political Science*, *43*(1), 43–58. doi:10.1080/10361140701842565

Vargo, S., & Lusch, R. (2004). Evolving to a New Dominant Logic for Marketing. *Journal of Marketing*, *68*(1), 1–17. doi:10.1509/jmkg.68.1.1.24036

Warnick, B., Xenos, M., Endres, D., & Gastil, J. (2005). Effects of campaign-to-user and text-based interactivity in political candidate campaign web sites. *Journal of Computer-Mediated Communication*, *10*(3).

Wring, D. (1997). Reconciling marketing with political science: Theories of political marketing. *Journal of Marketing Management*, *13*(7), 651–663. doi:10.1080/0267257X.1997.9964502

Yannas, P. (2005). Political Marketing in Greece Is Ready for Take-Off. *Journal of Political Marketing*, *4*(1), 1–15. doi:10.1300/J199v04n01_01

KEY TERMS AND DEFINITIONS

Online Engagement: A two-way interactive communication process using online technologies that aims to benefits those involved.

Online Presence: A collection of online technologies and channels (such as web sites, blogs, emails, social media accounts etc.) that can be used to interactively communicate once existence over the Internet.

Political Marketing: A set of activities, processes or political institutions used by political organisations, candidates and individuals to create, communicate, deliver and exchange promises of value with voter consumers, political party stakeholders and society at large.

Social Media: Mobile and web-based technologies to create highly interactive platforms via which individuals and communities share, co-create, discuss, and modify user-generated content.

Chapter 8
Using Social Media in the Workplace:
How "Lenovo Central" Brings Employees Together

Karen Mishra
Meredith College, USA

Khaner Walker
Lenovo, USA

Aneil Mishra
East Carolina University, USA

ABSTRACT

This chapter examines the internal communication practices of Lenovo, a $34 billion Fortune Global 500 technology company, and the world's second-largest PC vendor. In particular, this study examines how this company uses social media as a method of internal communications in fostering employee engagement. Internal communications is generally led by marketing or PR professionals with expertise in human resources, public relations, marketing, social media, and/or employee engagement. One new way that companies are extending internal communication is by developing the use of their company intranets. Intranets can support an organization by sharing accurate company information on a timely basis. This chapter describes how Lenovo has developed and uses its Lenovo Central intranet to engage employees in its mission and vision.

INTRODUCTION

This chapter examines the internal communication practices of a Lenovo, a $34 billion multinational technology company. This case study examines the development, intent and use of *Lenovo Central,* its company intranet. The case study also analyzes how it uses and publishes internal communication with employees in ways that enhance employee engagement. This chapter will introduce the role of internal communication, how social media

DOI: 10.4018/978-1-4666-6182-0.ch008

can support such communication, and Lenovo's success with *Lenovo Central.* The chapter also discusses the managerial implications for other firms interested in implementing an intranet in order to improve internal communication and foster employee engagement.

LITERATURE REVIEW

The Role of Internal Communication

The practice of internal communication can enhance an organizational culture by promoting employee engagement through open communication (Cahill, 1995; Deloitte, 2013; Harrison, 2013). Employees typically prefer to receive more communication from their superiors as it promotes their willingness to be involved in solving problems in the organization. Research has consistently argued for and empirically found that greater sharing of information by the organization serves to enhance employee empowerment, including a greater sense of impact on the organization and a greater sense of meaning (Mishra, & Spreitzer, 1998; Spreitzer & Mishra, 1999; Siegall & Gardner, 2000; Mills & Ungson 2003). Similar arguments and findings exist for the positive effect of communication within an organization on employee engagement (Kress, 2006; Saks 2006). Welch & Jackson (2007) identified internal communication as crucial for achieving employee engagement. A 2007/2008 Watson Wyatt study found that "Firms that communicate effectively are four times as likely to report high levels of employee engagement as firms that communicate less effectively."

Most recently, a Deloitte culture survey (2013) found that 50% of employees feel that "regular and candid communication" leads to a "culture of meaningful purpose." In addition, internal marketing "enables the firm to serve the needs of the customer (DeBussy, Ewing & Pitt, 2003: p. 150)." As reported in the Deloitte survey on culture and beliefs (2013), only 57% of employees who are happy at work said that their bosses talked about culture with them. Saks (2006) emphasized the need for clear and consistent communications with employees in order to achieve employee engagement, and suggested that employees who are more engaged will have a more positive relationship with their employer. Yet, managers seem to have less time to communicate, due to their demanding jobs (Robson & Tourish, 2005).

Effective internal communication can improve the trust between employees and management within an organization (DeBussy, Ewing & Pitt, 2003; Gavin & Mayer, 2005; Zeffane, Tipu, & Ryan, 2011). In one study (Robson & Tourish, 2005), employees identified a need for more internal communications, including face-to-face meetings, more openness, greater listening, improved email communication, more appreciation, an improved newsletter, and communications training in order to empower and engage employees. Often, however, top managers feel that communication with external constituents is more important than communication with internal ones (Therkelsen & Fiebich, 2003). In a more recent study of retail employees (Mishra & Boynton, 2009) found that those managers that take time for face-to-face meetings, listen, and provide feedback for employees on a regular basis, build strong trusting relationships with those employees and feelings of loyalty to both the local retail establishment and the larger corporate entity, as well.

Research has shown that there is strong link between trust and open communication within an organization (Mishra, 1996; Mishra, Schwartz & Mishra, 2011). Chia (2005) argued that "trust and commitment are byproducts of processes and policies which are designed to make the relationship satisfactory for both parties, such as open, appropriate, clear and timely communication" (p. 7). Trust between leaders and their employees, in terms of openness and concern, can be conveyed through empathic communication (Mishra & Mishra, 1994; 2013). Mishra (1996) found that "the extent to which the trusted person engages in undistorted communication then reinforces the trust (in terms of openness) placed in him or her" (p. 276). More generally, Dolphin (2005) argued that "sound relationships can only be developed on the basis of trust and reliable information (p. 185)."

A recent study examined how social media can enhance the way companies build an engaged workforce (Towers Watson, 2013). It found that only 56% of companies are using social media to build a sense of community with its workforce, such as sharing information with employees about culture, teambuilding or innovation (Towers Watson, 2013). This study also found that only 23% of organizations are effective at building a shared experience with their remote workforce (Towers Watson, 2013). Collaboration sites, such as a company intranet, are one way to build a shared experience. Web 2.0 technologies, such as an intranet, allow a firm to connect employees, customers, and partners (Lee, 2011). This study found that only 45% of companies surveyed actually use such a site and of those, just less than 35% found them effective (Towers Watson, 2013).

Increasingly, companies are developing intranets and other types of internal social media in order to keep employees apprised of the internal communications of the organization (Nakata, Zhu & Izberk-Bilgin, 2011). This is occurring as marketing and IT are increasingly working together to improve the communication networks of the organization (Nakata, Zhu & Izberk-Bilgin, 2011). Griffith & Harvey (2001) advised that "To reap the benefits of strong relational networks in the global marketplace, effective inter-organizational communications need to be established among members of the network (p. 88)." As internal communications executive Heather Lowe of Lenovo noted, "I made the conscious decision to come back into internal communication after having always worked in external, because I believe that the message should start with internal (H. Lowe, personal communication, May 5, 2013)." The Deloitte survey (2013) found that 45% of executives feel social media will enhance culture, yet only 27% of employees agree. One of the reasons executives feel positively about social media is that 38% of them believe it increases transparency in the organization, but again, only 17% of employees agree (Deloitte, 2013). The reason for this discrepancy between executives and employees needs to be understood.

Heather Lowe, Senior Manager Internal Communications, said that the most pressing challenge for her team is to "build a social media hub that can be used internally in an effective way, because then people can check it any time no matter where they are on the globe." She believes that the focus should be on short messages, such as using a video, so that when there are employees who speak many languages, it is easier for them to understand. In addition, it is critical to make sure that the internal messages mesh with the external messages about the brand. In fact, the internal communication team noted that several years ago, *Lenovo Central* was weak and people didn't think of it as a first resource of information. People didn't believe information about the company unless it was in their inbox or hand-delivered to them. Using the social media functionality of the redesigned *Lenovo Central* allowed the internal communications team to draw more people to that resource.

In addition, a global company has the added challenge of communicating in a way that respects not only corporate culture, but ethnic culture. One reason global communications fail, is that managers are not aware of "local sensitivities" (Mounter, 2003: p. 268). Khaner Walker, Sr. Manager of Communications at Lenovo also found this, noting that in the eastern part of the world, an employee values honor, so they want updates from their direct manager in order to show respect, but some managers aren't equipped to deliver updates. This is where the intranet can help augment a manager's ability to share information across the organization (Lee, 2011). In addition, when communicating with non-native English speakers, it is critical to listen, be sensitive to organizational needs, and promote a dialogue with global stakeholders (Mounter, 2003).

How the Intranet Supports Internal Communication

Marketing communications departments typically rely on a variety of channels to share company information, including intranets (internet services specifically for employee use) in order to share corporate and employee knowledge (Ruppel & Harrington, 2002; DeBussy, Ewing & Pitt, 2003). These intranets are also presumed to influence and be influenced by corporate culture as they develop and are adopted throughout the organization (Su & Contractor, 2011). Ruppel & Harrington (2002) found that "intranet implementation is facilitated by a culture that emphasizes an atmosphere of trust and concern for other people (ethical culture), flexibility and innovation (developmental culture), and policies, procedures and information management (hierarchical culture)". Lee (2011) noted that companies can "enhance the value of existing traditional businesses (p.9)" by using Web 2.0 "to complement existing company capabilities by integrating multiple Web 2.0 platforms (p. 11)" with social networks that connect employees, such as a company intranet. "The survival of emerging Web 2.0-based business models depend on attracting existing businesses as customers, contributors, and users (p. 13)."

Skok & Goldstein (2007) advocated for using a knowledge management (KM) strategy that focuses on expert, knowledge activities and group activities. In addition, they thought a champion would best "motivate management and staff, and to overcome possible barriers to management buy-in and a knowledge silo culture (p. 327)." One study found that new media, particularly the introduction of intranets, do positively impact internal marketing communications in the workplace (DeBussy, Ewing & Pitt, 2004) by increasing transparency and enhancing information flows. In addition, this study confirmed that intranets contribute toward two-way communication in the workplace, resulting in a more democratized workplace.

Finally, the intranet signals that employees are important stakeholders with equal access to information. A study of consultants by Su & Contractor (2011) found that "the organizational intranets in the consulting teams contained both tacit (e.g., skill learning, sales and marketing) as well as explicit (e.g., articles, deliverables, sand policies) information." The Towers Watson study (2013) agreed, finding that "remote workers are looking for clear communication, integrity and coaching from their managers."

In addition to improving information sharing, intranets are also ways to improve social capital as well. One recent study found that intranets are especially important for socializing new employees into an organization as well as serving as an organizational knowledge tool to retain employees (Chu & Chu, 2011). Specifically, Chu & Chu (2011) found that "the newcomers' adoption of intranet techniques has significant effects on socialization regarding how well they master their job, define their role, learn about their organization's culture and goals, and become socially integrated (p. 1175)." Radick (2011) noted a change in the use of intranets, "Whereas the intranet used to be focused on connecting people to information, it's now about connecting people to people."

Heather noted that their internal communications efforts, both electronic and face-to-face, should be transparent and trustworthy:

People can see through corporate BS. If it's got that tone, (then) they're not really saying what they mean, – so it's just important to be as plainspoken as you can and to be as transparent as you can. I know a lot of organizations try to hold information back and think 'oh, we're not ready to say that', but to the extent that you can give away as much as you know, it will go a long way towards creating that climate of trust.

In addition, it is not just her team that has this responsibility, but the executive leadership at Lenovo that have this responsibility: "That's how you gain trust: your leaders go out there face-to-face, and be as visible and as open to taking questions as they can. They should provide as much information as they feel they can without compromising the business."

RESEARCH QUESTION

This exploratory study of internal communication professionals and their internal customers seeks to understand the role of internal communications in a multinational technology company with locations around the globe. This study focuses on the role of the company intranet in its internal communications strategy to share information, foster employee engagement, and facilitate brand ambassadorship for Lenovo. This study used exploratory, semi-structured interviews conducted with managers responsible for public relations and/or internal communication at their firm (see interview questions in Appendix A), as well as employees who utilize the company intranet on a daily basis (see interview questions sin Appendix B).

METHOD

The first author and research assistant conducted all interviews in person. Each conversation was recorded, transcribed, and analyzed to understand how and what executives think about internal communications at Lenovo. Eight Lenovo executives participated in this study. Four of the participants work in internal communications for Lenovo at the headquarters in Morrisville, North Carolina. Four executives, also located at the North American headquarters in Morrisville, North Carolina, use the intranet on a daily basis; two from the accounting department and two from inside sales. A snowball technique was used in obtaining interview subjects for this study. One of the accountants is an MBA student of the first author and referred the first author to the second accountant. The inside sales executives were both alums of the first author. This was appropriate for this study because some degree of trust is helpful between the researcher and the interviewee to understand their role in internal communication (Atkinson & Flint, 2001).

The interview questions for the internal communications staff specifically asked how they execute internal communications at Lenovo (see Appendix A). The interview questions for the accounting and sales executives asked how they feel internal communications are accessible and useful to them at Lenovo (see Appendix B).

The interviews were conducted asking about internal communications in general, to understand Lenovo's best practices. At the completion of the interviews, the dominant theme of each interview was how *Lenovo Central* was such an important source of information to each employee on a daily basis, as well as how much *Lenovo Central* dominated the time and effort of the internal communications executives. Thus, *Lenovo Central* became the most important internal communication vehicle for the Lenovo internal communication team and thus, the focus of this study.

INTERVIEW FINDINGS

The internal communication executives interviewed for this study are:

1. Nancy Liang, Director, Global Internal Communications
2. Khaner Walker, Senior Manager Communications
3. Kelly Reid, Senior Global Communications & Content Strategist
4. Heather Lowe, Senior Communications Manager

The accounting and inside sales executives interviewed for this study are:

1. Kim Marut, North America Balance Sheet Lead Accountant
2. Marian Lakin, Monetization Controller
3. Joanna Still, Inside Sales Rep
4. Stephanie Mack, Inside Account Manager

The primary theme that emerged from these interviews on internal communications practices was the importance of *Lenovo Central*, the company's intranet, in their daily work lives.

RESULTS

Lenovo's Success with its Intranet, *Lenovo Central*

Khaner Walker is the Senior Manager of Communications at Lenovo in Raleigh, North Carolina. One of his primary roles is to support many different departments via *Lenovo Central*, the company intranet. Through his extensive background and work experience in journalism and public relations, Khaner has a unique vision for how *Lenovo Central* can provide timely, accurate, and critical content for employees across the globe. His goal is "to grow *Lenovo Central's* reach and usefulness for employees, along with enabling more interaction with employees (social postings on their own "wall," creating their own image galleries, etc.)." He has found that the more *Lenovo Central* grows the more competitive and creative each department head becomes in getting out the most interesting content on their particular site within *Lenovo Central*. Khaner's previous work experience has proven to be an extremely effective preparation for seeking out important information for Lenovo employees to know about and then translate that information in a way that is timely, accurate, and compelling (K. Walker, personal communication, January 18, 2013).

Khaner's boss, Nancy Liang, is Director of Global Internal Communications at Lenovo (N. Liang, personal communication, June 28, 2013). She came to Lenovo with a Harvard MBA and six years of experience at Cummins, where she was she was director of Internal Communications. She leads a team of six employees for the $34 billion company, who do most of the work in communicating news to all Lenovo employees around the globe, including *Lenovo Central*. Nancy's personal philosophy for internal communications at Lenovo is PCPC: People, Content, Process, Channel.

In terms of *People*, it is important to Nancy that 1) messages are sent to the right set of stakeholders; and that 2) messages are sent from the correct manager. When it has been decided that a message will come directly from the top, Nancy is insistent that decisions are deliberately made to send messages from either Chairman and CEO Yang Yuanqing's company email or his personal email, depending on the message and the target audience. This is critical, as research has found that CEOs believe that communication coming directly from the top positively influence "employees' feelings towards work and the organization's bottom line (Pincus, Rayfield & Cozzens, 1991, p. 27)." The most recent research by the Edelman Trust Barometer (2014) confirms that "trust in the person leading the company is inextricably linked with trust in the company itself."

Nancy confirmed that this is true for Lenovo and for Chairman and CEO Yang Yuanqing, as well. When speaking to a class of MBA students at Meredith College in Raleigh, North Carolina (N. Liang, personal communication, October 28, 2013), she remarked that "YY", as she calls him, "reads everything that is on *Lenovo Central*". She said that this confirms for her and for her team that what they do is of utmost importance for the company. In addition, any new information or announcement coming from one of his Senior Vice Presidents, he wants on *Lenovo Central* within 24 hours of them speaking or writing about it (N. Liang, personal communication, October 28, 2013).

One of her team members, Kelly Reid, is senior manager of global internal communications. Kelly's job is to manage and curate content for *Lenovo Central* (K. Reid, personal communication, May 5, 2013). As far as *Content*, Kelly said that, "we know who our audience is for the most part. It's the 30,000 Lenovo employees around the world." Nancy feels, however, that it is important to craft the message in just the right way for the audience it is intended for. For instance, it is critical to know your audience and whether the message should be in English or Chinese or both. Kelly agreed, saying that "the most effective way to communicate a message to people of many languages is by combining art and copy, so it's in a poster form." Kelly added that, "I think the biggest challenge because it's the most important challenge is asking the question 'why are we sending this. Why are we communicating this to the audience?'"

When Nancy is strategizing about *Process*, her team gathers, curates, writes, produces, and monitors the information that is posted on *Lenovo Central*. This includes financial information, interviews, photos from events, links to articles written about Lenovo, and monitoring the mechanism to encourage employees to co-create content, as well. Her team also works with each department at Lenovo to make sure that their own portals are up-to-date and useful for their own teams. Khaner mentioned that he is finding that department heads are becoming more competitive with each other in the content that they publish, wanting to make sure that they are putting forth their best effort.

The most important *Channel* her team communicates through is *Lenovo Central*, where information is available 24/7. This channel comes complete with a new news banner that changes each day, a photo gallery, a video gallery from around the world, and a place on *Lenovo Central* for events, such as a recent London fashion show or the Chairman's CCTV award. There is also a spot on the front page of *Lenovo Central* where employees can co-create content by updating news themselves and share it with fellow employees. This is critical for helping employees feel like they are an important part of creating and building the Lenovo culture. Heather, Senior Manager Internal Communications mentioned that ideally, they are looking for employees to contribute more to this social media presence: "We're moving towards a social media-based system, where no one person has the burden of creating content. It's crowd-sourced, meaning everybody is feeding in their view of the organization into one central hub. It's built piece by piece instead of a team of five or seven people churning out masses of content for the rest." Kelly also stressed the importance of adding content to *Lenovo Central* for employees:

> *The most effective way to create a lasting message is by putting it on Lenovo Central or the community, which Lenovo Central has the news section and the community section, and having the person go and find it and read it. Because they discovered it on their own...we're trying to do is move away from email communications and start to build a sense of discovery on Lenovo Central.*

This social media aspect of *Lenovo Central* allows employees to share information internally. They can post to their "wall" and share news and updates, which also helps fellow employees see how users are connected back to the up-to-date HR directory so that everyone can see who they are, who they work for, and where they work in the organization.

One other important channel Lenovo uses is their annual kickoff event in April where Chairman and CEO Yang lays out the strategic plan for the year so that employees are kept informed on the mission and vision of the company. Chairman and CEO Yang and his top executives meet with employees in three places around the world to make sure that everyone has an opportunity to be involved. Top managers share messages about the strategic plan, the Lenovo brand, and the new Lenovo products. (See Figures 1 and 2)

Figure 1. Screenshot of Lenovo Central homepage
Copyright 2014. Reprinted with permission.

It is important to understand how *Lenovo Central* impacts its intended audience, as well. For example, the accounting employees use *Lenovo Central* to get up-to-date information they need on employees from all over the world. When Kim, an accounting manager, needs an organizational chart for a group in China, she knows she can count on *Lenovo Central* to have the most current information (K. Marut, personal communication, February 26, 2013). This was particularly critical for her during a restructuring when people were moving to new positions, or especially in China, where people frequently leave the company for new positions. Toni, an accounting manager, also noted that this is critical because then she can rely on *Lenovo Central* to give her the most up-to-date information rather than rely on rumors, which are not necessarily accurate (A. Lakin, personal communication, March 15, 2013). Toni noted that *Lenovo Central* is very good at keeping her apprised of senior level changes in the organization. The one thing Toni would change about *Lenovo Central* would be for it to keep better track of lower-level moves, as her department regularly deals with folks from all levels of the organization, all over the world.

The sales function also values *Lenovo Central*. Joanna and Stephanie are both inside sales reps at Lenovo. They value this as something that helps keep them "in-the-loop". They find it up-to-date and organized. While they don't know who is behind *Lenovo Central*, they are impressed nonetheless at how timely the information is that they can rely on. This is especially important for them because their bosses are not always available on-site to provide them with this timely information in a face-to-face manner, so they know that they have access to company information regardless of whether or not they are able to meet with their supervisor on a regular basis to get company and employee information directly (J. Still, personal communication, March 15, 2013; S. Mack personal communication, March 20, 2013).

Challenges with *Lenovo Central*

Some of the employees noted that while they appreciate Lenovo Central, they have no idea who is in charge of it. This might be a problem if those employees need to utilize the intranet to share information throughout the company and don't know the official channels and/or people

Figure 2. Screenshot of Lenovo Central employee wall
Copyright 2014. Reprinted with permission.

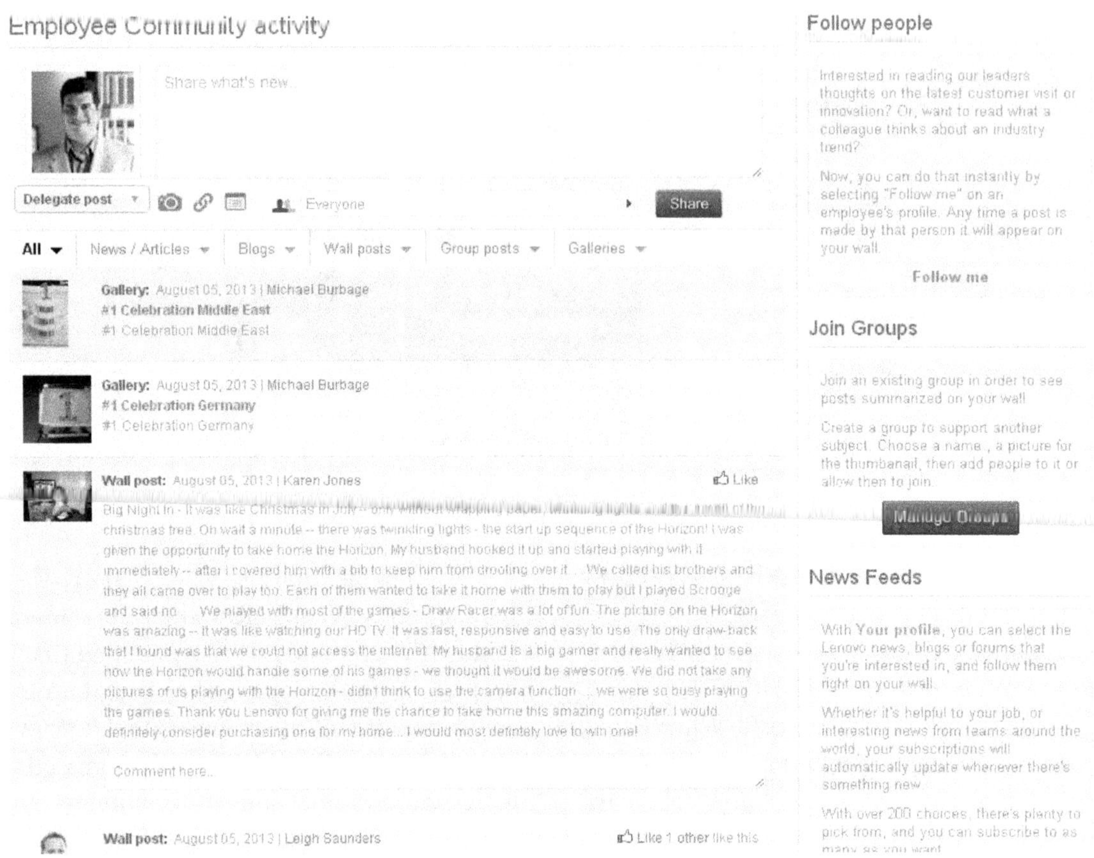

to go through to share that information. While the internal communications staff works hard behind the scenes, there might be an opportunity to be more visible to the employees who they are there to help.

Another challenge is communicating ethnic and/or cultural teachings through *Lenovo Central*. A couple of the employees interviewed expressed a desire for more exposure and communication around global culture to help them better understand how different cultures operate in the locations where Lenovo operates. They noted that since people are the core of the company, working all over the globe, it is important to understand those cultures because of who they are and where they're from.

The Larger Role of *Lenovo Central*

Khaner Walker, Senior Manager of Communications, summed up what he thinks is the role that *Lenovo Central* ultimately plays within Lenovo and in evangelizing the Lenovo brand.

I think our Intranet has had a key role in Lenovo's transformation from a PC company, to what we call a PC+ company (tablets, smartphones, smart TVs, etc.). This has been a major, substantive shift for Lenovo, considering our deep legacy in PCs from both Lenovo and IBM PC, and how our employees have enjoyed a considerable amount of success just from Lenovo's growing PC business (indeed we became the world's #1 PC company in early July).

But we realize the world is changing. The PC market as a whole is slowing down, and while Lenovo has been able to avoid this trend, we must innovate and push beyond our norms to realize our vision of becoming a lasting technology leader.

We use the Intranet on almost a daily basis to highlight Lenovo's PC+ strategy and expand upon what it means, what the company is doing, where we are launching new PC+ products, and where we will be launching.

Consider the viewpoint of an IBM employee who has been with the company for 15-20 years, or a Lenovo employee in China where they have enjoyed considerable PC success. This is more than introducing a new type of computer – this is a major, tremendously important shift in our company's strategy, which Lenovo Central has been the frontlines for internally. We use the Intranet to go beyond the strategy Yuanqing (our CEO) lays out on a PowerPoint slide – we bring it to life in a way employees can understand, see for themselves, and ultimately embrace.

A quick glance at yesterday's headlines from our Q1 earnings announcement highlights the success of this shift: "Lenovo Sells More Tablets and Phones than PCs, and That's Important" – Fast Co. "Lenovo, the world's largest PC maker, now sells more smartphones and tablets than computers." – NY Times.

The world's largest PC company now sells more phones and tablets than computers…an amazing shift – one that has happened much, much faster than we anticipated, and perhaps in large part due to a rapid, enthusiastic adoption internally.

I would argue that Lenovo Central's growing readership (more than 60,000 visits a month), increased views on videos that focus on PC+ products (compared to videos that focus on PCs), and my team's non-stop coverage of PC+ news plays a vital role in the company's successful transformation.

DISCUSSION AND CONTRIBUTIONS

Lenovo is a global company: is it possible for other multi-national corporations to incorporate its best practices in internal communication? There are some key takeaways.

1. **Make Daily Communication a Priority:** Even though top executives are busy, lower level employees crave information about the company, the strategy, and their fellow employees. Making information available (such as on a company intranet) prevents rumors and false information from taking over. Even when you as the manager don't have time to spend in daily face-to-face conversations with employees, an intranet can help fill in the information gaps. In addition, the more positive information employees have at their disposal, the better brand ambassadors they can be for the company when friends and neighbors ask about your brands and services.
2. **Establish One Global Language:** For the company to use so that everyone knows what to expect and how to receive internal communication messages. This helps to create a consistent message and delivery, as well. However, organizations should be flexible in their use of language, and consider incorporating a second key language, to keep all employees engaged in other parts of the world to avoid any major misunderstandings
3. **Share Cultural Information as Well as Company Information:** As organizations become more global in its employees and operations, it should find ways to help employees learn about what is culturally important and relevant about all employees in order to them in order to increase their

personal understanding of each other. This will help employees learn to appreciate the background and experience of fellow team members who work in other locations.

4. **Create a Dynamic Communications Vehicle:** (Such as a company intranet or daily email digest) to disseminate messages in a timely and interesting way to all employees. Make sure that this is a two-way communications vehicle, not just a one-way tool. Employees will feel more engaged if they have the opportunity to participate in and co-create communication efforts. If this is a two-way communications vehicle, employees will be more likely to remain engaged and utilize this as much as or more than email.
5. **Partner with HR:** To make sure that the HR directory is up-to-date and is tied into the communications system. This can help facilitate the exchange of timely and accurate information among a directory of global employees, as well as help build important relationships across cultural and country boundaries.
6. **Let Employees Know Who the Internal Communications Team is:** The team should be accessible to all employees so that they know who they can go to for up-to-date information as well as who can help them share new information with their colleagues.
7. **Share Brand Strategy:** By sharing strategic information with your employees, you can engage them in the vision of the company, its products, and the future direction of the company so that they become brand ambassadors for your company. Year after year, the Edelman Trust Barometer (2013; 2014) finds that consumers trust information from "someone like me" more than they trust information from traditional advertising. If your employees share brand information that they learn from the intranet, it will be much more powerful than any advertising campaign.

SHARING BRAND STRATEGY: THE YOGA COMPETITION

When Lenovo introduced its new Yoga tablet in fall 2013, the internal communications team decided to engage its employees in the introduction of this new product launch on *Lenovo Central.* Employees could win a Yoga tablet by posting their own yoga poses on *Lenovo Central.* The poses with the most "likes" got a new yoga tablet. This is a great example of engaging your employees in your new product and brand early, and then rewarding them with that product so that they will go out and be brand ambassadors with friends and neighbors for that product when it hits the market.

FUTURE RESEARCH DIRECTIONS

Companies like Lenovo using its intranet, *Lenovo Central*, represent a "best practice" in internal communications. Future research should study how many other Fortune Global 500 companies are actually using such an intranet in their own firms to allow employees to be kept up-to-date on all internal and external matters about their firm. In addition, future research should consider whether colleges are preparing future executives for this role in companies. Internal communications is a relatively new role in corporate communications, which may be why there are relatively few executives suited to take on this new challenge. Finally, future research should address whether or not Fortune Global 500 intranets are doing what Lenovo Central is doing, hosting its intranet in two languages, when this company has headquarters in both Beijing and North Carolina. The Director of Global Internal Communications speaks both Mandarin and English, which makes her uniquely qualified to manage an internet in both languages. How many other companies are thinking globally when they are developing their internal communications department and their intranets? Or is English the dominant language of business?

CONCLUSION

As a global technology leader, Lenovo is also leading the way in developing a world-class employee intranet, *Lenovo Central.* Designed to bridge cultures and languages, *Lenovo Central* is the place that employees state that they go to get up-to-date information about their colleagues and their company. Lenovo also uses its company intranet as a social media site to engage its employees with information about the company, to instill a sense of pride about the Lenovo brand, and to foster brand ambassadorship among its employees.

As companies grow and become more global in scope, this form of social media will be critical for crossing both geographic and socio-cultural boundaries, as well as engaging employees in acting as brand ambassadors, and sharing critical information about their company to their customers, neighbors, colleagues, and friends.

ACKNOWLEDGMENT

Thanks to Ms. Nancy Liang, Director of Global Internal Communications at Lenovo, for support of this study and to Ms. Amanda Baity, research assistant, for help in collecting data for this study.

REFERENCES

Atkinson, R., & Flint, J. (2001). Accessing hidden and hard-to-reach populations: Snowball research strategies. *Social Research Update, 33.*

Cahill, D. (1995). The managerial implications of the learning organization: A new tool for internal marketing. *Journal of Services Marketing*, *9*(4), 43–51. doi:10.1108/08876049510094513

Chia, J. (2005). *Measuring the immeasurable.* Retrieved from http://praxis.massey.ac.nz/fileadmin/Praxis/Files/Journal_Files/Evaluation_Issue/CHIA_ARTICLE.pdf#search=%22%20joy%20chia%20measuring%20the%20immeasurable%22

Chu, A., & Chu, R. (2011). The intranet's role in newcomer socialization in the hotel industry in Taiwan – Technology acceptance model analysis. *International Journal of Human Resource Management*, *22*(5), 1163–1179. doi:10.1080/09585192.2011.556795

De Bussy, N., Ewing, M., & Pitt, L. (2004). Stakeholder theory and internal marketing communications: A framework for analyzing the influence of new media. *Journal of Marketing Communications*, *9*(3), 147–161. doi:10.1080/1352726032000129890

Deloitte Core Beliefs and Culture Survey. (2013). Retrieved from http://www.deloitte.com/assets/Dcom-UnitedStates/Local%20Assets/Documents/us_leadership_2013corebeliefs&culturesurvey_051613.pdf

Dolphin, R. R. (2005). Internal communications: Today's strategic imperative. *Journal of Marketing Communications*, *11*(3), 171–190. doi:10.1080/1352726042000315414

Edelman Trust Barometer. (2013). Retrieved on 8/21/13 from http://www.edelman.com/insights/intellectual-property/trust-2013/

Edelman Trust Barometer. (2014). Retrieved on 1/22/14 from http://www.edelman.com/insights/intellectual-property/2014-edelman-trust-barometer/

Griffith, D. A., & Harvey, M. G. (2001). Executive insights: An intercultural communication model for use in global interorganizational networks. *Journal of International Marketing*, *9*(3), 87–103. doi:10.1509/jimk.9.3.87.19924

Harrison, A. G. (2013). Engagement ring: Building connections between employees and strategy. *Public Relations Tactics*, *20*(5), 16.

Kalla, H. K. (2005). Integrated internal communications: A multidisciplinary perspective. *Corporate Communications*, *10*(4), 302–314. doi:10.1108/13563280510630106

Kelemen, M., & Papasolomou, I. (2007). Internal marketing: A qualitative study of culture change in the UK banking sector. *Journal of Marketing Management*, *23*(7-8), 745–767. doi:10.1362/026725707X230027

Kress, N. (2005). Engaging your employees through the power of communication. *Workspan*, *48*(5), 26–36.

Lee, I. (2011). Overview of emerging web 2.0-based business models and web 2.0 applications in business: An ecological perspective. *International Journal of E-Business Research*, *7*(4), 1–16. doi:10.4018/jebr.2011100101

Mangold, W. G., & Faulds, D. J. (2009). Social media: The new hybrid element of the promotion mix. *Business Horizons*, *52*(4), 357–365. doi:10.1016/j.bushor.2009.03.002

Mills, P. K., & Ungson, G. (2003). Reassessing the limits of structural empowerment: Organizational constitution and trust as controls. *Academy of Management Review*, *28*(1), 143–153.

Mishra, A. K. (1996). Organizational responses to crisis: The centrality of trust. In R. Kramer, & T. Tyler (Eds.), *Trust in organizations* (pp. 261–287). Newbury Park, CA: Sage. doi:10.4135/9781452243610.n13

Mishra, A. K., & Mishra, K. E. (1994). The role of mutual trust in effective downsizing strategies. *Human Resource Management*, *33*(2), 261–279. doi:10.1002/hrm.3930330207

Mishra, A. K., & Mishra, K. E. (2013). *Becoming a trustworthy leader: Psychology & practice*. Routledge Press.

Mishra, A. K., & Spreitzer, G. M. (1998). Explaining how survivors respond to downsizing: The roles of trust, empowerment, justice and work redesign. *Academy of Management Review*, *23*(3), 567–588.

Mishra, K. E., & Boynton, L. (2009). Talk-the-talk: Using internal communication to build trust with employees. Paper presented at the International Public Relations Research Conference. Miami, FL.

Mishra, K. E., Schwarz, G. M., & Mishra, A. K. (2011). The evolution of trust and control as seen through an organization's human resources practices. In R. Searle (Ed.), *Trust and Human Resource Management*. Cheltenham, UK: Edward Elgar. doi:10.4337/9780857932006.00009

Mounter, P. (2003). Global internal communication: A model. *Journal of Communication Management*, *7*(3), 3. doi:10.1108/13632540310807412

Nakata, C., Zhu, Z., & Izberk-Bilgin, E. (2011). Integrating marketing and information services functions: A complementarity and competence perspective. *Journal of the Academy of Marketing Science*, *39*(5), 700–716. doi:10.1007/s11747-010-0236-z

Pincus, D. J., Rayfield, R. E., & Cozzens, M. D. (1991). The Chief Executive Officer's internal communications role: A benchmark program of research. In L. A. Grunig, & J. E. Grunig (Eds.), *Public Relations Research Annual* (Vol. 3, pp. 1–36). Hillsdale, NJ: Lawrence Earlbaum Associates.

Quirke, B. (2008). *Making the connections: Using internal communication to turn strategy into action*. Burlington, VT: Gower.

Radick, S. (2011). The power of social networks: Reviving the intranet. *Public Relations Tactics*, 18.

Robson, P., & Tourish, D. (2005). Managing internal communication: An organizational case study. *Corporate Communications*, *10*(3), 213–222. doi:10.1108/13563280510614474

Ruppel, C. P., & Harrington, S. J. (2001). Sharing knowledge through intranets: A study of organizational culture and intranet implementation. *Professional Communication*, *44*(1), 37–52. doi:10.1109/47.911131

Saks, A. M. (2006). Antecedents and consequences of employee engagement. *Journal of Managerial Psychology*, *21*(7), 600–619. doi:10.1108/02683940610690169

Siegall, M., & Gardner, S. (2000). Contextual factors of psychological empowerment. *Personnel Review*, *29*(6), 703–722. doi:10.1108/00483480010296474

Skok, W., & Goldstein, B. (2007). Managing organizational knowledge: Developing a strategy for a professional services company. *Strategic Change*, *16*(7), 327–339. doi:10.1002/jsc.805

Spreitzer, G. M., & Mishra, A. K. (1999). Giving Up Control Without Losing Control: Trust and Its Substitutes' Effects on Managers' Involving Employees in Decision Making. *Group & Organization Management*, *14*(2), 155–187. doi:10.1177/1059601199242003

Su, C., & Contractor, N. (2011). A Multidimensional Network Approach to Studying Team Members' Information Seeking From Human and Digital Knowledge Sources in Consulting Firms. *Journal of the American Society for Information Science and Technology*, *62*(7), 1257–1275. doi:10.1002/asi.21526

Therkelsen, D. J., & Fiebich, C. L. (2003). The supervisor: The linchpin of employee relations. *Journal of Communication Management*, *8*(2), 120–129. doi:10.1108/13632540410807592

Towers Watson Study. (2013, July 14). Retrieved from http://www.towerswatson.com/en/Insights/IC-Types/Survey-Research-Results/2013/05/Infographic-2013-Change-and-Communication-ROI-Study

Welch, M., & Jackson, P. R. (2007). Rethinking internal communication: A stakeholder approach. *Corporate Communications*, *12*(2), 177–198. doi:10.1108/13563280710744847

Zeffane, R., Tipu, S. A., & Ryan, J. C. (2011). Communication, commitment & trust: Exploring the triad. *International Journal of Business and Management*, *6*(6), 77–87. doi:10.5539/ijbm.v6n6p77

ADDITIONAL READING

Brown, B., Sikes, J., & Willmott, P. (2013). *Bullish on digital: McKinsey Global Survey Results*. McKinsey & Company.

Burgess, C. (2013). *The Social Employee: How Great Companies Make Social Media Work*. McGraw-Hill.

KEY TERMS AND DEFINITIONS

Employee Engagement: Employee engagement is "the degree to which an individual is attentive and absorbed in the performance of their roles (Saks, 2006, p. 602)."

Internal Communication: Internal communication is communication between the organization's leaders and one of its key publics: the employees (Dolphin, 2005). It is "social interaction through messages" (Kalla, 2005, p. 303) and reflects management's ability to build relationships between internal stakeholders at all levels within an organization (Welch & Jackson, 2007). Quirke (2008) noted that the role of internal communication is to "illuminate the connections between different pieces of information" (p. x), and its job is "to provide employees with the information they need to do their job" (p. x).

Intranet: internet services specifically for employee use in order to share corporate and employee knowledge (Ruppel & Harrington, 2002; DeBussy, Ewing & Pitt, 2003).

Lenovo Central: The company Intranet for Lenovo.

Lenovo: Lenovo is not just another technology company. We make the technology that powers the world's best ideas. We design tools for those who are driven by accomplishment. We are the company that powers the people who Do. The engine that helps them Do more. Do better. Do what's never been done. And we are united in the quest to help our users defy the impossible.

Social Media: Social media is also referred to as consumer-generated media. It includes online information created and/or shared by consumers about their favorite products and/or brands. "Social media encompasses a wide range of online, word-of-mouth forums including blogs, company-sponsored discussion boards and chat rooms, consumer-to-consumer e-mail, consumer product or service ratings websites and forums, Internet discussion boards and forums, moblogs (sites containing digital audio, images, movies, or photographs), and social networking websites, to name a few" (Mangold & Faulds, 2009).

Trust: Trust is defined as a willingness to be vulnerable to another person or party based on some positive expectations regarding the other party's intentions and/or behaviours (Mishra & Mishra, 1994).

APPENDIX A: INTERVIEW QUESTIONS FOR INTERNAL COMMUNICATION EXECUTIVES

1. Tell me about your role in communications at Lenovo.
2. What is your biggest challenge in developing relevant and timely communications in a global company?
3. What is the most effective way to share one message to people in different places?
4. What is the most effective way to share one message to people who speak different languages?
5. How does Lenovo's culture affect the way you choose to communicate across departmental or business borders?
6. How do marketing, communications and public relations work together to create organizational messages?
7. How do your organizational messages mesh with your external advertising messages?
8. Which come first, the external brand messages or the internal ones?
9. What role does the internet play in the way you communicate with employees?
10. What role does face-to-face communication play in the way you share messages about the company and the brand with employees?
11. What role does the immediate supervisor play in disseminating your messages?
12. If you could design an ideal communications system, what would it look like?
13. If you could design a new undergraduate communications class, what would it include?
14. What is the role does trust play in building open and transparent communications systems?
15. What is the role of the leader in building open and transparent communication systems?
16. As a recipient of those messages, what do you like about the communication process?
17. Is there anything you would change, if you could? Please elaborate.
18. Is there anything else you would like to share about this process?

APPENDIX B: INTERVIEW QUESTIONS FOR LENOVO EMPLOYEES

1. Tell me about how internal communications work at Lenovo.
2. How does Lenovo's culture affect the way you see that messages work across departmental or business borders?
3. Do you feel that your organizational messages mesh with your external advertising messages?
4. What role does the internet play in the way the organization communicates with employees?
5. What role does face-to-face communication play in the way your manager shares messages about the company and the brand with employees?
6. If you could design an ideal communications system, what would it look like?
7. What is the role does trust play in building open and transparent communications systems?
8. What is the role of the leader in building open and transparent communication systems?
9. As a recipient of those messages, what do you like about the communication process?
10. Is there anything you would change, if you could? Please elaborate.
11. Is there anything else you would like to share about this process?

Chapter 9
How Generation Y Perceives Social Networking Applications in Corporate Environments

Imed Boughzala
Telecom Ecole de Management, France

ABSTRACT

Organizations increasingly rely on corporate social networks and online communities to enhance socialization and knowledge sharing, collaboration, and value creation among coworkers. This chapter presents and analyzes results from a qualitative exploratory study conducted recently with a group of 24 graduate management students from a French business school. It contributes to a better understanding of how generation Y perceives the use of Social Networking (SN) applications inside businesses by drawing up a list of dos and don'ts. This study provides an ordered list of important adoption issues to consider when implementing and using CSN applications in businesses. It provides expectations and precautions for stakeholders to take into account for best use, compared to users (coworkers), managers, and the enterprise as a whole. A first list of guidelines, to favor the best adoption of these applications and to make their usage effective, is formulated.

INTRODUCTION

In 2005, the social aspect of the Web was emphasized by Tim O'Reilly (2005) to highlight the value of socialization related to people connections, content sharing and co-creation through social networks. Internet user is no longer considered as an information consumer but more as a content producer. To the point that in 2006 Time magazine titled its coverage "You." (*Yes, you. You control the Information Age. Welcome to your world*). Indeed, this magazine used to devote coverage to the person of the year since the late 1920s.

The idea was to highlight that internet users from that year (2006) will have the control over the information thanks to the Social Web (2.0), by expressing freely themselves on the web and interacting directly with others. This marks in somewhat a break with the traditional web.

Today, integrating Web 2.0 applications (i.e. social media) in businesses provides many opportunities to improve interaction, knowledge

DOI: 10.4018/978-1-4666-6182-0.ch009

sharing and collaboration among employees, also with customers and partners. These applications are becoming a popular medium for people interaction, content sharing (Constant et al., 1994; Davenport and Prusak, 1998; Cramton, 2001) and open collaboration (Coleman & Levine, 2008). Currently, to take profit from their potential, companies increasingly rely on corporate social networking (CSN) applications (in the continuum of Intranet efforts) to enhance the communication and increase the density of connections and sharing among coworkers to drive business value and innovation (Chesbrough & Appleyard, 2007; Sena & Sena, 2008).

According to many authors (Dudezert et al., 2009; Hershatter & Epstein, 2010; Boughzala, 2007-2012a; Deal et al., 2010; Gorman et al., 2004), the new generation of hypermodern employees (i.e. Generation Y) has developed new habits and behaviors at work. They use, on a daily basis, Web 2.0 applications (blogs, wikis, Really Simple Syndication (RSS) feeds, SN applications/services, folksonomy, podcasting, tagging, mashups, etc) in the private arena and, therefore, consider that such applications for self-organizing, sharing and collaboration are the best tools to work. Social networks and online communities are for them the best resources to solve problems collectively, to get connections and partnerships and thus to take advantage of the collective intelligence (Smith & Duin, 1994; Malone et al., 2009). This generation wants to choose by it-self the tools and devices it deems fit to use (notion of self-care, Bitner et al., 2002). This is part of larger organizational issues, called BYOD (Bring Your Own Device), BYOA (Bring Your Own Application, Ballagas et al., 2004) or more BYOB (Bring Your Own Behavior, Gunnarsson, 2012).

Researchers and practitioners to date have mostly assumed that people from this generation Y (Dudezert et al., 2009; Hershatter & Epstein, 2010), because of their massive use of social media in the private arena, would be willing to accept and use them more easily and quickly in corporate environment under what we call Enterprise 2.0 (Crumpacker & Crumpacker, 2007; Deal et al., 2010). However, to the best of our knowledge, there is no empirical work which has been reported on this issue confirming this assumption on the ground. Nobody can affirm today that generation Y would be the driver of this technology adoption in corporate environment considering their technology readiness (Parasuraman, 2000).

This chapter tries to address this gap by answering the following research questions: how the use of CSN applications is perceived by the generation Y? To what extent people from this generation are willing to adopt and use them within a corporate environment? And, what should be the best and worst use according to them?

The method adopted for this study is based on a qualitative exploratory study through an enriched Delphi method (Briggs et al., 2003). Twenty four graduate management students from a French business school were invited to participate voluntarily to a directed brainstorming session, using a Group Support System (GSS), in order to gather their statements and opinions. This study provided an ordered list of important adoption issues to consider when implementing and using CSN applications in businesses.

The purpose of this chapter is to contribute to a better understanding of the perception of generation Y with regard to CSN applications by drawing up a list of dos and don'ts. It provides important expectations and precautions to take into account by stakeholders for a best use, compared to users (coworkers), managers and the enterprise at whole.

The rest of this chapter is structured as follows: Section 2 briefly describes research background in terms of concepts (Web 2.0, generation Y and SN applications) and some related works and theories. Section 3 describes the research method that has been used in this exploratory study. Results are presented in section 4. Based on our findings, we discuss in section 5 their accordance with the technology acceptance and adoption models and theories; and present some guidelines associated with best CSN applications deployment and usage. The conclusion discusses contributions, limitations and future research directions.

BACKGROUND

Web 2.0 and Knowledge Sharing

Web 2.0 (O'Reilly, 2005) is one major change that is being transforming work practices and more widely the organization at whole. In fact, new usages for information and knowledge sharing have emerged with the advent of Web 2.0 applications, giving rise to the Enterprise 2.0 concept (Anderson, 2007). Enterprise 2.0 - a new culture of technology usage here - refers to "the use of Web 2.0, emergent social software platforms within companies, or between companies and their partners or customers" as defined initially by McAfee (2006).

Web 2.0 is a combination of applications (Blog, Wiki, Podcast, RSS feeds, Tagging, Social networks…); new values related to the use of these applications (user as producer, collective intelligence, perpetual beta, extreme ease if use) and standardized technology behind these applications (Ajax, XML, Open API, Microformats, Flash/Flex) (O'Reilly, 2005; Anderson, 2007).

Web 2.0 applications, also called social media, are intuitive, user-friendly, social centered, flexible and less formal than traditional information systems (Kaplan & Haenlein, 2010). Latter researchers have classified social media into six categories including collaborative projects (e.g. Wikipedia), blogs and microblogs (e.g. Twitter), content communities (e.g. Youtube), social networking sites/systems (SNSs) (e.g. Facebook), virtual game worlds (e.g. World of Warecraft) and virtual social worlds (e.g. Second Life). Used initially in the private arena, they are increasingly disseminated within professional spheres, regardless of organization type or field of activities (Boughzala, 2010a-2011). They are very useful for self-expression, social networking and interaction, and skills and talents identification. They are a good opportunity for companies to improve best practices' sharing, and to encourage open collaboration, crowdsourcing and co-creation (AIIM, 2009; Gorman et al., 2004).

Indeed, knowledge sharing among coworkers through web 2.0 applications remains the primary objective to reach for companies before hoping their collaboration and value co creation. Knowledge sharing is a volitional action by which knowledge is made known to other people (Davenport and Prusak, 1998; Cramton, 2001). This can be seen from two angles – a) the knowledge one considers sharing; and b) the person or people with whom one contemplates sharing it. Thus, an individual may deem a given body of knowledge to be highly sharable with someone, but not sharable with another (Bock et al., 2005; Boughzala and Briggs, 2012b). Social networks and online communities are very important for knowledge sharing and creation (Rheingold, 1993). Cummings (2003) posits that knowledge sharing is the means by which an organization obtains access to its own and other organizations' knowledge. Bresman et al. (1999) argued that individuals will only participate willingly in knowledge sharing once they share a sense of identity (or belonging) with others.

Social Networking Applications

One of the most interesting, rich and extremely popular web 2.0 applications is SN applications (mobile apps, sites, services or platforms) for developing and supporting online social network communities, and share user-created contents (Kim et al., 2010). Boyd and Ellison (2007) define them "as web-based services that allow individuals to (1) construct a public or semi-public profile

Figure 1. The honeycomb framework of social media (Kietzmann et al., 2011)

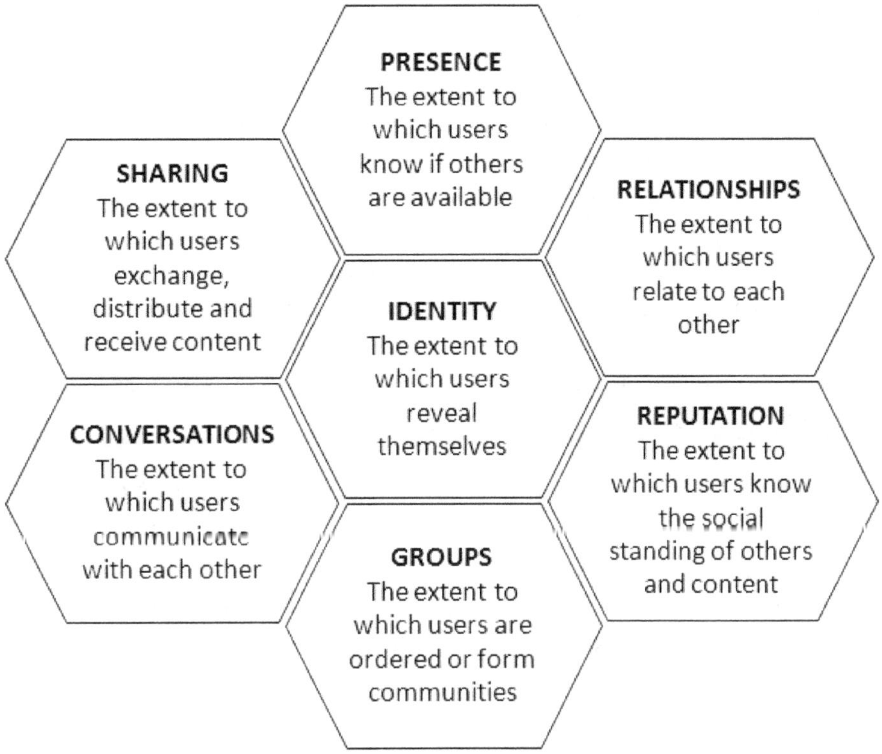

within a bounded system, (2) articulate a list of other users with whom they share a connection, and (3) view and traverse their list of connections and those made by others within the system." For Richter and Koch (2008 p. 87), social networking services/sites (SNSs) "are application systems that offer users functionalities for identity management and enable furthermore to keep in touch with other users."

Kaplan and Haenlein (2010) categorize SNS by four different terms: (1) self-presentation, (2) self-disclosure, (3) social presence, and (4) media richness in terms of the amount of information to be transmitted at time intervals. Later, Kietzmann et al. (2011) describe a categorization, called the honeycomb framework of social media, which is able to categorize SNS using seven functional building blocks (i.e. functionalities): Identity, Presence, Sharing, Relationships, Conversations, Reputation, Groups (Figure 1).

Generation Y

Another change related to the transformation of the organization is social that came with the arrival on the job market of the new generation of employees – the Generation Y (Anonymous editorial, 1993) ("Why" – i.e., eager of sense-making), Gen Y, Yers, Net Generation, Digital Natives or Milenials (Gorman et al., 2004; Forrester Consulting, 2006; Dudezert et al., 2009). A new generation of younger, college- and university-educated workers born between 1978 and 1995 and grown up with the Internet. This generation succeeds to the generation X (anonymous) which came after and is less known than, the baby boomers. According to Forrester Consulting (2006) and others (Broadbridge et al., 2009, Hershatter & Epstein, 2010), these employees are looking continuously for new technology and are eager to simply and quickly find good information/knowledge, anytime and anywhere and from any device; and are very autonomous and intuitive, not intimidated by knowledge complexity and organizational hierarchy (Boughzala, 2010b – 2012a). This new generation already upsets the traditional organization and sometimes confuses the professional sphere with the private one (Kowske et al., 2010). It is also a good opportunity for her to integrate enthusiastic and creative employees. The generation Y is characterized by a new culture – Culture 2.0 – of awareness, technology usage, knowledge sharing, mass collaboration and open innovation (Chesbrough & Appleyard, 2007).

CSN Applications and Generation Y

As young people from the generation Y are accustomed nowadays to meet and converse on Facebook, MySpace, Flickr and other similar SN applications, companies have realized the importance of social networking and started deploying and using their own SN platforms (Sena & Sena, 2008). Social networking within a corporate environment is an efficient way to link remotely located people with specific competency domains in large organizations (e.g. IBM, Disney, Accenture, Redbull), to create a sustainable relationship and maintain them. This social aspect makes the CSN applications an attractive opportunity for knowledge-intensive organizations (Richter & Riemer, 2009).

Sena and Sena (2008) argue that CSN applications "are primarily used to build trust and share knowledge on a peer to peer basis rather than through documents subject to information obsolescence." A study led by SelectMinds (2008) revealed that private and secure CSNs provide substantial savings for the company. "This study examined the financial contributions of CSN solutions in 60 leading, global organizations. The report revealed that a better connected workforce through CSN technology can yield significant financial contributions to organizations" (Sena & Sena, 2008). Key findings of the study include:

- 10.3% increase in productivity contributions;
- 8.8% increase in retention contributions; and
- 11.7% increase in new business.

Therefore, for many companies the adoption of CSN applications by workers and their incorporation into their daily workspace are becoming big challenges (Grady, 2008). They count on the contribution of generation Y, with relation to its alleged readiness, to lead this change and be the driver of this technology adoption.

The Technology Adoption Research

Technology is evolving and with this a big challenge for designers and managers to understand how and why people adopt or do not adopt new technology. The technology acceptance/adoption is one of the most important issues in the management information systems (MIS) area. The Theory of Reasoned Action (Fishbein and Ajzen, 1975) and the Theory of Planned Behavior (Ajzen, 1991) have been used successfully to assess technology adoption. TRA states that there are four constructs that a user has in actual behavior since the behavioral intention is positively influenced by beliefs, attitude, normative beliefs and subjective norm. TPB states that the attitude toward the behavior, subjective norm, and perceived behavioral control determine behavior intention and in consequence behavior.

Many studies have been carried out and many theories and models were provided to explain this social phenomenon, such as Technology Acceptance Model (TAM, Davis, 1989), Technology Readiness and Acceptance Model (TRAM, Parasuraman 2000), TAM 2 (Venkatesh & Davis, 2000), TAM 3 (Venkatesh & Bala, 2008), Unified Theory of Acceptance and Use of Technology (UTAUT, Venkatesh et al., 2003) and UTAUT 2 (Venkatesh et al., 2012). These cognitive-based models try to explain the behavioral intention to use a technology according to main two variables: the perceived ease of use and perceived usefulness; and other external variables such as social influence, performance expectancy, effort expectancy, voluntariness of use, experience, age, subjective norm, image, job relevance, output quality, computer self-efficacy, computer playfulness, hedonic motivation, habit, etc.

TAM is an adaptation of TRA and proposes that the acceptance of a technology in the workplace is influenced by the perceived usefulness and ease of use for the technology use (Davis 1989). TRAM includes individual beliefs to understand how people embrace and use new technologies for home and work measured by optimism, innovativeness, discomfort and insecurity (Parasuraman 2000). UTAUT provides a model to assess the likelihood of adoption for a new technology; it emerged from eight different technology acceptance models (Venkatesh et al. 2003). (Figures 2 & 3)

Furthermore according to DeLone and McLean (1992-2003), the success of an information system (IS) deployment is conditioned by the intention to use, the use and satisfaction of its users, which are conditioned by the quality of information, system and service. (Figure 4)

Figure 2. Technology acceptance models (TAM, TAM 2 vs. TAM 3)

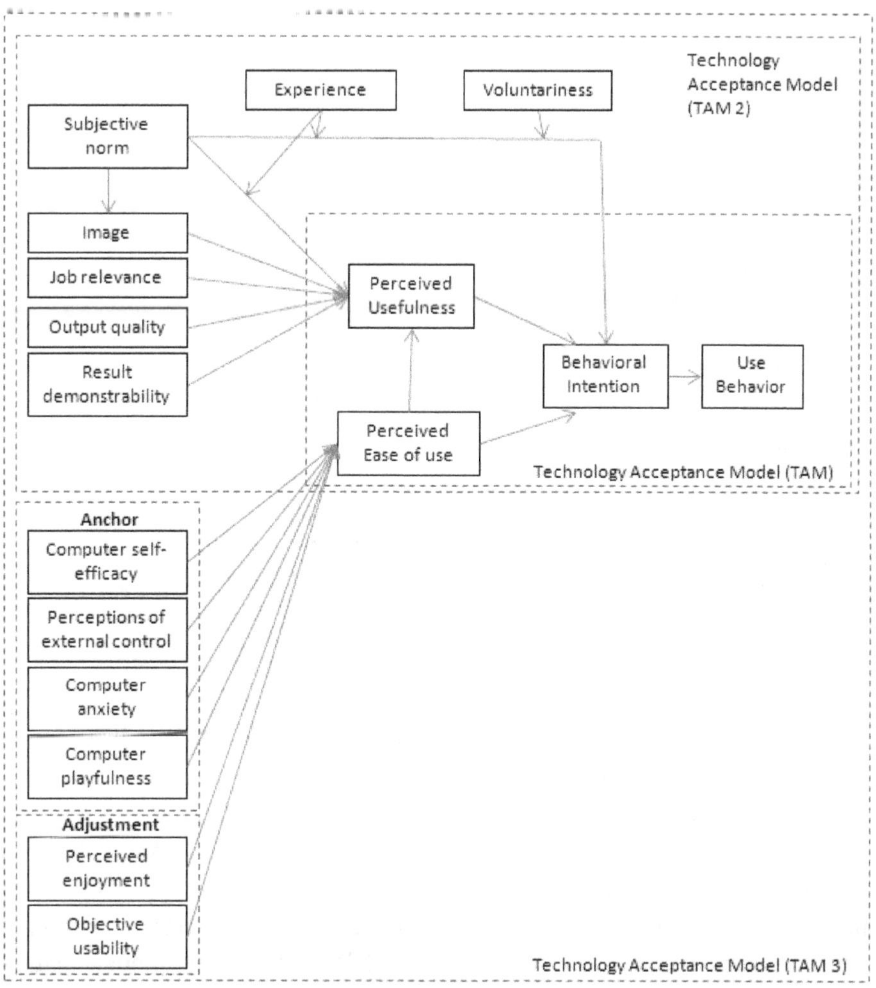

Figure 3. Unified theory of acceptance and use of technology (UTAUT 2 vs. UTAUT)

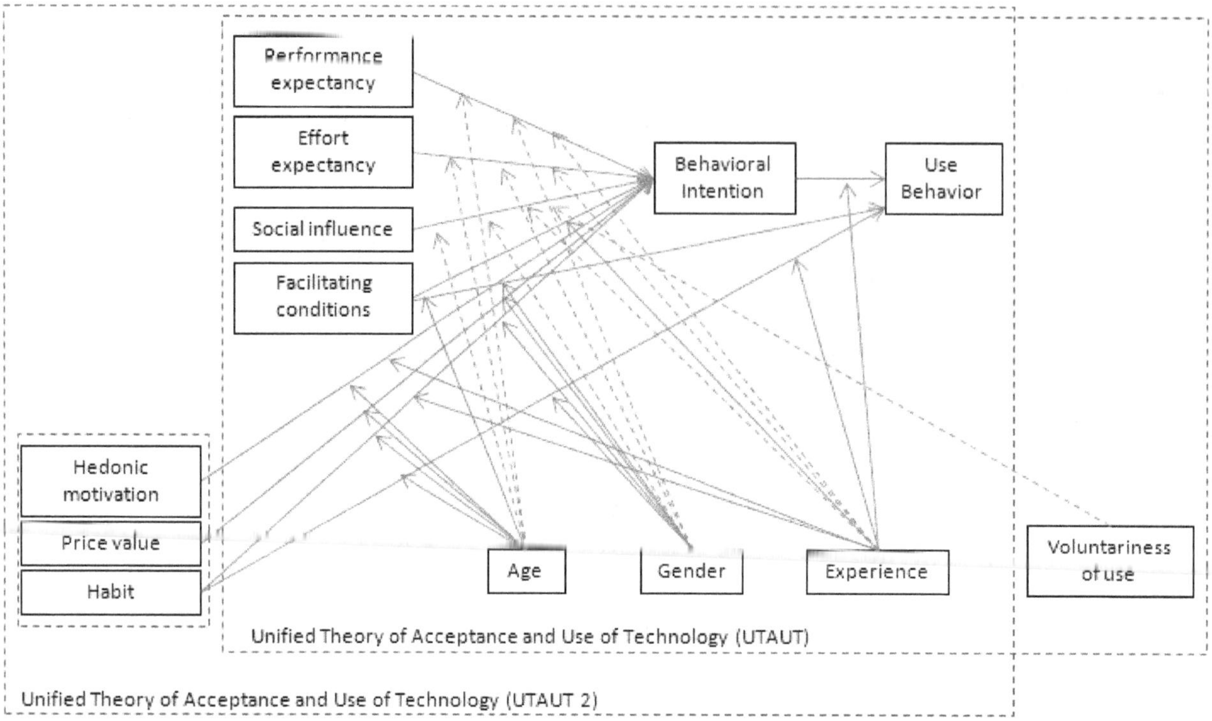

Figure 4. Model of Information Systems Success (DeLone and McLean, 2003)

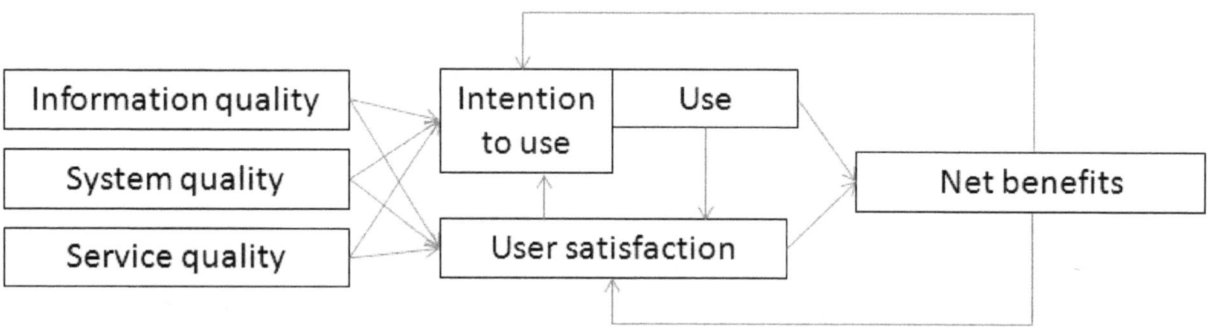

This chapter does not detail these models that are sources of inspiration to interpret the results of this exploratory study for explaining the acceptance and adoption of SN applications within a corporate environment by generation Y. This study comes as a prior step before a future quantitative confirmatory research.

RESEARCH METHOD

In order to address the aforementioned research gap, we carried out a qualitative exploratory study based on a Delphi approach, enriched by the use of the think Lets-based modeling (Briggs et al., 2003). Twenty four graduate management students (from the generation Y) from a French business school participated an electronic brainstorming around one main question: what do you think about Enterprise 2.0 through the use of SN applications within a corporate environment?, and five sub-questions:

- To what extent could CSN applications be used?
- What are benefits in the use of CSN applications compared to businesses and compared to you?
- What are the dos and don'ts to make their deployment successful?
- How you should use them (dos and don'ts)?
- How managers should use them (dos and don'ts)?

Delphi studies are regularly used in Information Systems studies when a consensus needs to be achieved among domain experts on a topic where idea generation is required (Keil et al., 2002). While Delphi studies are normally survey-based (Schmidt et al., 2001), we used a GSS and a well-structured facilitation process based on the use of thinkLets (Briggs et al., 2003). GSS is a suite of software tools designed to support collective problem solving, including the generation of ideas, reducing, organizing, and evaluating idea sets (Fjermestad and Hiltz, 1999). ThinkLets are pre-packaged thinking activities (facilitation techniques) that create predictable, repeatable patterns of collaboration among people working toward a goal. They facilitate information emergence and sharing among participants and assist the facilitators in controlling the reflection process to converge on relevant proposals. They are used to streamline collaboration during brainstorming sessions, rapid decision-making, creativity … (Vreede et al., 2009). Each participant in a GSS session uses a computer to submit ideas and votes to the group, to make selections, to organize ideas, or to write draft texts. Using GSS, all participants can contribute simultaneously, and may generate and evaluate ideas anonymously, while participating in well-structured deliberation processes (Briggs et al., 2003). The use of a GSS allowed us to collect extensive and well organized group collaboration results. It also served for the development of a synthesis report summarizing the results of the process.

The Participants

In June 2012, students of a GSS course (the objective of the course is to learn how to use a GSS (a technology for supporting group work) in order to run electronic brainstorming and solve problem collectively) were invited to participate in a study at the author's business school. In order to motivate them, students who volunteered to participate in the study received an extra credit. They were asked to answer the above questions through an

Table 1. Delphi study participant demographic data

Study data
• Total of participants: 24 • Nationality: 19 French, 3 Tunisian, 1 Senegalese, 1 Chinese • Educational background: all participants are Management Graduate students
• Youngest participant in Age: 20
• Oldest participant in Age: 23 • Age average: 21
• Males: 13
• Females: 11
• Business experience: at least a 6 months internship

electronic brainstorming. Demographics of the study participants are provided in Table 1.

The Brainstorming Process

The brainstorming process consisted of several activities in which the participants were asked to engage during a 180 minute period followed by 90 minute open discussion. A summarized agenda and research process follows:

- After an introductory presentation by the facilitator on Enterprise 2.0 and CSN applications in particular, and the scope of the brainstorming, participants were asked to anonymously generate ideas around the main question and five sub questions (40 minutes).
- Participants were then assigned to six subgroups and asked to reduce, clarify and organize collectively generated ideas into unique statements around one of the six questions (40 minutes). The goal was to converge on similar ideas, remove non-related ones, and reword those insufficiently clear. For the main general question and first sub question, statements have to be ordered in one list. For the second sub question, statements have to be classified around two themes: benefits compared to businesses and benefits compared to the generation Y. For the three other sub questions, statements have to be classified in terms of dos and don'ts.
- Participants then rejoined as a single group. Each subgroup presented and explained to the group which statements were selected for their respective question (40 minutes).
- Participants were then asked to individually and anonymously rate the relevance of each statement on a 5-point Likert-type scale, with '5' representing a very relevant statement and '1' a least relevant statement relating to each of the questions (20 minutes).
- The voting scores were then presented to all participants in a raw format to stimulate a discussion of the results (statement by statement), and to allow the reformulation of statements when necessary, to clarify ratings' standard deviations and so to build a collective consensus (40 minutes).

To end the brainstorming, we conducted after a 15 minute break an open discussion for 90 minutes with participants about the brainstorming results. We aimed to deepen understanding on how to make the deployment of CSN applications successful according to them. A list of guidelines was generated to favor the best adoption of these applications and make their usage effective.

Moreover, a research assistant audio recorded all the session and made field notes about oral statements during the meeting. In addition, participants recorded their key contributions on Post-it notes, and gave them to the research team at the end of the session. The facilitator made also field notes immediately following each step of the process.

RESULTS

To the main question, "what do you think about Enterprise 2.0 through the use of SN applications within a corporate environment?", participants made several statements. Here, in a decreasing order, quotes which had the higher votes (greater Mean and smaller Standard Deviation):

- "I don't want to have my colleagues among my friends' contacts." This confirms that they are aware of the need to separate between business and private spheres, contrary to the preconceived schemes advanced in the literature.
- "I'm afraid to speak freely thorny issues within a corporate environment, unless it

is anonymous." This means that they are afraid about what they could say on a network or blog informally be used against them later by the enterprise. To ensure the freedom of expression, they suggest that the communication would be anonymous on critical subjects. It would be here a form of self-censorship that is contrary to their supposed culture 2.0.

- "My private social network is sufficient for me." This is similar to say that the CSN applications would not necessarily be of a great contribution to their professional activities. An assertion contrary to an almost obviousness for managers.
- "I'm afraid of opinion-based discrimination." There is here distrust toward the enterprise and managers expressed by this generation. They think that spontaneity sometimes could be a disadvantage.
- "I want to be trained first and know the usage charter." Here, this generation does not feel well prepared/trained to use these applications in a professional setting. She therefore requires training and to know the terms of the usage charter. She believes that this latter should exist to frame well this professional use.
- "I want to use my personal PC / mobile device and own tools." Here, the interest in the BYOD and BYOA are confirmed. We can interpret that by its practical side (keeping the same device and application for both business and private uses) and/or the mistrust in enterprise side (tracking/control that the enterprise could do).
- "I use them [CSN applications] if I see a benefit or personal value." This statement shows the pragmatism (realism) of this generation in its continuous search for sense-making and recognition.

To the sub question 1, "To what extent could CSN applications be used?" participants made several statements. 8 statements in an ordered list have been elicited and consolidated. Table 2 summarizes the statements deemed most relevant by participants.

The Cronbach's alpha (α) for this question equals 0.88 (> 0.7), indicating a certain homogeneity in the participants' responses relative to the understanding of these statements – this is the same for all the other questions.

To the sub question 2, "What are the benefits in the use of CSN applications compared to businesses and compared to you?", participants made several statements. 8 statements for each theme have been elicited and consolidated. Table 3 summarizes the statements deemed most relevant by participants. These statements generally show that this generation is very well aware of the benefit of using CSN applications. Some statements are personal benefit oriented beyond their usefulness for performing the professional activity.

To the sub question 3, "What are the dos and don'ts to make their deployment successful?",

Table 2. Main usage of CSN applications (α=0.88)

1. Connection 2. Social awareness 3. Information and knowledge sharing
4. Forming or participating (to) groups
5. Reputation and self-advertising
6. Recruitment
7. Daily spontaneous reporting 8. Crowdsourcing: collaboration and problem solving

Table 3. Benefits from the CSN applications' usage (α=0.94)

Benefits Compared to Businesses
1. Give a better outside image
2. Surf on a new fashion: advertising and display
3. Communicate better on its objectives, products and services
4. Disseminate internally information content
5. Distribute job offers and recruit
6. Provoke Buzz around activities
7. Stimulate open innovation among coworkers
8. Promote cohesion between coworkers and integrate better new employees
Benefits Compared to Generation Y
1. Give a better self-image and valorize his/her skills
2. Find a job or new mission internally
3. Increase his/her employability and mobility
4. Get help to solve problems faster
5. Be well informed about what happen inside the enterprise in Pull mode (through a wall of activity monitoring)
6. Build a own professional network
7. Know more about coworkers (skills, activities, etc)
8. Co-create value

Table 4. Business usage (α=0.89)

Dos
1. Ensure data security and compliance with privacy
2. Allow creating extra-professional groups and keep them informal
3. Create an internal reputation index (e.g. R-index) and an endorsement system
4. Make of CSNs instruments for a participative management (debates, referenda, contests, voting…)
5. Create a mentoring system for new employees
6. Provide multi devices applications with the same quality as those used in the private sphere (e.g. Facebook, MySpace)
7. Associate a skills search engine
Don'ts
1. Control abusively their usage with deep statistics
2. Emerge a false spontaneity (self censorship, continuous picture control, fear to open up, fear to be judged)
3. Information overload (too much shared information)
4. Provide less interesting content
5. No animation of communities (no community management)
6. Keep tracking usage and analyze it without the knowledge of workers
7. Do not provide a rewarding system

participants made several statements. 7 statements for each theme have been elicited and consolidated. Table 4 summarizes the statements considered as the most relevant according to the participants. These statements show to which extent this generation gives importance for a good management of these applications. For them, they should remain informal social spaces rather than controlled ones.

To the sub question 4, "How you should use them (dos and don'ts)?", participants made several statements. 5 statements for each theme have been elicited and consolidated. Table 5 summarizes the statements considered as the most relevant according to the participants. These statements show at somewhat a lack of spontaneity (for not saying a simulation) and a lot of prudence in their use.

To the sub question 5, "How managers should use them (dos and don'ts)?", participants made several statements. 6 statements for each theme have been elicited and consolidated. Table 6 summarizes the statements considered as the most relevant according to the participants. These statements show a strong need for recognition and rewarding expressed by this generation. She is also very aware of the limitations of the usage of CSN applications.

DISCUSSION AND IMPLICATIONS

The findings of this exploratory study go up a gap between what they declared during the brainstorming and stereotypes commonly relayed on their technology usage in the academic and managerial literature (self-care, confusion of private and professional spheres, easy technology adoption, strong technical skills and less need for training being instinctive). These findings cast doubt compared to their adoption and waited potential in the diffusion of Enterprise 2.0 (particularly here CSN applications) within businesses.

In summary, key findings of this study show that:

- People from the generation Y are prudent with regard to their CSN use in a corporate environment, and suspicious about the real managerial intentions.
- They consider that socialization between coworkers must remain out of the hierarchical control.
- Private data protection is becoming a big priority for them.
- Security is briefly mentioned without insistence. It seems obvious for them to trust businesses with regard to their IS.
- The quality of the used technologies should be enough good for motivating their usage.
- They are not specially prepared for the CSN use, and their private use of social

Table 5. Generation Y usage (α=0.93)

Dos
1. Do not associate the professional profile to the private one
2. Fill well his/her professional profile (skills, experience, interests…)
3. Get noticed by the hierarchy and other employees: having followers
4. Choose the right interest groups and communities
5. Remain always professional in his/her communication (talk)
Don'ts
1. Talk about confidential things and customers
2. Disparage the enterprise, his/her manager/business unit, colleagues, client or future internal employer
3. Use the same SN application than in private arena
4. Share compromising content (photos, videos…)
5. Confuse the professional space with the private one

Table 6. Manager usage (α=0.85)

Dos
1. Shorten the hierarchical distance (direct access, more trust, more empowerment, more democracy)
2. Encourage and reward collaborators
3. Provide a transversal competence
4. Animate without imposing the participation
5. Know how to interest others
6. Lead by the example
Don'ts
1. Think only of profitability and amortization (the yield)
2. Control abusively the participation of collaborators
3. Use it to assess their skills
4. Observe without participating
5. Compel people to use it
6. Do not predict time for collaborators for that use

media is not a guarantee for an optimized professional use. They hope that others stop thinking that all of them are geeks.

- Their interest in CSN is individualistic and mostly opportunistic: building their professional network, taking care of their reputation, being recognized, increasing their employability, finding new opportunities of mobility, etc.

Through all results of this study, we find almost all the functional building blocks of the honeycomb framework of social media cited above (see Figure 1).

When we consider the technology acceptance and adoption research models (cited above i.e. TAM, UTAUT…) in this study, several variables explaining the intention of the generation Y to use CSN applications are addressed such as:

1. The perceived ease of use is cited when this generation claims for a prior training and a clear usage charter;
2. The perceived usefulness seems more related to the personal benefit rather than the execution of the professional activity;
3. The motivation and habit are mentioned when they insist on the quality of the technology since they are already very familiar with good quality technology in terms of HCI and features (e.g. authoring, tagging, sharing, connecting, voting, rating, commenting, etc);
4. The voluntariness of use is suggested by not to compel people to use these applications;
5. The effort expectancy is mentioned through the time prediction for collaborators to use these applications;
6. The experience seems essential since this generation ask for creating a mentoring system for new employees;
7. The image is mentioned several times through statements both for business and for users. For generation Y, that use could help for a better self-image and valorizing his/her skills;
8. The computer self-efficacy refers to a person judgment about his/her ability to use technology. Here generation Y assumes a need of a prior training since its private use of social media is not a guarantee for an optimized professional use.

However, if we consider the DeLone and McLean' model of IS success (DeLone & McLean, 1992-2003) (here the CSN applications deployment and use) only the open discussion was useful to get more statements and correlates to explain the intention to use the CSN applications and the satisfaction of the generation Y related to the quality of information (participants cited e.g. availability, accuracy, reliability, relevance, updatedness…), quality of system (i.e. the CSN applications should of a good quality in terms of HCI and features, participants cited e.g. compliance with standards, customization, user friendly, awareness, VoIP availability…) and quality of service (participants cited e.g. speed, bugs free, accessibility, interoperability with other applications and devices (mobile ones), technical support…).

In addition, a list of five guidelines, to favor the best adoption of these applications and make their usage effective, was formulated from this open discussion through the participants' statements:

1. Making users aware of benefits of these applications by using good internal communication.
2. Forecasting an action plan for change management including training of users and using companionship techniques.
3. Establishing a charter regulating the use of these applications.
4. Identifying champions to manage "formally" and sustain the use of these applications.
5. Creating a system of rewarding and recognition to motivate participation and contribution.

CONCLUSION AND PERSPECTIVES

In this chapter, we report on an exploratory study to understand how generation Y perceives CSN applications usage. It was based on qualitative approach and discussed important adoption issues to consider when implementing and using CSN applications within a corporate environment.

Despite being exploratory, the results of this study brought important insights toward answering the addressed research questions. They enabled us to provide important expectations and precautions to take into account by stakeholders for a best use, compared to users, managers and the enterprise at whole according to a set of young people from the generation Y.

Our contribution is both theoretical and practical as we propose an empirical evidence to explain the acceptance and adoption of CSN applications. The results should be of interest to academic researchers in the MIS area, and practitioners interested in CSN applications deployment and usage. The research contributes to collaboration processes and technology, social networks and online communities' literature, theory and practice through the development of first guidelines to favor the best adoption of these applications and make their usage effective. From a practical viewpoint, these findings suggested by this study may be useful to predict and explain variations in the attitudes and actions of people from the generation Y toward using CSN applications in terms of motivation, engagement, quality and continuance use. From a research viewpoint, this could justify the application of one of the adoption models or the building of a new research model related to that specific issue to provide evidence of proof of value and proof of use in the field.

Practitioners and researchers, however, should interpret these findings with caution, and regard this study as preliminary, rather than definitive. In fact, there are some limitations related to this work. First, the study is limited by the amount of knowledge the author has access to in terms of managerial literature. There are possibly other initiatives and case studies that can be related to issues discussed in this chapter. The second limitation concerns possible bias in the sampling method. Our analysis is based on a set of statements considered as relevant by a small – although significant – sample of students but not practitioners. The composition of this sample, in terms of users' knowledge and usage of SN applications, depends directly on the group of participants. Furthermore, the elicited statements resulted from only one group of students in a particular cultural context (participants have the same educational background and are mostly French by birth [79.16%]).

Further field studies and explorations are required in other settings and cultural contexts to validate and expand the findings. In the near future, a quantitative research using structural equation modeling (SEM) will be launched to analyze this social phenomenon by the theory and validate the correlation between some acceptance variables. The research model will be based on the previous technology acceptance/adoption models and theories.

In conclusion, this study could inspire other researchers in assessing new initiatives in the social web era such as through open sourcing or crowdsourcing online (open) communities.

REFERENCES

AIIM. (2009). *Collaboration and enterprise 2.0 - Work-meets-play or the future of business?* Retrieved from http://www.aiim.org/research/collaboration-enterprise20-research.aspx

Ajzen, I. (1991). The theory of planned behaviour. *Organizational Behavior and Human Decision Processes*, *50*(2), 179–211. doi:10.1016/0749-5978(91)90020-T

Anderson, P. (2007). What is web 2.0? Ideas, technologies and implications for education. *JISC Technology and Standards Watch*, *60*(1), 64.

Ballagas, R., Rohs, M., Sheridan, J. G., & Borchers, J. (2004). BYOD: Bring Your Own Device. Paper presented at the UbiComp 2004 Workshop, Sixth International Conference on Ubiquitous Computing. Nottingham, UK.

Bitner, M., Ostrom, A., Meuter, M., & Clancy, A. (2002). Implementing successful self-service technologies. *Academy of Management Journal*, *16*(4).

Bock, G.-O., Zmud, R. W., Kim, Y.-G., & Lee, J.-N. (2005). Behavioral intention formation in knowledge sharing: Examining the roles of extrinsic motivators, social-psychological factors and organizational climate. *Management Information Systems (MIS). Quarterly*, *29*(1), 87–111.

Boughzala, I. (2007). *Ingénierie de la collaboration: Théories, technologies et pratiques*. Paris, France: Hermès - Lavoisier.

Boughzala, I. (2010). *Mise en perspective de l'e-collaboration comme outil de transformation de l'organisation*. HDR Sciences de Gestion, Université de Nantes.

Boughzala, I. (2011). Collaboration 2.0 through the new organization transformation. In *Knowledge Management 2.0: Organizational Models and Enterprise Strategies*. Hershey, PA: IGI Global. doi:10.4018/978-1-61350-195-5.ch001

Boughzala, I. (2012). *Collaboration engineering: A contribution to its foundations through the 2.0 era*. Saarbrücken, Germany: Lambert Academic Publishing.

Boughzala, I., & Briggs, R. O. (2012). A value frequency model of knowledge sharing: An exploratory study on knowledge sharability in cross-organizational collaboration. *Electronic Markets*, *22*(1), 9–19. doi:10.1007/s12525-011-0080-0

Boughzala, I., & Limayem, M. (2010). The new generation of Knowledge Management for the Web 2.0 Age: KM 2.0. In *Encyclopedia of E-Business Development and Management in the Digital Economy*. Hershey, PA: IGI Global. doi:10.4018/978-1-61520-611-7.ch122

Boyd, D., & Ellison, N. (2007). Social network sites: Definition, history, and scholarship. *Journal of Computer-Mediated Communication, 13*(1), 210–230. doi:10.1111/j.1083-6101.2007.00393.x

Bresman, H., Birkenshaw, J., & Nobel, R. (1999). Knowledge transfer in international acquisitions. *Journal of International Business Studies, 30*(3), 439–462. doi:10.1057/palgrave.jibs.8490078

Briggs, R. O., de Vreede, G. J., & Nunamaker, J. F. Jr. (2003). Collaboration Engineering with ThinkLets to Pursue Sustained Success with Group Support Systems. *Journal of Management Information Systems, 19*(4), 31–64.

Broadbridge, A., Maxwell, G., & Ogden, S. (2009). Selling Retailing to Generation Y Graduates: Recruitment Challenges and Opportunities. *International Review of Retail, Distribution and Consumer Research, 19*(4), 405–420. doi:10.1080/09593960903331394

Chesbrough, H. W., & Appleyard, M. M. (2007). Open innovation and strategy. *California Management Review, 50*(1), 57–77. doi:10.2307/41166416

Coleman, D., & Levine, S. (2008). *Collaboration 2.0: Technology and best practices for successful collaboration in a web 2.0 world*. Happy About.

Constant, D., Keisler, S., & Sproull, L. (1994). What's mine is ours, or is it? A study of attitudes about information sharing. *Information Systems Research (Informs), 5*(4), 400–421. doi:10.1287/isre.5.4.400

Consulting, F. (2006). *Is Europe Ready for the Millennials? Innovate to meet the needs of the emerging generation*. Retrieved from http://www.ffpress.net/Kunden/XER/Downloads/XER87000/XER87000.pdf

Cramton, C. D. (2001). The mutual knowledge problem and its consequences for dispersed collaboration. *Organization Science, 12*(3), 346–371. doi:10.1287/orsc.12.3.346.10098

Crumpacker, M., & Crumpacker, J. (2007). Succession planning and generational stereotypes: Should HR consider age-based values and attitudes a relevant factor or a passing fad? *Public Personnel Management, 36*(4), 349–369.

Cummings, J. (2003). *Knowledge sharing: A review of the literature*. Washington, DC: World Bank Operations Evaluation Department. Retrieved from http://ieg.worldbankgroup.org/Data/reports/knowledge_eval_literature_review.pdf

Davenport, T. H., & Prusak, L. (1998). *Working knowledge: How organizations manage what they know*. Harvard Business School Press.

Davis, F. (1989). Perceived usefulness, perceived ease of use and user acceptance of information technology. *Management Information Systems Quarterly, 13*(3), 318–340. doi:10.2307/249008

de Vreede, G. J., Briggs, R., & Massey, A. (2009). Collaboration Engineering: Foundations and Opportunities. *Journal of the Association for Information Systems, 10*(3), 121–137.

Deal, J., Altman, J., David, G., & Rogelberg, S. (2010). Millennials at work: What we know and what we need to do (if anything). *Journal of Business and Psychology, 25*(2), 191–199. doi:10.1007/s10869-010-9177-2

DeLone, W. H., & MacLean, E. R. (1992). Information systems success: The quest for the dependent variable. *Information Systems Research, 3*(1), 60–95. doi:10.1287/isre.3.1.60

DeLone, W. H., & McLean, E. R. (2003). The DeLone and McLean model of information systems success: A ten-year update. *Journal of Management Information Systems, 19*(4), 9–30.

Dudezert, A., Boughzala, I., & Mounoud, E. (2009). *Comment intégrer la génération Millennials à l'entreprise? Management: Enjeux de demain* (pp. 323–334). Paris: Vuibert.

Editorial, A. (1993). Adverting Age. *Midwest Region*, *64*(36), 16.

Fishbein, M., & Ajzen, I. (1975). *Belief, attitude, intention and behavior: An introduction to theory and research*. Reading, MA: Addison-Wesley.

Fjermestad, J., & Hiltz, S. R. (1999). An assessment of group support systems experimental research: Methodology and results. *Journal of Management Information Systems*, *15*(3), 7–150.

Gorman, P., Nelson, T., & Glassman, A. (2004). The millenial generation: A strategic opportunity. *Organizational Analysis*, *12*(3), 255–270.

Grady, B. (2008). *Corporate America embraces social networking*. Information and Learning Company.

Gunnarsson, M. (2012). *BYOB (Bring Your Own Behavior) is a Driving Factor in the Adoption of Enterprise Mobility Applications*. Retrieved from http://blogs.ifsworld.com/2012/10/byob-bring-your-own-behavior-is-a-driving-factor-in-the-adoption-of-enterprise-mobility-applications/

Hershatter, A., & Epstein, M. (2010). Millennials and the world of work: An organization and management perspective. *Journal of Business and Psychology*, *25*(2), 211–223. doi:10.1007/s10869-010-9160-y

Howe, J. (2006). The rise of crowdsourcing: A definition. *Wired, 14*.

Kaplan, A. M., & Haenlein, M. (2010). Users of the world, unite! The challenges and opportunities of Social Media. *Business Horizons*, *53*(1), 59–68. doi:10.1016/j.bushor.2009.09.003

Keil, M., Tiwana, A., & Bush, A. (2002). Reconciling user and project manager perceptions of IT project risk: A Delphi study. *Information Systems Journal*, *12*(2), 103–119. doi:10.1046/j.1365-2575.2002.00121.x

Kietzmann, J. H., Hermkens, K., McCarthy, I. P., & Silvestre, B. S. (2011). Social Media? Get Serious! Understanding the functional building blocks of Social Media. *Business Horizons*, *54*(3), 241–251. doi:10.1016/j.bushor.2011.01.005

Kim, W., Jeong, O.-R., & Lee, S.-W. (2010). On social websites. *Information Systems Journal*, *35*(2), 215–236. doi:10.1016/j.is.2009.08.003

Kowske, B., Rasch, R., & Wiley, J. (2010). Millennials' (lack of) attitude problem: An empirical examination of generational effects on work attitudes. *Journal of Business and Psychology*, *25*(2), 265–279. doi:10.1007/s10869-010-9171-8

Malone, T. W., Laubacher, R., & Dellarocas, C. (2009). *Harnessing crowds: Mapping the genome of collective intelligence* (Working Paper No. 2009-001). MIT Center for Collective Intelligence.

McAfee, A. P. (2006). Enterprise 2.0: The Dawn of Emergent Collaboration. *Sloan Management Review*, *47*(3), 21–28.

O'Reilly, T. (2005). *What Is Web 2.0 Design Patterns and Business Models for the Next Generation of Software*. Retrieved from http://oreilly.com/web2/archive/what-is-web-20.html

Parasuraman, A. (2000). Technology Readiness Index (TRI), a multiple-item scale to measure readiness to embrace new technologies. *Journal of Service Research*, *2*(4), 307–320. doi:10.1177/109467050024001

Rheingold, H. (1993). *The virtual community: Homesteading on the electronic frontier*. Reading, MA: Addison-Wesley.

Richter, A., & Koch, M. (2008). Functions on Social Networking Services. In Proceedings of 8th International Conference on the Design of Cooperative Systems. Academic Press.

Richter, A., & Riemer, K. (2009). Corporate Social Networking Sites – Modes of Use and Appropriation through Co-Evolution. Paper presented at the 20th Australasian Conference on Information Systems. Melbourne, Australia.

Schmidt, R., Lyytinen, K., Keil, M., & Cule, P. (2001). Identifying software project risks: An international delphi study. *Journal of Management Information Systems*, *17*(4), 5–36.

SelectMinds. (2008). *Corporate Social Networking: SelectMinds Benchmarking Study*. Retrieved from www.selectminds.com

Sena, J., & Sena, M. (2008). Corporate social networking. *Issues in Information Systems*, *9*(2), 227–231.

Smith, J., & Duin, A. (1994). *Collective intelligence in computer-based collaboration*. L. Erlbaum Asso. Publishers.

Venkatesh, V., & Bala, H. (2008). Technology Acceptance Model 3 and a Research Agenda on Interventions. *Decision Sciences*, *39*(2), 273–315. doi:10.1111/j.1540-5915.2008.00192.x

Venkatesh, V., & Davis, F. D. (2000). A Theoretical Extension of the Technology Acceptance Model: Four Longitudinal Field Studies. *Management Science*, *46*(2), 186–204. doi:10.1287/mnsc.46.2.186.11926

Venkatesh, V., Morris, M. G., Davis, G. B., & Davis, F. D. (2003). User Acceptance of Information Technology: Toward a unified view. *Management Information Systems (MIS). Quarterly*, *27*(3), 425–478.

Venkatesh, V., Thong, J. Y. L., & Xu, X. (2012). Consumer acceptance and use of information technology: Extending the unified theory of acceptance and use of technology. *Management Information Systems (MIS). Quarterly*, *36*(1), 157–178.

KEY TERMS AND DEFINITIONS

Collective Intelligence: Refers to knowledge created from human interactions and interpersonal networking.

Corporate Social Networking: The use of social networking applications at the corporate level.

Enterprise 2.0 or Enterprise Social Software: The use of Web 2.0, emergent social software platforms within companies, or between companies and their partners or customers.

Generation Y: A new generation of younger, college- and university-educated workers born between 1980 and 2000 and grown up with the Internet, also known as Gen Y, Yers, Digital Natives, Net Generation or Millennials.

Online Community: A virtual community that exists online and whose members enable its existence through taking part in membership ritual.

Social Network: A social structure made up of a set of social actors (such as individuals or organizations) and a complex set of the dyadic ties between these actors.

Technology Adoption: To which extent an organization adopts a new technology and to which extent users are willing to accept using a new technology.

Web 2.0: The second generation of web development and design based on social software – also called Social Media.

Chapter 10
Social Media Opportunities for Market-Driven Firms

Elisa Arrigo
University of Milan – Bicocca, Italy

ABSTRACT

The emergence of social media has provided a new and essential way to reach customers. In fact, in many industries, more and more firms are seeking to approach social media for business purposes; thus, it becomes essential to understand how social platforms can be managed for corporate decision-making. The aim of this chapter is to give a better understanding of social media in the strategic management field; no study to date has examined the role of social media in market-driven firms. In particular, a novel conceptual framework is proposed to show how the integrated management of social media provides several opportunities to market-driven firms. First of all, social media enables market-driven firms to acquire data and information that is useful for monitoring the competitive environment. In addition, social media allows firms to develop greater customer knowledge and to improve customer relationships by attracting new customers and by engaging old ones.

INTRODUCTION

The advent of social media, "a group of internet-based applications that build on the ideological and technological foundations of Web 2.0 and that allow the creation and exchange of User Generated Content" (Kaplan & Haenlein, 2010, p. 61), has produced new ways to communicate, collaborate and share contents. Social media have been adopted by many firms using them to interact with customers everywhere on the global market. In fact, the accelerating complexity of demand and the increasing competitive rivalry have induced many firms to compete on a global landscape; and the advent of Internet and digital technologies (Chaffrey *et al.*, 2009) have assumed an important role in developing a worldwide presence.

Today every firm, regardless of its geographic location, operates in a dynamic and changing environment and only the firms that are able to quickly recognize the events impacting their business can successfully survive in this kind of competitive arena (Brondoni, 2012).

Market-Driven Management (Ohmae, 1990; Day, 1990, 1999; Narver & Slater, 1990; Kohli & Jaworski, 1990; Webster, 1994; Best, 2009;

DOI: 10.4018/978-1-4666-6182-0.ch010

Lambin, 2007) has emerged as one of the best strategic approaches for competing in current hyper-competitive markets. It is a business philosophy with the main purpose of creating superior customer value in direct and continuous confrontation with the competitors (Brondoni, 2009). In fact, the value perceived by customers of each firm's offer must be higher, compared to that of competitors' goods; thus, market-driven firms are involved in continual processes of identification of market changes, which could translate into customer value determinants.

In this context, social media can be very useful for firms. First of all, they can serve as an important inbound marketing channel, by influencing potential customers and empowering past customers to share their experiences (Ang, 2011; Laroche *et al.*, 2013; Sashi, 2012; Stone *et al.*, 2013). Secondly, social media allow for a wide variety of activities, including global information access, discussion groups and file transfer facilities, all of which impact business strategies (Kietzmann *et al.*, 2011; Fill, 2009; Chaffrey *et al.*, 2009; DiStaso *et al.*, 2012; Vuori *et al.*, 2012).

The purpose of this theoretical chapter, primarily based on the literature review, is to examine the role of social media in improving market-driven firms' competitiveness by attracting new customers, by communicating to a global audience and by monitoring competitor strategies. In fact, despite the growing popularity of social media in the academic literature, there is a relative lack of research on the benefits provided by social media management to the firms that adopt a strategic market orientation. We want to fill this gap by proposing a novel conceptual framework of analysis of social media opportunities for market-driven firms.

The chapter is structured as follows: after the introduction, section 2 analyzes the theoretical background on market-driven management and social media; section 3 describes the proposed framework on the opportunities of social media management for market-driven firms; section 4 provides future research directions; and finally, section 5 draws conclusions with managerial implications.

BACKGROUND

Market-Driven Management Literature Review

The academic literature on Market-Driven Management has grown rapidly in the last few years. Peter Drucker (1954) is considered one of the precursors of the concept of "*market orientation*" because he affirmed that the purpose of a business is to create a satisfied customer and the customer is still considered the core-focus of every market-driven firm (Best, 2009). However, the two papers that build the foundation of market orientation and constitute the basis of the following research studies are surely the papers of Kohli and Jaworski and Narver and Slater, both published in 1990.

According to Narver and Slater (1990), market-driven management has two core components: customer orientation and competitor orientation. To create superior customer value continuously, the former emphasizes the activity of analyzing and understanding target customers, and the latter focuses on the monitoring and examination of strengths and weaknesses of rivals. Moreover, an inter-functional coordination optimizes the acquisition of information about customers and rivals and coordinates the use of corporate resources and activities of the entire organization.

The management of information is of crucial relevance for market-driven firms and, in fact, Kohli and Jaworski (1990) define a market orientation as the firm's ability to generate, disseminate and use superior information about its customers and competitors. The key corporate processes of this approach are: the market intelligence mechanisms and the continuous dissemination of the collected data; their examination and processing; and finally, the appropriate and anticipated satisfaction of the market's needs.

A market orientation fosters the collection of data regarding customers, competitors and environmental trends. However, it is not simply a question of collecting a great deal of information, but of generating new knowledge and innovation through interaction with other players on the market. Consequently, the information acquired from the market acts as a platform that can generate future activities only if the firm develops mechanisms of learning. These latter simplify the acquisition, interpretation and incorporation of the knowledge generated in the corporate procedures (Baker & Sinkula, 1999).

As argued by Baker and Sinkula (2002), a learning orientation derives from the presence of values in the corporate culture that push the market-driven firm to proactively strive to acquire new knowledge. The marketing information processing activities are based also on the firm's degree of market orientation: the more a firm focuses on studying its competitors and customers, the greater its tendency to process a wealth of information will be.

Besides the ability to generate, disseminate and use superior information about customers and competitors, market-driven firms are characterized by a set of cultural values and beliefs that put customers' requests first (Deshpandé & Webster, 1989).

Notably, Best (2009) states that a market orientation is achievable through a corporate culture focused on the customers and the competitive scenario. In addition, market-driven management requires a reorganization of the firm around markets rather than around products and the definition of new performance metrics that can assess the market-driven strategies.

Lambin (2007) also recognizes the importance of the corporate culture, defining the market orientation as the business philosophy involving all levels within the organization and all participants in the market (customers, competitors, distributors, prescribers and the macro-marketing environment). In particular, for Lambin, market-driven management represents the fourth stage of the evolution of the marketing concept oriented to the corporate culture. It follows: the "*passive marketing*" (oriented to the product); the "*operational marketing*" (oriented to the sales); and the "*strategic marketing*" (oriented to the analysis of the customer). The cultural dimension is therefore emphasized in market-driven firms that, consequently, collect information about the expectations and the needs of all the participants in the market and utilize it to plan their strategies.

Hence, a market-driven firm becomes part of a system of corporate relations that provides better access to information about all the players on the competitive scene (Arrigo, 2009). In this way, according to Day (1990), market-driven firms build a greater ability to sense environmental trends in advance with respect to their competitors. As a result, they can more accurately formulate the strategies to win rivals and to satisfy customers.

Market-driven firms are also able to create strong relationships with market actors, first of all, the customers. In fact, they develop particular capabilities (Teece, 2009) to accomplish various functions: sensing opportunities or threats from environmental trends; responding to the modifications in the competitive scenario by combining resources in a different way or acquiring new ones from the outside; and choosing the best internal configuration in order to deliver the greatest customer value.

However, few of these capabilities are *distinctive capabilities* that lead the firm to outperform the competition (Day, 1994). A distinctive capability, as illustrated by Tracey *et al.* (2005), is based on superiority in process management, diffusion of learning and knowledge management and provides a big contribution to the creation of greater customer value. Only if the distinctive capability is specific for one firm and cannot be easily imitated, easily transferred between firms or easily substituted for another capability, it becomes a source of competitive advantage.

Three main types of distinctive capabilities characterize market-driven firms: inside-out capabilities, outside-in capabilities and spanning capabilities. In particular, the *outside-in capabilities* relate the corporate strategies to the analysis and interpretation of the external environment as they are activated by customer needs, competitive challenges and external opportunities. Market-driven firms outclass the competitors in two distinctive outside-in capabilities that allow the anticipation and the rapid reconfiguration of corporate activities: the *market sensing capability* and the *customer linking capability*.

Through the "*market sensing capability*", firms learn about competitors and other key market players, aiming to recognize the environmental trends and to modify them. Instead the "*customer linking capability*" consists of the ability to create and manage collaborative relationships with customers. Thanks to these capabilities, market-driven firms are able to scan each zone or player of their market periphery (competitors, customers, intermediaries, retailers, influencers and the macro-environment trends). They do not simply react to the competitors' moves or to the customers' requests, but they anticipate them, employing an outside-in management (Arrigo, 2012).

The outside-in management results in better knowledge of the competitive environment and furthermore, it makes the periphery of the market less obscured (Saka-Helmhout, 2011). In this direction, the analysis of every signal from the markets, such as new offerings from competitors and new or latent needs of customers, becomes decisive for the corporate success; market-driven firms must develop new ways and procedures to control all signals. Social media can represent a powerful tool in this sense as we will describe in the following paragraphs.

Social Media Literature Review

The advent of interactive digital media has heavily modified the market structure. It has transformed the firm and consumer relationship from the traditional Web 1.0 to the new interactive Web 2.0 environment where customers have an active role sharing, creating, discussing and modifying contents (DesAutels, 2011).

Web 2.0 faces firms with new challenges and new opportunities for reaching and staying in contact with their markets, learning about the needs and opinions of their customers as well as interacting with them in a direct and personalised way. Web 2.0 refers to the collection of open-source, interactive and user controlled online applications that can help share the experiences, facts and opinions of the users as participants in business and social processes. In fact, Web 2.0 applications support the creation of informal users' networks that facilitate the flow of information and knowledge (Constantinides & Fountain, 2008, p. 233).

Social media are relatively new media formats and, as there are hundreds of different social media platforms, few accepted classifications exist to distinguish them. Kaplan and Haenlein (2010) have offered one of the first classifications of social media on the basis of two dimensions: social presence/media richness and self-presentation/self-disclosure. The first dimension is related to the media research field and refers to the degree of social presence and media richness, i.e. how much the communication between partners is influential and avoids ambiguity and uncertainty. Instead, the self-presentation/self-disclosure component is related to the field of social processes and depends on the extent of required self-disclosure and on the types of potential self-presentation.

On the basis of these two dimensions, social media can be differentiated in: blogs, social networking sites, virtual social worlds, collaborative projects, content communities, and virtual game worlds (Kaplan & Haenlein, 2010).

Blogs (or Web logs) are web pages usually managed by one person/user that provide interaction with others by adding comments or opinions. They are the most known and fastest-growing category of Web 2.0 applications and they are quite risky because customers can complain online about the company's products and damage the brand reputation.

Social networking sites are applications in which users create personal information profiles that are accessible to other users for the exchange of personal contents and communication. The most known social network is Facebook with millions of users worldwide. Often companies have their own pages and people can sign up to become a fan. It is an efficient way for firms to offer discounts and special promotions and to display ads.

In *virtual social worlds*, the users, in the form of avatars, choose how to behave in a virtual life, interacting freely with other avatars without restrictions. In virtual worlds firms can implement various marketing strategies related both to marketing communication and marketing research purposes. Second Life is the most famous virtual social world where users build content and sell it to others through Linden Dollars.

Collaborative projects enable the creation of particular types of content by many end-users. These applications are based on the idea that only the joint effort of many users could lead to the best outcome. An example of a collaborative project is Wikipedia, considered the first source of information by many users.

Content communities are applications based on media content sharing between users. They can contain videos (e.g. YouTube), photos (e.g. Instagram), texts, PowerPoint presentations (e.g. Slideshare) and their popularity makes them very attractive for firms that often build inside a company page.

At last, *virtual game worlds* are applications in which users appear as avatars and act according to specific game rules (e.g. *World of Warcraft*). From a company's perspective, they can be used for marketing communication campaigns through the placement of the product within the game.

In all these social media the participants (and specifically customers and firms) share information, insights and experiences. According to Miller *et al.* (2009), the relevance of social media lies exactly in the interaction between consumers and the community and in the immediate, interactive and low-cost communications.

Social applications enhance the power of online communities in many ways (Kane *et al.*, 2009). First of all, among users they promote deep relationships that are richer than in the past, since the communications are more frequent and intimate. Social media also enable to quickly mobilize the online community for a specific event; this is very helpful for firms that want to understand the customers' response to a specific promotion or deal. Moreover, within social media and especially in content communities and collaborative projects, the knowledge generated by members is aggregated into documents or web pages that are frequently updated and corrected by other members.

Since customers use social media to communicate with one another, these conversations can be seen as an extension of the traditional word of mouth communication, recognized by the customers as one of the most truthful forms of communication (Fill, 2009). In traditional marketing communication the firm controls the content, the timing and the frequency of the communication. Instead, in digital communication it is the customer that searches for information about the firm and its products and becomes himself a new source of opinions and conversations. Consequently, the customer is a vehicle of information and firms must engage him in order to successfully exploit the new forms of marketing communications.

More specifically, social media are considered a hybrid element of the promotion mix (Mangold & Faulds, 2009) because they join aspects of the traditional integrated communication mix (i.e. the communication from the firm towards its market), to a "highly magnified form of word-of-mouth" among customers whereby firms cannot manage either the content or the frequency of this communication.

From a firm's point of view, social media allow to obtain many benefits (Michaelidou *et al.*, 2011) besides building direct relationships with customers. In fact, through social media the firm can: increase the traffic toward a company website; recognize new business opportunities; deliver commercial and institutional contents; and collect feedback from customers.

Because of the multitude of social media and networks available, firms are now testing different applications in many social platforms. Weinberg and Pehlivan (2011) speak about the "*social media mix*" in order to highlight the need for every firm to strategically choose the different types of social media platforms to use.

According to Kietzmann *et al.* (2011), every social medium performs different tasks related to seven functional blocks:

- **Identity:** the degree to which users reveal their personal information and identities,
- **Conversations:** the extent to which users communicate with others,
- **Sharing:** the extent to which users exchange, distribute and receive contents,
- **Presence:** the extent to which users can know if others are available,
- **Relationships:** the degree to which users relate to each other,
- **Reputation:** the extent to which users know the social status of others,
- **Groups:** the extent to which users can form communities.

By analysing each block, firms can monitor and understand how social media applications vary in order to develop an efficient social media strategy and to optimise the return of their presence. Having identified the building blocks, firms need to develop strategies (called the "4Cs") to monitor and respond to different social media activities. The 4C strategies are:

- **Cognize:** understanding the social media landscape;
- **Congruity:** defining particular strategies in order to meet the firm's objectives with social media functionalities;
- **Curate:** listening to social media conversations;
- **Chase:** environmental scanning to understand the speed of conversations and the information flows (Kietzmann *et al.*, 2011).

SOCIAL MEDIA MANAGEMENT IN MARKET-DRIVEN FIRMS

As we have described before, market-driven management is a corporate strategy that presupposes a continuous benchmarking with competitors (*competitor orientation*) and a focus on customers' needs and satisfaction (*customer orientation*).

Market-driven firms are able to sense and recognize the market trends (*market sensing capability*) and to profitably relate with customers (*customer linking capability*). To succeed in a dynamic and fast changing competitive environment, these firms need to adopt new ways of working, supporting collaboration and knowledge sharing inside the organization. Outside they need to relate and strengthen their ties with customers, besides having an in depth knowledge of the competitive environment.

In this context we suggest that social media management can provide many advantages to market-driven firms with regard to both the customer orientation and the competitor orientation. To this end, we propose a novel conceptual framework on the *Social Media Opportunities for Market-Driven Firms* (as shown below in Figure 1), showing how the active and strategic management of social media enables market-driven firms to increase their competitiveness through the

Figure 1. The proposed framework of "Social Media Opportunities for Market-Driven Firms"

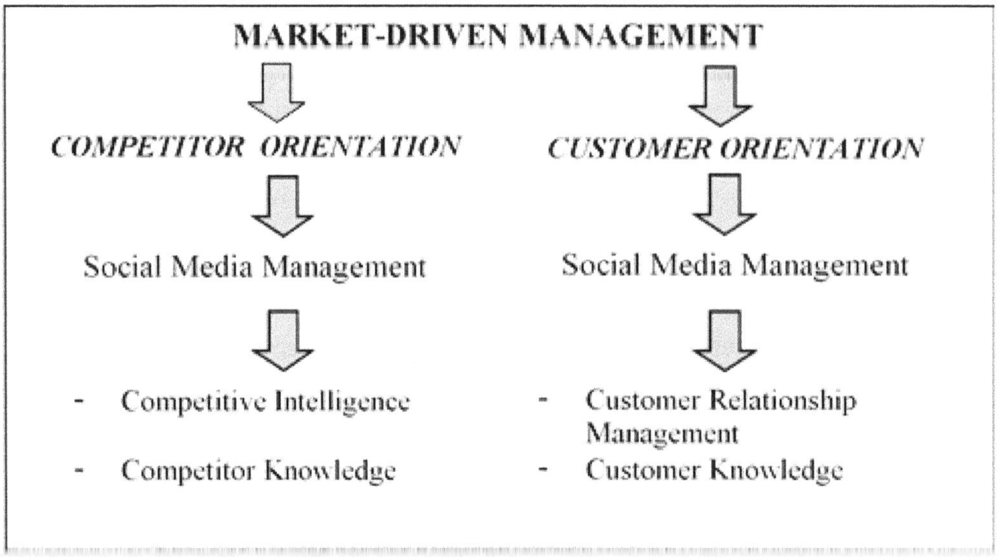

improvement of their customer relationships and a better monitoring and understanding of competitors' strategies. In fact, social media contain many data and information about the rivals and consent direct comparisons of customers with regard to different competing offers. In addition, social media management offers the possibility to connect with current and potential customers seeking their active involvement in business strategies. We know that the ability of a firm to create and maintain close relationships with its customers is recognized as a durable basis of competitive advantage (Day, 1999).

In the next paragraphs, we will examine the benefits provided to market-driven firms by social media management, analysing them in relation to the two core orientations of market-driven management:

- **Competitor Orientation:** considering social platforms as competitive media useful for monitoring the competitive environment and the competitor strategies;
- **Customer Orientation:** studying social media as a marketing medium for enhancing customer knowledge and customer relationships.

Social Media and Competitor Orientation in Market-Driven Firms

Market-driven firms need to assess the risks and opportunities of the competitive scenario, by making decisions based on a set of processes in order to gather data and to convert it into knowledge and then to utilize it inside the organization. Furthermore, these firms must develop in depth knowledge of competitors in order to anticipate their strategies and to succeed in the market. Social media enable market-driven firms to monitor the competitive environment through the competitive intelligence activity and to acquire information about their competitors.

Social Media and Competitive Intelligence

Competitive intelligence is a "combination of defining, gathering and analyzing intelligence about products, customers, competitors and any aspect of the environment needed to support executives and managers in making strategic decisions for an organization" (Dey *et al.*, 2011, p. 1). It differs from industrial espionage because competitive intelligence is considered as a legal business practice with focus on the monitoring of the external competitive environment.

Competitive intelligence usually employs both primary and secondary sources from customers, suppliers, retailers, media, and competitors in order to analyze the present environmental conditions, as well as their projection into the future. It can be categorized into strategic intelligence and tactical intelligence, depending on whether it is used for making long-term or short-term decisions (Vuori, 2011).

The first studies the future evolution of the firm's competitiveness inside the industry, estimating its prospective competitive positioning and delineating the strategies to achieve it. Thus, strategic intelligence must identify potential weaknesses and warning signals within the organization. Instead, tactical intelligence is based on the examination of the current market situation, and consequently, it is able to affect short-term decisions. It gathers and analyzes data and information related to the description of the profile of competitors and of the market structure (for example: the competitors operating in the market; the prices they set for the products; the marketing promotions they carry out; new product launches; their technology investments, etc.).

In the past, market analysts primarily focused competitive intelligence on facts and reports often made for other aims by third-parties or public institutions. At present, market-driven firms cannot limit their research and knowledge only to these data. In fact, a large amount of information and knowledge is required to successfully operate and several activities need to take place in order to make the right decisions.

Information technologies and social media make a big contribution, since the information necessary to face competitive challenges is moving quickly from published and proprietary sources to open social platforms (Harrysson *et al.*, 2012). Market-driven firms can search in social media to identify and discover facts and data helpful for developing new strategies in order to achieve a competitive advantage.

As argued by Dey *et al.* (2011), due to the enormous availability and accessibility of data and news on the web, firms need to create tools and procedures that make it less complex for analysts engaged in competitive intelligence to gather data and to process information. In fact, in order to collect large amounts of relevant data, every firm must have various data sources.

Thus, market-driven firms must monitor many web resources on online trading sites, financial news websites, digital newspapers and industry association websites. Using internet search engines, they must search in entertainment websites like: discussion groups, blogs, review websites, social networks. It is important to identify specific people and their conversations; they can be experts or trend spotters who have accurate information. In so doing, firms can eliminate the costs of extensive searches and engage a network of experts (Harrysson *et al.*, 2012).

A practical technique used in social media competitive analysis is text mining that derives information from written texts by using methods such as entity extraction, clustering, categorization and sentiment analysis. Using text mining for competitive intelligence purposes allows to analyze a big quantity of textual data quickly and to accomplish richer analysis to support decision makers. This process includes four main steps:

- **Data Processing:** pre-processing input texts into the specific format for additional analysis;
- **Concept Extraction:** the identification and extraction of pertinent concepts and terms by an initial text analysis;
- **Narrative Analysis:** the development of an automated solution;

- The creation of a conceptual taxonomy (Dai *et al.*, 2011).

Through competitive intelligence and text mining, market data are transformed into new corporate knowledge, since information is organised in a way that makes it significant for the firm. Other free internet tools to track social media conversations in real time are:

- Google Alerts allow to monitor what is said on the internet about a specific keyword.
- Social Mention allows to systematize the results by sentiment, influencers, sources, keywords, and tags and export them in an excel file that is easy to manage.
- Twitter Search is similar to Google alerts and focuses on Twitter conversations (Robison, 2011).

Social Media and Competitor Knowledge

Social media conversations help to understand the evolution of customer trends, as well as to monitor competitors' strategies. With the collected data market-driven firms are able to react to competitors' moves quickly, reorganizing their market strategies in order to be ready for action.

In particular, by conducting a social media competitive analysis (He *et al.*, 2013), a market-driven firm can obtain insights about the relative strengths and weaknesses, knowing better competitors and learning from them. In fact, to increase the competitive advantage and successfully assess the competitive environment, market-driven firms need to supervise and analyze not only the customer-generated content on their own social media sites, but also the information on competitors' social media sites.

Social media contain significant information about product appreciations, consumer opinions and attitudes, different brand powers, competitors' offers and promotions, but also competitors' announcements about their vision or strategies. Once the data have been gathered, market-driven firms must analyze, extract contents that are helpful for their purposes and disseminate and share these latter inside the organization, with non-stop continuous monitoring of the web sources.

Social technologies play a surprising role also in how information is analyzed and distributed. In fact, new analytic methods can be structured to derive insights from social media. For example, to isolate important messages or conversations about the firm and to understand their relevance in establishing realistic competitive benchmarks, specific social media metrics have been developed (Hoffman & Fodor, 2010).

Quantitative metrics, for example, are: the number of followers or fans; the number and frequency of postings; the amount of "liking" or tweets; the response timing, etc. However, qualitative metrics and techniques are also necessary to evaluate what is said in the conversations and to understand the attitude and opinions of customers. Every firm should use these measurements to compare their social media strategy against competitors' strategies.

Market-driven firms can monitor the frequency of customer postings on their social media pages and on those of competitors; or they can measure the number of "liking" on their posts; moreover, also the level of interaction that characterizes their own posts is an important metric.

Again, market-driven firms can examine the correlation existing between social media findings (consumer opinions, satisfaction, comments) and corporate events or competitors' strategies, such as price discounts or other promotional strategies. Competitive analysts can use social platforms to collect what is known about new developments or features of their products thanks to the fact that the firm's software developers have shared online information about a particular technology. Thus, through social media management, firms can easily expand their market and knowledge of competitors.

Figure 2. Social Media Management and Customer Orientation in Market-Driven Firms

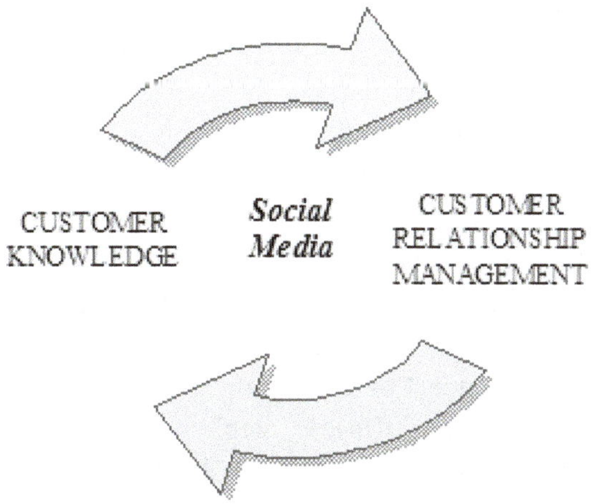

Social Media and Customer Orientation in Market-Driven Firms

Customer orientation is at the core of traditional marketing management; it implies a commitment to understanding and satisfying customers' needs, creating value for customers and anticipating new customer expectations. As market-driven firms have a strong focus on customers, they stay in close contact with them in order to deliver higher levels of satisfaction and build superior customer retention (Day, 2011).

The interactive nature of social media is relevant in this field because it involves customers in content generation and also in value creation. Nowadays, more and more firms are adopting social media to meet the growing number of customers using them for socializing, receiving information, comparing prices and product features and entertaining themselves. However, frequently these firms treat social media platforms as independent of each other; instead they should view their approach to social media as an integrated strategy in which customer engagement is central.

With regard to customer orientation, as shown in Figure 2, social media enable market-driven firms to interact with customers, strengthening their brands and moreover developing superior customer knowledge, through the social intelligence process.

An integrated management of social media pushes market-driven firms to develop a sort of "*virtuous circle*" in which through the customer knowledge generated from the social intelligence activity, firms define new social media strategies that can engage and satisfy customers.

Social Media and Customer Relationship Management

Sashi (2012) defines customer engagement as the focus "on satisfying customers by providing superior value than competitors to build trust and commitment in long-term relationships" (p. 260); thus, it is strictly related to the customer linking capability of market-driven firms.

In order to achieve customer engagement with social media management, market-driven firms must facilitate the customers' transition through seven different stages: connection, interaction, satisfaction, retention, commitment, advocacy and engagement (Sashi, 2012). First of all, firms must enter into contact with customers in order to interact with them. Only then, the customers can be satisfied, and only if they have been satisfied can the relationships be maintained in the long term, having developed a stronger commitment. In the next steps, customers will become brand advocates and lastly, engaged customers.

In all these stages, social media alter the roles of buyers and sellers. In fact, in the traditional market exchange, the seller has full control of the marketing mix tools; instead, in the virtual market, social media allow customers to participate in the marketing decisions and, consequently, the seller no longer has the unique prerogative. Within the social media, customers are free to connect both with other customers and non-customers, influencing these latter and pushing them into a new customer engagement cycle.

This is particularly relevant from a brand management perspective (Pentina *et al.*, 2013). Through social media, market-driven firms develop and reinforce their brands, creating a profound relationship with customers based on shared values. In social platforms, customers exchange information and share opinions, freely expressing their points of view. By generating contents online, they add value and become brand advocates who can positively influence other customers.

Moreover, in the social media environment every time people use applications designed by or about a specific brand, the firm gains exposure to their brand and, subsequently, the positive associations of the brand are strengthened and enhanced in customers' minds (Laroche *et al.*, 2013). In effect, it is proved that social media have a powerful effect on brand reputation: satisfied and loyal consumers communicate their positive attitudes toward the brand or toward the social applications created by the firm to new potential customers both offline and online (Kim & Ko, 2012).

In particular, online reviews are considered very helpful in information-sharing among customers for brand awareness purposes (Park & Allen, 2013). However, two managerial approaches are common in managing online reviews:

- **Problem Solving:** Ex post online reviews are seen as a mechanism for resolving complaints quickly, efficiently and discreetly in order to safeguard the firm's reputation, showing the corrective actions taken;
- **Strategic Approach:** online reviews are used to engage the customers more, improving operational efficiency and effectiveness and creating innovations.

Only firms adopting the strategic vision of the second approach will benefit from the social media as an efficient way of safeguarding and enhancing their brand reputation.

Furthermore, in order to preserve the accumulated brand equity, market-driven firms can try to influence customer conversations through a series of methods such as:

- The provision of platforms of networking where people who are interested in a topic can join these networks and converse inside them. In this way, firms can easily monitor what is said about them and can use these platforms to publicize their products or to communicate new promotions.
- The use of blogs to engage customers: firms can ask their customers to write feedback about products. Feedback helps to develop the sense of community that can appear as a virtual place where honest communications are present and the customers are engaged.
- The use of online and offline promotional tools to engage customers: for example, showing the use of the product with figures, films or online games (or better advergames) for entertaining customers on the social media.
- The provision of informative contents on product usage.
- Making customers become special for example offering products, coupons and special deals.
- The design of products in which the communicative element is well planned, and

every component can be discussed by customers as a talking-point (Mangold & Faulds, 2009).

Thus, through social media applications and platforms, market-driven firms can reach customers and promote the customer engagement in many ways. In so doing, they improve and reinforce their customer relationships.

Social Intelligence and Customer Knowledge

Social media support market-driven firms in customer knowledge management through a multi-way communication between firms and their customers. This digital communication has higher levels of efficiency than traditional communication channels (Chua & Banerjee, 2013).

In fact, the openness and participation properties of social media enable firms to communicate and offer descriptions for customers about their products and in micro-blogging services they can draw knowledge from customers. Through the analysis of social media and the accumulation of customer data, market-driven firms can comprehend how customers react to new offers and how customer trends evolve over a specific period of time.

Moreover, thanks to the interactivity of social media applications, market-driven firms can actively collaborate with customers in co-creating new products that respond more to customers' desires. Customers pay increased attention to product attributes and many commercially relevant products were initially conceptualized by lead users rather than firms. In addition, market-driven firms can engage customers in online surveys during the idea generation phase in new product development.

In corporate forums, for example, firms can publish contents about the existing product with the aim to understand customer opinions, purchase intentions, and suggested product improvements. Online communities also provide a relevant source for corporate information gathering because they deal with topics that interest firms. Thus, collecting data and information from online communities, firms become familiar with customers' tastes and preferences and also with customers' complaints and criticism. It is also possible to analyze the psychology of the customers from different points of view: mind-set evolution, value shifts, needs, expectations, etc.

Besides, on their company website, market-driven firms can better know customers' behaviors, monitoring which webpages (and products) are the most visited, and with the information collected, useful web analytics are built (Tonkin *et al.*, 2010).

For example, through an efficient management of social media and the creation of the social network www.mystarbucksidea.com (Sigala, 2011), the well-known coffee company Starbucks informs customers everyday about the latest products and events and, at the same time, analyzes their needs and expectations. The firm has also been able to redefine the roles of its customers that become active contributors of innovation, as evaluators and creators of new ideas. Lastly, it has succeeded in combating customers' reluctance towards knowledge sharing, promoting their engagement and paying attention to complaints (Chua & Banejeree, 2013).

Moreover, thanks to the social intelligence activity, firms obtain new customer knowledge by combining the information acquired by the social media with information coming from the traditional customer intelligence activity. Stone and Wookcock (2013) propose the process of "*Social Intelligence Customer Experience Optimisation*", describing four key-strategies that firms can follow in using social marketing approaches: customer acquisition and activation; customer retention and maintenance; customer penetration/share; and efficiency in customer management.

Through the social intelligence activities, market-driven firms can identify which are the most profitable customer groups, define special value propositions for them and implement personalized digital communications. They can understand customers' interests and expectations, their past and current buying behaviors; on the basis of the data acquired they can deliver the contents and entertainment most respondent to their customers' features and behaviors, retaining the customer base. In addition, market-driven firms can increase their market share with promotional offers on new products to loyal customers and with samples calling new customers to action.

Finally, social intelligence helps firms in reducing marketing and sales costs and in eliminating the risk of failure. In fact, customers use social media to find a description of the firm or of the product features, to search for information about new products or company news, to write feedback on their experiences, and to solve questions or doubts.

Firms can give the responsibility of collecting data to a group of employees that monitor the social media or, more efficiently, they can use software or services that regularly search social media electronically (Close, 2012), as we described in the previous paragraph about social media and competitor orientation.

For example, in their Facebook "Page Insights", firms can know the number of times that each webpage tab (ex: Timeline, Info Tab, Photo Tab) was viewed and they can also find demographic information about their fans. In fact, a specific section of the Facebook account (the "Your Fans section") provides the following information about the people who like their webpage: gender and age (based on the data people enter in their personal timelines), countries and cities (based on their IP address when they use Facebook); and languages (based on their default language setting). Furthermore, firms collect information about how their audience is engaging with their posts and can see the kinds of posts (ex: photos, links) that have the highest average reach and engagement.

In Twitter firms can also measure the number of followers per week and how much followers interact with firms' accounts daily. Some Twitter metrics are: follower growth (per day, week or month); follower quality and engagement; reach; traffic; and the conversion rate (the number of users that signed up for a service or bought a company product).

FUTURE RESEARCH DIRECTIONS

In this chapter we have attempted to propose a conceptual framework on the role of social media in market-driven firms, delineating the main social media opportunities. It is an initial effort that requires further research to better understand every specific opportunity provided by social media management. Thus, a qualitative research based on multiple case studies of market-driven firms could be accomplished in order to analyse how they manage their social media presence and, above all, how they assess it. A content analysis of customer posts and contributions on selected firms' social networks could help to understand how customers interact and participate in firms' promotional activities.

From a business point of view, an interesting research area also regards the threats of social media for market-driven firms. We have focused on the social media opportunities, but social media can also represent a threat for firms enjoying powerful brand equity. In fact, the transparency of social media could be very dangerous because firms cannot control one-to-many consumer conversations.

Moreover, future research could examine the mix of social media focusing on the social media applications chosen by market-driven firms. There are a variety of social media solutions that can be used effectively to support marketing. Which are the best in a market-driven perspective?

Lastly, another important future research area could be an industrial analysis, in order to test if market-driven firms of particular business sectors benefit more from social media management with respect to firms pertaining to other sectors.

Thus, social media management offers several important future research directions for academics in order to investigate all their aspects with a positive influence on business activities and to integrate social media into business strategies.

CONCLUSION

In the past few years the use of social media has quickly increased and social media have become a vital component of the modern web as they enable the creation of data reflecting personal opinions. Recent research studies have also considered social media to be an important way to reach customers for business purposes. In effect, social media have caused many changes in the relationship existing between the firms and the market: they have expanded the nature of competition and the sources of information, but above all, they have empowered the customers. These latter have evolved from simple content readers to content publishers and now they expect to be active participants in the marketing exchange; they want firms to listen, to engage and to respond. Thus, firms must develop new effective social media strategies in order to capture customers' attention.

In this chapter we have analysed the opportunities provided by the management of social media for firms adopting a market orientation. We have proposed a conceptual framework on "*Social Media Opportunities for Market-Driven Firms*" with the aim of contributing to a better understanding of social media in the strategic management field. In fact, no study to date has investigated the role of social media management in improving the competitiveness of market-driven firms.

By reviewing the main academic research studies on social media in a market-driven perspective, the proposed framework suggests that an active presence and a strategic use of social media can provide many benefits to market-driven firms. In fact, the pressure for customer value improvement pushes these firms to utilize all sources of information in order to understand how customers are changing and what competitors are doing.

More specifically, with regard to the necessary focus on competitors, social media help market-driven firms to overcome some limits of the traditional intelligence gathering, which typically involved collecting information from public and proprietary sources. New social media software lets firms rapidly, and sometimes automatically, accumulate accurate information from digital sources. In addition, through social media competitive intelligence, firms can develop in depth knowledge of their competitive environment.

With regard to customer orientation, market-driven firms can improve their customer relationships by being active and engaging their customers via social media; and by monitoring in real time what is said about them in social applications, they can improve their customer knowledge. Social media increase marketing's ability to move consumers from the awareness state to the engagement, consideration, loyalty and advocacy one. Thus, social media are very relevant also in a brand enhancement perspective.

Consequently, business managers should develop best practices related to the social media management. In this direction, first of all, managers should fully understand what social media are, the various forms they can take, and how to engage customers through them. They must be aware of two elements: customers have much greater control over their online experiences than the firm can imagine or manage; the social media environment is highly dynamic and quickly evolving, therefore, they always need to monitor social platforms and be familiar with their advancement.

Market-driven firms engaging in social media management, besides developing their own social media presence, should define or acquire efficient systems to regularly search online to gather information in social media. Appropriate guidelines and standards for the use of social media by employees should also be defined; employees should be responsible for their postings and respect the legal and professional framework.

Marketing managers should know precisely what is said about their brands in social media, how frequently it is being said and in which particular social media platform. At the same time, they should monitor social media platforms of competitors in order to effectively assess the competitive environment by performing a social media competitive analysis. Conversation tracking also allows to develop in depth knowledge on competitors' offers and on their social media strategies in order to react with the best competitive response.

Business managers should catch the opportunities offered by the emergence of social media related both to the monitoring of competitive environment and to the enhancement of customer relationships. They should also recognize that only the combination of both traditional and social media strategies allows firms to develop integrated marketing strategies to reach consumers and to influence them.

Furthermore, as the development of a social media presence and its management are expensive, market-driven firms need to develop specific performance metrics for social media applications in order to measure the return of the social media investment. However, besides the traditional returns on the company's investment (such as sales and sales revenues), managers should assess consumer behaviors and motivations, measuring how social media investments engage the customers with the brands.

REFERENCES

Ang, L. (2011). Is SCRM really a good social media strategy? *Journal of Database Marketing & Customer Strategy Management*, *18*(3), 149–153. doi:10.1057/dbm.2011.22

Arrigo, E. (2009). Market-driven management, global competition and corporate responsibility. *Symphonya: Emerging Issues in Management*, *1*, 51–67. doi: doi:10.4468/2009.1.06arrigo

Arrigo, E. (2012). Alliances, open innovation and outside-in management. *Symphonya: Emerging Issues in Management*, *2*, 53–65. doi: doi:10.4468/2012.2.05arrigo

Baker, W. E., & Sinkula, J. M. (1999). Learning orientation, market orientation, and innovation: Integrating and extending models of organizational performance. *Journal of Market-Focused Management*, *4*(4), 295–308. doi:10.1023/A:1009830402395

Baker, W. E., & Sinkula, J. M. (2002). Market orientation, learning orientation and product innovation: Delving into the organization's black box. *Journal of Market-Focused Management*, *5*(1), 5–23. doi:10.1023/A:1012543911149

Best, R. J. (2009). *Market-based management* (5th ed.). London, UK: Prentice Hall.

Brondoni, S. M. (2009). Market-driven management, competitive customer value and global networks. *Symphonya: Emerging Issues in Management*, *1*, 8–25. doi: doi:10.4468/2009.1.02brondoni

Brondoni, S. M. (Ed.). (2012). *Market-driven management and corporate growth*. Turin, Italy: Giappichelli.

Chaffrey, D., Ellis-Chadwick, F., Mayer, R., & Johnston, K. (2009). *Internet marketing: Strategy, implementation and practice* (4th ed.). Harlow, UK: Prentice Hall.

Chua, A. Y. K., & Banerjee, S. (2013). Customer knowledge management via social media: The case of Starbucks. *Journal of Knowledge Management*, *17*(2), 237–249. doi:10.1108/13673271311315196

Close, A. G. (2012). *Online consumer behaviour: Theory and research in social media, advertising, and e-tail*. New York: Routledge.

Constantinides, E., & Fountain, S. J. (2008). Web 2.0: Conceptual foundations and marketing issues. *Journal of Direct, Data and Digital Marketing Practice*, *9*(3), 231–244. doi:10.1057/palgrave.dddmp.4350098

Dai, Y., Kakkonen, T., & Sutinen, E. (2011). MinEdec: A decision-support model that combines text-mining technologies with two competitive intelligence analysis methods. *International Journal of Computer Information Systems and Industrial Management Applications*, *3*, 165–173.

Day, G. S. (1990). *The market-driven organization*. New York, NY: Free Press.

Day, G. S. (1994). The capabilities of market-driven organizations. *Journal of Marketing*, *58*(4), 37–52. doi:10.2307/1251915

Day, G. S. (1999, Fall). Creating a market-driven organization. *Sloan Management Review*, 11–22.

Day, G. S. (2011). Closing the marketing capabilities gap. *Journal of Marketing*, *75*(4), 183–195. doi:10.1509/jmkg.75.4.183

DesAutels, P. (2011). UGIS: Understanding the nature of user-generated information systems. *Business Horizons*, *54*(3), 185–192. doi:10.1016/j.bushor.2010.12.003

Deshpandé, R., & Webster, F. E. (1989). Corporate culture and marketing: Defining the research agenda. *Journal of Marketing*, *53*(1), 3–15. doi:10.2307/1251521

Dey, L., Haque, S. M., Khurdiya, A., & Shroff, G. (2011). Acquiring competitive intelligence from social media. In Proceedings of the 2011 Joint Workshop on Multilingual OCR and Analytics for Noisy Unstructured Text Data. ACM. DOI:10.1145/2034617.2034621

DiStaso, M. W., & McCorkindale, T. (2012). Social media: Uses and opportunities in public relations. *Global Media Journal*, *5*(2), 75–82.

Drucker, P. F. (1954). *The practice of management*. New York, NY: Harper & Brothers.

Fill, C. (2009). *Marketing communications: Interactivity, communities and content* (5th ed.). London: Prentice Hall.

Harrysson, M., Metayer, E., & Sarrazin, H. (2012, November). How 'social intelligence' can guide decisions. *The McKinsey Quarterly*, 1–9.

He, W., Zha, S., & Li, L. (2013). Social media competitive analysis and text mining: A case study in the pizza industry. *International Journal of Information Management*, *33*(3), 464–472. doi:10.1016/j.ijinfomgt.2013.01.001

Hoffman, D. L., & Fodor, M. (2010). Can you measure the ROI of your social media marketing? *MIT Sloan Management Review*, *52*(1), 41–49.

Kane, G. C., Fichman, R. G., Gallaugher, J., & Glaser, G. (2009). Community relations 2.0. *Harvard Business Review*, *87*(11), 45–50. PMID:19891388

Kaplan, A. M., & Haenlein, M. (2010). Users of the world, unite! The challenges and opportunities of social media. *Business Horizons*, *53*(1), 59–68. doi:10.1016/j.bushor.2009.09.003

Kietzmann, J. H., Hermkens, K., McCarthy, I. P., & Silvestre, B. S. (2011). Social media? Get serious! Understanding the functional building blocks of social media. *Business Horizons*, *54*(3), 241–251. doi:10.1016/j.bushor.2011.01.005

Kim, A. J., & Ko, E. (2012). Do social media marketing activities enhance customer equity? An empirical study of luxury fashion brand. *Journal of Business Research*, *65*(10), 1480–1486. doi:10.1016/j.jbusres.2011.10.014

Kohli, A. K., & Jaworski, B. J. (1990, April). Market orientation: The construct, research propositions, and managerial implications. *Journal of Marketing*, *54*(2), 1–18. doi:10.2307/1251866

Lambin, J. J. (2007). *Market-driven management: Strategic and operational marketing*. London: MacMillan.

Laroche, M., Mohammad, R. H., & Richard, M.-O. (2013). To be or not to be in social media: How brand loyalty is affected by social media? *International Journal of Information Management*, *33*(1), 76–82. doi:10.1016/j.ijinfomgt.2012.07.003

Mangold, W. G., & Faulds, D. J. (2009). Social media: The new hybrid element of the promotion mix. *Business Horizons*, *52*(3), 357–365. doi:10.1016/j.bushor.2009.03.002

Michaelidou, N., Siamagka, N. T., & Christodoulides, G. (2011). Usage, barriers and measurement of social media marketing: An exploratory investigation of small and medium b2b brands. *Industrial Marketing Management*, *40*(7), 1153–1159. doi:10.1016/j.indmarman.2011.09.009

Miller, K. D., Fabian, F., & Lin, S. J. (2009). Strategies for online communities. *Strategic Management Journal*, *30*(3), 305–322. doi:10.1002/smj.735

Narver, J. C., & Slater, S. F. (1990, October). The effect of a market orientation on business profitability. *Journal of Marketing*, *54*(4), 20–35. doi:10.2307/1251757

Ohmae, K. (1990). Managing in a borderless world. *Harvard Business Review*, 151–161. PMID:10292934

Park, S., & Allen, J. P. (2013). Responding to online reviews: Problem solving and engagement in hotel. *Cornell Hospitality Quarterly*, *54*(1), 64–73. doi:10.1177/1938965512463118

Pentina, I., Zhang, L., & Basmanova, O. (2013). Antecedents and consequences of trust in a social media brand: A cross-cultural study of Twitter. *Computers in Human Behavior*, *29*(4), 1546–1555. doi:10.1016/j.chb.2013.01.045

Robison, N. (2011). *4 free tools for social media competitive analysis*. Retrieved August 20, 2013, from http://blog.socialmediahq.com/4-free-tools-for-social-media-competitive-analysis/

Saka-Helmhout, A. (2011). Learning from the periphery: Beyond the transnational model. *Critical Perspectives on International Business*, *7*(1), 48–65. doi:10.1108/17422041111103831

Sashi, C. M. (2012). Customer engagement, buyer-seller relationships and social media. *Management Decision*, *50*(2), 253–273. doi:10.1108/00251741211203551

Sigala, M. (2011). Social networks and customer involvement in new service development (NSD): The case of www.mystarbucksidea.com. *International Journal of Contemporary Hospitality Management, 24*(7), 966-990

Stone, M., & Woodcock, N. (2013). Social intelligence in customer engagement. *Journal of Strategic Marketing*, *21*(5), 394–401. doi:10.1080/0965254X.2013.801613

Teece, D. J. (2009). *Dynamic capabilities and strategic management*. Oxford, UK: Oxford University Press.

Tonkin, S., Whitmore, C., & Cutroni, J. (2010). *Performance marketing with Google analytics: Strategies and techniques for maximizing online ROI*. Hoboken, NJ: Wiley Publishing, Inc.

Tracey, M., Lim, J., & Vonderembse, M. A. (2005). The impact of supply-chain management capabilities on business performance. *Supply-Chain Management: An International Journal*, *10*(3), 179–191. doi:10.1108/13598540510606232

Vuori, V. (2011). *Social media changing the competitive intelligence process: Elicitation of employees' competitive knowledge*. (Thesis for Degree of Doctor of Science in Technology). Tampere University of Technology, Tampere, Finland.

Vuori, W., & Okkonen, J. (2012). Refining information and knowledge by social media applications. *VINE: The Journal of Information and Knowledge Management System*, *42*(1), 117–128. doi:10.1108/03055721211207798

Webster, F. E. (1994). *Market-driven management*. Hoboken, NJ: John Wiley and Sons.

Weinberg, B. D., & Pehlivan, E. (2011). Social spending: Managing the social media mix. *Business Horizons*, *54*(3), 275–282. doi:10.1016/j.bushor.2011.01.008

ADDITIONAL READING

Baird, C. H., & Parasnis, G. (2011). From social media to social customer relationship management. *Strategy and Leadership*, *39*(5), 30–37. doi:10.1108/10878571111161507

Bradley, S., Kim, C., Kim, J., & Lee, I. (2012). Toward an evolution strategy for the digital goods business. *Management Decision*, *50*(2), 234–252. doi:10.1108/00251741211203542

De Valck, K., van Bruggen, G. H., & Wierenga, B. (2009). Virtual communities: A marketing perspective. *Decision Support Systems*, *47*(3), 185–203. doi:10.1016/j.dss.2009.02.008

Evans, D. (2012). *Social media marketing: An hour a day* (2nd ed.). Hoboken, New Jersey: John Wiley & Sons, Inc.

Evans, D., & McKee, J. (2010). *Social media marketing. The next generation of business engagement*. Hoboken, New Jersey: John Wiley & Sons, Inc.

Fisher, T. (2009). ROI in social media: A look at the arguments. *Journal of Database Marketing & Customer Strategy Management*, *16*(3), 189–195. doi:10.1057/dbm.2009.16

Garver, M. S. (2003). Best practices in identifying customer-driven improvement opportunities. *Industrial Marketing Management*, *32*(6), 455–466. doi:10.1016/S0019-8501(02)00238-9

Gilbert, E., & Karahalios, K. (2009). Predicting tie strength with social media. 27th International Conference on Human Factors in Computing Systems – CHI, 211-220. doi:10.1145/1518701.1518736

Hadcroft, P., & Jarrat, D. (2007). Market orientation: An interative process of customer and market engagement. *Journal of Business-To-Business Marketing*, *14*(3), 21–57. doi:10.1300/J033v14n03_02

Hanna, R., Rohm, A., & Crittenden, V. L. (2011). We're all connected: The power of the social media eco system. *Business Horizons*, *54*(3), 265–273. doi:10.1016/j.bushor.2011.01.007

Heller Baird, C., & Parasnis, G. (2011). From social media to social customer relationship management. *Strategy and Leadership*, *39*(5), 30–37. doi:10.1108/10878571111161507

Henning-Thurau, T., Malthouse, E. C., Friege, C., Gensler, S., Lobschat, L., Rangaswamy, A., & Skiera, B. (2010). The impact of new media on customer relationships. *Journal of Service Research*, *13*(3), 311–330. doi:10.1177/1094670510375460

Huston, L., & Sakkab, N. (2006). Connect and develop. Inside Procter & Gamble's new model for innovation. *Harvard Business Review*, (March): 1–9.

Kalampokis, E., Tambouris, E., & Tarabanis, K. (2013). Understanding the predictive power of social media. *Internet Research*, *23*(5), 544–559. doi:10.1108/IntR-06-2012-0114

Kane, G. C., Fichman, R. G., Gallaugher, J., & Glaser, G. (2009). Community relations 2.0. *Harvard Business Review*, *87*(11), 45–50. PMID:19891388

Kaplan, A. M., & Haenlein, M. (2011). Two hearts in three-quarter time: How to waltz the social media/viral marketing dance. *Business Horizons*, *54*(3), 253–263. doi:10.1016/j.bushor.2011.01.006

Lamore, P. R., Berkowitz, D., & Farrington, P. A. (2013). Proactive/responsive market orientation and marketing-Research and development intergration. *Journal of Product Innovation Management*, *30*(4), 695–711. doi:10.1111/jpim.12024

Libai, B., Bolton, R., Bugel, M. S., De Ruyter, K., Gotz, O., Risselada, H., & Stephen, A. T. (2013). Customer-to-customer interactions: Broadening the scope of word of mouth research. *Journal of Service Research*, *13*(3), 267–282. doi:10.1177/1094670510375600

Liu, Q. B., Karahanna, E., & Watson, R. T. (2011). Unveiling user-generated content: Designing websites to best present customer reviews. *Business Horizons*, *54*(3), 231–240. doi:10.1016/j.bushor.2011.01.004

Meerman Scott, D. (2010). *The new rules of marketing and PR: How to use social media, blogs, news releases, online video, and viral marketing to reach buyers directly*. Hoboken, New Jersey: John Wiley & Sons, Inc.

Narver, J. C., Slater, S. F., & Tietje, B. (1998). Creating a market orientation. *Journal of Market-Focused Management*, *2*(3), 241–255. doi:10.1023/A:1009703717144

Parent, M., Plangger, K., & Bal, A. (2011). The new WTP: Willingness to participate. *Business Horizons*, *54*(3), 219–229. doi:10.1016/j.bushor.2011.01.003

Pitt, L. F., & Berthon, P. (2011). Just when you thought it was safe to go back into the web: Marketing meets Web 2.0, social media, and creative consumers. *Business Horizons*, *54*(3), 181–183. doi:10.1016/j.bushor.2010.12.002

Powell, G., Groves, S., & Dimos, S. (2011). *ROI of social media: How to improve the return on your social marketing investment*. Hoboken, New Jersey: John Wiley & Sons, Inc.

Qualman, E. (2013). *Socialnomics: How social media transforms the way we live and do business*. Hoboken, New Jersey: John Wiley & Sons, Inc.

Safko, D. L. (2010). *The social media bible: tactics, tools, and strategies for business success*. Hoboken, New Jersey: John Wiley & Sons, Inc.

Senders, A., Govers, R., & Neuts, B. (2013). Social media affecting tour operators' customer loyalty. *Journal of Travel & Tourism Marketing*, *30*(1-2), 41–57. doi:10.1080/10548408.2013.750993

Sterne, J. (2010). *Social media metrics: how to measure and optimize your marketing investment*. Hoboken, New Jersey: John Wiley & Sons, Inc.

Tuonimen, M., Rajala, A., & Moller, K. (2004). Market-driving versus market-driven: Divergent roles of market orientation in business relationships. *Industrial Marketing Management*, *33*, 2017–2217.

Vorhies, D. W., Harker, M., & Rao, C. P. (1999). The capabilities and performance advantages of market-driven firms. *European Journal of Marketing*, *33*(11/12), 1171–1202. doi:10.1108/03090569910292339

Vuori, V., & Okkonen, J. (2011). Knowledge sharing motivational factors of using an intra-organizational social media platform. *Journal of Knowledge Management*, *16*(4), 2012.

Webber, R. (2012). Beyond likes, fans, and followers: How social media can drive real business objectives. *Cost Management*, *26*(3), 6–14.

KEY TERMS AND DEFINITIONS

Business Opportunities in Social Media: Benefits and advantages that a firm obtains from the management of social media.

Competitive Advantage: A favorable business condition that allows to outperform the competitors.

Competitive Analysis: An assessment of the strengths and weaknesses of current and potential competitors and of the environmental trends.

Customer Engagement: The continuous involvement of customers in the firm's activities and strategies.

Customer Relationship Management: The development and coordination of business strategies to advantageously interact with current and future customers, building solid relationships with them.

Market-Driven Management: A business philosophy with strategic focus on the market in which both customer satisfaction and continuous comparison with competitors are central in developing corporate strategies.

Social Media Management: The organization of actions and strategies developed in order to coordinate the social media activities.

Social Media Tools: The different typologies of social media applications constituting the social media mix.

Chapter 11
Web 2.0 and Social Media in Today's Business World

Edward T. Chen
University of Massachusetts – Lowell, USA

ABSTRACT

Social media technology is an innovative way for businesses to collaborate, network, and provide a mechanism for individuals to interact. When social media technology is used effectively, it can be a powerful tool for businesses to market themselves and obtain important data on their customers and competitors. Given the importance and public nature of today's consumer opinions, it is vital for companies to present themselves effectively on social media. Some companies and their employees are not familiar with this form of technology and do not realize the massive amount of data social media sites can generate. Therefore, companies need to develop a social media policy and educate their employees on how to analyze and respond to the data produced from social media. This chapter studies Web 2.0 tools and social media in today's business world and provides guidelines of adopting social media for organizations.

INTRODUCTION

Social media and Web 2.0 tools have the potential to greatly affect many facets of an organization. From upper management decision-making down to the delivery of the service or product, Web 2.0 applications and social media have the ability to greatly affect organizational structure. Furthermore, customers have the ability to interact with multiple functional units of the organization and its members in real time. Companies want to find a way to differentiate themselves and connect with customers. Through social media and Web 2.0 tools, businesses can deliver a better, more specific product tailored to the needs of their customers (Armstrong & Gao, 2010; Blanchard, 2011; Mayfield, 2008; Pentina, Prybutok, & Zhang, 2008).

Social media and Web 2.0 tools can assist an organization to achieve sales goals through expanded marketing and expanding their brand presence to potential customers. Web 2.0 and social media applications allow businesses to achieve organizational objectives through a higher level of information sharing (Bateman, Valentine, & Rittenburg, 2013; Harridge-March & Quinton, 2009; Subramani & Rajagopalan, 2003). Compa-

DOI: 10.4018/978-1-4666-6182-0.ch011

nies seeking to expand their presence can turn to Web 2.0 and social media applications. These tools allow customers to easily interact with companies from devise running on multiple platforms. Social media technology provides today's consumers with an easy way to voice their opinions and experiences, positive or negative, online for the entire world to see. Other consumers can reply and react to these posts leaving businesses with an enhanced or tarnished image (McAfee, 2009; Pentina, et al., 2008; Taylor, Lewin, & Strutton, 2011).

Businesses are becoming more competitive and efficient within their markets. Businesses need to ensure that company policies are prepared to handle the security and privacy concerns that could arise from the use of these technologies. Organizations must work to overcome potential issues when they open themselves up to Web 2.0 and social media tools. Businesses integrating Web 2.0 applications within their organization need to be prepared to properly train employees to ensure that these technologies are best utilized within their organization. If implemented correctly, Web 2.0 and social media can improve collaboration among employees. Furthermore, Web 2.0 and social media have helped to facilitate a new way consumers interact with brands, and the way that businesses respond to these interactions (Bhattacharjee, Gopal, & Sanders, 2003; Mayfield, 2008; Harridge-March & Quinton, 2009).

Software packages and applications are available to manage data associated with social media. Companies can use these solutions to help them not only collect the data but respond to consumer concerns and issues so consumers know their opinions are being heard and taken seriously. Gone are the days of a company being solely in charge of its reputation and image. A company's choice is not whether they are participating in social media it is what role they will play in it.

How Web 2.0 and Social Media Work

Web 2.0 is an often misunderstood term. Web 2.0 consists of a number of interesting terms and concepts such as social media, wikis, tagging, blogs, social bookmarks, and podcasting, to name a few. These technologies are based on the concept that the Internet is their platform for operating. Programs such as HTML, JavaScript, AJAX (Asynchronous JavaScript), and RIA (Rich Internet Applications). Web 2.0 technologies such as social media are able to perform their operations on an individual or client's machine. This concept is known as "client side" technologies. This idea of using the Internet as the platform, allows software to be delivered through one's browser (O'Reilly, 2005). Google's Chrome browser and Mozilla's Firefox allow individual to install plug-ins directly to the programs. Web 2.0 applications are integrated into the user's experience. An example of this specific technology is Tweetdeck. The famous social media site allows users to arrange Twitter feeds in a browser with customizable columns, Tweet filters, and the capability to manage multiple Twitter accounts all at once. Users are able to fully integrate their browsing experience and share pertinent information with other users in real time. Twitter allows users to schedule tweets to be posted at specific times to suit their audience.

Web 2.0 Technologies

Web 2.0 technologies are advancements from Web 1.0, where communication between the client-side browser and the server containing the content required a request and a response type of interaction. In Web 1.0 a client requested a specific page and the server responded with the content in a read-only way (Anderson, 2007). Innovations such as broadband Internet and the above mentioned HTML, JavaScript, AJAX, and RIA have allowed users to transition to a more service-based web experience rather than a dependence on the software (O'Reilly, 2005). Google Docs is a good example of this service-based Web 2.0 technology. Users create, share, and store documents on Google's servers, which do not require software to be installed on their personal computers. Unlike traditional document software such as Microsoft Office, Google Docs uses the web as its platform. The client-side system uses JavaScript programming language to update the documents, which are housed on Google's servers rather than the client's PC. This technology creates a more seamless user experience for the client as this communication is happening asynchronously. JavaScript manipulates Google Docs' HTML code, which in turn provides updated content to the user without him or her having to refresh their browser.

Wikis

Wikis are another example of Web 2.0 technologies that allow users to contribute, delete, or correct site content all via a web browser. Similar to Google Docs, information is stored on databases, which users can call upon to alter using a rich-text editor. Service providers use variations in technology to maintain control over their contents. For example, Google's email service uses its own task-specific browser plug-in. The website Wikipedia is a perfect example of a wiki technology. Through the use of Java and ActiveX, contributors to this website are able to edit the contents of the site in real time. These controls are embedded into web-based applications and give users the freedom to call upon the data and make changes as they see fit. Recently, Wikipedia introduced safeguards to regulate who can make changes. An example of Wikipedia's safeguards is the use of pending-changes. The Wikipedia reviewer community has the opportunity to review edits to content before the changes go live.

Crowdsourcing

This technology allowing users to act independently of each other but collectively has created a huge resource to the user community. Crowd knowledge or "crowdsourcing" has spawned organizations to utilize the power of problem-solving on a large scale (Surowiecki, 2005). Wikis have provided the opportunity for a huge influx of user-generated content (UGC). The video-sharing web site YouTube is another great example of user-generated content. Contributors upload video files to YouTube's servers. The videos then are made available for viewing by anyone. The success of these types of sites has been attributed to the rise of Rich Internet Application (RIA) and Web-Oriented Architecture (WOA) technologies, which have allowed the end users, or "client-side", to generate much more of the content. YouTube has thrived as a business based solely on user-generated content (Daugherty, Eastin, & Bright, 2008).

Rich Internet Application (RIA) and Web-Oriented Architecture (WOA)

With the rise of Rich Internet Application (RIA) and Web-Oriented Architecture (WOA) technologies, the fundamental way in which people communicate has shifted. In Web 1.0, users merely called upon pages instead of creating and interacting with user-generated content. The development of social media sites such as Facebook, Twitter, and LinkedIn have allowed users to utilize these technologies and communicate with each other in ways that Web 1.0 could not facilitate. Users are able to upload and share messages and pictures in real time with other users on the same network. Furthermore, users create a richer experience through mass participation. The more users these social networks have, the greater the experience for the users. For example, the social media site, LinkedIn, allows users to connect with people in the same industry they are in. LinkedIn utilizes the information users provide in order to create a better experience. LinkedIn will suggest people for the user to connect with and will also suggest user-generated groups to join. The members, all of who have a common business interest or experience, facilitate these LinkedIn groups (Daugherty, Eastin, & Bright, 2008; Leung, 2010).

User-Generated Content

With the advent of social networks, we have seen companies collect their consumers' user-generated content and harvest it in a way that has allowed the companies to generate profit. The information provided by LinkedIn users, which allows them to have a better user connection, also allows LinkedIn to direct specific adverting to the users by capturing and harvesting their information. Companies such as Facebook are paring consumers' posts and activities that are included their profiles with an ad. Sponsored stories and advertisements are directed only towards the people that the user had originally allowed to see the post or activity. If a Facebook user "Likes" the university of interest, the user, or one of the user's friends, may see a targeted ad for a related topic such as collegiate attire (Taylor, et al., 2011).

Tagging

One way that social media users share information is through the Web 2.0 tool of tagging. Tagging allows users to collectively classify and find information. Looking at Facebook, users can "tag" pictures of other users, labeling their name, which in turn allows the company to compile a database of shared pictures of that user. The term folksonomy is a Web 2.0 term used to describe the collaboration of users managing and categorizing tags. The website 43 Things is an example of folksonomy at work. This website is based on users describing forty-three things that one wishes to achieve in their life. From the exotic to the mundane, users tag topics that allow other users to search for them based on their interest. Users can describe how they achieved the shared goal and help others to complete their list (Chai, Das, & Rao, 2011; Tapscott & Williams, 2006).

Virtual Teams

Not all Web 2.0 activities are fun and games. Many businesses have utilized social media and Web 2.0 technologies to generate profits and to facilitate employee learning and collective thinking. Virtual teams are an example of a Web 2.0 technology that businesses have been able to take advantage of in the workplace. By providing the tools necessary for team members to collaborate and share knowledge, businesses are helping to contribute to the performance of their employees by increasing motivation and willingness to work towards a common goal (Gibson & Cohen, 2003). For a team to be effective, all members must have a clear understanding of the shared goal. Virtual team technology works as a facilitator in helping organizations achieve their goals and objectives. Living and working in a global economy, it is essential for businesses to galvanize their shared goals. In virtual teams, users communicate electronically, giving organizations the opportunity to procure the best talent regardless of one's geographical location (Chai, Das, & Rao, 2011; Schlenkrich & Upfold, 2009).

SOPA and PIPA

Stop Online Piracy Act (SOPA) and Protect IP Act (PIPA) are two bills that have been introduced by the United States Senate. The goal of these bills is to address the concern of content piracy that has become associated with many of the Web 2.0 technologies discussed. Websites such as YouTube are based on user-generated contents. These sites allow and encourage users to upload their own video content. These sites have encountered users releasing copyrighted material such as music, movies, and television shows without proper authorization. The entertainment industry complains that they are losing millions of dollars a year because of digital piracy on these and other sites. SOPA (Stop Online Piracy Act) and PIPA (Protect IP Act) have not yet become laws and have encountered resistance among the web's major players. Many Internet companies argue that these bills could require individual's Internet provider to block websites that are involved in digital file sharing (Bhattacharjee, Gopal, & Sanders, 2003; Newman, 2012).

To voice their concerns over SOPA, websites such as Wikipedia and Wired.com went "dark" on January 18, 2012 for 24 hours. The websites did not allow any content to be viewed in order to give users a better understanding of what could occur if bills such as SOPA passed. Similarly, the major Internet player, Google, posted an anti-SOPA link on its homepage on the same day. It is important for web users to be aware of the impact these bills could have on their ability to search the Internet and use shared knowledge and data in both their work and play. Many of the Web 2.0 technologies are designed to facilitate mass participation. Ideally, these websites get better and better when more people use and contribute to them. If these web sites are constricted, the idea of the Internet evolving into a larger-scale web of openness and sharing could be inhibited (Daugherty, Eastin, & Bright, 2008; Subramani & Rajagopalan, 2003).

Mashup

Exploring another Web 2.0 staple, Mashup, draws upon discussions of Internet piracy and some of the hurdles users could face in the wake of PIPA and SOPA. Mashups are websites that combine data from multiple sources. Open API technologies that are characteristic of Web 2.0 technology such as JavaScript, allow these sites to integrate data and functions. The creators of the sites do not have to do it themselves. This innovation has allowed sites such as Google Earth and Trulia to utilize data from multiple sources to create a unique site of their own. Trulia combines public information on homes sales, property taxes, and satellite imaging to create mapping of recently sold residences, homes that are for sale, and estimated values. Tools like Trulia have altered the way users experience the Internet and will continue to frequent the site in the near future. As technology improves, it will be interesting to see how the reuse of free data and open source software will improve Internet users' experiences. It will be important to address both privacy concerns as we saw with Facebook and piracy concerns from major media and publishing entities (Newman, 2012).

Architecture and participation are at the center of Web 2.0 technologies. The impact of this technology has the ability to have profound impacts on organizational effectiveness. Virtual teams have allowed organizations to collaborate in real time without members necessarily having to even see each other face-to-face. Members are able to share ideas and work to achieve common goals in an open and collaborative environment. Web 2.0 offers businesses the ability to increase efficiency and effectiveness of their operations. Businesses seeking to decrease operating expenses can utilize virtual teams to save on travel expenses if project members are not located near each other (Bell, 2009; Schlenkrich & Upfold, 2009).

Really Simple Syndication (RSS)

Web 2.0 technologies have created innovative solutions to basic operating needs. Really Simple Syndication (RSS) is an example of how business can increase their effectiveness within the marketplace. RSS tools are essentially Internet feeds of news or blog sources, pushing data to an RSS reader. Users can subscribe to feeds based on their interest. These feeds can update information regularly and readers simply need to visit the URL of the feed. This one-stop-shop is not only convenient for readers, but also for businesses. Businesses can publish RSS readers on their websites, which allow the organization to add new content. Those websites with updated contents allow key words to be searchable by Google, Bing, Yahoo!, and other major search engines.

Greater web traffic can be directed to businesses' websites by keywords from an RSS feed. Many companies purchase online advertising models such as the Pay Per Click (PPC). A company's advertisement is shown on web sites or search engine results with related content. Companies pay for the advertisement when users click on the ad. Sites that have agreed to show the ads are paid a percentage of the revenue or a fee. Organizations can save money with RSS feeds by not having to pay for PCC ads and other online advertising models. Thus, the organization can redirect funds and resources to another initiate of the organization.

SOCIAL MEDIA APPLICATIONS

According to Lannin and Scott (2013), the types of sites that fall under the category of social media include, but are not limited to, SNSs (e.g., Facebook, MySpace, LinkedIn, Google+), publishing media (e.g., Wordpress, Blogger, Wikipedia), content sharing (e.g., Pinterest, YouTube, Flickr, Digg, Last.fm), discussion (e.g., Yahoo Messenger, Google Talk, Skype), microblogging (e.g., Twitter, Tumblr, Posterous), live streaming (e.g., Friendfeed, Lifestream), live casting (e.g., Live stream), and virtual worlds.

In order to determine which applications are most appropriate for business use, it is imperative that the business owners understand what each application is, how it works, how to engage customers and how to measure effectiveness. According to Nielson's 2012 "The Social Media Report", the top 10 social networking sites, in order of size, are: 1. Facebook, 2. Blogger, 3. Twitter, 4. Wordpress, 5. LinkedIn, 6. Pinterest, 7. Google+, 8. Tumblr, 9. Myspace, and 10. Wikia. For the theme of this book, we discuss and describe the top 6 and the YouTube below. Furthermore, each application will be examined as part of one of the following broader site categories: SNS, blogs, microblogs, and content sharing.

Social Networking Sites

SNS are defined by Boyd and Ellison (2007) as web-based services that allow individuals to (1) construct a public or semi-public profile within a bounded system, (2) articulate a list of other users with whom they share a connection, and (3) view and traverse their list of connections and those made by others within the system. The nature and nomenclature of these connections may vary from site to site.

Facebook

Facebook is an online SNS. It was developed in 2004 by Mark Zuckerburg. According to Facebook's 2013 Annual Report, their mission is "make the world more open and connected." Facebook has over 1 billion users and over 618 million daily active users. They create value for their users by allowing them to connect and share with friends, express themselves, discover and learn and stay connected everywhere. Facebook is free to join. Upon entry, the user will see a timeline that allows users to display and organize memorable posts and photos in chronological order. There is also a news feed. The news feed is at the core of the user's home page and is a list of posts and stories from the user's friends. There is also a photo and video section which allows users to post photos and videos and share via "tagging" with others. In 2012, Facebook purchased Instagram. Instagram is a mobile-based photo sharing application, thus allowing users to upload photos instantly from their smart phones or tablets. Given that personal privacy is an issue for most users, it is important to note that the user can modify security settings for more privacy. Once a personal page is created, the user can create a business page (aka, Fan Pages).

The business user can then encourage "friends" to "like" their page. This allows others to view the user's posts, photos, videos and likes.

Facebook creates value for the business user with reach, relevance and engagement. Facebook ads can be purchased that target specific demographics; thereby, creating custom audiences. The user can choose to pay per click (CPC) or per thousand impressions (CPM) and can set a daily budget. Facebook provides ad analytics to enable tracking of the ad performance. This allows the business owners to modify the ad as needed. Effectiveness is measured via ad analytics, as well as data outlining users to the site, number of "likes", comments, posts and shares. Furthermore, the business owner can track the number of visitors to the company website that arrive from their Facebook page. Facebook is effective for business owners because it allows them to reach their target customers with a personal approach in a cost effective manner. In addition, 51% of consumers said they were more likely to buy a product after becoming a fan on Facebook (Narayanan et al., 2012).

LinkedIn

LinkedIn is a professional networking site. According to the LinkedIn company website, their mission is "to connect the world's professionals to make them more productive and successful." LinkedIn currently has over 225 million members in over 200 countries (About LinkedIn, 2013). Once registered, the user can setup a profile, complete with resume details, including employment and education experience. Once a profile is created, the user can begin to grow their professional network by inviting others to join their network. In addition to a personal page, the user can establish a business page. LinkedIn creates analytics for business pages that collects data on who is visiting your page and provides the user recommendations on other companies to follow. Other social networking sites include Google+ and MySpace. Other professional networking sites include Biznik.com, EFactor.com and meetingwave.com.

Blogs

According to Walker (2003), "a weblog, or blog, is a frequently updated website consisting of dated entries arranged in reverse chronological order so the most recent post appears first. Examples of genre exist on a continuum from confessional online diaries to logs tracking specific topics or activities through links and commentary." In order to be an effective blog, the commentary option should be made available in order to invite a conversation with the public (Garden, 2002).

Blogger

Blogger started in 1999 and was bought by Google in 2002 (Gillmor, 2003). As of 2012, Blogger had 58 million unique US PC users (Nielsen, 2012) . Blogger is a free to use online site that allows users to create their own blog, a site where users can publish their thoughts while engaging others. Once entering blogger, users can take a tour to learn more about the product features. The user can customize the look of their blog page and post photos and/or videos to each post. In addition, the user can earn money if they choose to participate in the AdSense program. This program places relevant ads on the user's blog post and Google/Blogger pays the user a portion of the proceeds. Followers are encouraged by adding a "Followers Gadget" to the page asking others to follow their blog. According to Lackie and LeMasney (2007), Blogger is the best choice for the minimalist, end user, slow adopter, non-adapter, conservative computer user, or basic blogger.

Wordpress

Wordpress is a free blogging engine, similar to Blogger, but Wordpress can be installed locally or used online. Wordpress has over 30 million users

(Nielsen, 2012). According to Lackie and LeMasney (2007), Wordpress is the best choice for the technologist, system administrator, programmer, experimenter, or experienced blogger. Wordpress allows users to blog, post, upload photos and follow other blogs. Wordpress provides analytics to view statistics about followers and viewers. Other blog sites include Bloglines, Flickr and Yahoo360.

Microblogs

Twitter

Twitter can be referred to as a filterblog or microblog. Similar to a blog, Twitter is used to quickly share a thought, picture or link, but with 140 characters or less. As of 2012, Twitter had over 500 million users, 140 active users (Narayanan et al., 2012). Twitter is a free service. Once an account is set up, the user enters to a central home page. The user can choose to send a message, "tweet", or follow others. Once the user develops a list of individuals to follow, a stream will appear on the home page with tweets from the individuals the users are following. The user can then resend, "re-tweet", a message from a person they are following to their followers or reply directly to that person. The "at sign", "@", is used to connect with another Twitter follow. Hashtags, "#", are used to bring attention to a particular topic and allow people to search for streams within Twitter about a specific topic. For example, if the user is talking about manufacturing, #manufacturing would be entered in the tweet. Then, others can search Twitter for "manufacturing" to find others talking about that particular topic.

Twitter provides analytics for companies to track follower demographics and activity. Twitter also offers promoted Tweets, which is a cost based service that makes posts for visible. Twitter statistics are impressive and important for business owners to take note. According to Narayanan et al. (2012), more than half of the active Twitter users follow companies, brands, or products, 79% of US Twitter users are more likely to recommend brands they follow, and 67% of US Twitter users are more likely to buy from brands they follow. Other Microblogs include GoogleReader, Tumblr and Bloglines.

Content Sharing

Pinterest

Pinterest is a photo sharing site. Quite simply, it is a pin board. After becoming a member, the user can share photos of interest on their virtual pin board. Pinterest has over 27 million unique PC visitors (Nielsen, 2012). A key benefit is that Pinterest reportedly drives more web traffic to other sites than Google+, LinkedIn, and YouTube combined (Fox, 2012). That is staggering and the main reason why business owners should be "pinning". The user should begin with at least 5 pin boards and add pins on a regular basis to attract followers. Pinterest etiquette suggests that the user always credit the source. The business owner should include Pin Buttons on their company website, so customers can pin easily. The business Pinterest board should be a mix of self-promotion and personal creativity. In addition, it is encouraged to download the Pinterest app so to pin photos from business functions and events and post to other social media sites as well (Peregrin, 2012). Effectiveness can be measured by the number of followers, re-pins and traffic to the company website. Other photo sharing and photo blog sites include Picasa, Flickr.

YouTube

Although a video site did not qualify for a top 10 spot in Nielson's 2012 "The Social Media Report", YouTube has become the second largest search engine only next to Google since 2013. We believe that video sharing can be important for small businesses and deserved a mention. YouTube is a video blogging site. It was started in 2005 and in 2006 was bought by Google. According to Narayanan, et al. (2012), YouTube has over 800 million unique visitors every month and those users can watch and rate videos. It is a powerful free tool that businesses can utilize to create their own public channel. YouTube also offers free analytics that can provide information on who are the viewers and what are their demographics. Other video sites include Google Video and IFILM.

It is important to note that many of these applications may fall into numerous categories. For example, although Facebook is best known as a social networking site, it is also a professional networking site, microblog and photo sharing site. The applications were categorized based on their main function.

HOW SOCIAL MEDIA PRESENCE AFFECTS COMPANIES

Web 2.0 and social media have allowed companies to tailor products and services to customers' needs and interests. There have been numerous changes in the way businesses can utilize information through these innovative technologies. Web 2.0 and social media create a paradigm shift in the way organizations operate and collaborate. User-generated content and crowd sourcing have filled the Internet with new content as well as the perception of how information can be shared (Surowiecki, 2005; Whitla, 2009). Massive data collection for business analytics by social media sites, such as Facebook and LinkedIn, has created shifts in business models. Advertisements targeting users' interest are made possible from large networks of information sharing (Subramani & Rajagopalan, 2003).

Businesses have been able to use the Internet as their platform to deliver services through the browser rather than traditional means. Companies can readily use Google Docs to generate invoices, training materials, and company memos without having to license expensive software such as Microsoft Office. Furthermore, with the integration of Web 2.0 services such as social media, companies can interact and collaborate in a more cohesive manner with its consumers and employees (Gallivan, Spitler, & Koufaris, 2005; Nambisan & Baron, 2007; Pentina, et al., 2008; Taylor, et al., 2011).

It is important to note that company technology must stay current to trends and service enhancements. Technology is constantly evolving. It is imperative that an organization be aware of the types of technology that are pertinent to their industry. They need to know how to take advantage of them. Organizations should focus on budgetary measures to ensure appropriate funds are allocated to electronic equipment updating and information technology staff. Companies always face the threat of a larger, better funded, and better organized entrant into their marketplace. A competitive advantage can be sustained if an organization is current on the trends of its consumers and available service enhancements. An organization may wish to update their website by integrating Facebook, LinkedIn, YouTube, and Flickr icons on their site. Users can click on a number of interactive Web 2.0 services to enhance their experience and connect to the organization in a way that is relatable and enjoyable to them (Nambisan & Baron, 2007).

A company can expand its brand presence through the use of Web 2.0 and social media. Sites such as Facebook, Twitter, and LinkedIn, can be utilized by businesses to connect with individuals seeking the types of goods or services they provide. The fast-food chain McDonalds uses Twitter to offer giveaways such as t-shirts, in order to strum-up customer interest. McDonalds also lists that they have a presence on Twitter in order to listen and respond to customer feedback. Companies must also be aware that overexposure could lead to a devalued brand or distain for their products. Twitter followers could become fed up with constant promotions or one member's feed tweeting too often. Users can became over saturated with information that is not of immediate interest to them. Thus, a brand's novelty could wear off. Despite the risks, companies are willing to pay to have millions of Twitter followers (Johnson, 2009).

With the utilization of Web 2.0 and social media within the workplace, companies must be aware that positive feedback is not always guaranteed. Websites such as Yelp have developed to allow users to review local restaurants and businesses. The site facilitates open communication between the business owner and its customers. Organizations benefit from having an online presence on these sites. They must be prepared to receive negative feedback. It is not always possible to please every consumer. Owners need to be aware of this fact and furthermore be prepared to address these reviews (Pentina, et al., 2008).

Yelp gives owners the opportunity to respond to customer feedback and turn the situation it into a positive one by taking the reviews as constructive criticism. Thus, business owners who are dependent on word-of-mouth advertising from this site have the opportunity to win customers back and show their desire to create a positive brand experience. Many businesses that receive negative feedback offer the dissatisfied customers discount or free service as well as a heart-felt apology. The website TripAdvisor allows travelers to not only converse about recent destinations and vacation experiences, but to review hotels and upload personal pictures of the facilities. Resort mangers have been quick to respond to hotel patrons' experiences and ratings of their facilities. Web 2.0 has helped to facilitate a new way consumers interact with brands and the way that businesses respond to these interactions (Parra-López, Bulchand-Gidumal, Gutiérrez-Taño, & Díaz-Armas, 2011; TripAdvisor, 2013).

SOCIAL MEDIA STRATEGY

Business strategy drives organizational and information systems strategy; therefore, overall business strategy also drives social media strategy. It is imperative that any social media strategy is linked with the company's objectives and goals. What does the company want to achieve from social media? Who do they want to engage? How will they measure effectiveness? A social media strategy can only be developed once those questions are answered.

According to Mergel (2013), all successful social media strategies need to clearly outline why, who, what, how, for whom, where, and did it work. The company needs to clearly outline who will oversee the social media strategy, determine the roles and responsibilities, decide on the content, who will provide the content and to whom they will share it. Then the company can begin to decide which of the social media applications are most appropriate for them. For a company just beginning to develop a social media strategy, a good place to start would be the use of a SNS and microblog, such as Facebook and Twitter. Finally, the company needs to ensure there are quantitative and qualitative measures in place to determine effectiveness.

After the strategic decisions are made, social media tactics and campaigns can be established. A good social media strategy will work to engage others in meaningful dialogue online, setup a conversational calendar and drive customers to the company website. According to French, Laberge and Magill (2012), customer engagement can be encouraged and improved via 5 steps. First, a customer engagement summit should be held with the purpose of aligning managers on the vision of engagement and decide the activities needed to engage customers. Second, a customer engagement council should be formed and should meet regularly. The purpose is to bring together all the forms of engagement, sales, services, marketing, product management, etc. to ensure alignment. Third, a chief content officer should be appointed to manage all the engagement touch points to ensure appropriate implementation of the strategy. Fourth, a listening center should be established.

Many companies spend time creating content but fail to monitor what is said about them on social media. This allows the company to quickly respond to both positive and negative feedback and foster a customer relationship. Lastly, the company needs to evaluate the total engagement budget. It is important to look at the business in its entirety to determine what is being spent on engagement. Then, create a plan to maximize efforts and minimize waste.

Now that a chief content officer has been identified, that individual can begin to generate a conversational calendar that would include content timing of posts and themes, as well as the social applications that will be used. The calendar should include the topics for the month, the application being used and the author of the content. This will ensure that all the applications are showcasing collaborative content. Many small businesses can get to this point. They establish a plan, setup a calendar and work to develop content. But, they fall short because they fail to development meaningful content that truly engages the customer. According to Schlinke and Crain (2013), in order to develop meaningful content, it is important to "act like a journalist". The chief content officer should know about the social media applications, build an editorial calendar, view the content from the reader's perspective, interview customers in their demographic, inform and educate readers, give a balanced assessment and be honest. In addition, the content should make sense for the brand.

Many companies start with a company website. With any social media strategy, it is important to ensure the website is fully integrated. First, the business owner needs to assess the website. The website needs to load quickly, be easy to view on a mobile device, be easy to navigate, be up-to-date, include current copyright, ensure that social media links are easily accessible and contain clear contact information. The hub and spoke model is often used to grow social media presence with the website acting as the hub and the spokes being the different social media applications. The website is 100% controlled by the business; whereas, the social media applications may change over time. Therefore, the company can completely control the website and continuously improve it. The website is where your customers will ultimately purchase your products and see the face of your brand; the social media applications, also called "spokes," are what help drive the customers there. Keep in mind the traffic along the spokes should run both ways to ensure engagement (Andzulis, Panagopoulos, & Rapp, 2012).

USING SOCIAL MEDIA TO INCREASE SALES AND DECREASE COSTS

Organizations can reduce operating costs by utilizing user-generated content and encouraging self-regulation. Many websites will advertise their Yelp reviews on their webpages. Yelp has created HTML code that businesses can plug into their webpage so that a live stream of the more positive reviews can be seen. As a consequence, businesses have real-life consumer reviews at their disposal. An organization could utilize these reviews by directing interested consumers to the reviews. Companies could cut costs on advertising or redirect advertising in a way that is more efficient and continually updated by a third party, for free (Taylor, et al., 2011).

Many Web 2.0 sites such as Wikipedia, YouTube, and Facebook allow users to flag inappropriate content and encourage self-regulation on their sites. Organizations can utilize user interest in creating a cohesive and high-quality experience. Wikipedia is not only based on the premise of user contributions to create a free, multilingual, online encyclopedia, but it also solicits volunteers to monitor these entries and contributions. Creating a substantially user-managed site reduces IT costs and the expense of hiring employees to do this work. Furthermore, it is not just externally facing Web 2.0 sites that are user-regulated. Through the use of Web 2.0 tools, company applications can be self-managed by employees and the users of the product.

The benefits to user-regulated applications and websites are well noted. However, in May 2005, Wikipedia encountered a significant blow to its self-regulated style. The Wikipedia biography incident known as, the Seigenthaler incident, occurred and lasted for four months. A Wikipedia entry on John Seigenthaler, Robert Kennedy's administrative assistant in the 1960's, falsely stated that he was thought to be directly involved in both John F. Kennedy and Robert Kennedy's assassination among other things (Seigenthaler, 2005). The author of the entry was anonymous. Wikipedia was unable to trace who had written the entry. An anti-Wikipedia activist, Daniel Brandt, was able to trace the IP address to a business in Nashville, Tennessee. An employee at the Nashville address, named Brain Chase, later came forward and admitted to making the Wikipedia entry (Terdiman, 2005). The Seigenthaler incident highlights the ways in which organizations must be aware of both the benefits and pitfalls of this new online paradigm. With a wealth of users and consumers contributing to site content, businesses must ensure that they are prepared to handle inaccurate and negative feedback.

Web 2.0 tools allow customers to more easily interact with companies. This can be accomplished through the integration on multiple platforms. Drawing data from one source, users can navigate through information that is of particular interest to them (Murugesan, 2007). When data is pulled from multiple sites, such as seen on Trulia's website, users benefit more from the aggregation of multiple data sources. Paralleling this integration of multiple data sources, consumers can pull data on organizations through the use of companies integrating their information on multiple platforms. A green cleaning company may set up a Twitter account to give eco-friendly cleaning tips, a Flickr account to allow consumers to see before and after pictures of homes they have cleaned, a YouTube video to display a promotional commercial, and a blog to detail the company's use of green products and the role they are playing in saving the environment. Through the use of multiple Web 2.0 applications, an organization can reach multiple users in a way that best relates to the user's interest (Nambisan & Baron, 2007; Trulia, 2013).

PRIVACY CONCERNS

It should be noted that while Web 2.0 innovations have created architecture for user-friendly business practices and experiences; privacy issues for companies can arise (Lanois, 2010; McDonald & Cranor, 2008). Hacking organizations have targeted not only major U.S. corporations, but also the United States government. Companies have been eager to utilize the convenience and cost benefits of cloud computing and Web 2.0 tools such as social media, cloud gaming, and Google Docs (Miller, 2008; Shimba, 2010).

Organizations need to implement and review policies for social media and Internet use for company employees. Ensuring that there are multiple safeguards in place such as two-step user verification and clear guidelines on the use of both personal and company Internet use can help to reduce privacy breaches. Consumers usually trust companies with their personal data. Users are able to make online purchases with their banking and credit card information utilizing Web 2.0 technologies. Other types of Non-Public Personal Information (NPPI) such as consumers' email addresses, phone numbers, and home addresses are utilized by organizations for various purposes (Rosenblum, 2007).

This personal information must be stored using the highest level of security whether it is in the "cloud" or on individual devices. Wireless application protocol (WAP) is commonly used in mobile web payment sites to integrate Web 2.0 applications onto devices such as mobile phones or tablets. WAP payments are usually secured on 128 bit encrypted websites and bill credit cards or online wallets directly, adding an additional layer of security for these consumer transactions. Companies have been able to use Web 2.0 technologies to provide more convenient tools for its employees and customers to safeguard their privacy. Businesses must be knowledgeable in the security of these technologies and be able to educate their consumers in order to take full advantage of these social media tools (McDonald & Cranor, 2008; Shimba, 2010).

MANAGERIAL CONSIDERATIONS OF WEB 2.0 AND SOCIAL MEDIA

Web 2.0 technology and social media can increase internal communication within an organization. Collaborative Web 2.0 tools such as social media and document sharing applications like Google Docs facilitate an interconnected work environment. Kirkman, Rosen, Tesluk, and Gibson (2004) conducted a study to explore how technological advances utilized in the workplace have benefited employees and their consumers. They found that highly empowered virtual teams were associated with significantly higher levels of process improvement and customer satisfaction than were less empowered teams. Empowering team members, and in turn improving customer satisfaction, have been key benefits of Web 2.0 technology in the workplace (Siebdrat, Hoegl, & Ernst, 2009).

With advances in Web 2.0 use in the workplace, businesses need to consider data protection. There could be security threats to the organization and its customers. Organizations should set specific guidelines for its employees to follow when handling Non Public Personal Information (NPPI) of its customers. It is important for organizations to properly train their employees to be aware of privacy settings and safety measures to take when utilizing social media and other Web 2.0 tools. Lack of training can lead to improper sharing of personal or company data without necessary malicious intention (Rosenblum, 2007; Subramani & Rajagopalan, 2003).

User trust and Internet privacy concern may affect the use of social media sites for social interaction. Dwyer, Hiltz, and Passerini (2007) found that users from Facebook and MySpace expressed similar levels of concern regarding Internet privacy. Facebook members were more trusting of the site and its members and more willing to include identifying information in their profile (McDonald & Cranor, 2008). They indicate that privacy within a social media site is not often expected and it is undefined. Users should make themselves aware of privacy settings within social networks such as Facebook or Twitter. Social media sites record all interactions and retain them for potential use in social data mining and business analytics. The study mentions the idea that social interactions take place face-to-face daily outside of the Internet without leaving a trace of lingering data. It would make sense that users would be preconditioned to not necessarily having privacy concerns when engaged in on-line social interactions. Organizations should encourage employees of using social media, both in and out of the workplace, to be aware of information sharing. Disclosing personal information such as email addresses or real name to their friends and communities on the social media sites may become a piece of information of business analytics and data mining (Subramani & Rajagopalan, 2003; Zhang, Sun, Zhu, & Fang, 2010).

It is not just Non-Public Personal Information of employees and customers that can be unintentionally shared. Company trade secrets and strategies can become publicly available without proper safeguards. For example, detailed plans of the United States Embassy being built in Baghdad, Iraq, appeared online in breach of security measure taken to protect the project. The website of the Kansas City, Missouri-based architectural firm that was contracted to design the compound accidently released the computer generated renderings without authorization (Lee, 2007). Clearly, in the midst of the Iraqi war, the United States State Department would not want this information to be widely available to the public. This incident highlights the importance of educating all employees of the importance of sensitive data and adhering to company IT policies. These cases illustrate the real-world implications of data breaches in a technologically advanced society.

It should be noted that the State Department incident was not suspected to be malicious. The Better Business Bureau encourages company review postings by consumers and former employees regularly as a risk management strategy. A disgruntled employee could harm a company's brand and customer base through data breaches. An irritated employee could illegally release consumer NPPI or write inaccurate information on social media sites while in possession of company Web 2.0 tools. Former employees can also do this through Web 2.0 blogs or social media sites such as LinkedIn. Confidentiality agreement between employees and the organization could prevent employees from ranting and raving about the organization on social media sites but not absolutely from information leakage.

TECHNICAL ISSUES AND BUSINESS IMPLICATIONS

It is essential to highlight both the positives and negatives of Web 2.0 tools and social media. One important benefit of Web 2.0 applications is the ability for the technology to ease consumers' lives. Consumers are able to integrate the technology on multiple platforms such as their smartphones or tablets and access information on the road or in the workplace. Businesses can utilize the convenience factor for customers by developing their Web 2.0 technologies in a way that appeals to their direct customers (Harridge-March & Quinton, 2009). Consumers seeking convenience and efficiency can place orders for goods on their mobile devices using applications developed by technology-based retail companies such as Amazon.com and Overstock.com. Smaller start-up companies can easily interact with local customers through Yelp and Twitter and create a user-friendly experience to enhance brand interaction.

Organizations will need IT experts to help facilitate the use of Web 2.0 applications within a business. For example, a small food truck business in Los Angeles selling fresh, organic juices has employed a web developer to create an application that would allow potential customers to track the juice truck's location. Customers can see the route the truck will take for the day, and can plan their purchase accordingly. The company, Juice on the Loose, also fully integrates Web 2.0 tools on their web page. Juice on the Loose provides a link to their Yelp page and integrates live feeds of their Twitter and Facebook pages all on their homepage (Pentina, et al., 2008; Juice on the Loose, 2013).

Organizations shall define how they will adopt social media and Web 2.0 technologies. By defining how they will adopt these technologies, companies can lay the proper groundwork for current and future operations (Ross, Weill, & Robertson, 2006). Pearlson and Saunders (2013) suggest several architectural principles such as ease of use, speed and quality, buying over building, innovation, data security, and data quality to organizations when adopting innovative IT technologies like Web 2.0 tools. It requires an in-depth knowledge of IT infrastructure and architecture to ensure that Web 2.0 tools and social media are best utilized to support business applications.

IBM has implemented Technology Adoption Programs (TAP) in order to remain competitive and on the forefront of innovation. IBM states that community participation in its TAP strategy is a critical element for the program to succeed. Alkalay, et al. (2007) points out that TAP could not work if IBM did not have an active community of emerging technology enthusiasts who can effectively collaborate using Web 2.0 tools. IBM supports the TAP community within the

IBM intranet. IBM is working to utilize new technological innovations in a user-driven and self-governing manner.

Organizations do not necessarily adopt Web 2.0 tools because of their novelty. There are other managerial considerations for IBM and various organizations adopting Web 2.0 applications within their work environments. Adaptability of the technology, standardization, scalability, and return on investment (ROI) should be on the Web 2.0 project plan. Actual costs of IT infrastructure such as server rooms and website development can be accounted for. It is important to measure the benefits of Web 2.0 technology such as brand loyalty and employee retention. Businesses can remain relevant to their customers and attract employees through financial investment to their commitments to innovative technology like Web 2.0 applications. Corporate policies must adapt and be open to evolving social media procedures for its employees. Allowing social media use by employees during office hours could create an open environment of dialogue and an innovative atmosphere within an organization. It is also important for companies to train their employees on the distinction of social media between company business and personal use (Harridge-March & Quinton, 2009). Web 2.0 and social media applications provide companies with the ability to interact with consumers and suppliers. Not all users are well versed to this technology. There can be user control issues such as one's inability to understand full privacy settings on social media sites or how to create a wiki entry (Zhang, et al., 2010).

BEST PRACTICES AND THE FUTURE OF SOCIAL MEDIA

According to the Flynn (2012), there are 113 social media best practices described for the following categories: legal risks, record management, regulatory risks, privacy and security risks, blog risks, mobile device risks, policy audits, writing effective policy, content management risks, employee training and reputation management. An example of a best practice for legal risks, states "because the law has not kept pace with social media, it's essential for employers implementing rules, policies, and procedures to help manage behavior, mitigate risk, and maximize legal compliance". Further an example of a best practice for employee training includes, "you cannot expect an untrained workforce to be compliant. Educate everyone who works on behalf of your organization". These 113 social media best practices are informative and practical and should be considered when designing social media strategy.

According to Strømmen-Bakhtiar (2012), the future of social media is highly uncertain. Further, if both the online communities and civil societies are not careful and do not act in concert to inform and educate the public; there is a great chance that the social media will become another tool for control, propaganda and surveillance of the citizenry. However, social media is growing, interesting, dynamic and complex. The type and number of social media applications grow and change daily. It is important that businesses continuously educate themselves and choose to use those applications that make the best fit for their business. Understanding the applications, incorporating them into a sound social media strategy that fits in with the company's overall business goals and measuring their effectiveness will help ensure long term success (Strømmen-Bakhtiar, 2012).

Web 2.0 applications can easily face obstacles because they are client-sided technologies. With the convenience of being able to interact with members in real time through virtual teams or social networks, it is important to notes that all of the information must be presented through a browser. The dependency on programming languages and browser-based applications can potentially stifle Web 2.0 technology from evolving. These types of technologies use a great amount of Internet bandwidth. For example, the video sharing sites

YouTube, Vevo, and Hulu allow users to stream media such as music, videos, television shows, and movies all over the Internet. Currently, Web 2.0 service providers use many proprietary technologies to maintain control over their contents. Google's email service uses its own task-specific browser plug-ins and Wikipedia uses self-developed wiki technology. All of this information is passed on to the user through the use of web applications like JavaScript. Google is developing a programming language called Google Dart in order to relieve dependency on JavaScript. Looking forward, Web 3.0 technologies should seek to solve such dependencies of browser applications (Bhattacharjee, Gopal, & Sanders, 2003).

Future technological infrastructure and applications must address the implications of many users accessing these large resources. Since users of many Web 2.0 applications and social media sites are able to contribute to and edit the contents of websites, one must ask if all of this information is positively contributing to the wealth of information on the Internet. One may argue that websites are filling up with useless or inaccurate information, which are polluting the Internet. However, it is the dependence on user contributions that are facilitating many of the great works that are coming out of Web 2.0 technology. For example, OpenStreetMap is building a free public-domain street map of the entire world through the compilation of local street maps made by their residents. The residents use GPS tracking to create the maps and upload the data to OpenStreetMap for the company to create a single large-scale map. Similarly, Inrix's Dust Network is tracking over 500,000 vehicles in the United States in order to provide real-time data on highway congestion (Goodchild, 2007). In both of these situations, the companies are dependent on volunteers to provide information in order to develop their products. Without the contribution of well-meaning users, these products would take additional time and money, or perhaps might not have developed at all.

CONCLUSION

The development of Web 2.0 and social media applications has been revolutionary to the ways in which we interact with one another. Our society has seen cultural shifts in which we view information sharing and our privacy. Web 2.0 applications have the ability to reach into almost every facet of our lives. An example of this has been the use of Web 2.0 to teach in higher education settings. Web 2.0 is facilitating a wealth of information sharing and creating unique user-experiences not previously seen in our society. Businesses have been able to utilize Web 2.0 applications to help enhance employee learning and collective thinking. Employees and customers are able to collaborate and share knowledge more easily.

Businesses are helping to contribute to the performance of their employees by increasing their motivation and willingness to work towards a common goal. Research has found that employees use Web 2.0 tools and social media for search and discovery of work-related information. Blogs, bookmarks, and wikis represent new repositories of information generated by employees. It has become increasingly important for organizations to provide internal social media tools to retain employees and increase internal communication among them. Companies are able to retain employees by bridging generational gaps through rich communications in social media. Many younger employees communicate primarily through Web 2.0 applications such as social networks and blogs. Companies that do not support the infrastructure or development of Web 2.0 technologies could suffer by having its employees move critical information outside of a company's firewall.

Web 2.0 and social media continually evolve for both personal and work benefits. Thus, social media organizations must stay current and relevant to provide effective tools to meet the needs of its individual and corporate users. Similarly, organizations will also benefit if they too evolve in this new social paradigm. From the sales front to human resources, companies have the opportunity to expand their market presence by interacting more gracefully with their customers through the use of Web 2.0 and social media applications.

Businesses are opening themselves up to new ways of interacting with stakeholders and thus becoming more competitive and efficient in their markets. Businesses implementing Web 2.0 applications within their organization need to train employees to properly use these technologies. Businesses should have a company IT policies, which are primed to handle the privacy and security concerns. Negative feedback generated from the use of these Web 2.0 and social media technologies can be handled carefully in a timely manner.

Furthermore, companies must also define their objectives with Web 2.0 technologies. Operating in a global economy, it is essential for businesses to galvanize their shared goals. If implemented correctly, Web 2.0 applications provide functions for greater internal communication within the organization as well as the external communication with customers and community. Web 2.0 tools allow businesses to collect suggestions and tailor their products to specific clientele. Through better communication using Web 2.0 and social media tools, businesses have benefited from employee retention and customer royalty. Thus, Web 2.0 and social media tools are becoming influential factors in an organization's sustainable business model and strategic management.

REFERENCES

Alexander, B., & Levine, A. (2008). Web 2.0 storytelling emergence of a new genre. *Educause Review Online, 43*(2).

Alkalay, A., Almond, C., Bloom, J., Chow, A., Peters, F., Rogers, R., & Wyble, C. (2007). *Supporting Innovators and Early Adopters A Technology Adoption Program Cookbook.* IBM International Technical Support Organization. Retrieved September 10, 2013 from http://www.redbooks.ibm.com/redpapers/pdfs/redp4374.pdf

Anderson, P. (2007). What is Web 2.0? Ideas, technologies and implications for education. *JISC Technology and Standards Watch*, 1-64.

Andzulis, J. M., Panagopoulos, N. G., & Rapp, A. (2012). A review of social media and implications for the sales process. *Journal of Personal Selling & Sales Management, 32*(3), 305–316. doi:10.2753/PSS0885-3134320302

Armstrong, C. L., & Gao, F. (2010). Now tweet this: How news organizations use Twitter. *Electronic News, 4*(4), 218–235. doi:10.1177/1931243110389457

Bateman, C. R., Valentine, S., & Rittenburg, T. (2013). Ethical decision making in a peer-to-peer file sharing situation: The role of moral absolutes and social consensus. *Journal of Business Ethics, 115*(2), 229–240. doi:10.1007/s10551-012-1388-1

Bell, A. (2009). *Exploring web 2.0: Second generation interactive tools -blogs, podcasts, wikis, networking, virtual worlds, and more*. Washington, DC: Katy Crossing Press.

Bhattacharjee, S., Gopal, R. D., & Sanders, G. L. (2003). Digital music and online sharing: Software piracy 2.0. *Communications of the ACM, 46*(7), 107–111. doi:10.1145/792704.792707

Blanchard, O. (2011). *Social Media ROI: Managing and Measuring Social Media Efforts in Your Organization.* Boston, MA: Pearson Education, Inc.

Boyd, D. M., & Ellison, N. B. (2007). Social network sites: Definition, history, and scholarship. *Journal of Computer-Mediated Communication, 13*(1), 210–230. doi:10.1111/j.1083-6101.2007.00393.x

Chai, S., Das, S., & Rao, H. R. (2011). Factors affecting bloggers' knowledge sharing: An investigation across gender. *Journal of Management Information Systems, 28*(3), 309–342. doi:10.2753/MIS0742-1222280309

Daugherty, T., Eastin, M., & Bright, L. (2008). Exploring consumer motivations for creating user-generated content. *Journal of Interactive Advertising, 8*(2), 1–24. doi:10.1080/15252019.2008.10722139

Dwyer, C., Hiltz, S., & Passerini, K. (2007). Trust and privacy concern within social networking sites: a comparison of Facebook and Myspace. In *Proceedings of the Thirteenth Americas Conference on Information Systems*. Keystone, CO: Academic Press. Retrieved September 10, 2013 from http://csis.pace.edu/~dwyer/research/DwyerAMCIS2007.pdf

Flynn, N. (2012). *The social media handbook: Policies and best practices to effectively manage your organization's social media presence, posts, and potential risks*. San Francisco, CA: Pfeiffer.

Fox, Z. (2012). *Pinterest drives more traffic than Google+, YouTube and LinkedIn combined*. Retrieved February 11, 2014 from http://mashable.com/2012/02/01/pinterest-traffic-study/

French, T., LaBerge, L., & Magill, P. (2012). Five 'no regrets' moves for superior customer engagement. *The McKinsey Quarterly*, (3): 119–125.

Gallivan, M. J., Spitler, V. K., & Koufaris, M. (2005). Does information technology training really matter? A social information processing analysis of coworkers' influence on IT usage in the workplace. *Journal of Management Information Systems, 22*(1), 153–192.

Garden, M. (2012). Defining blog: A fool's errand or a necessary undertaking. *Journalism, 13*(4), 483–499. doi:10.1177/1464884911421700

Gibson, C., & Cohen, S. (2003). *Virtual teams that work: Creating conditions for virtual team effectiveness*. San Francisco, CA: Jossey-Bass.

Gillmor, D. (2003). Google buys Pyra: Blogging goes big-time. *EJournal*. Retrieved January 20, 2014 from http://web.archive.org/web/20031008161432/http://weblog.siliconvalley.com/column/dangillmor/archives/000802.shtml

Goodchild, M. (2007). Citizens as voluntary sensors: Spatial data infrastructure in the world of Web 2.0. *International Journal of Spatial Data Infrastructures Research, 2*, 24–32.

Harridge-March, S., & Quinton, S. (2009). Virtual snakes and ladders: Social networks and the relationship marketing loyalty ladder. *The Marketing Review, 9*(2), 171–181. doi:10.1362/146934709X442692

Johnson, S. (2009). How Twitter will change the way we live. *Time Magazine*. Retrieved September 10, 2013 from http://content.time.com/time/magazine/article/0,9171,1902818,00.html

Juice On The Loose. (2013). Retrieved September 10, 2013 from http://www.juiceloosela.com

Kirkman, B., Rosen, B., Tesluk, P., & Gibson, C. (2004). The impact of team empowerment on virtual team performance: The moderating role of face-to-face interaction. *Academy of Management Journal, 47*(2), 175–192. doi:10.2307/20159571

Lackie, R. J., & LeMasney, J. W. (2007). Blogger, WorldPress.com, and their pseudoblog alternatives: A comparison of focus, features, and feel. *Journal of Library Administration, 46*(3/4), 139–180.

Lannin, D. G., & Scott, N. A. (2013). Social networking ethics: Developing best practices for the new small world. *Professional Psychology, Research and Practice*, *44*(3), 135–141. doi:10.1037/a0031794

Lanois, P. (2010). Caught in the Clouds: The Web 2.0, cloud computing, and privacy? *Northwestern Journal of Technology and Intellectual Property*, *9*(2), 29–49.

Lee, M. (2007). Baghdad embassy plans turn up online. *The Huffington Post*. Retrieved September 10, 2013 from http://www.huffingtonpost.com/huff-wires/20070531/baghdad-embassy-plans/

LinkedIn. (2013). *About LinkedIn*. Retrieved February 11, 2014 from http://www.linkedin.com/about-us

Mayfield, A. (2008). *What is Social Media?* iCrossing eBook. Retrieved September 10, 2013 from http://www.icrossing.co.uk/fileadmin/uploads/eBooks/What_is_Social_Media_iCrossing_ebook.pdf

McAfee, A. (2009). *Enterprise 2.0: New Collaborative Tools for Your Organization's Toughest Challenges*. Boston, MA: Harvard Business School Press.

McDonald, A. M., & Cranor, L. F. (2008). The cost of reading privacy policies. *ACM Transactions on Computer-Human Interaction*, *4*(3), 1–22. doi:10.1145/1314683.1314684

Mergel, I. (2013). Designing a social media strategy to fulfill your agency's mission. *Public Management*, *42*(1), 26–29.

Miller, M. (2008). *Cloud computing: Web-based applications that change the way you work and collaborate*. Indianapolis, IN: Queue Publishers.

Murugesan, S. (2007). Understanding web 2.0. *IT Professional*, *9*(4), 34–41. doi:10.1109/MITP.2007.78

Nambisan, S., & Baron, R. A. (2007). Interactions in virtual customer environments: Implications for product support and customer relationship management. *Journal of Interactive Marketing*, *21*(2), 42–62. doi:10.1002/dir.20077

Narayanan, M., Asur, S., Nair, A., Rao, S., Kaushik, A., & Mehta, D. et al. (2012). Social media and business. *Vikalpa: The Journal for Decision Makers*, *37*(4), 69–111.

Newman, J. (2012, January 17). SOPA and PIPA: Just the Facts. *PC World*. Retrieved September 10, 2013 from http://www.pcworld.com/article/248298/sopa_and_pipa_just_the_facts.html

Nielson. (2012). *The Social Media Report*. Retrieved from http://www.nielsen.com/content/dam/corporate/us/en/reports-downloads/2012-Reports/The-Social-Media-Report-2012.pdf

O'Reilly, T. (2005). *What is Web 2.0: Design Patterns and Business Models for the Next Generation of Software*. O'Reilly Media.

Parra-López, E., Bulchand-Gidumal, J., Gutiérrez-Taño, D., & Díaz-Armas, R. (2011). Intentions to use social media in organizing and taking vacation trips. *Computers in Human Behavior*, *27*(2), 640–654. doi:10.1016/j.chb.2010.05.022

Pearlson, K., & Saunders, C. (2013). *Managing and Using Information Systems* (5th ed.). Hoboken, NJ: John Wiley & Sons.

Pentina, I., Prybutok, V. R., & Zhang, X. (2008). The role of virtual communities as shopping reference groups. *Journal of Electronic Commerce Research*, *9*(2), 114–136.

Peregrin, T. (2012). Pin it to win it: Using Pinterest to promote your niche services. *Journal of the Academy of Nutrition and Dietetics*, *112*(12), 1930–1934. doi:10.1016/j.jand.2012.09.026 PMID:23174679

Rosenblum, D. (2007). What anyone can know: The privacy risks of social networking sites. *IEEE Security and Privacy*, *5*(3), 40–49. doi:10.1109/MSP.2007.75

Ross, J., Weill, P., & Robertson, P. (2006). *Enterprise Architecture as Strategy*. Boston, MA: Harvard Business School Press.

Schlenkrich, L., & Upfold, C. (2009). A guideline for virtual team managers: The key to effective social interaction and communication. *The Electronic Journal of Information Systems Evaluation*, *12*(1), 109–118.

Schlinke, J., & Crain, S. (2013). Social media from an integrated marketing and compliance perspective. *Journal of Financial Service Professionals*, *67*(2), 85–92.

Seigenthaler, J. (2005). A false Wikipedia 'biography'. *USA Today*. Retrieved September 10, 2013 from http://usatoday30.usatoday.com/news/opinion/editorials/2005-11-29-wikipedia-edit_x.htm

Shimba, F. (2010). *Cloud computing: Strategies for cloud computing adoption*. Dublin, Ireland: Dublin Institute of Technology.

Siebdrat, F., Hoegl, M., & Ernst, H. (2009). How to manage virtual teams. *MIT Sloan Management Review*, *50*(4), 63–68.

Strømmen-Bakhtiar, A. (2012). An essay on the emerging political economy and the future of the social media. In *Proceedings of 6th IEEE International Conference on Digital Ecosystems Technologies (DEST)*. IEEE. doi:10.1109/DEST.2012.6227941

Subramani, M., & Rajagopalan, B. (2003). Knowledge-Sharing and Influence in online social networks via viral marketing. *Communications of the ACM*, *46*(12), 300–307. doi:10.1145/953460.953514

Surowiecki, J. (2005). *The Wisdom of Crowds*. New York: Anchor.

Tapscott, D., & Williams, A. D. (2006). *Wikinomics: How Mass Collaboration Changes Everything*. London: Penguin Group.

Taylor, D. G., Lewin, J. E., & Strutton, D. (2011). Friends, fans, and followers: Do ads work on social networks? *Journal of Advertising Research*, *51*(1), 258–275. doi:10.2501/JAR-51-1-258-275

Terdiman, D. (2005). In search of the Wikipedia prankster. *CNETNews.com*. Retrieved September 10, 2013 from http://news.cnet.com/In-search-of-the-Wikipedia-prankster/2008-1029_3-5995977.html

TripAdvisor. (2013). Retrieved September 10, 2013 from http://www.tripadvisor.com

Trulia. (2012). Retrieved September 10, 2013 from http://www.trulia.com

Walker, J. (2003). *Final Version of Weblog Definition*. Retrieved from jilltxt.net/archives/blog_theorising/final_version_of_weblog_definition.html

Whitla, P. (2009). Crowdsourcing and its application in marketing activities. *Contemporary Management Research*, *5*(1), 15–28.

Zhang, C., Sun, J., Zhu, X., & Fang, Y. (2010). Privacy and security for online social networks: Challenges and opportunities. *IEEE Network*, *24*(4), 13–18. doi:10.1109/MNET.2010.5510913

ADDITIONAL READING

Baxter, G. J., & Connolly, T. M. (2013), The 'state of art' of organizational blogging, The Learning Organization, 20(20, 104-117.

Berthon, P. R., Pitt, L. F., Plangger, K., & Shapiro, D. (2012). *Marketing meets Web 2.0, social media, and creative consumers: implications for international marketing strategy*. Business.

Bilgram, V., Brem, A., & Voigt, K. I. (2008). User-centric innovations in new product development—systematic identification of lead users harnessing interactive and collaborative online-tools. *International Journal of Innovation Management*, *12*(03), 419–458. doi:10.1142/S1363919608002096

Bright, L., & Daugherty, T. (2012). Does customization impact advertising effectiveness? An exploratory study of consumer perceptions of advertising in customized online environments. *Journal of Marketing Communications*, *18*(1), 19–37. doi:10.1080/13527266.2011.620767

Chou, W., Prestin, A., Lyons, C., & Wen, K. (2013). Web 2.0 for health promotion: Reviewing the current evidence. *American Journal of Public Health*, *103*(1), e9–e18. doi:10.2105/AJPH.2012.301071 PMID:23153164

Constantinides, E., & Fountain, S. J. (2008). Web 2.0: Conceptual foundations and marketing issues. *Journal of Direct. Data and Digital Marketing Practice*, *9*(3), 231–244. doi:10.1057/palgrave.dddmp.4350098

Dwyer, P. (2007). Measuring the value of electronic word of mouth and its impact in consumer communities. *Journal of Interactive Marketing*, *21*(2), 63–79. doi:10.1002/dir.20078

Horizons, *55*(3), 261–271.

Kaiser, S., & Muller-Seitz, G. (2009). Acknowledging the innate impact of an information technology for engaging people in knowledge work: The case of weblog technology. *International Journal of Networking and Virtual Organizations*, *6*(1), 4–21. doi:10.1504/IJNVO.2009.022480

Lee, D., Kim, H. S., & Kim, J. K. (2011). The impact of online brand community type on consumer's community engagement behaviors: Consumer created vs. marketer-created online brand community in online social networking web sites. *Cyberpsychology, Behavior, and Social Networking*, *14*(1/2), 59–63. doi:10.1089/cyber.2009.0397 PMID:21329444

Lee, D., Kim, H. S., & Kim, J. K. (2012). The role of self-construal in consumers' electronic word of mouth (eWOM) in social networking sites: A social cognitive approach. *Computers in Human Behavior*, *28*(3), 1054–1062. doi:10.1016/j.chb.2012.01.009

Ramani, G., & Kumar, V. (2008). Interaction orientation and firm performance. *Journal of Marketing Management*, *72*(1), 27–45. doi:10.1509/jmkg.72.1.27

Rudman, R. J. (2010). Incremental risks in Web 2.0 applications. *The Electronic Library*, *28*(2), 210–230. doi:10.1108/02640471011033585

Song, F. W. (2010). Theorizing Web 2.0. *Information Communication and Society*, *13*(2), 249–275. doi:10.1080/13691180902914610

Standing, C., & Kiniti, S. (2011). How can organizations use wikis for innovation? *Technovation*, *31*(7), 287–295. doi:10.1016/j.technovation.2011.02.005

KEY TERMS AND DEFINITIONS

Crowdsourcing: The act of outsourcing a task to the generally undefined public often via the Internet without compensation.

Mashup: A term used in the Web 2.0 community to describe a webpage or a web application that uses content from more than one source to create a single new service displayed in a single graphical interface.

Really Simple Syndication (RSS): Also called Web feeds. It is a method by which web content can be easily and quickly distributed when it is changed or newly entered into a web site or web log.

Social Media: A marketing and sales applications to interact with customers and to manage brand reputation.

User-Generated Content (UGC): Published data or media that an unpaid contributor has provided to a web site. The published information might be a photo, video, blog or discussion forum post, poll response or comment made through a social media web site.

Virtual Team: Whose members are interact primarily through electronic communications to coordinate their activities and complete their tasks. Members of a virtual team may be within the same building or across continents.

Web-Oriented Architecture: is a style of software architecture that extends service-oriented architecture (SOA) to web-based applications, and is sometimes considered to be a light-weight version of SOA.

Chapter 12
Re-Conceptualizing Relational Integrated Marketing Communications from the Perspective of Social CRM

Kanghyun Yoon
University of Central Oklahoma, USA

Jeanetta D. Sims
University of Central Oklahoma, USA

ABSTRACT

As a new emerging trend, social Customer Relationship Management (social CRM) can be defined as the business practice of promoting voluntary customer engagement activities driven by social media into the value creation process in order to build long-term co-beneficial relationships with target customers as the ultimate end-goal of customer relationship management. Following the spirit of social CRM, this chapter is intended to propose conceptual guidelines for the design of effective relational integrated marketing communications strategies, including message and media strategies, with particular focus on the promotion of opinion leaders' voluntary engaged efforts with others in a typical social network setting. By implanting the power of social media in relational integrated marketing communications strategies, marketers are able to put the "relationship" back into CRM in order to restore its true meaning – building better long-term relationships with customers.

INTRODUCTION

As a new emerging trend, social customer relationship management (social CRM) can be defined as the business practice of promoting voluntary customer engagement activities driven by a mix of social media into the value creation process to build long-term co-beneficial relationships with target customers under the umbrella of customer relationship management (see Yoon & Sims, 2013, in press). The opening of this new field is possible since social media have paved new ways that allow target customers to create user-generated content across multiple platforms, to build their personal

DOI: 10.4018/978-1-4666-6182-0.ch012

social networks through rich interactive experiences with others, and to build better relationships with the firm using two-way communication channels (Hennig-Thurau et al., 2010). With the widespread adoption of social media, it becomes imperative for firms to capitalize on the benefits of social media for building and managing better long-term relationships with customers, along with improving financial performance, such as social return on investment.

Even with lots of marketers' attention on successful relationship-building processes however, there has been a lack of marketers making concrete alignment between the relationship-building process and integrated marketing communications practices from a relational integrated marketing communications (IMC) perspective. As expected, social CRM practices should start with the implementation of detailed relational communication processes to encourage voluntary engagement of target customers—specifically, those who are opinion leaders—into the value creation process as the core of any CRM practice (Boulding et al., 2005; Payne & Frow, 2005). Consequently, it is necessary to re-conceptualize the role of relational IMC practices in the relationship-building process under the umbrella of social CRM, which capitalizes on the power of social media to create better interactive experiences.

Thus, following the spirit of social CRM, this book chapter proposes a conceptual framework which allows marketers to design effective relational IMC strategies, including message and media strategies, especially relying on the voluntary engaged efforts of opinion leaders driven by social media in any social network setting.

A key feature of our proposed conceptual guidelines is as follows: By implanting the power of social media in relational IMC strategies, marketers are able to put the 'relationship' back into the true meaning of CRM since the locus of any CRM practice is on building better relationships with customers. As one major tenant, this book chapter first uses the *Model of Consumer Dynamics in Status (MCDS)* which accounts for consumer heterogeneity in the customer life cycle (Yoon & Kang, 2011; Yoon & Sims, 2013, in press). Accounting for consumer heterogeneity in marketing implies that marketers will engage in a personalization or customization efforts to meet the unmet needs of individual target customers. Consequently, marketers are able to design and implement a personalized relationship-building process depending on the unique life cycle patterns of individual customers.

Second, we utilize the *Integrated Communication Process Model* which incorporates mass media and interpersonal communication channels—especially using social media—occurring between marketers, opinion leaders and opinion seekers as social entities in any social network (Yoon & Sims, 2013, in press). Given the two-way interactive IMC channels, firms especially consider how to promote the voluntary engaged activities of opinion leaders—such as word-of-mouth, referral, recommendation, reviewing activities, and so on—as manifestations of customer social engagement in social networks. In addition, social CRM allows marketers to reshape the current direction of IMC from a relational perspective.

Third, in order to design relational IMC strategies in a personalized relationship-building process, along with specific message and media strategies, we employ the *Relationship Development or Escalation Model* suggested by Knapp (1978). Knapp's model, from the field of interpersonal communication, highlights how human beings develop personal relationships with each other in personal social networks.

Finally, considering that the true meaning of social CRM practices is the completed process of building and maintaining long-term relationships with target customers, CRM practitioners need to develop new metrics for diagnosing the performance of building better relationships with customers including the creation of various forms of social engagement activities into the value creation process (Gronroos & Voima, 2013). For this matter, we introduce a new concept called *relational or relationship equity* (RE), which captures a summation of current and future potential value for the entire relationship-building process with the firm. RE differs from the concepts of brand equity or customer equity, since these measures are associated with assessing monetary values for the firm.

This chapter is organized as follows. First, we provide a brief review of literature on social CRM, traditional marketing communications practices, and relationship-building processes, along with marketing metrics. In the next section, we discuss fundamental issues related to the implementation of relational IMC activities for social CRM and provide some guidelines of how to resolve all the issues mentioned. Then, we close our discussions after tackling some issues related to relational IMC and social CRM for future research.

CONCEPTUAL BACKGROUND

In order to propose a conceptual framework for relational IMC strategies—including message and media strategies—from the perspective of social CRM, it is necessary to align the main aspects of relational IMC strategies with the core of social CRM principles. For this task, we provide a brief review of literature on three selected areas: social CRM, traditional and relational IMC, and relationship building.

From Traditional CRM to Social CRM

Over the past several decades, marketers have witnessed a fundamental change in marketing perspective from transaction orientation driven by the exchange paradigm (Bagozzi, 1974; Hunt, 1983; Kotler, 1972) to relationship orientation driven by the loyalty building and value creation paradigm (Berry, 1983; Gronroos, 1990; Sheth & Parvatiyar, 1995; Sheth & Uslay, 2007; Vargo & Lusch, 2004). Relationship marketing and customer relationship management have been major disciplines in marketing since Levitt (1960) offered a new argument of meeting customer needs as the center of various types of marketing activities. Note that while the exchange paradigm is represented by value distribution and is outcome-oriented, the relationship orientation toward building long-term customer loyalty is characterized as value creation and is process-oriented (Sheth & Parvatiyar, 1995; Sheth & Uslay, 2007).

Driven by a new relational-focused orientation, marketing scholars and practitioners have shown their growing interest in customer relationship management as a strategic approach which utilizes the benefits of customer information—especially, behavioral purchasing patterns—in firms' internal databases in order to meet major principles of the relationship perspective (Boulding et al., 2005; Payne & Frow, 2005). Consequently, an organized effort of attracting, retaining, and growing target customers in a co-satisfying relationship process has been a top priority for firms. For clarity, refer to the following comprehensive definition of CRM as suggested by Payne and Frow (2005)

CRM is a strategic approach concerned with creating improved shareholder value through the development of appropriate relationships with key customers and customer segments. CRM unites the potential of relationship marketing strategies and IT [information technology] to create profitable, long-term relationships with customers and other key stakeholders. CRM provides enhanced opportunities to use data and information to both understand customers and co-create value with them. This requires a cross-functional integration of processes, people, operations and marketing capabilities that is enabled through information, technology and applications. (p. 168)

Despite its attractive potential, however, the future of traditional CRM has not been promising since its implemented outcomes are contradictory to the original expectations of CRM practitioners.

A typical observation is that most CRM projects have not delivered the expected return on investment (Srinivasan & Moorman, 2005). One possible reason for this unfavorable situation might be this: firms have considered how to maximize the company profit at the firm perspective, instead of how to promote customer engagement—based on the identification of consumer needs—into the process of building and maintaining long-term co-beneficial relationships with customers as the fundamental expectation of CRM efforts. Specifically, marketers have taken advantage of collected, customer-related information in internal databases and identified, attracted, and retained target customers in order to maximize customer lifetime value as the proxy of firm's profitability.

Driven by the shortcomings of traditional CRM strategies, marketers have recently turned their attention to social media as a new source of promoting customer engagement in the value creation process of CRM. To complement the pitfalls of traditional CRM practices, marketers have started considering how to capitalize on emerging social media—specifically, creating various forms of voluntary engaged activities as measures of customer engagement such as word-of-mouth, recommendations, posting reviews, Facebook 'likes', and so on—and to make use of the personal social network resources of target customers as opinion leaders in any social network setting. Consequently, a mix of social media with traditional CRM practices, called *social CRM*, has emerged into the surface of business practices as one new direction of traditional CRM strategy, after recognizing the power of social media and its potential for social engagement creation. CRM practitioners have also considered the development of social metrics—called *social analytics*—to diagnose the effectiveness of social CRM efforts (Hoffman & Fodor, 2012).

According to Lithium Technologies (2009), simply speaking, social CRM is a new business strategy and practical approach that combines the power of online communities, broader social networks around opinion leaders, and traditional CRM practices. As an expert in the CRM field, Paul Greenberg (2009) also provides a nice definition of social CRM as "the business strategy of engaging customers through social media with the goal of building trust and brand loyalty". In this book chapter, we borrow the social CRM definition of Yoon and Sims (2013, in press) as "a strategic business practice to build and manage long-term profitable relationships with customers by creating more customer engagement into the value creation process with the firm using social network systems."

Major Changes in Traditional IMC Practices

Traditional IMC strategies have mainly focused on efforts of communicating the value proposition of a firm's offerings with target customers using various types of promotional mix elements such as advertising, sales promotion, public relations, personal selling, and direct marketing. These promotional mix elements were used to most typically accomplish the three promotional goals of informing, persuading, and reminding. However, the surge of a new relational paradigm and corresponding CRM practices—combined with the emergence of social media—has paved new directions for relational IMC efforts.

In recent years, it is possible to observe three major transitions in the practice of IMC strategies: 1) change from a transactional to a relational IMC perspective; 2) transition from a one-way to two-way communication process; and 3) emerging role of social media for customer engagement in the value creation process. We briefly discuss key aspects of these three major transitions in IMC practices under the umbrella of social CRM.

From Transactional to Relational IMC. Traditional IMC efforts can be regarded as a marketer-oriented communication process in the sense that firms have focused on the acceleration of diffusion processes—as an aggregated outcome of all individual buyers' completed adoption decisions—for a specific brand/product within a target market. Stated differently, marketers have designed transaction-oriented IMC strategies to promote instant purchases by target customers using a mix of promotional elements, especially using mass media and sales promotional activities. Consider one typical transaction-oriented definition of IMC as follows: *IMC is the concept and process of strategically managing audience-focused, channel-centered, and result-driven brand communication programs over time* (Kliatchko, 2005, p. 21).

By arguing that "communication is the human activity that links people together and creates relationships," Duncan and Moriarty (1988, p. 2) propose a communication-based model to discuss how a communication process can be the foundation of any relationship marketing effort. Since then, marketers have witnessed major changes in their transactional IMC perspective and at the same time, have paid attention to relational IMC practices (Andersen, 2001; Finne & Gronroos, 2009; Lindberg-Repo & Gronroos, 2004). In order to make the entire acceleration of one offering's diffusion process relational with a target market using various types of promotional elements, marketers need to re-conceptualize the role of traditional IMC practice in the value creation process as the core of social CRM efforts.

From a One-Way to Two-Way Communication Process. It can be argued that traditional IMC efforts have been driven by one-way communication channels since the firms' efforts to gather receivers' feedback are not emphasized well and since the traditional communication process does not include interpersonal channels between receivers and others to account for word-of-mouth activities, as one part of social contagion. For details, refer to Belch and Belch's (2007) *Model of the Communication Process* (see their Figure 5-1), which consists of the sender and receiver as the major participants in the communication process, and message and channel as two communication tools, with the feedback channel. Over the years, this model has been used for the design of various types of IMC strategies from the firm's standpoint.

In fact, scholars in mass communication have shown the power of interpersonal communication activities through a two-way communication process. For instance, a study in *The People's Choice* (Lazarsfeld, Berelson, & Gaudet, 1944) indicates that informal and interpersonal contacts have much stronger influence on voting behaviors during presidential election campaigns than exposure to radio or newspaper as major sources of influence. Driven by this finding, Katz and Lazarsfeld (1955; Katz, 1957) later proposed the two-step flow theory of mass communication. In addition, marketers have posited that the diffusion of innovations is a function of two driving forces, such as the use of mass media targeting for innovators via mass communication channels and word-of-mouth activities between innovators and followers, as potential buyers, via interpersonal communication channels (Bass, 1969; Rogers, 1962). In marketing, scholars have investigated the power of interpersonal communication channels—mainly driven by an abundant amount of data—in the diffusion and adoption process (Godes & Mayzlin, 2004; Iyengar, Van den Bulte, & Valente, 2011; Manchanda, Xie, & Youn, 2008; Watts & Dodds, 2007).

The two-step flow of communication theory (Katz & Lazarsfeld, 1955) postulates that promotional information initiating from mass media by marketers moves in two distinct stages. First, individuals, as opinion leaders, who pay close attention to main messages delivered by mass media receive the information. Then, the opinion leaders pass on their own interpretations, along with the actual media content, to their friends and nearby neighbors. Thus, the two-step flow theory has improved our understanding of how mass media and interpersonal communication influence the decision-making of opinion leaders as well as their interpersonal behaviors on opinion seekers. In addition, this theory refines the ability to predict the influence of media messages on audience behaviors and helps explain why certain media campaigns may have failed to alter audience attitudes and behaviors.

Social Media and Customer Engagement. In recent years, social media as a new marketing channel have paved new opportunities for attracting new buyers, retaining existing customers to make them loyal, and improving various types of the firm's performance indicators. In addition, social media have been playing a major role in implementing advanced promotional strategies, which rely on a mix of various types of promotional elements including social media as an additional promotional element (Armelini & Villanueva, 2011; Kaplan & Haenlein, 2010; Mangold & Faulds, 2009).

From the relationship-building perspective, social media represent a unique blending of new technological platforms, social interaction, and customer engagement within any social network. For instance, users are voluntarily submitting recommendation comments, posting personal photos and videos, and pressing 'likes' in Facebook, often accompanied by other types of feedback called *consumer-generated content*, on new social media platforms. As an example, one can view the Facebook fan page of Coca-Cola, which has more than 80 million 'likes' and was established not by the company, but by brand-enthusiasts. Social media also provide new opportunities for users to be involved in genuine online conversations with others about their mutual interests based on personal thoughts and experiences (i.e., one Coca-Cola Facebook fan posted, "I love Diet Coke....AWESOME"). Finally, social media become useful tools for allowing opinion leaders to exercise high levels of opinion leadership—i.e., creating various forms of voluntary engagement activities—by influencing the behavioral patterns of opinion seekers as potential buyers over the diffusion process.

In summary, social media have great potential to accelerate the diffusion process of a firm's offerings as new innovations, to encourage the efforts of opinion leaders on influencing opinion seekers, and to create various forms of engaged efforts into the value creation process in a typical social network setting. Despite social media's emerging popularity, however, firms are wary to invest the time to participate in social media, because it remains unproven if social media engagement translates into increased sales. In other words, marketers should consider how to cultivate reciprocal relationships with customers and appropriate interactions with customers within the social networks in order to build long-term relationships from the perspective of social CRM.

Putting all of the above ideas together, we provide a summary picture which depicts the entire two-way communication process—possibly using a mix of multiple communication channels—from sellers to opinion leaders and finally to opinion seekers in a typical social network setting from the perspective of social network theory. The summary picture is shown in Figure 1. Following the spirit of the two-way flow of communication theory, this picture allows marketers to understand the key aspect of mass communication channels between firms as the senders and opinion leaders as the receivers. Specifically, marketers are able to understand how opinion leaders pay close attention to mass media, respond to mass media, and respond to media messages when they are received. Second, this picture makes it possible for marketers to understand how opinion leaders pass their own interpretations, along with the actual media content, to friends and neighbors within their personal social networks. The term 'personal influence' refers to the process of intervening between the media's direct message and the audience's ultimate reaction to that message. It is well-known that opinion leaders are quite influential in getting people to change their attitudes and behaviors. Finally, this Figure allows

Figure 1. A two-way flow of communication in social network settings

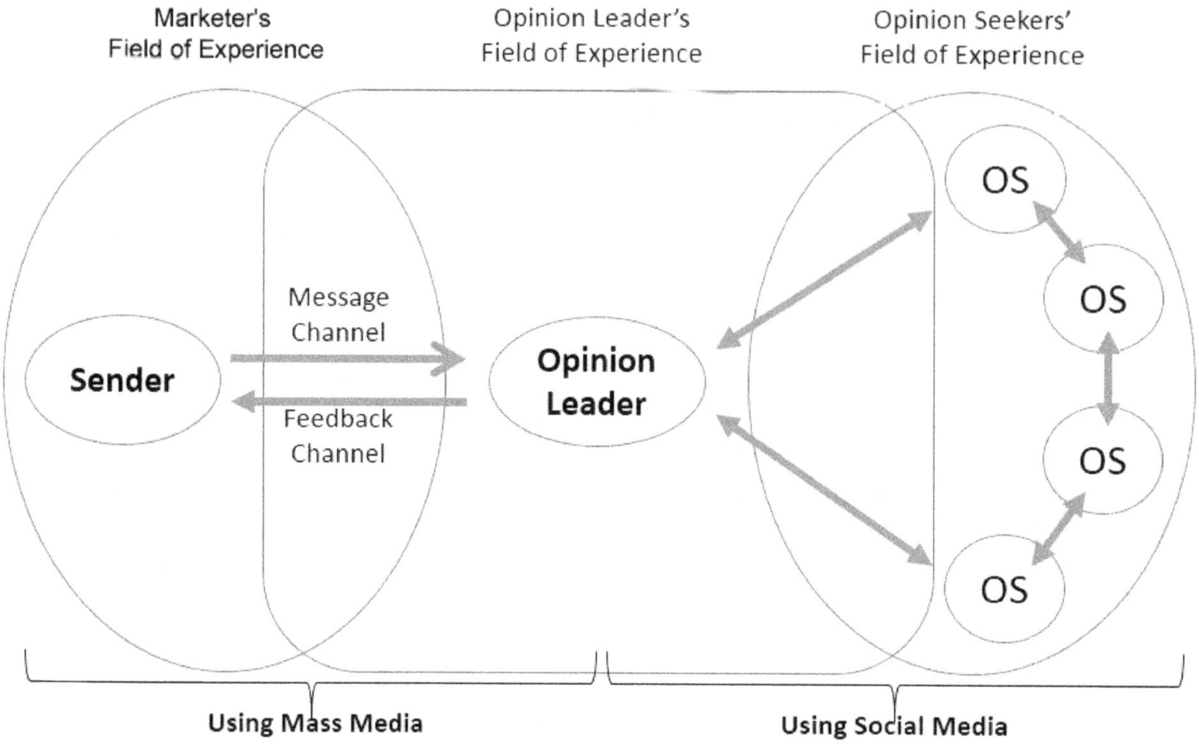

marketers to understand how opinion leaders construct and utilize their own personal networks before exercising various forms of their unique opinion leadership.

Developing Ongoing Relationships with Customers

Considering the relationship-building process as the ultimate direction of any social CRM practice, marketers have been interested in understanding how human beings develop personalized favorable relationships with others as the social entities in any social network setting. Marketers' efforts of building long-term profitable relationships with target customers and ultimately making customers loyal for business purposes can be understood in this social network context. A review of literature indicates that marketers are able to borrow fruitful insights from three areas of disciplines such as business to consumer (B2C) consumer marketing, business to business (B2B) industrial marketing, and interpersonal communication.

The first type of insight comes from the perspective of the loyalty formation/building process prevalent in the B2C marketing area. Given the assumption that customer loyalty is the ultimate status of any entire relationship-building process, marketers in consumer marketing have identified several ways to make customers loyal. For instance, Payne (1994), Christopher et al. (1998), and Christopher, Payne, and Ballantyne (2002) developed the concept of *Relationship Ladder*—also called *Customer Loyalty Ladder*—from the relationship marketing perspective. This framework implies that customers can move from one level of loyalty to the next following the stages of prospect, customer, client, supporter, advocate, and partner depending on the level of customer engagement. Given this underlying assumption, the major task of relationship marketing strategy is to bring customers as high up the ladder as possible, since greater benefits accrue to the company at the higher level of loyalty. In addition, assuming that loyalty is an outcome of attitudinal formation processes, which rely on the three cognitive, affective, and conative components of attitude, Oliver (1997, 1999) identifies four types of cognitive, affective, conative, and action loyalty in the loyalty formation phase.

A second type of insight is related to the seller-buyer relationship-building process prevailing in the B2B industrial marketing area. Specifically, industrial marketing practitioners have been interested in figuring out how to build favorable relationships between sellers and buyers in the B2B context. Industrial marketers have proposed various types of models which consist of a variety of relationship stages and of triggering factors moving the relationship from one stage to the next in the relationship-building process. Selected studies are those of Ford (1980), Dwyer et al. (1987), Frazier (1983), Heide (1994), Miller and Parks (1982), and Narayandas and Rangan (2004). Proposing a compound model which captures various stages of the relationship development process between seller and buyer, Andersen (2001) identifies four stages—such as pre-relationship, negotiation, relationship development, and termination, depending on the degree of mutual adaptation—via marketing communications efforts.

Finally, scholars in interpersonal communication also provide various types of models and theoretical explanations regarding the relationship development and dissolution/ deterioration process (Altman & Taylor, 1973; Avtgis, West, & Anderson, 1998; Taylor & Altman, 1987). Selected are two noticeable models: *Relationship Development Staircase Model* suggested by Knapp (1978) and *Relationship Development Elevator Model* by Beebe, Beebe, and Richmond (2002). Assuming that two basic common phases are relationship development and deterioration, both models have attempted to describe the ongoing progression of any relationship between two human beings over time. For clarity, we provide a summary table which compares several selected models for the relationship-building process with respect to detailed steps, underlying assumptions, and other key features in Table 1.

MAIN FOCUS OF THE CHAPTER

For the successful implementation of relational IMC strategies within the spirit of social CRM, marketers first need to re-conceptualize the true essence of relational IMC practices from the relational perspective and then consider proper guidelines for its implementation and performance control. To accomplish this goal, we discuss the following issues: 1) what is meant by the process of building and maintaining personal relationships with target customers with respect to consumer heterogeneity in customer life cycle, 2) how to trigger customers' voluntary engaged activities into the value creation process with the execution of relational IMC strategies, 3) how to capitalize on the personal social networks of target customers—called opinion leaders in the two-way flow of communication process—using a mix of mass and social media, and 4) what kinds of metrics are required to diagnose the effectiveness of any relational IMC and social CRM practices. Later, by combining all of these issues together, this book chapter attempts to provide relevant solutions and recommendations for the design of relational IMC strategies.

ISSUES, CONTROVERSIES, AND PROBLEMS

Issue 1: Identification of a Personalized Relationship-Building Process

The design of relational IMC strategies should start with the understanding of how individual customers build and maintain their personal

Table 1. Summary of selected relationship-building models in major disciplines

Types of Selected Models	Customer Loyalty Ladder Model Payne (1994, 1998)	Customer Loyalty Formation Model Oliver (1997, 1999)	Seller-Buyer Relationship Building Model Andersen (2001)	Relationship Development Staircase Model Knapp (1978)	Relationship Development Elevator Model Beebe, Beebe, & Richmond (2002)
Stages of Relationship Development Process	Prospect ↓ Customer ↓ Client ↓ Supporter ↓ Advocate ↓ Partner	Cognitive Loyalty ↓ Affective Loyalty ↓ Conative Loyalty ↓ Action Loyalty	Pre-relationship ↓ Negotiation ↓ Relationship development ↓ Termination phase	Initiating ↓ Experimenting ↓ Intensifying ↓ Integrating ↓ Bonding	Preinteraction Awareness ↓ Initiation ↓ Exploration ↓ Intensification ↓ Intimacy
Key Aspects of Selected Models	Customer loyalty is related to the evolving status of commitment of target customers over time.	Customer loyalty is defined as a deeply held commitment to rebuy or repatronize a preferred product consistently.	Relationships in the B2B industrial marketing area go through three phases prior to the fourth phase of termination.	Relationships in the interpersonal communication area have five stages that progress toward bonding	Relationships in the interpersonal communication area begin with low-level awareness and progress toward intimacy.
Underlying Assumption	It assumes that the key to success in service business lies with concentrating on and retaining existing customers.	It starts with the perspective of attitude formation processes.	It starts from a marketing communications perspective.	It starts from an interpersonal dyad between two human beings.	It starts from an interpersonal dyad between two human beings.

relationships with the firm and others over their life cycle in a social network setting. Stated differently, considering that the true meaning of social CRM efforts is the well-being of all entities in the social networks—i.e., firms as providers, target customers as main buyers, and neighbors and friends as potential buyers—in the CRM or relationship marketing perspective, marketers need to understand and design a personalized relationship-building process with individual target customers. For instance, marketers are able to be interested in making any customers loyal in a relationship-building process which consists of several steps such as creating new trials, retaining existing relationships, making them loyal, and if possible, terminating the ongoing relationships.

Contrary to this assumption, traditional CRM practices have mainly focused on the maximization of individual customers' monetary values driven by the transactional exchange process, instead of emphasizing the creation of customer values for the well-being of all entities in social networks. One typical example is the efforts of firms for maximizing individual customers' customer lifetime value (CLV) and separating high-valued customers from the group of low-valued ones for target purposes (Gupta, Lehmann, & Stuart, 2004; Kumar & Rajan, 2009; Reinartz & Kumar, 2002).

In order to successfully implement various types of social CRM practices; however, CRM practitioners need to return to the original principles of CRM and be involved in a personalized relationship-building process with various types of members in any social network. One way to achieve this goal is to address "potential heterogeneity in customer behavior" (Boulding et al. 2005; Kumar, 2008) and design customized CRM programs depending on the status of individual target customers in the life cycle. Target customers are likely to change their status as they make a series of purchases over the life cycle in a relationship-building process or as they shift through adoption and loyalty building processes from the perspective of diffusion of innovation and adoption (Dodson & Muller, 1978; Hahn, Park, Krishnamurthi, & Zoltners, 1994). For instance, marketers are able to design personalized marketing strategies depending on an individual customer's status in the stages of acquisition, retention, and attrition (Kumar, 2008). Stated differently, CRM practitioners need to consider when and how target customers become adopters and later loyal to a specific market offering from the relationship-building perspective (Reichheld, 1993). In fact, Reinartz, Thomas, and Kumar (2005) argue that marketers need to allocate firm resources into acquisition and retention strategies to maximize customer profitability.

To execute the personalized relationship-building process for social CRM strategies, marketers need to understand how target customers change their loyalty status over their life cycle by utilizing the gathered behavioral information in firms' databases. For this matter, this book chapter proposes one conceptual framework—called *Model of Consumer Dynamics in Status (MCDS)* suggested by Yoon and Kang (2011) and Yoon and Sims (2013, in press)—which describes how target customers become an adopter and later a loyal customer during the relationship-building process. The details of this conceptual framework are shown in Figure 2.

Note that our proposed framework is different from the one suggested by Kumar (2008). For the details of Kumar's framework, refer to Figure 1-5 in his book (Kumar 2008, p. 9). Kumar discusses various types of topics such as acquiring profitable customers, retaining current customers for profitability, allocating resources, and managing customer referral behaviors, among other topics, depending on the customer life cycle framework. In contrast, our framework enables CRM practitioners to attract, retain, and grow customers—with personalized CRM practices—after accounting for consumer heterogeneity in consumer dynamics, given the presence of a firm's internal database.

One major advantage of using this conceptual framework is to allow CRM practitioners to consider important customer-oriented insights and relevant metrics—as a set of challenging tasks. For instance, marketers can understand when and how potential buyers (PBs) make a purchase decision to become first-time buyers (FTBs) or adopters given the presence of marketing stimuli offered by the competing firms. Then, marketers are likely to consider when and why the FTBs stop making additional purchases, make a first-repeat purchase with the same brand, or switch to one of the competing brands before becoming one of my repeat customers (MRCs). Finally, marketers may review when and why MRCs make a series of repeat purchases with my brand and ultimately become emotionally committed and loyal customers given the presence of marketing efforts such as loyalty programs toward the goals of relationship marketing. Of course, marketers are also able to consider how to attract competitors' repeat customers (CRCs) as the main part of attraction strategy. Given the proposed framework MCDS, we are able to identify major marketing goals and relevant metrics—as the guidelines—when targeting four types of consumer groups toward the goal of making them loyal and ultimately, an ambassador, as shown in Table 2.

Issue 2: Design of Relational IMC Practices for Relationship Building

From the standpoint of relationship building for social CRM, marketers should also align the spirit of traditional IMC practices with that of relationship marketing, resulting in *relational IMC*. Considering that social CRM efforts are one typical branch for relationship marketing,

Figure 2. Model of consumer dynamics in status (MCDS)

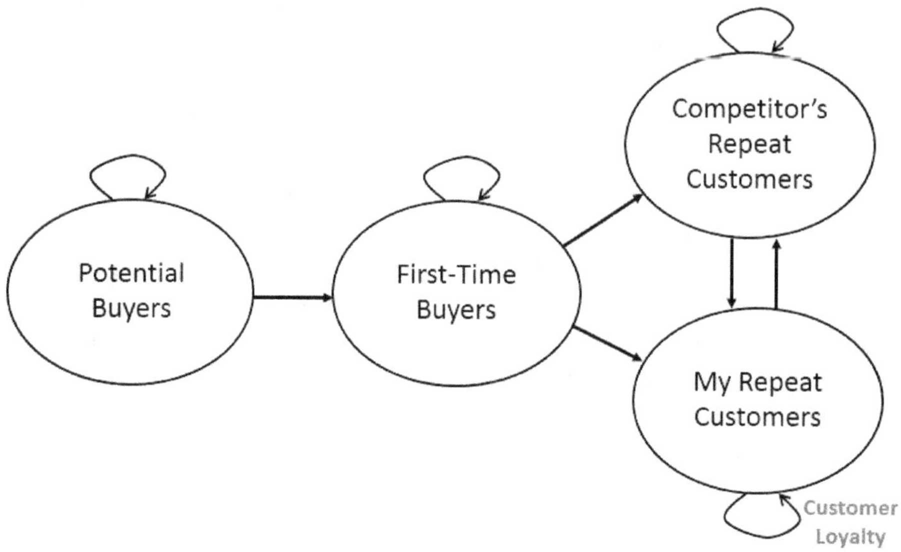

Gronroos (2006) argues that current directions of any marketing activities are not truly aligned with the original meaning of "managing customer relationships" in a proper manner. Given one marketing definition of the American Marketing Association, he specifically pinpoints that the phrase 'creating, communication and delivering value ... for managing customer relationships' needs to be re-conceptualized and operationalized properly in the context of IMC practices.

In addition, it is necessary for marketers to remember that an essence of social CRM practice is the value creation process which is to be driven by voluntary customer engagement activities using an effective mix of traditional mass and new social media (Gronroos, 2004; Yoon & Sims, 2013, in press). Given this assumption, one important question is how to promote target customers' voluntary engaged activities—called customer engagement—into the value creation process using relational IMC practices which relies on effective message and media strategies. Thus, the true meaning of social CRM can be secured when firms promote target customers' voluntary execution of their engaged activities into the value creation and loyalty-building process by taking advantage of two-way relationship communication channels including social media as the new hybrid element of the promotional mix (Mangold & Faulds, 2009). We can consider three following issues regarding the design of relational IMC strategies including message and media efforts for the long-term, relationship-building process.

Two-Way Communication Process. It has been assumed that one typical goal of IMC activities is the acceleration of the diffusion process for a company's brand within a target market given the efforts of mass and interpersonal communication with a mix of mass media and word-of-mouth strategies (Bass, 1969; Rogers, 1962). Despite this assumption, traditional IMC efforts can be regarded as marketer-oriented and transaction-oriented communication (Sheth & Parvatiyar, 1995) since two-way interaction activities between firms as the provider and customers as the receiver are not emphasized much and the traditional communication process does not highlight the role of customers' word-of-mouth activities in a typical social network. One reason for this situation might come from the extensive use of

Table 2. Marketing goals and metrics for each type of customer group

Transition Patterns	Marketing Goals	Examples of Marketing Activities	Relevant Metrics
Unknown Buyers (UBs) → Potential Buyers (PBs)	▪ Identifying a list of potential customers as target; ▪ Developing specific profiles of potential customers for future prediction	STP activities for segmenting, targeting, and positioning purposes; e-newsletters; a series of direct mailings and calls	Size of market potential; number of potential buyers
Potential Buyers (PBs) → First Time Buyers (FTBs)	▪ Developing purchase intentions after increasing the awareness, knowledge, liking, and preference levels; ▪ Maximizing the number of trials from potential customers as the paying customers	A series of welcome emails, conversion OTM, and e-newsletters; a series of conversion DMs and emails	Awareness level; knowledge level; intention level; conversion rate; churn rate
First Time Buyers (FTBs) → My Repeat Customers (MRCs)	▪ Maximizing overall satisfaction with the firm's offerings; ▪ Reinforce an overall positive attitude; ▪ Increasing the likelihood to make a first repeat purchase	Surveys for measuring satisfaction; coupons for repeat purchase; frequent calls for managing ongoing relationships	Satisfaction level, conversion rate; churn rate; effectiveness of promotional campaigns
My Repeat Customers (MRCs) → My Loyal Customers (LCs)	▪ Increasing the likelihood to stay as a repeat customer; ▪ Prevent them from switching to other competing offerings; ▪ Making them loyal by increasing their emotional attachment level	Loyalty programs; programs for increasing emotional attachment; interactive Website designs allowing firm/product ratings and comments	Repeat purchase rate; level of customer loyalty; commitment level, level of emotional attachment; level of ratings; tone of comments
My Loyal Customers (LCs) → Ambassadors	▪ Increasing an overall bonding level with the firm and its offerings; ▪ Increasing the number of engaged activities for the firm; ▪ Making them an ambassador of the firm	Bonding formation programs; programs for creating customer referral, WOM, recommendations, and other engagement activities; frequently updated and content-rich social media platforms	Customer retention rate; Level of customer bonding; Number of customer engagement activities; frequency of social media platform interactions

the traditional communication process model for the design of IMC strategy. As evidence, refer to many IMC textbooks including the one by Belch and Belch (2007).

For the success of social CRM practice, marketers should equip themselves with a new perspective toward the new roles of IMC practices in the value creation and long-term relationship-building process with target customers. As mentioned previously, marketers should change their perspective from transaction to relational IMC based on two-way, not one-way, communication processes within a typical social network. In addition, they should attempt to promote customers' voluntary engaged efforts into the value creation process as the proxy of building long-term relationships with customers.

To achieve this goal, we propose *the Integrated Communication Process Model* which consists of mass media and interpersonal communication channels between marketers, opinion leaders, and opinion seekers (Yoon & Sims, 2013, in press). This proposed model is rooted in the principles of two-step flow of communication (Katz, 1957; Lazarsfeld, Berelson, & Gaudet, 1944). However, there are additional merits in the use of this model. First, it recaptures the true essence of two-way communication between three types of typical social entities in any social network. Second, it highlights the key roles of opinion leaders in the creation of social contagion activities within their personal networks using various types of social media. Considering that one critical element of social CRM practices is customer engagement into the value creation process, opinion leaders may take a critical role of disseminating a firm's value proposition to opinion seekers as the ambassador from the perspective of social network theory. The essence of our proposed integrated communication process model is highlighted in Figure 1.

Given this picture, social CRM practitioners need to consider how to build and manage relationships with customers using two-way communication channels and how to promote social engagement of customers into the value creation process by showing non-transactional behaviors such as word-of-mouth as well as influencing behaviors and inputting knowledge for customer engagement, particularly utilizing various types of social media. In addition to initiating social engagement of customers, social CRM practitioners should consider a plan to routinely engage in social media monitoring of relevant customer interactions that may or may not be initiated by the firm.

New Relational IMC Efforts for Relationship Building. As mentioned previously, an ultimate goal of any CRM effort is to build and maintain long-term relationships with customers via relational IMC strategies in a two-way communication process which is designed to promote various types of social engagement activities among opinion leaders into the value creation process. Note that typical examples of engaged activities of opinion leaders are non-transactional behaviors of word-of-mouth, recommendation, and reviewing activities. In order to make traditional IMC practices relational from the perspective of the relationship-building process, marketers may conduct two following key tasks: 1) Design and implement a series of relational IMC programs in order to build and manage long-term relationships with opinion leaders and 2) monitor how opinion leaders exercise opinion leadership with social entities in their social networks using various types of social media.

First, the design of relational IMC efforts relies upon the status changes of opinion leaders—depending on a series of successive purchases—over the customer life cycle and at each transition in the MCDS. Specifically, marketers should design and implement relational IMC programs (Andersen, 2001; Duncan & Moriarty, 1988; Finne & Gronroos, 2009; Lindberg-Repo & Gronroos, 2004) so that opinion leaders become loyal and an ambassador of the firms. Second, by utilizing the personal network resources in a social network setting, opinion leaders may make a huge influence on opinion seekers via their voluntary engaged activities of recommendation, creating positive word-of-mouth, reviews, creating content in a blog, and creating referrals, among other activities. However, all of the communication process should be based on a two-way communication process with customers.

For this matter, we introduce Knapp's (1978) framework for relationship building which allows marketers to create a series of transitional status of target customers over the life cycle using relational IMC activities. In the relationship interaction stages, Knapp's stages represent the most complete possible progression of any relationship between two social entities. The model consists of 10 stages, five that describe "coming together" and five that describe "coming apart." The stages of relational development or "coming together" are initiating, experimenting, intensifying, integrating, and bonding, while the deterioration or "coming apart" stages are differentiating, circumscribing, stagnating, avoiding, and terminating (Fox, Warber, & Makstaller, 2013; Knapp, 1978).

Knapp's (1978) model carries with it several assumptions about the progression of any relationship through the stages in an interpersonal communication process. Movement through all the stages in the model occurs in a systematic, sequential fashion which may be in any direction. Although relationship movement up, down, and sideways on the "staircase" is an ongoing and changing process, researchers are able to classify the relationships at any given time. Thus, Knapp represents his model metaphorically as a dual staircase upon which relationships ascend, descend, and stabilize. Although other similar models and modified versions exist, Knapp's original conception is clear and intuitively compelling with movement through stages explained in terms of social exchange theory (Blau, 1964;

Cropanzano & Mitchell 2005; Homans, 1961; Thibaut & Kelley, 1959).

In order to design relational IMC strategies to promote engaged activities into the value creation process using various types of relational IMC programs and ultimately, build and maintain long-term personalized relationships with target customers—especially opinion leaders—in a social network setting, it is recommended that social CRM practitioners combine the concept of Knapp's (1978) relationship development process with the proposed *Model of Consumer Dynamics in Status* to account for consumer heterogeneity over the customer life cycle. For example, CRM practitioners may focus on how to build new relationships with potential buyers, while promoting their engagement at the same time by using persuasive IMC strategies with a well-designed value proposition of the offered brand in the personalized relationship-building process.

Power of Customer Engagement in Social Network. There have been only a handful of studies in the academic field with respect to guidelines for its implementation since this discipline is at an early stage (Bagozzi, 1994; Mosadegh & Behboudi, 2011; Woodcock, Green, & Starkey, 2011). The growth of social media implies that the firm can no longer control the relationship-building process with customers as traditional IMC strategies suggest. Instead, firms need to embrace this shift and develop new guidelines for the implementation of social CRM, which facilitates collaborative experiences with customers in the value creation process, consequently translating the entire relationship-building process with customers into a co-beneficial one.

One figure suggested by Reichheld and Sasser (1990, p. 108) indicates the power of customer loyalty and referral behaviors of loyal customers on company performance. Since then, marketers have paid lots of attention to the role of customer engagement in the value (co-)creation process as the core of typical CRM practices. One major reason that the concept of customer engagement (CE) is important is because the promotion of voluntary engaged efforts of customers as opinion leaders—via a series of relational IMC efforts—plays a key role in generating both transactional and non-transactional outcomes in any personal social network. One typical example of transactional outcomes is customer referrals (Kumar, Petersen, & Leone, 2010; Ryu & Feick, 2007), while examples of non-transactional outcomes are word-of-mouth, reviewing, or recommendation behaviors to others (Godes & Mayzlin, 2004, 2009; de Matos & Rossi, 2008; Chen & Xie, 2008). As a result, it is possible to argue that the popular customer lifetime value (CLV) measure, as the proxy of company profitability (Brodie et al., 2011; Kumar et al., 2010), be replaced with the measure of relationship equity (RE) including customer engagement as one component when diagnosing the value of individual customers in a relationship-building process.

Recognizing the fact that customer engagement is a major driving force to maximize the effectiveness of social CRM practices, marketing scholars take it as one of critical research priority (refer to a list of research priorities for the period of 2010-2012 by Marketing Science Institute (2010). Take a look at the definition of CE as suggested by Brodie et al. (2011) shown below:

Customer engagement (CE) is a psychological state that occurs by virtue of interactive, cocreative customer experiences with a focal agent/object (e.g., a brand) in focal service relationships. It occurs under a specific set of context-dependent conditions generating differing CE levels; and exists as a dynamic, iterative process within service relationships that cocreate value. CE plays a central role in a nomological network governing service relationships in which other relational concepts (e.g., involvement, loyalty) are antecedents and/or consequences in iterative CE processes. It is a multidimensional concept subject to a context- and/or stakeholder-specific expression of relevant cognitive, emotional and/ or behavioral dimensions.

The above proposed definition implies that any voluntary engaged efforts of customers are likely to occur when they have ongoing relationship-building experiences with the firm in a dynamic, interactive, and co-beneficial process of value creation. In addition, it plays a key role in the creation of transaction and non-transactional outcomes when customers exercise the active and voluntary roles of opinion leadership to other friends and neighbors within their personal social networks as competitive resources for firms. Thus, it can be suggested that CE represents a strategic imperative for building long-term relationships with customers—via relational IMC efforts—and creating various types of company performances (Bijmolt et al., 2010; Brodie, Hollebeek, Juric, & Ilic, 2011; van Doorn et al., 2010, Verhoef, Renartz, & Krafft, 2010).

New Message and Media Strategy for Relational IMC. As expected, two key parts of any IMC strategy are message and media strategies. Marketers also need to make both traditional message and media strategies relational following the spirit of social CRM practices. To align relational IMC practices with the perspective of social CRM, marketers should consider new message and media strategies—which utilize various types of social media as a new promotional mix—from the perspective of building long-term relationships with target audiences for the design of relational IMC strategy.

Regarding the message strategy, the central effort of traditional IMC strategies is to deliver designed communication messages related to the value proposition of market offering via the selected mix of various types of media, but mainly mass media. Typically, most of IMC practices have been centered on three types of promotional goals—i.e., informing, persuading, and reminding (Belch & Belch, 2007). One traditional approach for the design of an effective message strategy is driven by the Six-Segment Strategy Wheel (Taylor, 1999). This model starts with the structure of the human brain and assumes that the left- and right-hand side of the wheel represents the transmission and ritual views of communication. Depending on two types of views, marketers are suggested to choose one of six segments—i.e., ration, acute need, and routine for representing the transmission view and ego, social, and sensory for the ritual view—and design an effective message strategy depending on the choice of one segment or multiple segments.

However, traditional message design efforts have been silent on how to build long-term relationships with target customers. Specifically, most traditional efforts for message strategies have focused on the ultimate persuasion of opinion leaders into lead-to-sales outcomes without much focus on the process of building and managing further relationships with opinion leaders and their interpersonal activities with opinion seekers in a social network. Thus, marketers should consider new directions of message strategies within the context of social CRM and relational IMC practices. For instance, marketers may consider heterogeneous message strategies targeting two types of opinion leaders and opinion seekers, depending upon their status over the customer life cycle. Also, they may focus on the promotion of opinion leaders' engaged efforts into the value creation process in the social network setting. In summary, marketers should consider how to realign the roles of existing message strategies on the relationship-building and value creation process.

In an attempt to deliver customized messages based on the value proposition of the firm's market offerings and promote the voluntary engaged efforts of opinion leaders into the value creation process, marketers are likely to use social media as an additional new promotional element. In this book chapter, we mainly focus on the role of social media as a tool to build ongoing relationships with target customers in a direct manner and opinion seekers in an indirect manner using relational IMC efforts. In addition, we also focus on encouraging their social engagement activities in the value creation process in the relationship-building process.

The emergence of online advertising and social media as prominent promotion vehicles has prompted marketers to strategically shift their focus to online and social media. However, it is essential to recognize that traditional media advertising are still effective and marketers need to balance online and traditional offline media for the achievement of relational IMC goals. Remember that several scholars explore major differences between the effectiveness of online and traditional media advertising on several marketing dimensions (Chao, Corus, & Li, 2012; Kaplan & Haenlein, 2010).

Issue 3: New Metric of Relational Equity (RE) for Social CRM

The final challenge that marketers may face is what kinds of metrics should be utilized for measuring the effectiveness of social CRM efforts for the entire relationship-building process. Traditionally, marketers have utilized financial and behavioral measures such as the number of units sold, dollar amount of sales, "churn" rate as a percentage of the customer base, and customer retention rate, among others (Lehman & Winer, 2005; Winer, 2001). In addition, recent popular metrics that marketers have utilized are return-on-investment, customer lifetime value, and customer equity (Gupta & Zeithaml, 2006).

Considering the true meaning of social CRM practices, however, marketers should develop new metrics to measure the outcomes of building long-term relationships with target customers. One suggested metric is *relational* or *relationship equity* as an indicator of whether or not the entire relationship-building process is managed effectively over the entire life cycles of individual target customers (Iyer, Sharma, & Bejou, 2006; Sawhney & Zabin, 2002; Raimondo, Miceli, & Costabile, 2008). In the domain of social CRM, marketers also need to measure the effort of customer engagement and sentiment—as social CRM metrics which are driven by social media during the interpersonal communication processes between opinion leaders and opinion seekers—in the perspective of dual creation of values for the firm and customers (Etlinger, 2011). Since social analytics is a new discipline, a lack of guidelines exists on how to measure the performance of social CRM activities, and this study attempts to provide new guidelines for social CRM implementation.

Relationship equity is different from the traditional popular concepts of brand equity and customer equity. By definition, the concept of customer equity refers to "the total of the discounted lifetime values summarized over all of the firm's current and potential customers" (Rust, Lemon, & Zeithaml, 2004, p. 101). Strictly speaking, both brand equity and customer equity measures represent the standpoint of the sellers' interests in a sense that both captures the financial performances, i.e., monetary equity, of each brand and all individual customers that the firm has. Stated differently, brand equity and customer equity do not capture how well the firms are doing in building co-beneficial relationships with individual customers in the long run which might be driven by their voluntary engaged activities within the boundary of a typical social network. By definition, RE refers to "customer perceptions of the proportionality between her or his own benefit-cost ratio and the provider's benefit-cost ratio within a continuous relationship" (Raimondo, Miceli, & Costabile, 2008, p. 145).

Apparently, marketing scholars and practitioners should update the dimensionality and underlying structure of this new social CRM metric, called relational or relationship equity, because the concept needs to capture how well marketers are able to develop co-beneficial long-term relationships with target customers under the umbrella of social CRM and also represent the degree of customers' voluntary engaged activities—i.e., customer engagement—in the value creation process coupled with an effective mix of traditional mass and social media. In conclusion, combined with the essence of relational marketing practices, any social CRM practice should consider the maximization of relational or relationship equity.

Regarding the dimensionality of this new metric, called relation or relationship equity (RE), marketers are able to consider several subdimensions. First, it is posited that RE consists of two types of transactional and non-transactional value. The transactional value is represented by customer lifetime value (CLV), while the non-transactional value mainly representing customer engagement value (CEV, Kumar et al., 2010) is characterized with customer referral value or CRV (which is the ability of a customer to refer others to the firm), customer influence value or CIV (which is the ability of a customer to influence others concerning the firm), and customer knowledge value or CKV (which is the amount of information and understanding that a customer has about the firm). Following the principles of Kumar et al. (2010), we thus attempt to develop relevant metrics for CLV, CRV, CIV, and CKV, depending on customer types in their life cycle. We also identify marketing cost-related metrics in the perspective of return-on–marketing-investment.

SOLUTIONS AND RECOMMENDATIONS

From the standpoint of social CRM, our guidelines for relational IMC practices are rooted on three conceptual frameworks following a holistic approach: 1) the *Model of Consumer Dynamics in Status* which describes how customers change their status over the life cycle to account for consumer heterogeneity; 2) the *Integrated Communication Process Model* which highlights interactions between social entities such as providers, opinion leaders, and opinion seekers in a social network setting (refer to Borgatti & Halgin, 2011; Burt, Kilduff, & Tasselli, 2013; and Granovetter, 1973 for social network theory) and the engagement activities of opinion leaders into the value creation process—using an optimal mix of mass and social media—in a two-way communication process (Yoon & Sims, 2013, in press); and 3) Knapps' (1978) *Relationship Escalation Model* which describes how it is possible for opinion leaders to build and maintain ongoing interpersonal relationships with the firm and other social entities in a specific personal social network setting. Importantly, all of the relationship-building processes need to be directed toward the maximization of relational or relationship equity (RE) following the spirit of social CRM activities.

Given this setting, we provide specific recommendations for the design of relational IMC strategies—including new message and media strategies, along with key metrics, as major parts of any IMC strategy—within the boundary of social CRM practices. Especially, we focus on the role of opinion leadership—via various forms of engaged activities as typical outcomes of customer engagement—toward opinion seekers in any personal social network in an attempt to build and manage personalized long-term relationships. The success of the value co-creation process relies heavily upon customers' efforts and involvement. The value co-creation effectively leads to greater interdependence among main actors, which in turn builds trust and sustainable relationships in any social network setting. Remember that cooperation is as prevalent in economic activity as in the relationship-building process. We first discuss specific solutions in three areas and finally provide a summary table which combines all of the discussed suggestions.

Designing Personalized Relationship-Building Processes

In order to build and manage personalized relationship processes with target customers, it is necessary to design relational IMC strategies depending on the concept of consumer heterogeneity over the customer life cycle. For this task, this study introduces the *Model of Consumer Dynamics in Status* which describes how individual customers change their loyalty status over time as they make a series of purchases (Yoon & Kang, 2011; Yoon & Sims, 2013, in press). This concept is very important since the essence of social CRM focuses on the relationship-building process and marketers are able to design customized messages and media strategies depending on the types of target customers. As mentioned previously, Kumar (2008) also identifies three stages such as acquisition, retention, and attrition over the life cycle, but it starts from the perspective of customer lifetime value.

For identifying personalized relationship-building processes, this study identifies four different stages of customer status—specifically, potential buyers (PBs), first-time buyers (FTBs), my repeat customers (MRCs), and loyal customers (LCs)—following the spirit of the original *Model of Consumer Dynamics in Status (MCDS)*. Note that this suggested framework does include the loyalty status of my repeat customers and exclude the status of competitors' repeat customers (CRCs). A series of four different stages of customer status over the lifetime is depicted in Figure 3.

It is necessary for social CRM practitioners to figure out specific marketing goals and relevant metrics when targeting each type of customer group at different stages of the life cycle. Refer to Table 2 for the details of marketing goals, examples of marketing activities, and relevant metrics. Remember that Table 2 includes one more type of customer status, i.e., targeting unknown buyers (UBs) for the sake of readers.

When targeting potential buyers (PBs), social CRM practitioners need to make them first-time buyers (FTBs). In order to achieve this company goal, marketers are able to complete the first type of specific marketing goal such as increasing buyer awareness, knowledge, like or preference, and intention levels following the essence of the consumer response process (Belch & Belch, 2007). Then, marketers are likely to generate the maximum number of trials from all potential buyers to make them FTBs. For this matter, marketers are able to utilize various types of promotional campaigns such as welcome emails, direct mail, mass communication channels, and so on. For example, Ann Taylor Loft offers frequent promotional emails with prominently-featured sales promotions and products to entice shoppers toward a first-time purchase.

When targeting first-time buyers (FTBs), social CRM practitioners need to make them my repeat customers (MRCs). In order to achieve this goal, they may consider the completion of the following activities: 1) maximizing their overall satisfaction with the firm's offerings, 2) reinforcing an overall positive attitude toward the firm and its offerings, and 3) increasing the likelihood to make a first repeat purchase. For this matter, marketers are able to measure the level of customer satisfaction, use different types of promotional campaigns, and so on. For example, following a purchase, Amazon.com sends emails and frequently updates its Facebook page with links to products on its website in an effort to share relevant content with customers that will generate a repeat purchase.

When targeting my repeat customers (MRCs), it is important for social CRM practitioners to make them loyal customers (LCs). In order to achieve this goal, marketers are able to complete 1) the first specific goal of increasing the likelihood to stay as a repeat customer, 2) the second specific goal of preventing them from switching to other competing offerings, and 3) the third specific goal of making them truly loyal by enhancing their emotional attachment to the firm and its offerings. Major examples of marketing activities for this matter are loyalty programs, matching behaviors, any programs for enhancing emotional attachment, and so on. As an example of building emotional attachment, the Twitter feed for Hershey's Kisses stimulates repeat activity through providing chocolate images and recipes to followers. Also, Virgin America attempts to move customers to

Figure 3. Personalized relationship-building process over customer life cycle

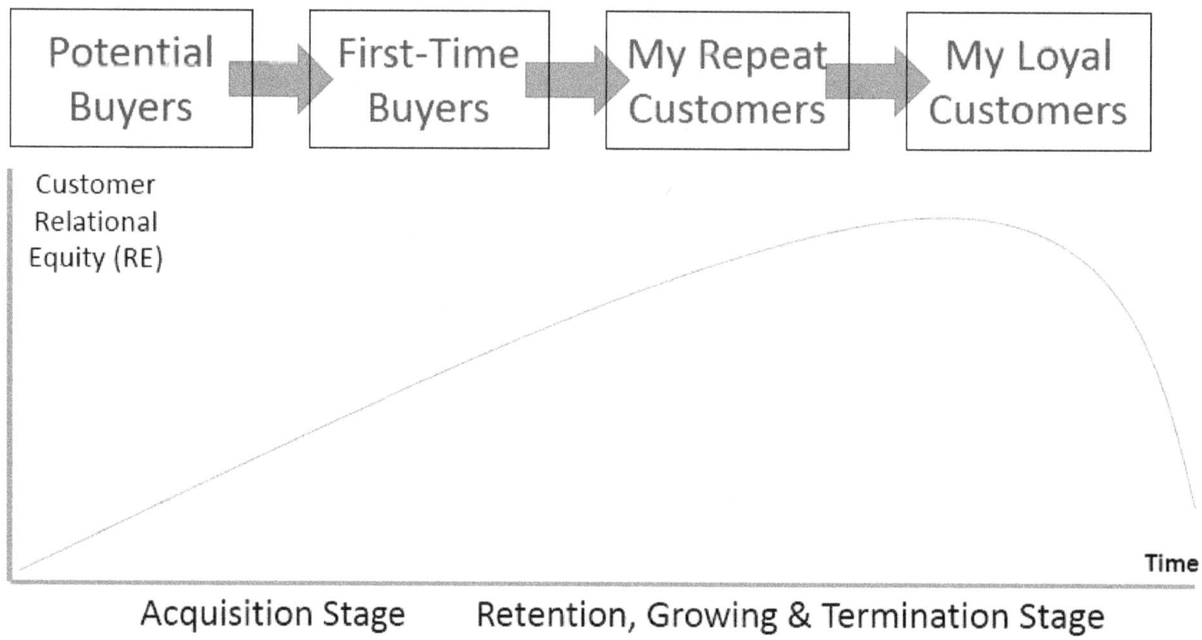

greater loyalty through using Twitter to offer money-saving promotions to followers.

When targeting loyal customers (LCs), social CRM practitioners need to make them an ambassador of the firm. Traditionally, marketers have shown a lack of interest on this matter. Recognizing the power of word-of-mouth and the importance of referral behaviors among existing retained customers, marketers have started changing their attitude toward this marketing opportunity. Thus, marketing practitioners are able to 1) complete the first specific goal of increasing the level of customers' overall bonding with the firm, 2) increase the number of voluntary engaged activities among opinion leaders using their personal social networks, and 3) make customers an ambassador of the firm. Major examples of marketing activities can be any programs that enhance the bonding formation process, creating customer referrals, WOM, recommendation, and reviewing activities among others.

Remember that in this study, an ultimate goal of any social CRM practice—depending on the strong execution of relational IMC strategies—is the maximum creation of various forms of voluntary social engagement activities by opinion leaders toward opinion seekers in any social network setting. As a contemporary example, consider how the Pinterest social media platform is being used by companies to engage customers in voluntary activities. To stimulate loyal customers using Pinterest, companies, like Ikea and Chobani offer a breakdown of pin boards, with their products categorized based on user interest for customers to voluntarily keep pinning. Providing followers with product-relevant pin boards via this social media platform creates a high level of customer engagement in this social network setting.

Relational IMC Strategies and Social Engagement

This book chapter utilizes the suggestions of Knapp's (1978) *Relationship Development or Escalation Model* in order to design relational and personalized IMC strategies depending on each type of customer group at different stages of the customer life cycle as shown in Table 2. The specific guidelines for the customized relational IMC strategies by customer type are as follows.

When Targeting Potential Buyers (PBs). An overall effort of targeting potential buyers can be related to the *initiating* and *experimenting* stages in Knapp's (1978) model. Key aspects of both stages are provided. The *initiating* stage is: very short and sometimes as short as less than 15 seconds in human relationships; in this stage, human interactions are concerned with creating very favorable impressions of each other; and thus, human beings may use standard greetings or observe each other's appearance or behavioral aspects. The *experimentation* stage consists of: individuals asking multiple questions in order to gain information about each other and decide if they wish to continue the relationship; and in fact, many relationships do not progress further than this point.

Given the explanation of these relational stages, IMC practitioners first should be able to start creating new contacts with potential buyers to create favorable impressions, to introduce a new value proposition of the firm's offerings and to build new relationships with them for the first time. Then, marketers are able to share further offering-related information with potential buyers using feedback channels in a two-way communication process. Regarding message strategy, marketers are able to highlight the essence of value proposition for the firm's marketing offering. And with respect to media strategy, marketers are able to listen to target customers' opinions for identifying their unmet needs and for identifying appropriate contact points using a mix of mass media communication channels including selected social media.

When Targeting First-Time Buyers (FTBs). The *intensifying* stage in Knapp's (1978) model is related to the efforts of targeting FTBs. Key aspects of this stage are: self-disclosure or self-expression becomes more common; the human relationships become less formal; the individuals begin to see each other as valued or talented individuals; and statements are made about the level of commitment, along with trust, that each one has to the relationship.

Given the above relational stage, IMC practitioners should be able to create self-disclosure behaviors of first-time buyers, if possible, to generate their interactions and to make less formal relationships with them. Remember that at this point, many of the FTBs should be satisfied with the firm's offerings as the key condition of this status. For this matter, message strategies may highlight how effective high levels of a firm's commitment and trust are to further enhance relationships with FTBs, and media strategies may depend on frequent use of social media in a rather informal relationship environment.

When Targeting Current Repeat Customers (CRCs). The efforts of targeting the CRCs can be related to the *integrating* stage in Knapp's model. Key aspects of this stage are as follows: human beings are able to become a valuable pair to each other; they begin to do things together to create valuable outcomes; importantly, others begin to see them as a pair loyal to each other; and thus, a shared relational identity starts to build at this stage.

When considering the major direction of relational IMC strategies, marketers should be able to enhance current customer loyalty based on the value co-creation process with current repeat customers, coupled with emotional attachment efforts. Thus, target customers should feel that they and the firm already have become a valuable pair to each other at this stage and should also show a high level of togetherness. In this case, message strategy needs to focus on the efforts of highlighting the opportunity of being involved into the value co-creation process and the creation of emotional attachment to the firm and its offerings. Media strategy also focuses on the design of a mix of mass and social media which cultivates more interactions with target customers to enhance true customer loyalty.

When Targeting My Loyal Customers (LCs). The efforts of targeting LCs can be related to the *bonding* stage in Knapp's model. Key aspects of this stage are as follows: a formal, sometimes legal, announcement of the relationship is made; examples include a marriage and best friend ritual in human relationships, or a partnership agreement in business relationships; however, few relationships actually reach this level or stage.

As this stage represents the major direction of relational IMC strategies, marketers should be able to create strong partnerships with existing loyal customers since most loyalty measures in practice are driven by behavioral outcomes, implying a lack of attitudinal loyalty (Dick & Basu, 1994; Yoon & Tran, 2011). In addition, marketers need to be involved in the bonding formation process, while focusing on the value co-creation process with loyalty customers, coupled with the generation of various forms of their voluntary engaged activities as opinion leaders. Regarding message strategy, marketers are able to highlight the importance of voluntary customer engagement activities for helping each other in a personal social network setting. With respect to media strategy, marketers are able to induce opinion leadership for further social engagement efforts using a mix of various types of social media.

Relationship Equity as a New Metric for Social CRM

The success of any social CRM practice, along with relational IMC strategies, depends on the effectiveness of an overall relationship building and maintenance process over the customer life cycle. In this regard, social CRM practitioners need to develop new metrics which represent how effectively the firm executes personalized relationship-building processes with individual target customers, instead of using customer lifetime value or customer equity from the firm's standpoint of monetary value.

For this matter, this study proposes the concept of relational or relationship equity (RE) as mentioned previously. The relational equity is an overarching metric which diagnoses the effectiveness of any social CRM practice since it consists of various types of specific measures at different stages of the customer life cycle, along with Knapp's relationship development process, as shown in Table 1 and Figure 3. In other words, marketers are able to diagnose the performance of different relational IMC and other marketing strategies at different stages as target customers make a series of successive purchases until becoming a loyal customer and an ambassador of the firm.

For the new relational equity metric, the effectiveness of building long-term relationships with target customers can be measured in terms of three sources such as relational IMC efforts for relationship building, customer engagement, and cost for relationship-building process. Typical examples of relational IMC-related metrics can be levels of awareness, knowledge, liking, preference, intention, and trial or purchase, following the stages in the hierarchy-of-effects model or consumer response process (Belch & Belch, 2007). Also, various types of metrics for relationship building in Knapp's relationship development process can be considered. Examples of metrics for relationship building and customer engagement include the following: level of customer impression; customer knowledge value (CKV, Kumar et al. 2010); customer influence value (CIV, Kumar et al. 2010), which can be represented by number of reviews and frequency of posting opinions on blogs or frequency of pressing 'like' in Facebook; customer sentiment; customer referral value (CRV, Kumar et al. 2010); customer lifetime value (CLV); customer commitment; perceived togetherness; level of customer bonding, and so on. Finally, metrics for the cost of relationship building are new customer acquisition cost (CAC), social media cost, reward program cost, matching cost, and advertising cost per customer, among others.

Summary of Proposed Guidelines for Relational IMC Strategies

Given the breadth of discussion thus far, we provide the summary of our proposed guidelines for relational IMC strategies—under the umbrella of social CRM—which are designed to build and mpersonalized long-term relationships with individual customers over the life cycle. Depending on types of customer groups over the life cycle such as potential buyers, first-time buyers, my repeat customers, and loyal customers, specifically, this summary table provides key information about major goals for targeting strategy, underlying principles of marketing strategies, key challenges for social CRM, and major directions for relational IMC strategies along with message strategy, media strategy, and relevant metrics. The summary information is shown in Table 3.

FUTURE RESEARCH DIRECTIONS

From a holistic approach, this book chapter has thus far shed light on very relevant concepts and united them into an integrative conceptual framework as the guideline for designing effective relational IMC programs under the umbrella of social CRM. In order to make any relational IMC practices successful, however, CRM practitioners need to consider the following issues in detail for future research. One issue that marketers first need to consider is the fact that no consensus has been reached on a commonly accepted definition of what a relationship is in a commercial context and of what relationship marketing or loyalty marketing is (Gronroos, 2006; Harker 1999), even though Palmartier (2008) provides a comprehensive list of relationship marketing definitions. Following are several selected issues for future research.

Heterogeneous Relationship-Building Processes

Marketing practitioners have been interested in making customers loyal in the long run. In this context, consumer heterogeneity represents the starting point for personalization or customization in order to meet the unique unmet needs of individual customers and understand their personal behavioral patterns. In the past, the efforts of firms' loyalty formation processes have tended to be marketer-oriented in the sense that the loyalty concept comes from the standpoint of the firm. Instead, marketers should understand unique and personalized relationship-building processes—by accounting for consumer heterogeneity in the relationship building—for each of individual target customers, and put this knowledge into the design of personalized relationship-building strategy. As a guideline, this chapter introduces Knapp's (1978) model to shed light on how firms build long-term relationships with customers over time. This is one issue for future research since marketers need to investigate how to build and maintain personalized relationships with individual customers using this suggested framework.

Storytelling Approach for Customer Engagement in Marketing Communications

Among marketing practitioners and scholars, the topic of customer engagement has been a hot topic. For instance, recent issues in the *Journal of Service Research* cover various types of issues related to customer engagement (Brodie et al., 2011; Kumar et al., 2010; van Doorn, et al., 2010; Verhoef, Reinartz, & Krafft, 2010;). The Marketing Science Institute (MSI) also noted this topic as one of the hot research priorities for the period of 2010-2012 due to its significant impact on company performance.

In this chapter, it is argued that one necessary requirement for making social CRM practices

Table 3. Guidelines for relational IMC practices and metrics by customer type

Evaluation Criterion	Targeting Potential Buyers	Targeting First-Time Buyers	Targeting My Repeat Customers	Targeting My Loyal Customers
Major Goal for Targeting Strategy	Transforming them into first-time buyers (FTBs)	Transforming them into my repeat customers (MRCs)	Transforming them into brand loyal patrons of the firm or its offerings	Transforming them into ambassadors of the firm
Underlying Principles of Marketing Strategies	Acquiring potential buyers based on adoption/diffusion and two-way relational IMC processes	Retaining first-time buyers based on repeat, renewal or replacement processes	Growing my repeat customers based on the loyalty formation process	Developing their partnerships with the firm based on the bonding formation process
Key Challenges in the Value Creation Process for social CRM	Designing and communicating the value proposition for building new relationships	Diagnosing current value proposition for creating repeat behaviors and maximizing overall satisfaction	Sharing personal emotions attached to the firm's offerings with others for enhancing existing customer loyalty	Creating voluntary content creation activities, using personal social networks, for enhancing the quality of value creation process
Major Directions of Relational IMC Practices for Building Long-Term Relationships	Creating new relationships with PBs based on new value proposition at the stages of: ▪ Initiating: Creating contacts to introduce value proposition of the firm's offerings ▪ Experimenting: Sharing further information using two-way feedback channels ▪ Intensifying: n/a ▪ Integrating: n/a ▪ Bonding: n/a	Creating continued relationships with my FTBs using assessed satisfaction results at the stages of: ▪ Initiating: Reminding FTBs with current value proposition of the firm's offerings ▪ Experimenting: Addressing dissatisfied features in the value proposition ▪ Intensifying: Creating self-disclosure behaviors for trust and commitment ▪ Integrating: n/a ▪ Bonding: n/a	Enhancing sustained loyalty of MRCs based on emotional-oriented value proposition at the stages of: ▪ Initiating: Reminding MRCs with enhanced value proposition of the firm's offerings ▪ Experimenting: Addressing how to grow with the firm ▪ Intensifying: Creating emotionally-enhanced behaviors for increasing customer loyalty ▪ Integrating: Increasing the level of togetherness with the firm and its offerings ▪ Bonding: n/a	Creating strong partnerships with MRCs based on bonding-oriented value proposition at the stages: ▪ Initiating: Reminding LCs with enhanced value proposition of the firm's offerings ▪ Experimenting: Addressing how to help each other ▪ Intensifying: Creating emotionally-enhanced behaviors for increasing customer bonding level ▪ Integrating: Increasing the level of togetherness with the firm and its offerings ▪ Bonding: Voluntarily exchanging relevant, interesting content using personal social networks
Major Focus of Message Strategy	Highlighting value proposition of the firm's offerings to start a new relationship building process	Highlighting the firm's commitment and trust as the continuation of further enhanced relationships	Highlighting the creation of emotional attachments to the firm and its offerings	Highlighting the importance of voluntary engaged efforts with others in personal social networks
Major Focus of A Mix of Mass & Social Media Strategy	Listening to customer opinions for identifying target customers' unmet needs with two-way feedback channels	Gathering customer complaints and feedbacks for improving overall customer satisfaction	Interacting with customers in a loyalty building process to create brand loyalty for the firm's offerings	Inducing opinion leaderships for social engagement as an ambassador in their personal social networks
Suggested Metrics for Relational or Relationship Equity	Measuring the effectiveness of building new relationships with potential buyers using: ▪ Metrics for relational IMC: Levels of customer awareness, liking or preference, intention, trial, etc. ▪ Metrics for relationship building and customer engagement: Level of customer impression, customer knowledge, customer sentiment, etc. ▪ Metrics for relationship building cost: New customer acquisition cost using mass media advertising, free samples, price discounts, etc.	Measuring the effectiveness of satisfaction enhancement programs with new trials using: ▪ Metrics for relational IMC: Level of customer satisfaction, number of complaints, lead-to-sales, etc. ▪ Metrics for relationship building and customer engagement: Level of customer commitment/ trust, customer knowledge, customer sentiment, number of customer referrals, customer lifetime value, etc. ▪ Metrics for relationship enhancement cost: Customer retention cost, price discounts, advertising on mass media, social media, and emails, etc.	Measuring the effectiveness of loyalty building programs with my existing repeat customers using: ▪ Metrics for relational IMC: Customer retention rate, customer attrition rate, etc. ▪ Metrics for relationship building and customer engagement: Level of customer loyalty, customer commitment, togetherness with the firm, customer lifetime value, etc. ▪ Metrics for loyalty formation cost: Customer churn rate, loyalty program cost, matching cost, advertising cost on social media, etc.	Measuring the effectiveness of bond building and customer engagement programs using: ▪ Metrics for relational IMC: Customer retention rate, customer attrition rate, etc. ▪ Metrics for relationship building and customer engagement: Level of customer bonding with the firm, number of referral, recommendation, WOM, and reviewing activities, customer lifetime value, etc. ▪ Metrics for bonding formation cost: Rewarding cost for social engagement, advertising on social media, etc.

successful is to properly exercise the customer engagement or social engagement of participants into the value creation process (Gronroos & Voima, 2013) in any social network setting. The reason is simple: the voluntary engagement of target customers makes the participants an owner of the value co-creation process with any marketing activities. Also, the efforts of value co-creation processes depend on a greater interdependence among main key actors—such as firms, opinion leaders, and opinion seekers in the social networks—resulting in building trust and commitment, and also sustaining co-beneficial relationships. In this regard, the task of conceptualizing the role of customer engagement, along with the identification of its proper metrics, is one important issue for future research.

A storytelling approach may boost interaction and social engagement activities of opinion leaders with others in the social networks. Studies in human psychology have found that if individuals are told something through narrative, they are more likely to relate to the message, absorbing it further, and remaining engaged from start to finish (Robertson, 2013). In this regard, marketers may utilize storytelling approaches to make opinion leaders more engaged into the value creation process (Papadatos, 2006; Woodside, 2010; Woodside, Sood, & Miller, 2008;).

Development and Utilization of Personal Social Networks

The success of customer engagement also depends on how to trigger the voluntary engaged efforts of opinion leaders influencing opinion seekers in the social networks. In this regard, social CRM practitioners need to understand how opinion leaders form their own personal social networks and exercise their opinion leadership using their own personal networks in order to create various types of engagement activities such as referrals, word-of-mouth activities, recommendations, reviews, and so on—combined with the use of social media.

For this matter, social network analysis (SNA) can be helpful. SNA is referred to as the study of human relationships between social entities in any social network setting by means of graph theory methodology (Burt, Kilduff, & Tasselli, 2013; Wasserman & Faust, 1994;). The amount of research on SNA has grown considerably in the past decades. However, this area still leaves a lot to be unpacked. With the methodological utilization of the graph theory, it is possible for marketers to investigate how opinion leaders construct their personal networks and utilize them for creating various forms of social engagement activities with others (Chapman, 2011; Uzzi & Dunlap, 2005).

Regarding the definition of social network, two well-known network theories have been used to identify the characteristic elements of network theorizing: Granovetter's strength of weak ties theory (Granovetter, 1973) and Burt's structural holes theory (Burt, 1973). Both theories share an underlying theoretical model—labeled the network flow model—from which we derive additional implications about relationship building and social engagement processes. Also, future research can include additional discussions on the possibility of another fundamental model, called the bond model, the merits of model-based network theorizing for facilitating the generation of new theory, and endogeneity in network theorizing. Nowadays, marketers are able to identify the network building and managing processes of opinion leaders in the social networks mainly driven by the presence of so-called big data (McKinsey Global Institute, 2011).

Re-Conceptualizing the Role of Products in Value Creation Process

Even though this chapter discusses the essence of relational IMC practices in the context of social CRM, it should be noted that the efforts of building long-term relationships with customers start with the provision of market offerings or products which include needs-satisfying features. Traditionally, products have been regarded as the 'means' for reaching consumers or end users or the tools for creating various types of exchange processes from the perspective of goods-dominant logic (Vargo & Lusch, 2004). However, marketers need to understand the fundamental roles of market offerings—as the means of creating voluntary engaged activities of target customers with others—in the value creation process. One main reason is that end users are the ones who actually perceive or determine the final values of the offerings (Gronroos, 2006). In this regard, it is necessary to re-conceptualize the role of any product in the value creation process while simultaneously attempting to build and maintain long-term relationships with customers over the life cycle.

CONCLUSION

In the context of social CRM practices, relational IMC is a new marketing communications approach which is focused on the building and maintaining of co-beneficial relationships with target customers, i.e., opinion leaders, in a two-way interactive communication process, mainly targeting their exercise of voluntary engagement efforts into the value creation process in a social network setting. In this regard, this book chapter has attempted to provide the guidelines for personalized relational IMC practices, depending on the heterogeneous status of individual customers over the customer life cycle. Especially, we have considered how to put the true meaning of 'Relationship' back into social CRM practices (Fournier & Avery, 2011).

To prepare useful guidelines, we specifically discuss how individual customers build and maintain long-term relationships with others by borrowing Knapp's (1978) suggested concepts prevailing in the interpersonal communication area in a loyalty building process. We also discuss how to implant the relationship perspective into the traditional transaction-oriented IMC processes. Putting all together, we prepare our guidelines by discussing how to design relational IMC strategies through promoting voluntary customer engagement activities into the value creation process using various types of traditional mass and new social media.

The major contribution of this chapter has been providing a framework for specific message and media strategies that allow marketers to design, implement, and manage the communication processes associated with social CRM practices with the overall aim of making consumers loyal through IMC activities with both traditional and new social media. This framework is characterized by two key features. First, the social CRM strategy is based on consumer heterogeneity in purchasing experience as consumers change their status in *the Model of Consumer Dynamics in Status* as shown in Figure 2. Using these strategies, marketers are able to provide customized marketing and IMC programs, depending on the needs as well as characteristics of the target group of consumers. Second, this chapter allows marketers to capitalize on various types of traditional mass media and new social media in an attempt to accelerate the diffusion process of a specific brand or offering, based on the integrated communication process as shown in Figure 1.

This chapter is not without its limitations. Since the manuscript mentions just guidelines and conceptual frameworks along with anecdotal examples, it lacks some evidential support from empirical studies. However, once an underlying framework for social CRM has been developed (as is provided in this chapter), scholars can design empirical studies to test the framework against the backdrop of real-life occurrences.

Welcome to the new world of social CRM and relational IMC! In the era of new social CRM, it is necessary for us as social CRM practitioners to have a more extensive framework of new relational IMC practices in order to induce a full level of customer engagement into the value creation process, to make customers emotionally attached to the company brand or product offering, and ultimately, to develop and manage long-term co-beneficial relationships with target customers in any social network setting. The conceptual framework of this book chapter should provide effective guidelines for social CRM and relational IMC practitioners as they usher in this new era and as they engage in efforts to re-conceptualize traditional IMC modes of thought with the unique role and metrics of social media. By moving toward a more relationship-building perspective that incorporates the status of individual customers over the life cycle, it is believed that relational IMC practitioners will be more poised for the new social CRM.

REFERENCES

Altman, I., & Taylor, D. (1973). *Social penetration: The development of interpersonal relationships*. New York: Holt.

Andersen, P. H. (2001). Relationship development and marketing communication: An integrative model. *Journal of Business and Industrial Marketing*, *16*(3), 167–182. doi:10.1108/08858620110389786

Armelini, G., & Villanueva, J. (2011). The power of word of mouth: Adding social media to the marketing mix. *IESEinsight*, *9*, 29–36.

Avtgis, T. A., West, D. V., & Anderson, T. L. (1998). Relationship stages: An inductive analysis identifying cognitive affective, and behavioral dimensions of Knapp's relational stages model. *Communication Research Reports*, *15*(3), 280–287. doi:10.1080/08824099809362124

Bagozzi, R. P. (1974). Marketing as an organized behavioral system of exchange. *Journal of Marketing*, *38*(4), 77–81. doi:10.2307/1250397

Bagozzi, R. P. (1994). Interactions in small groups: The social relations model. In J. N. Sheth, & A. Parvatiyar (Eds.), *Relationship marketing: Theory, methods, and applications*. Atlanta: Emory University, Center for Relationship Marketing.

Bass, F. M. (1969). A new product growth model for consumer durables. *Management Science*, *15*(5), 215–227. doi:10.1287/mnsc.15.5.215

Beebe, S. A., Beebe, S. J., & Richmond, M. V. (2002). *Interpersonal communication: Relating to others* (3rd ed.). Boston, MA: Allyn & Bacon.

Belch, G. E., & Belch, M. A. (2007). *Advertising and promotion: An integrated marketing communications perspective* (7th ed.). Boston, MA: McGraw-Hill Irwin.

Berry, L. L. (1983). Relationship marketing. In L. L. Berry, G. L. Shostack, & G. Upah (Eds.), *Emerging perspective on services marketing* (pp. 25–28). Chicago: American Marketing Association.

Bijmolt, T. H. A., Leeflang, P. S. H., Block, F., Eisenbeiss, M., Hardie, B. G. S., Lemmens, A., & Saffert, P. (2010). Analytics for customer engagement. *Journal of Service Research*, *13*(3), 341–356. doi:10.1177/1094670510375603

Blau, P. M. (1964). *Exchange and power in social life*. New York: John Wiley.

Borgatti, S. P., & Halgin, D. S. (2011). On network theory. *Journal of Organization Science*, *22*, 1157–1167.

Boulding, W., Staelin, R., Ehret, M., & Johnston, W. J. (2005). A customer relationship management roadmap: What is known, potential pitfalls, and where to go. *Journal of Marketing*, *69*(4), 155–166. doi:10.1509/jmkg.2005.69.4.155

Brodie, R. J., Hollebeek, L. D., Juric, B., & Ilic, A. (2011). Customer engagement: Conceptual domain, fundamental propositions, and implications for research. *Journal of Service Research*, *14*(3), 252–271. doi:10.1177/1094670511411703

Burt, R. S. (1973). *Structural holes: The social structure of competition*. Cambridge, MA: Harvard University Press.

Burt, R. S., Kilduff, M., & Tasselli, S. (2013). Social network analysis: Foundations and frontiers on advantage. *Annual Review of Psychology*, *64*(1), 527–547. doi:10.1146/annurev-psych-113011-143828

Chao, C., Corus, C., & Li, T. (2012). Balancing traditional media and online advertising strategy. *International Journal of Business, Marketing, &. Decision Sciences*, *5*(1), 12–24.

Chapman, C. (2011). How to use social networking to build your own network. *British Journal of Administrative Management*, *73*, 14–15.

Chen, Y., & Xie, J. (2008). Online consumer review: Word-of-mouth as a new element of marketing communication mix. *Management Science*, *54*(3), 721–739. doi:10.1287/mnsc.1070.0810

Christopher, M., Payne, A., & Ballantyne, D. (2002). *Relationship marketing: Creating stakeholder value*. Oxford, UK: Butterworth-Heinemann.

Christopher, M., Payne, A., Peck, H., & Clark, M. (1998). *Relationship marketing for competitive advantage: Winning and keeping customers*. Oxford, UK: Elsevier Science Ltd.

Cropanzano, R., & Mitchell, M. S. (2005). Social exchange theory: An interdisciplinary review. *Journal of Management, 31*(6), 874–900. doi:10.1177/0149206305279602

de Matos, C. A., & Rossi, C. A. V. (2008). Word-of-mouth communications in marketing: A meta-analytic review of the antecedents and moderators. *Journal of the Academy of Marketing Science, 36*(4), 578–596. doi:10.1007/s11747-008-0121-1

Dick, A. S., & Basu, K. (1994). Customer loyalty: Toward an integrated conceptual framework. *Journal of the Academy of Marketing Science, 22*(2), 99–113. doi:10.1177/0092070394222001

Dodson, J. A., & Muller, E. (1978). Models of new product advertising and word-of-mouth. *Management Science, 24*(15), 1568–1578. doi:10.1287/mnsc.24.15.1568

Duncan, T., & Moriarty, S. E. (1988). A communication-based marketing model for managing relationships. *Journal of Marketing, 62*(2), 1–13. doi:10.2307/1252157

Dwyer, F. R., Schurr, P., & Oh, S. (1987). Developing buyer-seller relationships. *Journal of Marketing, 51*(2), 11–27. doi:10.2307/1251126

Etlinger, S. (2011). *A framework for social analytics*. Altimeter Group.

Finne, A., & Gronroos, C. (2009). Rethinking marketing communication: From integrated marketing communications to relationship communication. *Journal of Marketing Communications, 15*(2-3), 179–195. doi:10.1080/13527260902757654

Ford, D. (1980). Buyer/seller relationships in international industrial markets. *European Journal of Marketing, 14*(5), 339–354. doi:10.1108/EUM0000000004910

Fournier, S., & Avery, J. (2011). Putting the 'relationship' back into CRM. *MIT Sloan Management Review, 52*(3), 63–72.

Fox, J., Warber, K. M., & Makstaller, D. C. (2013). The role of Facebook in romantic relationship development: An exploration of Knapp's relational stage model. *Journal of Social and Personal Relationships, 30*(6), 771–794. doi:10.1177/0265407512468370

Frazier, G. L. (1983). Interorganizational exchange behavior in marketing channels: A broadened perspective. *Journal of Marketing, 47*(4), 68–78. doi:10.2307/1251400

Godes, D., & Mayzlin, D. (2004). Using online conversation to study word-of-mouth communication. *Marketing Science, 23*(4), 545–560. doi:10.1287/mksc.1040.0071

Godes, D., & Mayzlin, D. (2009). Firm-created word-of-mouth communication: Evidence from a field test. *Marketing Science, 28*(4), 721–739. doi:10.1287/mksc.1080.0444

Granovetter, M. S. (1973). The strength of weak ties. *American Journal of Sociology, 78*(6), 1360–1380. doi:10.1086/225469

Greenberg, P. (2009). Time to put a stake in the ground on social CRM. *ZDNet—Social CRM: The Conversation Blog*.

Gronroos, C. (1990). From marketing mix to relationship marketing: Towards a paradigm shift in marketing. *Management Decision, 32*(2), 4–20. doi:10.1108/00251749410054774

Gronroos, C. (2004). The relationship marketing process: Communication, interaction, dialogue, and value. *Journal of Business and Industrial Marketing, 19*(2), 99–113. doi:10.1108/08858620410523981

Gronroos, C. (2006). On defining marketing: Finding a new roadmap for marketing. *Marketing Theory, 6*(4), 395–417. doi:10.1177/1470593106069930

Gronroos, C., & Voima, P. (2013). Critical service logic: Making sense of value creation and co-creation. *Journal of the Academy of Marketing Science, 41*(2), 133–150. doi:10.1007/s11747-012-0308-3

Gupta, D., & Zeithaml, D. (2006). Customer metrics and their Impact on financial performance. *Marketing Science, 25*(6), 718–739. doi:10.1287/mksc.1060.0221

Gupta, S., Lehmann, D. R., & Stuart, J. A. (2004). Valuing customers. *JMR, Journal of Marketing Research, 41*(1), 7–18. doi:10.1509/jmkr.41.1.7.25084

Hahn, M., Park, S., Krishnamurthi, L., & Zoltners, A. A. (1994). Analysis of new product diffusion using a four-segment trial-repeat model. *Marketing Science, 13*(3), 224–247. doi:10.1287/mksc.13.3.224

Harker, M. J. (1999). Relationship marketing defined? An examination of current relationship marketing definitions. *Marketing Intelligence & Planning, 17*(1), 13–20. doi:10.1108/02634509910253768

Heide, J. (1994). Interorganizational governance in marketing channels. *Journal of Marketing, 58*(1), 71–85. doi:10.2307/1252252

Hennig-Thurau, T., Malthouse, E. C., Friege, C., Gensler, S., Lobschat, L., Rangaswamy, A., & Skiera, B. (2010). The impact of new media on consumer relationships. *Journal of Service Research, 13*(3), 311–330. doi:10.1177/1094670510375460

Hoffman, D. L., & Fodor, M. (2012). Can you measure the ROI of your social media marketing? *MIT Sloan Management Review, 52*(1), 41–49.

Homans, G. C. (1961). *Social behavior: Its elementary forms*. New York: Harcourt Brace.

Hunt, S. D. (1983). General theories and the fundamental explanada of marketing. *Journal of Marketing, 47*(4), 9–17. doi:10.2307/1251394

Iyengar, R., Van den Bulte, C., & Valente, T. W. (2011). Opinion leadership and social contagion in new product diffusion. *Marketing Science, 30*(2), 195–212. doi:10.1287/mksc.1100.0566

Iyer, G. R., Sharma, A., & Bejou, D. (2006). Developing relationship equity in international markets. *Journal of Relationship Marketing, 5*(1), 3–20. doi:10.1300/J366v05n01_02

Kaplan, A. M., & Haenlein, M. (2010). Users of the world, unite! The challenges and opportunities of social media. *Business Horizons, 53*(1), 59–68. doi:10.1016/j.bushor.2009.09.003

Katz, E. (1957). The two-step flow of communication: An up-to-date report on an hypothesis. *Public Opinion Quarterly, 21*(1), 61–78. doi:10.1086/266687

Katz, E., & Lazarsfeld, P. F. (1955). *Personal Influence*. New York: The Free Press.

Kliatchko, J. G. (2005). Towards a new definition of integrated marketing communications (IMC). *International Journal of Advertising, 24*(1), 7–34.

Knapp, M. L. (1978). *Interpersonal communication and human relationships*. Boston, MA: Allyn & Bacon.

Kotler, P. (1972). A generic concept of marketing. *Journal of Marketing, 36*(2), 46–54. doi:10.2307/1250977

Kumar, V. (2008). *Managing customers for profit: Strategies to increase profits and build loyalty*. Pearson Prentice-Hall.

Kumar, V., Aksoy, L., Donkers, B., Venkatesan, R., Wiesel, T., & Tillmanns, S. (2010). Undervalued or overvalued customers: Capturing total customer engagement value. *Journal of Service Research, 13*(3), 297–310. doi:10.1177/1094670510375602

Kumar, V., Petersen, J. A., & Leone, R. P. (2010). Driving profitability by encouraging customer referrals: Who, when, and how. *Journal of Marketing, 74*(5), 1–17. doi:10.1509/jmkg.74.5.1

Kumar, V., & Rajan, B. (2009). Profitable customer management: Measuring and maximizing customer lifetime value. *Management Accounting Quarterly, 10*(3), 1–18.

Lazarsfeld, P. F., Berelson, B., & Gaudet, H. (1944). *The people's choice: How the voter makes up his mind in a presidential campaign*. New York: Columbia University Press.

Lehmann, D. R., & Winer, R. S. (2005). *Analysis for marketing planning* (6th ed.). Boston, MA: McGraw-Hill.

Levitt, T. (1960). Marketing myopia. *Harvard Business Review, 38*, 45–60.

Lindberg-Repo, K., & Gronroos, C. (2004). Conceptualising communication strategy from a relational perspective. *Industrial Marketing Management, 33*(3), 229–239. doi:10.1016/j.indmarman.2003.10.012

Lithium Technologies. (2009). *Powering the customer network with social CRM*. Lithium Technologies.

Manchanda, P., Xie, Y., & Youn, N. (2008). The role of targeted communication and contagion in product adoption. *Marketing Science, 27*(6), 961–976. doi:10.1287/mksc.1070.0354

Mangold, W. G., & Faulds, D. J. (2009). Social media: The new hybrid elements of the promotion mix. *Business Horizons, 52*(4), 357–365. doi:10.1016/j.bushor.2009.03.002

Marketing Science Institute. (2010). *Marketing Science Institute 2010-2012 Research Priorities*. Cambridge, MA: Marketing Science Institute.

McKinsey Global Institute. (2011). *Big data: The next frontier for innovation competition and productivity*. Research Rcport.

Miller, G., & Parks, M. (1982). Communication in dissolving relationships. In S. Duck (Ed.), *Personal Relationships 4: Dissolving Personal Relationships*. New York: Academic Press.

Mosadegh, M. J., & Behboudi, M. (2011). Using social network paradigm for developing a conceptual framework in CRM. *Australian Journal of Business and Management Research, 18*, 50–64.

Narayandas, D., & Rangan, V. K. (2004). Building and sustaining buyer-seller relationships in mature industrial markets. *Journal of Marketing, 68*(3), 63–77. doi:10.1509/jmkg.68.3.63.34772

Oliver, R. L. (1997). *Satisfaction: A behavioral perspective on the consumer*. Boston, MA: McGraw-Hill.

Oliver, R. L. (1999). Whence consumer loyalty? *Journal of Marketing, 63*, 33–44. doi:10.2307/1252099

Palmatier, R. W. (2008). *Relationship marketing*. Marketing Science Institute.

Papadatos, C. (2006). The art of storytelling: How loyalty marketers can build emotional connections to their brands. *Journal of Consumer Marketing, 20*(4), 297–308.

Payne, A. (1994). Relationship marketing: Making the customer count. *Managing Service Quality, 4*(6), 29–31. doi:10.1108/EUM0000000003939

Payne, A., & Frow, P. (2005). A strategic framework for customer relationship management. *Journal of Marketing, 69*(4), 167–176. doi:10.1509/jmkg.2005.69.4.167

Raimondo, M. A., Miceli, C. N., & Costabile, M. (2008). How relationship age moderates loyalty formation: The increasing effect of relational equity on customer loyalty. *Journal of Service Research*, *11*(2), 142–160. doi:10.1177/1094670508324678

Reichheld, F. F. (1993, March-April). Loyalty-based management. *Harvard Business Review*, 64–73.

Reichheld, F. F., & Saaser, W. E. Jr. (1990, September-November). Zero defections: Quality comes to services. *Harvard Business Review*, 105–111.

Reinartz, W., & Kumar, V. (2002, July). The mismanagement of customer loyalty. *Harvard Business Review*, 86–94.

Reinartz, W., Thomas, J. S., & Kumar, V. (2005). Balancing acquisition and retention resources to maximize customer profitability. *Journal of Marketing*, *69*(1), 63–79. doi:10.1509/jmkg.69.1.63.55511

Robertson, D. (2013, Quarter 1). Storytelling is key to engagement. *Market Leader*, 17.

Rogers, E. M. (1962). *Diffusion of Innovations*. Glencoe, IL: Free Press.

Rust, R. T., Lemon, K. N., & Zeithaml, V. A. (2004). Return on marketing: Using customer equity to focus marketing strategy. *Journal of Marketing*, *68*(1), 109–127. doi:10.1509/jmkg.68.1.109.24030

Ryu, G., & Feick, L. (2007). A penny for your thoughts: Referral reward programs and referral likelihood. *Journal of Marketing*, *71*(1), 84–94. doi:10.1509/jmkg.71.1.84

Sawhney, M., & Zabin, J. (2002). Managing and measuring relational equity in the network economy. *Journal of the Academy of Marketing Science*, *30*(4), 313–332. doi:10.1177/009207002236908

Sheth, J. N., & Parvatiyar, A. (1995). The evolution of relationship marketing. *International Business Review*, *4*(4), 397–418. doi:10.1016/0969-5931(95)00018-6

Sheth, J. N., & Uslay, C. (2007). Implications of the revised definition of marketing: From exchange to value creation. *Journal of Public Policy & Marketing*, *26*(2), 302–307. doi:10.1509/jppm.26.2.302

Srinivasan, R., & Moorman, C. (2005). Strategic firm commitments and rewards for customer relationship management in online retailing. *Journal of Marketing*, *69*(4), 193–200. doi:10.1509/jmkg.2005.69.4.193

Taylor, D., & Altman, I. (1987). Communication in interpersonal relationships: Social penetration processes. In M. Roloff, & G. Miller (Eds.), *Interpersonal processes: New directions in communication research*. Newbury Park, CA: Sage.

Taylor, R. E. (1999, November-December). A six-segment message strategy wheel. *Journal of Advertising Research*, 7–17.

Thibault, J. W., & Kelley, H. H. (1959). *The social psychology of groups*. New York: John Wiley.

Uzzi, B., & Dunlap, S. (2005). How to build your network. *Harvard Business Review*, *83*(12), 53–60.

van Doorn, J., Lemon, K. N., Mittal, V., Nass, S., Pick, D., Pirner, P., & Verhoef, P. C. (2010). Customer engagement behavior: Theoretical foundations and research directions. *Journal of Service Research*, *13*(3), 253–266. doi:10.1177/1094670510375599

Vargo, S. L., & Lusch, R. F. (2004). Evolving to a new dominant logic for marketing. *Journal of Marketing*, *68*(1), 1–17. doi:10.1509/jmkg.68.1.1.24036

Verhoef, P. C., Reinartz, W. J., & Krafft, M. (2010). Customer engagement as a new perspective in customer engagement. *Journal of Service Research, 13*(3), 247–252. doi:10.1177/1094670510375461

Wasserman, S., & Faust, K. (1994). *Social network analysis: Methods and applications*. New York: Cambridge University Press. doi:10.1017/CBO9780511815478

Watts, D. J., & Dodds, P. S. (2007). Influentials, networks, and public opinion formation. *The Journal of Consumer Research, 34*(4), 441–458. doi:10.1086/518527

Winer, R. S. (2001). A framework for customer relationship management. *California Management Review, 43*(4), 89–105. doi:10.2307/41166102

Woodcock, N., Green, A., & Starkey, M. (2011). Social CRM as a business strategy. *Journal of Database Marketing & Customer Strategy Management, 18*(1), 50–64. doi:10.1057/dbm.2011.7

Woodside, A. G. (2010). Brand-consumers storytelling theory and research: Introduction to a psychology and marketing special issue. *Psychology and Marketing, 25*(6), 521–540.

Woodside, A. G., Sood, S., & Miller, K. E. (2008). When consumers and brands talk: Storytelling theory and research in psychology and marketing. *Psychology and Marketing, 25*(2), 97–145. doi:10.1002/mar.20203

Yoon, K., & Kang, H. (2011). *The role of consumer heterogeneity on the design of loyalty program.* (Unpublished thesis). Long Island University, Long Island, NY.

Yoon, K., & Sims, J. D. (2013). Integrating social media and traditional CRM: Toward a conceptual framework for social CRM practices. In A. Ayanso, & K. Lertwachara (Eds.), *Harnessing the power of social media and web analytics: Techniques, tools, and applications*. Academic Press.

Yoon, K., & Tran, T. V. (2011). Revisiting the relationship between consumer loyalty and price sensitivity: The moderating role of deal-proneness. *Journal of Marketing Theory and Practice, 19*(3), 293–306. doi:10.2753/MTP1069-6679190303

ADDITIONAL READING

Ang, L. (2010). Community relationship management and social media. *Database Marketing & Customer Strategy Management, 18*(1), 31–38. doi:10.1057/dbm.2011.3

Baird, C. H., & Gautam, P. (2011). *From social media to social CRM: What customers want – Part I* IBM Global Business Services White Paper retrieved from http://www-935.ibm.com/services/us/gbs/thoughtleadership/ibv-social-crm-whitepaper.html

Baird, C. H., & Gautam, P. (2011). *From social media to Social CRM: Reinventing the customer relationship – Part II*. IBM Global Business Services White Paper retrieved from http://www-935.ibm.com/services/us/gbs/thoughtleadership/ibv-social-crm-whitepaper.html

Knapp, M. L., Ellis, D. G., & Williams, B. A. (1980). Perceptions of communication behavior associated with relationship terms. *Communication Monographs, 47*(4), 262–278. doi:10.1080/03637758009376036

Tarasi, C. O. (2007). Managing customer relationships. In N. K. Malhotra (Ed.), *Review of marketing research* (Vol. 3, pp. 3–38). Emerald Group Publishing Limited. doi:10.1108/S1548-6435(2007)0000003005

Wong, D. (2013). *A collection of 101 companies rocking it on social media.* HubSpot e-book retrieved March 7, 2014 from http://cdn1.hubspot.com/hub/53/101-Companies-Rocking-Social-media-HubSpotv5.pdf

KEY TERMS AND DEFINITIONS

Customer Engagement: As a psychological state, this happens when individual customers have ongoing experiences with a firm in a dynamic, interactive, and co-creative process of value.

Customer Heterogeneity: This term describes the degree to which individual customers are unique and different from each other in a defined target market.

Customer Relationship Management (CRM): This is a firm's strategic approach to build and maintain long-term relationships with customers—based on the co-creation process of dual values—from the perspective of relationship marketing.

Integrated Communication Process: Unlike the traditional communication process which focuses on the communication efforts of firms with customers using mass media, this process emphasizes the perspective of a two-step communication process which includes mass media—i.e., between a firm and an opinion leader—and interpersonal communication functions—i.e., between an opinion leader and opinion seekers.

Model of Consumer Dynamics in Status: As a new conceptual framework, this model describes how each potential buyer becomes a first-time buyer, and then becomes a my or competitor repeat customer before becoming a loyal one, depending on a series of successive purchases over the stages of the customer life cycle. This model is introduced to account for consumer heterogeneity when implementing a personalized relationship-building process.

Relational Integrated Marketing Communications (IMC): Considering the fact that communication is a human activity that links people together and creates relationships, this concept focuses on the firm's efforts of building and maintaining co-beneficial relationships with target audiences using various types of promotional elements including social media in the context of a two-way communication process.

Relationship Development or Escalation Model: Suggested by Knapp (1978), this model explains the progression of any relationship between two social entities through stages that involve coming together or apart. This model is based on interpersonal communication processes and consists of 10 stages—five stages of initiating, experimenting, intensifying, integrating, and bonding for "coming together" and five stages of differentiating, circumscribing, stagnating, avoiding, and terminating for "coming apart."

Relationship Equity (RE): This provides an indication of whether the entire relationship-building process is managed effectively over the entire life cycles of individual target customers. Specifically, it captures a summation of current and future potential value for the entire relationship-building process with the firm.

Social CRM: This concept is a strategic business practice to build and maintain long-term profitable relationships with customers by creating more voluntary customer engagement into the value creation process with the firm using social network systems. Social CRM is an outcome of combining traditional CRM practices with social media.

Social Media: This term refers to the collection of media which allow people to interact by creating, sharing, and exchanging user-generated content in virtual communities and social networks.

Traditional Integrated Marketing Communications (IMC): This concept focuses on communicating the value proposition of a firm's offerings with target customers using various types of promotional mix elements such as advertising, sales promotion, public relations, personal selling, and direct marketing.

Chapter 13
The Role of Social Media in the Knowledge-Based Organizations

Kijpokin Kasemsap
Suan Sunandha Rajabhat University, Thailand

ABSTRACT

This chapter introduces the role of Social Media (SM) in Knowledge-Based Organizations (KBOs), thus explaining the concept of KBOs, the difference between KBOs and non-KBOs, the concept of Knowledge Management (KM), the concept of SM, the importance of SM to KBOs, the application of SM in the KBOs, and the challenges of SM in the KBOs. This chapter explains the significance of SM for organizational development and adaptation to the business architecture in order to create knowledge integration environment in the KBOs. SM enables the creation of knowledge value chain to customize information and delivery for a technological business growth. Firms need to be connected to their technological business environment through SM because interacting with external sources of knowledge can effectively improve their capabilities about industry benchmark and competitive advantage. Understanding the role of SM in the KBOs will significantly enhance the organizational performance and achieve business goals in the global business environments.

INTRODUCTION

The need for techniques and management models for regional knowledge-based management remains topical, and it is on the increase (Zhao & Ordóñez de Pablos, 2011; Sotarauta, Horlings, & Liddle, 2012). The role of knowledge has been studied from the managerial perspective in several streams of academic literature, and no common title for the wide knowledge-related research field exists (Lönnqvist & Laihonen, 2013). KM has become one of the most important trends in modern businesses across the globe (Pandey & Dutta, 2013). A general goal of KM is to improve the systematic handling of knowledge and potential knowledge within the organization (Heisig, 2009). KM is becoming an important leverage point for organizations used to lift their efficiency, innovation, and competitive abilities (Rowley, 1999; Davenport & Prusak, 2000). Organizations that

DOI: 10.4018/978-1-4666-6182-0.ch013

implement KM recognize knowledge as the basis for competitiveness and as the key to business success (Drucker, 1993; Nonaka & Takeuchi, 1995). According to Thierauf and Hoctor (2006) and Handzic (2009), the fundamental purpose of KM is to collect, organize, and process knowledge into a form that is useful to all employees. An important role in KM is played by applications that exist in the organization such as intranet, enterprise resource planning (ERP), and customer relationship management (CRM). Such applications store transactions and customer data values for business decision making (Turban & Volonino, 2011). SM is defined as a series of technological innovation in terms of both hardware and software that facilitates inexpensive content creation, interaction, and interoperability by online users (Berthon, Pitt, Plangger, & Shapiro, 2012). SM involves social relations among people who have some types of relationship (Wellman, 2001). SM is about the way that users can share without provoking dissatisfaction (Lyons, 2008). This chapter introduces the role of SM in the KBOs, thus explaining the concept of KBOs, the difference between KBOs and non-KBOs, the concept of KM, the concept of SM, the importance of SM to KBOs, the application of SM in the KBOs, and the challenges of SM in the KBOs.

BACKGROUND

Nicholas and Rowlands (2011) categorized SM tools in eight categories: social networking, blogging, microblogging, collaborative authoring, social tagging and bookmarking, scheduling and meeting tools, conferencing, and image or video sharing. In addition, Gu and Widen-Wulff (2010) categorized SM tools for scholarly communication into eight different categories: blogs, mini blogs, RSS (rich site summary), wikis, tagging, social networks, multimedia sharing, and online documents. SM tools are convenient for sharing knowledge in a bottom-up process, whereas traditional KM tools are designed mainly for knowledge and information sharing with a top-down focus such as distribution derived by management (Grace, 2009; Bertoni & Chirumalla, 2011). Definition and classification of SM techniques are classified as blogs, micro blogs, social networks, media sharing content, social bookmarking, and voting sites (Boyd & Ellison, 2008; Singh, Veron-Jackson, & Cullinane, 2008). In addition, Machin-Mastromatteo (2011) stated that SM is used to refer to websites or software applications, which allows the publication or posting of users' content and the interactions between their users. SM techniques are related to Facebook, Google +, Twitter, Tumblr, and Pinterest (Machin-Mastromatteo, 2011). SM differs from traditional computer-mediated communications in three primary ways: a shift in the locus of activity from the desktop to the web (meaning greater accessibility); a shift in the locus of value production from the firm to the consumer (deriving from increased interaction/interactivity); and a shift in the locus of power away from the firm to the consumer (Berthon et al., 2012).

THE ROLE OF SOCIAL MEDIA IN THE KNOWLEDGE-BASED ORGANIZATIONS

This section introduces the concept of KBOs, the difference between KBOs and non-KBOs, the concept of KM, the concept of SM, the importance of SM to KBOs, the application of SM in the KBOs, and the challenges of SM in the KBOs.

Concept of Knowledge-Based Organizations

Drucker (1998) noted a new organizational form which he named the information-oriented organization. Features of KBOs include building of social and cognitive relations between employees, who have influenced the information sharing across the organization. The result of those social and cognitive relations can be seen in creating knowledge as the added value (Drucker, 1998). Nonaka (1998) indicated the importance of rapid response to customer needs and the creation of innovative products. Creating knowledge depends on exploiting tacit knowledge of each employee within the organization (Nonaka, 1998). The higher rates of implementing information technology (IT) increase the importance of techno-social interactions. The effect is visible in decreasing hierarchical relations. The organizational relations become flatter (Nonaka & Takeuchi, 1995). Organizations can have particular capabilities for knowledge creation, sharing and application which confer them a comparative advantage in terms of economic efficiency, compared to other institutional forms as markets (Madhok & Osegowitsh, 2000). Firms are the open systems for working with knowledge and for developing ongoing processes of organizational learning (Lavie, 2006; Sirmon, Hitt, & Ireland, 2007). External learning, or knowledge acquisition from external sources, has been recognized as one of the critical means for knowledge and capability reconfiguration to achieve a firm's strategic renewal (Lavie, 2006). In addition, learning from external sources allows the firm to expand its knowledge base, enhance the recognition of opportunities and threats, and grant access to new market and technological capabilities (Danneels, 2008; Narteh, 2008). These advantages of external knowledge acquisition are especially worthwhile in high-technology industries where dynamic environments may cause obsolescence in firm's current knowledge and capabilities (Uotila, Maula, Keil, & Zahra, 2009). Openness and external learning are critical in this kind of knowledge environments (Sirmon et al., 2007) for taking advantage of the geographic benefits of industrial districts or clusters (Sammarra & Biggiero, 2008; Whittington, Owen-Smith, & Powel, 2009). Knowledge-intensive clusters speed the pace of innovation for firms as knowledge developed within organizations. Although inter-organizational knowledge procedures appear in all industries, their intensity and effects of knowledge are enhanced by spatial proximity (Whittington et al., 2009).

Sveiby (2001) stated that strategic factors for creating KBOs are intellectual capital and intangible assets. Zack (2003) indicated that most of what organizations produce has hidden assets of the organization. Zack (2003) defined invisible asset as knowledge about what the organization produces, how an organization is organized, and for what reasons. Furthermore, Zack (2003) considered KBOs in terms of process, place, purpose, and perspective:

1. **Process:** This term includes the application of the existing knowledge and the creation of knowledge. Knowledge sharing within an organization provides the benefit based on past knowledge. The increased teamwork creates new knowledge and emerges opportunities for experimentation and learning.
2. **Place:** The KBOs, people, and resources create and apply knowledge by the continued interaction. The organization is seeking for knowledge wherever, and connects with anyone who can help it to learn.
3. **Purpose:** The organization should establish an organizational culture that will enable the knowledge sharing, the exploitation, and the use of organizational knowledge in everyday business. To ensure performing of these KM processes, an organization uses information technology and web technology.
4. **Perspective:** The organization holds its knowledge-oriented image regardless of the service or a product that is provided by it. Organizational knowledge and learning are the primary criteria for evaluating work organization, location, and relationships with customers. It is what, and how it learns from the customers.

Mahesh and Suresh (2009) identified three groups of KBOs based on a knowledge perspective.

1. The first group includes manufacturing organizations, which have been involved in their structure through some knowledge-intensive functions (Mahesh & Suresh, 2009). Knowledge-intensive work is limited to individual parts of the organization such as research and development (R&D) departments. A narrow group of employees creates knowledge-based decisions and a knowledge value chain within KM context. Social and cognitive distance is lower among the employees in departments and higher at the entire level of organization (Mahesh & Suresh, 2009).
2. The second group includes the consulting firms, legal firms, and technology organizations which are belong to the organizations where knowledge often constitutes a major part of the output. The knowledge value chain depends on the ability of processing employees' specialized knowledge in the organization (Mahesh & Suresh, 2009). Social and cognitive distance is smaller in all parts of the organization (Mahesh & Suresh, 2009).
3. The third group consists of organizations with information and communication technology (ICT) and consumer packaged goods (CPG) (Mahesh & Suresh, 2009). This group refers to organizations with a diverse business network, thus producing a wide range of the customized business and technology products and services. These organizations depend on high technology and innovation, thus leading to perceptive distance between the middle level and the bottom level in an organizational hierarchy (Mahesh & Suresh, 2009).

Difference between KBOs and Non-KBOs

Knowledge-based resources differ from other firm's resources in several ways which make their integration, development and transfer difficult (Martinkenaite, 2012). Firstly, knowledge may be difficult to codify and articulate as it is accumulated in the minds of individuals, developed through experience and refined by practice (Grant, 1996). Tacit nature of knowledge-based resources is also reflected in collective action that is governed by organizational routines, structures, and cultures (Zander & Kogut, 1995). Because tacit knowledge cannot be written down or captured in explicit form, it creates ambiguity as to what causal connections between actions and outcomes are. In addition, an ambiguous nature of knowledge inhibits the abilities of a recipient to acquire and utilize it (Simonin, 1999). Secondly, knowledge-based resources are subject to the high level of social complexity. Knowledge-based resources reflect a system of many unique and interdependent technologies, individual and team-based experiences and organizational routines that are combined for the development of organizational capabilities (Kogut & Zander, 1992). Furthermore, organizational knowledge in the KBOs resides in the communities of practice and relationships among groups of individuals (Brown & DuGuid, 1992). That hinders the comprehension of a totality of an asset and, subsequently, prevents its transferability (Chakravarthy, McEvily, Doz, & Rau, 2003). Finally, organizational knowledge in the KBOs is embedded in broader institutional context (Kostova, 1999). Organizational knowledge in the KBOs reflects a particular set of shared norms, beliefs and ways of doing things that pose unlearning barriers to the recipient, primarily due to its unwillingness to abandon existing organizational practices and acquire new ones (Szulanski, 2000).

Concept of Knowledge Management

KM can be defined as the set of activities involved in discovering, capturing, sharing, and applying knowledge to enhance, in a cost-effective fashion, the impact of knowledge on the unit's goal achievement (Beccerra-Fernandez

& Sabherwal, 2010). Knowledge is considered the most important resource in organizations (Choe, 2004). Knowledge must be refreshed by the organization, and therefore, knowledge networks are needed to ensure employees have opportunities to share knowledge (McGurk & Baron, 2012). Labedz, Cavaleri, and Berry (2011) stated that KM processes that have been integrated into work processes can be used to correct dysfunctional organizational behavior. Knowledge has been used as an effective tool to improve the firm's functioning (Zaim, Ekrem, & Selim, 2007; Perez-Lopez & Alegre, 2012). KM has been shown to be a powerful ingredient in the success of organizations (Davenport & Prusak, 1998; Desouza & Awazu, 2006). KM is aimed at getting people to efficiently innovate, collaborate, and make correct decisions by focusing on high-quality knowledge (Plessis, 2005).

The goal of KM is to improve the internal knowledge processes; and all information needed for corporate decisions can be available and efficiently used (Parker & Nitse, 2006). Knowledge is widely recognized as a strategic asset in improving organizational performance (Sharma & Djiaw, 2011). KM provides the processes and structures to create, capture, analyze, and act on information which helps organizations to manage continuous change in a highly dynamic environment (Lim & Klobas, 2000). KM is crucial for maintaining and gaining competitive advantage (Fugate, Stank, & Mentzer, 2009; Kiessling, Richey, Meng, & Dabic, 2009; Massa & Testa, 2009; Huang & Lai, 2012), as it supports more effective knowledge acquisition and transfer (McKinlay, 2005). KM practice is the most effective aspect when it is considered strategically, and aligned with business objectives (Davenport, De Long, & Beers, 1998; Greiner, Bohmann, & Krcmar, 2007). KM practice is available for improving the performance of the creative activities (Bettiol, Di Maria, & Grandinetti, 2012). Current literature in the field of KM focuses on certain industries: the public sector (Chong, Salleh, Ahmad, & Sharifuddin, 2011; Salleh, Chong, Syed Ahmad, & Syed Ikhsan, 2012; Ferguson, Burford, & Kennedy, 2013), non-governmental organizations (Corfield, Paton, & Little, 2013), the banking industry (Dutt, Qamar, & Jha, 2011; Bidmeshgipour, Ismail, & Omar, 2012; Oluikpe, 2012), small and medium-sized enterprises (SMEs) (Durst & Edvardsson, 2012), manufacturing organizations (Birasnav & Rangnekar, 2010), and human service and professional services firms (Austin, Ciaassen, Vu, & Mizrahi, 2008; Palte, Hertlein, Smolnik, & Riempp, 2011).

KM systems can be categorized as the following groups: groupware, document management systems, expert systems, semantic networks, relational and object oriented databases, simulation tools, and artificial intelligence (Gupta & Sharma, 2004). KM can be defined as a systematic approach that provides efficient disciplines and procedures to enable knowledge to grow and create knowledge value chain for organizations (Rao, 2002; Sajeva, 2010). As knowledge is the core element of KM, organizational competitiveness depends on how knowledge is applied, exploited, and integrated (Sajeva, 2010). Marques and Simon (2006) found a strong and positive relationship between the adoption of KM process and organizational performance. Chadha and Kapoor (2010) stated that knowledge transferred and shared within an organization can considerably affect its competitive ability and business performance. KM is considered to be effective if it contributes to increase in productivity by making the right information to the right people (Gunasekaran & Ngai, 2007). In addition, Singh, Shankar, Narain, and Kumar (2006) stated that the cornerstone to the long-term survival of a firm is recognizing the value of the knowledge that is a key to the innovative thinking and investment. When knowledge is delivered and distributed in an organization, its potential values will eventually appear (Davenport & Prusak, 1998). Johannessen, Olsen, and Olaisen (1999) combined organizational vision with KM. Johannessen et al. (1999) indicated that organizational vision leads to knowledge creation; and knowledge creation leads to organizational creation and integrates knowledge utilization. In addition, new product development (NPD) is considered as a KM concept (Arora, 2002). Knowledge is easily stored because it may be codified, while the relational perspective recognizes the contextual and relational aspects of knowledge which can make knowledge difficult to share outside the specific location where the knowledge is developed (Hayes & Walsham, 2003).

Concept of Social Media

SM refers to online services that support social interactions among SM users through highly accessible and scalable web-based publishing techniques (Dutta, 2010), in order to co-create, find, share, and evaluate the online information repository (Kaplan & Haenlein, 2010). SM is a group of internet-based applications that build on the ideological and technological foundations of Web 2.0; and the internet-based applications allow the exchange of user-generated content (Kaplan & Haenlein, 2010). A typical classification of SM includes collaborative projects (i.e. Wikipedia), blogs, user-generated content communities (i.e., Flickr, YouTube, and Youku/Toduo), social networking sites (i.e., Facebook and Cyworld), virtual game worlds (i.e. EverQuest), and virtual social worlds (i.e. Second Life) (Kaplan & Haenlein, 2010). Facebook can be used to inspire discussions among relevant interest groups related to academic interaction and participation in a more personalized way (Saw, Abbott, Donaghey, & McDonald, 2013). In addition, YouTube can be used to introduce new information, concepts, and services at the point of SM need (Saw et al., 2013). In addition, Kietzmann, Hermkens, McCarthy, and Silvestre (2011) have focused their SM attention delivered by mobile and web-based technologies, which create interactive SM platforms (i.e., Facebook, LinkedIn, Ingram, Orkut, Twitter, and Quora). SM provides and creates fresh opportunities for organizations, communities, and individuals (i.e., blogs and podcasts) (Kietzmann et al., 2011).

According to Musser and O'Reilly (2007), SM platforms and tools exhibit the following key characteristics:

1. To enable web users to do more than retrieve information. SM platform enables users to actively interact with the content as well as its creators. This is the foundation of user-generated content.
2. To enable web users to execute applications straight from their browsers; and control data on the SM platform.
3. To add value to the SM content. This SM facility leads to a seamless exchange of information, thus building a strong body of knowledge called collective intelligence.
4. To utilize simple interfaces without requirement of specialized knowledge to apply.
5. To decentralize SM without center of control under conventional media systems.
6. To use open technology standards that rapidly grow into open ecosystems of the loosely coupled applications built on open data and reusable components.
7. To permit appropriate solutions to evolve in response to real world usage and needs. SM platform recognizes the fact that real success comes from cooperation.

Importance of Social Media to Knowledge-Based Organizations

SM has the potential to support multi-way communication between organizations and their customers at relatively lower costs (Gallaugher & Ransbotham, 2010). Academic attention has utilized SM in online business and e-commerce websites such as Amazon.com and eBay.com (Levy, 2009; Chua, 2011). According to SM platform, the benefits of using SM platform should be implicit so that the reciprocity in knowledge sharing and ease of use are the key factors that make or break the SM success (Vuori & Okkonen, 2012). Development of Web 2.0 and SM creates information on transactions and customer data (Hanna, Rohm, & Crittenden, 2011). SM has become an important source of knowledge, and enables the creation of the value chain content (Nahapiet & Sumantra, 1998; Von Krogh, 2012). Knowledge is available not only inside the organization, but also outside of the organization. Kumar and Bhagwat (2010) stated that SM enables firms to acquire knowledge similar to that of expensive focus groups, but at a fraction of the cost in mass numbers. The SM approach can yield higher margins since organizations offer relevant information about an individual's or its business partners (Solis, 2010; Weinberg & Pehlivan, 2011). In addition, social networking allows not only access, transfer and sharing of knowledge, but also the creation of relationships between users of social networking as new components communicate with each other (O'Dell & Hubert, 2011). The potential value of social communication channels is in the anticipation of the quality and access of knowledge for both individuals and organization (O'Dell & Hubert, 2011). SM allows instant transfers of video and picture material, thus maintaining SM-related blogs (Mangold & Faulds, 2009). SM gives rise to the joint efforts of the public, thus resulting in a new database of information and knowledge (Mangold & Faulds, 2009). The design and structure of SM links the development of digital media technologies (i.e. digital signage) with the decline in prices, thus facilitating the transfer of information on events (i.e., corporate television and video portals) (Mangold & Faulds, 2009). SM helps build brand awareness, visibility, reputation, knowledge sharing, customer acquisition and retention, low cost promotions, NPD, and CRM (Kaplan & Haenlein, 2010).

Application of Social Media in the Knowledge-Based Organizations

SM is effectively applied by the ways of external knowledge acquisition in the KBOs. Organizations need to carry out an explorative learning that enables them to reconfigure their capabilities base (Danneels, 2008). External knowledge acquisition by firms may be considered as a key element for explorative learning development (Lavie, 2006). In the clustered regions, external knowledge acquisition enables firms to leverage the benefits of the networks of social relations in which they are embedded (Whittington et al., 2009). In industries with high technological dynamism, firms face a greater risk that their core technological capabilities become rapidly obsolete (Uotila et al., 2009). In addition, changes in customers' demands may negatively affect the value of current marketing capabilities. Regulatory or institutional changes in the organizational industry may vary the value of technological knowledge and marketing knowledge. According to environmental dynamism, firms need an ongoing reconfiguration of their knowledge base in order to be adapted to their environment (Danneels, 2008). Regarding the resource-based view (RBV) and the knowledge-based view (KBV) of the firm, organizational capabilities and core competences are based on knowledge (Khamseh & Jolly, 2008). The generation of new organizational capabilities will require the acquisition of new knowledge, or that explorative learning to take place (Danneels, 2008; Uotila et al., 2009).

The core competency of the knowledge-intensive service networks can be seen in the ability to combine the distinctive competencies of the network partners with the external factor in order to produce unique services for the customer (Evanschitzky, Ahlert, Blaich, & Kenning, 2007). The knowledge-intensive service networks can be a simultaneous combination of competencies of the network partners. In addition, a knowledge transfer will enable the network partners to permanently execute certain tasks. One may imagine a typical merger and post-merger integration project. In the process of a merger, experts in management, post-merger integration, law, and finance are required to work together by pooling their asymmetric resources in order to successfully merge two firms. Specialized knowledge (i.e., knowledge about strategy and markets of the merging companies, knowledge about contract law, and knowledge about finance) is necessary for successfully completing the process (Evanschitzky et al., 2007). This knowledge is often provided by management consultants, investment banks, and law firms. These firms sometimes work together on a contract basis, but other times the specialized firms may form a network.

Against the backdrop of recent trends in web technologies, making profitable use of SM is at the top of the agenda for many organizations (Levy, 2009). The application of SM is useful in work context, especially when embedded to other information systems (Grossman, 2008; Levy, 2009; Razmerita, Kirchner, & Sudzina, 2009). SM applications enable the employees to participate in collaboration, thus contributing to organizational information flows in an informal manner (Wagner & Bolloju, 2005; Schneckenberg, 2009), achieved by linking complementary organizations and respective organizations with their distributors and customers (Nahapiet & Sumantra, 1998; Von Krogh, 2012). Organizations can add the knowledge value chain in the form of providing high-value public information, which can enable organizational clients to make better decisions (Dowson, 2005). In 2004, online SM platforms got a large push, when Facebook announced the concept to give people the power to share and make the world more open and connected (Lin, Greissler, Ehrlich, & Shoop, 2011). Use of SM is constantly growing; and organizations use SM for self-promotion, distribution, and the exchange of information. In addition, the use of SM will increase the return on investment (ROI) of SM; and the use of SM will lead to higher added value in the KBOs (Hoffman & Fodor, 2010).

According to knowledge policy, the use of SM in marketing communication in the KBOs will increase the reliability of the information and the general perception of loyalty to the brand and the organization's good name (Von Krogh, 2012). In addition, users express their opinions, criticisms, and straight communication (Andre, Bernstein, & Luther, 2012). A capacity to adapt SM is conditional with changes in organizational behavior regarding the initiation and adaptation of technological innovations (Smit & Wandel, 2006). SM plays an increasingly important role in global advertising strategy as it penetrates into daily lives and business practices (Okazaki & Taylor, 2013). SM has the opportunity to capitalize on the social networking capability to bring people together, image transferability which enables marketers to build the brand with larger audiences than ever before, and personal extensibility which allows interactions and relationships to be built over much larger geographic boundaries than ever before (Okazaki & Taylor, 2013). SM phenomenon may be indicative of emerging global cultures with an emphasis on modernity, technology, freedom, and individual choice (Steenkamp, 2001). In addition, organizations can benefit from implementing SM in their enterprises as part of organizational knowledge-driven frameworks; employees' productivity and efficiency can grow by adopting SM (Levy, 2009; Paroutis & Al Saleh, 2009).

Challenges of Social Media in the Knowledge-Based Organizations

The modern wave of communication brings challenges and risks in developing new communication channels between organizations and customers. Customers want organizations to engage, respond, and listen to their opinions. SM opens the channels of communication among stakeholders such as businesses, universities, research institutes, suppliers, customers, users, and competitors. SM services have distinct technical features that release passion among SM users to engage in knowledge sharing (Paroutis & Saleh, 2009). There is a need to raise the awareness of SM to information users and policymakers of the potential exploitation of information resources for implementing SM architecture (Vaccaro & Madsen, 2009). SM provides better opportunities for KBOs to acquire strategic priority position, thus enhancing the benefits from the use of IT (Porter, 2001). In addition, SM offers opportunities to strengthen customer relationships by encouraging customers to engage with their brands (Van Doorn, Lemon, Mittal, Nass, Pick, Pirner, & Verhoef, 2010; Verhoef, Reinartz, & Krafft, 2010) and by fostering online brand or user communities (Goldenberg, Han, Lehmann, & Hong, 2009; Libai, Bolton, Bugel, De Ruyter, Gotz, Risselada, & Stephen, 2010; Stephen & Toubia, 2010), which can strengthen brand equity and increase customer lifetime value (CLV). The purpose of social networking between organizations is the tendency to develop and implement technology solutions and processes that will increase the added value in organization and bring added value to the customer in the form of utility value (Moeller, 2010). In addition, Trusov, Bucklin, and Pauwels (2009) stated that the referrals on social network sites have substantially longer carryover effects than traditional advertising, and produce substantially higher response elasticity. SM characteristics (i.e., YouTube, Facebook, and Twitter) have been effectively used to distribute healthcare information to communities at large, especially teens and young adults (Vance, Howe, & Dellavalle, 2009).

The expansion of online SM portals and blogs increases the quality and quantity of communication among Web 2.0 users, which are the potential customers. Such communication is often rich in opinions on the quality of products or services (Weinberg & Pehlivan, 2011). In addition, social networks grow in different business environments and strongly influence the changes in society, technology, and business practice (Evans, 2008). Customers prefer to get information from friends and other personal contacts (Susskind, 2002). KBOs should be aware that the customers, as users of internet tools, are becoming the new marketers with extensive opinion-leading talks about the brand (Brown, 2010), with viral marketing as an important marketing tool for the organization (Ferguson, 2008; Kaplan & Haenlein, 2010). Viral marketing develops the triadic relationships among organization, customer, and the community as a result of customer exchange of messages based on similar personal characteristics and needs (Palmer & Koenig-Lewis, 2009). Furthermore, SM does not require expensive and complex technical implementations, but it impacts organizational culture changes and adaptation of knowledge processes (Chui, Miller, & Roberts, 2009). Sustainable development and increased uncertainty in the business environment force companies to inflict a constant reconstruction of a comprehensive infrastructure as a strategic goal (Antonelli, 2003; Kaplan & Mikes, 2012). The renewal of SM is based on a more flexible organizational structure (internal environment) including the introduction of modern technologies for the implementation of relationship marketing and renovation of the technological innovations (Antonelli, 2003; Kaplan & Mikes, 2012).

An organization has to establish a policy for customer intelligence and suppliers and develop a marketing strategy that provides market positioning and design of brand loyalty (Li, Xie, & Xu, 2011). KM resources constitute social capital, which occurs in two forms as an internal adhesive to create the organizational culture and as an external agent relationship (Bonabeau, 2009). In addition, the increase of the financial and non-financial performance leads to higher added value in knowledge companies (Wirtz, Schilke, & Ullrich, 2010). KBOs can invest in developing their own SM platform, which can be the way of informing the customers about organizational strategy, and getting ideas for product or service development (Fuchs & Schreier, 2011). An organizational culture is closely associated with creating a knowledge value chain in organization (Garwin, 1998; Othman & Sheehan, 2011). Organizations have to reach decisions on strategies to increase the added values (i.e., takeover, accumulation, and divestment) with a consensus with partners (Moeller, 2010). Organizations have to add SM to their overall recruitment strategy to meet the goals of being cost-effective, targeted, and strategic; remaining competitive; and sourcing top talent (Madia, 2011). For successful participation to occur in the knowledge value chain, organizations and employees have to identify common goals and trust each other (Moeller, 2010). Organizations must ensure that the flow of information through SM is properly secured, and that they will not lose their knowledge (Von Krogh, 2012). Individuals are connected through SM; and the social relationship between individuals can be an opportunity for organizations to transfer the knowledge (Ali, 2011; Ballantine & Stephenson, 2011; Smith, 2011). For example, the marketing leaders can use SM to gather information from consumers in a potentially continuous business trend (Palmer & Koenig-Lewis, 2009; Kaplan & Haenlein, 2010; Kozinets, De Valck, Wognicki, & Wilner, 2010; Campbell, Pitt, Parent, & Berthon, 2011).

FUTURE RESEARCH DIRECTIONS

Future research directions should broaden the perspectives of different types of SM to be utilized in the KBOs. In addition, future research should study a greater understanding of SM and other KM-related variables (i.e., knowledge-sharing behavior, knowledge creation, organizational learning, learning orientation, and motivation to learn) in the KBOs.

CONCLUSION

This chapter introduced the role of SM in the KBOs, thus explaining the concept of KBOs, the difference between KBOs and non-KBOs, the concept of KM, the concept of SM, the importance of SM to KBOs, the application of SM in the KBOs, and the challenges of SM in the KBOs. This chapter explained the significance of SM for organizational development and adaptation to the business architecture in order to create knowledge integration environment in the KBOs. In the new economy, SM emergence has a strong and positive influence on the development of modern communication and business growth. With expanded SM during the innovative economy, there are the qualitative steps in the communication and transmission of information. SM has changed the focus on KM from managing the knowledge to providing the access to knowledge in the KBOs (Von Krogh, 2012). An inexpensive media campaign utilizing SM method reaches a relatively large volume of potential consumers in the business world. Organizations should be aware of the risks that they are exposed because of SM technology. SM allows access to data and video information to a broad range of potential consumers. The marketing communication strategy using SM allows both a permanent presence in the information technology ecosystem and quick responses to any negative responses to the public. Organizations have to recognize the value of knowledge sharing and the significance of SM, and set up departments for making knowledge-related policy and the effective management of SM. SM enables the creation of knowledge value chain to customize information and delivery for a technological business growth. Firms need to be connected to their technological business environment through SM because interacting with external sources of knowledge can effectively improve their capabilities about industry benchmark and competitive advantage. Understanding the role of SM in the KBOs will significantly enhance the organizational performance and achieve business goals in the global business environments.

REFERENCES

Ali, H. (2011). Exchanging value within individuals' networks: Social support implications for health marketers. *Journal of Marketing Management, 27*(3-4), 316–335. doi:10.1080/0267257X.2011.547075

Andre, P., Bernstein, M., & Luther, K. (2012). What makes a great tweet? *Harvard Business Review, 90*(5), 36–37.

Antonelli, C. (2003). *The economics of innovation, new technologies, and structural change*. London, UK: Routledge.

Arora, R. (2002). Implementing KM – A balanced scorecard approach. *Journal of Knowledge Management, 6*(3), 240–249. doi:10.1108/13673270210434340

Austin, M. J., Ciaassen, J., Vu, C., & Mizrahi, P. (2008). Knowledge management: Implications for human service organizations. *Journal of Evidence-Based Social Work, 5*(1-2), 361–389. doi:10.1300/J394v05n01_13 PMID:19064454

Ballantine, P. W., & Stephenson, R. J. (2011). Help me, I'm fat! Social support in online weight loss networks. *Journal of Consumer Behaviour, 10*(6), 332–337. doi:10.1002/cb.374

Beccerra-Fernandez, I., & Sabherwal, R. (2010). *Knowledge management: Systems and processes*. London, UK: M. E. Sharpe.

Berthon, P. R., Pitt, L. F., Plangger, K., & Shapiro, D. (2012). Marketing meets Web 2.0, social media, and creative consumers: Implications for international marketing strategy. *Business Horizons, 55*(3), 261–271. doi:10.1016/j.bushor.2012.01.007

Bertoni, M., & Chirumalla, K. (2011). Leveraging Web 2.0 in new product development: Lessons learned from a cross-company study. *Journal of Universal Computer Science, 17*(4), 548–564.

Bettiol, M., Di Maria, E., & Grandinetti, R. (2012). Codification and creativity: Knowledge management strategies in KIBS. *Journal of Knowledge Management, 16*(4), 550–562. doi:10.1108/13673271211246130

Bidmeshgipour, M., Ismail, W. K. W., & Omar, R. (2012). Knowledge management and organizational innovativeness in Iranian banking industry. *Knowledge Management and E-Learning, 4*(4), 481–499.

Birasnav, M., & Rangnekar, S. (2010). Knowledge management structure and human capital development in Indian manufacturing industries. *Business Process Management Journal, 16*(1), 57–75. doi:10.1108/14637151011017949

Bonabeau, E. (2009). Decisions 2.0.: The power of collective intelligence. *MIT Sloan Management Review, 50*(2), 45–52.

Boyd, D. M., & Ellison, N. B. (2008). Social network sites: Definition, history, and scholarship. *Journal of Computer-Mediated Communication, 13*(1), 210–230. doi:10.1111/j.1083-6101.2007.00393.x

Brown, E. (2010). *Working the crowd: Social media marketing for business*. Swindon, UK: British Informatics Society Limited.

Brown, J. S., & Duguid, P. (1992). Organizational learning and communities of practice: Toward a unified view of working, learning and innovation. *Organization Science, 2*(1), 40–57. doi:10.1287/orsc.2.1.40

Campbell, C., Pitt, L. F., Parent, M., & Berthon, P. R. (2011). Understanding consumer conversations around ads in a web 2.0 world. *Journal of Advertising, 40*(1), 87–102. doi:10.2753/JOA0091-3367400106

Chadha, S. K., & Kapoor, D. (2010). A study on knowledge management practices of auto component manufacturing companies in Ludhiana City. *The IUP Journal of Knowledge Management*, *8*(1-2), 68–76.

Chakravarthy, B., McEvily, S., Doz, Y., & Rau, D. (2003). Knowledge management and competitive advantage. In M. Easterby-Smith, & M. Lyles (Eds.), *The Blackwell handbook of organizational learning and knowledge management* (pp. 305–323). Malden, MA: Blackwell.

Choe, J. M. (2004). The consideration of cultural differences in the design of information systems. *Information & Management*, *41*(5), 669–688. doi:10.1016/j.im.2003.08.003

Chong, S. C., Salleh, K., Ahmad, S. N. S., & Sharifuddin, S. I. (2011). Knowledge management implementation in a public sector accounting organization: An empirical investigation. *Journal of Knowledge Management*, *15*(3), 497–512. doi:10.1108/13673271111137457

Chua, A. Y. K. (2011). How Web 2.0 supports customer relationship management in Amazon. *International Journal of Electronic Customer Relationship Management*, *5*(3-4), 288–304. doi:10.1504/IJECRM.2011.044693

Chui, M., Miller, A., & Roberts, P. R. (2009). Six ways to make Web 2.0. work. *The McKinsey Quarterly*, *1*, 2–7.

Corfield, A., Paton, R., & Little, S. (2013). Does knowledge management work in NGOs? A longitudinal study. *International Journal of Public Administration*, *36*(3), 179–188. doi:10.1080/01900692.2012.749281

Danneels, E. (2008). Organizational antecedents of second-order competences. *Strategic Management Journal*, *29*(5), 519–543. doi:10.1002/smj.684

Davenport, T. H., De Long, D. W., & Beers, M. C. (1998). Successful knowledge management projects. *Sloan Management Review*, *39*(2), 43–57.

Davenport, T. H., & Prusak, L. (1998). *Working knowledge: Managing what your organization knows*. Boston, MA: Harvard Business School Press.

Davenport, T. H., & Prusak, L. (2000). *Working knowledge: How organisations manage what they know*. Boston, MA: Harvard Business School Press.

Desouza, K. C., & Awazu, Y. (2006). Knowledge management at SMEs: Five peculiarities. *Journal of Knowledge Management*, *10*(1), 32–43. doi:10.1108/13673270610650085

Dowson, R. (2005). *Developing knowledge-based client relationships*. Burlington, VT: Elsevier.

Drucker, P. (1993). *Post-capitalist society*. Oxford, UK: Butterworth-Heinemann.

Drucker, P. (1998). The coming of the new organization. In P. Drucker (Ed.), *Harvard Business Review on knowledge management* (pp. 1–19). Boston, MA: Harvard Business School Press.

Durst, S., & Edvardsson, I. R. (2012). Knowledge management in SMEs: A literature review. *Journal of Knowledge Management*, *16*(6), 879–903. doi:10.1108/13673271211276173

Dutt, H., Qamar, F., & Jha, V. S. (2011). A research to identify knowledge orientation in Indian commercial banks. *International Journal of Knowledge Management Studies*, *4*(4), 389–418. doi:10.1504/IJKMS.2011.048435

Dutta, S. (2010). What's your personal social media strategy? *Harvard Business Review*, *88*(11), 127–130. PMID:21049685

Evans, D. (2008). *Social media marketing: An hour a day*. Indianapolis, IN: John Wiley & Sons.

Evanschitzky, H., Ahlert, D., Blaich, G., & Kenning, P. (2007). Knowledge management in knowledge-intensive service networks - A strategic management approach. *Management Decision*, *45*(2), 265–283. doi:10.1108/00251740710727287

Ferguson, R. (2008). Word of mouth and viral marketing: Taking the temperature of the hottest trends in marketing. *Journal of Consumer Marketing*, *25*(3), 179–182. doi:10.1108/07363760810870671

Ferguson, S., Burford, S., & Kennedy, M. (2013). Divergent approaches to knowledge and innovation in the public sector. *International Journal of Public Administration*, *36*(3), 168–178. doi:10.1080/01900692.2012.749278

Fuchs, C., & Schreier, M. (2011). Customer empowerment in new product development. *Journal of Product Innovation Management*, *28*(1), 17–32. doi:10.1111/j.1540-5885.2010.00778.x

Fugate, B. S., Stank, T. P., & Mentzer, J. T. (2009). Linking improved knowledge management to operational and organizational performance. *Journal of Operations Management*, *27*(3), 247–264. doi:10.1016/j.jom.2008.09.003

Gallaugher, J., & Ransbotham, S. (2010). Social media and customer dialog management at Starbucks. *MIS Quarterly Executive*, *9*(4), 197–212.

Garwin, C. (1998). Building a learning organization. In P. Drucker (Ed.), *Harvard Business Review on knowledge management* (pp. 47–80). Boston, MA: Harvard Business School Press.

Goldenberg, J., Han, S., Lehmann, D. R., & Hong, J. W. (2009). The role of hubs in the adoption process. *Journal of Marketing*, *73*(2), 1–13. doi:10.1509/jmkg.73.2.1

Grace, T. P. L. (2009). Wikis as a knowledge management tool. *Journal of Knowledge Management*, *13*(4), 64–74. doi:10.1108/13673270910971833

Grant, R. M. (1996). Toward a knowledge-based theory of the firm. *Strategic Management Journal*, *17*(1), 109–122. doi:10.1002/smj.4250171110

Greiner, M. E., Bohmann, T., & Krcmar, H. (2007). A strategy for knowledge management. *Journal of Knowledge Management*, *11*(6), 3–15. doi:10.1108/13673270710832127

Grossman, M. (2008). An emerging global knowledge management platform: The case of iBridge. *VINE: The Journal of Information and Knowledge Management Systems*, *38*(4), 525–534. doi:10.1108/03055720810917750

Gu, F., & Widen-Wulff, G. (2010). Scholarly communication and possible changes in the context of social media: A Finnish case study. *The Electronic Library*, *29*(6), 762–776. doi:10.1108/02640471111187999

Gunasekaran, A., & Ngai, E. W. (2007). Knowledge management in 21st century manufacturing. *International Journal of Production Research*, *45*(11), 2391–2418. doi:10.1080/00207540601020429

Gupta, J., & Sharma, S. (2004). *Creating knowledge based organization*. Boston, MA: Idea Group Publishing.

Handzic, M. (2009). Evaluating knowledge management's effectiveness for decision support: Preliminary results. In R. W. King (Ed.), *Knowledge management and organizational learning* (pp. 237–252). New York, NY: Springer-Verlag. doi:10.1007/978-1-4419-0011-1_15

Hanna, R., Rohm, A., & Crittenden, L. V. (2011). We are all connected: The power of the social media ecosystem. *Business Horizons*, *54*(3), 265–273. doi:10.1016/j.bushor.2011.01.007

Hayes, M., & Walsham, G. (2003). Knowledge sharing and ICTs: A relational perspective. In M. Easterby-Smith, & M. A. Lyles (Eds.), *The Blackwell handbook of organizational learning and knowledge management* (pp. 54–57). Malden, MA: Blackwell.

Heisig, P. (2009). Harmonisation of knowledge management: Comparing 160 KM frameworks around the globe. *Journal of Knowledge Management*, *13*(4), 4–31. doi:10.1108/13673270910971798

Hoffman, L. D., & Fodor, M. (2010). Can you measure the ROI of your social media marketing? *MIT Sloan Management Review*, *52*(1), 41–49.

Huang, L. S., & Lai, C. P. (2012). An investigation on critical success factors for knowledge management using structural equation modeling. *Technology Management*, *40*, 24–30.

Johannessen, J. A., Olsen, B., & Olaisen, J. (1999). Aspects of innovation theory based knowledge management. *Journal of International Management*, *19*(2), 121–139.

Kaplan, M. A., & Haenlein, M. (2010). Users of the world, unite! The challenges and opportunities of social media. *Business Horizons*, *53*(1), 59–68. doi:10.1016/j.bushor.2009.09.003

Kaplan, S. R., & Mikes, A. (2012). Managing risks: A new framework. *Harvard Business Review*, *90*(6), 49–60.

Khamseh, H. M., & Jolly, D. (2008). Knowledge transfer in alliances: Determinant factors. *Journal of Knowledge Management*, *12*(1), 37–50. doi:10.1108/13673270810852377

Kiessling, T. S., Richey, R. G., Meng, J., & Dabic, M. (2009). Exploring knowledge management to organizational performance outcomes in a transitional economy. *Journal of World Business*, *44*(4), 421–433. doi:10.1016/j.jwb.2008.11.006

Kietzmann, H. J., Hermkens, K., McCarthy, P. I., & Silvestre, S. B. (2011). Social media? Get serious! Understanding the functional building blocks of social media. *Business Horizons*, *54*(3), 241–251. doi:10.1016/j.bushor.2011.01.005

Kogut, B., & Zander, U. (1992). Knowledge of the firm, combinative capabilities, and the replication of technology. *Organization Science*, *3*(3), 383–397. doi:10.1287/orsc.3.3.383

Kostova, T. (1999). Transnational transfer of strategic organizational practices: A contextual perspective. *Academy of Management Review*, *24*(2), 308–324.

Kozinets, R. V., De Valck, K., Wognicki, A. C., & Wilner, S. J. S. (2010). Networked narratives: Understanding word-of-mouth marketing in online communities. *Journal of Marketing*, *74*(1), 71–89. doi:10.1509/jmkg.74.2.71

Kumar, V., & Bhagwat, Y. (2010). Listen to the customer. *Marketing Research*, *22*(2), 14–19.

Labedz, C., Cavaleri, S., & Berry, G. (2011). Interactive knowledge management: Putting pragmatic policy planning in place. *Journal of Knowledge Management*, *15*(4), 551–567. doi:10.1108/13673271111151956

Lavie, D. (2006). Capability reconfiguration: An analysis of incumbent responses to technological change. *Academy of Management Review*, *31*(1), 153–174. doi:10.5465/AMR.2006.19379629

Levy, M. (2009). Web 2.0 implications on knowledge management. *Journal of Knowledge Management*, *13*(1), 120–134. doi:10.1108/13673270910931215

Li, M. B., Xie, S. Q., & Xu, X. (2011). Recent development of knowledge-based systems, methods and tools for one-of-a-kind production. *Knowledge-Based Systems*, *24*(7), 1108–1119. doi:10.1016/j.knosys.2011.05.005

Libai, B., Bolton, R., Bugel, M. S., De Ruyter, K., Gotz, O., Risselada, H., & Stephen, A. T. (2010). Customer-to-customer interactions: Broadening the scope of word of mouth research. *Journal of Service Research*, *13*(3), 267–282. doi:10.1177/1094670510375600

Lim, D., & Klobas, J. (2000). Knowledge management in small enterprises. *The Electronic Library*, *18*(6), 420–432. doi:10.1108/02640470010361178

Lin, D., Greissler, P., Ehrlich, S., & Shoop, E. (2011). IDEA: A framework for a knowledge-based enterprise 2.0. *Journal of Universal Computer Science*, *17*(4), 515–531.

Lönnqvist, A., & Laihonen, H. (2013). Managing regional development: A knowledge perspective. *International Journal of Knowledge-Based Development*, *4*(1), 50–63. doi:10.1504/IJKBD.2013.052493

Lyons, D. (2008). Facebook's roar becomes a meow. *Newsweek, 152*(16), E22.

Machin-Mastromatteo, J. D. (2011). *Exploring users' information behavior in social networks: A contribution to the understanding of the use of social networks*. Saarbrucken, Germany: Lambert Academic Publishing.

Madhok, A., & Osegowitsh, T. (2000). The international biotechnology industry: A dynamic capabilities perspective. *Journal of International Business Studies*, *31*(2), 325–335. doi:10.1057/palgrave.jibs.8490909

Madia, S. A. (2011). Best practices for using social media as a recruitment strategy. *Strategic HR Review*, *10*(6), 19–24. doi:10.1108/14754391111172788

Mahesh, K., & Suresh, K. J. (2009). Knowledge criteria for organization design. *Journal of Knowledge Management*, *13*(4), 41–51. doi:10.1108/13673270910971815

Mangold, G. W., & Faulds, J. D. (2009). Social media: The new hybrid element of the promotion mix. *Business Horizons*, *52*(4), 357–365. doi:10.1016/j.bushor.2009.03.002

Marques, D. P., & Simon, F. J. G. (2006). The effect of knowledge management practices on firm performance. *Journal of Knowledge Management*, *10*(3), 143–156. doi:10.1108/13673270610670911

Martinkenaite, I. (2012). Antecedents of knowledge transfer in acquisitions. *Baltic Journal of Management*, *7*(2), 167–184. doi:10.1108/17465261211219796

Massa, S., & Testa, S. (2009). A knowledge management approach to organizational competitive advantage: Evidence from the food sector. *European Management Journal*, *27*(2), 129–141. doi:10.1016/j.emj.2008.06.005

McGurk, J., & Baron, A. (2012). Knowledge management: Time to focus on purpose and motivation. *Strategic HR Review*, *11*(6), 316–321. doi:10.1108/14754391211264776

McKinlay, A. (2005). Knowledge management. In S. Ackroyd, R. Batt, & P. Thompson (Eds.), *The Oxford handbook of work and organization* (pp. 242–262). Oxford, UK: Oxford University Press.

Moeller, K. (2010). Partner selection, partner behavior, and business network performance: An empirical study of German business networks. *Journal of Accounting and Organizational Change*, *6*(1), 27–51. doi:10.1108/18325911011025687

Musser, J., & O'Reilly, T. (2007). *Web 2.0 principles and practices*. O'Reilly Media Inc. Retrieved February 15, 2014, from http://oreilly.com/radar/web2report.csp

Nahapiet, J., & Sumantra, G. (1998). Social capital, intellectual capital and the organizational advantage. *Academy of Management Review*, *23*(2), 242–266.

Narteh, B. (2008). Knowledge transfer in developed-developing country interfirm collaborations: A conceptual framework. *Journal of Knowledge Management*, *12*(1), 78–91. doi:10.1108/13673270810852403

Nicholas, D., & Rowlands, I. (2011). Social media use in the research workflow. *Information Services & Use*, *31*(1-2), 61–83.

Nonaka, I. (1998). The knowledge-creating company. In P. Drucker (Ed.), *Harvard Business Review on knowledge management* (pp. 21–46). Boston, MA: Harvard Business School Press.

Nonaka, I., & Takeuchi, H. (1995). *The knowledge-creating company: How Japanese companies create the dynamics of innovation*. Oxford, UK: Oxford University Press.

O'Dell, C., & Hubert, C. (2011). *The new edge in knowledge: How knowledge management is changing the way we do business*. Hoboken, NJ: John Wiley & Sons.

Okazaki, S., & Taylor, C. R. (2013). Social media and international advertising: Theoretical challenges and future directions. *International Marketing Review*, *30*(1), 56–71. doi:10.1108/02651331311298573

Oluikpe, P. (2012). Developing a corporate knowledge management strategy. *Journal of Knowledge Management*, *16*(6), 862–878. doi:10.1108/13673271211276164

Othman, R., & Sheehan, T. N. (2011). Value creation logics and resource management: A review. *Journal of Strategy and Management*, *4*(1), 5–24. doi:10.1108/17554251111110096

Palmer, A., & Koenig-Lewis, N. (2009). An experiential, social network-based approach to direct marketing. *Direct Marketing: An International Journal*, *3*(3), 162–176. doi:10.1108/17505930910985116

Palte, R., Hertlein, M., Smolnik, S., & Riempp, G. (2011). The effects of a knowledge management strategy on KM performance in professional services firms. *International Journal of Knowledge Management*, *7*(1), 16–34. doi:10.4018/jkm.2011010102

Pandey, S. C., & Dutta, A. (2013). Role of knowledge infrastructure capabilities in knowledge management. *Journal of Knowledge Management*, *17*(3), 435–453. doi:10.1108/JKM-11-2012-0365

Parker, R. K., & Nitse, S. P. (2006). Competitive intelligence gathering. In D. G. Schwartz (Ed.), *Encyclopedia of knowledge management* (pp. 44–50). London, UK: Idea Group. doi:10.4018/978-1-59140-573-3.ch007

Paroutis, S., & Al Saleh, A. (2009). Determinants of knowledge sharing using Web 2.0 technologies. *Journal of Knowledge Management*, *13*(4), 52–63. doi:10.1108/13673270910971824

Perez-Lopez, S., & Alegre, J. (2012). Information technology competency, knowledge processes and firm performance. *Industrial Management & Data Systems*, *112*(4), 644–662. doi:10.1108/02635571211225521

Plessis, M. D. (2005). Drivers of knowledge management in the corporate environment. *International Journal of Information Management*, *25*(3), 193–202. doi:10.1016/j.ijinfomgt.2004.12.001

Porter, E. M. (2001). Strategy and the internet. *Harvard Business Review*, *79*(3), 62–78. PMID:11246925

Rao, M. (2002). *Knowledge management tools and techniques: Practitioners and experts evaluate KM solutions*. Amsterdam, The Netherlands: Elsevier.

Razmerita, L., Kirchner, K., & Sudzina, F. (2009). Personal knowledge management: The role of Web 2.0 tools for managing knowledge at individual and organizational levels. *Online Information Review*, *33*(6), 1021–1039. doi:10.1108/14684520911010981

Rowley, J. (1999). What is knowledge management? *Library Management*, *20*(8), 416–419. doi:10.1108/01435129910291175

Sajeva, S. (2010). The analysis of key elements of socio-technical knowledge management system. *Economics and Management*, *15*, 765–774.

Salleh, K., Chong, S. C., Syed Ahmad, S. N., & Syed Ikhsan, S. O. (2012). Learning and knowledge transfer performance among public sector accountants: An empirical survey. *Knowledge Management Research and Practice*, *10*(2), 164–174. doi:10.1057/kmrp.2011.46

Sammarra, A., & Biggiero, L. (2008). Heterogeneity and specificity of inter-firm knowledge flows in innovation networks. *Journal of Management Studies*, *45*(4), 800–829. doi:10.1111/j.1467-6486.2008.00770.x

Saw, G., Abbott, W., Donaghey, J., & McDonald, C. (2013). Social media for international students – It's not all about Facebook. *Library Management*, *34*(3), 156–174. doi:10.1108/01435121311310860

Schneckenberg, D. (2009). Web 2.0 and the empowerment of the knowledge worker. *Journal of Knowledge Management*, *13*(6), 509–520. doi:10.1108/13673270910997150

Sharma, R. S., & Djiaw, V. (2011). Realising the strategic impact of business intelligence tools. *VINE - The Journal of Information and Knowledge Management Systems*, *41*(2), 113-131.

Simonin, B. (1999). Ambiguity and the process of knowledge transfer in strategic alliances. *Strategic Management Journal*, *20*(7), 595–623. doi:10.1002/(SICI)1097-0266(199907)20:7<595::AID-SMJ47>3.0.CO;2-5

Singh, M. D., Shankar, R., Narain, R., & Kumar, A. (2006). Survey of knowledge management practices in Indian manufacturing industries. *Journal of Knowledge Management*, *10*(6), 110–128. doi:10.1108/13673270610709251

Singh, T., Veron-Jackson, L., & Cullinane, J. (2008). Blogging: A new play in your marketing game plan. *Business Horizons*, *51*(4), 281–292. doi:10.1016/j.bushor.2008.02.002

Sirmon, D. G., Hitt, M. A., & Ireland, R. D. (2007). Managing firm resources in dynamic environments to create value: Looking inside the black box. *Academy of Management Review*, *32*(1), 273–292. doi:10.5465/AMR.2007.23466005

Smit, B., & Wandel, J. (2006). Adaptation, adaptive capacity and vulnerability. *Global Environmental Change*, *16*(3), 282–292. doi:10.1016/j.gloenvcha.2006.03.008

Smith, K. T. (2011). Digital marketing strategies that Millennials find appealing, motivating, or just annoying. *Journal of Strategic Marketing*, *19*(6), 489–499. doi:10.1080/0965254X.2011.581383

Solis, B. (2010). *Engage! The complete guide for brands and businesses to build, cultivate, and measure success in the new web*. Hoboken, NJ: John Wiley & Sons.

Sotarauta, M., Horlings, L., & Liddle, J. (2012). *Leadership and change in sustainable regional development*. London, UK: Routledge.

Steenkamp, J. B. E. M. (2001). The role of national culture in international marketing research. *International Marketing Review*, *18*(1), 30–44. doi:10.1108/02651330110381970

Stephen, A. T., & Toubia, O. (2010). Deriving value from social commerce networks. *JMR, Journal of Marketing Research*, *47*(2), 215–228. doi:10.1509/jmkr.47.2.215

Susskind, A. M. (2002). I told you so! Restaurant customers' word-of-mouth communication patterns. *Cornell Hospitality Quarterly*, *43*(2), 75–85. doi:10.1177/0010880402043002008

Sveiby, E. K. (2001). A knowledge based theory of the firm to guide in strategy formulation. *Journal of Intellectual Capital*, *2*(4), 344–358. doi:10.1108/14691930110409651

Szulanski, G. (2000). The process of knowledge transfer: A diachronic analysis of stickiness. *Organizational Behavior and Human Decision Processes*, *82*(1), 9–27. doi:10.1006/obhd.2000.2884

Thierauf, R. J., & Hoctor, J. J. (2006). *Optimal knowledge management: Wisdom management systems concepts and applications*. London, UK: Idea Group. doi:10.4018/978-1-59904-016-5

Trusov, M., Bucklin, R. E., & Pauwels, K. (2009). Effects of word-of-mouth versus traditional marketing: Finding from an internet social networking site. *Journal of Marketing*, *73*(5), 90–102. doi:10.1509/jmkg.73.5.90

Turban, E., & Volonino, L. (2011). *Information technology for management: Improving strategic and operational performance*. Hoboken, NJ: John Wiley & Sons.

Uotila, J., Maula, M., Keil, T., & Zahra, S. A. (2009). Exploration, exploitation, and financial performance: Analysis of S&P 500 corporations. *Strategic Management Journal*, *30*(2), 221–231. doi:10.1002/smj.738

Vaccaro, A., & Madsen, P. (2009). Transparency: The new ICT-driven ethics? *Ethics and Information Technology*, *11*(2), 113–122. doi:10.1007/s10676-009-9190-1

Van Doorn, J., Lemon, K. N., Mittal, V., Nass, S., Pick, D., Pirner, P., & Verhoef, P. C. (2010). Customer engagement behavior: Theoretical foundations and research directions. *Journal of Service Research*, *13*(3), 247–252. doi:10.1177/1094670510375599

Vance, K., Howe, W., & Dellavalle, R. (2009). Social internet sites as a source of public health information. *Dermatologic Clinics*, *27*(2), 113–136. doi:10.1016/j.det.2008.11.010 PMID:19254656

Verhoef, P. C., Reinartz, W., & Krafft, M. (2010). Customer engagement as a new perspective in customer management. *Journal of Service Research*, *13*(2), 247–252. doi:10.1177/1094670510375461

Von Krogh, G. (2012). How does social software change knowledge management? Toward a strategic research agenda. *The Journal of Strategic Information Systems*, *21*(2), 154–164. doi:10.1016/j.jsis.2012.04.003

Vuori, V., & Okkonen, J. (2012). Knowledge sharing motivational factors of using an intra-organizational social media platform. *Journal of Knowledge Management*, *16*(4), 592–603. doi:10.1108/13673271211246167

Wagner, C., & Bolloju, N. (2005). Supporting knowledge management in organisations with conversational technologies: Discussion forums, weblogs and wikis. *Journal of Database Management*, *16*(2), i–viii.

Weinberg, D. B., & Pehlivan, E. (2011). Social spending: Managing the social media mix. *Business Horizons*, *54*(3), 275–282. doi:10.1016/j.bushor.2011.01.008

Wellman, B. (2001). Computer networks as social networks. *Science*, *293*(14), 2031–2034. doi:10.1126/science.1065547 PMID:11557877

Whittington, K. B., Owen-Smith, J., & Powel, W. W. (2009). Networks, propinquity, and innovation in knowledge-intensive industries. *Administrative Science Quarterly*, *54*(1), 90–122. doi:10.2189/asqu.2009.54.1.90

Wirtz, W. B., Schilke, O., & Ullrich, S. (2010). Implications of the Web 2.0. for creating value on the internet. *Long Range Planning*, *43*(2-3), 272–290. doi:10.1016/j.lrp.2010.01.005

Zack, H. M. (2003). Rethinking the knowledge-based organization. *MIT Sloan Management Review*, *44*(4), 67–71.

Zaim, H., Ekrem, T., & Selim, Z. (2007). Performance of knowledge management practices: A casual analysis. *Journal of Knowledge Management*, *11*(6), 54–67. doi:10.1108/13673270710832163

Zander, U., & Kogut, B. (1995). Knowledge and the speed of the transfer and imitation of organizational capabilities: An empirical test. *Organization Science*, *6*(1), 76–92. doi:10.1287/orsc.6.1.76

Zhao, J., & Ordóñez de Pablos, P. (2011). Regional knowledge management: The perspective of management theory. *Behaviour & Information Technology*, *30*(1), 39–49. doi:10.1080/0144929X.2010.492240

ADDITIONAL READING

Abril, P. S., Levin, A., & Del Riego, A. (2012). Blurred boundaries: Social media privacy and the twenty-first century employee. *American Business Law Journal*, *49*(1), 63–124. doi:10.1111/j.1744-1714.2011.01127.x

Alhabash, S., Park, H., Kononova, A., Chian, Y., & Wise, K. (2012). Exploring the motivation of Facebook use in Taiwan. *Cyberpsychology, Behavior, and Social Networking*, *15*(6), 304–311. doi:10.1089/cyber.2011.0611 PMID:22703036

Argote, L. (2013). *Organizational learning: Creating, retaining, and transferring knowledge*. New York, NY: Springer-Verlag. doi:10.1007/978-1-4614-5251-5

Baird, H. C., & Parasnis, G. (2011). From social media to social customer relationship management. *Strategy and Leadership*, *30*(5), 30–37. doi:10.1108/10878571111161507

Bebensee, T., Helms, R., & Spruit, M. (2011). Exploring Web 2.0 applications as a mean of bolstering up knowledge management. *Electronic Journal of Knowledge Management*, *9*(1), 1–9.

Borges, R. (2013). Tacit knowledge sharing between IT workers: The role of organizational culture, personality, and social environment. *Management Research Review*, *36*(1), 89–108. doi:10.1108/01409171311284602

Brown, V. R., & Vaughn, E. D. (2012). The writing on the (Facebook) wall: The use of social network sites in hiring decisions. *Journal of Business and Psychology*, *26*(2), 219–225. doi:10.1007/s10869-011-9221-x

Chai, S., & Kim, M. (2012). A socio-technical approach to knowledge contribution behavior: An empirical investigation of social networking sites users. *International Journal of Information Management*, *32*(2), 118–126. doi:10.1016/j.ijinfomgt.2011.07.004

Chen, Y., Fay, S., & Wang, Q. (2011). The role of marketing in social media: How online consumer reviews evolve. *Journal of Interactive Marketing*, *25*(2), 85–94. doi:10.1016/j.intmar.2011.01.003

Chikandiwa, S. T., Contogiannis, E., & Jembere, E. (2013). The adoption of social media marketing in South African banks. *European Business Review*, *25*(4), 365–381. doi:10.1108/EBR-02-2013-0013

Chu, S., & Choi, S. M. (2011). Electronic word-of-mouth in social networking sites: A cross-cultural study of the United States and China. *Journal of Global Marketing*, *24*(3), 263–281. doi:10.1080/08911762.2011.592461

Chua, A. Y. K., & Banerjee, S. (2013). Customer knowledge management via social media: The case of Starbucks. *Journal of Knowledge Management*, *17*(2), 237–249. doi:10.1108/13673271311315196

Comunello, F., & Anzera, G. (2012). Will the revolution be tweeted? A conceptual framework for understanding the social media and the Arab Spring. *Islam & Christian-Muslim Relations*, *23*(4), 1–18. doi:10.1080/09596410.2012.712435

Connell, J., & Voola, R. (2013). Knowledge integration and competitiveness: A longitudinal study of an industry cluster. *Journal of Knowledge Management*, *17*(2), 208–225. doi:10.1108/13673271311315178

DeAndrea, D. C., Ellison, N. B., LaRose, R., Steinfield, C., & Fiore, A. (2012). Serious social media: On the use of social media for improving students' adjustment to college. *The Internet and Higher Education*, *15*(1), 15–23. doi:10.1016/j.iheduc.2011.05.009

Denford, J. S. (2013). Building knowledge: Developing a knowledge-based dynamic capabilities typology. *Journal of Knowledge Management*, *17*(2), 175–194. doi:10.1108/13673271311315150

Dooley, J., Jones, S., & Iverson, D. (2012). Web 2.0: An assessment of social marketing principles. *Journal of Social Marketing*, *2*(3), 207–221. doi:10.1108/20426761211265195

Dwyer, C. (2011). Privacy in the age of Google and Facebook. *IEEE Technology and Society Magazine*, *30*(3), 58–63. doi:10.1109/MTS.2011.942309

Espinoza, G., & Juvonen, J. (2011). The pervasiveness, connectedness and intrusiveness of social network sites. *Cyberpsychology, Behavior, and Social Networking*, *14*(12), 705–709. doi:10.1089/cyber.2010.0492

Grant, K. (2011). Knowledge management, an enduring but confusing fashion. *Electronic Journal of Knowledge Management*, *9*(2), 117–131.

Kaplan, A. M. (2012). If you love something, let it go mobile: Mobile marketing and mobile social media 4x4. *Business Horizons*, *55*(2), 129–139. doi:10.1016/j.bushor.2011.10.009

Käpylä, J. (2012). Towards a critical societal knowledge management. *Journal of Intellectual Capital*, *13*(3), 288–304. doi:10.1108/14691931211248873

Kittinger, R., Correia, C. J., & Irons, J. G. (2012). Relationship between Facebook use and problematic internet use among college students. *Cyberpsychology, Behavior, and Social Networking*, *15*(6), 324–327. doi:10.1089/cyber.2010.0410 PMID:22703039

Lee, J., & Fink, D. (2013). Knowledge mapping: Encouragements and impediments to adoption. *Journal of Knowledge Management*, *17*(1), 16–28. doi:10.1108/13673271311300714

Lee, M. R., & Lan, Y. (2011). Toward a unified knowledge management model for SMEs. *Expert Systems with Applications*, *38*(1), 729–735. doi:10.1016/j.eswa.2010.07.025

Lerro, A., Iacobone, A. F., & Schiuma, G. (2012). Knowledge assets assessment strategies: Organizational value, processes, approaches and evaluation architectures. *Journal of Knowledge Management*, *16*(4), 563–575. doi:10.1108/13673271211246149

Machin-Mastromatteo, J. D. (2012). Participatory action research in the age of social media: Literacies, affinity spaces and learning. *New Library World*, *113*(11-12), 571–585. doi:10.1108/03074801211282939

Matayong, S., & Mahmood, A. K. (2013). The review of approaches to knowledge management system studies. *Journal of Knowledge Management*, *17*(3), 472–490. doi:10.1108/JKM-10-2012-0316

Milewicz, C., & Saxby, C. (2013). Leaders' social media usage intentions for in-bound customer communications. *Management Research Review*, *36*(9), 849–867. doi:10.1108/MRR-03-2012-0049

Mills, A. M., & Smith, T. A. (2011). Knowledge management and organizational performance: A decomposed view. *Journal of Knowledge Management*, *15*(1), 156–171. doi:10.1108/13673271111108756

Muntinga, D. G., Moorman, M., & Smit, E. G. (2011). Introducing COBRAs: Exploring motivations for brand-related social media use. *International Journal of Advertising*, *30*(1), 13–46. doi:10.2501/IJA-30-1-013-046

Myers, P. S. (2012). *Knowledge management and organizational design*. London, UK: Routledge.

Panahi, S., Watson, J., & Partridge, H. (2012). Social media and tacit knowledge sharing: Developing a conceptual model. *World Academy of Science. Engineering and Technology, 64*, 1095–1102.

Pentina, I., Koh, A. C., & Le, T. T. (2012). Adoption of social networks marketing by SMEs: Exploring the role of social influences and experience in technology acceptance. *International Journal of Internet Marketing and Advertising, 7*(1), 65–82.

Ponte, D., & Simon, J. (2011). Scholarly communication 2.0: Exploring researchers' opinions on Web 2.0 for scientific knowledge creation, evaluation, and dissemination. *Serials Review, 37*(3), 149–156. doi:10.1080/00987913.2011.10765376

Rabeh, H. A. D., Jimenéz-Jimenéz, D., & Martínez-Costa, M. (2013). Managing knowledge for a successful competence exploration. *Journal of Knowledge Management, 17*(2), 195–207. doi:10.1108/13673271311315169

Ruiz-Jiménez, J. M., & Fuentes-Fuentes, M. (2013). Knowledge combination, innovation, organizational performance in technology firms. *Industrial Management & Data Systems, 113*(4), 523–540. doi:10.1108/02635571311322775

Schiuma, G. (2012). Managing knowledge for business performance improvement. *Journal of Knowledge Management, 16*(4), 515–522. doi:10.1108/13673271211246103

Scott-Kennel, J., & Von Batenburg, Z. (2012). The role of knowledge and learning in internationalization of professional service firms. *Service Industries Journal, 32*(10), 1667–1678. doi:10.1080/02642069.2012.665897

Serenko, A., Bontis, N., & Hull, E. (2011). Practical relevance of knowledge management and intellectual capital scholarly research: Books as knowledge translation agents. *Knowledge and Process Management, 18*(1), 1–9. doi:10.1002/kpm.363

Shirazi, F. (2013). Social media and the social movements in the Middle East and North Africa – A critical discourse analysis. *Information Technology & People, 26*(1), 28–49. doi:10.1108/09593841311307123

Sigala, M. (2012). Social networks and customer involvement in new service development (NSD), The case of www.mystarbucksidea.com. *International Journal of Contemporary Hospitality Management, 24*(7), 966-990

Siong, C. C., Salleh, K., Syed, N. S., & Syed-Ikhsan, S. O. (2011). KM implementation in a public sector accounting organization: An empirical investigation. *Journal of Knowledge Management, 15*(3), 497–512. doi:10.1108/13673271111137457

Smith, A. N., Fischer, E., & Yongjian, C. (2012). How does brand-related user-generated content differ across YouTube, Facebook, and Twitter? *Journal of Interactive Marketing, 26*(2), 102–113. doi:10.1016/j.intmar.2012.01.002

Tenopir, C., Volentine, R., & King, D. W. (2013). Social media and scholarly reading. *Online Information Review, 37*(2), 193–216. doi:10.1108/OIR-04-2012-0062

Vuori, V., & Okkonen, J. (2012). Refining information and knowledge by social media applications – Adding value by insight. *VINE - The Journal of Information and Knowledge Management Systems, 42*(1), 117-128.

Wallace, D. P., Fleet, C. V., & Downs, L. J. (2011). The research core of the knowledge management literature. *International Journal of Information Management, 31*(1), 14–20. doi:10.1016/j.ijinfomgt.2010.10.002

Zhang, Z. (2011). Customer knowledge management and the strategies of social software. *Business Process Management Journal*, *17*(1), 82–106. doi:10.1108/14637151111105599

Zheng, S., Zhang, W., Wu, X., & Du, J. (2011). Knowledge- based dynamic capabilities an innovation in networked environments. *Journal of Knowledge Management*, *15*(8), 1035–1051. doi:10.1108/13673271111179352

KEY TERMS AND DEFINITIONS

Communications: All means of symbolic or verbal communication that people and machines use to make contact and share information.

Information: Data that is presented within a context that gives it meaning and relevance.

Information Technology: Set of tools, processes, and associated equipment employed to collect, process, and present information.

Knowledge: The sum of what is known and resides in the intelligence and the competence of people.

Knowledge Base: Organized repository of knowledge (in a computer system or an organization) consisting of concepts, data, objectives, requirements, rules, and specifications.

Knowledge Management: Strategies and processes designed to identify, value, and share an organization's intellectual assets to enhance its performance and competitiveness.

Media: Communication channels through which news, education, and data are distributed.

Organization: A social unit of people that is structured and managed to meet a need or to pursue collective goals.

Social Media: Primarily internet or cellular phone-based application and tools to share information among people.

Chapter 14
Social Media for Business Model Improvement

In Lee
Western Illinois University, USA

ABSTRACT

This chapter reviews some of the major business applications of social media and discusses how social media applications are used to support business model improvement. Social media offers business organizations an array of innovative ways to interact with their employees, customers, partners, and other stakeholders. Consumers have easy ways of interacting with companies and their employees in real time with various social media embedded devices. Managers are realizing that social media affects a wide spectrum of business activities from building product or brand awareness to after-sales services. Therefore, it is crucial for companies to analyze their social media applications, develop a plan to continually monitor their advancements, and quickly respond to the social media needs of customers. For practitioners, this chapter provides managerial guidelines for social media applications for business model improvement.

1. INTRODUCTION

Recently, the Web paradigm shifted from a business-centered focus to user-centered one. This paradigm shift has become known as "Web 2.0", coined by Tim O'Reilly in 2004 (O'Reilly, 2007). Web 2.0 refers to a website that has evolved beyond Web 1.0 and features user-created-content and online communities that allow website visitors to interact dynamically with the site. While technological distinctions between Web1.0 and Web 2.0 are often not clear in some areas, the social and technological environment for positive user participation and interactivity epitomizes Web 2.0.

Social media embodies the principles of Web 2.0 and is continuously evolving and offers business model improvement tools and support business processes, knowledge management, customer relationship management, and partner relationship management. Despite the lack of a comprehensive framework for the use of social media applications for business improvement, businesses are eager to use them. Managers are already active users of the various social media technologies such as social networks and blogs.

DOI: 10.4018/978-1-4666-6182-0.ch014

Managers are realizing that social media affects a wide spectrum of business activities from building product or brand awareness to after-sales services. For example, investing in social media applications will enhance relationships with customers and provide the opportunity to better understand the customer needs. Therefore, it is crucial for companies to analyze their social media applications, develop a plan to continually monitor their advancements, and quickly respond to the social media needs of customers.

The main purposes of this chapter are to explore emerging social media applications and to discuss social media applications for business model improvement. This study proceeds as follows: Section 2 presents a literature review on social media and business models. Section 3 explores social media applications for business model improvement. Section 4 discusses managerial guidelines for social media applications for business model improvement.

2. LITERATURE REVIEW

2.1 Types of Social Media Tools

Companies are beginning to capitalize on social media tools in a variety of ways. Many businesses integrate a variety of social media tools into their core business processes to achieve competitive advantage. Users contribute to the development of content through writing comments and recommendations on Google, Yahoo, and Facebook, submitting videos on YouTube, co-designing games like The Sims, creating avatars in virtual environments like Second Life, or developing open source codes for Linux. High-profile companies, from P&G to GM to IBM to Cisco, have all adopted social media tools, and exert to derive strong competitive advantages from it.

Many companies are expanding social media efforts to capture customer data and leverage it to generate instantaneous, custom-tailored customer experiences (Bughin et al., 2008). For example, Amazon uses data generated from site visitors in order to provide targeted product suggestions to other site visitors. For a potential purchaser who is interested in a certain product, Amazon lists products that other purchasers of the same product also looked at or may be interested in. Netflix aggregates and analyzes subscriber movie preferences in order to provide accurate online movie recommendations. Businesses can leverage social media technologies in order to dynamically collaborate with customers and partners in efforts to generate new design innovations (Brown, 2008). This section introduces five types of social media tools for businesses.

2.1.1 Social Networking Services

Many companies leverage social networking services (SNS) such as Facebook and Google+ to increase productivity in the workplace. SNS are web-based services that allow individuals to (1) construct a public or semi-public profile within a bounded system, (2) articulate a list of other users with whom they share a connection, and (3) view and traverse their list of connections and those made by others within the system (Boyd & Ellison, 2007). SNS facilitate recruiting and connecting potential contributors for distributed innovation processes. As recruiting tools, SNS enable recruiters to view the manner in which candidates behave in an online setting and the type of people they socialize with. Job seekers use SNS such as LinkedIn to network with professionals for internship and job opportunities. Companies can also use SNS to engage in direct market research and maintain a positive relationship with customers. LinkedIn's new service, Company Groups, allows a company's employees to participate in a single internal web forum where they can talk to one another, share ideas, and ask company-related questions.

2.1.2 Collaborative Platform

Collaborative platforms allow users to post, delete, or update contents via a web browser. Internal corporate wikis can be used as a collaborative platform tool to tap the expertise of a large group. For businesses, wikis serve as an excellent collaborative platform for collective intelligence and can facilitate innovations (Tapscott & Williams, 2007). For example, Nokia has been using internal wikis for engineers to solve product-design problems. Internal wikis are increasingly used by companies such as Adobe Systems, Amazon.com, Disney, Intel, Pixar, and Microsoft. External corporate wikis enable companies to have the opportunity to derive collaboration from the public that participates in wiki-based projects. By allowing consumers to contribute ideas revolving around the company's products, the company can not only develop a core consumer base, but can also create values for any consumer that can benefit from the collaborative works. Sun Microsystems' Sun Wikis is a directory of wiki spaces where contributors inside and outside of Sun Microsystems can share information with each other and contribute ideas to the wikis.

Social media has also led to collective intelligence. For example, prediction markets tools can help aggregate a vast amount of information from employees within organizations to better guide company actions. An example of this is the sales forecast at HP through prediction markets (Chen & Plott, 2002). HP pioneered prediction markets in sales forecasting and expanded it to several business units. HP is working towards a commercial launch of the implementation of it as a product. Procter & Gamble, through its 'Connect and Develop' platform opened to inputs from company alumni, current employees, and even customers, has successfully secured a large stream of new product innovations (Huston & Sakkab, 2006). While Procter & Gamble's best innovations had come from connecting ideas among employees, after analyzing the performance of a small number of products they had acquired from external sources, they realized that external connections could produce highly profitable innovations as well. Its 'Connect and Develop' platform taps into the creative ideas of innovators and others from the outside would.

2.1.3 Blogs

Blogs (short for weblogs) are online journals that are characterized by short entries and regular updates. Blogs are inherently flexible and can be used for a variety of purposes, ranging from posting personal opinions to corporate knowledge management initiatives and customer relationship management. Personal or public blog sites are used to host blogs and the posted messages can be distributed to other sites or readers via RSS (Really Simple Syndication). WordPress is a popular blog hosting site available to individuals and companies.

One of the most useful features of blogs is the functionality that allows readers to comment on each post often called an open thread. This feature enables readers to engage in an open dialogue for every post. The collective comments and links on blogs form a clustered network termed the blogosphere. A variety of public blogging services are available to individuals and companies. For example, Twitter is the most popular social networking and microblogging service firm. Members of Twitter post text-based messages of up to 140 characters displayed on the author's profile page and delivered to the author's subscribers who are known as followers.

The publication of a blog enables the company to interact directly with consumers. Leading companies like Intel, IBM, P&G, Ford, and Cisco are all early adopters of corporate blogs. While the blog can be used for public relations, it can also be used to promote new products and receive consumer feedback to products and services. Senior management can also utilize internal and external blogs to make announcements and seek inputs from various stakeholders. Internal corporate blogs offer a communication channel for individual employees to express themselves, ask advices from colleagues, and discuss ideas with each other. Internal blog sites can be used as a knowledge repository to store key information, expert knowledge and experience, and as a connection point among employees.

2.1.4 Social Bookmarking

Social bookmarking is the process of adding, annotating, editing, and sharing bookmarks with others via social bookmarking websites. An empirical analysis of the complex dynamics of social bookmarking has shown that a consensus around stable distributions and shared vocabularies emerge, even in the absence of a centrally controlled vocabulary (Halpin et al., 2007). Companies are increasingly using bookmarking sites like Delicious, Reddit, Digg, and StumbleUpon to promote new products and services and also to save, organize, and remember the web pages users find interesting on the web. Social bookmarking utilizes tagging to collectively classify and find web pages. For example, at Digg, users can "tag" web pages, labeling their name, which in turn allows the company to catalog shared tags of users.

2.1.5 Media Sharing

Media sharing is a social media application that enables users to create, store, and share their multimedia files (photos, videos, sounds) with others. Media sharing websites allow users to upload their photos, videos, and sounds to the sites that can be accessed from anywhere via web browsers. There are the main two forms of media sharing sites: videos and photos. Instagram, Pinterest, and Flickr are popular photo-sharing sites. YouTube is a powerful video sharing site that companies can utilize to create their own video publication channel. YouTube also offers free analytics that can provide information on users' viewing habits and their demographics. YouTube has become the second largest search engine only next to Google since 2013.

2.2 Business Models

Mayo and Brown (1999) argue that a company should design key interdependent systems that create and sustain a competitive business. Many successful ventures have been created based on innovative business models that provide unique values to customers. A business model should be reasonably simple, logical, measurable, comprehensive, and operationally meaningful (Morris et al., 2005). In the literature, a business model is defined as a statement (Stewart & Zhao, 2000), a system of interdependent activities (Zott & Amit, 2010) an articulation (Teece, 2010), the organization (Timmers, 1999), a representation of management thinking and practice (Chararbaghi et al., 2003), and a method (Afuah & Tucci, 2003; Rappa, 2004).

A number of studies have presented the logically interrelated components of a business model. For example, Morris et al. (2005) suggest six fundamental components: value proposition, customer, internal processes/competencies, external positioning, economic model, and personal/investor factors. Johnson et al. (2008) propose four interlocking elements: customer value proposition, profit formula, key resources, and key processes. Like the definition of the business model, there exists no general agreement on the required components of a business model. Table 1 summarizes various definitions and components of a business model developed by the prior studies.

In sum, all these definitions share a common idea: it concerns what is produced and sold, how, and to whom it is sold. How is the value of the product or service derived? To derive essential components among the business models, we categorized the various components into groups based on their underlying similarity and identified six major categories: value proposition, organizational

Table 1. Definitions and components of a business model

Study	Definition	Components
Timmers (1998)	An architecture for the product, service and information flows, including a description of the various business actors and their roles; a description of the potential benefits for the various business actors; a description of the sources of revenues.	Business actors and their roles, benefits, and sources of revenues
Amit & Zott (2001)	The content, structure, and governance of transactions designed so as to create value through the exploitation of business opportunities	The content, structure, and governance of transactions
Chesbrough & Rosenbloom (2002)	The business model is the heuristic logic that connects technical potential with the realization of economic value.	Value proposition, market segment, value chain structure, revenue generation and margins, position in the value network, and competitive strategy
Dubosson-Torbay, Osterwalder, & Pigneur (2002)	A business model is nothing else than the architecture of a firm and its network of partners for creating, marketing and delivering value and relationship capital to one or several segments of customers in order to generate profitable and sustainable revenue streams.	The products and services, the relationship capital, the infrastructure and the network of partners, and the financial aspects
Afuah & Tucci (2003)	The method by which a firm builds and uses its resources to offer its customers better value than its competitors and to make money doing so.	Customer value, scope, pricing, revenue sources, connected activities, implementation, capabilities, and sustainability
Morris et al. (2005)	A business model is a concise representation of how an interrelated set of decision variables in the areas of venture strategy, architecture, and economics are addressed to create sustainable competitive advantage in defined markets.	Value proposition, customer, internal processes/competencies, external positioning, economic model, and personal/investor factors
Shafer et al. (2005)	A business model is a representation of a firm's underlying core logic and strategic choices for creating and capturing value within a value network.	core logic and strategic choices for creating and capturing value
Johnson et al. (2008)	A business model consists of four interlocking elements that, taken together, create and deliver value.	Customer value proposition (CVP), profit formula, key resources, and key processes
Teece (2010)	A business model articulates the logic, the data and other evidence that support a value proposition for the customer, and a viable structure of revenues and costs for the enterprise delivering that value.	The design or architecture of value creation, delivery and capture mechanisms

governance, market scope, networked activities, resources, and sustainability.

Many previous studies analyzed the business model in a relatively static point of view. However, the static view has limitations in describing the evolutionary nature of the business model. Business model evolution is viewed as a fine-tuning process involving intended and emergent changes both between and within its core components (Demil & Lecocq, 2010). In the dynamic view of the business model, the business model transforms itself over time and manifests its evolution with the dynamic adjustment of the components in interaction with the environments. Different types of accumulated resources interact with each other and with other parts of the firm's infrastructure, thereby creating unique combinations that will vary within the firm, and which produce and determine the firm's idiosyncratic set of capabilities (Kor & Mahoney, 2000). With a new set of capabilities, the company can build new value propositions and tap new markets.

3. SOCIAL MEDIA FOR BUSINESS MODEL IMPROVEMENT

While there exists an abundance of studies on the classifications, theories, and operations of business models, little attention has been given to a social media's impact on the business model improvement. We identified the six logically related business model components categorized in the previous section: value proposition, organizational governance, market scope, networked activities, resources, and sustainability. Many companies utilize social media tools to strengthen their existing business models. Understanding how social media applications can improve the value of existing businesses is a prerequisite to successful social media development. Specifically, we discuss how social media can be used to improve each component of a business model. Various real-world examples are provided to illustrate the use of social media for business model improvement.

3.1 Value Proposition

Value proposition refers to a description of the customer problem and needs, the solution that addresses the problem and needs, and the value of this solution from the customer's perspective. Social media is changing the value proposition dynamics between the company and customers. Customer-centric social media enhances the company's ability to offer better valued products/services by engaging customers in the value creation process as well as in the value consumption process. The customers are equipped with various online social networking applications and investigative knowledge and tools about products and services. Furthermore, customers' expectations for better value of the products and services are ever increasing due to increased competition among sellers. In this business environment, sustaining any value proposition at a long term is a difficult task and listening to customers' changing needs is a necessity business activity.

To enhance value proposition to customers, companies began to use social networking services (SNS) in a variety of ways. First, SNS are used to solicit feedback on customers' product experiences and assess their preferences. By creating a social network with customers and seeking innovative ideas from customers about the company's products, a company can find ways to enhance the value proposition. Second, SNS connect employees with customers to provide customized value to individual customers. According to Lynch (2009), Texas Instruments (TI) noticed a problem in its customer service department in 2004, the main customers of which are engineers who buy and use some of the company's most technical products. To respond to customer questions more effectively, TI decided to build "E2E," which stands for engineers to engineers. Launched in 2008, E2E became a private social networking site where TI engineers interact with customer engineers. E2E proved to be a transparent portal where customer engineers and TI engineers could share best practices that help enhance TI's value proposition to customers. Opening the innovation process to final customers is a new variant of Open Innovation (Chesbrough, 2003) and is a potential source of value proposition. For example, Nokia hosts a corporate wiki forum where users are free to express their views about Nokia products. Nokia uses the ideas contributed by the users in developing their new value proposition which is a next generation product.

3.2 Organizational Governance

Governance is formally defined as "systems and processes that ensure the overall direction, effectiveness, supervision and accountability of an organization" (Cornforth, 2003). Organizational governance typically decides the size of the organization, the type of the organizational structure, and organizational policies. There is no one-size-fits-all type of governance structure. The members of the governance structure may include internal stakeholders such as staff and owners and external stakeholders such as community leaders and government officials. It is expected that governance structures evolve over time with changing environments.

Social media is increasingly recognized as an essential tool for governance by the senior members of an organization. According to a 2012 IBM study of over 1,700 CEOs in 64 countries, CEOs see social media as a tool for collaboration and relationship-building in the service of innovation and the creative exchange of ideas. The senior management's responsibility is to ensure that its company develops a comprehensive social media strategy and policies. The senior management needs to raise the right questions concerning the company's approach to the issue, test management's assumptions, and ensure that management creates and implements an effective social media strategy, policies, and practices (Chaher & Spellman, 2013).

According to 2012 Social Media Survey conducted by Stanford University's Rock Center for Corporate Governance in conjunction with The Conference Board (Larcker et al., 2012), nearly two-thirds of respondents (65%) of the executives and board members use social media for personal purposes, and 63% for business purposes. Of those who use social media, 80% have a LinkedIn account and 68% have a Facebook account, indicating top managers are familiar with social media. However, only 24% of senior managers and 8% of directors receive reports containing summary information and metrics from social media. These results show that more proactive roles are still required at the top management.

The executives and board members set the overall tone for social media development. Since social media is widely used for business and communication activities of the individual employees, it becomes important for the executives and board members to build clear and transparent guidelines to encourage creative and productive use of social media. They needs to analyze any major incidents involving publicly disseminated complaints, allegations or other negative comments about the company, as these increasingly appear to have an impact on corporate value (Katz & McIntosh, 2013).

3.3 Market Scope

Market scope determines specific market segments for the products or services that have appealing value propositions to the target groups. The market scope will be determined by a number of factors such as the particular social mission, needs of the market, competition in the market, and human and financial resources. A precise market segmentation study can be conducted by geography (e.g., cities, states, regions, and counties), demographics (e.g., age, income, gender, family size, occupation, education, and ethnicity), and psychographics (e.g., lifestyles, beliefs, values, interest, activities, and attitude).

SNS can be used in a variety of ways to promote products and services in the target market. For example, Coca-Cola developed a section called MyCoke at the virtual world There.com. This section features large promotional displays, Coke-branded virtual clothing, and activities for consumers (Nasco et al., 2010). Procter and Gamble launched a "My Talking Stain Tide Commercial Contest" inviting consumers to create new ads for their product. McDonalds uses Twitter to offer giveaways such as T-shirts in an effort to market their fast foods. McDonalds also uses Twitter in order to communicate with customers. All these social media activities help the companies reach target customers effectively.

3.4 Networked Activities

A corporate value network is concerned about improvement of any network activities among suppliers, manufacturers, distributors, and retailers that add value to products/services. The significance and weight of value network partners are measured based on the magnitude of their value addition to products/services in different stages towards the final products. That is, the higher value the partner generates, the greater the role that partner plays in the network. The high-value partner needs special attention in value network management.

The difficulty of managing networked activity lies in the fact that it is heavily focused on the external processes, while having little visibility and/or control of these external processes. Social media enables value network partners to share information in a timely, interactive, and visible manner. Therefore, the process visibility increases and network process control is better managed. Furthermore, social media is more human-centric than traditional applications. Social media adds a human element to the technical network activities by engaging employees in multiple businesses in a more interactive manner. A company-owned private blog site enables the company to interact directly with partners, enhancing the power of the human element in the processes.

Social media enables companies to extend their boundaries. For example, Groupon is partnering with multiple merchant reputation sites such as Yelp and TripAdvisor. By expanding the networked activities with the strategic partners this way, their sales potentials increase significantly. Social media also brings small and medium-sized enterprises into the value network, which otherwise would not have been possible without social media. Easy-to-access social media tools lowered technological and resource barriers for many small and medium-sized enterprises, and their activities in the value network have become more visible. The visibility of global network activities is also more enhanced as social media enhances global communications and information sharing.

3.5 Resources

This component provides a conceptually grounded framework for assessing sustainable and developmental resources, and enables these resources to be examined in terms of the opportunities and threats for establishing sustainable competitive advantages. From a resource-based view, every firm has a unique set of resources that the firm can leverage to exploit opportunities and counter threats (Wernerfelt, 1984). Since not all resources are equal in creating sustainable competitive advantages, many researchers focused on identifying advantage-creating resources. Barney (1986, 1991) suggested that the advantage-creating resources must be firm-specific, rare, and difficult to imitate. In a changing environment, a company must continuously invent and upgrade their resources if they are to maintain a competitive advantage and growth.

Social media helps develop financial, technical, and operational resources in organizations. Social media facilitates creating, storing, refining, and sharing informational resources. Knowledge management, training, ERP, research and development, and human resources are areas where social media applications can be used to enhance various resources. Senior management needs to use social media to empower employees. Social networking services are used to support recruiting activities and connect potential contributors for distributed innovation processes (Cash et al., 2008). For example, social media is involved in the co-creation of new products with customers. According to Bughin et al. (2008), one in ten participants in the online community Second Life are already involved in co-creating with companies in different ways (testing prototypes or participating in design of new products), and 60% of the participants in this community say that they are willing to experiment with co-creation.

3.6 Sustainability

Sustainability is concerned with the development of the ways a company can gain a sustainable competitive advantage in the market. This component lays a ground work for how a company will attempt to develop a sustainable competitive advantage and use it to improve its competitive position in the market. Since 2010, sustainability has been widely implemented in businesses due to increased environmental awareness. Sustainability is becoming an integral part of a business model in a drive to achieve long-term corporate growth and profitability and fulfill environmental and social responsibilities at the same time.

Businesses have embraced social media for their sustainability initiatives and it is likely that more businesses will incorporate social media into their sustainability initiatives. Social networking services and blogs have already been used to promote corporate sustainability to their employees and solicit ideas from outside. For example, IBM's Smarter Planet is a website devoted to communicating its sustainability initiatives. General Electric is using social media to find innovative solutions to sustainability dilemmas. Starbucks brought its BetaCup Challenge to a website that crowdsources ideas from the public in order to find a sustainable solution to the coffee cup.

Social media is often used by consumers to speak out against business practices and the speed of information dissemination in social media is stupendous. Businesses that ignore their social responsibility can quickly become a target of the Consumer Watchdog. In April, 2012, to protest the hike of healthcare rates in California, supporters of Consumer Watchdog used Facebook and blogs to sign the petition to demand the justification of health care rates. It is now imperative for manufacturers of environmentally hazardous materials to keeping track of social media sites to monitor consumers' uptake on social and environmental issues.

4. GUIDELINES FOR SOCIAL MEDIA APPLICATIONS FOR BUSINESS MODEL IMPROVEMENT

Based on the survey of social media practices, this section presents guidelines for social media implementation to achieve business model improvement.

4.1 Social Media should not just be a Part of Marketing Strategy, but a Part of an Enterprise-Wide Business and IT Strategy

It should be noted that social media affect the entire spectrum of business functions beyond just marketing. Social media is an integral part of IT strategy as well as marketing strategy. Lederer and Mendelow (1989) suggest that alignment of IT with strategy increases the likelihood of developing systems more critical to the organization. As the role of IT in business strategy development increases, the alignment will lead to a more competitive and profitable organization (Galliers, 1991). To enhance the potential benefits of social media, it is critical to analyze the impacts of social media on the entire organization and develop a coherent set of unique applications for their business strategy, since there is no uniform set of social media applications to all businesses.

4.2 Develop a Change Management Plan

Managing organizational change is a difficult task, but essential to make a new social media implementation successful. There is a chance to fail in the social media endeavors if not carefully developed and managed. Skepticism exists as to how social media for businesses can truly be exploited, either because the technology is too complex, or because major organizational bottlenecks of hierarchy and control exist (Davenport, 2007). High profile cases of failures of social media adoption exist. For example, Cambrian House failed in its crowdsourcing model. While operating a fully open architecture for collaboration, no one in the company had taken the full responsibility for idea development, leading to limited business development opportunities. This case shows the importance of communication and employee participation in the social media projects.

To facilitate the change management process, a company needs to appoint managers who can champion social media initiatives, to gain senior management support, to set achievable social media goals, and to communicate the change management to employees. The establishment of an appropriate change management program will minimize the failure rates or disappointing performance of social media adoption. In addition, investments in staff training are necessary to develop the competence of employees. It is generally assumed that training leads to improved competence. In addition, an appropriate work load assessment needs to be conducted in order not to burden employees in using and managing job-related social media applications.

4.3 A Well-Planned Enterprise-Wide Social Media Architecture needs to be Established for Content Development and Management

As social media becomes part of business strategy, companies are being challenged to support a variety of high-volume bandwidth-intensive social media applications. For companies, the architecture needs to address which media to use, how often to monitor and audit them, what contents, and who are the creators and consumers of the contents (e.g., employee or customers, potential customers, or general public). Companies need to redesign their website to improve the usability, aesthetics, and interactivity (Constantinides, 2004), and develop mechanisms to seamlessly integrate social media into existing business processes.

4.4 A Well-Planned Social Media Metric Needs to be Established for Performance Measurement

Many companies integrate social media into their business operations, but ignore the use of social media metrics to measure the performance. It is imperative to identify key performance metrics, establish the target values, and generate periodic performance reports. It is also important to prioritize key performance metrics. In order to establish target performance of various social media applications, competitors' performance metrics can be benchmarked. Key performance metrics include the number of social connections and followers, the number of reviews and review scores for products, the number of posts and reposts at blogs, the number of comments, response time to comments, social media development costs, and conversion rates (e.g., email subscriptions, and downloads).

4.5 Maintain Security Standards and Control Content Exposure

In seeking to gain value from social media endeavors, companies must be aware of the risks associated with these technologies. While social media inherently connects employees within the company and may connect the company to outsiders, companies must maintain tight security standards in order to prevent unauthorized access or the spread of harmful computer viruses (Dinger & Grover, 2010). Companies need to be aware of the data security issues, legal issues related to unintended disclosure of company data, and privacy issues. Recently, the US Securities and Exchange Commission (SEC) said it may file a law suit against Netflix and its CEO Reed Hastings over a post the CEO made on Facebook in July, 2012. In July, Mr. Hastings posted three lines stating that "Netflix monthly viewing exceeded 1 billion hours for the first time ever in June." This post raised the issue of whether it was privately disclosed information or not. Some claim that the SEC is in essence saying that Facebook is not a "public" website. SEC's Regulation FD, adopted in 2000, requires public companies to make full and fair public disclosure of material non-public information. The SEC believed that figure was material information that should have been disclosed in a press release or regulatory filing. This case illustrates the potential legal ramification of content posted on the social networking sites. In order to encourage proper access and usage of social media applications, companies need to establish social media security and usage policies and requires users to understand them.

REFERENCES

Afuah, A., & Tucci, C. (2003). *Internet Business Models and Strategies*. Boston: McGraw-Hill/ Irwin.

Amit, R., & Zott, C. (2001). Value creation in e-business. *Strategic Management Journal*, *22*(6/7), 493–520. doi:10.1002/smj.187

Barney, J. B. (1986). Strategic factor markets: Expectations, luck, and business strategy. *Management Science*, *32*(10), 1231–1241. doi:10.1287/mnsc.32.10.1231

Barney, J. B. (1991). Firm resources and sustained competitive advantage. *Journal of Management*, *17*(1), 99–120. doi:10.1177/014920639101700108

Boyd, D. M., & Ellison, N. B. (2007). Social network sites: definition, history, and scholarship. *Journal of Computer-Mediated Communication*, *13*(1), 210–230. doi:10.1111/j.1083-6101.2007.00393.x

Brown, T. (2008). Design thinking. *Harvard Business Review*, *86*, 84–92. PMID:18605031

Bughin, J. R., Chui, M., & Johnson, B. (2008). The next step in open innovation. *The McKinsey Quarterly*, (4): 112–122.

Cash, J. J. I., Earl, M. J., & Morison, R. (2008). Teaming up to crack innovation & enterprise integration. *Harvard Business Review*, *86*, 90–100. PMID:19009723

Chaher, S., & Spellman, J. D. (2013). *Corporate governance and social media: A brave new world for board directors*. The Global Corporate Governance Forum. Retrieved on March 5, 2014 from http://www.ifc.org/wps/wcm/connect/topics_ext_content/ifc_external_corporate_site/global+corporate+governance+forum/publications/private+sector+opinion/pso+27+cg+and+social+and+media

Chararbaghi, K., Fendt, C., & Willis, R. (2003). Meaning, legitimacy and impact of business models in fast-moving environments. *Management Decision*, *41*(4), 372–382. doi:10.1108/00251740310468013

Chen, K., & Plott, C. (2002). *Information aggregation mechanisms: Concept, design and implementation for a sales forecasting problem* (Working Paper 1131). California Institute of Technology, Division of the Humanities and Social Sciences.

Chesbrough, H. (2003). *Open innovation: The new imperative for creating and profiting from technology*. Boston: Harvard Business School Press.

Chesbrough, H., & Rosenbloom, R. S. (2002). The role of the business model in capturing value from innovation: Evidence from Xerox Corporation's technology spin-off companies. *Industrial and Corporate Change*, *11*(3), 529–555. doi:10.1093/icc/11.3.529

Constantinides, E. (2004). Influencing the online consumer's behaviour: The web experience. *Journal of Internet Research*, *14*(2), 111–126. doi:10.1108/10662240410530835

Cornforth, C. (2003). *The governance of public and non-profit organisations: What do boards do?* Oxon, UK: Routledge Taylor & Francis Group. doi:10.4324/9780203167571

Corporation, I. B. M. (2012). *Leading through connections: Insights from the global chief executive officer study*. Retrieved on March 5, 2014 from http://www-935.ibm.com/services/us/en/c-suite/ceostudy2012/

Davenport, T. (2007). Why enterprise 2.0 won't transform organizations. *Harvard Business Review*. Retrieved January 2009, from http://discussionleader.hbsp.com/davenport/2007/03/why_enterprise_20_wont_transfo.html

Demil, B., & Lecocq, X. (2010). Business model evolution: In search of dynamic consistency. *Long Range Planning*, *43*(2/3), 227–246. doi:10.1016/j.lrp.2010.02.004

Dinger, M., & Grover, V. (2010). The web 2.0 trend: Implications for the modern business. In *Encyclopedia of E-Business Development and Management in the Global Economy*. Hershey, PA: IGI Global. doi:10.4018/978-1-61520-611-7.ch117

Dubosson-Torbay, M., Osterwalder, A., & Pigneur, Y. (2002). E-business model design, classification, and measurements. *Thunderbird International Business Review*, *44*(1), 5–23. doi:10.1002/tie.1036

Galliers, R. D. (1991). Strategic information systems planning: Myths, reality and guidelines for successful implementation. *European Journal of Information Systems*, *1*(1), 55–64. doi:10.1057/ejis.1991.7

HalpinH.RobuV.ShepherdH. (2007). The complex dynamics of collaborative tagging. In Proceedings of the 16th International Conference on the World Wide Web (WWW'07). Banff, Canada: ACM Press. 10.1145/1242572.1242602

Huston, L., & Sakkab, N. (2006). Connect and develop: Inside Procter & Gamble's new model for innovation. *Harvard Business Review*, *84*(3), 1–8.

Johnson, M. W., Christensen, C. M., & Kagermann, H. (2008). Reinventing your business model. *Harvard Business Review*, *86*(12), 59–67.

Katz, D. A., & McIntosh, L. A. (2013). Corporate governance update: The board, social media and regulation FD. *New York Law Journal*. Retrieved on March 5, 2014 from http://www.wlrk.com/webdocs/wlrknew/WLRKMemos/WLRK/WLRK.22371.13.pdf

Kor, Y., & Mahoney, J. T. (2000). Penrose resource-based approach: The process and product of research creativity. *Journal of Management Studies*, *37*(1), 109–139.

Larcker, D. F., Larcker, S. M., & Tayan, B. (2012). *What do corporate directors and senior managers know about social media?* Retrieved on March 5, 2014 from http://www.gsb.stanford.edu/sites/default/files/documents/TCB_DN-V4N20-12.Social_Media.pdf

Lederer, A., & Mendelow, A. (1989). Co-ordination of information systems plans with business plans. *Journal of Management Information Systems*, *6*(2), 5–19.

Lynch, C. G. (2009). TI's web 2.0 success story: Better customer service. *CIO*. Retrieved June 1, 2010, from http://www.cio.com/article/496338/TI_s_Web_2.0_Success_Story_Better_Customer_Service

Mayo, M. C., & Brown, G. S. (1999). Building a competitive business model. *Ivey Business Journal*, *63*(3), 18–23.

Morris, M., Schindehutte, M., & Allen, J. (2005). The entrepreneur's business model: Toward a unified perspective. *Journal of Business Research*, *58*(6), 726–735. doi:10.1016/j.jbusres.2003.11.001

Nasco, S. A., Boostrom, R. E. Jr, & Coker, K. K. (2010). Virtual commerce. In *Encyclopedia of E-Business Development and Management in the Global Economy*. Hershey, PA: IGI Global. doi:10.4018/978-1-61520-611-7.ch116

O'Reilly, T. (2007). What is web 2.0: Design patterns and business models for the next generation of software. *Communications & Strategies*, *65*, 17–37.

Rappa, M. (2004). *Business Models on the Web*. Retrieved July 25, 2006 from http://digitalenterprise.org/models/models.html

Shafer, S. M., Smith, H. J., & Linder, J. (2005). The power of business models. *Business Horizons*, *48*(3), 199–207. doi:10.1016/j.bushor.2004.10.014

Stewart, D. W., & Zhao, Q. (2000). Internet marketing, business models, and public policy. *Journal of Public Policy & Marketing*, *19*(2), 287–296. doi:10.1509/jppm.19.2.287.17125

Tapscott, D., & Williams, A. D. (2007). *Wikinomics: How Mass Collaboration Changes Everything*. New York: Penguin.

Teece, D. J. (2010). Business models, business strategy and innovation. *Long Range Planning*, *43*(2/3), 172–194. doi:10.1016/j.lrp.2009.07.003

Timmers, P. (1998). Business models for electronic markets. *Electronic Markets*, *8*(2), 3–8. doi:10.1080/10196789800000016

Wernerfelt, B. (1984). A resource-based view of the firm. *Strategic Management Journal*, *5*(2), 170–180. doi:10.1002/smj.4250050207

Zott, C., & Amit, R. (2010). Business model design: An activity system perspective. *Long Range Planning*, *43*(2/3), 216–226. doi:10.1016/j.lrp.2009.07.004

ADDITIONAL READING

Baird, C. H., & Parasnis, G. (2011). From social media to social customer relationship management. *Strategy and Leadership*, *39*(5), 30–37. doi:10.1108/10878571111161507

Cayzer, S. (2004). Semantic blogging and decentralized knowledge management. *Communications of the ACM*, *47*(12), 47–52. doi:10.1145/1035134.1035164

Correa, T., Hinsley, A. W., & De Zuniga, H. G. (2010). Who interacts on the Web?: The intersection of users' personality and social media use. *Computers in Human Behavior*, *26*(2), 247–253. doi:10.1016/j.chb.2009.09.003

Culnan, M. J., McHugh, P. J., & Zubillaga, J. I. (2010). How large U.S. companies can use twitter and other social media to gain business value. *MIS Quarterly Executive*, *9*(4), 243–259.

Drury, G. (2008). Opinion piece: Social media: Should marketers engage and how can it be done effectively? *Journal of Direct. Data and Digital Marketing Practice*, *9*(3), 274–277. doi:10.1057/palgrave.dddmp.4350096

Fillis, I., Johannson, U., & Wagner, B. (2003). A conceptualisation of the opportunities and barriers to e-business developemnt in the smaller firm. *Journal of Small Business and Enterprise Development*, *10*(3), 336–341. doi:10.1108/14626000310489808

Gallaugher, J., & Ransbotham, S. (2010). Social media and customer dialog management at Starbucks. *MIS Quarterly Executive*, *9*(4), 197–212.

Haythornthwaite, C. (2005). Social networks and Internet connectivity effects. *Information Communication and Society*, *8*(2), 125–147. doi:10.1080/13691180500146185

Kietzmann, J. H., Hermkens, K., McCarthy, I. P., & Silvestre, B. S. (2011). Social media? Get serious! Understanding the functional building blocks of social media. *Business Horizons*, *54*(3), 241–251. doi:10.1016/j.bushor.2011.01.005

Lee, S., Hwan, T., & Lee, H. H. (2006). Corporate blogging strategies of the Fortune 500 companies. *Management Decision*, *44*(3), 316–334. doi:10.1108/00251740610656232

Mangold, W. G., & Faulds, D. J. (2009). Social media: The new hybrid element of the promotion mix. *Business Horizons*, *52*(4), 357–365. doi:10.1016/j.bushor.2009.03.002

McAfee, A. P. (2006). Enterprise 2.0: The dawn of emergent collaboration. *Sloan Management Review*, *47*(3), 21–28.

Nambisan, S., & Nambisan, P. (2008). How to profit from a better virtual customer environment, *MIT Sloan Management Review*, 53-61.

Singh, T., Veron-Jackson, L., & Cullinane, J. (2008). Blogging: A new play in your marketing game plan. *Business Horizons*, *51*(4), 281–292. doi:10.1016/j.bushor.2008.02.002

Wagner, C. (2004). Wiki: A technology for conversational knowledge management and group collaboration. CAIS, 13, 265-289.

KEY TERMS AND DEFINITIONS

Business Model: A decision-making framework for developing logically coherent activities to support value creation and formulating strategies to sustain competitive advantages.

Governance: Systems and processes that ensure the overall direction, effectiveness, supervision and accountability of an organization.

Media Sharing: A social media application that enables users to create, store, and share their multimedia files (photos, videos, sounds) with others.

Social Bookmarking: The process of adding, annotating, editing, and sharing bookmarks with others.

Sustainability: The development of the ways a company can gain a sustainable competitive advantage in the market.

Value Proposition: A description of the customer problem and needs, the solution that addresses the problem and needs, and the value of this solution from the customer's perspective.

Compilation of References

Aberdeen Group. (2008). *Social media monitoring and analysis: Generating consumer insights from online conversation.* Retrieved September 1, 2013 from http://robertoigarza.files.wordpress.com/2008/10/rep-social-media-monitoring-and-analysis-aberdeen-group-2008.pdf

Abosag, I., Roper, S., & Hind, D. (2012). Examining the relationship between brand emotion and brand extension among supporters of professional football clubs. *European Journal of Marketing, 46*(9), 1233–1251. doi:10.1108/03090561211247810

Adams, J., Khan, H. T. A., Raeside, R., & White, D. (2007). *Research Methods for Graduate Business and Social Science Students.* New Delhi: Response.

Afuah, A., & Tucci, C. (2003). *Internet Business Models and Strategies.* Boston: McGraw-Hill/Irwin.

Agre, P. E. (2002). Real-Time Politics: The Internet and the Political Process. *The Information Society, 18*(5), 311–331. doi:10.1080/01972240290075174

Aharony. (2009). Librarians and information scientist in the blogosphere: An exploratory analysis. *Library and Information Science Research,* (31), 174-181.

AIIM. (2009). *Collaboration and enterprise 2.0 - Work-meets-play or the future of business?* Retrieved from http://www.aiim.org/research/collaboration-enterprise20-research.aspx

Ajzen, I. (1991). The theory of planned behaviour. *Organizational Behavior and Human Decision Processes, 50*(2), 179–211. doi:10.1016/0749-5978(91)90020-T

Alam, I. (2006). Removing the fuzziness form the fuzzy front-end of service innovations through customer interactions. *Industrial Marketing Management, 35*(4), 468–480. doi:10.1016/j.indmarman.2005.04.004

Alam, I., & Perry, C. (2002). A customer-oriented new service development process. *Journal of Services Marketing, 16*(6), 515–534. doi:10.1108/08876040210443391

Alavi, M., Kayworth, T. R., & Leidner, D. E. (2006). An Empirical Examination of the Influence of Organizational Culture on Knowledge Management Practices. *Journal of Management Information Systems, 22*(3), 191–224. doi:10.2753/MIS0742-1222220307

Alden, D. L., Hoyer, W. D., & Lee, C. (1993). Identifying global and culture-specific dimensions of humor in advertising: A multinational analysis. *Journal of Marketing, 57*(2), 64–75. doi:10.2307/1252027

Alexander, B., & Levine, A. (2008). Web 2.0 storytelling emergence of a new genre. *Educause Review Online, 43*(2).

Algesheimer, R., Dholakia, U. M., & Herrmann, A. (2005). The social influence of brand community: Evidence from European car clubs. *Journal of Marketing, 69*(3), 19–34. doi:10.1509/jmkg.69.3.19.66363

Ali, H. (2011). Exchanging value within individuals' networks: Social support implications for health marketers. *Journal of Marketing Management, 27*(3-4), 316–335. doi:10.1080/0267257X.2011.547075

Alkalay, A., Almond, C., Bloom, J., Chow, A., Peters, F., Rogers, R., & Wyble, C. (2007). *Supporting Innovators and Early Adopters A Technology Adoption Program Cookbook.* IBM International Technical Support Organization. Retrieved September 10, 2013 from http://www.redbooks.ibm.com/redpapers/pdfs/redp4374.pdf

Allee, V. (2000). Reconfiguring the value network. *The Journal of Business Strategy*, *21*(4), 36–39. doi:10.1108/eb040103

Allsop, D. T., Bassett, B. R., & Hoskins, J. A. (2007). Word of mouth research: Principles and applications. *Journal of Advertising Research*, *47*(4), 398–411. doi:10.2501/S0021849907070419

Altman, I., & Taylor, D. (1973). *Social penetration: The development of interpersonal relationships*. New York: Holt.

Amit, R., & Zott, C. (2001). Value creation in e-business. *Strategic Management Journal*, *22*(6/7), 493–520. doi:10.1002/smj.187

Amoroso, D., & Orita, A. (2010). A Study of Anonymity of Social Media Use in Japan and the United States. In *Proceedings of National Conference JASMIN 2010*. Matsuyama, Japan: Japan Society for Management Information.

Amoroso, D., Amoroso, N., & Orita, A. (2011). Social Media Use by American-born versus Japanese-born Respondents: Is There a Difference? In *Proceedings of National Conference JASMIN 2011*. Matsuyama, Japan: Japan Society for Management Information.

Amoroso, D. L., & Ogawa, M. (2013). Comparing Mobile and PC Internet Adoption Factors of Loyalty and Satisfaction with Online Shopping Consumers. *International Journal of E-Business Research*, *9*(2), 24–45. doi:10.4018/jebr.2013040103

Andersen, P. H. (2001). Relationship development and marketing communication: An integrative model. *Journal of Business and Industrial Marketing*, *16*(3), 167–182. doi:10.1108/08858620110389786

Anderson, P. (2007). What is Web 2.0? Ideas, technologies and implications for education. *JISC Technology and Standards Watch*, 1-64.

Anderson, S. (2008). Using social networks to market. *Rough Notes*, *151*(2), 114–115.

Andre, P., Bernstein, M., & Luther, K. (2012). What makes a great tweet? *Harvard Business Review*, *90*(5), 36–37.

Andzulis, J. M., Panagopoulos, N. G., & Rapp, A. (2012). A review of social media and implications for the sales process. *Journal of Personal Selling & Sales Management*, *32*(3), 305–316. doi:10.2753/PSS0885-3134320302

Ang, L. (2011). Is SCRM really a good social media strategy? *Journal of Database Marketing & Customer Strategy Management*, *18*(3), 149–153. doi:10.1057/dbm.2011.22

Annetta, L. (2008). Video games in education: Why they should be used and how they are being used. *Theory into Practice*, *47*(3), 229–239. doi:10.1080/00405840802153940

Antonelli, C. (2003). *The economics of innovation, new technologies, and structural change*. London, UK: Routledge.

Argyris, C. (1977). Double loop learning in organizations. *Harvard Business Review*, *55*(5), 115–125.

Armelini, G., & Villanueva, J. (2011). The power of word of mouth: Adding social media to the marketing mix. *IESEinsight*, *9*, 29–36.

Armstrong, C. L., & Gao, F. (2010). Now tweet this: How news organizations use Twitter. *Electronic News*, *4*(4), 218–235. doi:10.1177/1931243110389457

Arora, R. (2002). Implementing KM – A balanced scorecard approach. *Journal of Knowledge Management*, *6*(3), 240–249. doi:10.1108/13673270210434340

Arrigo, E. (2009). Market-driven management, global competition and corporate responsibility. *Symphonya: Emerging Issues in Management*, *1*, 51–67. doi: doi:10.4468/2009.1.06arrigo

Arrigo, E. (2012). Alliances, open innovation and outside-in management. *Symphonya: Emerging Issues in Management*, *2*, 53–65. doi: doi:10.4468/2012.2.05arrigo

Ashworth, C. J. (2013). *Empowering small firms: Value and impact of social media communication innovation in pure-play SME retail marketing*. Paper presented at the EURAM Conference 2013. Istanbul, Turkey.

Ashworth, C. J. (2012). Marketing and organisational development in e-SMEs: Understanding survival and sustainability in growth-oriented and comfort-zone pure-play enterprises in the fashion retail industry. *The International Entrepreneurship and Management Journal, 8*(2), 165–201. doi:10.1007/s11365-011-0171-6

Atkinson, R., & Flint, J. (2001). Accessing hidden and hard-to-reach populations: Snowball research strategies. *Social Research Update, 33*.

Aula, P. (2010). Social media, reputation risk and ambient publicity management. *Strategy and Leadership, 38*(6), 43–49. doi:10.1108/10878571011088069

Austin, M. J., Ciaassen, J., Vu, C., & Mizrahi, P. (2008). Knowledge management: Implications for human service organizations. *Journal of Evidence-Based Social Work, 5*(1-2), 361–389. doi:10.1300/J394v05n01_13 PMID:19064454

Avtgis, T. A., West, D. V., & Anderson, T. L. (1998). Relationship stages: An inductive analysis identifying cognitive affective, and behavioral dimensions of Knapp's relational stages model. *Communication Research Reports, 15*(3), 280–287. doi:10.1080/08824099809362124

Bagozzi, R. P. (1974). Marketing as an organized behavioral system of exchange. *Journal of Marketing, 38*(4), 77–81. doi:10.2307/1250397

Bagozzi, R. P. (1994). Interactions in small groups: The social relations model. In J. N. Sheth, & A. Parvatiyar (Eds.), *Relationship marketing: Theory, methods, and applications*. Atlanta: Emory University, Center for Relationship Marketing.

Baird, C., & Parasnis, G. (2011). From social media to social customer relationship management. *Strategy and Leadership, 39*(5), 30–37. doi:10.1108/10878571111161507

Baird, D. E., & Fisher, M. (2005). Neomillennial User Experience Design Strategies: Utilizing Social Networking Media To Support Always on Learning Styles. *Journal of Educational Technology Systems, 34*(1), 5–32. doi:10.2190/6WMW-47L0-M81Q-12G1

Baker, E. W., Al-Gahtani, S. S., & Hubona, G. S. (2010). Cultural impacts on acceptance and adoption of information technology in a developing Country. *Journal of Global Information Management, 18*(3), 35–58. doi:10.4018/jgim.2010070102

Baker, W. E., & Sinkula, J. M. (1999). Learning orientation, market orientation, and innovation: Integrating and extending models of organizational performance. *Journal of Market-Focused Management, 4*(4), 295–308. doi:10.1023/A:1009830402395

Baker, W. E., & Sinkula, J. M. (2002). Market orientation, learning orientation and product innovation: Delving into the organization's black box. *Journal of Market-Focused Management, 5*(1), 5–23. doi:10.1023/A:1012543911149

Baldwin, C., Hienerth, C., & von Hippel, E. (2006). How user innovations become commercial products: A theoretical investigation and case study. *Research Policy, 35*(9), 1291–1313. doi:10.1016/j.respol.2006.04.012

Ballagas, R., Rohs, M., Sheridan, J. G., & Borchers, J. (2004). *BYOD: Bring Your Own Device*. Paper presented at the UbiComp 2004 Workshop, Sixth International Conference on Ubiquitous Computing. Nottingham, UK.

Ballantine, P. W., & Stephenson, R. J. (2011). Help me, I'm fat! Social support in online weight loss networks. *Journal of Consumer Behaviour, 10*(6), 332–337. doi:10.1002/cb.374

Bampo, M., Ewing, M. T., Mather, D. R., Stewart, D., & Wallace, M. (2008). The effects of the social structure of digital networks on viral marketing performance. *Information Systems Research, 19*(3), 273–290. doi:10.1287/isre.1070.0152

Banbersta, M. (2010, June). The success factors of the Social Network Sites Twitter. *Applied Sciences*.

Barney, J. B. (1986). Strategic factor markets: Expectations, luck, and business strategy. *Management Science, 32*(10), 1231–1241. doi:10.1287/mnsc.32.10.1231

Barney, J. B. (1991). Firm resources and sustained competitive advantage. *Journal of Management, 17*(1), 99–120. doi:10.1177/014920639101700108

Baskerville, R. &Wood-Harper, A.T. (1996). *A taxonomy of action research methods* (Working paper). Institute of Informatics and Management Accounting, Copenhagen Business School.

Bass, F. M. (1969). A new product growth model for consumer durables. *Management Science*, *15*(5), 215–227. doi:10.1287/mnsc.15.5.215

Bastone, J. (2010, August 17). Evaluate social media by listening, leveraging and engaging. *Direct: Magazine of Direct Marketing*. Retrieved February 12, 2014 from http://www.chiefmarketer.com/web-marketing/evaluate-social-media-by-listening-leveraging-and-engaging-17082010

Bateman, C. R., Valentine, S., & Rittenburg, T. (2013). Ethical decision making in a peer-to-peer file sharing situation: The role of moral absolutes and social consensus. *Journal of Business Ethics*, *115*(2), 229–240. doi:10.1007/s10551-012-1388-1

Batra, R., & Ray, M. L. (1986). Affective responses mediating acceptance of advertising. *The Journal of Consumer Research*, *13*(2), 234–249. doi:10.1086/209063

Bauer, H. H., Grether, M., & Leach, M. (2002). Building customer relations over the internet. *Industrial Marketing Management Journal*, *31*(2), 155–163. doi:10.1016/S0019-8501(01)00186-9

Bean, J. (2010). BP: Delivering on the brand promise (?). *Slideshare.net*. Retrieved May 3, 2011, from http://www.slideshare.net/JustinCBean/bp-a-marketing-case-study

Beatty, R. C., Shim, J. P., & Jones, M. C. (2001). Factors influencing corporate web site adoption: A time-based assessment. *Information & Management*, *38*(6), 337–354. doi:10.1016/S0378-7206(00)00064-1

Beccerra-Fernandez, I., & Sabherwal, R. (2010). *Knowledge management: Systems and processes*. London, UK: M. E. Sharpe.

Beebe, S. A., Beebe, S. J., & Richmond, M. V. (2002). *Interpersonal communication: Relating to others* (3rd ed.). Boston, MA: Allyn & Bacon.

Beer, D. (2008). Social network(ing) sites…revisiting the story so far: A response to Danah Boyd & Nicole Ellison. *Journal of Computer-Mediated Communication*, *13*(2), 516–529. doi:10.1111/j.1083-6101.2008.00408.x

Beinggirl - Proctor and Gamble. (2011). *Beinggirl.co.in*. Retrieved May 3, 2011, from http://www.beinggirl.co.in/main/home.php

Belch, G. E., & Belch, M. A. (2007). *Advertising and promotion: An integrated marketing communications perspective* (7th ed.). Boston, MA: McGraw-Hill Irwin.

Bell, A. (2009). *Exploring web 2.0: Second generation interactive tools -blogs, podcasts, wikis, networking, virtual worlds, and more*. Washington, DC: Katy Crossing Press.

Bello, D. C., Etzel, M. J., & Pits, R. E. (1983). The communication effects of controversial sexual content in television programs and commercials. *Journal of Advertising*, *3*(12), 32–42. doi:10.1080/00913367.1983.10672846

Bennett, J., Owers, M., Pitt, M., & Tucker, M. (2010). Workplace impact of social networking. *Property Management*, *28*(3), 138–148. doi:10.1108/02637471011051282

Bernoff, J., & Li, C. (2008). Harnessing the power of the oh-so-social-web. *MIT Sloan Management Review*, *49*(3), 36–42.

Berry, L. L. (1983). Relationship marketing. In L. L. Berry, G. L. Shostack, & G. Upah (Eds.), *Emerging perspective on services marketing* (pp. 25–28). Chicago: American Marketing Association.

Berthon, P. R., Pitt, L. F., Plangger, K., & Shapiro, D. (2012). Marketing meets Web 2.0, social media, and creative consumers: Implications for international marketing strategy. *Business Horizons*, *55*(3), 261–271. doi:10.1016/j.bushor.2012.01.007

Bertoni, M., & Chirumalla, K. (2011). Leveraging Web 2.0 in new product development: Lessons learned from a cross-company study. *Journal of Universal Computer Science*, *17*(4), 548–564.

Best, R. J. (2009). *Market-based management* (5th ed.). London, UK: Prentice Hall.

Bettiol, M., Di Maria, E., & Grandinetti, R. (2012). Codification and creativity: Knowledge management strategies in KIBS. *Journal of Knowledge Management*, *16*(4), 550–562. doi:10.1108/13673271211246130

Bhattacharjee, S., Gopal, R. D., & Sanders, G. L. (2003). Digital music and online sharing: Software piracy 2.0. *Communications of the ACM*, *46*(7), 107–111. doi:10.1145/792704.792707

Bidmeshgipour, M., Ismail, W. K. W., & Omar, R. (2012). Knowledge management and organizational innovativeness in Iranian banking industry. *Knowledge Management and E-Learning*, *4*(4), 481–499.

Bijmolt, T. H. A., Leeflang, P. S. H., Block, F., Eisenbeiss, M., Hardie, B. G. S., Lemmens, A., & Saffert, P. (2010). Analytics for customer engagement. *Journal of Service Research*, *13*(3), 341–356. doi:10.1177/1094670510375603

Binhammer, R. (2009). How Dell took social media mainstream. Smartblogs.com/socialmedia. Retrieved May 3, 2011, from http://smartblogs.com/socialmedia/2009/10/02/how-dell-took-social-media-mainstream/

Birasnav, M., & Rangnekar, S. (2010). Knowledge management structure and human capital development in Indian manufacturing industries. *Business Process Management Journal*, *16*(1), 57–75. doi:10.1108/14637151011017949

Bitner, M., Ostrom, A., Meuter, M., & Clancy, A. (2002). Implementing successful self-service technologies. *Academy of Management Journal*, *16*(4).

Blanchard, O. (2011). *Social Media ROI: Managing and Measuring Social Media Efforts in Your Organization*. Boston, MA: Pearson Education, Inc.

Blau, P. M. (1964). *Exchange and power in social life*. New York: John Wiley.

Bock, G.-O., Zmud, R. W., Kim, Y.-G., & Lee, J.-N. (2005). Behavioral intention formation in knowledge sharing: Examining the roles of extrinsic motivators, social-psychological factors and organizational climate. *Management Information Systems (MIS). Quarterly*, *29*(1), 87–111.

Bonabeau, E. (2009). Decisions 2.0.: The power of collective intelligence. *MIT Sloan Management Review*, *50*(2), 45–52.

Booth, N., & Matic, J. A. (2011). Mapping and leveraging influencers in social media to shape corporate brand perceptions. *Corporate Communications: An International Journal*, *16*(3), 184–191. doi:10.1108/13563281111156853

Borgatti, S. P., & Halgin, D. S. (2011). On network theory. *Journal of Organization Science*, *22*, 1157–1167.

Borroff, R. (2000). Viral Markcting. *Precision Marketing*, *20*, 12.

Boughzala, I. (2007). *Ingénierie de la collaboration: Théories, technologies et pratiques*. Paris, France: Hermès - Lavoisier.

Boughzala, I. (2010). *Mise en perspective de l'e-collaboration comme outil de transformation de l'organisation*. HDR Sciences de Gestion, Université de Nantes.

Boughzala, I. (2011). Collaboration 2.0 through the new organization transformation. In *Knowledge Management 2.0: Organizational Models and Enterprise Strategies*. Hershey, PA: IGI Global. doi:10.4018/978-1-61350-195-5.ch001

Boughzala, I. (2012). *Collaboration engineering: A contribution to its foundations through the 2.0 era*. Saarbrücken, Germany: Lambert Academic Publishing.

Boughzala, I., & Briggs, R. O. (2012). A value frequency model of knowledge sharing: An exploratory study on knowledge sharability in cross-organizational collaboration. *Electronic Markets*, *22*(1), 9–19. doi:10.1007/s12525-011-0080-0

Boughzala, I., & Limayem, M. (2010). The new generation of Knowledge Management for the Web 2.0 Age: KM 2.0. In *Encyclopedia of E-Business Development and Management in the Digital Economy*. Hershey, PA: IGI Global. doi:10.4018/978-1-61520-611-7.ch122

Boulding, W., Staelin, R., Ehret, M., & Johnston, W. J. (2005). A customer relationship management roadmap: What is known, potential pitfalls, and where to go. *Journal of Marketing*, *69*(4), 155–166. doi:10.1509/jmkg.2005.69.4.155

Bowers-Brown, J., & Gunter, B. (2002). Political parties' use of the Web during the 2001 general election. *Aslib Proceedings*, *54*(3), 166–176. doi:10.1108/00012530210441719

Boyd, D. M., & Ellison, N. B. (2008). Social network sites: Definition, history and scholarship. *Journal of Computer-Mediated Communication*, *13*(2), 210–230.

Brabham, D. C. (2010, November). The effectiveness of crowdsourcing public participation in a planning context. *SSRN Working Paper Series*.

Bresman, H., Birkenshaw, J., & Nobel, R. (1999). Knowledge transfer in international acquisitions. *Journal of International Business Studies*, *30*(3), 439–462. doi:10.1057/palgrave.jibs.8490078

Briggs, R. O., de Vreede, G. J., & Nunamaker, J. F. Jr. (2003). Collaboration Engineering with ThinkLets to Pursue Sustained Success with Group Support Systems. *Journal of Management Information Systems*, *19*(4), 31–64.

Brindley, L. (2006). Re-defining the library. *Library Hi Tech. Bradford*, *24*(4), 484–495. doi:10.1108/07378830610715356

Broadbridge, A., Maxwell, G., & Ogden, S. (2009). Selling Retailing to Generation Y Graduates: Recruitment Challenges and Opportunities. *International Review of Retail, Distribution and Consumer Research*, *19*(4), 405–420. doi:10.1080/09593960903331394

Brodie, R. J., Hollebeek, L. D., Juric, B., & Ilic, A. (2011). Customer engagement: Conceptual domain, fundamental propositions, and implications for research. *Journal of Service Research*, *14*(3), 252–271. doi:10.1177/1094670511411703

Brogan, C., & Bastone, J. (2014). Acting on customer intelligence from social media. *AMA Marketing Effectiveness Online Seminar Series*. Retrieved February 12, 2014 from https://www.sas.com/offices/NA/canada/en/resources/whitepaper/wp_21122.pdf

Brogan, C. (2010). Social media 101. In *Media*. Hoboken, NJ: John Wiley & Sons.

Brondoni, S. M. (2009). Market-driven management, competitive customer value and global networks. *Symphonya: Emerging Issues in Management*, *1*, 8–25. doi: doi:10.4468/2009.1.02brondoni

Brondoni, S. M. (Ed.). (2012). *Market-driven management and corporate growth*. Turin, Italy: Giappichelli.

Brown, E. (2010). *Working the crowd: Social media marketing for business*. Swindon, UK: British Informatics Society Limited.

Brown, J. J., & Reingen, P. H. (1987). Social ties and word-of-mouth referral behavior. *The Journal of Consumer Research*, *14*(3), 350–362. doi:10.1086/209118

Brown, J. S., & Duguid, P. (1992). Organizational learning and communities of practice: Toward a unified view of working, learning and innovation. *Organization Science*, *2*(1), 40–57. doi:10.1287/orsc.2.1.40

Brown, J. S., & Duguid, P. (2001). Knowledge and organization: A social-practice perspective. *Organization Science*, *12*(2), 198–213. doi:10.1287/orsc.12.2.198.10116

Brown, M. R., Bhadury, R. K., & Pope, N. K. L. (2010). The impact of comedic violence on viral advertising effectiveness. *Journal of Advertising*, *39*(1), 49–65. doi:10.2753/JOA0091-3367390104

Brown, R., Hayton, J., Sandy, C., & Brown, P. (1977). *Small businesses - Strategy for survival*. London: Wilton House Publications.

Brown, S., Kozinets, R. V., & Sherry, J. F. Jr. (2003). Teaching old brands new tricks: Retro branding and the revival of brand meaning. *Journal of Marketing*, *67*(3), 19–33. doi:10.1509/jmkg.67.3.19.18657

Brown, T. (2008). Design thinking. *Harvard Business Review*, *86*, 84–92. PMID:18605031

Bruhn, M., Schoenmueller, V., & Schafer, D. B. (2012). Are social media replacing traditional media in terms of brand equity creation? *Management Research Review*, *35*(9), 770–790. doi:10.1108/01409171211255948

Bryman, A., & Bell, E. (2007). *Business research methods*. Oxford, UK: Oxford University Press.

Bughin, J. R., Chui, M., & Johnson, B. (2008). The next step in open innovation. *The McKinsey Quarterly*, (4): 112–122.

Bühler, A., & Nufer, G. (2010). *Relationship marketing in sports*. Oxford, UK: Butterworth-Heinemann.

Burson-Marsteller. (2010). Burson-Marsteller 2010 Fortune Global 100 Social Media Study. *The Burson-Marsteller Blog*. Retrieved April 7, 2011, from http://www.burson-marsteller.com/Innovation_and_insights/blogs_and_podcasts/BM_Blog/Lists/Posts/Post.aspx?ID=160

Burson-Marsteller. (2012). Burson-Marsteller 2011 Fortune Global 100 Social Media Study - Update. *The Burson-Marsteller Blog*. Retrieved July 4, 2012, from http://www.burson-marsteller.com/Innovation_and_insights/blogs_and_podcasts/BM_Blog/default.aspx

Burt, R. S. (1973). *Structural holes: The social structure of competition*. Cambridge, MA: Harvard University Press.

Burt, R. S., Kilduff, M., & Tasselli, S. (2013). Social network analysis: Foundations and frontiers on advantage. *Annual Review of Psychology*, *64*(1), 527–547. doi:10.1146/annurev-psych-113011-143828

Butler, P., & Harris, P. (2009). Considerations on the evolution of political marketing theory. *Marketing Theory*, *9*(2), 149–164. doi:10.1177/1470593109103022

Cahill, D. (1995). The managerial implications of the learning organization: A new tool for internal marketing. *Journal of Services Marketing*, *9*(4), 43–51. doi:10.1108/08876049510094513

Campbell, C., Pitt, L. F., Parent, M., & Berthon, P. R. (2011). Understanding consumer conversations around ads in a web 2.0 world. *Journal of Advertising*, *40*(1), 87–102. doi:10.2753/JOA0091-3367400106

Carr, P. L. (2009). From innovation to transformation: A review of the 2006-7 serials literature. *Library Resources & Technical Services*, *53*(1), 3–15. doi:10.5860/lrts.53n1.3

Cash, J. J. I., Earl, M. J., & Morison, R. (2008). Teaming up to crack innovation & enterprise integration. *Harvard Business Review*, *86*, 90–100. PMID:19009723

Cassell, C., Buehring, A., Symon, G., & Johnson, P. (2006). Qualitative methods in management research: An introduction to the themed issue. *Management Decision*, *44*(2), 161–166. doi:10.1108/00251740610650166

Castronovo, C., & Huang, L. (2012). Social media in an alternative marketing communication model. *Journal of Marketing Development and Competitiveness*, *6*(1), 117–134.

Centeno, C., Wainer, L., Misuraca, G., Punie, Y., & Broster, D. (2009). *Key findings, future prospects, and policy challenges. Joint Research Centre Institute for Prospective Technological Studies*. Luxembourg: Office for Official Publications for the European Communities.

Chadha, S. K., & Kapoor, D. (2010). A study on knowledge management practices of auto component manufacturing companies in Ludhiana City. *The IUP Journal of Knowledge Management*, *8*(1-2), 68–76.

Chadwick, S., & Beech, J. (2007). Introduction: The marketing of sport. In *The marketing of sport* (pp. 3–22). Harlow, UK: Pearson Education.

Chadwick, S., Garford, W., Guimaraes, G., & O'Reilly, D. (2008). The formation, organisation and management of MyFootballClub: Implications for marketing practice. *Journal of Direct. Data and Digital Marketing Practice*, *10*(2), 150–160. doi:10.1057/dddmp.2008.29

Chaffrey, D., Ellis-Chadwick, F., Mayer, R., & Johnston, K. (2009). *Internet marketing: Strategy, implementation and practice* (4th ed.). Harlow, UK: Prentice Hall.

Chaher, S., & Spellman, J. D. (2013). *Corporate governance and social media: A brave new world for board directors*. The Global Corporate Governance Forum. Retrieved on March 5, 2014 from http://www.ifc.org/wps/wcm/connect/topics_ext_content/ifc_external_corporate_site/global+corporate+governance+forum/publications/private+sector+opinion/pso+27+cg+and+social+and+media

Chai, S., Das, S., & Rao, H. R. (2011). Factors affecting bloggers' knowledge sharing: An investigation across gender. *Journal of Management Information Systems*, *28*(3), 309–342. doi:10.2753/MIS0742-1222280309

Chakravarthy, B., McEvily, S., Doz, Y., & Rau, D. (2003). Knowledge management and competitive advantage. In M. Easterby-Smith, & M. Lyles (Eds.), *The Blackwell handbook of organizational learning and knowledge management* (pp. 305–323). Malden, MA: Blackwell.

Chaney, P. (2009). *The Digital Handshake: Seven Proven Strategies to Grow Your Business Using Social Media*. Hoboken, NJ: John Wiley & Sons Inc.

Chan, Y. Y. Y., & Ngai, E. W. T. (2011). Conceptualising electronic word-of-mouth activity: An input-process-output perspective. *Marketing Intelligence & Planning*, *29*(5), 488–516. doi:10.1108/02634501111153692

Chao, C., Corus, C., & Li, T. (2012). Balancing traditional media and online advertising strategy. *International Journal of Business, Marketing, &. Decision Sciences, 5*(1), 12–24.

Chapman, C. (2011). How to use social networking to build your own network. *British Journal of Administrative Management, 73*, 14–15.

Chararbaghi, K., Fendt, C., & Willis, R. (2003). Meaning, legitimacy and impact of business models in fast-moving environments. *Management Decision, 41*(4), 372–382. doi:10.1108/00251740310468013

Chattopadhyay, A., & Basu, K. (1990). Humor in advertising: The moderating role of prior brand evaluation. *JMR, Journal of Marketing Research, 27*(4), 466–476. doi:10.2307/3172631

Chen, K., & Plott, C. (2002). *Information aggregation mechanisms: Concept, design and implementation for a sales forecasting problem* (Working Paper 1131). California Institute of Technology, Division of the Humanities and Social Sciences.

Chen, S. (2009). Corporate Responsibilities in Internet-Enabled Social Networks. *Journal of Business Ethics, 90*(S4), 523–536. doi:10.1007/s10551-010-0604-0

Chen, Y., & Xie, J. (2008). Online consumer review: Word-of-mouth as a new element of marketing communication mix. *Management Science, 54*(3), 721–739. doi:10.1287/mnsc.1070.0810

Chesbrough, H. W. (2003). *Open innovation: The new imperative for creating and profiting from technology*. Harvard Business School Press.

Chesbrough, H. W., & Appleyard, M. M. (2007). Open innovation and strategy. *California Management Review, 50*(1), 57–77. doi:10.2307/41166416

Chesbrough, H., & Rosenbloom, R. S. (2002). The role of the business model in capturing value from innovation: Evidence from Xerox Corporation's technology spin-off companies. *Industrial and Corporate Change, 11*(3), 529–555. doi:10.1093/icc/11.3.529

Chia, J. (2005). *Measuring the immeasurable*. Retrieved from http://praxis.massey.ac.nz/fileadmin/Praxis/Files/Journal_Files/Evaluation_Issue/CHIA_ARTICLE.pdf#search=%22%20joy%20chia%20measuring%20the%20immeasurable%22

Chiu, H.-C., Hsieh, Y.-C., Kao, Y.-H., & Lee, M. (2007). The determinants of email receivers' disseminating behaviors on the internet. *Journal of Advertising Research, 47*(4), 524–534. doi:10.2501/S0021849907070547

Choe, J. M. (2004). The consideration of cultural differences in the design of information systems. *Information & Management, 41*(5), 669–688. doi:10.1016/j.im.2003.08.003

Chong, S. C., Salleh, K., Ahmad, S. N. S., & Sharifuddin, S. I. (2011). Knowledge management implementation in a public sector accounting organization: An empirical investigation. *Journal of Knowledge Management, 15*(3), 497–512. doi:10.1108/13673271111137457

Christodoulides, G. (2009). Branding in the post-internet era. *Marketing Theory, 9*(1), 141–144. doi:10.1177/1470593108100071

Christodoulides, G., Jevons, C., & Bonhomme, J. (2012). Memo to marketers: Quantitative evidence for change. How user-generated content really affects brands. *Journal of Advertising Research, 52*(1), 53–64. doi:10.2501/JAR-52-1-053-064

Christopher, M., Payne, A., & Ballantyne, D. (2002). *Relationship marketing: Creating stakeholder value*. Oxford, UK: Butterworth-Heinemann.

Christopher, M., Payne, A., Peck, H., & Clark, M. (1998). *Relationship marketing for competitive advantage: Winning and keeping customers*. Oxford, UK: Elsevier Science Ltd.

Chu, A., & Chu, R. (2011). The intranet's role in newcomer socialization in the hotel industry in Taiwan – Technology acceptance model analysis. *International Journal of Human Resource Management, 22*(5), 1163–1179. doi:10.1080/09585192.2011.556795

Chua, A. (2002). The influence of social interaction on knowledge creation. *Journal of Intellectual Capital, 3*(4), 375–392. doi:10.1108/14691930210448297

Chua, A. Y. K. (2011). How Web 2.0 supports customer relationship management in Amazon. *International Journal of Electronic Customer Relationship Management, 5*(3-4), 288–304. doi:10.1504/IJECRM.2011.044693

Chua, A. Y. K., & Banerjee, S. (2013). Customer knowledge management via social media: The case of Starbucks. *Journal of Knowledge Management, 17*(2), 237–249. doi:10.1108/13673271311315196

Chui, M., Miller, A., & Roberts, P. R. (2009). Six ways to make Web 2.0. work. *The McKinsey Quarterly, 1*, 2–7.

Churchill, N. C., & Lewis, V. L. (1983, May-June). The five stages of small business growth. *Harvard Business Review*, 30–50.

Clark, L., & Roberts, S. (2010). Employer's Use of Social Networking Sites: A Socially Irresponsible Practice. *Journal of Business Ethics, 95*(4), 507–525. doi:10.1007/s10551-010-0436-y

Clawson, T. (2012, July 11). Email's social evolution. *Marketing*, S8-S9.

Cline, T. W., Altsech, M. B., & Kellaris, J. J. (2003). When does humor enhance or inhibit ad responses? The moderating role of the need for humor. *Journal of Advertising, 32*(3), 31–45. doi:10.1080/00913367.2003.10639134

Close, A. G. (2012). *Online consumer behaviour: Theory and research in social media, advertising, and e-tail*. New York: Routledge.

Coleman, D., & Levine, S. (2008). *Collaboration 2.0: Technology and best practices for successful collaboration in a web 2.0 world*. Happy About.

Colliander, J., & Wien, A. H. (2013). Trash talk rebuffed: consumers' defense of companies criticized in online communities. *European Journal of Marketing, 47*(10), 1733–1757. doi:10.1108/EJM-04-2011-0191

Constant, D., Keisler, S., & Sproull, L. (1994). What's mine is ours, or is it? A study of attitudes about information sharing. *Information Systems Research (Informs), 5*(4), 400–421. doi:10.1287/isre.5.4.400

Constant, D., Sproull, L., & Kiesler, S. (1996). The kindness of strangers: The usefulness of electronic weak ties for technical advice. *Organization Science, 7*(2), 119–135. doi:10.1287/orsc.7.2.119

Constantinides, E. (2004). Influencing the online consumer's behaviour: The web experience. *Journal of Internet Research, 14*(2), 111–126. doi:10.1108/10662240410530835

Constantinides, E., & Fountain, S. J. (2008). Web 2.0: Conceptual foundations and marketing issues. *Journal of Direct. Data and Digital Marketing Practice, 9*(3), 231–244. doi:10.1057/palgrave.dddmp.4350098

Consulting, F. (2006). *Is Europe Ready for the Millennials? Innovate to meet the needs of the emerging generation*. Retrieved from http://www.ffpress.net/Kunden/XER/Downloads/XER87000/XER87000.pdf

Conway, M., & Dorner, D. (2004). An evaluation of New Zealand political party websites. *Information Research, 9*(4).

Cooke, M., & Buckley, N. (2008). Web 2. 0, social networks and the future of market research. *International Journal of Market Research, 50*(2), 267–293.

Corfield, A., Paton, R., & Little, S. (2013). Does knowledge management work in NGOs? A longitudinal study. *International Journal of Public Administration, 36*(3), 179–188. doi:10.1080/01900692.2012.749281

Cornforth, C. (2003). *The governance of public and non-profit organisations: What do boards do?* Oxon, UK: Routledge Taylor & Francis Group. doi:10.4324/9780203167571

Corporation, I. B. M. (2012). *Leading through connections: Insights from the global chief executive officer study*. Retrieved on March 5, 2014 from http://www-935.ibm.com/services/us/en/c-suite/ceostudy2012/

Coulter, K. S., & Roggeveen, A. (2012). Like it or not: Consumer responses to word-of-mouth communications in online social networks. *Management Research Review, 35*(9), 878–899. doi:10.1108/01409171211256587

Coursaris, C., & Papagiannidis, S. (2009). Online political marketing in Greece: An evaluation of the 2007 national elections and two case studies. *Computers in Human Behavior, 25*(4), 853–861. doi:10.1016/j.chb.2008.10.002

Cramton, C. D. (2001). The mutual knowledge problem and its consequences for dispersed collaboration. *Organization Science, 12*(3), 346–371. doi:10.1287/orsc.12.3.346.10098

Creswell, J. W., & Miller, D. L. (2000). Determining validity in qualitative inquiry. *Theory into Practice*, *39*(3), 124–130. doi:10.1207/s15430421tip3903_2

Cropanzano, R., & Mitchell, M. S. (2005). Social exchange theory: An interdisciplinary review. *Journal of Management*, *31*(6), 874–900. doi:10.1177/0149206305279602

Cross, R., & Sproull, L. (2004). More Than an Answer: Information Relationships for Actionable Knowledge. *Organization Science*, *15*(4), 446–462. doi:10.1287/orsc.1040.0075

Crumpacker, M., & Crumpacker, J. (2007). Succession planning and generational stereotypes: Should HR consider age-based values and attitudes a relevant factor or a passing fad? *Public Personnel Management*, *36*(4), 349–369.

Cruz, D., & Fill, C. (2008). Evaluating viral marketing: Isolating the key criteria. *Marketing Intelligence & Planning*, *26*(7), 743–758. doi:10.1108/02634500810916690

Cummings, J. (2003). *Knowledge sharing: A review of the literature*. Washington, DC: World Bank Operations Evaluation Department. Retrieved from http://ieg.worldbankgroup.org/Data/reports/knowledge_eval_literature_review.pdf

Curran, J., & Blackburn, R. A. (2001). *Researching the Small Enterprise*. London: Sage Publications.

Curran, K., O'Hara, K., & O'Brien, S. (2011). The role of Twitter in the world of business. *International Journal of Business Data Communications and Networking*, *7*(3), 1–15. doi:10.4018/jbdcn.2011070101

Cyert, R. M., & Williams, J. R. (1993). Organizations, decision making and strategy: Overview and comment. *Strategic Management Journal*, *14*(S2), 5–10. doi:10.1002/smj.4250141003

Czepiel, J. A. (1990). Service encounters and service relationships: Implications for research. *Journal of Business Research*, *20*(1), 13–21. doi:10.1016/0148-2963(90)90038-F

Dadashzadeh, M. (2010). Social Media In Government : From e-Govemment To eGovemance. *Journal of Business and Economic Research*, *8*(11), 81–87.

Dahl, D. W., Sengupta, J., & Vohs, K. D. (2009). Sex in advertising: Gender differences and the role of relationship commitment. *The Journal of Consumer Research*, *36*(2), 215–231. doi:10.1086/597158

Dai, Y., Kakkonen, T., & Sutinen, E. (2011). MinEdec: A decision-support model that combines text-mining technologies with two competitive intelligence analysis methods. *International Journal of Computer Information Systems and Industrial Management Applications*, *3*, 165–173.

Danneels, E. (2008). Organizational antecedents of second-order competences. *Strategic Management Journal*, *29*(5), 519–543. doi:10.1002/smj.684

Das, B., & Sahoo, J. (2011). Social Networking Sites – A Critical Analysis of Its Impact on Personal and Social Life. *International Journal of Business and Social Science*, *2*(14), 222–228.

Datta, P. R., Chowdhury, D. N., & Chakraborty, B. R. (2005). Viral marketing: New form of word-of-mouth through internet. *Business Review (Federal Reserve Bank of Philadelphia)*, *3*(2), 69–75.

Daugherty, T., Eastin, M., & Bright, L. (2008). Exploring consumer motivations for creating user-generated content. *Journal of Interactive Advertising*, *8*(2), 1–24. doi:10.1080/15252019.2008.10722139

Davenport, T. (2007). Why enterprise 2.0 won't transform organizations. *Harvard Business Review.* Retrieved January 2009, from http://discussionleader.hbsp.com/davenport/2007/03/why_enterprise_20_wont_transfo.html

Davenport, T. H., De Long, D. W., & Beers, M. C. (1998). Successful knowledge management projects. *Sloan Management Review*, *39*(2), 43–57.

Davenport, T. H., & Prusak, L. (1998). *Working knowledge: How organizations manage what they know*. Harvard Business School Press.

Davis, F. (1989). Perceived usefulness, perceived ease of use, and user acceptance of information technology. *Management Information Systems Quarterly*, *13*(3), 319–340. doi:10.2307/249008

Davis, F., & Venkatesh, V. (2004). Toward Pre-prototype User Acceptance Testing of New Information Systems: Implications for Software Project Management. *IEEE Transactions on Engineering Management*, *51*(1), 31–46. doi:10.1109/TEM.2003.822468

Davison, H., Maraist, C., & Bing, M. (2011). Friend or Foe? The Promise and Pitfalls of Using Social Networking Sites for HR Decisions. *Journal of Business and Psychology*, *26*(2), 153–159. doi:10.1007/s10869-011-9215-8

Day, G. S. (1990). *The market-driven organization*. New York, NY: Free Press.

Day, G. S. (1994). The capabilities of market-driven organizations. *Journal of Marketing*, *58*(4), 37–52. doi:10.2307/1251915

Day, G. S. (1999, Fall). Creating a market-driven organization. *Sloan Management Review*, 11–22.

Day, G. S. (2011). Closing the marketing capabilities gap. *Journal of Marketing*, *75*(4), 183–195. doi:10.1509/jmkg.75.4.183

De Burgh, H., Carson, D., & Gilmore, A. (2000). SME marketing management competencies. *International Business Review*, *9*(3), 363–382. doi:10.1016/S0969-5931(00)00006-8

De Bussy, N., Ewing, M., & Pitt, L. (2004). Stakeholder theory and internal marketing communications: A framework for analyzing the influence of new media. *Journal of Marketing Communications*, *9*(3), 147–161. doi:10.1080/1352726032000129890

de Matos, C. A., & Rossi, C. A. V. (2008). Word-of-mouth communications in marketing: A meta-analytic review of the antecedents and moderators. *Journal of the Academy of Marketing Science*, *36*(4), 578–596. doi:10.1007/s11747-008-0121-1

de Vreede, G. J., Briggs, R., & Massey, A. (2009). Collaboration Engineering: Foundations and Opportunities. *Journal of the Association for Information Systems*, *10*(3), 121–137.

Deal, J., Altman, J., David, G., & Rogelberg, S. (2010). Millennials at work: What we know and what we need to do (if anything). *Journal of Business and Psychology*, *25*(2), 191–199. doi:10.1007/s10869-010-9177-2

Dean, D., & Croft, R. (2001). Friends and relations: Long-term approaches to political campaigning. *European Journal of Marketing*, *35*(11/12), 1197–1216. doi:10.1108/EUM0000000006482

Deephouse, D. L. (2000). Media Reputation as a Strategic Resource: An Integration of Mass Communication and Resource-Based Theories. *Journal of Management*, *26*(6), 1091–1112. doi:10.1177/014920630002600602

Deloitte Core Beliefs and Culture Survey. (2013). Retrieved from http://www.deloitte.com/assets/Dcom-UnitedStates/Local%20Assets/Documents/us_leadership_2013corebeliefs&culturesurvey_051613.pdf

Deloitte. (2012). *Fan power: Football money league*. Sports Business Group.

DeLone, W. H., & MacLean, E. R. (1992). Information systems success: The quest for the dependent variable. *Information Systems Research*, *3*(1), 60–95. doi:10.1287/isre.3.1.60

DeLone, W. H., & McLean, E. R. (2003). The DeLone and McLean model of information systems success: A ten-year update. *Journal of Management Information Systems*, *19*(4), 9–30.

Demil, B., & Lecocq, X. (2010). Business model evolution: In search of dynamic consistency. *Long Range Planning*, *43*(2/3), 227–246. doi:10.1016/j.lrp.2010.02.004

Derbaix, C., & Vanhamme, J. (2003). Inducing word-of-mouth by eliciting surprise – A pilot investigation. *Journal of Economic Psychology*, *24*(1), 99–116. doi:10.1016/S0167-4870(02)00157-5

DesAutels, P. (2011). UGIS: Understanding the nature of user-generated information systems. *Business Horizons*, *54*(3), 185–192. doi:10.1016/j.bushor.2010.12.003

Deshpandé, R., & Webster, F. E. (1989). Corporate culture and marketing: Defining the research agenda. *Journal of Marketing*, *53*(1), 3–15. doi:10.2307/1251521

Desouza, K. C., & Awazu, Y. (2006). Knowledge management at SMEs: Five peculiarities. *Journal of Knowledge Management*, *10*(1), 32–43. doi:10.1108/13673270610650085

Dholakia, R. R., & Kshetri, N. (2004). Factors Impacting the Adoption of the Internet among SMEs. *Small Business Economics, 23*(4), 311–322. doi:10.1023/B:SBEJ.0000032036.90353.1f

Dholakia, U. M., & Durham, E. (2010). One Café Chain's Facebook Experiment. *Harvard Business Review, 88*(3), 26.

Dick, A. S., & Basu, K. (1994). Customer loyalty: Toward an integrated conceptual framework. *Journal of the Academy of Marketing Science, 22*(2), 99–113. doi:10.1177/0092070394222001

Dinger, M., & Grover, V. (2010). The web 2.0 trend: Implications for the modern business. In *Encyclopedia of E-Business Development and Management in the Global Economy*. Hershey, PA: IGI Global. doi:10.4018/978-1-61520-611-7.ch117

DiStaso, M. W., & McCorkindale, T. (2012). Social media: Uses and opportunities in public relations. *Global Media Journal, 5*(2), 75–82.

Divol, R., Edelman, D., & Sarrazin, H. (2012). Demystifying social media. *McKinsey Quarterly*. Retrieved September 13, 2013, from http://www.mckinsey.com/insights/marketing_sales/demystifying_social_media

Dobele, A., Lindgreen, A., Beverland, M., Vanhamme, J., & van Wijk, R. (2007). Why pass on viral messages? Because they connect emotionally. *Business Horizons, 50*(4), 291–304. doi:10.1016/j.bushor.2007.01.004

Dobele, A., Toleman, D., & Beverland, M. (2005). Controlled infection! Spreading the brand message through viral marketing. *Business Horizons, 48*(2), 143–149. doi:10.1016/j.bushor.2004.10.011

Dodgson, M. (1993). Organizational learning: A review of some literatures. *Organization Studies, 14*(3), 375–394. doi:10.1177/017084069301400303

Dodson, J. A., & Muller, E. (1978). Models of new product advertising and word-of-mouth. *Management Science, 24*(15), 1568–1578. doi:10.1287/mnsc.24.15.1568

Dolphin, R. R. (2005). Internal communications: Today's strategic imperative. *Journal of Marketing Communications, 11*(3), 171–190. doi:10.1080/1352726042000315414

Dowson, R. (2005). *Developing knowledge-based client relationships*. Burlington, VT: Elsevier.

Droge, C., Stanko, M. A., & Pollitte, W. A. (2010). Lead Users and Early Adopters on the Web: The Role of New Technology Product Blogs. *Journal of Product Innovation Management, 27*(1), 66–82. doi:10.1111/j.1540-5885.2009.00700.x

Drucker, P. (1993). *Post-capitalist society*. Oxford, UK: Butterworth-Heinemann.

Drucker, P. (1998). The coming of the new organization. In P. Drucker (Ed.), *Harvard Business Review on knowledge management* (pp. 1–19). Boston, MA: Harvard Business School Press.

Drucker, P. F. (1954). *The practice of management*. New York, NY: Harper & Brothers.

DTI. (2007). *What does the DTI recognise as a small and medium-sized enterprise (SME)?* Department of Trade and Industry. Retrieved from http://www.dti.gov.uk

Dubosson-Torbay, M., Osterwalder, A., & Pigneur, Y. (2002). E-business model design, classification, and measurements. *Thunderbird International Business Review, 44*(1), 5–23. doi:10.1002/tie.1036

Dudezert, A., Boughzala, I., & Mounoud, E. (2009). *Comment intégrer la génération Millennials à l'entreprise? Management: Enjeux de demain* (pp. 323–334). Paris: Vuibert.

Duguid, P. (2005). The Art of Knowing: Social and Tacit Dimensions of Knowledge and the Limits of the Community of Practice. *The Information Society, 21*(2), 109–118. doi:10.1080/01972240590925311

Dunbar, R. I. M. (1992). Neocortex size as a constraint on group size in primates. *Journal of Human Evolution, 22*(6), 469–493. doi:10.1016/0047-2484(92)90081-J

Duncan, C. P., & Nelson, J. E. (1985). Effects of humor in a radio advertising experiment. *Journal of Advertising, 14*(2), 33–64. doi:10.1080/00913367.1985.10672944

Duncan, T., & Moriarty, S. E. (1988). A communication-based marketing model for managing relationships. *Journal of Marketing, 62*(2), 1–13. doi:10.2307/1252157

Dunn, B. J. (2010, December). How I Did It ... Best Buy's CEO on Learning to Love Social Media. *Harvard Business Review*.

Durst, S., & Edvardsson, I. R. (2012). Knowledge management in SMEs: A literature review. *Journal of Knowledge Management*, *16*(6), 879–903. doi:10.1108/13673271211276173

Dutta, S. (2010). What's your personal social media strategy? *Harvard Business Review*, *88*(11), 127–130. PMID:21049685

Dutt, H., Qamar, F., & Jha, V. S. (2011). A research to identify knowledge orientation in Indian commercial banks. *International Journal of Knowledge Management Studies*, *4*(4), 389–418. doi:10.1504/IJKMS.2011.048435

Dwyer, C., Hiltz, S., & Passerini, K. (2007). Trust and privacy concern within social networking sites: a comparison of Facebook and Myspace. In *Proceedings of the Thirteenth Americas Conference on Information Systems*. Keystone, CO: Academic Press. Retrieved September 10, 2013 from http://csis.pace.edu/~dwyer/research/DwyerAMCIS2007.pdf

Dwyer, F. R., Schurr, P., & Oh, S. (1987). Developing buyer-seller relationships. *Journal of Marketing*, *51*(2), 11–27. doi:10.2307/1251126

Easterby-Smith, M., Thorpe, R., & Lowe, A. (2002). *Management research - An introduction*. London: Sage Publications.

Edelman Trust Barometer. (2013). Retrieved on 8/21/13 from http://www.edelman.com/insights/intellectual-property/trust-2013/

Edelman Trust Barometer. (2014). Retrieved on 1/22/14 from http://www.edelman.com/insights/intellectual-property/2014-edelman-trust-barometer/

Edelman, D. (2010, December). Branding in The Digital Age: You're Spending Your Money In All the Wrong Places. *Harvard Business Review*.

Editorial, A. (1993). Adverting Age. *Midwest Region*, *64*(36), 16.

Edosomwan, S., Prakasan, K., Kouame, D., Watson, J., & Seymour, T. (2011). The History of Social Media and its Impact on Business. *Journal of Applied Management and Entrepreneurship*, *16*(3), 79–91.

Eisenhardt, K. M. (1989). Building theories from case study research. *Academy of Management Review*, *14*, 532–550.

Eisenhardt, K. M., & Graebner, M. A. (2007). Theory building from cases: Opportunities and challenges. *Academy of Management Journal*, *50*(1), 25–32. doi:10.5465/AMJ.2007.24160888

Eisenhardt, K. M., & Santos, F. M. (2002). Knowledge-Based View: A New Theory of Strategy? In A. M. Pettigrew, H. Thomas, & R. Whittington (Eds.), *Handbook of Strategy and Management* (pp. 139–164). London: Sage Publications Ltd.

Eisenhardt, K. M., & Zbaracki, M. J. (1992). Strategic decision making. *Strategic Management Journal*, *13*(S2), 17–37. doi:10.1002/smj.4250130904

Erdoğmuşa, İ. E., & Çiçek, M. (2012). The impact of social media marketing on brand loyalty. *Procedia: Social and Behavioral Sciences*, *58*, 1353–1360. doi:10.1016/j.sbspro.2012.09.1119

Ertimur, B., & Gilly, M. C. (2012). So Whaddya think? Consumers create ads and other consumers critique them. *Journal of Interactive Marketing*, *26*(3), 115–130. doi:10.1016/j.intmar.2011.10.002

Etlinger, S. (2011). *A framework for social analytics*. Altimeter Group.

Evanschitzky, H., Ahlert, D., Blaich, G., & Kenning, P. (2007). Knowledge management in knowledge-intensive service networks - A strategic management approach. *Management Decision*, *45*(2), 265–283. doi:10.1108/00251740710727287

Evans, D. (2008). *Social media marketing: An hour a day*. Indianapolis, IN: John Wiley & Sons.

Evening Herald. (2014, February 8). *Twitter usage drops*. Retrieved from http://www.herald.ie/lifestyle/twitter-usage-drops-29989318.html

Facebook. (2013). *Over 1 billion people now on Facebook*. Retrieved from https://www.facebook.com

Farrell, H., & Drezner, D. W. (2008). The power and politics of blogs. *Public Choice*, *134*(1-2), 15–30. doi:10.1007/s11127-007-9198-1

Fashion United. (2013). Retrieved from http://www.fashionunited.co.uk/facts-and-figures-in-the-uk-fashion-industry

Fattah, H. M. (2000). Viral marketing is nothing new. *Technology Marketing Intelligence*, *20*(10), 1–4.

Feick, L. F., & Price, L. L. (1987). The market maven: A diffuser of marketplace information. *Journal of Marketing*, *51*(1), 83–97. doi:10.2307/1251146

Ferguson, R. (2008). Word of mouth and viral marketing: Taking the temperature of the hottest trends in marketing. *Journal of Consumer Marketing*, *25*(3), 179–182. doi:10.1108/07363760810870671

Ferguson, S., Burford, S., & Kennedy, M. (2013). Divergent approaches to knowledge and innovation in the public sector. *International Journal of Public Administration*, *36*(3), 168–178. doi:10.1080/01900692.2012.749278

Fidelman, M. (2011). 5 Reasons Why Dell Is The World's Most Social Company. www.businessinsider.com. Retrieved June 11, 2011, from http://www.businessinsider.com/is-dell-the-worlds-most-social-company-scorecard-2011-6?utm_source=twbutton&utm_medium=social&utm_term=&utm_content=&utm_campaign=sai-contributor

Fill, C. (2009). *Marketing communications: Interactivity, communities and content* (5th ed.). London: Prentice Hall.

Fillis, I., Johansson, U., & Wagner, B. (2003). A conceptualisation of the opportunities and barriers to e-business development in the smaller firm. *Journal of Small Business and Enterprise Development*, *10*(3), 336–344. doi:10.1108/14626000310489808

Finkelstein, S., & Hambrick, D. C. (1990). Top-management-team tenure and organizational outcomes: The moderating role of managerial discretion. *Administrative Science Quarterly*, *35*(3), 484–503. doi:10.2307/2393314

Finne, A., & Gronroos, C. (2009). Rethinking marketing communication: From integrated marketing communications to relationship communication. *Journal of Marketing Communications*, *15*(2-3), 179–195. doi:10.1080/13527260902757654

Fischer, E., & Reuber, A. R. (2010). Social interaction via new social media: (How) can interactions on Twitter affect effectual thinking and behavior? *Journal of Business Venturing*, *26*(1), 1–18. doi:10.1016/j.jbusvent.2010.09.002

Fishbein, M., & Ajzen, I. (1975). *Belief, attitude, intention and behavior: An introduction to theory and research*. Reading, MA: Addison-Wesley.

Fisher, D., & Smith, S. (2011). Co-creation is chaotic: What it means for marketing when no one has control. *Marketing Theory*, *11*(3), 325–250. doi:10.1177/1470593111408179

Fjermestad, J., & Hiltz, S. R. (1999). An assessment of group support systems experimental research: Methodology and results. *Journal of Management Information Systems*, *15*(3), 7–150.

Floyd, S. W., & Wooldridge, B. (1999). Knowledge Creation and Social Networks in Corporate Entrepreneurship: The Renewal of Organizational Capability. *Entrepreneurship. Theory into Practice*, *23*(3).

Flynn, N. (2012). *The social media handbook: Policies and best practices to effectively manage your organization's social media presence, posts, and potential risks*. San Francisco, CA: Pfeiffer.

Fogg, B. J., Marshall, J., Laraki, O., Osipovich, A., Varma, C., Fang, N., et al. (2001). *What makes Web sites credible? A report on a large quantitative study*. Paper presented at the SIGCHI Conference on Human Factors in Computing Systems. Seattle, WA. doi:10.1145/365024.36503710.1145/365024.365037

Fombrun, C., & Shanley, M. (1990). What's in a name? Reputation building and corporate strategy. *Academy of Management Journal*, *33*(2), 233–258. doi:10.2307/256324

Ford, D. (1980). Buyer/seller relationships in international industrial markets. *European Journal of Marketing*, *14*(5), 339–354. doi:10.1108/EUM0000000004910

Fornell, C., & Larcker, D. (1981). Evaluating Structural Equation Models with Unobservable Variables and Measurement Error. *JMR, Journal of Marketing Research, 18*(1), 39–50. doi:10.2307/3151312

Forrester Research, Inc. (2011). *Listening and engaging in the digital marketing age*. Retrieved August 31, 2013 from http://i.dell.com/sites/content/corporate/secure/en/Documents/listening-and-engaging-in-the-digital-marketing-age.pdf

Foscht, T., Swoboda, B., & Morschett, D. (2006). Electronic commerce-based internationalisation of small, niche-oriented retailing companies: The case of Blue Tomato and the snowboard industry. *International Journal of Retail & Distribution Management, 34*(7), 556–572. doi:10.1108/09590550610673626

Fournier, S., & Avery, J. (2011). Putting the 'relationship' back into CRM. *MIT Sloan Management Review, 52*(3), 63–72.

Fournier, S., & Avery, J. (2011). The uninvited brand. *Business Horizons, 54*(3), 193–207. doi:10.1016/j.bushor.2011.01.001

Fox, Z. (2012). *Pinterest drives more traffic than Google+, YouTube and LinkedIn combined*. Retrieved February 11, 2014 from http://mashable.com/2012/02/01/pinterest-traffic-study/

Fox, J., Warber, K. M., & Makstaller, D. C. (2013). The role of Facebook in romantic relationship development: An exploration of Knapp's relational stage model. *Journal of Social and Personal Relationships, 30*(6), 771–794. doi:10.1177/0265407512468370

Franke, N., Keinz, P., & Schreier, M. (2008). Complementing mass customization toolkits with user communities: How peer input improves customer self-design. *Journal of Product Innovation Management, 25*(6), 546–559. doi:10.1111/j.1540-5885.2008.00321.x

Franke, N., & Piller, F. (2004). Value creation by toolkits for user innovation and design: The case of the watch market. *Journal of Product Innovation Management, 21*(6), 401–415. doi:10.1111/j.0737-6782.2004.00094.x

Frazier, G. L. (1983). Interorganizational exchange behavior in marketing channels: A broadened perspective. *Journal of Marketing, 47*(4), 68–78. doi:10.2307/1251400

French, T., LaBerge, L., & Magill, P. (2012). Five 'no regrets' moves for superior customer engagement. *The McKinsey Quarterly*, (3): 119–125.

Frow, P., & Payne, A. (2007). Special issue papers. Towards the 'perfect' customer experience. *Brand Management, 15*(2), 89–101. doi:10.1057/palgrave.bm.2550120

Fuchs, C., & Schreier, M. (2011). Customer empowerment in new product development. *Journal of Product Innovation Management, 28*(1), 17–32. doi:10.1111/j.1540-5885.2010.00778.x

Fugate, B. S., Stank, T. P., & Mentzer, J. T. (2009). Linking improved knowledge management to operational and organizational performance. *Journal of Operations Management, 27*(3), 247–264. doi:10.1016/j.jom.2008.09.003

Fulk, J., & DeSanctis, G. (1995). Electronic Communication and Changing Organizational Forms. *Organization Science, 6*(4), 337–349. doi:10.1287/orsc.6.4.337

Gaasterland, M. (2009). Most products are like tampons. *Blog: Social Media Tactics You can Trust*. Retrieved from http://www.michielgaasterland.com/case-studies/most-products-are-like-tampons/

Gadekar, R., Thakur, K., & Ang, P. H. (2011). Web sites for e-electioneering in Maharashtra and Gujarat, India. *Internet Research, 21*(4), 435–457. doi:10.1108/10662241111158317

Gaines-Ross, L. (2010, December). Reputation Warfare. *Harvard Business Review*, 70–77.

Gallaugher, J., & Ransbotham, S. (2010). Social media and customer dialog management at Starbucks. *MIS Quarterly Executive, 9*(4), 197–212.

Galliers, R. D. (1991). Strategic information systems planning: Myths, reality and guidelines for successful implementation. *European Journal of Information Systems, 1*(1), 55–64. doi:10.1057/ejis.1991.7

Gallivan, M. J., Spitler, V. K., & Koufaris, M. (2005). Does information technology training really matter? A social information processing analysis of coworkers' influence on IT usage in the workplace. *Journal of Management Information Systems, 22*(1), 153–192.

Garden, M. (2012). Defining blog: A fool's errand or a necessary undertaking. *Journalism*, *13*(4), 483–499. doi:10.1177/1464884911421700

Garwin, C. (1998). Building a learning organization. In P. Drucker (Ed.), *Harvard Business Review on knowledge management* (pp. 47–80). Boston, MA: Harvard Business School Press.

Gelb, B. D., & Pickett, C. M. (1983). Attitude-toward-the-ad: Links to humor and to advertising effectiveness. *Journal of Advertising*, *12*(2), 34–42. doi:10.1080/00913367.1983.10672838

Georgi, D., & Mink, M. (2013). eCCIq: The quality of electronic customer-to customer interaction. *Journal of Retailing and Consumer Services*, *20*(1), 11–19. doi:10.1016/j.jretconser.2012.08.002

Gibson, C., & Cohen, S. (2003). *Virtual teams that work: Creating conditions for virtual team effectiveness*. San Francisco, CA: Jossey-Bass.

Gibson, R. K., Rommele, A., & Ward, S. (2003). German Parties and Internet Campaigning in the 2002 Federal Election. *German Politics*, *12*(1), 79–108. doi:10.1080/09644000412331307534

Gibson, R., & Ward, S. (2000). A proposed methodology for studying the function and effectiveness of party and candidate websites. *Social Science Computer Review*, *18*(3), 301–319. doi:10.1177/089443930001800306

Gil De Zúñiga, H., Puig-I-Abril, E., & Rojas, H. (2009). Weblogs, traditional sources online and political participation: An assessment of how the internet is changing the political environment. *New Media & Society*, *11*(4), 553–574. doi:10.1177/1461444809102960

Gil de Zúñiga, H., Veenstra, A., Vraga, E., & Shah, D. (2010). Digital Democracy: Reimagining Pathways to Political Participation. *Journal of Information Technology & Politics*, *7*(1), 36–51. doi:10.1080/19331680903316742

Gilbert, E., & Karahalios, K. (2009). Predicting tie strength with social media. In *Proceedings of the 27th International Conference on Human Factors in Computing Systems* (CHI '09). ACM.

Gillmor, D. (2003). Google buys Pyra: Blogging goes big-time. *EJournal*. Retrieved January 20, 2014 from http://web.archive.org/web/20031008161432/http://weblog.siliconvalley.com/column/dangillmor/archives/000802.shtml

Gioia, D. A., & Chittipeddi, K. (1991). Sensemaking and sense-giving in strategic change initiation. *Strategic Management Journal*, *12*(6), 433–448. doi:10.1002/smj.4250120604

Godes, D., & Mayzlin, D. (2004). Using online conversation to study word-of-mouth communication. *Marketing Science*, *23*(4), 545–560. doi:10.1287/mksc.1040.0071

Godes, D., & Mayzlin, D. (2009). Firm-created word-of-mouth communication: Evidence from a field test. *Marketing Science*, *28*(4), 721–739. doi:10.1287/mksc.1080.0444

Goldenberg, J., Han, S., Lehmann, D. R., & Hong, J. W. (2009). The role of hubs in the adoption process. *Journal of Marketing*, *73*(2), 1–13. doi:10.1509/jmkg.73.2.1

Goodchild, M. (2007). Citizens as voluntary sensors: Spatial data infrastructure in the world of Web 2.0. *International Journal of Spatial Data Infrastructures Research*, *2*, 24–32.

Gorman, P., Nelson, T., & Glassman, A. (2004). The millenial generation: A strategic opportunity. *Organizational Analysis*, *12*(3), 255–270.

Goulding, C., Shankar, A., & Canniford, R. (2013). Learning to be tribal: Facilitating the formation of consumer tribes. *European Journal of Marketing*, *47*(5/6), 813–832. doi:10.1108/03090561311306886

Grace, T. P. L. (2009). Wikis as a knowledge management tool. *Journal of Knowledge Management*, *13*(4), 64–74. doi:10.1108/13673270910971833

Grady, B. (2008). *Corporate America embraces social networking*. Information and Learning Company.

Granovetter, M. (1973). The Strength of Weak Ties. *American Journal of Sociology*, *78*(6), 1360–1380. doi:10.1086/225469

Granovetter, M. (1983). The strength of weak ties: A network theory revisited. *Sociological Theory*, *1*, 201–233. doi:10.2307/202051

Grant, R. M. (1996). Toward a knowledge-based theory of the firm. *Strategic Management Journal*, *17*(1), 109–122. doi:10.1002/smj.4250171110

Grant, R. M. (1996b). Prospering in dynamically-competitive environments: Organizational capability as knowledge integration. *Organization Science*, *7*(4), 375–387. doi:10.1287/orsc.7.4.375

Grant, W. J., Moon, B., & Grant, J. B. (2010). Digital Dialogue? Australian Politicians' use of the Social Network Tool Twitter. *Australian Journal of Political Science*, *45*(4), 579–604. doi:10.1080/10361146.2010.517176

Gray, E. R., & Balmer, J. M. T. (1998). Managing Corporate Image and Corporate Reputation. *Long Range Planning*, *31*(5), 695–702. doi:10.1016/S0024-6301(98)00074-0

Greenberg, P. (2009). Time to put a stake in the ground on social CRM. *ZDNet—Social CRM: The Conversation Blog*.

Green, D., & Gerber, A. (2003). The underprovision of experiments in political science. *The Annals of the American Academy of Political and Social Science*, *589*(1), 94–112. doi:10.1177/0002716203254763

Greiner, M. E., Bohmann, T., & Krcmar, H. (2007). A strategy for knowledge management. *Journal of Knowledge Management*, *11*(6), 3–15. doi:10.1108/13673270710832127

Griffith, D. A., & Harvey, M. G. (2001). Executive insights: An intercultural communication model for use in global interorganizational networks. *Journal of International Marketing*, *9*(3), 87–103. doi:10.1509/jimk.9.3.87.19924

Grimes, S. (2013). The rise and stall of social media listening. *Information Week*, *1361*, 5–6.

Grönoos, C. (1994). From Marketing Mix to Relationship Marketing: Towards a paradigm shift in marketing. *Management Decision*, *32*(2), 4–20. doi:10.1108/00251749410054774

Grönroos, C. (1997). Value-driven relational marketing: From products to resources and competencies. *Journal of Marketing Management*, *13*(5), 407–419. doi:10.1080/0267257X.1997.9964482

Gronroos, C. (2004). The relationship marketing process: Communication, interaction, dialogue, and value. *Journal of Business and Industrial Marketing*, *19*(2), 99–113. doi:10.1108/08858620410523981

Gronroos, C. (2006). On defining marketing: Finding a new roadmap for marketing. *Marketing Theory*, *6*(4), 395–417. doi:10.1177/1470593106069930

Gronroos, C., & Voima, P. (2013). Critical service logic: Making sense of value creation and co-creation. *Journal of the Academy of Marketing Science*, *41*(2), 133–150. doi:10.1007/s11747-012-0308-3

Grossman, M. (2008). An emerging global knowledge management platform: The case of iBridge. *VINE: The Journal of Information and Knowledge Management Systems*, *38*(4), 525–534. doi:10.1108/03055720810917750

Gu, F., & Widen-Wulff, G. (2010). Scholarly communication and possible changes in the context of social media: A Finnish case study. *The Electronic Library*, *29*(6), 762–776. doi:10.1108/02640471111187999

Guglielmo, C. (2009). Dell Rings Up $ 6. 5 Million in Sales Using Twitter. *Bloomberg.com*. Retrieved May 3, 2011, from http://www.bloomberg.com/apps/news?pid=newsarchive&sid=akXzD_6YNHCk

Gummerus, J., Veronica, L., Weman, E., & Pihlstrom, M. (2012). Customer engagement in a Facebook brand community. *Management Research Review*, *35*(9), 857–877. doi:10.1108/01409171211256578

Gummesson, E. (1994). Making relationship marketing operational. *International Journal of Service Industry Management*, *5*(5), 5–20. doi:10.1108/09564239410074349

Gummesson, E. (2000). *Qualitative methods in management research*. London: Sage Publications.

Gummesson, E. (2005). Qualitative research in marketing: Road-map for a wilderness of complexity and unpredictability. *European Journal of Marketing*, *39*(3/4), 309–327. doi:10.1108/03090560510581791

Gummesson, E. (2006). Qualitative research in management: Addressing complexity, context and persona. *Management Decision*, *44*(2), 167–179. doi:10.1108/00251740610650175

Gunasekaran, A., & Ngai, E. W. (2007). Knowledge management in 21st century manufacturing. *International Journal of Production Research*, *45*(11), 2391–2418. doi:10.1080/00207540601020429

Gundlach, H., & Neville, B. (2012). Authenticity: Further theoretical and practical development. *Journal of Brand Management*, *19*(6), 484–499. doi:10.1057/bm.2011.51

Gunnarsson, M. (2012). *BYOB (Bring Your Own Behavior) is a Driving Factor in the Adoption of Enterprise Mobility Applications*. Retrieved from http://blogs.ifsworld.com/2012/10/byob-bring-your-own-behavior-is-a-driving-factor-in-the-adoption-of-enterprise-mobility-applications/

Gupta, D., & Zeithaml, D. (2006). Customer metrics and their Impact on financial performance. *Marketing Science*, *25*(6), 718–739. doi:10.1287/mksc.1060.0221

Gupta, J., & Sharma, S. (2004). *Creating knowledge based organization*. Boston, MA: Idea Group Publishing.

Gupta, S., Lehmann, D. R., & Stuart, J. A. (2004). Valuing customers. *JMR, Journal of Marketing Research*, *41*(1), 7–18. doi:10.1509/jmkr.41.1.7.25084

Guthrie, G. (2010). *Basic Research Methods*. New Delhi: SAGE Publications.

Hackworth, B. A., & Kunz, M. B. (2010). Health care and social media: Building relationships via social networks. *Academy of Health Care Management Journal*, *6*(1), 55–69.

Hahn, K. H., & Kim, J. (2009). The effect of offline brand trust and perceived internet confidence on online shopping intention in the integrated multi-channel context. *International Journal of Retail & Distribution Management*, *37*(2), 126–141. doi:10.1108/09590550910934272

Hahn, M., Park, S., Krishnamurthi, L., & Zoltners, A. A. (1994). Analysis of new product diffusion using a four-segment trial-repeat model. *Marketing Science*, *13*(3), 224–247. doi:10.1287/mksc.13.3.224

Halliday, S., & Vrusias, B. (2011). *The spread and spread of word of web: Towards understanding how marketers can interact with social networks*. Paper presented at the Academy of Marketing Conference 2011. Liverpool, UK.

HalpinH.RobuV.ShepherdH. (2007). The complex dynamics of collaborative tagging. In Proceedings of the 16th International Conference on the World Wide Web (WWW'07). Banff, Canada: ACM Press. 10.1145/1242572.1242602

Hambrick, D. C., & Mason, P. A. (1984). Upper echelons: The organization as a reflection of its top managers. *Academy of Management Review*, *9*(2), 193–206.

Handzic, M. (2009). Evaluating knowledge management's effectiveness for decision support: Preliminary results. In R. W. King (Ed.), *Knowledge management and organizational learning* (pp. 237–252). New York, NY: Springer-Verlag. doi:10.1007/978-1-4419-0011-1_15

Hanna, R., Rohm, A., & Crittenden, L. V. (2011). We are all connected: The power of the social media ecosystem. *Business Horizons*, *54*(3), 265–273. doi:10.1016/j.bushor.2011.01.007

Harker, M. J. (1999). Relationship marketing defined? An examination of current relationship marketing definitions. *Marketing Intelligence & Planning*, *17*(1), 13–20. doi:10.1108/02634509910253768

Harker, M. J., & Egan, J. (2006). The past, present and future of relationship marketing. *Journal of Marketing Management*, *22*(1-2), 215–242. doi:10.1362/026725706776022326

Harridge-March, S., & Quinton, S. (2009). Virtual snakes and ladders: Social networks and the relationship marketing loyalty ladder. *The Marketing Review*, *9*(2), 171–181. doi:10.1362/146934709X442692

Harrigan, P. (2011). *Modelling CRM in the social media age*. Paper presented at the Academy of Marketing Conference 2011. Liverpool, UK.

Harrison, A. G. (2013). Engagement ring: Building connections between employees and strategy. *Public Relations Tactics*, *20*(5), 16.

Harrison, J. S., & Freeman, R. E. (1999). Stakeholders, Social Responsibility, and Performance: Empirical Evidence and Theoretical Perspectives. *Academy of Management Journal*, *42*(5), 479–485. doi:10.2307/256971

Harrysson, M., Metayer, E., & Sarrazin, H. (2012, November). How 'social intelligence' can guide decisions. *The McKinsey Quarterly*, 1–9.

Hart, S. L. (1992). An integrative framework for strategy-making processes. *Academy of Management Review*, *17*(2), 327–351.

Hassan, S., & Li, F. (2005). Evaluating the usability and content usefulness of web sites: A benchmarking approach. *Journal of Electronic Commerce in Organizations*, *3*(2), 46–67. doi:10.4018/jeco.2005040104

Hassenzahl, M., & Tractinsky, N. (2006). User experience – A research agenda. *Behaviour & Information Technology*, *25*(2), 91–97. doi:10.1080/01449290500330331

Hathi, S. (2010). How social networking increase collaboration at IBM. *SCM Features*, *14*(1), 32–35.

Hayes, M., & Walsham, G. (2003). Knowledge sharing and ICTs: A relational perspective. In M. Easterby-Smith, & M. A. Lyles (Eds.), *The Blackwell handbook of organizational learning and knowledge management* (pp. 54–57). Malden, MA: Blackwell.

Healy, J. C., & McDonagh, P. (2013). Consumer roles in brand culture and value co-creation in virtual communities. *Journal of Business Research*, *66*(9), 1528–1540. doi:10.1016/j.jbusres.2012.09.014

Heide, J. (1994). Interorganizational governance in marketing channels. *Journal of Marketing*, *58*(1), 71–85. doi:10.2307/1252252

Heine, S., Lehman, D., Markus, H., & Kitayama, S. (2010). Is there a universal need for positive self-regard? *Psychological Review*, *106*(4), 766–794. doi:10.1037/0033-295X.106.4.766 PMID:10560328

Heisig, P. (2009). Harmonisation of knowledge management: Comparing 160 KM frameworks around the globe. *Journal of Knowledge Management*, *13*(4), 4–31. doi:10.1108/13673270910971798

Hendry, J. (2000). Strategic decision making, discourse, and strategy as social practice. *Journal of Management Studies*, *37*(7), 955–978. doi:10.1111/1467-6486.00212

Henneberg, S. C. (2004). The views of an advocatus dei: Political marketing and its critics. *Journal of Public Affairs*, *4*(3), 225–243. doi:10.1002/pa.187

Henneberg, S. C. (2008). Leading or Following? *Journal of Political Marketing*, *5*(3), 29–46. doi:10.1300/J199v05n03_02

Hennig-Thurau, T., Gwinner, K. P., Walsh, G., & Gremler, D. D. (2004). Electronic word-of-mouth via consumer-opinion platforms: What motivates consumers to articulate themselves on the internet? *Journal of Interactive Marketing*, *18*(1), 38–52. doi:10.1002/dir.10073

Hennig-Thurau, T., Malthouse, E., Friege, C., Gensler, S., Lobschat, L., Rangaswamy, A., & Skiera, B. (2010). The impact of new media on customer relationships. *Journal of Service Research*, *13*(3), 311–330. doi:10.1177/1094670510375460

Herring, S. C. (2008). Questioning the generational divide: Technological exoticism and adult constructions of online youth identity. In D. Buckingham (Ed.), *Youth, Identity, and Digital Media* (pp. 71–92). Cambridge, MA: The MIT Press.

Hershatter, A., & Epstein, M. (2010). Millennials and the world of work: An organization and management perspective. *Journal of Business and Psychology*, *25*(2), 211–223. doi:10.1007/s10869-010-9160-y

He, W., Zha, S., & Li, L. (2013). Social media competitive analysis and text mining: A case study in the pizza industry. *International Journal of Information Management*, *33*(3), 464–472. doi:10.1016/j.ijinfomgt.2013.01.001

Hinde, R. A. (1979). *Towards understanding relationships*. London, UK: Academic Press.

Hodgkinson, G. P., & Johnson, G. (1994). Exploring the Mental Models of Competitive Strategists: The Case for a Processual Approach. *Journal of Management Studies*, *31*(4), 525–552. doi:10.1111/j.1467-6486.1994.tb00629.x

Hoffman, D. L., & Fodor, M. (2010). Can you measure the ROI of your social media marketing? *MIT Sloan Management Review*, *52*(1), 41–49.

Hofstede, G., Hofstede, G., & Minkov, M. (2010). *Cultures and Organizations: Software of the Mind*. New York: McGraw-Hill.

Homans, G. C. (1961). *Social behavior: Its elementary forms*. New York: Harcourt Brace.

Hopkins, J. L. (2012). Can Facebook be an effective mechanism for generating growth and value in small businesses? *Journal of Systems and Information Technology, 14*(2), 131–141. doi:10.1108/13287261211232153

Horovitz, B. (2013). *Horovitz: Best and worst ads of 2013.* Retrieved 6th January 2014 from http://www.usatoday.com/story/money/business/2013/12/23/top-five-ads-of-2013-commercials-advertisements-year-end/4045173/

Howe, J. (2006). The rise of crowdsourcing: A definition. *Wired, 14.*

Hsu, C., & Lin, J. (2008). Acceptance of blog usage: The roles of technology acceptance, social influence and knowledge sharing motivation. *Information & Management, 45*(1), 65–74. doi:10.1016/j.im.2007.11.001

Huang, C.-C., Lin, T.-C., & Lin, K.-J. (2009). Factors affecting pass-along email intentions (Paeis), integrating the social capital and social cognition theories. *Electronic Commerce Research and Applications, 8*(3), 160–169. doi:10.1016/j.elerap.2008.11.001

Huang, L. S., & Lai, C. P. (2012). An investigation on critical success factors for knowledge management using structural equation modeling. *Technology Management, 40*, 24–30.

Hughes, A., & Dann, S. (2009). Political marketing and stakeholder engagement. *Marketing Theory, 9*(2), 243–256. doi:10.1177/1470593109103070

Hung, K. H., & Li, S. Y. (2007). The influence of eWOM on virtual consumer communities: Social capital, consumer learning, and behavioral outcomes. *Journal of Advertising Research, 47*(4), 485–495. doi:10.2501/S002184990707050X

Hung, S.-Y., Kang, T.-C., Yen, D. C., Huang, A. H., & Chen, K. (2012). A Cross-Cultural Analysis of Communication Tools and Communication Outcomes. *Journal of Global Information Management, 20*(3), 55–83. doi:10.4018/jgim.2012070103

Hunt, S. D. (1983). General theories and the fundamental explanada of marketing. *Journal of Marketing, 47*(4), 9–17. doi:10.2307/1251394

Huston, L., & Sakkab, N. (2006). Connect and develop: Inside Procter & Gamble's new model for innovation. *Harvard Business Review, 84*(3), 1–8.

Hutchins, E. L. D., Hollan, J., & Norman, D. A. (1985). Direct Manipulation Interfaces. *Human-Computer Interaction, 1*(4), 311–338. doi:10.1207/s15327051hci0104_2

Hutzschenreuter, T., & Kleindienst, I. (2006). Strategy-Process Research: What Have We Learned and What Is Still to Be Explored. *Journal of Management, 32*(5), 673–720. doi:10.1177/0149206306291485

Ilinitch, A. Y., D'Aveni, R. A., & Lewin, A. Y. (1996). New organizational forms and strategies for managing in hypercompetitive environments. *Organization Science, 7*(3), 211–220. doi:10.1287/orsc.7.3.211

Inforrm. (2013). Social media: more Twitter usage statistics. *International Forum for Responsible Media (Inforrm).* Retrieved from http://inforrm.wordpress.com/2013/11/19/social-media-more-twitter-usage-statistics

Israel, S. (2009). *Twitterville: How businesses can thrive in the new global neighborhoods.* Penguin.

Ito, M., Davidson, C., Jenkins, H., Lee, C., Eisenberg, M., & Weiss, J. (2008). Youth online authorship. In D. Buckingham (Ed.), *Youth, identity, and digital media.* Cambridge, MA: The MIT Press.

Iyengar, R., Van den Bulte, C., & Valente, T. W. (2011). Opinion leadership and social contagion in new product diffusion. *Marketing Science, 30*(2), 195–212. doi:10.1287/mksc.1100.0566

Iyer, G. R., Sharma, A., & Bejou, D. (2006). Developing relationship equity in international markets. *Journal of Relationship Marketing, 5*(1), 3–20. doi:10.1300/J366v05n01_02

Jackson, N. (2006). Dipping their big toe into the blogosphere: The use of weblogs by the political parties in the 2005 general election. *ASLIB Proceedings: New Information Perspectives, 58*(4), 292-303.

Jackson, T. (2010). Case Study: United Airlines Loses Millions on Social Media. *Social Media Risk.com.* Retrieved May 3, 2011, from http://socialmediarisk.com/2010/03/case-study-united-airlines-loses-millions-on-social-media/

Jeppesen, L. B., & Molin, M. (2003). Consumers as co-developers: Learning and innovation outside the firm. *Technology Analysis and Strategic Management, 15*(3), 363–383. doi:10.1080/0953732031000160153l

Johannessen, J. A., Olsen, B., & Olaisen, J. (1999). Aspects of innovation theory based knowledge management. *Journal of International Management, 19*(2), 121–139.

Johnson, S. (2009). How Twitter will change the way we live. *Time Magazine*. Retrieved September 10, 2013 from http://content.time.com/time/magazine/article/0,9171,1902818,00.html

Johnson, G. J., Bruner, G. C. II, & Kumar, A. (2006). Interactivity and its facets revisited: Theory and empirical test. *Journal of Advertising, 35*(4), 35–52. doi:10.2753/JOA0091-3367350403

Johnson, J. C., & Weller, S. C. (2002). Elicitation techniques for interviewing. In J. F. Gubrium, & J. A. Holstein (Eds.), *Handbook of interview research: Context and method* (pp. 491–514). London: Sage Publications.

Johnson, M. W., Christensen, C. M., & Kagermann, H. (2008). Reinventing your business model. *Harvard Business Review, 86*(12), 59–67.

Judge, T., Erez, A., Bono, J., & Thoresen, C. (2002). Are measures of self-esteem, neuroticisocial media, locus of control, and generalized self-efficacy indicators of a common core construct? *Journal of Personality and Social Psychology, 83*(3), 693–710. doi:10.1037/0022-3514.83.3.693 PMID:12219863

Juice On The Loose. (2013). Retrieved September 10, 2013 from http://www.juiceloosela.com

Jurvetson, S., & Draper, T. (1997). *Viral marketing phenomenon explained*. Retrieved April 15th, 2013, from http://www.dfj.com/news/article_26.shtml

Kalamas, M., Mitchell, T., & Lester, D. (2009). Modeling social media use: Bridging the communication gap in higher education. *Journal of Advertising Education, 13*(1), 44–57.

Kalla, H. K. (2005). Integrated internal communications: A multidisciplinary perspective. *Corporate Communications, 10*(4), 302–314. doi:10.1108/13563280510630106

Kalnes, Ø. (2009). Norwegian Parties and Web 2.0. *Journal of Information Technology & Politics, 6*(3-4), 251–266. doi:10.1080/19331680903041845

Kane, G. C., Fichman, R. G., Gallaugher, J., & Glaser, G. (2009). Community relations 2.0. *Harvard Business Review, 87*(11), 45–50. PMID:19891388

Kane, K., Robinson-Combre, J., & Berge, Z. (2010). Tapping into social networking: Collaborating enhances both knowledge management and e-learning. *Journal of Information and Knowledge Management Systems, 40*(1), 62–70.

Kanter, B., & Fine, A. H. (2010). The networked nonprofit. In *Seven*. San Francisco: Jossey-Bass, John Wiley & Sons.

Kaplan, A., & Haenlein, M. (2010). Users of the world, unite! The challenges and opportunities of Social Media. *Business Horizons, 53*(1), 59–68. doi:10.1016/j.bushor.2009.09.003

Kaplan, S. R., & Mikes, A. (2012). Managing risks: A new framework. *Harvard Business Review, 90*(6), 49–60.

Karabell, S. (2010). Just a pretty face(book)? Social media tries to come of age. *INSEAD Knowledge*. Retrieved March 17, 2011, from http://knowledge.insead.edu/contents/social-networking-wpp-google.cfm?vid=419

Katz, D. A., & McIntosh, L. A. (2013). Corporate governance update: The board, social media and regulation FD. *New York Law Journal*. Retrieved on March 5, 2014 from http://www.wlrk.com/webdocs/wlrknew/WLRKMemos/WLRK/WLRK.22371.13.pdf

Katz, E. (1957). The two-step flow of communication: An up-to-date report on an hypothesis. *Public Opinion Quarterly, 21*(1), 61–78. doi:10.1086/266687

Katz, E., & Lazarsfeld, P. F. (1955). *Personal Influence*. New York: The Free Press.

Kaupins, G., & Park, S. (2010). Legal and Ethical Implications of Corporate Social Networks. *Employee Responsibilities and Rights Journal, 23*(2), 83–99. doi:10.1007/s10672-010-9149-8

Keil, M., Tiwana, A., & Bush, A. (2002). Reconciling user and project manager perceptions of IT project risk: A Delphi study. *Information Systems Journal, 12*(2), 103–119. doi:10.1046/j.1365-2575.2002.00121.x

Kelemen, M., & Papasolomou, I. (2007). Internal marketing: A qualitative study of culture change in the UK banking sector. *Journal of Marketing Management*, *23*(7-8), 745–767. doi:10.1362/026725707X230027

Keller, K. L. (1993). Conceptualizing, measuring, and managing customer-based brand equity. *Journal of Marketing*, *57*(1), 1–22. doi:10.2307/1252054

Keller, K. L. (2009). Building strong brands in a modern marketing communications environment. *Journal of Marketing Communications*, *15*(2), 139–155. doi:10.1080/13527260902757530

Kemp, S. (2014). *Social, digital & mobile worldwide in 2014*. Retrieved from http://wearesocial.net/blog/2014/01/social-digital-mobile-worldwide-2014

Khamseh, H. M., & Jolly, D. (2008). Knowledge transfer in alliances: Determinant factors. *Journal of Knowledge Management*, *12*(1), 37–50. doi:10.1108/13673270810852377

Kiessling, T. S., Richey, R. G., Meng, J., & Dabic, M. (2009). Exploring knowledge management to organizational performance outcomes in a transitional economy. *Journal of World Business*, *44*(4), 421–433. doi:10.1016/j.jwb.2008.11.006

Kietzmann, J. H., Hermkens, K., McCarthy, I. P., & Silvestre, B. S. (2011). Social media? Get serious! Understanding the functional building blocks of social media. *Business Horizons*, *54*(3), 241–251. doi:10.1016/j.bushor.2011.01.005

Kim, A. J., & Ko, E. (2012). Do social media marketing activities enhance customer equity? An empirical study of luxury fashion brand. *Journal of Business Research*, *65*(10), 1480–1486. doi:10.1016/j.jbusres.2011.10.014

Kim, H.-S., & Jin, B. (2006). Exploratory study of virtual communities of apparel retailers. *Journal of Fashion Marketing and Management*, *10*(1), 41–55. doi:10.1108/13612020610651114

Kim, S., & Jones, C. (2009). Online shopping and moderating role of offline brand trust. *Direct Marketing: An International Journal*, *3*(4), 282–300. doi:10.1108/17505930911000874

Kim, W., Benedetto, C. A. D., & Lancioni, R. A. (2011). The effects of country and gender differences on consumer innovativeness and decision processes in a highly globalized high-tech product market. *Asia Pacific Journal of Marketing and Logistics*, *23*(5), 714–744. doi:10.1108/13555851111183101

Kim, W., Jeong, O.-R., & Lee, S.-W. (2010). On social websites. *Information Systems Journal*, *35*(2), 215–236. doi:10.1016/j.is.2009.08.003

King, N. (1998). Template analysis. In G. Symon, & C. Cassell (Eds.), *Qualitative methods and analysis in organisational research: A practical guide*. London: Sage Publications.

Kirby, J., & Marsden, P. (2006). *Connected marketing: The viral, buzz and word of mouth revolution*. Oxford, UK: Elsevier.

Kirkman, B., Rosen, B., Tesluk, P., & Gibson, C. (2004). The impact of team empowerment on virtual team performance: The moderating role of face-to-face interaction. *Academy of Management Journal*, *47*(2), 175–192. doi:10.2307/20159571

Kiron, D., Palmer, A., Phillips, N., & Kruschwitz, N. (2012b). Social Business: What Companies Really Doing?, *MIT Sloan Management Review Research Report*.

Kiron, D., Palmer, A., Phillips, N., & Kruschwitz, N. (2012a). What Managers Really Think About Social Business. *MIT Sloan Management Review*, *53*(4), 51–60.

Kliatchko, J. G. (2005). Towards a new definition of integrated marketing communications (IMC). *International Journal of Advertising*, *24*(1), 7–34.

Knapp, M. L. (1978). *Interpersonal communication and human relationships*. Boston, MA: Allyn & Bacon.

Kogut, B., & Zander, U. (1992). Knowledge of the firm, combinative capabilities, and the replication of technology. *Organization Science*, *3*(3), 383–397. doi:10.1287/orsc.3.3.383

Kohli, A. K., & Jaworski, B. J. (1990, April). Market orientation: The construct, research propositions, and managerial implications. *Journal of Marketing*, *54*(2), 1–18. doi:10.2307/1251866

Kor, Y., & Mahoney, J. T. (2000). Penrose resource-based approach: The process and product of research creativity. *Journal of Management Studies*, *37*(1), 109–139.

Kostova, T. (1999). Transnational transfer of strategic organizational practices: A contextual perspective. *Academy of Management Review*, *24*(2), 308–324.

Kotadia, H. (2009). *Definition: What is Social CRM?* Social CRM and Business.

Kotler, P. (1972). A generic concept of marketing. *Journal of Marketing*, *36*(2), 46–54. doi:10.2307/1250977

Kotzaivazoglou, I. (2011). Political marketing in the Greek context: Does market orientation exist? *International Review on Public and Nonprofit Marketing*, *8*(1), 41–56. doi:10.1007/s12208-011-0070-0

Kowske, B., Rasch, R., & Wiley, J. (2010). Millennials' (lack of) attitude problem: An empirical examination of generational effects on work attitudes. *Journal of Business and Psychology*, *25*(2), 265–279. doi:10.1007/s10869-010-9171-8

Kozinets, R. V., de Valck, K., Wojnicki, A. C., & Wilner, S. J. (2010). Networked narratives: Understanding word-of-mouth marketing in online communities. *Journal of Marketing*, *74*(2), 71–89. doi:10.1509/jmkg.74.2.71

Kress, N. (2005). Engaging your employees through the power of communication. *Workspan*, *48*(5), 26–36.

Kuhn, M. (2007). Interactivity and Prioritizing the Human: A code of Blogging Ethics. *Journal of Mass Media Ethics*, *22*(1), 18–36. doi:10.1080/08900520701315244

Kumar, V. (2008). *Managing customers for profit: Strategies to increase profits and build loyalty*. Pearson Prentice-Hall.

Kumar, V., Aksoy, L., Donkers, B., Venkatesan, R., Wiesel, T., & Tillmanns, S. (2010). Undervalued or overvalued customers: Capturing total customer engagement value. *Journal of Service Research*, *13*(3), 297–310. doi:10.1177/1094670510375602

Kumar, V., & Bhagwat, Y. (2010). Listen to the customer. *Marketing Research*, *22*(2), 14–19.

Kumar, V., & Mirchandani, R. (2012). Increasing the ROI of social media marketing. *MIT Sloan Management Review*, *54*(1), 55–61.

Kumar, V., Petersen, J. A., & Leone, R. P. (2010). Driving profitability by encouraging customer referrals: Who, when, and how. *Journal of Marketing*, *74*(5), 1–17. doi:10.1509/jmkg.74.5.1

Kumar, V., & Rajan, B. (2009). Profitable customer management: Measuring and maximizing customer lifetime value. *Management Accounting Quarterly*, *10*(3), 1–18.

Kwak, H., Lee, C., Park, H., & Moon, S. (2010). What is Twitter, a social network or a news media? In *Proceedings of the 19th International Conference on World Wide Web* (pp. 591–600). Academic Press. doi:10.1145/1772690.177275110.1145/1772690.1772751

Labedz, C., Cavaleri, S., & Berry, G. (2011). Interactive knowledge management: Putting pragmatic policy planning in place. *Journal of Knowledge Management*, *15*(4), 551–567. doi:10.1108/13673271111151956

Lackie, R. J., & LeMasney, J. W. (2007). Blogger, WorldPress.com, and their pseudoblog alternatives: A comparison of focus, features, and feel. *Journal of Library Administration*, *46*(3/4), 139–180.

Lambin, J. J. (2007). *Market-driven management: Strategic and operational marketing*. London: MacMillan.

Lannin, D. G., & Scott, N. A. (2013). Social networking ethics: Developing best practices for the new small world. *Professional Psychology, Research and Practice*, *44*(3), 135–141. doi:10.1037/a0031794

Lanois, P. (2010). Caught in the Clouds: The Web 2.0, cloud computing, and privacy? *Northwestern Journal of Technology and Intellectual Property*, *9*(2), 29–49.

Lappas, G., Chatzopoulos, S., & Yannas, P. (2008). Parliamentary Candidates Running on the Web for the 2004 Greek National Elections. *Journal of Political Marketing*, *7*(3-4), 256–277. doi:10.1080/15377850802008327

Larceneux, F. (2007). Buzz et recommandations sur internet: Quels effets sur le box-office? *Recherche et Applications en Marketing*, *22*(3), 45–64. doi:10.1177/076737010702200304

Larcker, D. F., Larcker, S. M., & Tayan, B. (2012). *What do corporate directors and senior managers know about social media?* Retrieved on March 5, 2014 from http://www.gsb.stanford.edu/sites/default/files/documents/TCB_DN-V4N20-12.Social_Media.pdf

Laroche, M., Mohammad, R. H., & Richard, M.-O. (2013). To be or not to be in social media: How brand loyalty is affected by social media? *International Journal of Information Management, 33*(1), 76–82. doi:10.1016/j.ijinfomgt.2012.07.003

Larson, K., & Watson, R. T. (2011). *The value of social media: Toward measuring social media strategies.* Paper presented at the 32nd International Conference on Information Systems (ICIS). Shanghai, China.

LaTour, M. S., & Henthorne, T. L. (1994). Ethical judgments of sexual appeals in print advertising. *Journal of Advertising, 23*(3), 81–91. doi:10.1080/00913367.1994.10673453

Lavie, D. (2006). Capability reconfiguration: An analysis of incumbent responses to technological change. *Academy of Management Review, 31*(1), 153–174. doi:10.5465/AMR.2006.19379629

Lazarsfeld, P. F., Berelson, B., & Gaudet, H. (1944). *The people's choice: How the voter makes up his mind in a presidential campaign.* New York: Columbia University Press.

Lederer, A., & Mendelow, A. (1989). Co-ordination of information systems plans with business plans. *Journal of Management Information Systems, 6*(2), 5–19.

Lee, M. (2007). Baghdad embassy plans turn up online. *The Huffington Post.* Retrieved September 10, 2013 from http://www.huffingtonpost.com/huff-wires/20070531/baghdad-embassy-plans/

Lee, G. K., & Cole, R. E. (2003). From a firm-based to a community-based model of knowledge creation: The case of the Linux kernel development. *Organization Science, 14*(6), 633–649. doi:10.1287/orsc.14.6.633.24866

Lee, I. (2011). Overview of emerging web 2.0-based business models and web 2.0 applications in business: An ecological perspective. *International Journal of E-Business Research, 7*(4), 1–16. doi:10.4018/jebr.2011100101

Lee, W., Xiongb, L., & Hu, C. (2012). The Effect of Facebook Users' Arousal and Valence on Intention to Go to the Festival: Applying an Extension of the Technology Acceptance Model. *International Journal of Hospitality Management, 31*(3), 819–827. doi:10.1016/j.ijhm.2011.09.018

Lehmann, D. R., & Winer, R. S. (2005). *Analysis for marketing planning* (6th ed.). Boston, MA: McGraw-Hill.

Leng, G. S., Lada, S., & Muhammad, M. Z. (2011). An Exploration of Social Networking Sites (SNS) Adoption in Malaysia Using Technology Acceptance Model (TAM), Theory of Planned Behavior (TPB) and Intrinsic Motivation. *Journal of Internet Banking and Commerce, 16*(2), 2–27.

Levinthal, D. A., & March, J. G. (1993). The myopia of learning. *Strategic Management Journal, 14*(S2), 95–112. doi:10.1002/smj.4250141009

Levitt, T. (1960). Marketing myopia. *Harvard Business Review, 38*, 45–60.

Levy, M. (2009). Web 2.0 implications on knowledge management. *Journal of Knowledge Management, 13*(1), 120–134. doi:10.1108/13673270910931215

Li, C. (2009). *The world's most valuable brands. Who's most engaged? ENGAGEMENTdb: Ranking the top 100 global brands.* Retrieved February 9, 2014 from http://www.altimetergroup.com/2009/07/engagementdb.html

Libai, B., Bolton, R., Bugel, M. S., De Ruyter, K., Gotz, O., Risselada, H., & Stephen, A. T. (2010). Customer-to-customer interactions: Broadening the scope of word of mouth research. *Journal of Service Research, 13*(3), 267–282. doi:10.1177/1094670510375600

Li, M. B., Xie, S. Q., & Xu, X. (2011). Recent development of knowledge-based systems, methods and tools for one-of-a-kind production. *Knowledge-Based Systems, 24*(7), 1108–1119. doi:10.1016/j.knosys.2011.05.005

Lim, D., & Klobas, J. (2000). Knowledge management in small enterprises. *The Electronic Library, 18*(6), 420–432. doi:10.1108/02640470010361178

Lin, D., Greissler, P., Ehrlich, S., & Shoop, E. (2011). IDEA: A framework for a knowledge-based enterprise 2.0. *Journal of Universal Computer Science, 17*(4), 515–531.

Lindberg-Repo, K., & Gronroos, C. (2004). Conceptualising communication strategy from a relational perspective. *Industrial Marketing Management, 33*(3), 229–239. doi:10.1016/j.indmarman.2003.10.012

Lin, F., Liu, C.-W., & Kuo, I.-H. (2013). Moderating Effect of Perceived Usefulness on the Relationship between Ease of Use, Attitude toward Use and Actual System Use. *International Journal of Organizational Innovation, 5*(3), 180–191.

Lin, K.-Y., & Lu, H.-P. (2011). Why People Use Social Networking Sites: An Empirical Study Integrating Network Externalities and Motivation Theory. *Computers in Human Behavior, 27*(3), 1152–1161. doi:10.1016/j.chb.2010.12.009

LinkedIn. (2013). *About LinkedIn.* Retrieved February 11, 2014 from http://www.linkedin.com/about-us

LipikaD. S.MirajulH.ArpitK.GautamS. (2011). Acquiring competitive intelligence from social media. In Proceedings of the 2011 Joint Workshop on Multilingual OCR and Analytics for Noisy Unstructured Text Data. ACM. DOI:

Lipsman, A., Mudd, G., Rich, M., & Bruich, S. (2012, March). The power of like: How brands reach (and influence) fans through social media. *Journal of Advertising Research, 52*(1), 40–52. doi:10.2501/JAR-52-1-040-052

Lithium Technologies. (2009). *Powering the customer network with social CRM.* Lithium Technologies.

Liu, F., Cheng, H., & Li, J. (2009). Consumer responses to sex appeal advertising: A cross-cultural study. *International Marketing Review, 26*(4/5), 501–520. doi:10.1108/02651330910972002

Liu-Thompkins, Y. (2012). Seeding viral content: The role of message and network factors. *Journal of Advertising Research, 52*(4), 465–478. doi:10.2501/JAR-52-4-465-478

Liu-Thompkins, Y., & Rogerson, M. (2012). Rising to stardom: An empirical investigation of the diffusion of user-generated content. *Journal of Interactive Marketing, 26*(2), 71–82. doi:10.1016/j.intmar.2011.11.003

Lombardot, É. (2007). La nudité en publicité: Quelle influence sur l'attention portée à l'annonce et la fonction mémorielle de la marque? *Recherche et Applications en Marketing, 22*(4), 23–41. doi:10.1177/076737010702200401

Lönnqvist, A., & Laihonen, H. (2013). Managing regional development: A knowledge perspective. *International Journal of Knowledge-Based Development, 4*(1), 50–63. doi:10.1504/IJKBD.2013.052493

Luck, E. M., Beaton, J., & Moffatt, J. J. (2010). *The social media (r)evolution: Obama's political campaign.* Paper presented at the 2010 Global Marketing Conference. Tokyo, Japan.

Lutz, R. J., MacKenzie, S. B., & Belch, G. (1983). Attitude toward the ad as a mediator of advertising effectiveness: Determinants and consequences. *Advances in Consumer Research. Association for Consumer Research (U. S.), 10*, 532–539.

Lynch, C. G. (2009). TI's web 2.0 success story: Better customer service. *CIO.* Retrieved June 1, 2010, from http://www.cio.com/article/496338/TI_s_Web_2.0_Success_Story_Better_Customer_Service

Lyons, D. (2008). Facebook's roar becomes a meow. *Newsweek, 152*(16), E22.

Maarek, P. (1995). *Political Marketing and Communication.* John Libbey & LTD Publishers.

Machin-Mastromatteo, J. D. (2011). *Exploring users' information behavior in social networks: A contribution to the understanding of the use of social networks.* Saarbrucken, Germany: Lambert Academic Publishing.

MacInnis, D., & Jaworski, B. (1988). Information processing from advertisements: Toward an integrative framework. *Journal of Marketing, 53*(4), 1–23. doi:10.2307/1251376

MacKenzie, S. B., & Lutz, R. J. (1989). An empirical examination of the structural antecedents of attitude toward the ad in an advertising pretesting context. *Journal of Marketing, 53*(2), 48–65. doi:10.2307/1251413

MacKenzie, S. B., Lutz, R. J., & Belch, G. (1986). The role of attitude toward the ad as a mediator of advertising effectiveness: A test of competing explanations. *JMR, Journal of Marketing Research, 23*(2), 130–143. doi:10.2307/3151660

Maclaren, P., & Catterall, M. (2012). Researching the social web: Marketing information from virtual communities. *Marketing Intelligence & Planning*, *20*(6), 319–326. doi:10.1108/02634500210445374

Madhok, A., & Osegowitsh, T. (2000). The international biotechnology industry: A dynamic capabilities perspective. *Journal of International Business Studies*, *31*(2), 325–335. doi:10.1057/palgrave.jibs.8490909

Madia, S. A. (2011). Best practices for using social media as a recruitment strategy. *Strategic HR Review*, *10*(6), 19–24. doi:10.1108/14754391111172788

Magnusson, P. (2003). Benefits of involving users in service. *European Journal of Innovation Management*, *6*(4), 228–238. doi:10.1108/14601060310500940

Mahesh, K., & Suresh, K. J. (2009). Knowledge criteria for organization design. *Journal of Knowledge Management*, *13*(4), 41–51. doi:10.1108/13673270910971815

Makadok, R., & Barney, J. B. (2001). Strategic factor market intelligence: An application of information economics to strategy formulation and competitor intelligence. *Management Science*, *47*(12), 1621–1638. doi:10.1287/mnsc.47.12.1621.10245

Malone, T. W., Laubacher, R., & Dellarocas, C. (2009). *Harnessing crowds: Mapping the genome of collective intelligence* (Working Paper No. 2009-001). MIT Center for Collective Intelligence.

Manchanda, P., Xie, Y., & Youn, N. (2008). The role of targeted communication and contagion in product adoption. *Marketing Science*, *27*(6), 961–976. doi:10.1287/mksc.1070.0354

Mangold, W. G., & Faulds, D. J. (2009). Social media: The new hybrid element of the promotion mix. *Business Horizons*, *52*(4), 357–365. doi:10.1016/j.bushor.2009.03.002

Mantere, S., & Vaara, E. (2008). On the Problem of Participation in Strategy: A Critical Discursive Perspective. *Organization Science*, *19*(2), 341–358. doi:10.1287/orsc.1070.0296

March, J. G. (1991). Exploration and exploitation in organizational learning. *Organization Science*, *2*(1), 71–87. doi:10.1287/orsc.2.1.71

Marketing Science Institute. (2010). *Marketing Science Institute 2010-2012 Research Priorities*. Cambridge, MA: Marketing Science Institute.

Marques, D. P., & Simon, F. J. G. (2006). The effect of knowledge management practices on firm performance. *Journal of Knowledge Management*, *10*(3), 143–156. doi:10.1108/13673270610670911

Martinkenaite, I. (2012). Antecedents of knowledge transfer in acquisitions. *Baltic Journal of Management*, *7*(2), 167–184. doi:10.1108/17465261211219796

Massa, S., & Testa, S. (2009). A knowledge management approach to organizational competitive advantage: Evidence from the food sector. *European Management Journal*, *27*(2), 129–141. doi:10.1016/j.emj.2008.06.005

Mayfield, A. (2008). *What is Social Media?* iCrossing eBook. Retrieved September 10, 2013 from http://www.icrossing.co.uk/fileadmin/uploads/eBooks/What_is_Social_Media_iCrossing_ebook.pdf

Mayo, M. C., & Brown, G. S. (1999). Building a competitive business model. *Ivey Business Journal*, *63*(3), 18–23.

McAfee, A. P. (2006, Spring). Enterprise 2.0: The dawn of emergent collaboration. *MIT Sloan Management Review*, 21–28.

McAfee, A. (2009). *Enterprise 2.0: New Collaborative Tools for Your Organization's Toughest Challenges*. Boston, MA: Harvard Business School Press.

McCarthy, E. J. (1960). *Basic marketing*. Columbus, OH: McGraw-Hill/Irwin.

McCarthy, J., Rowley, J., Ashworth, C. J., & Pioch, E. (2014). Managing brand presence through social media: The case of UK football clubs. *Internet Research*, *24*(2), 181–204. doi:10.1108/IntR-08-2012-0154

McCracken, G. (1988). *The long interview*. Newbury Park, CA: Sage Publications. doi:10.4135/9781412986229

McDonald, A. M., & Cranor, L. F. (2008). The cost of reading privacy policies. *ACM Transactions on Computer-Human Interaction*, *4*(3), 1–22. doi:10.1145/1314683.1314684

McGurk, J., & Baron, A. (2012). Knowledge management: Time to focus on purpose and motivation. *Strategic HR Review, 11*(6), 316–321. doi:10.1108/14754391211264776

McKinlay, A. (2005). Knowledge management. In S. Ackroyd, R. Batt, & P. Thompson (Eds.), *The Oxford handbook of work and organization* (pp. 242–262). Oxford, UK: Oxford University Press.

McKinsey Global Institute. (2011). *Big data: The next frontier for innovation competition and productivity*. Research Report.

McLean, R., & Wainwright, D. (2009). Social networks, football fans, fantasy and reality: How corporate and media interests are invading our life world. *Journal of Information. Culture and Ethics, 7*(1), 54–71.

Mergel, I. (2013). Designing a social media strategy to fulfill your agency's mission. *Public Management, 42*(1), 26–29.

Mezias, S. J., & Glynn, M. A. (1993). The three faces of corporate renewal: Institution, revolution, and evolution. *Strategic Management Journal, 14*(2), 77–101. doi:10.1002/smj.4250140202

Michaelidou, N., Siamagka, N. T., & Christodoulides, G. (2011). Usage, barriers and measurement of social media marketing: An exploratory investigation of small and medium b2b brands. *Industrial Marketing Management, 40*(7), 1153–1159. doi:10.1016/j.indmarman.2011.09.009

Miller, G., & Parks, M. (1982). Communication in dissolving relationships. In S. Duck (Ed.), *Personal Relationships 4: Dissolving Personal Relationships*. New York: Academic Press.

Miller, K. D., Fabian, F., & Lin, S. J. (2009). Strategies for online communities. *Strategic Management Journal, 30*(3), 305–322. doi:10.1002/smj.735

Miller, M. (2008). *Cloud computing: Web-based applications that change the way you work and collaborate*. Indianapolis, IN: Queue Publishers.

Mills, P. K., & Ungson, G. (2003). Reassessing the limits of structural empowerment: Organizational constitution and trust as controls. *Academy of Management Review, 28*(1), 143–153.

Mintzberg, H., Raisinghani, D., & Theoret, A. (1976). The structure of unstructured decision processes. *Administrative Science Quarterly, 21*(2), 246–275. doi:10.2307/2392045

Mishra, K. E., & Boynton, L. (2009). *Talk-the-talk: Using internal communication to build trust with employees*. Paper presented at the International Public Relations Research Conference. Miami, FL.

Mishra, A. K. (1996). Organizational responses to crisis: The centrality of trust. In R. Kramer, & T. Tyler (Eds.), *Trust in organizations* (pp. 261–287). Newbury Park, CA: Sage. doi:10.4135/9781452243610.n13

Mishra, A. K., & Mishra, K. E. (1994). The role of mutual trust in effective downsizing strategies. *Human Resource Management, 33*(2), 261–279. doi:10.1002/hrm.3930330207

Mishra, A. K., & Mishra, K. E. (2013). *Becoming a trustworthy leader: Psychology & practice*. Routledge Press.

Mishra, A. K., & Spreitzer, G. M. (1998). Explaining how survivors respond to downsizing: The roles of trust, empowerment, justice and work redesign. *Academy of Management Review, 23*(3), 567–588.

Mishra, K. E., Schwarz, G. M., & Mishra, A. K. (2011). The evolution of trust and control as seen through an organization's human resources practices. In R. Searle (Ed.), *Trust and Human Resource Management*. Cheltenham, UK: Edward Elgar. doi:10.4337/9780857932006.00009

Moeller, K. (2010). Partner selection, partner behavior, and business network performance: An empirical study of German business networks. *Journal of Accounting and Organizational Change, 6*(1), 27–51. doi:10.1108/18325911011025687

Moloney, K. (2004). *Is Political Marketing New Words or New Practice in UK Politics?* Paper presented at the PSA Conference. Lincoln, UK.

Moon, M. J. (2002). The Evolution of E-Government among Municipalities: Rhetoric or Reality? *Public Administration Review, 62*(4), 424–433. doi:10.1111/0033-3352.00196

Moore, G., & Benbasat, I. (1991). Development of an Instrument to Measure the Perceptions of Adopting New Information Technology Innovation. *Information Systems Research*, *2*(3), 192–222. doi:10.1287/isre.2.3.192

Morris, M., Schindehutte, M., & Allen, J. (2005). The entrepreneur's business model: Toward a unified perspective. *Journal of Business Research*, *58*(6), 726–735. doi:10.1016/j.jbusres.2003.11.001

Morrison, P. D., Roberts, J. H., & Midgley, D. F. (2004). The Nature of Lead Users and Measurement of Leading Edge Status. *Research Policy*, *33*(2), 351–362. doi:10.1016/j.respol.2003.09.007

Morrissey, B. (2008). Viral video hits blur the authenticity line. *Adweek*, *49*(37), 8.

Mosadegh, M. J., & Behboudi, M. (2011). Using social network paradigm for developing a conceptual framework in CRM. *Australian Journal of Business and Management Research*, *18*, 50–64.

Mounter, P. (2003). Global internal communication: A model. *Journal of Communication Management*, *7*(3), 3. doi:10.1108/13632540310807412

Muehling, D. D., & McCann, M. (1993). Attitude toward the ad: A review. *Journal of Current Issues and Research in Advertising*, *15*(2), 25–58. doi:10.1080/10641734.1993.10505002

Muniz, A. M. Jr, & O'Guinn, T. C. (2001). Brand community. *The Journal of Consumer Research*, *27*(4), 412–431. doi:10.1086/319618

Murugesan, S. (2007). Understanding web 2.0. *IT Professional*, *9*(4), 34–41. doi:10.1109/MITP.2007.78

Musser, J., & O'Reilly, T. (2007). *Web 2.0 principles and practices*. O'Reilly Media Inc. Retrieved February 15, 2014, from http://oreilly.com/radar/web2report.csp

Myers, M., Calantone, R., Page, T. Jr, & Taylor, C. (2000). Academic Insights: An Application of Multiple-Group Causal Models in Assessing Cross-Cultural Measurement Equivalence. *Journal of International Marketing*, *8*(4), 108–121. doi:10.1509/jimk.8.4.108.19790

Mylona, I. (2008). SMS in Everyday Political Marketing in Greece. *Journal of Political Marketing*, *7*(3-4), 278–294. doi:10.1080/15377850802008335

Nahapiet, J., & Sumantra, G. (1998). Social capital, intellectual capital and the organizational advantage. *Academy of Management Review*, *23*(2), 242–266.

Nakata, C., Zhu, Z., & Izberk-Bilgin, E. (2011). Integrating marketing and information services functions: A complementarity and competence perspective. *Journal of the Academy of Marketing Science*, *39*(5), 700–716. doi:10.1007/s11747-010-0236-z

Nambisan, S. (2002). Designing virtual customer environments for new product development: Toward a theory. *Academy of Management Review*, *27*(33), 392–413.

Nambisan, S., & Baron, R. A. (2007). Interactions in virtual customer environments: Implications for product support and customer relationship management. *Journal of Interactive Marketing*, *21*(2), 42–62. doi:10.1002/dir.20077

Nambisan, S., & Nambisan, P. (2008). How to Profit From a Better Virtual Customer Environment. *MIT Sloan Management Review*, *49*(3), 53–61.

Narayanan, M., Asur, S., Nair, A., Rao, S., Kaushik, A., & Mehta, D. et al. (2012). Social media and business. *Vikalpa: The Journal for Decision Makers*, *37*(4), 69–111.

Narayandas, D., & Rangan, V. K. (2004). Building and sustaining buyer-seller relationships in mature industrial markets. *Journal of Marketing*, *68*(3), 63–77. doi:10.1509/jmkg.68.3.63.34772

Narteh, B. (2008). Knowledge transfer in developed-developing country interfirm collaborations: A conceptual framework. *Journal of Knowledge Management*, *12*(1), 78–91. doi:10.1108/13673270810852403

Narver, J. C., & Slater, S. F. (1990, October). The effect of a market orientation on business profitability. *Journal of Marketing*, *54*(4), 20–35. doi:10.2307/1251757

Narver, J. C., Slater, S. F., & MacLachlan, D. L. (2004). Responsive and proactive market orientation and new-product success. *Journal of Product Innovation Management*, *21*(5), 334–347. doi:10.1111/j.0737-6782.2004.00086.x

Nasco, S. A., Boostrom, R. E. Jr, & Coker, K. K. (2010). Virtual commerce. In *Encyclopedia of E-Business Development and Management in the Global Economy*. Hershey, PA: IGI Global. doi:10.4018/978-1-61520-611-7.ch116

Newell, J. L. (2001). Italian Political Parties on the Web. *The Harvard International Journal of Press/Politics*, *6*(4), 60–87. doi:10.1177/108118001129172341

Newman, J. (2012, January 17). SOPA and PIPA: Just the Facts. *PC World*. Retrieved September 10, 2013 from http://www.pcworld.com/article/248298/sopa_and_pipa_just_the_facts.html

Newson, A., Houghton, D., & Patten, J. (2009). *Blogging and other social media: Exploiting the technology and protecting the enterprise*. Ashgate.

Nicholas, D., & Rowlands, I. (2011). Social media use in the research workflow. *Information Services & Use*, *31*(1-2), 61–83.

Nicolajsen, H. W., & Scupola, A. (2011). Investigating issues and challenges for customer involvement in business services innovation. *Journal of Business and Industrial Marketing*, *26*(5), 368–376. doi:10.1108/08858621111144424

Nielsen. (2012). *Global consumers' trust in 'earned' advertising grows in importance*. Retrieved September 1, 2013 from http://www.nielsen.com/us/en/press-room/2012/nielsen-global-consumers-trust-in-earned-advertising-grows.html

Nielson. (2012). *The Social Media Report*. Retrieved from http://www.nielsen.com/content/dam/corporate/us/en/reports-downloads/2012-Reports/The-Social-Media-Report-2012.pdf

Nonaka, I. (1991, November-December). The knowledge-creating company. *Harvard Business Review*, 96–104.

Nonaka, I. (1994). A dynamic theory of organizational knowledge creation. *Organization Science*, *5*(1), 14–37. doi:10.1287/orsc.5.1.14

Nonaka, I. (1998). The knowledge-creating company. In P. Drucker (Ed.), *Harvard Business Review on knowledge management* (pp. 21–46). Boston, MA: Harvard Business School Press.

Nonaka, I., & Takeuchi, H. (1995). *The knowledge-creating company: How Japanese companies create the dynamics of innovation*. Oxford, UK: Oxford University Press.

Nonaka, I., & Toyama, R. (2003). The knowledge-creating theory revisited: Knowledge creation as a synthesizing process. *Knowledge Management Research & Practice*, *1*(1), 2–10. doi:10.1057/palgrave.kmrp.8500001

Normann, R., & Ramirez, R. (1993, July-August). From value chain to value constellation: Designing interactive strategy. *Harvard Business Review*, 65–77. PMID:10127040

Nudd, T. (2013). The 20 most viral ads of 2013. *Adweek*. Retrieved 5th January 2014 from www.adweek.com/news-gallery/20-most-viral-ads-2013-154000#intro

Nunes, P. F., & Merrihue, J. (2007). *The Continuing Power of Mass Advertising The Continuing Power of Mass Advertising*. MIT Sloan Management Review.

O'Cass, A. (1996). Political marketing and the marketing concept. *European Journal of Marketing*, *30*(10/11), 37–53. doi:10.1108/03090569610149782

O'Dell, C., & Hubert, C. (2011). *The new edge in knowledge: How knowledge management is changing the way we do business*. Hoboken, NJ: John Wiley & Sons.

O'Guinn, T. C., & Muňiz, A. M. Jr. (2005). Communcal consumption and the brand. In D. G. Mick, & S. Ratneshwar (Eds.), *Inside consumption: Frontiers of research on consumer motives*. London: Routledge.

O'Reilly, T. (2005). *What Is Web 2.0 Design Patterns and Business Models for the Next Generation of Software*. Retrieved from http://oreilly.com/web2/archive/what-is-web-20.html

O'Reilly, T. (2006). Web 2.0 Compact Definition: Trying Again. *O'Reilly Radar Blog*. Retrieved April 8, 2011, from http://radar.oreilly.com/2006/12/web-20-compact-definition-tryi.html 05-04-2011

O'Reilly, K., & Marx, S. (2011). How young, technical consumers determine online WOM credibility. *Qualitative Market Research: An International Journal*, *14*(4), 330–359. doi:10.1108/13522751111163191

O'Sullivan, B. (2000). What you don't know won't hurt me. *Human Communication Research*, *26*(3), 403–431.

OgawaM.AmorosoD.MukahiT.TanabuM.SatoO. (2012). Social Media Use at Work: Comparison of the United States and Japan. In Proceedings of National Conference JASMIN 2012. Tokyo, Japan: Japan Society for Management Information.

Ogawa, S., & Piller, F. T. (2006). Reducing the risks of new product development. *MIT Sloan Management Review*, *47*(2), 65–71.

Ohmae, K. (1990). Managing in a borderless world. *Harvard Business Review*, 151–161. PMID:10292934

Okazaki, S., & Taylor, C. R. (2013). Social media and international advertising: Theoretical challenges and future directions. *International Marketing Review*, *30*(1), 56–71. doi:10.1108/02651331311298573

O'Leary, N., & Wasserman, T. (2010). Old Spice campaign smells like a sales success, too. *Brand Week*. Retrieved April 13th 2013, from http://www.brandweek.com/bw/content_display/news-and-features/direct/e3i45f1c709df-0501927f56568a2acd5c7b

Oliver, R. L. (1997). *Satisfaction: A behavioral perspective on the consumer*. Boston, MA: McGraw-Hill.

Oliver, R. L. (1999). Whence consumer loyalty? *Journal of Marketing*, *63*, 33–44. doi:10.2307/1252099

Oluikpe, P. (2012). Developing a corporate knowledge management strategy. *Journal of Knowledge Management*, *16*(6), 862–878. doi:10.1108/13673271211276164

Ormrod, R. P. (2005). A Conceptual Model of Political Market Orientation. *Journal of Nonprofit & Public Sector Marketing*, *14*(1-2), 47–64. doi:10.1300/J054v14n01_04

Osarenkhoe, A. (2006). Customer-centric strategy: A longitudinal study of implementation of a customer relationship management solution. *International Journal of Technology Marketing*, *1*, 115–144.

O'Shaughnessy, N. J. (2001). The marketing of political marketing. *European Journal of Marketing*, *35*(9/10), 1047–1057. doi:10.1108/03090560110401956

Osterholm, J. (2013). *Brand fandom: The modern market mavens of the digital age*. Retrieved August 31, 2013 from http://odmgrp.com/blog/2013/01/24/brand-fandom-the-modern-market-mavens-of-the-digital-age/

Othman, R., & Sheehan, T. N. (2011). Value creation logics and resource management: A review. *Journal of Strategy and Management*, *4*(1), 5–24. doi:10.1108/17554251111110096

Owyang, J. (2009). *The future of the social web: In five eras*. Retrieved April 24, 2012 from http://www.web-strategist.com/blog/2009/04/27/future-of-the-social-web/

Owyang, J. (2011). A Chronology Of Brands That Got Punk'D By Social. *Web Strategy*. Retrieved May 17, 2011, from http://www.web-strategist.com/blog/2008/05/02/a-chonology-of-brands-that-got-punkd-by-social-media/

Palmatier, R. W. (2008). *Relationship marketing*. Marketing Science Institute.

Palmer, A., & Koenig-Lewis, N. (2009). An experiential, social network-based approach to direct marketing. *Direct Marketing: An International Journal*, *3*(3), 162–176. doi:10.1108/17505930910985116

Palte, R., Hertlein, M., Smolnik, S., & Riempp, G. (2011). The effects of a knowledge management strategy on KM performance in professional services firms. *International Journal of Knowledge Management*, *7*(1), 16–34. doi:10.4018/jkm.2011010102

Pandey, S. C., & Dutta, A. (2013). Role of knowledge infrastructure capabilities in knowledge management. *Journal of Knowledge Management*, *17*(3), 435–453. doi:10.1108/JKM-11-2012-0365

Papadatos, C. (2006). The art of storytelling: How loyalty marketers can build emotional connections to their brands. *Journal of Consumer Marketing*, *20*(4), 297–308.

Papagiannidis, S., Coursaris, C., & Bourlakis, M. (2012). Do websites influence the nature of voting intentions? The case of two national elections in Greece. *Computers in Human Behavior*, *28*(2), 300–307. doi:10.1016/j.chb.2011.09.013

Parasuraman, A. (2000). Technology Readiness Index (TRI), a multiple-item scale to measure readiness to embrace new technologies. *Journal of Service Research*, *2*(4), 307–320. doi:10.1177/109467050024001

Parker, R. K., & Nitse, S. P. (2006). Competitive intelligence gathering. In D. G. Schwartz (Ed.), *Encyclopedia of knowledge management* (pp. 44–50). London, UK: Idea Group. doi:10.4018/978-1-59140-573-3.ch007

Park, S., & Allen, J. P. (2013). Responding to online reviews: Problem solving and engagement in hotel. *Cornell Hospitality Quarterly, 54*(1), 64–73. doi:10.1177/1938965512463118

Paroutis, S., & Al Saleh, A. (2009). Determinants of knowledge sharing using Web 2.0 technologies. *Journal of Knowledge Management, 13*(4), 52–63. doi:10.1108/13673270910971824

Parra-López, E., Bulchand-Gidumal, J., Gutiérrez-Taño, D., & Díaz-Armas, R. (2011). Intentions to use social media in organizing and taking vacation trips. *Computers in Human Behavior, 27*(2), 640–654. doi:10.1016/j.chb.2010.05.022

Parrott, G., Roomi, M. A., & Holliman, D. (2010). An analysis of marketing programmes adopted by regional small and medium-sized enterprises. *Journal of Small Business and Enterprise Development, 17*(2), 184–203. doi:10.1108/14626001011041201

Parvatiyar, A., & Sheth, J. N. (2001). Customer relationship management: Emerging practice, process, and discipline. *Journal of Economic and Social Research, 3*(2), 1–34.

Patton, M. Q. (2002). *Qualitative research & evaluation methods* (3rd ed.). London: Sage.

Payne, A. (1994). Relationship marketing: Making the customer count. *Managing Service Quality, 4*(6), 29–31. doi:10.1108/EUM0000000003939

Payne, A. F., Storbacka, K., & Frow, P. (2008). Managing the co-creation of value. *Journal of the Academy of Marketing Science, 36*(1), 83–96. doi:10.1007/s11747-007-0070-0

Payne, A., & Frow, P. (2005). A strategic framework for customer relationship management. *Journal of Marketing, 69*(4), 167–176. doi:10.1509/jmkg.2005.69.4.167

Pearlson, K., & Saunders, C. (2013). *Managing and Using Information Systems* (5th ed.). Hoboken, NJ: John Wiley & Sons.

Pentina, I., Prybutok, V. R., & Zhang, X. (2008). The role of virtual communities as shopping reference groups. *Journal of Electronic Commerce Research, 9*(2), 114–136.

Pentina, I., Zhang, L., & Basmanova, O. (2013). Antecedents and consequences of trust in a social media brand: A cross-cultural study of Twitter. *Computers in Human Behavior, 29*(4), 1546–1555. doi:10.1016/j.chb.2013.01.045

Peregrin, T. (2012). Pin it to win it: Using Pinterest to promote your niche services. *Journal of the Academy of Nutrition and Dietetics, 112*(12), 1930–1934. doi:10.1016/j.jand.2012.09.026 PMID:23174679

Perez-Lopez, S., & Alegre, J. (2012). Information technology competency, knowledge processes and firm performance. *Industrial Management & Data Systems, 112*(4), 644–662. doi:10.1108/02635571211225521

Perry, C. (1998). Processes of a case study methodology for postgraduate research in marketing. *European Journal of Marketing, 32*(9/10), 785–802. doi:10.1108/03090569810232237

Peters, K., Chen, Y., Kaplan, A. M., Ognibeni, B., & Pauwels, K. (2013). Social media metrics - A framework and guidelines for managing social media. *Journal of Interactive Marketing, 27*(4), 281–298. doi:10.1016/j.intmar.2013.09.007

Petrescu, M., & Korgaonkar, P. (2011). Viral advertising: Definitional review and synthesis. *Journal of Internet Commerce, 10*(3), 208–226. doi:10.1080/15332861.2011.596007

Pettigrew, A. M. (1992). The character and significance of strategy process research. *Strategic Management Journal, 13*(S2), 5–16. doi:10.1002/smj.4250130903

Pfeffer, J., & Sutton, R. I. (2000). The Knowing-Doing Gap: How Smart Companies Turn Knowledge into Action. *Administrative Science Quarterly, 46*, 558.

Phelps, J. E., Lewis, R., Mobilio, L., Perry, D., & Raman, N. (2004). Viral marketing or electronic word-of-mouth advertising: Examining consumer responses and motivations to pass along e-mail. *Journal of Advertising Research, 44*(4), 333–348.

Piller, F. T., & Walcher, D. (2006). Toolkits for Idea Competitions: A Novel Method to Integrate Users in New Product Development. *R & D Management*, *36*(3), 307–318. doi:10.1111/j.1467-9310.2006.00432.x

Pincus, D. J., Rayfield, R. E., & Cozzens, M. D. (1991). The Chief Executive Officer's internal communications role: A benchmark program of research. In L. A. Grunig, & J. E. Grunig (Eds.), *Public Relations Research Annual* (Vol. 3, pp. 1–36). Hillsdale, NJ: Lawrence Earlbaum Associates.

Plessis, M. D. (2005). Drivers of knowledge management in the corporate environment. *International Journal of Information Management*, *25*(3), 193–202. doi:10.1016/j.ijinfomgt.2004.12.001

Poetz, M. K., & Schreier, M. (2012). The value of crowdsourcing: Can users really compete with professionals in generating new product ideas? *Journal of Product Innovation Management*, *29*(2), 245–256. doi:10.1111/j.1540-5885.2011.00893.x

Pookulangare, S., & Koesler, K. (2011). Cultural influence on consumers' usage of social networks and its impact on online purchase intentions. *Journal of Retailing and Consumer Services*, *18*(4), 348–354. doi:10.1016/j.jretconser.2011.03.003

Porter, C. E., & Donthu, N. (2008). Cultivating Trust and Harvesting Value in Virtual Communities. *Management Science*, *54*(1), 113–128. doi:10.1287/mnsc.1070.0765

Porter, E. M. (2001). Strategy and the internet. *Harvard Business Review*, *79*(3), 62–78. PMID:11246925

Porter, L., & Golan, G. J. (2006). From Subservient Chickens to Brawny Men: A comparison of viral advertising to television advertising. *Journal of Interactive Advertising*, *6*(2), 30–38.

Porter, M. E. (1987). From competitive advantage to corporate strategy. *Harvard Business Review*, *65*, 43–59.

Prabhu, D. (2006). KM Tigers. *Inside Knowledge*, *9*(9).

Prahalad, C. K., & Ramaswamy, V. (2004). Co-creating unique value with customers. *Strategy and Leadership*, *32*(3), 4–9. doi:10.1108/10878570410699249

Prahalad, C. K., & Ramaswamy, V. (2004). Co-creation experiences: The next practice in value creation. *Journal of Interactive Marketing*, *18*(3), 5–14. doi:10.1002/dir.20015

Prandelli, E., Sawhney, M., & Verona, G. (2008). *Collaborating with customers to innovate*. Edward Elgar. doi:10.4337/9781848442917

Prandelli, E., Verona, G., & Raccagni, D. (2006). Diffusion of Web-Based Product Innovation. *California Management*, *48*(4), 109–135. doi:10.2307/41166363

Qualman, E. (2009). *Socialnomics: How social media transforms the way we live and do business*. John Wiley & Sons, Incorporated.

Quirke, B. (2008). *Making the connections: Using internal communication to turn strategy into action*. Burlington, VT: Gower.

Radick, S. (2011). The power of social networks: Reviving the intranet. *Public Relations Tactics*, 18.

Raimondo, M. A., Miceli, C. N., & Costabile, M. (2008). How relationship age moderates loyalty formation: The increasing effect of relational equity on customer loyalty. *Journal of Service Research*, *11*(2), 142–160. doi:10.1177/1094670508324678

Rajagopalan, N., Rasheed, A. M. A., & Dutta, D. K. (1993). Strategic decision processes: Critical review and future directions. *Journal of Management*, *19*(2), 349–384. doi:10.1177/014920639301900207

Rao, M. (2002). *Knowledge management tools and techniques: Practitioners and experts evaluate KM solutions*. Amsterdam, The Netherlands: Elsevier.

Rappa, M. (2004). *Business Models on the Web*. Retrieved July 25, 2006 from http://digitalenterprise.org/models/models.html

Rayport, J. F. (1996). The virus of marketing. *Fast Company*. Retrieved May 20th 2013, from http://www.fastcompany.com/magazine/06/virus.html

Razmerita, L., Kirchner, K., & Sudzina, F. (2009). Personal knowledge management: The role of Web 2.0 tools for managing knowledge at individual and organizational levels. *Online Information Review*, *33*(6), 1021–1039. doi:10.1108/14684520911010981

Rechtin, M. (2009). Fiesta viral marketing: First, Ford built awareness of its upcoming small car, next, it shows off features. *Automotive News*, *84*, 6–7.

Reichert, T., Heckler, S. E., & Jackson, S. (2001). The effects of sexual social marketing appeals on cognitive processing and persuasion. *Journal of Advertising*, *30*(1), 13–27. doi:10.1080/00913367.2001.10673628

Reichheld, F. F. (1993, March-April). Loyalty-based management. *Harvard Business Review*, 64–73.

Reichheld, F. F., & Saaser, W. E. Jr. (1990, September-November). Zero defections: Quality comes to services. *Harvard Business Review*, 105–111.

Reid, A. (2005, February). Viral advertising campaigns. *Campaign*, 14.

Reinartz, W., Krafft, M., & Hoyer, W. D. (2004). The customer relationship management process: Its measurement and impact on performance. *JMR, Journal of Marketing Research*, *41*(3), 293–305. doi:10.1509/jmkr.41.3.293.35991

Reinartz, W., & Kumar, V. (2002, July). The mismanagement of customer loyalty. *Harvard Business Review*, 86–94.

Reinartz, W., Thomas, J. S., & Kumar, V. (2005). Balancing acquisition and retention resources to maximize customer profitability. *Journal of Marketing*, *69*(1), 63–79. doi:10.1509/jmkg.69.1.63.55511

Rheingold, H. (1993). *The virtual community: Homesteading on the electronic frontier*. Reading, MA: Addison-Wesley.

Richter, A., & Koch, M. (2008). Functions on Social Networking Services. In *Proceedings of 8th International Conference on the Design of Cooperative Systems*. Academic Press.

Richter, A., & Riemer, K. (2009). *Corporate Social Networking Sites – Modes of Use and Appropriation through Co-Evolution*. Paper presented at the 20th Australasian Conference on Information Systems. Melbourne, Australia.

Robertson, D. (2013, Quarter 1). Storytelling is key to engagement. *Market Leader*, 17.

Robinson, S. (2006). Using games and clickers to encourage students to study and participate. *Academy of Educational Leadership*, *11*(2), 25–29.

Robison, N. (2011). *4 free tools for social media competitive analysis*. Retrieved August 20, 2013, from http://blog.socialmediahq.com/4-free-tools-for-social-media-competitive-analysis/

Robson, P., & Tourish, D. (2005). Managing internal communication: An organizational case study. *Corporate Communications*, *10*(3), 213–222. doi:10.1108/13563280510614474

Rogers, E. M. (1962). *Diffusion of Innovations*. Glencoe, IL: Free Press.

Rohm, A., Velitchka, D., Kaltcheva, G., & Milne, R. (2013). A mixed-method approach to examining brand-consumer interactions driven by social media. *Journal of Research in Interactive Marketing*, *7*(4), 295–311. doi:10.1108/JRIM-01-2013-0009

Rosenblum, D. (2007). What anyone can know: The privacy risks of social networking sites. *IEEE Security and Privacy*, *5*(3), 40–49. doi:10.1109/MSP.2007.75

Ross, J., Weill, P., & Robertson, P. (2006). *Enterprise Architecture as Strategy*. Boston, MA: Harvard Business School Press.

Rowley, J. (1999). What is knowledge management? *Library Management*, *20*(8), 416–419. doi:10.1108/01435129910291175

Rowley, J., Kupiec-Teahan, B., & Leeming, E. (2007). Customer community and co-creation: A case study. *Marketing Intelligence & Planning*, *25*(2), 136–146. doi:10.1108/02634500710737924

Ruppel, C. P., & Harrington, S. J. (2001). Sharing knowledge through intranets: A study of organizational culture and intranet implementation. *Professional Communication*, *44*(1), 37–52. doi:10.1109/47.911131

Rust, R. T., Lemon, K. N., & Zeithaml, V. A. (2004). Return on marketing: Using customer equity to focus marketing strategy. *Journal of Marketing*, *68*(1), 109–127. doi:10.1509/jmkg.68.1.109.24030

Rust, R. T., & Oliver, R. W. (1994). The death of advertising. *Journal of Advertising*, *23*(4), 71–77. doi:10.1080/00913367.1943.10673460

Rutherford, L. L. (2008). Building participative library services: The impact of social software use in public libraries. *Library Hi Tech*, *26*(3), 41. doi:10.1108/07378830810903337

Ryu, G., & Feick, L. (2007). A penny for your thoughts: Referral reward programs and referral likelihood. *Journal of Marketing*, *71*(1), 84–94. doi:10.1509/jmkg.71.1.84

Sajeva, S. (2010). The analysis of key elements of socio-technical knowledge management system. *Economics and Management*, *15*, 765–774.

Saka-Helmhout, A. (2011). Learning from the periphery: Beyond the transnational model. *Critical Perspectives on International Business*, *7*(1), 48–65. doi:10.1108/17422041111103831

Saks, A. M. (2006). Antecedents and consequences of employee engagement. *Journal of Managerial Psychology*, *21*(7), 600–619. doi:10.1108/02683940610690169

Salleh, K., Chong, S. C., Syed Ahmad, S. N., & Syed Ikhsan, S. O. (2012). Learning and knowledge transfer performance among public sector accountants: An empirical survey. *Knowledge Management Research and Practice*, *10*(2), 164–174. doi:10.1057/kmrp.2011.46

Sammarra, A., & Biggiero, L. (2008). Heterogeneity and specificity of inter-firm knowledge flows in innovation networks. *Journal of Management Studies*, *45*(4), 800–829. doi:10.1111/j.1467-6486.2008.00770.x

Sampedro, V., & Perez, F. S. (2008). The 2008 Spanish General Elections: Antagonistic Bipolarization Geared by Presidential Debates, Partisanship,and Media Interests. *The International Journal of Press/Politics*, *13*(3), 336–344. doi:10.1177/1940161208319293

Santos, S. (2011). Why Social Media is Disruptive. www.thesocialcustomer.com. Retrieved May 17, 2011, from http://thesocialcustomer.com/shawn-santos/34382/why-social-media-disruptive

Sashi, C. M. (2012). Customer engagement, buyer-seller relationships and social media. *Management Decision*, *50*(2), 253–273. doi:10.1108/00251741211203551

Saunders, M., Lewis, P., & Thornill, A. (2007). *Research methods for business students* (4th ed.). Harlow, UK: Pearson.

Saw, G., Abbott, W., Donaghey, J., & McDonald, C. (2013). Social media for international students – It's not all about Facebook. *Library Management*, *34*(3), 156–174. doi:10.1108/01435121311310860

Sawhney, M., & Zabin, J. (2002). Managing and measuring relational equity in the network economy. *Journal of the Academy of Marketing Science*, *30*(4), 313–332. doi:10.1177/009207002236908

Scammell, M. (1999). Political Marketing: Lessons for Political Science. *Political Studies*, *47*(4), 718–739. doi:10.1111/1467-9248.00228

Schau, H. J., Muñiz, A. M. Jr, & Arnould, E. J. (2009). How brand community practices create value. *Journal of Marketing*, *73*(5), 30–51. doi:10.1509/jmkg.73.5.30

Schlenkrich, L., & Upfold, C. (2009). A guideline for virtual team managers: The key to effective social interaction and communication. *The Electronic Journal of Information Systems Evaluation*, *12*(1), 109–118.

Schlinke, J., & Crain, S. (2013). Social media from an integrated marketing and compliance perspective. *Journal of Financial Service Professionals*, *67*(2), 85–92.

Schmidt, R., Lyytinen, K., Keil, M., & Cule, P. (2001). Identifying software project risks: An international delphi study. *Journal of Management Information Systems*, *17*(4), 5–36.

Schmidt, S., & Ralph, D. (2011). Social Media: More Available Marketing Tools. *Business Review (Federal Reserve Bank of Philadelphia)*, *18*(2), 37–43.

Schneckenberg, D. (2009). Web 2.0 and the empowerment of the knowledge worker. *Journal of Knowledge Management*, *13*(6), 509–520. doi:10.1108/13673270910997150

Schultz, D. E. (1999). Integrated marketing communications and how it relates to traditional media advertising. In J. P. Jones (Ed.), *The Advertising Business: Operations, Creativity, Media Planning, Integrated Communications* (pp. 325–338). London, UK: Sage. doi:10.4135/9781452231440.n34

Schultz, D. E., & Peltier, J. (2013). Social media's slippery slope: challenges, opportunities and future research directions. *Journal of Research in Interactive Marketing*, *7*(2), 86–99. doi:10.1108/JRIM-12-2012-0054

Schweidel, D. A., & Moe, W. W. (2012, October). The perils of 'selective listening' in social media monitoring: Sentiment and venue choice in social media posting behavior. *SSRN Working Paper Series*.

Schweidel, D. A., Moe, W. W., & Boudreaux, C. (2011). *Social media intelligence: Measuring brand sentiment from online conversations*. Retrieved February 12, 2014 from http://ssrn.com/abstract=1874892 or http://dx.doi.org/10.2139/ssrn.1874892

Scott, C. M., Klein, D., & Bryant, J. (1990). Consumer response to humor in advertising: A series of field studies using behavioral observation. *The Journal of Consumer Research*, *16*(4), 498–501. doi:10.1086/209235

Scott, J. (2000). *Social network analysis: A handbook* (2nd ed.). London: Sage Publications.

Scupola, A., & Nicolajsen, H. W. (2010). Service innovation in academic libraries: Is there a place for the customers? *Library Management*, *31*(4/5), 304–318. doi:10.1108/01435121011046362

Scupola, A., & Nicolajsen, H. W. (2013). Library perceptions of using social software such as blogs in the idea generation phase of service innovations: Lessons from an experiment. In *Organizational Change and Information Systems - Working and living together in new ways (LNISO)* (pp. 137–145). Berlin: Springer. doi:10.1007/978-3-642-37228-5_14

Seb, J. (2012, November 15). Brands delve deeper into crowdsourcing. *Marketing Week*, 6.

Seigenthaler, J. (2005). A false Wikipedia 'biography'. *USA Today*. Retrieved September 10, 2013 from http://usatoday30.usatoday.com/news/opinion/editorials/2005-11-29-wikipedia-edit_x.htm

SelectMinds. (2008). *Corporate Social Networking: SelectMinds Benchmarking Study*. Retrieved from www.selectminds.com

Sena, J., & Sena, M. (2008). Corporate social networking. *Issues in Information Systems*, *9*(2), 227–231.

Severn, J., Belch, G. E., & Belch, M. A. (1990). The effects of sexual and non-sexual advertising appeals and information level on cognitive processing and communication effectiveness. *Journal of Advertising*, *19*(1), 14–22. doi:10.1080/00913367.1990.10673176

Sevin, E., Kimball, S., & Khalil, M. (2011). Listening to president Obama: A short examination of obama's communication practices. *The American Behavioral Scientist*, *55*(6), 803–812. doi:10.1177/0002764211406847

Shafer, S. M., Smith, H. J., & Linder, J. (2005). The power of business models. *Business Horizons*, *48*(3), 199–207. doi:10.1016/j.bushor.2004.10.014

Shama, A. (1976). The marketing of political candidates. *Journal of the Academy of Marketing Science*, *4*(4), 764–777. doi:10.1007/BF02729836

Shang, R.-A., Chen, Y.-C., & Liao, H.-J. (2006). The value of participation in virtual consumer communities on brand loyalty. *Internet Research*, *16*(4), 365–379. doi:10.1108/10662240610690025

Sharma, R. S., & Djiaw, V. (2011). Realising the strategic impact of business intelligence tools. *VINE - The Journal of Information and Knowledge Management Systems*, *41*(2), 113-131.

Shaw, S., & Fairhurst, D. (2008). Engaging a new generation of graduates. *Education + Training*, *50*(5), 366–378. doi:10.1108/00400910810889057

Sherer, S. A., Kohli, R., Yao, Y., & Cederlund, J. (2011). Do Cultural Differences Matter in IT Implementation? A Multinational's Experience with Collaborative Technology. *Journal of Global Information Management*, *19*(4), 1–17. doi:10.4018/jgim.2011100101

Sheth, J. N., & Parvatiyar, A. (1995). The evolution of relationship marketing. *International Business Review*, *4*(4), 397–418. doi:10.1016/0969-5931(95)00018-6

Sheth, J. N., & Uslay, C. (2007). Implications of the revised definition of marketing: From exchange to value creation. *Journal of Public Policy & Marketing*, *26*(2), 302–307. doi:10.1509/jppm.26.2.302

Shimba, F. (2010). *Cloud computing: Strategies for cloud computing adoption*. Dublin, Ireland: Dublin Institute of Technology.

Shirey, T. (2010). BP and Social Media. *WebpageFX Weekly*. Retrieved May 3, 2011, from http://www.webpagefx.com/blog/business-advice/bp-and-social-media/

Shukla, T. (2010). Factors affecting 'internet marketing' campaigns with reference to viral and permission marketing. *The IUP Journal of Management Research, 9*(1), 26–37.

Sicilia, M., & Palazon, M. (2008). Brand communities on the internet: A case study of Coca-Cola's Spanish virtual community. *Corporate Communications: An International Journal, 13*(3), 255–270. doi:10.1108/13563280810893643

Siebdrat, F., Hoegl, M., & Ernst, H. (2009). How to manage virtual teams. *MIT Sloan Management Review, 50*(4), 63–68.

Siegall, M., & Gardner, S. (2000). Contextual factors of psychological empowerment. *Personnel Review, 29*(6), 703–722. doi:10.1108/00483480010296474

Sigala, M. (2011). Social networks and customer involvement in new service development (NSD): The case of www.mystarbucksidea.com. *International Journal of Contemporary Hospitality Management, 24*(7), 966-990

Silva, C. (2010, May). Social Media Customer Leaders: Some Early Performance Data. *Harvard Business Review*.

Simonin, B. (1999). Ambiguity and the process of knowledge transfer in strategic alliances. *Strategic Management Journal, 20*(7), 595–623. doi:10.1002/(SICI)1097-0266(199907)20:7<595::AID-SMJ47>3.0.CO;2-5

Simpson, M., Padmore, J., & Newman, N. (2012). Towards a new model of success and performance in SMEs. *International Journal of Entrepreneurial Behaviour & Research, 18*(3), 264–285. doi:10.1108/13552551211227675

Singh, M. D., Shankar, R., Narain, R., & Kumar, A. (2006). Survey of knowledge management practices in Indian manufacturing industries. *Journal of Knowledge Management, 10*(6), 110–128. doi:10.1108/13673270610709251

Singh, T., Veron-Jackson, L., & Cullinane, J. (2008). Blogging: A new play in your marketing game plan. *Business Horizons, 51*(4), 281–292. doi:10.1016/j.bushor.2008.02.002

Sinickas, A. (2010/2011). Who needs surveys when you can scan social media? *SCM, 15*(1), 11.

Sirmon, D. G., Hitt, M. A., & Ireland, R. D. (2007). Managing firm resources in dynamic environments to create value: Looking inside the black box. *Academy of Management Review, 32*(1), 273–292. doi:10.5465/AMR.2007.23466005

Skok, W., & Goldstein, B. (2007). Managing organizational knowledge: Developing a strategy for a professional services company. *Strategic Change, 16*(7), 327–339. doi:10.1002/jsc.805

Smit, B., & Wandel, J. (2006). Adaptation, adaptive capacity and vulnerability. *Global Environmental Change, 16*(3), 282–292. doi:10.1016/j.gloenvcha.2006.03.008

Smith, A. (2012, April 20). Three amazing crowdsourcing campaigns. *Social Media Today*. Retrieved September 1, 2013 from http://socialmediatoday.com/alex-smith/492666/three-amazing-crowdsourcing-campaigns

Smith, J. (2013). The most unforgettable ad campaigns of 2013. *Forbes*. Retrieved 5th January 2014 from www.forbes.com/sites/jacquelynsmith/2013/12/17/the-most-unforgettable-ad-campaigns-of-2013/print/

Smith, A. N., Fischer, E., & Yongjian, C. (2012). How does brand-related user-generated content differ across YouTube, Facebook, and Twitter? *Journal of Interactive Marketing, 26*(2), 102–113. doi:10.1016/j.intmar.2012.01.002

Smith, J., & Duin, A. (1994). *Collective intelligence in computer-based collaboration*. L. Erlbaum Asso. Publishers.

Smith, K. T. (2011). Digital marketing strategies that Millennials find appealing, motivating, or just annoying. *Journal of Strategic Marketing, 19*(6), 489–499. doi:10.1080/0965254X.2011.581383

Smith, T., Coyle, J. R., Lightfoot, E., & Scott, A. (2007). Reconsidering models of influence: The relationship between consumer social networks and word-of-mouth effectiveness. *Journal of Advertising Research, 47*(4), 387–397. doi:10.2501/S0021849907070407

Social Bakers. (2014). *United Kingdom Facebook Statistics Online*. Retrieved from http://www.socialbakers.com/facebook-statistics/united-kingdom

Social Media Examiner. (2013). Retrieved January 3, 2014 from http://www.socialmediaexaminer.com/social-media-marketing-industry-report-2013/

Solis, B. (2010). *Engage! The complete guide for brands and businesses to build, cultivate, and measure success in the new web*. Hoboken, NJ: John Wiley & Sons.

Solman, G. (2008a). Levi's likes the style of new viral videos. *Brandweek*, *49*(20), 4.

Solman, G. (2008b). Viral video success changes Levi's plans. *Adweek*, *49*(17), 6.

Sørensen, F., Mattsson, J., & Sundbo, J. (2010). Experimental methods in innovation research. *Research Policy*, *39*(3), 313–320. doi:10.1016/j.respol.2010.01.006

Sotarauta, M., Horlings, L., & Liddle, J. (2012). *Leadership and change in sustainable regional development*. London, UK: Routledge.

Southgate, D., Westoby, N., & Page, G. (2010). Creative determinants of viral video viewing. *International Journal of Advertising*, *29*(3), 349–368. doi:10.2501/S0265048710201221

Spender, J. C. (1996). Making knowledge the basis of a dynamic theory of the firm. *Strategic Management Journal*, *17*(S2), 45–62. doi:10.1002/smj.4250171106

Spender, J. C., & Grant, R. M. (1996). Knowledge and the firm: Overview. *Strategic Management Journal*, *17*(S2), 5–9. doi:10.1002/smj.4250171103

Spenner, P. (2010, December). Why You Need a New-Media Ringmaster. *Harvard Business Review*, 78–80.

Spreitzer, G. M., & Mishra, A. K. (1999). Giving Up Control Without Losing Control: Trust and Its Substitutes' Effects on Managers' Involving Employees in Decision Making. *Group & Organization Management*, *14*(2), 155–187. doi:10.1177/1059601199242003

Srinivasan, R., & Moorman, C. (2005). Strategic firm commitments and rewards for customer relationship management in online retailing. *Journal of Marketing*, *69*(4), 193–200. doi:10.1509/jmkg.2005.69.4.193

Stanbouli, K. (2003). Marketing viral et publicité. *Revue Française du Marketing*, *192/193*, 97–106.

Stavros, C., & Westberg, K. (2009). Using triangulation and multiple case studies to advance relationship marketing theory. *Qualitative Market Research: An International Journal*, *12*(3), 307–320. doi:10.1108/13522750910963827

Steenkamp, J. B. E. M. (2001). The role of national culture in international marketing research. *International Marketing Review*, *18*(1), 30–44. doi:10.1108/02651330110381970

Steinert-Threlkeld, T. (2009). Following Zappos.com. *ZDNet*. Retrieved May 3, 2011, from http://www.jmorganmarketing.com/wp-content/uploads/2010/01/ZDNet-Zappos-SR.pdf

Stephen, A. T., & Toubia, O. (2010). Deriving value from social commerce networks. *JMR, Journal of Marketing Research*, *47*(2), 215–228. doi:10.1509/jmkr.47.2.215

Sterne, J. (2010). Social Media Metrics: How to Measure and Optimize Your Marketing Investment. In *Media* (Vol. 3). Hoboken, NJ: John Wiley & Sons.

Sternthal, B., & Craig, S. (1973). Humor in advertising. *Journal of Marketing*, *37*(4), 12–18. doi:10.2307/1250353

Stewart, D. W., & Pavlou, P. A. (2002). From consumer response to active consumer: Measuring the effectiveness of interactive media. *Journal of the Academy of Marketing Science*, *30*(4), 376–396. doi:10.1177/009207002236912

Stewart, D. W., & Zhao, Q. (2000). Internet marketing, business models, and public policy. *Journal of Public Policy & Marketing*, *19*(2), 287–296. doi:10.1509/jppm.19.2.287.17125

Steyer, A., Garcia-Bardidia, R., & Quester, P. (2007). Modélisation de la structure sociale des groupes de discussion sur internet: Implications pour le contrôle du marketing viral. *Recherche et Applications en Marketing*, *22*(3), 29–44. doi:10.1177/076737010702200303

Stiles, P. (2001). The Impact of the Board on Strategy: An Empirical Examination. *Journal of Management Studies*, *38*(5), 627–650. doi:10.1111/1467-6486.00252

Stone, M., & Woodcock, N. (2013). Social intelligence in customer engagement. *Journal of Strategic Marketing*, *21*(5), 394–401. doi:10.1080/0965254X.2013.801613

Strömbäck, J. (2007). Political Marketing and Professionalized Campaigning. *Journal of Political Marketing*, *6*(2-3), 49–67. doi:10.1300/J199v06n02_04

Strømmen-BakhtiarA. (2012). An essay on the emerging political economy and the future of the social media. In Proceedings of 6th IEEE International Conference on Digital Ecosystems Technologies (DEST). IEEE. 10.1109/DEST.2012.6227941

Strutton, D., Taylor, D. G., & Thompson, K. (2011). Investigating generational differences in e-WOM behaviors: For advertising purposes, does X = Y? *International Journal of Advertising*, *30*(4), 559–586. doi:10.2501/IJA-30-4-559-586

Stubbart, C. I. (1989). Managerial cognition: A missing link in strategic management research. *Journal of Management Studies*, *26*(4), 325–347. doi:10.1111/j.1467-6486.1989.tb00732.x

Subramani, M., & Rajagopalan, B. (2003). Knowledge-Sharing and Influence in online social networks via viral marketing. *Communications of the ACM*, *46*(12), 300–307. doi:10.1145/953460.953514

Su, C., & Contractor, N. (2011). A Multidimensional Network Approach to Studying Team Members' Information Seeking From Human and Digital Knowledge Sources in Consulting Firms. *Journal of the American Society for Information Science and Technology*, *62*(7), 1257–1275. doi:10.1002/asi.21526

Supporters Direct and Substance. (2010). *The Social and Community Value of Football*. Author.

Surowiecki, J. (2005). *The Wisdom of Crowds*. New York: Anchor.

Susskind, A. M. (2002). I told you so! Restaurant customers' word-of-mouth communication patterns. *Cornell Hospitality Quarterly*, *43*(2), 75–85. doi:10.1177/001088040204300208

Sveiby, E. K. (2001). A knowledge based theory of the firm to guide in strategy formulation. *Journal of Intellectual Capital*, *2*(4), 344–358. doi:10.1108/14691930110409651

Swanepoel, C., Lye, A., & Rugimbana, R. (2009). Virally inspired: A review of the theory of viral stealth marketing. *Australasian Marketing Journal*, *17*(1), 9–15. doi:10.1016/j.ausmj.2009.01.005

Sweeney, J. (2010). *Man United – into the red*. Retrieved from http://www.bbc.co.uk/iplayer/episode/b00snmrj/Panorama_Man_United_Into_the_Red/

Szulanski, G. (2000). The process of knowledge transfer: A diachronic analysis of stickiness. *Organizational Behavior and Human Decision Processes*, *82*(1), 9–27. doi:10.1006/obhd.2000.2884

Tan, K. (2010). Why social media are absolutely crucial to businesses. *INSEAD Knowledge*. Retrieved March 17, 2011, from http://knowledge.insead.edu/contents/networking-social-media-crampton-100513.cfm?vid=415

Tapp, A., & Clowes, J. (2002). From carefree casuals to professional wanderers: Segmentation possibilities for football supporters. *European Journal of Marketing*, *36*(11/12), 1248–1269. doi:10.1108/03090560210445164

Tapscott, D., & Williams, A. D. (2006). *Wikinomics: How Mass Collaboration Changes Everything*. London: Penguin Group.

Taylor, D. G., Lewin, J. E., & Strutton, D. (2011). Friends, fans, and followers: Do ads work on social networks? *Journal of Advertising Research*, *51*(1), 258–275. doi:10.2501/JAR-51-1-258-275

Taylor, D., & Altman, I. (1987). Communication in interpersonal relationships: Social penetration processes. In M. Roloff, & G. Miller (Eds.), *Interpersonal processes: New directions in communication research*. Newbury Park, CA: Sage.

Taylor, R. E. (1999, November-December). A six-segment message strategy wheel. *Journal of Advertising Research*, 7–17.

Teece, D. J. (2009). *Dynamic capabilities and strategic management*. Oxford, UK: Oxford University Press.

Teece, D. J. (2010). Business models, business strategy and innovation. *Long Range Planning*, *43*(2/3), 172–194. doi:10.1016/j.lrp.2009.07.003

Tellis, G. J. (2004). *Effective advertising: Understanding when, how, and why advertising works*. Thousand Oaks, CA: Sage Publications.

Terdiman, D. (2005). In search of the Wikipedia prankster. *CNET News.com.* Retrieved September 10, 2013 from http://news.cnet.com/In-search-of-the-Wikipedia-prankster/2008-1029_3-5995977.html

Therkelsen, D. J., & Fiebich, C. L. (2003). The supervisor: The linchpin of employee relations. *Journal of Communication Management, 8*(2), 120–129. doi:10.1108/13632540410807592

Thibault, J. W., & Kelley, H. H. (1959). *The social psychology of groups*. New York: John Wiley.

Thierauf, R. J., & Hoctor, J. J. (2006). *Optimal knowledge management: Wisdom management systems concepts and applications*. London, UK: Idea Group. doi:10.4018/978-1-59904-016-5

Thomas, D., & Barlow, M. (2011). *The executive's guide to enterprise social media strategy*. Hoboken, NJ: John Wiley & Sons Inc.

Thompson, C. (2010). To click with youth, GMC pitches go viral. *Automotive News, 84*, 4.

Thorbjørnsen, H., Supphellen, M., Nysveen, H., & Pedersen, P. E. (2002). Building brand relationships online: A comparison of two interactive applications. *Journal of Interactive Marketing, 16*(3), 17–34. doi:10.1002/dir.10034

Tikkanen, H., Hietanen, J., Henttonen, T., & Rokka, J. (2009). Exploring virtual worlds: Success factors in virtual world marketing. *Management Decision, 47*(8), 1357–1381. doi:10.1108/00251740910984596

Timmers, P. (1998). Business models for electronic markets. *Electronic Markets, 8*(2), 3–8. doi:10.1080/10196789800000016

Tonkin, S., Whitmore, C., & Cutroni, J. (2010). *Performance marketing with Google analytics: Strategies and techniques for maximizing online ROI*. Hoboken, NJ: Wiley Publishing, Inc.

Towers Watson Study. (2013, July 14). Retrieved from http://www.towerswatson.com/en/Insights/IC-Types/Survey-Research-Results/2013/05/Infographic-2013-Change-and-Communication-ROI-Study

Towner, T. L., & Dulio, D. A. (2012). New Media and Political Marketing in the United States: 2012 and Beyond. *Journal of Political Marketing, 11*(1-2), 95–119. doi:10.1080/15377857.2012.642748

Tracey, M., Lim, J., & Vonderembse, M. A. (2005). The impact of supply-chain management capabilities on business performance. *Supply-Chain Management: An International Journal, 10*(3), 179–191. doi:10.1108/13598540510606232

Trammell, K. D., & Keshelashvili, A. (2005). Examining the New Influencers: A Self-Presentation Study of A-List Blogs. *Journalism & Mass Communication Quarterly, 82*(4), 968–982. doi:10.1177/107769900508200413

TripAdvisor. (2013). Retrieved September 10, 2013 from http://www.tripadvisor.com

Trulia. (2012). Retrieved September 10, 2013 from http://www.trulia.com

Truong, H. (2010). The top ten successful viral ads of all time by AdAge. *DigiWave*. Retrieved 11th March 2013, from http://www.thedigiwave.com/2010/11/top-ten-viral-ads-of-all-time.html

Trusov, M., Bucklin, R. E., & Pauwels, K. (2009). Effects of word-of-mouth versus traditional marketing: Finding from an internet social networking site. *Journal of Marketing, 73*(5), 90–102. doi:10.1509/jmkg.73.5.90

Tsai, J. (2009). Video is more than viral: Forget YouTube sensations and wardrobe malfunctions. *CRM Magazine, 13*, 36–42.

Tsoukas, H., & Vladimirou, E. (2001). What is organizational knowledge? *Journal of Management Studies, 38*(7), 973–993. doi:10.1111/1467-6486.00268

Turban, E., & Volonino, L. (2011). *Information technology for management: Improving strategic and operational performance*. Hoboken, NJ: John Wiley & Sons.

Tuten, T. L. (2008). *Advertising 2.0: Social media marketing in a web 2.0 world*. Westport, CT: Praeger.

Tyler, T. R. (2002). Is the internet changing social life? It seems the more things change, the more they stay the same. *The Journal of Social Issues, 58*(1), 195–205. doi:10.1111/1540-4560.00256

Underwood, R., Bond, E., & Baer, R. (2001). Building service brands via social identity: Lessons from the sports marketplace. *Journal of Marketing Theory and Practice*, *9*(1), 1–13.

Uotila, J., Maula, M., Keil, T., & Zahra, S. A. (2009). Exploration, exploitation, and financial performance: Analysis of S&P 500 corporations. *Strategic Management Journal*, *30*(2), 221–231. doi:10.1002/smj.738

Urquhart, C., & Vaast, E. (2012). *Building social media theory from case studies: A new frontier for IS research*. Paper presented at the 31st International Conference on Information Systems. Orlando, FL.

Utz, S. (2009). The (potential) benefits of campaigning via social network sites. *Journal of Computer-Mediated Communication*, *14*(2), 221–243. doi:10.1111/j.1083-6101.2009.01438.x

Uzzi, B., & Dunlap, S. (2005). How to build your network. *Harvard Business Review*, *83*(12), 53–60.

Vaccaro, A., & Madsen, P. (2009). Transparency: The new ICT-driven ethics? *Ethics and Information Technology*, *11*(2), 113–122. doi:10.1007/s10676-009-9190-1

Van De Ven, A. H. (1992). Suggestions for studying strategy process: A research note. *Strategic Management Journal*, *13*(S1), 169–191. doi:10.1002/smj.4250131013

van Doorn, J., Lemon, K. N., Mittal, V., Nass, S., Pick, D., Pirner, P., & Verhoef, P. C. (2010). Customer engagement behavior: Theoretical foundations and research directions. *Journal of Service Research*, *13*(3), 253–266. doi:10.1177/1094670510375599

Van Onselen, A., & Van Onselen, P. (2008). On message or out of touch? Secure web sites and political campaigning in Australia. *Australian Journal of Political Science*, *43*(1), 43–58. doi:10.1080/10361140701842565

Vance, K., Howe, W., & Dellavalle, R. (2009). Social internet sites as a source of public health information. *Dermatologic Clinics*, *27*(2), 113–136. doi:10.1016/j.det.2008.11.010 PMID:19254656

Vargo, S., & Lusch, R. (2004). Evolving to a New Dominant Logic for Marketing. *Journal of Marketing*, *68*(1), 1–17. doi:10.1509/jmkg.68.1.1.24036

Veeck, A. (2013, October). Beyond monitoring: Analyzing the content of social media data. *Quirks*, 74-75.

Venkatesh, V. (2000). Determinants of perceived ease of use: Integrating control, intrinsic motivation, and emotion into the technology acceptance model. *Information Systems Research*, *11*(4), 342–365. doi:10.1287/isre.11.4.342.11872

Venkatesh, V., & Bala, H. (2008). Technology Acceptance Model 3 and a Research Agenda on Interventions. *Decision Sciences*, *39*(2), 273–315. doi:10.1111/j.1540-5915.2008.00192.x

Venkatesh, V., & Davis, F. (1996). A model of the antecedents of perceived ease of use: Development and test. *Decision Sciences*, *27*(3), 451–481. doi:10.1111/j.1540-5915.1996.tb01822.x

Venkatesh, V., & Davis, F. D. (2000). A Theoretical Extension of the Technology Acceptance Model: Four Longitudinal Field Studies. *Management Science*, *46*(2), 186–204. doi:10.1287/mnsc.46.2.186.11926

Venkatesh, V., Morris, M. G., Davis, G. B., & Davis, F. D. (2003). User Acceptance of Information Technology: Toward a unified view. *Management Information Systems (MIS). Quarterly*, *27*(3), 425–478.

Venkatesh, V., Thong, J. Y. L., & Xu, X. (2012). Consumer acceptance and use of information technology: Extending the unified theory of acceptance and use of technology. *Management Information Systems (MIS). Quarterly*, *36*(1), 157–178.

Verhoef, P. C., & Langerak, F. (2002). Eleven misconceptions about customer relationship management. *Business Strategy Review*, *13*(4), 70–76. doi:10.1111/1467-8616.00235

Verhoef, P. C., Reinartz, W. J., & Krafft, M. (2010). Customer engagement as a new perspective in customer engagement. *Journal of Service Research*, *13*(3), 247–252. doi:10.1177/1094670510375461

Vivek, S. D., Beatty, S. E., & Morgan, R. M. (2012). Customer engagement: Exploring customer relationships beyond purchase. *Journal of Marketing Theory and Practice*, *20*(2), 127–145. doi:10.2753/MTP1069-6679200201 von Hippel, E. (1986). Lead users: A source of novel product concepts. *Management Science*, *32*(7), 91–805. doi:10.1287/mnsc.32.7.791

Von Krogh, G. (2012). How does social software change knowledge management? Toward a strategic research agenda. *The Journal of Strategic Information Systems*, *21*(2), 154–164. doi:10.1016/j.jsis.2012.04.003

Vuori, V. (2011). *Social media changing the competitive intelligence process: Elicitation of employees' competitive knowledge.* (Thesis for Degree of Doctor of Science in Technology). Tampere University of Technology, Tampere, Finland.

Vuori, V., & Okkonen, J. (2012). Knowledge sharing motivational factors of using an intra-organizational social media platform. *Journal of Knowledge Management*, *16*(4), 592–603. doi:10.1108/13673271211246167

Vuori, W., & Okkonen, J. (2012). Refining information and knowledge by social media applications. *VINE: The Journal of Information and Knowledge Management System*, *42*(1), 117–128. doi:10.1108/03055721211207798

Wagner, C., & Bolloju, N. (2005). Supporting knowledge management in organisations with conversational technologies: Discussion forums, weblogs and wikis. *Journal of Database Management*, *16*(2), i–viii.

Walker, J. (2003). *Final Version of Weblog Definition.* Retrieved from jilltxt.net/archives/blog_theorising/final_version_of_weblog_definition.html

Walters, S. (2013). Beyond listening: Six steps for integrating and acting on social media. *Business Intelligence Journal*, *18*(1), 13–17.

Warnick, B., Xenos, M., Endres, D., & Gastil, J. (2005). Effects of campaign-to-user and text-based interactivity in political candidate campaign web sites. *Journal of Computer-Mediated Communication*, *10*(3).

Wasserman, T. (2013). *The most-shared ads of 2013.* Retrieved 5th January 2014 from www.mashable.com/2013/11/21/these-are-the-most-shared-ads-of-2013/

Wasserman, S., & Faust, K. (1994). *Social network analysis: Methods and applications.* Cambridge University Press. doi:10.1017/CBO9780511815478

Wasserman, T. (2009). Marketing innovation of the decade: Viral videos. *Adweek*, *50*(44), 24.

Waters, R. D., Burnett, E., Lamm, A., & Lucas, J. (2009). Engaging stakeholders through social networking: How nonprofit organizations are using Facebook. *Public Relations Review*, *35*(2), 102–106. doi:10.1016/j.pubrev.2009.01.006

Watters, E. (2004). *Urban tribes: A generation redefines friendship, family, and commitment.* London: Bloomsbury Publishing.

Watts, D. J., & Dodds, P. S. (2007). Influentials, networks, and public opinion formation. *The Journal of Consumer Research*, *34*(4), 441–458. doi:10.1086/518527

Webster, F. E. (1994). *Market-driven management.* Hoboken, NJ: John Wiley and Sons.

Weick, K. E. (1993). The Collapse of Sensemaking in Organizations: The Mann Gulch Disaster. *Administrative Science Quarterly*, *38*(4), 628. doi:10.2307/2393339

Weick, K. E., Sutcliffe, K. M., & Obstfeld, D. (2005). Organizing and the process of sensemaking. *Organization Science*, *16*(4), 409–421. doi:10.1287/orsc.1050.0133

Weigelt, K., & Camerer, C. (1988). Reputation and corporate strategy: A review of recent theory and applications. *Strategic Management Journal*, *9*(5), 443–454. doi:10.1002/smj.4250090505

Weimann, G. (1983). The strength of weak conversational ties in the flow of information and influence. *Social Networks*, *5*(3), 245–267. doi:10.1016/0378-8733(83)90027-8

Weinberg, B. D., & Pehlivan, E. (2011). Social spending: Managing the social media mix. *Business Horizons*, *54*(3), 275–282. doi:10.1016/j.bushor.2011.01.008

Weinberger, M. G., & Gulas, C. S. (1992). The impact of humor in advertising: A review. *Journal of Advertising*, *21*(4), 35–59. doi:10.1080/00913367.1992.10673384

Weiss, A. M., Lurie, N. H., & MacInnis, D. J. (2008). Listening to strangers: Whose responses are valuable, how valuable are they, and why? *JMR, Journal of Marketing Research*, *45*(4), 425–436. doi:10.1509/jmkr.45.4.425

Welch, M., & Jackson, P. R. (2007). Rethinking internal communication: A stakeholder approach. *Corporate Communications*, *12*(2), 177–198. doi:10.1108/13563280710744847

Welker, C. B. (2002). The paradigm of viral communication. *Information Services & Use*, *22*, 3–8.

Wellman, B. (2001). Computer networks as social networks. *Science*, *293*(14), 2031–2034. doi:10.1126/science.1065547 PMID:11557877

Wernerfelt, B. (1984). A resource-based view of the firm. *Strategic Management Journal*, *5*(2), 170–180. doi:10.1002/smj.4250050207

Westley, F., & Mintzberg, H. (1989). Visionary leadership and strategic management. *Strategic Management Journal*, *10*(S1), 17–32. doi:10.1002/smj.4250100704

Whitla, P. (2009). Crowdsourcing and its application in marketing activities. *Contemporary Management Research*, *5*(1), 15–28.

Whittington, K. B., Owen-Smith, J., & Powel, W. W. (2009). Networks, propinquity, and innovation in knowledge-intensive industries. *Administrative Science Quarterly*, *54*(1), 90–122. doi:10.2189/asqu.2009.54.1.90

Williamson, B. (2009, July 24). Managing at a distance. *Business Week*.

Winer, R. S. (2001). A framework for customer relationship management. *California Management Review*, *43*(4), 89–105. doi:10.2307/41166102

Wirtz, W. B., Schilke, O., & Ullrich, S. (2010). Implications of the Web 2.0. for creating value on the internet. *Long Range Planning*, *43*(2-3), 272–290. doi:10.1016/j.lrp.2010.01.005

Wolfe, R. A. (1994). Organizational Innovation: Review, Critique and Suggested Research Directions. *Journal of Management Studies*, *31*(3), 405–431. doi:10.1111/j.1467-6486.1994.tb00624.x

Woodcock, N., Green, A., & Starkey, M. (2011). Social CRM as a business strategy. *Journal of Database Marketing & Customer Strategy Management*, *18*(1), 50–64. doi:10.1057/dbm.2011.7

Woodside, A. G. (2010). Brand-consumers storytelling theory and research: Introduction to a psychology and marketing special issue. *Psychology and Marketing*, *25*(6), 521–540.

Woodside, A. G., Sood, S., & Miller, K. E. (2008). When consumers and brands talk: Storytelling theory and research in psychology and marketing. *Psychology and Marketing*, *25*(2), 97–145. doi:10.1002/mar.20203

Wooldridge, B., & Floyd, S. W. (1990). The strategy process, middle management involvement, and organizational performance. *Strategic Management Journal*, *11*(3), 231–241. doi:10.1002/smj.4250110305

Wring, D. (1997). Reconciling marketing with political science: Theories of political marketing. *Journal of Marketing Management*, *13*(7), 651–663. doi:10.1080/0267257X.1997.9964502

Yang, K., & Jolly, L. (2009). The Effects of Consumer Perceived Value and Subjective Norm on Mobile Data Service Adoption between American and Korean Consumers. *Journal of Retailing and Consumer Services*, *16*(6), 502–508. doi:10.1016/j.jretconser.2009.08.005

Yannas, P. (2005). Political Marketing in Greece Is Ready for Take-Off. *Journal of Political Marketing*, *4*(1), 1–15. doi:10.1300/J199v04n01_01

Yin, R. K. (1994). *Case study research design and methods* (2nd ed., Vol. 5). Thousand Oaks, CA: Sage Publications.

Yin, R. K. (2009). *Case study research: Design and methods* (4th ed.). London: Sage.

Yoon, K., & Kang, H. (2011). *The role of consumer heterogeneity on the design of loyalty program*. (Unpublished thesis). Long Island University, Long Island, NY.

Yoon, K., & Sims, J. D. (2013). Integrating social media and traditional CRM: Toward a conceptual framework for social CRM practices. In A. Ayanso, & K. Lertwachara (Eds.), *Harnessing the power of social media and web analytics: Techniques, tools, and applications*. Academic Press.

Yoon, K., & Tran, T. V. (2011). Revisiting the relationship between consumer loyalty and price sensitivity: The moderating role of deal-proneness. *Journal of Marketing Theory and Practice*, *19*(3), 293–306. doi:10.2753/MTP1069-6679190303

Zack, H. M. (2003). Rethinking the knowledge-based organization. *MIT Sloan Management Review*, *44*(4), 67–71.

Zaim, H., Ekrem, T., & Selim, Z. (2007). Performance of knowledge management practices: A casual analysis. *Journal of Knowledge Management*, *11*(6), 54–67. doi:10.1108/13673270710832163

Zander, U., & Kogut, B. (1995). Knowledge and the speed of the transfer and imitation of organizational capabilities: An empirical test. *Organization Science*, *6*(1), 76–92. doi:10.1287/orsc.6.1.76

Zeffane, R., Tipu, S. A., & Ryan, J. C. (2011). Communication, commitment & trust: Exploring the triad. *International Journal of Business and Management*, *6*(6), 77–87. doi:10.5539/ijbm.v6n6p77

Zhang, C., Sun, J., Zhu, X., & Fang, Y. (2010). Privacy and security for online social networks: Challenges and opportunities. *IEEE Network*, *24*(4), 13–18. doi:10.1109/MNET.2010.5510913

Zhao, J., & Ordóñez de Pablos, P. (2011). Regional knowledge management: The perspective of management theory. *Behaviour & Information Technology*, *30*(1), 39–49. doi:10.1080/0144929X.2010.492240

Zott, C., & Amit, R. (2010). Business model design: An activity system perspective. *Long Range Planning*, *43*(2/3), 216–226. doi:10.1016/j.lrp.2009.07.004

About the Contributors

In Lee is a professor in the School of Computer Sciences at the College of Business and Technology at Western Illinois University (WIU) in the United States. He is the recipient of the 2013 Provost's Award for Academic Excellence in Scholarly Activities and a three-time winner of the Research Excellence Award in the College of Business and Technology at WIU. He is also a best paper winner and invited speaker at various conferences. He was a Keimyung Global Scholar during his sabbatical in 2009. He is the founding Editor-in-Chief of the *International Journal of E-Business Research.* He has published his research in such journals as *Journal of Small Business Management, Management Decision, Business Horizons, International Small Business Journal, Communications of the ACM, IEEE Transactions on Systems, Man, and Cybernetics, IEEE Transactions on Engineering Management, International Journal of Production Research, Computers and Education, Decision Support Systems, Computers and Operations Research, International Journal of Production Economics, Knowledge and Process Management, Computers in Human Behavior, Business Process Management Journal, Computers and Industrial Engineering*, and others. Prior to his academic career, he worked for a number of multinational corporations, as well as served as a consultant for various government agencies and private organizations. His current research interests include social media, social enterprise, Web technology development and management, investment strategies for computing technologies, and mobile services. He received his BBA from Keimyung University in South Korea, MBA from the University of Texas at Austin, and PhD in Business Administration from the University of Illinois at Urbana-Champaign in the United States.

* * *

Donald L. Amoroso is the Lowder Weil Endowed Chair of Innovation and Strategy in the College of Business at Auburn University Montgomery, Professor of Information Systems, Founder of Axcell LLC Consulting Group (focusing on innovation in strategy), and Research Fellow / Adjunct Professor at Asian Institute of Management in Manila, Philippines. He is working with colleagues at 12 Japanese and 6 Philippine universities to develop research on each of the components of the mobile ecosystem. Dr. Amoroso has consulted with over 60 international organizations (such as GE Japan, BMW Japan) working with CEOs and CIOs to develop strategic plans, marketing strategies, accounting and enterprise resource management systems, and projects for information technology. Dr. Amoroso received his MBA and PhD from the University of Georgia in 1984 and 1986, respectively, and has spent more than 25 years in higher education and industry. His experience included working in GE Capital as a director of Enterprise Solutions and with Solista/GartnerGroup as a consulting partner. Dr. Amoroso's current areas of research include strategy and leadership and mobile technologies, including Internet adoption, understanding consumer behavior using the Internet, online shopping, and music downloading. He has authored 67 articles and proceedings, written 5 books, presented at over 52 professional conferences and venues. He has published in 30 journals such as *Journal of Management Information Systems, Data Base,* and *Information & Management* and been on the editorial board of key journals including *Information Systems Management Journal.*

Elisa Arrigo, PhD, is Assistant Professor of Management at the Department of Economics, Management and Statistics (University of Milan-Bicocca, Italy). She holds a PhD in Marketing and Management from Milan-Bicocca University; during her PhD studies, she was a visiting scholar at Stockholm School of Business. She teaches Marketing and Marketing Communication in academic undergraduate and master courses. Her research interests lie primarily in Market-Driven Management, Corporate Social Responsibility, and Luxury and Fashion Management. She is currently involved in research projects related to the global marketing strategies of fashion and luxury firms with reference to the impact of digital technologies. She has published books, book chapters, and academic papers in referred national and international journals on various aspects of her research topics.

Catherine J. Ashworth has had a wide-ranging career, including over 10 years as an international marketing specialist in industries from environmental conditioning to high tech consumer products. Having moved into academia, Catherine's current teaching includes global/international and strategic marketing. Catherine also has a strong interest and experience in consumer psychology/behaviour, B2B/services marketing and communications. Catherine has a PhD in SME fashion e-retailing, examining success, organizational development, and sustainability strategies in both pure-play and clicks-and-mortar enterprises. Current research includes social media marketing and e-business development strategy. Catherine operates successfully as an e-business consultant engaging in Knowledge Transfer and Action Research Projects across the UK. She has assisted companies in industries such as anti-terror, chemicals, and professional work-wear to embed strategic/digital marketing capabilities which have led to considerable growth. Outside of academic work, Catherine is a keen salsa dancer and is also a qualified Clinical Hypnotherapist and NLP Practitioner.

Hartmut Behr is professor of international politics at Newcastle University (UK). He holds a PhD from the University of Cologne and a post-doc from the University of Jena (Germany). Professor Behr is the author of *Immigration Politics in the Nation State* (1998), *Deterritorialized Politics* (2004), and *A History of International Political Theory* (2010), as well as many articles in international and peer-reviewed journals. He is working at the moment on a new book on *Politics of Difference: Epistemologies of Peace*, which will appear shortly with Routledge.

Imed Boughzala is Associate Professor at the Department of Information Systems at the Business School of the Mines-Telecom Institute in Paris, France. He received a PhD in Computer Information Systems and HDR in Management respectively from the University of Paris VI Pierre & Marie Curie and the University of Nantes. His research's interests are related to e-collaboration, knowledge sharing, and crowdsourcing. During the last years, he has been experimenting with virtual learning, collaboration, and project management through 3D Virtual Worlds and Serious Games. Imed Boughzala is the author of several articles and books. He is member of the editorial board of *Information & Management.* In 2008 and 2009, he was visiting Professor at three universities for three successive semesters: Brunel West London University, University of Arkansas, and University of Nebraska at Omaha.

Edward T. Chen is Professor of Management Information Systems of Operations and Information Systems Department in the Manning School of Business at University of Massachusetts Lowell. Dr. Chen has published over 60 refereed research articles in scholarly journals such as *Information & Management, Journal of Computer Information Systems, Project Management, Comparative Technology Transfer and Society, Journal of International Technology and Information Management, International Journal of Innovation and Learning*, etc. Dr. Chen has served as vice-president, board director, track chair, and session chair of many professional associations and conferences. Professor Chen has also served as journal editor, editorial reviewer, and ad hoc reviewer for various academic journals. Dr. Chen has received the Irwin Distinguished Paper Award at the Southwestern Federation of Administrative Disciplines conference and the Best Paper Award at the International Conference on Accounting and Information Technology. His main research interests are in the areas of Project Management, Knowledge Management, Agile Software Development, and Green IT.

Ranjan Das is professor of strategic management at the Indian Institute of Management Calcutta. His research interests include strategic thinking, strategy development, strategy execution, and management of change, innovation, entrepreneurship, and leadership. As a strategic and general management consultant and as a facilitator for business and organizational transformation, apart from his extensive teaching experience, Prof. Das draws on over two and half decades of senior level industry experience including that of being a General Manager of an MNC, the Managing Director of a Indian Joint Sector Company, and an Entrepreneur cum Institution builder. Prof. Das has published several articles in reputed international journals and also authored several case studies pertaining to strategy and related areas. He has also authored/co-authored several books and book chapters relating to diversification, corporate restructuring, and entry strategies for MNCs.

Kijpokin Kasemsap received his BEng degree in Mechanical Engineering from King Mongkut's University of Technology Thonburi, his MBA degree from Ramkhamhaeng University, and his DBA degree in Human Resource Management from Suan Sunandha Rajabhat University. He is a Special Lecturer at Faculty of Management Sciences, Suan Sunandha Rajabhat University based in Bangkok, Thailand. He is a Member of International Association of Engineers (IAENG), International Association of Engineers and Scientists (IAEST), International Economics Development and Research Center (IEDRC), International Association of Computer Science and Information Technology (IACSIT), International Foundation for Research and Development (IFRD), and International Innovative Scientific and Research Organization (IISRO). He also serves on the International Advisory Committee (IAC) for International Association of Academicians and Researchers (INAAR). He has numerous original research articles in top international journals, conference proceedings, and book chapters on business management, human resource management, and knowledge management published internationally.

Karen M. Lancendorfer (PhD, Michigan State University) is Associate Professor of Marketing in the Haworth College of Business at Western Michigan University. She is also Director of the Advertising & Promotion Program, where she is the 2011-12 recipient of the WMU Distinguished Teaching Award and the 2012 Haworth College of Business Service Award. Her current research interests focus on political advertising, corporate image, and consumer behavior. Her work has been included in a number of publications including the *Journal of Business Research, Harvard International Journal of Press/Politics, Journal of Information Technology, Asian Journal of Communication, International Journal* *of Nonprofit and Voluntary Sector Marketing*, *Corporate Reputation Review*, *International Journal of E-Business Research*, and the *Journal of Political Marketing*, as well as in conference proceedings. She is the former associate editor for the *Journal of Interactive Advertising*, and the 2014 President-elect of the American Academy of Advertising.

Jeff McCarthy is a senior digital marketing specialist with over 15 years' experience in E-commerce, E-retail, M-commerce, interactive and direct marketing in B2B and B2C environments. Jeff's skills include social media, digital publishing and magazines, email marketing, SEO, PPC, mobile marketing, affiliate and database marketing. His specialties include sports marketing, mail order, online gaming, and sports betting. Having managed his own e-commerce business for several years, Jeff is now a highly experienced speaker/trainer for the CIM, IDM, E-consultancy organizations, alongside his successful teaching career at MMU. Jeff also provides in-company training for the CIM Academy. Jeff was also one of the first marketers to receive the IDM CPD Award (Feb 2006). Jeff is also an internationally published author in practitioner and academic journals (e.g. *Internet Research*; *Journal of Direct Data and Digital Marketing Practice*) and is currently researching the impact of social media on football clubs in the UK.

Aneil Mishra is the Thomas D. Arthur Professor of Leadership at East Carolina University in the College of Business. He is a global thought leader in the area of trustworthy leadership. He is the author of *Becoming a Trustworthy Leader: Psychology & Practice* (Routledge, 2013), which features leaders from Fortune 500 companies who have built trust with employees and customers through innovative and collaborative practices. He is an award-winning professor who has taught at Penn State University, Wake Forest University, Duke University, and Michigan State University. He was Associate Dean for Academic Affairs in the School of Business at North Carolina Central University and also the VP of Faculty and Curriculum for 2tor where he launched MBA@UNC. He currently consults with leaders and teams in Fortune 500 companies to help them build trust and build a culture of collaboration. Aneil's AB, cum laude in Economics, is from Princeton University and his PhD is from the University of Michigan Ross School of Business.

Karen Mishra is an assistant professor in the School of Business at Meredith College in Raleigh, North Carolina, where she teaches marketing, digital marketing, and global business. Her research focuses on how leaders build trust through internal communication with employees. She is the author of *Becoming a Trustworthy Leader: Psychology & Practice* (Routledge, 2013), which features leaders from Fortune 500 companies who have built trust with employees and customers through transparent communication. She has taught at Penn State, Wake Forest University, and Michigan State University. Prior to her teaching career, she was an account executive for the $75 million Pepsi Cola account for Johnson Controls Plastic Container Division. She currently consults with corporate leaders and teams to help them build their communication and collaboration skills. Karen's MBA is from the University of Michigan Ross School of Business and her PhD is from The University North Carolina at Chapel Hill.

Tsuneki Mukahi is a Professor of School of Management, Chukyo University in Japan. He teaches Information Systems and Information Management. He received his PhD from the Osaka Institute of Technology in Japan. His research focuses on Computer-Mediated Communication and Knowledge

Management. He has published papers in *Journal of Electronic Commerce in Organizations* and international conference proceedings such as Hawaii International Conference on System Sciences and Pacific Asia Conference on Information System. He has also published papers in refereed Japanese journals such as *Japan Society of Management Information Journal* and *Journal of Japan Industrial Management Association.*

Hanne Westh Nicolajsen holds a position as associate professor at the Department of Communication, Aalborg University in Copenhagen, Denmark. Her main research interest is organizational use of ICT focusing on the use of ICT in support of changed organizational practices in particular organizational practices of innovation, knowledge management, and learning. Recently, her focus has been divided between two areas. One area is user- and employee-driven innovation with focus on idea competitions and crowdsourcing within knowledge intensive organizations. Another stream of research—mainly driven by empirical experiments—is strengthening of problem-based learning and social learning processes within higher education.

Mikako Ogawa serves as an assistant professor at Research Center for Advanced Science and Technology, Tokyo University of Marine Science and Technology. Dr. Ogawa completed her PhD (Media and Governance) in 2010 followed by completing MBA in 2003 Keio University after working as a system engineer for 8 years. Her research areas include information sharing in the food supply chain, food traceability, and communication issues between food companies and consumer. She is a member of Association for Information Systems, Japan Society for Management Information, The Food System Research Association of Japan, the Japan Society of Foodservice Studies, and so on.

Kelley O'Reilly (PhD, Utah State University) is Assistant Professor of Sales and Business Marketing at Western Michigan University and the recipient of the 2013 Haworth College of Business Research Award. She has more than 20 years of executive-level experience in franchise retail and service businesses and her research interests are qualitative research methods, Customer Relationship Management (CRM), sales, and service quality. Her work has been included (or is forthcoming) in publications of *Organizational Research Methods, International Journal of Retail and Distribution Management, Journal of Research in Marketing and Entrepreneurship, Qualitative Market Research: An International Journal, International Journal of E-Business Research,* and *Journal of Relationship Marketing,* among others.

Savvas Papagiannidis is the David Goldman Professor of Innovation and Enterprise in the Newcastle University Business School, UK. He holds a PhD in Theoretical Physics and a second doctorate in Business Administration. Upon completion of his PhD, he joined the ebusiness@newcastle research team, working on a number of Internet-related research projects. His work has been published in several academic journals and presented at international conferences. His research aims to inform our understanding of how e-business technologies affect the social and business environment, organisational strategies and business models, and how these are implemented in terms of functional innovations. His work puts strong emphasis on innovation, new value creation, and exploitation of entrepreneurial opportunities within the context of different industries.

Maria Petrescu is an assistant professor of marketing at Nova Southeastern University. Her main research areas include digital marketing, social media and international marketing. Dr. Petrescu has participated in prestigious conferences, such as the American Marketing Association Summer Educators' Conference, the Academy of Marketing Science Conference, the AMS World Marketing Congress, and the Society for Marketing Advances Conference. She also published in journals such as the *Journal of Product and Brand Management*, the *Journal of Marketing Analytics*, and the *Journal of Internet Commerce* on topics such as online price dispersion, viral advertising, and cloud computing.

Jennifer Rowley is Professor of Information and Communications at Manchester Metropolitan University, and Editor of the *Journal of Further and Higher Education*. Teaching includes research methods, information and knowledge management, and management and marketing. Jenny provides students with a supportive learning structure whilst challenging individuals to push themselves beyond their own expectations. Jenny believes that teaching is not just about creating highly employable graduates; it involves contributing to creating someone who has the capacity to observe and analyse the world around them, to think for themselves, and to make difficult choices. Jenny's research interests are broad and ever-evolving and currently focus around digital information, learning environments, and marketing. In digital marketing, current interests include digital branding, social media marketing, and mobile marketing. When not working, Jenny enjoys spending time with family and friends, plus walking, gardening, and travelling, sometimes simultaneously!

Ada Scupola is a senior associate professor at the Department of Communication, Business, and Information Technologies, Roskilde University, Denmark. She holds a PhD in Social Sciences from Roskilde University, an MBA from the University of Maryland at College Park, USA, and a MSc from the University of Bari, Italy. She is the editor-in-chief of *The International Journal of E-Services and Mobile Applications*. Her main research interests include: innovation theory with focus on open innovation, user-driven innovation, and ICT-based innovation in specific sectors, such as facility management, libraries, and consulting services; adoption of Information and Communication Technologies (ICT) in teams and organizations and in organizational populations with special focus on SMEs; leadership and competences studies especially in relation to adoption of e-technologies; "sourcing" strategies (outsourcing and in-sourcing) with focus on supply chain management and role of Information and Communication Technologies (ICTs); impact studies of e-commerce on industrial structures; and the role of ICT in clusters.

Jeanetta D. Sims (PhD, University of Oklahoma) is an Associate Professor in the Marketing Department at the University of Central Oklahoma, where she teaches courses in business communication and marketing communications. She is Accredited in Public Relations (APR), and her research interests are in strategic communication, organizational diversity, and persuasion and social influence. Her scholarship has appeared in book chapter and journal publication formats including the *Journal of Communication, Journal of Public Relations Research, Human Communication Research, Communication Monographs, Communication Research, Atlantic Marketing Journal, Mass Communication & Society, Corporate Reputation Review, Council on Undergraduate Research Quarterly*, and *Still Searching for Our Mothers' Gardens: Experiences of New, Tenure-Track Women of Color in 'Majority' Institutions.*

T. Stamati has obtained a Degree in Informatics and Telecommunications from National and Kapodistrian University of Athens (Greece). She also holds an MPhil Degree in Information Systems from University of Manchester (UMIST) (UK), MBA Degree from Lancaster University Management School (UK), and PhD in Information Systems from National and Kapodistrian University of Athens (Greece). She has 15 years of experience in senior management positions in ICT companies of the Greek and European private sector. She is an adjunct professor in University of Athens. Her research interests focus on information systems, social media, innovation, and cloud computing.

S. Venkataraman is a Doctoral Research Fellow at the Indian Institute of Management Calcutta. His research interests include sustainability, entrepreneurship, corporate social media, and public-private partnerships. Venkataraman has a Master's degree in Business Management and has close to two decades of senior leadership experience in the financial sector and infrastructure advisory services sector in India, Africa, and the Caribbean. He was formerly the CEO of an international credit rating agency and has served as a consultant on African Development Bank, Asian Development Bank, and World Bank assignments.

Khaner Walker helps companies engage with people using the written word – storytelling by way of media pitches, ads, tweets, events, or internal notes to thousands of employees. He currently manages an amazing team of communications professionals at Lenovo, the world's largest PC company. Together, they plan comprehensive campaigns for multiple global business groups and the company as a whole. This includes anything from printed design, email, Intranet, video production, and event planning to testing batteries on lavaliers and holding the occasional boom microphone. In the past, he has led teams at one of the South's top PR agencies and managed communications for a private tech company on its way to an IPO. He has shared his knowledge with several non-profit boards he cares deeply about, and will continue doing so when finished with his MBA. He had the extreme luck of marrying an amazing woman, whom he met in Raleigh, NC – a place they are glad to call home. He received his undergrad from NC State University with a degree in Political Science.

Kanghyun Yoon is currently an Assistant Professor of Marketing at the University of Central Oklahoma. Yoon earned his BS and MS degrees from Hankuk University of Foreign Studies (Seoul, Korea), his MBA from Illinois Institute Technology (Chicago, IL, USA), and PhD from the University of Wisconsin (Milwaukee, WI, USA). His research interests are in the empirical modeling of consumers' decision-making, brand loyalty, customer satisfaction, online auctions, shopping value, and sustainability using econometric, Bayesian, and IO approaches. Dr. Yoon has published academic articles in several journals such as *Information Systems Research* and *Journal of Marketing Theory & Practice*, among others. He is also the author of a new online book called *Fundamentals of Customer-Driven Marketing*.

Index

R

S

T

U

V

W

www.ingramcontent.com/pod-product-compliance
Lightning Source LLC
LaVergne TN
LVHW060417300926
849162LV00006B/1449
* 9 7 8 1 4 6 6 6 6 1 8 2 0 *